PERSONALITY DISORDERS

301.00 Paranoid
301.21 Introverted
301.22 Schizotypal
301.50 Histrionic
301.81 Narcissistic
301.70 Antisocial
301.83 Borderline
301.82 Avoidant
301.60 Dependent
301.40 Compulsive
301.84 Passive-Aggressive
301.89 Other or mixed

PSYCHOSEXUAL DISORDERS

GENDER IDENTITY DISORDERS

302.50 Transsexualism
302.60 Gender identity disorder of childhood
302.85 Other gender identity disorder of
        adolescence or adult life

PARAPHILIAS

302.81 Fetishism
302.30 Transvestism
302.10 Zoophilia
302.20 Pedophilia
302.40 Exhibitionism
302.82 Voyeurism
302.83 Sexual masochism
302.84 Sexual sadism
302.89 Other

PSYCHOSEXUAL DYSFUNCTIONS

302.71 With inhibited sexual desire
302.72 With inhibited sexual excitement
        (frigidity, impotence)
302.73 With inhibited female orgasm
302.74 With inhibited male orgasm
302.75 With premature ejaculation
302.76 With functional dyspareunia
306.51 With functional vaginismus
302.79 Other

OTHER PSYCHOSEXUAL DISORDERS

302.01 Ego-dystonic homosexuality
302.90 Psychosexual disorder not elsewhere
        classified

DISORDERS USUALLY ARISING IN CHILDHOOD OR ADOLESCENCE

This section lists conditions that usually first manifest themselves in childhood or adolescence. Any appropriate adult diagnosis can be used for diagnosing a child.

MENTAL RETARDATION

317.00 Mild mental retardation
318.00 Moderate mental retardation
318.10 Severe mental retardation
318.20 Profound mental retardation
319.00 Unspecified mental retardation

PERVASIVE DEVELOPMENTAL DISORDERS

299.00 Infantile autism
299.80 Atypical childhood psychosis

SPECIFIC DEVELOPMENTAL DISORDERS

315.60 Specific reading disorder
315.10 Specific arithmetical disorder
315.32 Developmental language disorder
315.39 Developmental articulation disorder
307.60 Enuresis
307.70 Encopresis
315.50 Mixed
315.80 Other

ATTENTION DEFICIT DISORDERS

314.00 With hyperactivity
314.10 Without hyperactivity

CONDUCT DISORDERS

312.00 Undersocialized conduct disorder
        aggressive type
312.10 Undersocialized conduct disorder,
        unaggressive type
312.20 Socialized conduct disorder

ANXIETY DISORDERS OF CHILDHOOD OR ADOLESCENCE

309.21 Separation anxiety disorder
313.21 Shyness disorder
313.00 Overanxious disorder

OTHER DISORDERS OF CHILDHOOD OR ADOLESCENCE

313.22 Introverted disorder of childhood
313.81 Oppositional disorder
313.23 Elective mutism
313.83 Academic underachievement disorder

DISORDERS CHARACTERISTIC OF LATE ADOLESCENCE

309.22 Emancipation disorder of adoles-
        cence or early adult life
313.82 Identity disorder
309.23 Specific academic or work inhibition

EATING DISORDERS

307.10 Anorexia nervosa
307.51 Bulimia
307.52 Pica
307.53 Rumination
307.59 Atypical

SPEECH DISORDERS

307.00 Stuttering

STEREOTYPED MOVEMENT DISORDERS

307.21 Transient tic disorder
307.22 Chronic motor tic disorder
307.23 Tourette's disorder
307.20 Atypical tic disorder
307.30 Other

REACTIVE DISORDERS NOT ELSEWHERE CLASSIFIED

POST-TRAUMATIC STRESS DISORDER

308.30 Acute
309.81 Chronic

ADJUSTMENT DISORDERS

309.00 With depressed mood
309.24 With anxious mood
309.28 With mixed emotional features
309.82 With physical symptoms
309.30 With disturbance of conduct
309.40 With mixed disturbance of emotions
        and conduct
309.83 With withdrawal
309.89 Other

DISORDERS OF IMPULSE CONTROL NOT ELSEWHERE CLASSIFIED

312.31 Pathological gambling
312.32 Kleptomania
312.33 Pyromania
312.34 Intermittent explosive disorder
312.35 Isolated explosive disorder
312.39 Other impulse control disorder

OTHER DISORDERS

UNSPECIFIED MENTAL DISORDER (NON-PSYCHOTIC)

V40.90 Unspecified mental disorder
        (non-psychotic)

Note: The traditional neurotic subtypes are included in the Affective, Anxiety, Somatoform, and Dissociative Disorders.

FUNDAMENTALS OF ABNORMAL PSYCHOLOGY

FUNDAMENTALS OF ABNORMAL PSYCHOLOGY

FREDERICK MEARS
Texas Eastern University

ROBERT J. GATCHEL
University of Texas at Arlington and
University of Texas
Health Science Center at Dallas

**RAND McNALLY
COLLEGE PUBLISHING COMPANY**
Chicago

WITH LOVE TO OUR DAUGHTERS
Tammy Mears
Holly Mears
Jennifer Rose Gatchel

78 79 80 10 9 8 7 6 5 4 3 2 1

SPONSORING EDITOR Louise Waller
PROJECT EDITOR Geoffrey Huck
DESIGNERS Gary John Fedota, Kristin Nelson

PREFACE

We have both regularly taught a course in abnormal psychology over a period of years and, as a result, have seriously considered what undergraduate students want to know about abnormal behavior in writing this text. Students most often ask for definitions of the various kinds of abnormal behavior and the causes that underlie such behavior. Learning the essential features of the several types of psychopathology, and developing an understanding of the human experience that is part of a given psychological disturbance, allows students to appreciate what abnormality is, how it feels, and what it means to the individual involved. Also, how the various types of abnormal behavior are assessed and treated is another area of special interest to students.

We feel it is important to begin a discussion of this developing and changing field by providing a comprehensive overview that stresses the need for students to learn how to evaluate theories, research, and the issues of methodology in a critical manner. Only by developing such a critical faculty can students distinguish the value of new information. Is it purely speculative or will it be substantiated and supported at some level?

The major theoretical orientations of the field of abnormal psychology are comprehensively covered in this text. How social-learning, psychodynamic, phenomenological-existential, and biological theories have been used in assessment and treatment approaches is another important feature of the book. In order to include all of this material, each chapter in part II first discusses a major form of psychopathology, then describes symptoms, causes, assessment, treatment, and the prognosis for improvement. The discussion of a specific disorder covers all aspects of the disorder in one place. Many case studies provide illustrations of particular kinds of abnormal behavior and changes that can be brought about in such behavior.

The text is divided into three major parts. Beginning with an historical overview of the field, various theoretical points of view are surveyed, and then issues involved in the classification and assessment of abnormal behavior are given. The proposed reclassification of behaviors, the DSM-III, now being developed by the American Psychiatric Association, has been incorporated throughout the text wherever possible, and this has been compared with the older DSM-II.

Part II of the text reviews the major forms of psychopathology. Each chapter begins with important statistics associated with the disorder. These give the prevalence of the disorder, the usual age of onset, and the ratio of males to females who exhibit the disorder.

Part III considers psychological problems characteristic of specific ages from childhood to old age.

The initial drafts of the present text bear only slight resemblance to the final product. Extensive revisions were made based on the diverse and expert comments we received from colleagues who regularly teach abnormal psychology courses. We were especially aided in our writing task by the penetrating critiques and suggestions made by a number of colleagues who reviewed one or more of the chapters: Juris Draguns, Steen Halling, Richard McFall, Jacob Orlofsky, Robert P. Rugel, Leonard W. Sushinsky, and Andrea Weiland. A number of our talented students provided some illuminating comments: thanks to Marianne Clark, Elizabeth Gaas-Abrams, Sandy Snyder, and Anita Taunton-Blackwood. Also, Tricia Cogdell and Anne Williams assisted valuably with references.

We would also like to thank and acknowledge the great amount of help we received from the staff at Rand McNally: Charles H. Heinle, Geoffrey Huck, Barbara Simons, Gary Fedota, Jenny Gilbertson, Rebecca Strehlow, and, in particular, Louise Waller. Finally, special thanks are expressed to Mary Johnson, who provided secretarial assistance in organizing and typing the contents of the manuscript.

G.M.
R.G.

CONTENTS

PART 1

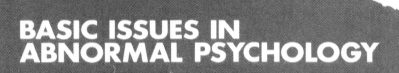

BASIC ISSUES IN
ABNORMAL PSYCHOLOGY

1

THE ROOTS OF ABNORMAL PSYCHOLOGY

OVERVIEW In this chapter, we will cover four basic topics concerning the historical roots of abnormal psychology. We will begin with the supernatural approach and then examine the early psychopathologies, the emergence of physical treatments, and the rise of psychological treatments. These sections cover a broad span of time, from before the time of ancient Greece to the present.

In the first section, we will examine ancient efforts to explain abnormal behavior, as well as primitive attempts at therapy. The topics of spirit intrusion (demonic possession) and shamanism comprise much of this introductory section. We will then discuss efforts to treat the mentally disturbed with rather humane physical therapies. The section concludes with a review of the Middle Ages and the revival of demonology. Spirit intrusion, the association of the mentally ill with the devil, and the relationship between witchcraft and insanity will be examined.

In the second section, we will discuss the early psychopathologies, setting the stage for the discussions of modern syndromes in later chapters. We will briefly trace the development of the following syndromes: anxiety, melancholia, mania, dementia, amentia, moral insanity, and hysteria. We will point out early descriptions of these syndromes, name changes that ensued, and, in some cases, early treatment strategies.

The third section focuses on the emergence of physical treatments—those methods widely and typically used to treat a wide variety of symptoms. For example, we will examine venesection (bleeding), bowel purging, and the use of early drugs. Also in this section we will describe the early lunatic asylum.

The fourth and final section examines the rise of psychological treatments (moral management). In this section we highlight three important individuals—Philippe Pinel, William Tuke, and Dorothea Dix—who fostered the growth of humane treatment for the mentally disturbed. We also trace the development of hypnotism from its roots with Mesmer to its evolution as a tool in psychotherapy. In the remaining parts of this section we will examine modern extensions of moral management: the state mental hospital and the community mental health center. The chapter concludes with an introduction to community psychology and a description of the functions and problems facing community mental health centers.

THE SUPERNATURAL APPROACH

DEMONIC POSSESSION AND SHAMANISM

For thousands of years, people have relied on the supernatural to explain the behavior of the mentally disturbed. Malevolent gods, demons, witches, werewolves, vampires, and even the moon and planets have been used to account for mental disorders. Imbedded in the folklore of many cultures is the notion that a person can be inhabited or possessed by supernatural forces. In Norse mythology, for example, mania, hysteria, hypnotism, and other odd behaviors were explained as manifestations of supernatural beings within the person. In Babylon, more than three thousand years ago, the Akkadians wrote extensively about the power of spirits and how they could possess a person. The mythology of the Far East contains similar beliefs about the spirit world and possession. For example, the fox was viewed as a supernatural creature having the power to reshape itself and enter the body of a man or woman, inducing madness. Other cultures also had their own feared animals or beings that they believed could possess and control people.

Without exception, the most feared and most widely acknowledged supernatural force was the devil. Known by such names as Satan, Lucifer, Leviathan, and Belphegor, the devil reigned supreme for centuries as the major provoker of madness. As we shall see, the demonologists of the Middle Ages provided volumes of literature describing the characteristics of possession by the devil and how such possession was to be treated.

An important point about spirit intrusion or demonic possession is that the possessed person was often viewed as being evil or nefarious. Madness was often associated with sin or estrangement from God. This is a significant point because the belief that the mentally disturbed were evil probably intensified the inhumane treatment characteristically administered to them. No doubt the belief that a madman was not just crazy but evil fostered the merciless and inhumane treatments that prevailed in early lunatic asylums.

Some years ago, Forest Clements (1932) detailed primitive peoples' views of disease and corresponding therapy. His findings bear directly on the supernatural view of mental disturbance. Table 1.1 lists five disease theories and five corresponding therapies as outlined by Clements. Category 3, spirit intrusion, is basically what we have been discussing. Although the other four disease theories played some role in accounting for

Cited in Ellenberger 1970, p. 5

DISEASE THEORY	THERAPY
1. Disease-object intrusion	Extraction of disease object (e.g., a splinter)
2. Loss of the soul	To find, bring back, and restore the lost soul
3. Spirit intrusion	a. Exorcism
	b. Mechanical extraction of the foreign spirit
	c. Transference of the foreign spirit into another living being
4. Breach of taboo	Confession, propitiation
5. Sorcery	Counter-magic

PRIMITIVE DISEASE THEORIES
Table 1.1

PRIMITIVE PSYCHOSURGERY— TREPHINING

One ancient surgical procedure used in expelling a spirit was trephining (or trepanning). Evidence from ancient skulls suggests that trephining was performed thousands of years ago, apparently as a therapeutic strategy. Briefly, trephining involved cutting or chipping out a sizable portion of the skull with a chisel or stone hammer. The operation produced a gaping hole through which a demon could escape—at least this notion is one possible reason for trephining, although there doubtless could have been other reasons for this crude surgical procedure. The photograph shows a patient from whose skull a large circular disc has been removed.

Trepanned skulls of prehistoric times have been found in Britain and France, in other parts of Europe, and in Peru. The practice still exists among tribal and aboriginal people in parts of Algeria, in Melanesia, and perhaps elsewhere, but it is fast becoming extinct.

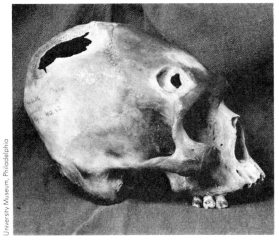

University Museum, Philadelphia

A trephined skull from Tacna, Peru. Trephination was performed as early as 5,000 years ago. A perforation was made in the skull with a sharp instrument. It is speculated that the operation was not always fatal.

the mentally disturbed, spirit intrusion was for many years the etiological model for madness.

From primitive times through the Middle Ages, spirit intrusion was dealt with or treated by various magical processes or pseudo-medical techniques. Ellenberger (1970) describes three principal methods used to expel intrusive spirits.

1. Expelling the spirit or demon by physical means—beating, bleeding, exposing the possessed to foul odors or loud noises, or having the possessed drink horrendous concoctions.
2. Transferring the spirit into the body of another creature—either the shaman or an animal.
3. Exorcising the spirit through ''psychic means.'' These include incantations, tricks, magic, or prayer.

The *shaman* played a major role in treating spirit intrusion, other diseases, and treatment in general. In broad terms, a shaman is a special priest, witch doctor, or medicine man who by magic supposedly acquires supernatural power that he uses to treat the sick person. In ancient times most therapy procedures (such as those described by Clements in table 1.1) were under the direction of a shaman.

In a typical scenario of shamanism, the priest-doctor excites himself into a wild frenzy and passes into a trance, at which time he acquires supernatural power and can then perform unearthly feats of healing (Wilson 1971). With the rise of Aegean civilization and the subsequent development of Roman civilization, shamanism and demonology gradually lessened. The Greco-Roman period provided humane therapies for the mentally disturbed and also offered physical explanations for mental disturbances.

THE MIDDLE AGES

The decline of the Greco-Roman era led to the deterioration of rationalism, accompanied by the disappearance of humane treatment of the ill and physical explanations for mental disturbances. Moreover, the Western world, after the collapse of the Roman empire, gradually became church-dominated. Many historians assert that the resurrection of demonology, in particular the notion of possession, was used by the church hierarchy to account for the many natural disasters that beset Europe during the Middle Ages. For example, it

THE DECLINE OF DEMONOLOGY

Belief in demonic possession and various brands of shamanism were prevalent prior to the time of Plato and the flourishing of Greek and Roman rationalism. But during the Greco-Roman era, numerous scientists and philosophers suggested that the supernatural played no part in mental disturbances. The Greek physician Hippocrates (460–377 B.C.) suggested that mental disorders probably had their origin in some brain dysfunction. He proposed, for example, that the brain might be affected by various imbalances of body fluids such as bile and blood.

Hippocrates also developed an early classification system of mental disorders that included encephalitis (then called "phrenitis"), mania, and melancholia. Moreover, he advocated therapy procedures quite apart from the magical procedures used for expelling spirits. For example, rest, a good diet, exercise, and other therapies unusual for this time were prescribed.

Hippocrates' classification systems, in addition to his humane treatment methods for the mentally disturbed, represented advanced thinking. But after the Greco-Roman period ended, the two major trends that emerged were a more vigorous use of the supernatural to account for mental disturbances and an increase in inhumane treatment of the mentally disturbed.

HANDBOOK OF THE WITCH-HUNTER

It was during the Middle Ages that a handbook for witch-hunters was published. This "divinely inspired" text, known as *Malleus Maleficarum* or "The Hammer of Witches" (1486), was perhaps the most sinister guide to terror and inhumanity ever written. As Robbins (1959) tells us, it had authority and credibility because its authors were two well-known and respected scholars: Johann Sprenger, who was Dean of Cologne University, and Heinrich Kraemer, who held high offices in the church. The text of Sprenger and Kraemer had three basic sections, each dealing with specific undertakings for the judge or hangman. The first part of the text stressed the enormity of witchcraft, and here Sprenger and Kraemer attempted to arouse the readers' fear of and hatred toward witches. To achieve this goal, the first section gave biblical quotes and commandments to demonstrate that God was forcibly opposed to witches and wished for their extermination. Absolutely, the word of God did convince and suggest to many that witches existed and should be destroyed (Exodus 22:18: "Thou shalt not suffer a witch to live," or Leviticus 20:27: "A man also or woman that hath a familiar spirit, or that is a wizard, shall surely be put to death: they shall stone them with stones; their blood shall be upon them").

In the second section, Sprenger and Kraemer examined methods for identifying possession and counteracting its effects and clearly described the symptoms of possession. Part three of the manuscript concerned itself with the procedures for examining and passing sentence on the accused person. In point of fact, to be absolutely positive that the charged person was a witch, it was always necessary to obtain a confession. Clearly, the horrors of this document rested in this section, which gave specific directions for extracting a confession by specific tortures: thumbscrewing, strappado (in which the victims were hoisted by a rope fastened to their wrists, with their arms tied behind their backs, and then dropped just short of the floor), whipping, binding, tearing the flesh with red-hot pincers, or pressing the accused into a spiked chair. Finally, the book described in all its gory detail the execution of the witch. The person was to be burned alive with green firewood, making for a very slow and agonizing death.

The abhorrent practices outlined in *Malleus Maleficarum* were not isolated cases. In England alone, the number of witch burnings was staggering. Robert Steele estimates that between 1603 and 1628, 70,000 people were burned as witches (Robbins 1959). In Germany, 100,000 people were burned, and historians suggest doubling this figure for the whole of Europe. (Robbins 1959)

From *The Encyclopedia of Witchcraft and Demonology*, by Russell Hope Robbins,
© 1959 by Crown Publishers. Used by permission of Crown Publishers

**It was widely held that witches poisoned
people by using killing ointment, a con-
coction made from roots, animals and
fish, snakes, and stones. In this seventeenth century woodcut, three witches
are about to rub killing ointment on a
sleeping woman.**

COTTON MATHER ON WITCHCRAFT

The devils, after a most preternatural manner, by
the dreadful judgment of heaven, took a bodily
possession of many people in Salem, and the
adjacent places; and the houses of the poor people began to be filled with the horrid cries of
persons tormented by evil spirits. These seemed
an execrable witchcraft in the foundation of this
wonderful affliction, and many persons, of divers
characters, were accused, apprehended, prose-
cuted upon the visions of the afflicted. For my
own part, I was always afraid of proceeding to
commit and condemn any person, as a confeder-
ate with affecting demons, upon so feeble an evidence as a spectral representative. Accordingly, I
ever testified against it, both publicly and privately.

From *The Diary of Cotton Mather*, 1692.

was an almost universal belief that the plague was
punishment sent by God for the wickedness of
people. Witches, however, also were blamed for
spreading the plague with their "killing ointments"
(Robbins 1959).

It is important to make a distinction between
early views of "insanity" and of "witchcraft." For
one, insanity was the best possible defense against
the charge of witchcraft (Robbins 1959). That is to
say, many accused of being a witch — a much more
serious charge — tried to convince their accusers
that they were not witches but rather were mad. In
fact, a witch was held responsible for causing

insanity in others. Thus two treatments existed: one
for the possessed (the insane) and another for the
witch. Treatment of possession consisted mainly of
such exorcistic rituals as incantation, prayer, sprin-
kling the possessed with holy water, placing charms
on the four corners of the bed of the possessed,
and blessing the bed. Although the treatment for
the possessed could be harsh at times, the objective
was rarely to kill the person. By contrast, witches
were to be punished and usually killed for their
deeds. Rather than being seen as insane — victims
of the devil — witches were viewed as willing ac-
complices of Satan.

THE EARLY PSYCHOPATHOLOGIES

Although possession was considered to be the most
extreme form of insanity or mental illness, for many
centuries physicians have documented a number of
milder symptoms equated with emotional disturbances. In this section we shall present the most
frequently reported symptoms of abnormal behavior recorded. It is interesting to note that many of
the symptoms reported by people today were also
reported thousands of years ago. In some cases,
the names of the clinical syndromes have changed;

in others they have been retained. We shall also
look at various treatment procedures that were
employed to treat these syndromes.

ANXIETY

Since the time of Hippocrates, persistent anxiety
(uneasiness, anguish, apprehension, or fearfulness)

has been mentioned by medical writers (Altschule 1976). During the Greco-Roman era the name of this symptom, called *anxiety* today, was ''angor'' or ''inquietude.'' It has been viewed in many different ways. At one extreme were those who viewed anxiety (angor) as a signal of insanity or madness. It was also sometimes viewed as a symptom of imbecility. At the other extreme were those who viewed anxiety as a symptom of situational stresses. Generally, however, many physicians from the sixteenth to the eighteenth century viewed anxiety as the basic symptom of mental illness.

During the nineteenth century, medical writers, in particular Heinrich Neumann (1814–1884), suggested that anxiety originated when an individual's needs or desires were frustrated. Sigmund Freud, as we shall see in chapter 3, apparently used Neumann's notions of anxiety to formulate the underpinnings of psychoanalysis. (In chapter 3, under psychoanalysis, we shall again discuss certain features of anxiety. A more formal presentation of anxiety and neurosis will be given in chapter 6.)

MELANCHOLIA (DEPRESSION)

Melancholia was one of the first recorded emotional disturbances. This reaction has generally signified a state of gloominess, despair, and depression. During the Greco-Roman era, the diagnostic label of ''melancholia'' was applied to those who ''weeped without reason.'' Greek physicians speculated that the disorder was caused by an imbalance of body fluids. Vomiting of black bile, for example, was believed to be related to feelings of sadness. Indeed, the term *melancholia* means ''black bile''—from the Greek *melas* ''black'' and *chole* ''bile.''

Numerous physical treatments were prescribed for melancholia in Greco-Roman times. Soaking the body in wine or diluted vinegar, applying plasters to the body, and drinking various herbs were typical therapeutic methods (Goshen 1967). A nonphysical or environmental treatment used in ancient Greece was *incubation*. This involved ''lying on the ground,'' specifically in a sacred cavern or cave. It was maintained that a supine person would ultimately sleep, and that during sleep the patient would receive an oracle or vision that would cure him or her (Ellenberger 1970).

In medieval times, melancholia was sometimes viewed as a symptom of possession. For example, one of the eleven indications of possession spelled out by Rouen (1644) was ''to be tired of living.'' Often melancholia was associated with suicide attempts and the loss of desire to live.

By the 1800s little had been written about the possible causes of melancholia. Instead, various clinicians were reporting new manifestations of melancholia. Refusal to eat, slowness of movement, and slow speech began to be viewed as other symptoms of this reaction. During the 1800s, Jean-Etienne Esquirol further suggested that a patient could be insane as well as depressed. He called this disorder *lypemania,* or partial insanity.

MANIA

Like melancholia, *mania* was also considered a major psychopathology in ancient times. Plato saw mania and ignorance as two major mental disorders, and Hippocrates and Galen added epilepsy to this list. In ancient Greece, *mania* referred to a condition in which a person went wild or mad. Aretus (second century A.D.) describes the syndrome in these words:

> [The manic would] . . . laugh, play, dance night and day. . . . Others have madness . . . with anger; and these sometimes rend their clothes and kill their keepers, and lay violent hands upon themselves.

Relative to modern classifications of bipolar affective disorders, Alexander of Tralles (A.D. 525–605) observed that some patients oscillated between mania and melancholia. In the 1800s, Falret, a French physician, observed a ''circular insanity'' (*folie circulaire*) in which mania alternated with melancholia.

For centuries, mania alone has signified a clinical form of delirium in which ideas run wildly together, judgment is impaired, and incoherence and great excitement prevail. John Haslam (1764–1844), a superintendent of the Bethlehem Asylum in London, described the manic person as one who had a ''succession of ideas . . . too rapid to be examined.'' As we shall see in chapter 8, these early accounts resemble recent clinical descriptions.

The treatment of mania has involved numerous physical remedies. In the Greco-Roman

HISTORICAL VIEWS OF MASTURBATION

[A] young man of fine physical development . . . wrote good verses and practiced masturbation to excess. [He] asked for medical advice . . . [and] was persuaded to try severe manual labor, he cleared six acres of heavily timbered beech and sugar tree bottoms . . . was cured and rose to distinction in civil life. (*New Orleans Medical and Surgical Journal*, 1855)

Today it is hard to believe that many individuals with great power and prestige, those who directed other people's lives, could have been so misguided where masturbation was concerned. Antimasturbation literature influenced not only the general public and clergy, but also physicians. The literature condemning masturbation began in 1700 with the publication of a book titled *Onania; or, the Heinous Sin of Self-Pollution and All Its Frightful Consequences.* In 1758 a French physician, S. D. Tissot, published a text (*Onan*) that also dealt with diseases induced by "onanism" or masturbation. Even major figures such as Benjamin Rush (1745–1813), the father of American psychiatry, supported antimasturbation writings (Spitz 1952).

The orgasm similarly was once looked on as a perverse phenomenon. As late as the 1890s, the Boston physician E. W. Cushing contended

that the process of having an orgasm was a disease and should be treated by asexualizing the patient by means of castration (Baker-Benfield 1976). (This was considered particularly the case for women who had orgasms.) Baker-Benfield (1976) hints that the rise of gynecology was, in part, an effort to control and asexualize women. One woman who had had a clitorectomy to correct the "disease of masturbation" made this statement:

My condition is all I could desire. I know and feel that I am well; I never think of self-abuse; it is foreign and distasteful to me. (Dunn 1987, cited in Baker-Benefield 1976)

In this general connection, Karlen (1971) notes that in the 1890s and early 1900s castrations and vasectomies were performed on feeble-minded children to lessen their masturbation. In 1899, Dr. Sharp of the Indiana State Reformatory claimed that severing the sperm ducts (vasectomy) gave the young male inmates "a more sunny disposition, brighter intellect [and ceased their] excessive masturbation."

Finally, Wilhelm Griesinger (1817–1868), like many other psychiatrists of that era, contended that masturbation during childhood led to insanity. Indeed, even schizophrenia was once labeled "masturbative insanity."

---

period, bathing, fasting, and drinking herbs were commonly prescribed. Incubation was the typical environmental treatment. During the Middle Ages and through the 1700s, bleeding and special drugs were employed. (In chapter 8, we will thoroughly review affective reactions, examining both mania and melancholia as well as bipolar reactions.)

DEMENTIA (THE THOUGHT DISORDER)

Dementia is one of the most ancient diagnostic labels (Altschule 1976). Both in the past, and to some extent in modern times, dementia refers to the inability to reason. The label further signifies that the person at one time did have reasoning

abilities, but later lost his or her intellectual functioning. By contrast, *amentia,* or mental retardation, implies that the person never had adequate intellectual skills.

In the early 1800s, Pinel used the term *dementia* to refer to schizophrenic or psychotic patients. Some time after this, John Haslam of London's Bethlehem Asylum described a subvariety of dementia characterized by progressive emotional deterioration and withdrawal. This particular syndrome was later named *hebephrenia.* Later still, in the middle of the 1800s, Benedict Morel coined the term "dementia praecox" to refer to a puberty-onset dementia (Sahakian 1975). This term finally fell into disuse, and the condition was renamed schizophrenia. (In chapter 9 we will review in detail schizophrenic syndromes, their etiol-

Alexander Morison in 1824 published this sketch of a "Female Idiot," with a large head and a "humoured expression." Apparently she was quite retarded, since Morison reports that she could not be taught to dress herself.

This picture from Morison is of "a Female labouring under partial insanity with depression." The depression, Morison tells us, was occasioned by the loss of a brother. She refused to eat, and would not speak or move for long periods. Two years later, she died.

ogy, and treatment. In chapters 14 and 18, we will also discuss dementia again; in those chapters, however, the term is used to refer to organic brain syndromes.)

AMENTIA (MENTAL RETARDATION)

Perhaps no syndrome has been described so thoroughly throughout history as mental retardation. It was described in ancient Greece and extensively throughout Europe during the Middle Ages. The mentally retarded, the demented, and a host of other individuals suffering diverse impairments often were treated similarly and confined to large asylums. But while mental retardation has been described since ancient Greece, it was not until the time of Jean Itard, Philippe Pinel, and Edouard Seguin that attempts were made to do more than confine the retarded. During the late 1700s and early 1800s, Seguin and the others made consistent efforts to rehabilitate the mentally retarded. Although Seguin believed that "idiots" were suffering from a prolonged infancy—a consequence, he thought, of nutritional deficiency during their neonatal period—he maintained that these people could be cured.

We should also note that many efforts were

made to classify retardates according to their level of intellectual functioning. The name for the syndrome also changed frequently. For centuries it was referred to as "amentia." Later these names were used: oligophrenia ("little mind"), idiocy, imbecility, feeble-mindedness, mentally handicapped, mentally deficient, mentally subnormal, and so on. (In chapter 15 we shall explore in detail modern views of mental retardation—how it is assessed, its levels and classifications, etiological theories, and remedial and preventive issues.)

MORAL INSANITY

Monomania was a broad diagnostic category used in the 1800s to refer to disorders in which the person appeared normal in almost every respect, except one area of deviance. Moral insanity (as well as nymphomania) was a prime illustration of monomania.

About 1837, an English psychiatrist, James Pritchard, coined the term moral insanity to refer to persons who were not insane in the classical sense. While the diagnostic terms of Pritchard's day included such labels as "dementia" and "amentia," there was no diagnostic category for those individuals who were insane with regard to ethics and morality. Pritchard recognized that those described with his new label could reason; that is, they did not hallucinate. Further, he was aware that they were not retarded or amented. But the morally insane repeatedly made poor judgments concerning their ethical conduct. According to Pritchard and other clinicians of that time, these individuals were criminally inclined and "commit every species of mischief. . . ." Cesare Lombroso (1836–1909) also dealt with the morally insane in his position as superintendent of an Italian prison. Lombroso proposed that the morally insane and criminals were "throwbacks" to prehistoric people.

Other than custodial care, no systematic treatment efforts were proposed to treat the morally insane. The lack of systematic therapy efforts may be traced to the belief that moral insanity was inherited.

The future of the diagnostic label "moral insanity" was limited. Later the term *psychopathic inferiority* replaced it, and this in turn gradually gave way to the diagnostic term *psychopathic personality*. This was shortened to *psychopath*; still more recently, the term *sociopath* has been widely used. (In chapter 13 we shall cover the concept of moral insanity as well as other antisocial patterns in contemporary life.)

HYSTERIA AND CONVERSION DISORDERS

Hysteria was one of the earliest and most frequently recorded emotional disorders. The Greeks, in particular, pointed out the elaborate symptoms that often accompanied this syndrome. They observed fits of crying, imaginary illnesses, and actual physical symptoms such as blindness and paralysis. According to Greek physicians, however, hysteria could only affect women. This unusual notion, which lasted for centuries, prompted them to name this disorder after women; the term refers to the uterus (*hystera*).

By the late 1700s hysteria was often referred to as *conversion disorder*. This name was used because it was observed that physical symptoms shifted or were converted into a different form. G. M. Burrows (1828), a major psychiatric writer of that day, maintained that many physical illnesses were hysteria in disguise. Epilepsy, mania, and a host of other disorders were viewed by some as forms of hysteria.

By the nineteenth century, hysteria or conversion disorders were generally thought to be a special type of organic brain disease. Standing against this view was the eminent French neurologist Jean-Martin Charcot (1825–1893). From his experiments with hypnotism, Charcot concluded that symptoms could also be shifted about the body in hysteric patients. This finding led him to the conviction that self-hypnotism played a part in the development of hysteria. That is, hysteria was seen as a psychologically induced reaction. (As we shall see in chapter 3, hysteria was to play a significant role in the development of Freud's theories of psychopathology. In chapter 6, we shall discuss hysteria and conversion disorders in more detail.)

EMERGENCE OF PHYSICAL TREATMENTS

Two new ways of handling the mentally ill arose after the Middle Ages—lunatic asylums and special methods of physical treatment. These approaches were alike in one important way: both were inhumane. As Skultan (1975) has written, one guiding principle in the treatment of the mad was to instill fear in them. The remorseless physical treatments that were applied, as well as the institutions themselves, achieved all too well that guiding principle.

Our objective in pointing out the bizarre conditions that prevailed during those times is to illustrate their unbelievable inhumanity and so help you appreciate the significance of the reforms they eventually provoked. Many of the same inhumane and unethical conditions persisted, however, and even today court cases are still attempting to deal with the constitutionality of involuntary commitment and forced treatment.

THE LUNATIC ASYLUMS

In 1257, St. Mary of Bethlehem Hospital was founded in London. Its principal function was to incarcerate a diverse group of social misfits: prostitutes, vagrants, beggars, feeble-minded adults and children, criminals, and, of course, the mad. The hospital became known as "Bedlam" (a slang pronunciation of "Bethlehem"), and its residents were called "Bedlamites." To be sure, it was a place of bedlam—a persistent scene of wild uproar

MALARIA THERAPY

Before the twentieth century, there was no truly effective physical treatment for any type of emotional disorder. Although there were many physical methods in addition to those discussed, none was effective in treating mental disorders from our perspective today.

But in the early twentieth century, a number of physical therapies were developed that purportedly did have therapeutic benefits with a few mental disorders. One of the earliest physical therapies was *malaria therapy*. In 1917, the Austrian neurologist von Jauregg (1857–1940) claimed he had developed a successful treatment for cerebral syphilis. Basically, the treatment involved injecting the patient with blood containing malaria parasites. (The blood had been withdrawn from human patients who had malaria.) After the blood was intramuscularly injected, the syphilitic patient had 10 to 12 fever bouts. As to why malaria therapy was effective in some cases, two explanations were proposed: the first one suggested that an increase in body heat due to fever killed the agents producing the syphilis; the second one suggested that malaria itself somehow produced body defenses that in turn killed the agents.

The discovery of malaria therapy was indeed significant, for it encouraged the search for other physical therapies to treat mental disorders. (Von Jauregg was, in fact, given the 1927 Nobel Prize for medicine.) In particular, it hastened the development of convulsive shock treatments. Manfred Sakel (1900–1957), in the late 1920s, began inducing convulsions and comas in schizophrenic patients by administering high doses of insulin. Malaria therapy slowly fell into disuse, but its emergence fostered numerous varieties of physical therapy.

and confusion. The therapeutic armamentarium of Bedlam included chaining the hands and ankles, beatings, forced nakedness, bleedings, isolation, and public ridicule and mockery. But to outsiders Bedlam was a circus, a place of entertainment. Londoners could spend a Sunday afternoon snickering and teasing the Bedlamites, and all for the price of one shilling (Bromberg 1975).

The lunatic asylum in London was matched by two other so-called hospitals in Paris, the Hospice de Bicêtre and the Hôpital de la Salpêtrière. Bicêtre was an asylum for male patients, and the Salpêtrière was for female patients. The conditions of these asylums resembled closely the unbelievably gruesome conditions at Bedlam. In short, these and most other early asylums were nothing short of barbaric prisons.

PHYSICAL TREATMENT METHODS

BLEEDING (VENESECTION) Between the seventeenth and nineteenth centuries there were many physical methods for treating the insane, but none was practiced more widely than bleeding. One casual view stated that inflammation of the brain, caused by black bile in the blood, resulted in insanity. Blood-letting or *venesection* (a procedure also used to treat physical disorders) was thus employed to reduce "impurities" in the blood. This practice continued well into the 1800s. In the venesection procedure, a vein was opened at the thumb or forefinger or under the tongue, and about 10 ounces of blood removed. Venesection was used to treat a variety of disorders, particularly mania and depression (Burrows 1828). Other physicians and psychiatrists during the 1800s bled patients by placing leeches on the anus. Nymphomania was treated "successfully" by application of leeches to the vulva (Burrows 1828). Even suicide, it was thought, could be prevented by bleeding. These methods were not used just in isolated cases, but were accepted medical procedures.

PURGING Cathartics and emetics were commonly administered as treatments for a variety of mental disorders. It was a commonly held medical belief that constipation provoked and prolonged insanity. Consequently, various methods of purging were applied. For example, at the Salpêtrière in Paris, forced enemas were given regularly. The patients were seated in a specially designed chair where cold water was ". . . propelled . . . full on the anus" (Burrows 1828). Not only were emetics given daily to insane patients to heal them, but in some cases they were given as punishment (Burrows 1828). Another method of purging was to induce vomiting.

OPIUM AND OTHER EARLY DRUGS   Perhaps no drug has been so extensively administered for mental illness as opium (and its derivative morphine). Derived from poppy seeds, opium was used by Hippocrates and other Greek physicians to treat emotional disorders, and so by the seventeenth century it was an established therapeutic agent. In

fact, opium derivatives continued to be given well into the twentieth century (Zilboorg and Henry 1941).

In addition to opium, many other drugs began to be used in the 1700s and 1800s. Tinctures of rhubarb, atropine (belladonna); camphor, and stramonium were gradually beginning to replace bleeding, bowel purging, and other primitive therapies. A little later, *chloral hydrate* (a synthetically produced sedative) and *barbiturates* began to supplant opium and the earlier drugs.

RISE OF PSYCHOLOGICAL TREATMENTS

MORAL MANAGEMENT

The connotation of the term *moral* has changed considerably since the nineteenth century (Skultan 1975). As it was used then, "moral" essentially meant "psychological" or "emotional." A "moral cause" referred to a mental illness that was psychologically induced. In terms of treatment, *moral management* involved using psychological methods more than purely physical methods. Hypnosis and psychotherapy were direct outgrowths of moral management. To some extent, moral management also involved efforts at treating patients with kindness.

Several individuals were important in the rise of moral management. Philippe Pinel, William Tuke, and Dorothea Dix, in particular, did much to humanize the large asylums in both Europe and the United States. In the main, most of the individuals involved in the moral management effort focused first on removing physical restraints. Physical restraints (chains and locked cells, for example) were a basic part of the earlier physical methods. A question often asked by those skeptical of restraint removal was this: "What mode of treatment will replace physical restraints?" Robert Hill, an advocate of moral treatment, stated: "Vigilant and unceasing attendance by day and night—kindness, occupation, and attention to health, cleanliness, and comfort. . . ." (Hill 1839)

PHILIPPE PINEL (1745–1826)   The French physician Philippe Pinel is remembered principally for his unchaining of the mental patients at Bicêtre and Salpêtrière, the Paris hospitals of which he was superintendent. On September 11, 1793, Pinel appealed to the commissioner of prisons to adopt a

new plan: removing the patients' physical restraints and taking the patients from their filthy dungeons. With great reluctance and skepticism the commissioner and warden went along with Pinel's plan. Indeed, the warden taunted Pinel, saying to him, "Are not you yourself crazy that you would unchain these beasts?" (Semelaigne 1894). Nevertheless, the chains were removed, and in their place was used Pinel's new drug: kindness (Bromberg 1975). To the amazement of Pinel's critics, many of the lunatics immediately improved. It was reported that a dazed madman, after being unchained, talked for the first time in years (Bromberg 1975). Pinel's demand was significant, for it started a new trend throughout much of Europe and the United States. He has often been credited with initiating moral management.

WILLIAM TUKE (1732–1822)   William Tuke, a Quaker tea merchant, devoted much of the latter part of his life to bringing about humanitarian reform in lunatic asylums in England. In 1792 Tuke founded the Retreat at York. It was opened to treat about 30 disturbed patients. In contrast to conditions in other asylums, patients at the York retreat were treated as guests, with kindness and respect. Therapeutically, physical treatment was discouraged, but manual labor and occupational therapy were considered beneficial.

DOROTHEA LYNDE DIX (1802–1887)   Although we have already noted the horrendous conditions in early asylums, it is important also to recognize that in the United States there were few asylums at all in the 1600s and 1700s. Dorothea Dix not only became involved in improving conditions in existing hospitals, but she also devoted much of her life to establishing new and better ones.

Philippe Pinel (1745–1826), liberating the patients at Salpêtrière Hospital.

Dorothea Dix, a former schoolteacher, began her crusade in 1841. After observing the sufferings of jailed "lunatics," Dix thereafter became a persistent advocate for proper care of the mentally ill. She wasted little time in trying to help mental patients, but went directly to legislators, even to the President. As a result of her efforts, much changed, and a new wave of concern followed her humanitarian strivings. Because of the monumental improvement in the conditions of asylums, and because of her fostering a new general awareness, Dorothea Dix has been credited with being the greatest social reformer in American history (APA 1944).

THE STATE HOSPITAL

During the 1800s, there was a gradual shift in the sources of funds to operate almshouses, prisons, and asylums. Public sources began to supplant private philanthropy. Massachusetts, for instance, by the 1830s began to consign money for the construction and operation of a large state mental hospital. The State Lunatic Hospital at Worcester, opened in 1833, was to become the prototype of the modern state hospital (Grob 1973).

From the 1800s to the 1960s, state hospitals

Dorothea Dix (1802–1887), a great social reformer, advocated humane treatment for the mentally ill.

HYPNOTISM: A MAJOR PSYCHOLOGICAL TREATMENT

No doubt many ancient shamans used trance states in their healing attempts. Although we have no evidence that hypnotism was practiced by ancient peoples, trance states were probably involved in religious rituals and healing ceremonies. The power of suggestion of the shaman and priests would seem to have been useful. The all-powerful healer, even in early Christian healings, used "the laying-on of hands." Normal objects could take on great healing qualities, it was assumed, if used by a powerful healer. Water, oil, the hands, and saliva were thought to have healing effects when applied with formal ritual by a powerful person. We can be reasonably sure that it was the suggestibility of the person healed, coupled with the commands of the healer, that produced positive results.

The exorcist-healer Johann Gassner (1727–1779), an Austrian priest, employed "the laying-on of hands" and trance induction to heal people. An immensely popular man, Gassner had a huge following who attended his public healings. Through inducing a trance state in a subject, Gassner would demonstrate how the symptoms expressed by the sick person could be shifted about. He maintained that the symptoms were often manifestations of the devil; thus his trance induction sought to purge the devil. Gassner's use of trance induction or suggestion is one of the earliest documented accounts of a rudimentary form of hypnotism.

At approximately the same time as Gassner was attempting to heal people, Franz Anton Mesmer (1733–1815), an Austrian physician, was also experimenting with trance states. Mesmer, unlike the exorcist Gassner, believed that "animal magnetism" existed throughout the universe and that the human body was susceptible to being influenced by magnetic forces. Mesmer demonstrated to many scientists and patients what he thought were magnetic forces within the body. He could lay his hands on various subjects, and particular symptoms or behaviors would appear. After convincing several people of the power of magnetism, Mesmer set up practice. Dr. Mesmer's clinic contained a great copper bath or tub with flooring covered with powdered glass. From the tub protruded metal rods and twists of wire that could be grasped by those watching the magnetizing. Mesmer would gravely touch each member of the audience with a magnetized iron wand (Bromberg 1975). Then he would touch the patient. One eyewitness wrote:

> Mesmer, dressed in a lilac coat, moved about, extending a magic wand . . . gazing steadily into their eyes, while he held both hands in his, bringing the middle fingers in immediate contact, to establish the communication. (DeCourmelles 1891, p. 8)

Eventually Mesmer's notions about animal magnetism were rejected by most medical people. Yet the apparent trance state induced by his procedures, the so-called "magnetic sleep," was still unexplained.

The middle and late 1800s witnessed the rise of a procedure very similar to mesmerism. This time it had a new name: hypnotism. Soon a few prominent physicians, including Hippolyte-Marie Bernheim (1840–1919) and Jean-Martin Charcot (1825–1893), began using hypnotism as a medical therapy. Neurological problems, hysteria, paralysis, epilepsy, and many other problems, medical as well as psychological, were treated by hypnotism. Charcot had contended that hysteria was somehow linked to self-hypnotism, and the idea of self-hypnotism and hysteria in general enhanced his belief in an unconscious mind.

Hypnotism, then, was the main psychological therapy of the 1800s. In Charcot's hypnotic demonstrations, many people witnessed how symptoms could be removed or shifted about by suggestion. In turn, many clinicians began to move from organic explanations of emotional disorders toward psychological ones. Thus hypnotism became the first formal psychotherapy. Soon new variants of hypnotism emerged. In Vienna, the physician Josef Breuer was encouraging his patients, under hypnosis, to talk about troubling events. Another young neurologist, Sigmund Freud, was also using hypnotism to get out pent-up emotions. The foundations of psychoanalysis had finally been established.

were the main source of custodial and therapeutic care for the mentally disturbed. For years the state hospital was the only resource for treatment (Pollack and Taube 1975). More recently, however, the resident population of state hospitals has been declining rather dramatically. For instance, in 1963, the resident population for state hospitals was approximately 500,000. By 1972 this figure had decreased to a little over 275,000 (Gottesman 1975; Pollack and Taube 1975). This represented a national decrease of about 40 percent.

While no single factor can explain this dramatic decrease, several causes have been suggested. For one, the introduction of psychoactive drugs has been suggested as a major reason why severely disturbed patients can continue treatment on an out-patient basis. For another, during the 1960s community mental health centers began to spring up across the country. These centers treated patients who previously would certainly have had to be treated in a state hospital (Gottesman 1975). We shall look briefly at the development of community psychology and the community mental health movement.

COMMUNITY PSYCHOLOGY AND COMMUNITY MENTAL HEALTH CENTERS

Community psychology has as its main goal the prevention of human problems through community and social intervention (Korchin 1976). In the main, this relatively new field models itself after public health medicine. Public health medicine, for example, provides services and information to people so that diseases will be prevented. Vaccinations and chlorination of water are two typical public health efforts. Similarly, community psychology approaches the problem of mental illness from the angle of prevention. Preventive efforts focus on altering the social environment or social institutions — schools, the family, and the like — so that the individual's vulnerability to stresses will be lessened.

In 1955, the Joint Commission on Mental Illness and Health recommended that construction of large state hospitals cease. In their place would be created regional community mental health centers that would provide comprehensive services. By "comprehensive services" the federal government meant such things as in-patient care, out-patient care, emergency care, partial hospitalization, and community consultation programs. Crit-

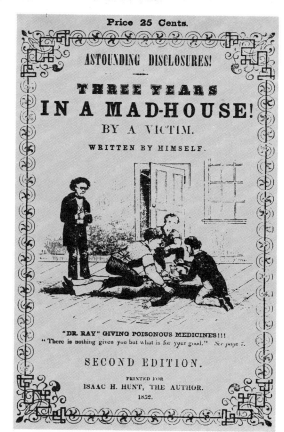

Isaac H. Hunt wrote this pamphlet, published in 1852, attacking current methods of treatment in mental hospitals.

ics, however, have suggested that not all these services are being provided.

Since the major thrust of community psychology is community intervention, let us examine briefly three major strategies. First is *crisis intervention*. In crisis intervention, short-term emergency psychotherapy or counseling is provided for those experiencing a temporary or situational problem. For example, a person contemplating suicide may call a "hot line" number to get immediate emotional support. Second is *community consultation*. Consultant services are provided to other agencies (schools or hospitals, for example) that may encounter individuals with problems. Generally, the consultant is either called in to work directly with troubled individuals or used for in-service education for other professionals. The third strategy, *use of paraprofessionals,* involves having people without formal training work in various mental health programs. The paraprofessionals themselves may have been, for instance, criminals, drug users, or child abusers who now wish to help other people with similar difficulties (Korchin 1976).

Although community mental health centers were in vogue between the 1960s and the late 1970s, during this span critics also voiced concern about the accomplishments of community psychology goals and the effectiveness of community centers. Shortly, after the community movement commenced, a study by Glassocote, Sanders, Forstenzer, and Foley (1964) suggested that most mental health centers were not complying with the original goals set forth by Congress, that is, "comprehensive services." This 1964 survey suggested that most centers were in fact providing typical services, for the most part standard psychotherapy. More recent surveys have also pointed out the lack of comprehensive services. For exam-

ple, it has been suggested that many centers did not emphasize a broad array of services (consultation, use of paraprofessionals), but were instead very traditional, medically dominated therapy centers (Chu and Trotter 1972).

We should note finally that empirical data are needed concerning the effectiveness of both community mental health therapy efforts and preventive strategies. Specifically, there is no evidence yet to suggest that these centers can prevent the development of psychopathologies (Cowen 1973). Although the enthusiasm for the goals of community psychology may have been somewhat thwarted in the 1970s, future investigation into the effectiveness of community programs needs to be undertaken so that the goals can be retained or redefined.

SUMMARY

1. Ancient people commonly believed that mental disturbances were due to demons and other supernatural forces. Spirit intrusion was the typical supernatural explanation for abnormal behavior. Ellenberger (1970) notes that there were many magical or pseudo-medical means for treating spirit intrusion. *Trephining* is one example of a pseudo-medical procedure. It involved removing a portion of the skull, thus allowing the spirit to escape.

2. During the Greco-Roman era there was a decline in the belief of spirit intrusion as an explanation for abnormal behavior. Hippocrates and other physicians of this time began to seek physical explanations for mental disturbances. For example, an imbalance of body fluids (humors) was thought to account for deviant behavior.

3. The Middle Ages witnessed the reemergence of demonology. Many church officials insisted that the plague and other plights of this period were the responsibility of witches and the devil. *Malleus Maleficarum,* a textbook for witch-hunters, described how to identify the possessed and the witch, and how to extract confessions. As a rule, the insane were believed to be possessed, but were not believed to be evil. The witch, on the other hand, was held responsible for the possession and so was

viewed as vile and wicked, but not usually considered mentally disturbed.

4. In addition to possession or spirit intrusion, there existed numerous ancient psychopathologies. *Anxiety* (or *angor*) was recorded as early as the Greco-Roman period. It was originally thought to be a sign of madness. Much later, anxiety became the hallmark of neurotic disorders. *Melancholia* was the term used for many centuries to refer to depression. Like anxiety, melancholia was observed thousands of years ago. During the Greco-Roman era, melancholia was thought to be caused by an excess of black bile. Ancient treatments for melancholia included incubation (reclining in a sacred cave) and the application of wine, vinegar, and plasters to the body.

5. *Mania* was another early psychopathology. The term referred to a condition in which a person became extremely excited, experienced a flight of ideas, and was for the most part uncontrollable. Early clinicians also noted that some individuals oscillated between mania and melancholia.

6. During the sixteenth and seventeenth centuries, several major books were written condemning masturbation. Many authors of these books stated that masturbation was not only evil, but also led to insanity and a host of other sexual perversions. Sexual

operations were performed increasingly during the eighteenth and nineteenth centuries to lessen masturbation and orgasms.

7. *Dementia* was an early psychopathology that referred to the inability to think or reason. Unlike the mentally retarded, demented people had reasoning ability at one point in their lives, but lost it. Psychotic people as well as brain-damaged individuals were most likely to be classified as being demented.

8. *Amentia,* along with other early terms such as idiocy and imbecility, referred to mental retardation. Although mental retardation has been observed since ancient times, it was not until the late 1700s that systematized efforts were made to rehabilitate and educate the retarded. Itard, Pinel, and Seguin, for example, were involved in helping retarded persons.

9. *Moral insanity* is a relatively recent diagnostic term, compared with the previously mentioned psychopathologies. It referred to those who were ''insane'' with regard to ethics and morality. Although these people did not hallucinate or have delusions, they exhibited poor judgment, lacked a ''conscience,'' and were often criminally inclined. The terms *sociopath* and *psychopath* evolved from moral insanity.

10. *Hysteria* (or conversion disorder) was first described by the Greeks. The term referred to a host of symptoms, principally those that mimicked actual organic disorders. Paralysis, blindness, and other seemingly physical symptoms were often hysterically induced. By the nineteenth century, hysteria was thought to be organically caused. Later, however, because of the work of Charcot, Bernheim, and Freud, hysteria gradually began to be viewed as a psychological problem. Hypnotism was often used to treat this reaction.

11. *Physical treatments* were increasingly used after the Middle Ages to treat mental disturbances. A wide variety of physical methods were applied indiscriminately to hospitalized patients. The lunatic asylum represented one form of physical treatment—physical restraint. Other common physical treatments were venesection (bleeding) and bowel purging. Many harsh and primitive physical methods not only were used as treatments, but also were intentionally employed as a form of punishment. Drugs such as opium and chloral hydrate were extensively given to the mentally disturbed during the 1800s.

12. *Psychological therapies* (stemming from *moral management*) arose in part as a reaction to the inhumane and ineffective physical methods. Moral management involved both removing physical restraints from hospitalized patients and treating these people with some degree of kindness. Individuals such as Pinel, Tuke, and Dix strongly advocated humane treatment for the mentally disturbed.

    Hypnotism was perhaps the first formal psychological therapy. It evolved from the special trance induction methods used by the exorcist Gassner and the physician Mesmer.

13. *The state hospital* replaced the lunatic asylum as a custodial setting for many mentally disturbed persons. The first state mental hospital was founded in the United States at Worcester, Mass., in 1833. From the early 1800s to the 1960s, state mental hospitals were the main source of custodial care and therapy for the mentally disturbed. But by the middle 1960s, *community mental health centers* were becoming increasingly common. *Crisis intervention, community consultation,* and use of *paraprofessionals* in a counseling capacity are distinctive features of community mental health programs.

Altschule, M. D. *The development of traditional psychopathology.* New York: Wiley, 1976.

Boyers, R., & Orrill, R. *R. D. Laing & antipsychiatry.* New York: Perennial Library, Harper & Row, 1971.

Rosen, G. *Madness in society.* Chicago: University of Chicago Press, 1968.

Starkey, M. L. *The devil in Massachusetts.* New York: Doubleday, 1961.

Szasz, T. S. *The age of madness.* Garden City, N. Y.: Anchor Books, 1973.

Von Bertalanffy, L. *Robots, men and mind.* New York: Braziller, 1967.

**RECOMMENDED
READINGS**

2

BIOLOGICAL PERSPECTIVES OF ABNORMAL BEHAVIOR

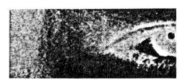
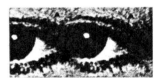

OVERVIEW   In this chapter we will discuss a number of viewpoints that relate biological factors and abnormal behavior. These approaches provide a framework for viewing the biological contributions that are dealt with in each of the chapters on clinical syndromes. Here we will examine four biological factors that have been used to account for abnormal behavior: body type, biochemistry, genetics, and brain defects. Several supplementary discussions are also included.

THE BIOLOGICAL PERSPECTIVE

The *biological perspective* refers to a group of viewpoints in which physical or organic factors are assumed to account for abnormal behavior. These physical or organic factors are termed *biological contributors*. They include such things as chemical imbalances in the central nervous system, lesions or structural damage to the central nervous system, genetic defects, viruses, bacteria, and malnutrition. We must stress that not all such biological factors are inherited. Chemical imbalances or damage to the brain, for example, may in some cases result from environmental conditions. Biological contributors, then, include all organic factors that induce abnormal behavior. The factors themselves may develop because of genetic endowment, environmental stresses, or a combination of both genetic and environmental contributions.

We should also emphasize that debate still rages about the relative importance of genetic endowment, prenatal hazards, or child-rearing practices in determining abnormal behavior. This section will not attempt to resolve this debate but will rather present the viewpoints and the research evidence that tends to support the biological perspective. Whenever possible, however, we will include methodological problems and various alternative ways of interpreting these data.

BODY TYPE AND ABNORMAL BEHAVIOR

The pseudo-sciences of physiognomy and phrenology were forerunners of the organic approach and the biological perspective in general. Physiognomy involved the assessing of an individual's personality by studying his or her facial expressions and structure. The eyes, the hair, the shape of the mouth, nose, chin, forehead, and even the eyelashes were studied, classified, and subsequently said to be linked with personality and abnormal behavior. Phrenology attributed personality traits to the conformation and "bumps" of the skull.

Proceeding directly from the work of physiognomists were the notions of criminal behavior proposed by Cesare Lombroso (1836–1909), an Italian criminologist-physician. Lombroso conducted a series of investigations on inmates of a military prison. From these investigations he concluded that individuals with particular body types or physiques were predisposed to violence, crime, and insanity. Lombroso maintained that criminals in general came from degenerate hereditary strains and that this degeneration was manifested in their physical traits.

Although Lombroso's notions were disputed even in his day, the direction of his investigations influenced the German psychiatrist Ernst Kretschmer (1884–1964). Kretschmer classified people according to three discrete physical groupings: thin (asthenic type), muscular (athletic type) and obese (pyknic type).

THE ORGANIC APPROACH

Substantial expansions in knowledge occurred during the nineteenth century, and much of this "information explosion" took place in the field of biology. Many of the nineteenth-century neurologists speculated that in a short time all mental illnesses would be explained by *neuropathology*, or disease of the nerves. That is, the neurologists of that day felt that understanding the degeneration of nerve cells would clear up much of the mystery surrounding mental disorders.

Supporting some of the early enthusiasm for neuropathology and mental illnesses was the fact that a few mental abnormalities do indeed have an underlying cellular disease. A major psychiatric breakthrough occurred when autopsies revealed pronounced impairment of brain tissue and spinal-cord wasting in certain patients who had been diagnosed as insane. In this particular disorder, a microscopic organism had destroyed brain tissue. This form of insanity was called *general paralysis of the insane* (GPI) and was manifested by marked personality changes, impulsivity, disorientation, memory impairments, delusions, hallucinations, and other symptoms. Although GPI had been differentiated from other insanities as early as the 1820s by Bayle and Calmiel, it was not until 1877 that Richard von Krafft-Ebing formally confirmed the connection between GPI and a syphilitic organism. GPI was later dropped as a term, and the disease was seen instead as one of the advanced stages of *cerebral syphilis*.

On the whole, general paralysis of the insane became the model for the organic approach. Its identification fostered the viewing of behavior disorders as mental *diseases*. Although a few other syndromes have been attributed directly to organic impairment, the discovery of the biological basis of general paralysis was a milestone for the organic approach.

Based on a large-scale study of psychotics, Kretschmer (1925) suggested that particular body types were highly associated with particular psychopathologies. For example, schizophrenics were rarely obese; the asthenic body type was associated with schizophrenia. Manic-depressive patients, by contrast, tended to be obese.

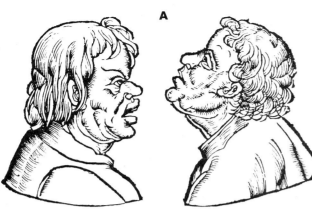

A

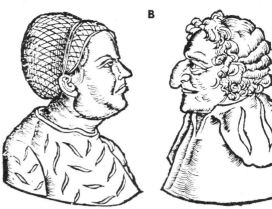

B

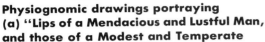

Physiognomic drawings portraying (a) "Lips of a Mendacious and Lustful Man, and those of a Modest and Temperate Man"; (b) "Nose of an Arrogant Woman, and that of a Magnanimous Man."

But Kretschmer's classification system of three discrete body types seemed unrealistic, and in the 1930s and 1940s, William Sheldon developed a more sophisticated system. Although Sheldon's system still used three main types—ectomorph (thin), mesomorph (muscular), and endomorph (obese)—the person being classified would be scored from one to seven on each type. A score of seven indicated the greatest degree of that particular body type component. Working with more than 3,500 mental patients at two large state hospitals, Sheldon also found an association between body type and psychiatric diagnosis. Sheldon (1940) held that the soft, round endomorphs were predisposed to manic-depressive illnesses; the thin, emaciated ectomorphs were more inclined to develop schizophrenia; and the muscular mesomorphs were less prone to mental disorders than the other two body types.

Although the inheritance of physique or body type no doubt has an effect on behavior, there is no evidence to suggest that body type in fact causes a specific psychopathology. Indeed, it is not clear how much effect environmental stress has on body type. Nonetheless, many correlational studies have also shown an association between psychiatric diagnosis and body type (Glueck & Glueck 1956; Walker 1962; Dutton 1964). The Dutton study, for example, showed that psychotic children are often below other children in weight, height, and skeletal maturity.

Great caution must be exercised in evaluating these investigations, mainly because there were numerous methodological problems. First, Kretschmer's methods for assessing physique were not reliable. Second, he did not control for age; schizophrenia, for example, typically has an early onset and appears at a time when people are thin because they are young. Sheldon's investigations solved some of the methodological problems of the Kretschmer studies, but other problems remained. The investigators who rated the person in regard to body type were also familiar with the rationale of Sheldon's theory. They may possibly have been inclined to make the body type fit the psychiatric diagnosis, or vice versa.

Aside from the methodological problems, a number of other questions remain to be answered: How does the environment affect physique or body type? After the onset of a particular syndrome, what changes occur in body type? Are certain social stereotypes or role expectations associated with various body types? Could various body types increase the possibility that the individual would learn certain kinds of behavior? For example, the muscular or mesomorphic person would appear to be more capable of learning aggressive behaviors than, say, the endomorphic person.

In sum, then, the high association found between body type and abnormal behavior may be a result of hereditary endowment that determines both body type and behavior. Or it may be a result of methodological errors. Or the high association may be due to other possibilities such as social expectation or learning. Nevertheless, there exists no conclusive proof that structural or morphological features of the body cause any psychopathology.

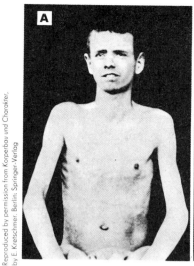  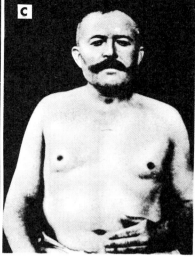

**Kretschmer's three body types:
(a) asthenic, (b) athletic, (c) pyknic.**

BIOCHEMISTRY AND ABNORMAL BEHAVIOR

The notion that chemicals can induce mental disturbances is ancient. As we mentioned in the first chapter, Hippocrates in the fourth century B.C. believed that depression was caused by bile, one of the four body "humors" of Greek biochemistry. In the nineteenth century it was commonly held that various forms of insanity were caused by poisons in the brain and body — this is why bleeding appeared to be a reasonable treatment. Pathological reactions to alcohol (as in Korsakoff's psychosis, for example) further reinforced the concept that chemicals could affect behavior and could induce mental disturbances.

The modern era of the biochemical view was probably introduced by the physiologist Walter B. Cannon (1871–1945). In about 1915, Cannon proposed that a hormone secreted by the adrenal medulla, *epinephrine,* was linked to the emotions of fear and rage. In the early 1940s came another big boost for the biochemical view. Albert Hofmann, a chemist employed by the Sandoz Drug Company of Switzerland, accidentally ingested a synthetic drug derived from ergot, a fungus that grows on grains. The drug was LSD-25. After ingesting this substance, Hofmann experienced profound distortions in thinking and complex hallucinations. Some time after this startling observation, the psychiatric community referred to the hallucination-inducing qualities of LSD as a new model for psychotic disorders.

The discovery that LSD and other drugs can mimic psychosis (the drugs are called *psychotomimetic compounds*) initiated research to find natural substances in the body that were similar to these compounds. In the 1950s it was established that *mescaline* bore a striking resemblance to the naturally occurring chemical epinephrine (Osmond & Smythies 1952). Osmond and his associates formulated a hypothesis that being subjected to stress increased epinephrine, which in turn predisposed an individual to develop psychotic reactions. Actually, much earlier, during the late 1930s, it had been noted that some individuals who had inhaled high levels of amphetamines developed a paranoid psychosis (Snyder 1974). Iversen and Iversen (1975), in this connection, noted that amphetamine addicts are often misdiagnosed as paranoid schizophrenics. In sum, drug-induced psychosis provided much support for the role of biochemistry in abnormal behavior.

Before continuing to explore the biochemical view, let us introduce several important terms that will be used throughout the text: *catecholamines* and *amines.* These terms will be used interchangeably in this text; these substances also are often called *neurotransmitters.* Simply put, catecholamines or amines are found in specific sites in the brain and contribute principally to nervous system transmission. The basic catecholamines are *epinephrine, norepinephrine, dopamine,* and *serotonin.* The last three are most often implicated in psychopathologies. For example, in chapter 8 we will review some evidence suggesting that lowered levels of norepinephrine are responsible for depression.

In addition to the discovery that particular drugs could induce psychotic-like behavior, more support for the biochemical approach came in the

METHODS OF BIOCHEMICAL RESEARCH

Three methods are commonly used to analyze chemical substances believed to play a role in abnormal behavior. First, body fluids such as urine or perspiration can be examined to determine the presence of the chemical in question. Certain varieties of mental retardation, for example, can be detected very early by analyzing the urine. In many other disorders, ranging from schizophrenia to hyperactivity, body fluids have been assessed to determine if there is a chemical basis or chemical reaction for the clinical syndrome. Second, brain tissue may be inspected to determine whether various neurotransmitter substances are depleted or oversupplied at specific brain areas. Third, normal subjects may be injected with a substance to determine whether their reactions resemble those of psychiatric subjects. The Swiss chemist who accidentally took LSD was one of the first to report that biochemical compounds could induce psychotic behavior.

The methodological problems involved in biochemical research can be highlighted by posing several questions: Are the chemical changes observed in body fluids a result of stress itself (the syndrome) or of the chemical agent? Could the diet of hospitalized psychiatric patients affect the excretions or other fluids that are assessed? Is the drug-induced behavior the same sort of behavior experienced by a person with the actual syndrome? These are just a few of the questions and issues that trouble drug research. Nonetheless, research in biochemistry has expanded our knowledge of the complex nature of psychopathology.

early 1950s when it was found that *iproniazid*, a drug once used to treat tuberculosis, could elevate the mood in many depressed patients. This substance apparently inhibited an enzyme called *monoamine oxidase* (MAO), which at high levels can produce depression. Apparently MAO alters norepinephrine levels.

In addition to the studies dealing with psychopathologies, many attempts have been made to clarify the biochemical bases of learning and memory. Several important studies have shown that environmental enrichment can alter anatomical as well as biochemical features in the brain (Bennett, Rosenzweig, & Diamond 1968; Rosenzweig, Bennett, & Diamond 1972). Similar studies have revealed that changes in brain chemistry accompany learning and performance (Hydén & Lange 1972). Conversely, it has been demonstrated that memory impairments can be induced by various chemicals (Squire & Davis 1975). Given these findings, it is reasonable to suggest that biochemistry is critically involved not only in psychopathologies but in behavior in general.

A few methodological problems commonly beset biochemical research. First, while the research mentioned here suggests that special environmental stresses can alter biochemistry, it could be argued just as reasonably that a stressful environment induces depression that in turn results in changes in biochemistry. Another flaw is the use of typical diagnostic categories and the assumption that those receiving the same diagnostic label will be similar in most respects. As we will see in many sections of this book, individuals with specific psychopathologies do not form a uniform group; that is, great individual differences exist, for example, among schizophrenics.

GENETICS AND ABNORMAL BEHAVIOR

Genetics refers to the study of heredity. This science attempts to demonstrate how physical or behavioral characteristics of offspring are acquired from their parents. *Physical genetics* involves the way heredity correlates with physical or biological qualities. The color of the eyes, skin, or hair, the blood type, and vulnerability to disease are some characteristics determined by physical genetics. *Behavioral genetics* involves the way in which behavior or psychological features are inherited although, strictly speaking, complex human behavior cannot be directly inherited. For both physical and behavioral genetics, the *gene* is the basic unit of hereditary transmission.

Genetic factors in human behavior were first studied systematically by the English biologist Sir Francis Galton. Galton was interested in discovering the relationship between intelligence and heredity. In 1869 Galton published a study in which he found that high intelligence tends to run in particular families. From his data, Galton concluded that high intelligence was an inherited

STUDYING HUMAN HEREDITY

Three typical methods of the genetic investigation of humans involve the study of families, of twins, and of adopted offspring.

Family risk studies assess each member of a family to determine whether the prevalence of a given psychopathology exceeds that found in the general population. Of critical importance in family risk studies is the requirement that the psychopathology considered be precisely defined. If this requirement is not met, meaningful comparisons with a norm cannot be made. Family risk studies make up much of the early literature of psychiatric genetics; schizophrenia was the psychopathology most often considered. (In the chapter on schizophrenia, we deal with some of the weaknesses of this method.)

Twin studies are more complex and methodologically sounder than family studies. For example, after the diagnostic data are obtained, identical twins who live in the same environment can be compared with respect to the syndrome in question. Comparisons also can be made between identical twins reared apart and between fraternal twins (two-egg twins). For schizophrenia, the concordance ratio for identical twins is much higher than the ratio for fraternal twins, which seems to suggest some genetic contribution. But another point is worthy of our attention.

Identical twins, in comparison with fraternal twins or normal siblings, have a greater risk of retardation and birth and pregnancy complications (Hanson & Gottesman 1976). This observation certainly raises some questions about identical twin studies and the genetic hypothesis because it is possible that trauma to the central nervous system (birth complications, for example), not genetic factors, predisposes twins to schizophrenia.

Another method for analyzing the contribution of genetics is to study children—particularly twins—who have been raised in foster homes. Termed the *adoptive method,* it permits the separation of biological and environmental influences. A number of meaningful comparisons can be made by employing this method. For example, we can determine whether the adopted child resembles his or her biological parents with regard to the disorder in question. The biological parents may be affected by the psychopathology and not the adoped child; or both the biological parents and the child may be affected. Other comparisons are also possible. In the main, though, the purpose is to determine the impact of genetic endowment in a different environment. (These methods also will be described more completely in the chapter on schizophrenia.)

characteristic. But as we know today, Galton had no way of knowing whether the intelligence was a result of the environments provided by the families or a result of hereditary factors. The fact that environment and heredity are so interwoven prompted the development of methods more sophisticated than the study of family trees.

Since Galton's time, the genetics of behavior has been extensively studied in animals. Numerous experimental investigations have permitted researchers to isolate particular behaviors and then inbreed animals so that these behaviors would be enhanced in the offspring. Dogs, monkeys, and rats have generally been used in genetic studies. In dogs, for instance, such behaviors as obedience, tameness or wildness, tendency to bite, emotionality, and barking capacity have a genetic component that can be transferred to the offspring (Scott

& Fuller 1965; Lerner 1968). In rats, Tryon (1963) demonstrated that skill in running a maze could be influenced by inbreeding. Dull strains of rats produced slow maze learners while bright strains produced fast maze learners. Years ago, Witt and Hall (1949) found that susceptibility to convulsions could be controlled through breeding animals with low or high seizure tendencies.

Although humans cannot be inbred for the sake of demonstrating the contribution of genetics or environment, several methods of research have been developed that provide us with some evidence concerning genetics and abnormal behavior.

In several of the later chapters we will review genetic studies that suggest there is a genetic contribution to psychopathology. Here we must mention that the mechanisms of genetic transmission and psychopathology are far from being completely understood. By contrast with typical Mendelian genetic transmission, in which independent, discrete characteristics are inherited, much of gene-influenced abnormal behavior possibly arises from what are known as *polygenic effects*. Simply put, polygenic effects are effects in the offspring that require both genetic factors and other physical or environmental stressors. That is, environmental factors combine with genetic factors to predispose the person to a psychopathology (Hanson & Gottesman 1976). Support for the existence of polygenic effects comes from examining concordance ratios for identical and fraternal twins. For identical twins the concordance rate for schizophrenia is not 100 percent; yet the rate for identical twins is much higher than that for fraternal twins. This suggests that both genetic and environmental contributions are required for schizophrenia. Other interpretations, however, such as the vulnerability of identical twins in general, stand in opposition to the polygenic effect. In sum, at this time the precise way in which inheritance influences psychopathology has not been determined. Further, only a few psychopathologies such as schizophrenia and the affective disorders have been studied extensively. Future research perhaps will distinguish environmental influences from genetic ones.

THE BRAIN AND ABNORMAL BEHAVIOR

Before examining the part that neuroanatomical defects play in psychopathology, we need to make an important introductory remark: Psychopathology is a complex phenomenon and does not appear to be the result of a single structural defect in the nervous system. The brain (as available evidence suggests) operates in a complex and reciprocally dependent manner. Little empirical support exists to show that a specific brain structure or brain site relates directly to a specific psychiatric diagnosis.

In many fields of brain research, investigations have been undertaken with the purpose of localizing specific brain functioning. For example, for more than 30 years, Karl Lashley tried to find the location or brain site of memory. Employing a procedure in which he surgically destroyed various brain sites, Lashley concluded that loss or retention of memory depends more on how much of the brain is impaired than on what area of the brain is impaired. This finding that the nervous system works as a whole is referred to as *mass action*. The concept of mass action does not support the belief

THE NERVOUS SYSTEM

To understand many of the theories proposed to account for abnormal behavior, it is useful and necessary to have a general understanding of the nervous system. Here we will discuss and illustrate the central nervous system; the peripheral nervous system; the autonomic nervous system; the cerebral hemispheres; and the frontal and temporal lobes.

Central nervous system. The *central nervous system* includes the brain and the spinal cord. The brain is the entire large mass of nervous tissue located beneath the skull. The spinal cord is also a mass of nervous tissue, but it occupies the vertebral canal. The three subdivisions of the brain are the *hindbrain, midbrain*, and *forebrain*.

Peripheral nervous system. Nerve fibers that lie outside the central nervous system—that is, outside the brain and spinal cord—make up the *peripheral nervous system*. The peripheral nervous system connects the central nervous system with the outside world via *receptors* and *effectors*.

Autonomic nervous system. The *autonomic nervous system* is a division of the peripheral nervous system. It is a motor system that regulates smooth muscles and glands. It operates below the level of awareness, although many of its effects are experienced consciously.

The autonomic nervous system has two subdivisions: the sympathetic division, and the parasympathetic division. Each of these divisions tends to dominate during various states or conditions.

For example, the *sympathetic division* is dominant during stress. Sympathetic predominance gives rise to numerous responses throughout the body: blood pressure increases; blood flow to the skeletal muscles is augmented; heart rate increases; sweat gland activity increases; but there is vasoconstriction (or a reduction) of blood flow to the intestines and other internal organs. Severe emotional stress triggers *sympathetic overarousal* or what is sometimes called the *stress response syndrome* (Horowitz 1976). This syndrome is highlighted by cardiovascular changes and subjective feelings: high heart rate (tachycardia), elevated blood pressure, restlessness and anxiety, sleep impairments, fatigue. Sympathetic overarousal may be induced by numerous conditions: military combat, rape, concentration camp experiences, bereavement, and many other situational stresses (Horowitz 1976).

On the other hand, *parasympathetic predominance* occurs usually under conditions of rest, eating, or relaxation. Heart rate, blood pressure, and other cardiovascular processes usually slow down somewhat. Benson (1975) maintains that parasympathetic dominance, or a type of "relaxation response," can be learned. He suggests that various meditational techniques can elicit the relaxation response—combating the stress response syndrome—thus resulting in positive physiologic changes.

Cerebral hemispheres. The largest sections of the brain are the two cerebral hemispheres. For our purposes, each cerebral hemisphere can be divided into four areas or *lobes*: the *frontal* lobe, the *parietal* lobe, the *temporal* lobe, and the *occipital* lobe. Because of their relevance to certain behavior problems, we will focus only on the frontal and temporal lobes.

Frontal lobes. In general, the frontal lobes are associated with motivation, personality, and affect. Alterations in the frontal lobe which are discussed in chapter 14 may produce marked changes in personality (Minckler 1972). *Psychosurgery* usually involves removing or disconnecting various pathways in the frontal lobe region. The most radical psychosurgical procedure is the *prefrontal lobectomy*, in which much of the entire frontal lobe is removed. In a *prefrontal topectomy*, only selected areas are ablated. Finally, in the *prefrontal lobotomy*, nerve fibers connecting the frontal lobes to the thalamus and limbic system are severed (Leukel 1976). These highly controversial procedures have been used to treat patients experiencing anxiety, obsessions, schizophrenia, and intractable pain (Chusid 1970). Both the ethics and the scientific bases of psychosurgery have been strongly challenged.

Temporal lobes. The temporal lobes are located on the side of the cerebral hemispheres. The left temporal lobe has been associated generally with language functions. Two specialized regions are *Broca's area* and *Wernicke's area*. Damage to Broca's area may produce speaking impairments, while damage to Wernicke's area may produce the inability to understand spoken language.

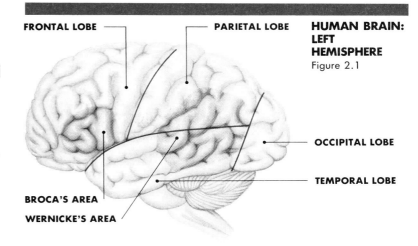

HUMAN BRAIN: LEFT HEMISPHERE
Figure 2.1

FRONTAL LOBE
PARIETAL LOBE
OCCIPITAL LOBE
TEMPORAL LOBE
BROCA'S AREA
WERNICKE'S AREA

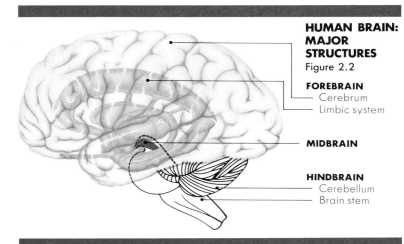

HUMAN BRAIN: MAJOR STRUCTURES
Figure 2.2

FOREBRAIN
— Cerebrum
— Limbic system
MIDBRAIN
HINDBRAIN
— Cerebellum
— Brain stem

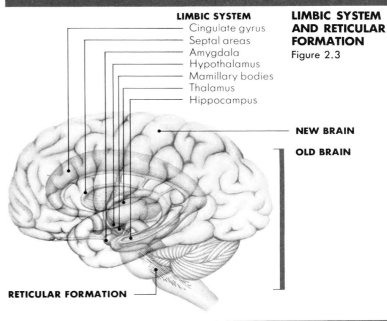

LIMBIC SYSTEM AND RETICULAR FORMATION
Figure 2.3

LIMBIC SYSTEM
— Cingulate gyrus
— Septal areas
— Amygdala
— Hypothalamus
— Mamillary bodies
— Thalamus
— Hippocampus
NEW BRAIN
OLD BRAIN
RETICULAR FORMATION

CRITICS OF THE MEDICAL MODEL

Several critics have voiced considerable opposition to the biological perspective in general. Specifically, these individuals strongly resist labeling behavior problems as "illnesses" or "diseases." To summarize their views: Psychopathology is not a medical issue, like cancer or heart disease, but rather an ethical, social, or existential issue. The biological perspective, and in particular the medical model, thus is viewed as naive, degrading, and unsupported by evidence.

Theodore Sarbin. As we noted in chapter 1, the insane person and the witch were viewed differently in the Middle Ages. While the insane were depicted as "sick," witches were depicted as evil. Theodore Sarbin (1966) gives a similar account as he traces the development of the term *sickness*:

> In my own historical search, the first metaphorical use of sickness to denote behavior deviations occurred in the 16th century. In an effort to save some hysterical nuns from the Inquisition—and probably influenced by the recently rediscovered writing of Galen—Teresa of Avila . . . declared that the nuns were not evil, but *comas enfermas* (as if sick). This declaration was made at the time of the rise of modern science . . . and of humanistic opposition to the excesses of the Inquisition. The new metaphor ultimately transferred the task of passing judgment on disordered persons from ecclesiastical authorities to medical practitioners. With the further development of Galenic medicine and the strengthening of the mind-body dualism, Teresa's *as if sick* became shortened to *sick*. . . . Thus the myth of [mental illness] was born. (Sarbin & Juhasz 1966, p. 3)

Sarbin views psychiatric syndromes, for the most part, not as illnesses but as "social roles." These roles are often forced on the person by his or her commitment to a hospital. Hospitalization, for instance, often provides "sick roles" which patients are expected to fill.

Thomas S. Szasz. Thomas Szasz has been one of the most outspoken critics of the medical model. Szasz has written at least five books in which he discusses the irrationality and immorality of labeling behavior problems as "mental illnesses." (His important works include *The Myth of Mental Illness, Ideology and Insanity, The Manufacture of Madness, the Second Sin, and The Age of Madness.*) Szasz, a psychiatrist, takes to task his own profession by declaring that psychiatry really involves moral problems and problems of personal responsibility, rather than medical problems. The thrust of his contention against psychiatry is that it has created mental illness. He suggests that early psychiatry made attempts to create new criteria for abnormal behaviors so that they could be called "illnesses." In his words:

> [In] modern medicine new diseases were *discovered*, in modern psychiatry they were invented. Paresis was *proved* to be a disease; hysteria was declared to be one. (Szasz 1961, p.12)

R. D. Laing. Since the early 1960s, R. D. Laing, a British psychiatrist, has been attacking traditional psychiatry and the medical model. Laing maintains that mental illness is not an illness per se, but rather a political, social economic, and ethical issue. Siegler, Osmond, and Mann (1971) say that Laing views traditional psychiatry as a type of conspiracy. In agreement with Sarbin's thoughts, Laing (1967) asserts:

that memory is localized. Rather, as Lashley says, the brain is remarkably linked together. Based on available data, and applying Lashley's principle, it seems that localizing schizophrenia, depression, or other psychopathologies in the brain is remote.

Two important brain systems, however, have been linked with certain behaviors and may be involved biologically in the contribution to psychopathology. These systems are the *limbic system* and the *reticular formation* (also called the reticular activating or reticular arousal system).

James Papez, in 1937, proposed a brain model to account for emotional behavior, called *Papez's circuit*. Papez's circuit involves a ring of brain structures located beneath the cerebral cortex. The brain structures comprising this neural circuit include the hypothalamus, thalamus, cingulate gyrus, mammillary bodies, hippocampus,

T. R. Sarbin is a critic of labeling individuals with psychiatric terms. He sees many so-called illnesses as social roles.

Thomas Szasz, a psychiatrist, believes that psychiatry has "invented" mental diseases by developing diagnostic criteria that deal mainly with moral issues rather than physical issues.

The person labeled is inaugurated not only into a role, but a career of patient, by the concerted action of coalition (a "conspiracy") of family, G.P., mental health officer, psychiatrists, nurses, psychiatric social workers, and often fellow patients. (p. 84)

Thus, for Laing the problem behavior in question is not the result of disease but of special interpersonal experiences. In a word, it is a role. Placing psychopathologies within a medical context, according to Laing, degrades the person experiencing the problem. Furthermore, hospitalization invalidates or discounts this individual's experience. And finally, what traditional psychiatric methods call "treatment," Laing says, is actually an attempt to get the person to abandon his or her subjective experiential viewpoint. (Siegler, Osmond, & Mann 1971)

While some criticisms of the medical model are valid, it would be risky to ignore the contributions of biological factors. In fact, the critics are speaking out more against the indiscriminate use of the labels "illness" and "disease" when applied to problematic behaviors than against the suggestion that certain behaviors may have a biological or biochemical underpinning.

amygdala, septal areas, and a few others. These brain formations taken together are today called the *limbic system*. (The word *limbic* means "border;" this system borders between the new brain and older primitive brain elements.)

The functions and structures of the limbic system have been studied extensively in both humans and animals. Clinical cases of human subjects with brain injuries, for example, have revealed some of the functions of this system. Animal experimentation has also disclosed some functions. Regarding humans, MacLean (1972, 1973, 1975) suggests that disruptions to the limbic system are linked to mood changes, distortions of perceptions (hallucinations), depersonalization, and delusions. Korsakoff's psychosis—a pathological reaction to alcohol—involves marked destruction of mammillary bodies in the limbic system. Damage to or bilateral removal of portions of the temporal lobe, which is connected to parts of the limbic system, produces a cluster of symptoms termed the Klüver-Bucy syndrome. The most striking features of this syndrome are visual hallucinations, hypersexuality, and compulsive behavior. Memory deficits, especially in older persons, appear to have part of their etiology in alterations in the limbic system.

Animal experimentations with the limbic system typically involve the removal of limbic structures and chemical or electrical stimulation of existing structures. Early studies on the hypothalamus suggested that this structure was highly involved in emotionality (Bard 1928; Hess 1928). More specifically, later studies showed that amygdala stimulation facilitated "affective rage" and flight (Hernandez-Peon, O'Flaherty, & Mazzuchelli-O'Flaherty 1967). Hyperemotionality and flight behavior can also be elicited by septal alterations (Slotnick, McMullen, & Fleischer 1974). Further, septal lesions have been reported to lower an animal's "rage threshold" (Brady & Nauta 1953). (In chapter 14, which deals with brain dysfunctions and sleep disorders, we will discuss the limbic system further.)

The second brain system involved is the *reticular formation* in the brain stem. This system extends from the thalamus downward to the top of the spinal cord. Extensive research has shown that the reticular formation is involved in sleep, memory, attention, and other vital functions. (Jones, Bobillier, & Jouvet 1969; Penfield & Jasper 1954). When the *raphe*, a brain stem mechanism, is destroyed, insomnia results (Carlson 1977). Clinical data also suggest that the reticular formation or other brain stem mechanisms may be involved in hyperactivity, sleep disorders, psychotic behavior, and autism (Frederiks 1969; Matthews & Miller 1972; Rosenzweig 1955; Rimland 1964; Kety 1971). Because some of these disorders involve overarousal, drugs that reduce arousal frequently act on the reticular formation. The phenothiazines and amphetamines, for example, may change the chemical features of the reticular formation.

So far, no firm empirical evidence has been found to demonstrate a direct link between psychopathology and structural defects of the reticular formation. The general difficulty of evaluating chemical and structural alterations in the brain, as well as the fact that other stresses could have produced the alterations, continues to lessen the authority of this form of research when it is applied to abnormal behavior. To conclude, it seems that far too little is known at this stage about the role of neuroanatomical structures and psychopathology. What appears to be certain, however, is that neuroanatomical, biochemical, and environmental factors intertwine in their contribution to abnormal behavior.

SUMMARY

1. The *biological perspective* deals with the association of biological factors and psychopathology. *Biological contributors* refer to biological factors that affect behavior. Damage to the brain, genetic defects, malnutrition, biochemical imbalances, and similar physical agents are examples of biological contributors.

2. One of the first efforts to show a relationship between biological contributors and psychopathology dealt with research into body types. Lombroso, Kretschmer, and Sheldon conducted studies examining the relationship between body type and abnormal behavior. Kretschmer and Sheldon's studies demonstrated that, for example, the thin body type was related to psychotic behavior. However, profound methodological problems have prevented the acceptance of body-type notions.

3. Numerous studies have examined the connection between biochemical disturbances and psychopathology. Drugs have been isolated or developed that can mimic psychotic reactions (psychotomimetic compounds). Other drugs can abate certain abnormal behaviors. Yet the methodological problems in biochemical research dealing with psychopathology do not always permit a cause-and-effect relationship to be established. For example, are the symptoms exhibited in a particular psychopathology the result of biochemical disturbances, or are the biochemical disturbances a result of the pyschopathology?

4. *Genetics* is the study of heredity. Physical

traits are passed on genetically to the offspring, and as certain breeding experiments with laboratory animals have suggested, behavioral tendencies can also be passed on. Determining whether specific human psychopathologies are a result of genetic endowment is exceedingly difficult. Three basic genetic methods have been used to aid in determining the contribution of genetic endowment: family risk studies, twin studies, and adoption studies. Family risk studies have revealed that various psychopathologies occur in particular families, but these may be a consequence of environmental factors. Twin studies, using identical twins separated shortly after birth, have been used to separate the effects of genetics and environment. In some cases, syndromes such as schizophrenia do have a high concordance ratio for identical twins, even if they are reared apart. Adoption studies have also been used to examine the effects of genetics and environment. These studies permit numerous comparisons; e.g., a foster child may be compared with his or her biological parents with respect to the incidence of a psychopathology.

5. Two general systems in the central nervous system have been linked with emotionality, arousal, and possibly certain syndromes. These systems are the *limbic system* and the *reticular formation*. The limbic system lies beneath the cerebral hemispheres and comprises many neural structures that have been shown to be involved in emotionality and other functions. The reticular formation, located in the brainstem, is involved in cortical arousal. Dysfunctions in this system have been associated with sleep impairments, hyperactivity, and other syndromes, but thus far, no direct empirical evidence has shown that reticular formation defects produce specific behavior disorders.

Delgado, J. M. R. *Physical control of the mind.* New York: Harper & Row, 1969.

Eccles, J. C. *The understanding of the brain.* New York: McGraw-Hill, 1977.

Malmo, R. B. *On emotions, needs, and our archaic brain.* New York: Holt, Rinehart & Winston, 1975.

Mark, V. H., & Ervin, F. R. *Violence and the brain.* New York: Harper & Row, 1970.

Pincus, J. H., & Tucker, G. J. *Behavioral neurology.* New York: Oxford University Press, 1974.

Snyder, S. H. *Madness and the brain.* New York: McGraw-Hill, 1974.

RECOMMENDED READINGS

3 PSYCHOSOCIAL PERSPECTIVES OF ABNORMAL BEHAVIOR

OVERVIEW In this chapter we will discuss a number of viewpoints or perspectives whose supporters maintain that abnormal behavior is mainly a function of psychological or sociological factors. We have grouped four broad approaches under this heading of "psychosocial perspectives." Although these viewpoints differ greatly on many issues, they share an essential similarity on one point: that abnormal behavior is a result of special environments.

The four perspectives are (1) the psychodynamic perspective, which includes classical psychoanalysis, neo-Freudianism, and transactional analysis; (2) the phenomenological and existential perspectives; (3) the learning perspective (behavioral model), examining three different learning theories; and (4) the sociological perspective, along with four subcategories dealing with different social influences.

Not all these viewpoints are given exactly the same coverage. For example, because of the detail of psychoanalytic and transactional analytic treatment, we examine these two treatment strategies here; the same also applies to the phenomenological-existential perspectives, in which context we discuss Carl Rogers's client-centered therapy and Frankl's logotherapy. On the other hand, because so many specialized techniques have been developed within the learning perspective, we will describe these in connection with the particular psychopathologies in Parts II and III.

Because of the significant differences in

focus, it is difficult to evaluate all these perspectives by the same criteria. For each one, however, we will mention some of the criticisms that theorists of other schools have made.

THE PSYCHODYNAMIC PERSPECTIVE

The first psychological approach we will consider is the *psychodynamic perspective,* one that comprises several personality theories and psychotherapeutic positions. The psychodynamic perspective maintains that psychological forces or energies within the person account for abnormal behavior. (The two parts of the term *psycho-dynamic* mean "mind"/"energies.") The psychodynamic theories we will consider include Freud's psychoanalysis; the analytic views of Adler, Sullivan, and Horney; and Berne's transactional analysis.

Although many psychodynamic theories exist, and each has its unique features, most tend to rely on the following assumptions (adapted from Rychlak 1973):

1. Traumatic childhood events are usually repressed or forced out of awareness.
2. Unconscious psychological forces determine most abnormal behaviors.
3. Traumatic childhood events greatly influence adult behavior.
4. The abnormal behavior engaged in (or the symptoms shown) by the adult or child are compensations for needs unmet during childhood. The symptoms may also enable the trauma to remain repressed.
5. The traumatic childhood event must be revealed to the person—that is, the event must be brought into awareness—before symptoms can be removed or the personality can develop adequately. ·

Psychonalysis involves three separate areas: a theory of personality, a theory of psychopathology, and a therapy or treatment procedure. We will examine each of these areas.

FREUD'S THEORY OF PERSONALITY

In addition to treating patients, Freud was interested in formulating a model of the human mind that would help others understand how the mind worked in general and how psychopathologies develop. In 1923, Freud made a significant revision in the personality theory that he had been developing for a number of years. During that year he renounced an early model of the mind, the topographical theory, in which he divided the mind into three regions (the preconscious, the conscious, and the unconscious). He settled instead for his new *structural model of personality,* an effort to describe the essential components of the human psyche or "psychic apparatus." The hypothetical structures of the mind were the *id,* the *ego,* and the *superego.*

THE ID In spite of his opposition to organic explanations of hysteria, Freud was chiefly a biological or organic theorist. He maintained that human beings were driven by a reservoir of inherited energies—instincts. The instincts that were of significance in his theory of personality were *eros* and *thanatos.* Eros involves instinctual forces represented by such things as sexuality and love; thanatos, on the other hand, is a destructive instinct, represented by aggression and death. Another part of eros is *libido,* which stands for all sexual energies. Freud contended that libido is responsible for pleasurable activities, motivating such behavior as sex and affection. Both of these instinctual drives—eros and thanatos—seek expression. Often they are fused together in activities, but at other times they are in opposition. Eros and thanatos also obey or follow the *pleasure principle.* That is, their goals are to seek pleasure and avoid pain. Both instincts, however, operate at an unconscious level.

Eros and thanatos, as well as other instincts, make up the *id,* which represents all instinctual drives. It is a reservoir of primitive strivings that obeys the pleasure principle. Although the id functions at an unconscious level, it nonetheless exerts profound influence on behavior.

THE EGO But the id has no capacity to alter the outside world. Freud therefore developed another

Sigmund Freud (1856–1939) is the father of psychoanalysis and was one of
the first to propose that mental illness
was psychologically induced.

This picture of Freud was taken during
his last years.

component that had the task of dealing with just
that. At birth, the id can only want or desire. What
is lacking is a way to influence the environment
directly so that the id's desires can be satisfied. The
function of the ego is to do the id's work with
respect to the outside world. Thus it is a sort of
mediator between the inside world of instincts and
the outside world. The ego attempts to obey the
reality principle, rather than the pleasure principle.
This means that external reality, not innate drive,
is the ego's main concern.

THE SUPEREGO   The superego is the third hypothetical component of Freud's model. Developmentally, it is the last to emerge. As the ego forms
out of the id, the superego forms out of the ego.
The superego represents a type of inner "parent"
or seat of morality for the person. It involves all
prohibitions and values. Most simply characterized, the superego is the "conscience." Its principal
functions are morally to evaluate and keep in check
the performance of the ego.

A PSYCHOANALYTIC THEORY
OF PSYCHOPATHOLOGY

Freud's theory of psychopathology deals chiefly
with his concept of the origin of neurosis. He
theorized that neurosis, hysteria in particular,
developed under certain circumstances, which are
summarized by Meissner, Mack, and Semrad
(1975, p. 542):

1. There is an inner conflict between drives and
   fear that prevents drive discharge.
2. Sexual drives are involved in these conflicts.
3. Conflict has not been worked through to a
   realistic solution. Instead, the drives that
   seek discharge have been expelled from
   consciousness through repression or
   another defense mechanism.
4. Repression merely succeeds in rendering
   the drives unconscious; it does not deprive
   them of their power and make them
   innocuous. Consequently, the repressed

EGO DEFENSE MECHANISMS

For Freud, conflict and anxiety were important psychodynamic stressors. That is, conflict and anxiety create additional tension that interferes with adaptive efforts. But the ego develops various mental tactics to reduce or terminate conflict and other intrapsychic stressors. Disturbing thoughts and impulses can be held at bay through the use of *ego defense mechanisms* (EDMs). EDMs consist of a set of mental operations that reduce psychic stress by bringing about a compromise among conflicting impulses, or by reducing the individual's awareness of certain painful and frustrating circumstances. EDMs have four basic characteristics:

1. EDMs usually operate below the level of awareness.
2. EDMs serve to protect the person from his or her own threatening impulses, which may break into the consciousness.
3. EDMs assist in helping the person attain portions of an unattainable goal—that is, substitute goals are accepted in place of the goals that are out of reach.
4. EDMs maintain a psychological equilibrium or homeostasis by denying, repressing, or distorting conflicts that may exist.

Defense mechanisms may also be classified in various ways. For example, repression, reaction formation, and displacement are conceived of as being neurotic defenses (Meissner, et al. 1975). In *repression,* the unwanted material is simply pushed out of awareness. A *reaction formation* is the handling of unacceptable impulses by acting out their opposites—for example, a man who fears his own homosexuality may beat up a "queer." *Displacement* involves shifting the instincts (aggressive or sexual) to a safe object—for example, a frustrated person who cannot safely hit an adult may displace his or her aggressions by striking a child. Defenses also can be classified as being immature or mature: *projection* (attributing one's own feelings to others); *regression* (returning to a previous adaptive tactic to handle stress); and *somatization* (converting stress into a bodily symptom) are referred to as immature EDMs. Some defense mechanisms that are considered mature are suppression, or the conscious postponement of attention; *sublimation,* or satisfying an impulse by turning it into a socially desired behavior (such as getting rid of aggression through contact sports); and *humor.* (Meissner et al. 1975)

tendencies/drives fight their way back to consciousness, disguised as neurotic symptoms.

5. An inner conflict leads to neurosis in adolescence or adulthood only if a neurosis or a rudimentary neurosis based on the same type of conflict existed in early childhood.

Freud's conceptions of psychopathology have two important features. First, as noted above, blocked sexual desires are repressed, and these repressed desires or conflicts continue to influence behavior via symptom formation. It is important to recognize here that Freud believed that the illness, or symptom formation (hysteria, for example), is actually an adaptive mechanism.

Freud also tried to explain psychotic behavior. He maintained that psychotic reactions result from a poorly developed ego. Moreover, because of overwhelming stress, the individual *regressed* or became *fixated* at an earlier level of ego development. The stress in the case of a schizophrenic, for example, was thought to be conflict about homosexuality (Munroe 1955). Paranoid delusions, according to Freud, are also rooted in sexual conflicts with a person of the same sex.

Freud gained considerable insight into psychopathology from his clinical studies with his patients. Many of his early patients were women diagnosed as hysterics; he saw only a few psychotics. Freud himself underwent a lengthy self-analysis from which he concluded that his own neurosis was based on traumatic childhood events that had been repressed. (Unfortunately, we do not know what these events were.) Nonetheless, Freud told a colleague, Wilhelm Fleiss, "The main patient who keeps me busy is myself."

PSYCHOANALYSIS: A THERAPY

Psychoanalysis is not only a theory of illness (neurosis) but also a therapeutic technique. We should stress that orthodox psychoanalysis, the original Freudian method, has undergone many changes over the years. Initially Freud tried hypnosis alone in an effort to eliminate conversions or hysteria. Then he adopted the *cathartic method* of Josef Breuer, in which the patient, under hypnosis, would try to "reenact" or relive traumatic childhood events. Later, Freud dropped hypnosis and the cathartic method and developed the basic tool of psychoanalytic therapy, *free association*.

In free association the patient says whatever comes into his or her mind. The analytic couch and the "silence of the analyst" encourage the patient to regress to the traumatic episodes, thus widening the patient's conscious awareness of the trauma and his or her unacceptable wishes.

Several other things of importance also occur during analysis. The analyst is involved with *interpretation* — explaining or "translating" free-associated thoughts, unconscious ones, to the patient so that he or she can understand them. Coltrera and Ross (1967) point out that Freud defined psychoanalysis as the art of interpretation.

Transference and *resistance* also occur during the analytic session. Transference takes place when the patient begins to relate to the analyst as if he or she were a parent figure. Indeed, the analyst's couch (the doctor sits behind the patient or out of sight) fosters transference. Gerhard Adler (1967) remarks:

> The reasons for the couch are well-enough known . . . the freedom of the patient to use the analyst for his transference fantasies, the creation of a "dependent" position facilitating the emergence of infantile material, assisting relaxation and an attitude conducive to free association. . . . (p. 344)

Resistance, on the other hand, occurs when the patient consciously attempts to prevent repressed material from being revealed in the session.

In sum, the principal goal of psychoanalysis was to bring unconscious material into the patient's awareness. Another goal was to have the patient "act out" or express repressed memories during analytic sessions, in particular during transference.

Freud thought that mental illness (neurosis) was caused by unconscious forces (traumatic childhood experiences and unacceptable sexual and aggressive impulses), so that venting and uncovering these forces should bring them under the control of the ego or conscious mind.

THE NEO-FREUDIANS

As Brown (1972) observed, the history of psychoanalysis has been distinguished by two major responses to Freud's biological assumptions (the libido theory) about human nature. First, there were the strict followers of Freud's dogma, who explored even further the notions of inborn aggression, infantile sexuality, and the death instinct. Melanie Klein (1882–1960), for example, represents this biological pole. Second, there were those who moved away from the libido theory. This splinter group is often referred to as the *neo-Freudians*. In the main, this second response to orthodox analytic theory focused on the importance of psychosocial determinants. It stressed interpersonal experiences as being crucial in the development of psychopathology. Among the neo-Freudians were such analysts as Alfred Adler, Karen Horney, Harry Stack Sullivan, Erik Erikson, and Erich Fromm.

ALFRED ADLER Sigmund Freud had a considerable following by the turn of the century. Numerous young doctors could be found at Freud's home listening to the master discuss his favorite subjects: unconscious motivation, the meaning of dreams, infantile sexuality, and the power of the id. Early disciples and junior colleagues included Carl Jung, Alfred Adler, Harry Stack Sullivan; later Freud was admired and almost worshiped by Otto Rank, Sandor Ferenczi, and many more. Soon, however, a few of his admirers began to question some of Freud's ideas. To generalize, Freud's dissenters were most opposed to his insistence on the importance of the id (libido theory) in determining behavior. The notion that humans were chiefly moved by repressed sexual energies was unacceptable to a few of his pupils. Adler was one of the more noteworthy dissenters, principally because he rejected much of the libido theory and the primacy of the id.

Adler could not embrace the notion of the primacy of biological instincts in determining men-

**Alfred Adler (1870–1937), an early fol-
lower of Freud, disagreed that sexual
instincts were the main forces determining behavior. Adler stressed the importance of the interpersonal milieu.**

**Harry Stack Sullivan (1892–1949) was
initially a strong supporter of Freud.
Later however, like Adler, he began to
emphasize the importance of the interpersonal environment.**

tal life and behavior. For Adler, it was early
environmental experiences that mattered most in
human development. In particular, the child's early
interpersonal encounters were of interest to Adler.
For example, overprotection, rejection or neglect,
and sibling rivalry were interpersonal stressors that
created many problems. Adler also suggested that,
in addition, the child is concerned about his or her
own physical appearance. Slight or severe physical
defects create interpersonal rejection, and inferior feelings often develop from constitutional
defects.

These points were shaped into Adler's concept of the *inferiority complex*, which was to play a
major role in his theory of personality and psychopathology. It was well known in traditional medicine that a defect or inferiority of an organ, the
heart, for example, would induce a "compensatory" reaction in the body. A damaged heart valve
created compensatory hypertrophy of the cardiac
muscle (Brown 1972). By the same token, Adler
suggested that a psychological defect or inferiority
also created an overcompensatory reaction. The

neglected child, for instance, would develop feelings of inferiority and later in life might devise
tactics to overcompensate for these feelings. "Becoming sick" or retreating into illnesses was one
kind of overcompensation. By becoming sick (or
pretending to be ill) the person could gain some
power, love, and control over significant others.
Whereas Freud held that we wish to satisfy instinctual urges, Adler contended that we strive for
superiority or conquest over our perceived feelings
of inadequacy. He saw neuroticism, frigidity, homosexuality, and numerous other behaviors as
compensatory efforts.

Adler's major influence on psychoanalysis
was his emphasis on the importance of interpersonal relations. As we shall see, he had a notable
influence not only on other psychoanalysts, but
also on other personality theorists and psychotherapists.

HARRY STACK SULLIVAN Another theorist
and therapist who moved away from Freud's libido
theory was Harry Stack Sullivan (1892–1949).

Sullivan maintained that psychiatry and psycho-analysis were actually the study of interpersonal relations. Personality development and psychopathology, he proposed, cannot be considered apart from the individual's relations with other people. Thus, mental disturbances, for the most part, stem from disturbed interpersonal relations. Schizophrenia, however, Sullivan's major interest, was viewed as a result of heavy reliance on repression.

Another feature of Sullivan's position was his use of the concept of *self*. For Sullivan the self was the individual's organized way of viewing life, a dynamic organization representing thoughts and feelings and the "I" or "me" experience. Sullivan proposed that the self emerges from the "reflected appraisal" of significant others—chiefly the parents. Sullivan also dealt with the idea that the self can evaluate itself—determine a self-esteem. Mental disturbances revolve around disturbances in self-esteem and other distortions in the self-system, such as unrealistic views about the self. This position closely resembles the phenomenological perspective.

CRITICISMS Critics have pointed out some methodological problems in psychoanalysis. (These criticisms also apply to transactional analysis, the next topic.) First, psychoanalysis and the psychodynamic view as a whole offer conceptions that are essentially untestable. That is, many of the topics considered in the psychodynamic perspective cannot be empirically verified. For example, Freud's descriptions of the libido, other structures, and intrapsychic energies are not based on his sense impressions—that is, what he could actually see—but rather on inferences. The id, ego, and superego, for instance, cannot be seen or measured. This feature of psychodynamic agents does not lead to or permit experimental analysis or causal analysis (Skinner 1953).

A second criticism of psychoanalysis involves its rationale concerning therapy. It has been contended that the main objective in therapy is not the elimination of the symptoms in question, but the development of insight. An abnormal behavior—say, intense anxiety—is not the principal concern; the concern is the self-realization of the trauma inducing the anxiety (insight) and the determination of why the patient decided to develop anxiety as a coping tactic. (We will discuss the question of the effectiveness of psychoanalysis in our discussion of neuroses in chapter 6.)

TRANSACTIONAL ANALYSIS (TA)

Eric Berne (1910–1970) was a psychiatrist trained in traditional psychoanalytic methods. Yet when Berne was 46 years old, after working 15 years to become a psychoanalyst, his application for membership as an analyst was rejected by the San Francisco Psychoanalytic Institute (Steiner 1974). This rejection evidently intensified his efforts to "add something new to psychoanalytic training" (Steiner 1974).

Berne developed *transactional analysis* (TA) principally as a technique for describing how people communicate with one another. (A *transaction* is a unit of social interaction.) TA departs quite markedly from psychoanalysis. Berne maintained that the primary needs of human beings were not sexual or aggressive, but the need to be noticed and recognized by others. That is, human beings have *recognition-hunger*. Social interactions and social interchanges among people are therefore aimed at fulfilling the need for recognition.

Berne was intrigued by René A. Spitz's reports that infants persistently deprived of human contact and unstimulating environments ultimately "sink into an irreversible decline . . ." For Berne and many other clinicians, the unstimulating environments of these early orphanages and institutions, and most importantly, maternal deprivation, resulted in the infants' progressive deterioration. The infants were not physically held or "stroked." But Berne proposed that just as the infant needs physical strokes and intimacy to survive, so do people at all stages within the life span. *Stroking* is the giving or imparting of recognition; the fundamental unit of recognition Berne called a *stroke*. Examples of strokes vary along a continuum of responses: physically holding or embracing someone, saying hello to someone, or verbally praising (or scolding) someone.

According to *transactional analysis*, people relate to each other to get strokes. Stroke-getting efforts may be normal and adaptive, or they may be destructive and unadaptive. Berne used the term *games* to describe ulterior or unconscious transactions between people that are designed to acquire strokes. The game has the advantage, like Freud's defense mechanisms, of achieving psychological equilibrium. Dependency needs, masochistic needs, sadistic needs, and many others can be satisfied through games. Games are thus designed

Fred Kaplan/Black Star

Eric Berne (1910–1970) was the founder of transactional analysis. Berne stressed the importance of being recognized and the influence of parental messages on the behavior of offspring.

to result in strokes; however, they vary in the degree of pathology.

Another important concept of TA is its use of three *ego states* in describing communication and psychological illness in general. An ego state is an inferred psychodynamic force, consisting of feelings and ways of thinking that correspond to overt behavior (Berne 1972). There are three ego states: *Parent, Adult,* and *Child.* They are made up of mental "tapes" that we play back on given occasions. These tapes were recorded chiefly during early childhood, but we play them back every day. In a real sense we are three persons, determined by the content of the ego states we possess.

The *Parent* ego state is a collection of neurological tapes of parental attitudes and feelings as recorded in childhood. Meininger (1973) notes:

> The Parent tape contains recordings of how mothers and fathers behave. . . . It enables us to respond immediately to a wide variety of situations in our daily lives without having to recalculate what is happening each time the same problem comes up. . . . The Parent tape provides a set of automatic responses for dealing with repetitive situations. (p. 18)

That is, in many situations we respond habitually

out of our Parent ego state, both in thinking and behaving.

The *Adult* ego state is the rational component. Unlike the other two ego states, the Adult appraises the environment objectively. Functionally, it resembles a computer.

The *Child* ego state represents feelings and ways of thinking that occurred early in our lives. Since we still retain the tapes of early childhood, we will at times emit behavior mediated by this ego state.

These three ego states can vary in their influence on behavior and thinking. That is, it is possible for one ego state to dominate behavior. For example, a particular person may respond often from a Child ego state: this person may at times be rebellious, destructive, or creative (Holloway, 1977).

In TA's theory of illness, *parental programming* or a *parental injunction* is viewed as the basic culprit. This programming occurs very early and involves particular messages and instructions given by the parents to the child. During the formative years, because of the programming, the child decides his or her future. Berne (1972) puts it this way:

> Each person decides in early childhood how he will live and how he will die, and that plan, which he carries in his head wherever he goes, is called his *script.* (p. 31)

A *script* is a collection of thoughts and feelings about how to live and is stored in the ego states.

Steiner (1974) states that a harmful script is a blueprint or life plan that is decided on very early in childhood as a result of parental injunctions. In contrast with such harmful scripts, Steiner (1974) describes the alternative:

> In a life course which develops normally, a decision of such importance as what one's identity is to be and what goals one will pursue would be made late enough in life so that a certain measure of knowledge informs the choice. In a situation where a youngster is under no unreasonable pressure, important decisions about life will occur no earlier than adolescence. (p. 69)

Stated simply, a *script decision* made very early will probably be more pathological than one made later.

The early script decision resembles a Greek

tragic drama in that it has a prologue, a climax, and a tragic ending. In connection with Freudian thought, the script resembles the *repetition compulsion*: the adult must repeat mentally or symbolically traumatic childhood events (Steiner 1974).

TA is, then, a psychodynamic approach. It assumes that events in the past — the script decision and the ego state tapes — determine behavior. Syndromes such as alcoholism, schizophrenia, paranoia, depression, and many others are a consequence of past instructions that continue to reverberate in a person's head. Treatment methods, to be consistent with this model of illness, should attempt first to analyze the script and the games played, and then to "reeducate" or "reparent" the person.

Transactional analysis as a therapy has not kept pace with transactional analysis as a descriptive system of interactions. Indeed, Berne, Steiner, Harris, and other prominent TA therapists have not placed as much emphasis on changing unadaptive behavior and thinking as on describing what the ineffective person does. An exception appears to be the work of Jacqui Lee Schiff. Jacqui and Aaron Schiff (Schiff, Fishman, Mellor, Schiff, & Schiff 1975) have reported success with schizophrenics. Briefly, they took schizophrenics into their home and, through a very detailed procedure, "regressed" their patients to early childhood and then *reparented* them; that is, they gave them new ego states or new tapes. Reparenting, the treatment for psychosis, involves erasing the original *Parent* tapes and replacing these tapes with new data (Schiff et al. 1975).

Several other points about TA should be mentioned. Since the major stressors are stroke deficits, game-playing, and the contamination and exclusion of the Adult ego state, transactional therapy often focuses on developing the person's awareness of his or her games or ways of getting strokes (insight), on establishing more of Adult, and on establishing a "stroke reserve." To achieve some of these objectives, the transactional therapist attempts to teach the client how to recognize his or her Parent, Adult, or Child messages. According to Harris (1969), the initial hours of therapy are spent helping the client become aware of his or her three ego states. The awareness of the P-A-C is made possible first by teaching the client the language of TA. TA is unusual in that it is one of the only therapy methods that attempts to establish a common language between client and therapist.

CRITICISMS   Transactional analysis, like psychoanalysis, is involved chiefly in describing inner states or psychodynamic forces. The criticism, again, has been that many of TA's claims are unproven and untestable. In therapy approaches, TA has borrowed many of its techniques from Gestalt therapy, and these do not always seem consistent with the theory of psychopathology forwarded by transactional analysis. Finally, the success of many of the treatments, such as the "reparenting" of schizophrenics, has not been verified by other investigators. Like psychoanalysis, however, transactional analysis has richly contributed to our view and understanding of people.

THE PHENOMENOLOGICAL-EXISTENTIAL PERSPECTIVE

The *phenomenological* and *existential* viewpoints, differ markedly from the psychodynamic views of psychoanalysis and transactional analysis. Although these perspectives do not deal as much with psychopathologies and traditional abnormalities, they do present interesting views of the causes of behavior and the stressors that humans encounter. We will also consider several therapy strategies for these perspectives.

PHENOMENOLOGY

Phenomenology is a philosophical viewpoint stemming mainly from the work of the German philosopher Edmund Husserl (1859–1938). Husserl, like so many other philosophers, was interested in ways to categorize or classify reality. Traditionally, some philosophers have stated that reality can be grouped into two forms: *matter* and *mind*. Other philosophers have denied the existence or importance of one or the other forms. Some, the *materialists*, said that only matter existed. Others, such as George Bishop Berkeley (1685-1753), stated that only ideas and mental events exist. This philosophy was called *immaterialism* or *idealism*. But even the most serious advocate of materialism, John Locke, admitted that human beings are never actually aware of anything but their own ideas and thoughts. Husserl's viewpoint of reality clearly borrowed from the immaterialist tradition. For Husserl and other phenomenologists, the importance, understanding, and meaning of reality do not rest primarily in what physically exists, but rather in how physical things "appear" to us in our consciousness. *Phenomenology* is, therefore, a system or philosophy of consciousness. Its principal concerns are how things appear to a "self." Indeed, the *self* is a significant feature of phenomenology, and consciousness is thought to be *intentionally* caused by some sort of inner inhabitant (Solomon 1972). Most phenomenologists argue that consciousness is not accidental but intentional (Wilson 1966).

Phenomenology, then, is not directly concerned with physical objects or occurrences, but rather with the "impressions" and sensations these things have in the consciousness. Unlike idealism or immaterialism, phenomenology does not deny the existence of matter and physical events. Rather, it gives primacy to the processes of consciousness and awareness.

For psychologists, phenomenology can provide a framework that considers the uniqueness of each person's consciousness. The British psychiatrist R. D. Laing, for example, relies on the phenomenological view to explain human behavior. He suggests that in studying the interactions between people, it is not only each person's behavior that is important, but also how each person interprets the other's behavior. Consider the example of a psychology lecturer who gives an hour lecture to a group of undergraduate students. The reality of this particular situation is that every student is exposed to the same lecture. But a survey of the students concerning their impressions suggests otherwise. Some students have no particular impressions of the professor; others think he was critical and sarcastic; still others think he was delightful and humorous. A rating of impressions shows that he was simultaneously dull, nasty, and great! How can

this be? Laing proposes that we often create or invent other people's behaviors to accommodate our inner frame of reference (Laing, Phillipson, and Lee 1966). Laing and his associates give us a few additional examples that illustrate how a particular behavior may be interpreted quite differently:

> I act in a way that is *cautious* to me, but *cowardly* to you. She sees herself as *vivacious*, but he sees her as *superficial*. He sees himself as *friendly*, she sees him as *seductive*. (p. 15)

Stated simply, it is not how we behave but how we are interpreted that is vital for the phenomenologist.

A few basic assumptions of the phenomenological perspective are listed here. This list, however, is a generalization; that is, phenomenological positions exist that do have different features.

1. Conscious experience is more important than unconscious experience in determining behavior.
2. Normal behavior or psychopathologies are a function of consciousness, perceptions, and interpretations of the social environment.
3. Reality is our "perceptual field."

The perspective of the phenomenological psychologist Carl Rogers provides a good contrast with the psychodynamic perspective in general. The major difference between the phenomenological view and the psychodynamic view lies in the importance given to past experience and unconscious motivation. Phenomenology stresses the present and conscious or willful processes. Rogers maintains just this; that immediate perceptual awareness, not unconscious forces, is of prime importance in understanding behavior.

CARL ROGERS An American clinical psychologist, Carl R. Rogers (1902–) has spent the major portion of his career developing a phenomenological view of humankind as well as a therapy procedure. Briefly, Rogers worked at Rochester Guidance Center in the 1930s, then became a psychology professor at Ohio State University during the 1940s. During his tenure at Ohio he published *Counseling and Psychotherapy*; later, in 1954, he published a second important work, *Client-oriented Therapy*. In both of these volumes Rogers reveals his phenomenological slant; the

Carl Rogers is the primary founder of client-centered therapy. Rogers believes that the quality of the therapeutic relationship is crucial in helping individuals to solve their problems.

central theme of his books is that human beings have an innate drive to express their inherent potentialities. This innate drive or motivation he calls the *actualizing tendency*. For Rogers, the actualizing tendency is what motivates and governs behavior. Its purpose is to fulfill all of the organism's needs, both physical and psychological. A second central feature of Rogers's writing involves the notion of phenomenology. Rogers maintains that the individual's perceptions of reality — subjective awareness — determine for the most part his or her behavior. Objective reality is of less concern. Also part of this second theme is Rogers's idea of the *phenomenal field*. As Freud used the concept of ego to represent a reality mediator, Rogers uses the phenomenal field. It includes all the perceptions and experiences occurring within the person, all the perceptions that are available to awareness. In short, this field defines and determines our subjective reality (Rogers 1951).

Another component of Rogers's phenomenological view is the *self*. As part of the phenomenal field, it is the hub of consciousness. The self is a developmental part of the phenomenal field that unfolds or develops as the child interacts with his or her environment. Through this interaction with an environment, the child discovers that he or she is separate from it. This discovery of separateness — "what is me," and "what is not me" — evolves into a self or self-concept. For the self to thrive,

THE EXISTENTIALIST VIEW

Summarizing the work of the existential phenomenologist Paul Ricoeur, Stewart and Mickunas (1974) list several characteristics of existentialism. Here we will examine two of these characteristics that in our estimation best illustrate the existential trend.

1. *Existentialism focuses on the importance of the body.* Existentialists recognize that we are not just mental or spiritual beings, but that, like all other creatures, we are physical beings. The physical element limits us; we are physically trapped in our bodies. The existential writer Gabreil Marcel declares, "I am bodily." Some of us, however, resolutely deny our "physicalness." But various realities break down this denial and eventually signal to us the importance of the body in our existence; for example, death, illness, and physical limitations are nagging reminders of our physicalness. In a challenging book, *The Denial of Death* (1972), Ernest Becker illustrates how we tenaciously deny our physicalness. He has written that we consciously attempt to distort and suppress our animal functioning (excrement, for example). Our abject finitude is caused by our physicalness, and this awareness sooner or later dashes our assurance of permanence and immortality. In Becker's words, the human character is a "vital lie." Human belief that we are principally mental is an illusion. Becker says:

Rogers believes that certain kinds of conditions are necessary.

Need for positive regard. In developing the ideas of transactional analysis, Berne asserted that human beings have "recognition-hunger." A need to be noticed, loved, stroked, and recognized is essential for physical as well as psychological survival. Similarly, Rogers proposes that we have a basic need to experience certain things: sympathy, warmth, respect, acceptance, and love from important people in our lives. That is, human beings have a *need for positive regard*.

Conditions of worth. Rogers has made it clear in his writings that people need to be positively valued (need for positive regard). But he has also noted that not everything we do will be regarded positively by others. Some of our behaviors

The person is both a self and a body, and from the beginning there is the confusion about where "he" really "is"—in the symbolic inner self or in the physical body. The inner self represents the freedom of thought, imagination, and infinite reach of symbolism. The body represents determinism and boundness. The child gradually learns that his freedom as a unique being is dragged back by the body and its appendages which dicate "what" he is. (Becker 1972, pp. 41–42)

In Becker's existential view, we wish to deny our creature consciousness (awareness of our physical body and its limitations). Existence is a dilemma because we are mortal animals, physical beings who also have consciousness of this mortality. For many existentialists, the human condition is tied to these facts.

2. Existentialism focuses on freedom and choice. All existentialists, recount Stewart and Mickunas (1974), maintain that to exist is to choose freely. But the choices in many cases must be made when too little information is available. Søren Kierkegaard (1813–1855), a Danish existential philosopher and theologian, noted that the great dilemma for human beings is that we are incapable of knowing anything that is ab-

solute or certain. The limitations of our knowledge are tragic because we are compelled to know particular things: For example, "How do I know there is a God?" The alternative is the risk of faith. But this is a leap into uncertainty. Nevertheless, a choice is what we must make.

Aside from choosing to believe or not to believe in a deity, choices must also be made elsewhere in our lives. Some of these choices we can later verify to see if they were the correct ones; but other choices we must make knowing we may never be sure whether they were right. "What is the purpose of my existence?" "Who am I?" The answer to these questions lies in choice, but we always feel the risk involved. We are condemned to choose and be free. Each of us is confronted with the "dreadful" freedom of choice, or at least we think so. Our plight is that existence and choosing are inescapable.

Existentialism, clearly, does not paint an optimistic or favorable picture of life. Pessimism pervades almost all existential writing. It is assumed that to be trapped in our bodies with our thoughts and to be doomed to choose are gloomy and futile prospects. Further, it is assumed that only ephemeral beliefs in purpose or meaning abate the human condition of existence.

are approved, but others are not valued. The person discovers that there are *conditions of worth*, that some of his actions are not valued. Finding that one is only conditionally worthy sets in motion the process of denial and distortion. According to Rogers, the child will separate or split off from his or her experience those behaviors or qualities that are not valued; in short, the person becomes closed to aspects of the self or of his or her behavior. Conditions of worth are stressors that are crippling for the person. They engender denial and distortion of experience, and this process creates a condition of stress called *incongruence*.

<u>Incongruence.</u> Rogers does not use typical diagnostic terms such as "anxiety disorders" or "psychotic disorders." Instead, he has used the labels *defensive behaviors* and *disorganized*

behaviors to refer respectively to neurotic-like reactions and more serious thought disturbances. For Rogers, both of these classes of behaviors entail *incongruence*.

Because of the need for positive regard, the individual may distort unpleasant awarenesses such as conditions of worth and may begin to "experience selectively." Incongruence emerges when an experience or thought is incompatible with one's self-concept or self-esteem. For instance, a woman who has very high self-esteem may picture herself as kind and thoughtful. She thinks: "I never feel badly toward people"; "I never hate anyone." Then someone infuriates her, and she thinks: "I despise that person." Here is the dilemma. Her self-concept or esteem tells her how she must feel, but some of her experiences conflict with that concept. This dilemma produces incongruence—incompatibility between self and experience.

Incongruence is a stressor because it leads to *defenses*. Rogers suggests that experiences that collide with our self-concept bring about defensive maneuvers. Consider another example: A person's conditions of worth may consist of beliefs that she will be loved and valued by others if she does not have sexual thoughts or desires. This introjected value, perhaps from her parents, clashes with her experiences of sexual desires. The resolution is a defensive maneuver. The defenses used for such incongruent events are *distortion* and *denial of experience*. Although both these defenses resemble Freud's ego defense mechanism called *repression*, Rogers, unlike Freud, believes that defenses are essentially crippling, that they are stumbling blocks in the way of achieving our inherent potential (Maddi 1972). In the most serious situations, disorganization of the self occurs. In this case the person is overwhelmed with incongruent experiences; not even the defenses help, and so the self-concept begins to collapse.

Anxiety and threat also are mentioned in Rogers's perspective. The phenomenal field may contain elements that anticipate incongruences between self and experience. This anticipation of incongruence is anxiety or threat.

Client-centered therapy. Rogers's approach to treatment was first called *nondirective counseling*. Later it was changed to *client-centered therapy*. Both names are descriptive and appropriate for Rogerian therapy. First, client-centered therapy does not violate the assumptions of phenomenology, for it relies most heavily on the assumption that consciousness is supreme in determining behavior. This means that the client is capable (possesses the inherent potential) of making correct choices in his or her life. Stated still another way, the *actualizing tendency* needs only certain kinds of support for the person to flourish independently. Indeed, the original name of Rogerian therapy, "nondirective counseling," suggests that the therapist refrains from imposing his or her values and goals on the client. The therapist's role is rather to unleash the client's inherent goodness and rightness by providing a special supportive therapeutic environment. (By contrast, psychoanalysis is a "directive" therapy. The therapist often gives advice and attempts to solve the patient's problems.) Rogers saw several problems with directive approaches to therapy. For one, he was troubled by the term "patient," and so introduced the term "client." For another, Rogers was convinced that

the client, not the therapist, should take responsibility for the direction of the therapy sessions.

On the whole, client-centered therapy focuses on the relationship between client and therapist. Therapeutic relationships attempt to foster: (1) responding with empathy, (2) being genuine, (3) listening attentively, (4) reflecting the client's feelings (pointing them out), and (5) promoting the client's attempts to work out his or her own problems.

THE EXISTENTIAL PERSPECTIVE

To understand the existential perspective, we should begin with the difficult task of defining "existentialism." Difficulties of definition arise first, because this perspective is not a specific doctrine or viewpoint, but rather a "trend" in philosophical thinking (Urmson 1960). Second, there are many kinds of existentialism (Stewart & Mickunas 1974). Third, existentialism is inseparably linked to phenomenology, and so the two terms are difficult to define apart from one another; indeed, existentialism is often referred to as *existential phenomenology*. With these three problems in mind, we will present a general view of existentialism as it relates to behavior.

EXISTENTIAL STRESSORS Existentialism does not directly involve mental disturbances or abnormal behavior. Rather, each of us is involved in a crisis. The crisis of existence is in part related to our physicalness and the necessity of choice. However, other existential stressors prevail. Perhaps the first stressor revealed by existential philosophers was "How are we to know anything for sure?" This question represents the doctrine of *scepticism*. Scepticism holds that there are certain important questions in our lives that we will never be able to answer.

Lack of information, not knowing, is an existential stressor. *Uncertainty* is often the name given to this condition. Years ago, existential philosophers pointed out what many modern psychologists have attempted to verify experimentally: that "control" and "predictability" over events in our lives are highly important. On a much bigger scale, existentialism deals with helplessness. The questions "What is the purpose of my existence?" "What will happen to me?" or "What is the sense of human existence?" are related to the modern topic of helplessness. The existentialist theologian Paul Tillich's concept of "nonbeing" is similarly related. For Tillich, anxiety is, at its fundamental level, the existential awareness of nonbeing. Anxiety and helplessness emerge when we reason that we cannot preserve our "self." *Meaninglessness* is a related existential stressor. The potential occurrence of nothingness, or the annihilation of self, mocks and leers at our feelings of meaning. Meaninglessness is the awareness that our existence is without reason. Sidney Jourard (1971) referred to conditions of meaninglessness as *dispiriting events.* Conditions that make us feel unimportant, worthless, or hopeless, lower our self-esteem, make us feel "that existence is absurd and meaningless . . ." are dispiriting events (Jourard 1971). Existential therapies aim at counterbalancing dispiriting events. Not knowing (skepticism), uncertainty, helplessness, anxiety, meaninglessness, and the like, are the focus of many existential therapies.

Logotherapy. There is no single existential therapy. It is more precise to speak of existential *therapies.* Considering this fact, we will examine a representative model of one existential therapy.

Viktor Frankl (1905–), a Viennese neuropsychiatrist, developed *logotherapy.* Frankl's form of existential therapy evolved out of his observations while in a concentration camp during World War II. During Frankl's imprisonment he witnessed the death and suffering of many of his friends as well as the death of his wife. As a physician in one of the camps, he almost daily encountered death, depression, and illness in his patients. But Frankl was intrigued by one of his observations: death came most rapidly to those who gave up hope and to those who saw no meaning to their suffering and existence. For Frankl, life is sustained by the "will-to-meaning." That is, having a purpose or goal is a vital ingredient for survival. Those in the camps who lost the "will-to-meaning" were the ones who gave up trying; they waited for the Red Cross to come; they failed to get involved in anything; they shriveled up and died. Frankl, as well as many other clinicians since then, have noted that many of those surviving concentration camp or POW experiences had some sort of involvement. Doctors, nurses, and clergy typically had a higher survival rate.

After the Nazi concentration camp experiences, Frankl refined his ideas about the importance of meaning and purpose. Logotherapy owed its inception to Frankl's assumption that human beings must have a sense of purpose and a will-to-meaning. Literally, *logotherapy* means a

"therapy of meaning." *Logo* implies both "spiritual" and "meaning." Briefly, the objectives of logotherapy entail:

1. Helping the person find meaning and purpose in life. Discovering the will-to-meaning is a goal.
2. Helping the person learn to take responsibility for his or her life; Frankl asserts that we are free and are capable of making choices.
3. Helping the person develop self-acceptance and self-realization.

Logotherapy, for the most part, does not focus specifically on trying to remove a symptom. Rather, the focus is on the person's attitude toward his or her symptom (Patterson 1973). In fact, in one logotherapy technique, *paradoxical intention,* the person is instructed to intensify the symptom he or she wishes to remove, a procedure that will, according to Frankl (1960), mobilize the "capacity of self-detachment." *De-reflection* is another procedure that resembles the stoic goal of logotherapy. In de-reflection the person is instructed to turn his or her awareness toward positive features of a negative situation. That is, de-reflection would attempt to persuade the person to reinterpret suffering to show that it may have meaning. This point is illustrated by Frankl:

> I should like to quote [the] . . . case of a colleague, an old general practitioner who turned to me because he still could not get over the loss of his wife who had died two years earlier. His marriage had been very happy and he was very depressed. I asked him quite simply: "Tell me, what would have happened if you had died instead of your wife, if she had survived you?" "That would have been terrible," he said. "Quite unthinkable. How my wife would have suffered!" "Well, you see," I answered, "your wife has been spared that, and it was you who spared her, though, of course, you must now pay by surviving and mourning her." In that very moment his mourning had been given a meaning—the meaning of sacrifice. The depression was overcome. (Wolberg 1967, p. 168)

CRITICISMS Critics point out that neither the phenomenological nor the existentialist perspective is compatible with the scientific or experimental method. Consciousness or the self, for instance, are not directly observable. Nor can one reliably measure "incongruence" or "actualizing tendency."

Critics of these perspectives also question the issue of *cause*. They say that psychology as a science is concerned with showing functional relationships between variables, or with demonstrating that some event or stimulus caused a behavior to happen. To do this, both the cause and the effect must be observable. The phenomenological-existential perspectives, however, hold that internal agents—the self or incongruence, for example—cause behavior in some instances. These causes cannot be observed. The question then arises: How do we know that the self is not caused by the person's environmental history? Indeed, what causes the self or other internal states to happen? Combs and Snygg (1959) say: "All behavior . . . is completely determined by . . . the perceptual field of the behaving organism . . ." (p. 20). But what causes the perceptual field to happen? Other theorists say it is a function of biological endowment or the environment, and so why talk about a mediating (inner) stage as a cause? Another example of this criticism argues that to say that Ann, a client, is defensive and not growing psychologically because she

has low self-esteem does not provide an answer. Why is her self-esteem low? The phenomenologist would answer, "Because she was not valued, stroked, or recognized." But the critics would say this answer deals with conditions in her social environment, not with internal perceptual fields. Why talk about her self or perceptual field as explanatory agents? Even in helping Ann therapeutically, a client-centered therapist would only be able to deal with Ann's environment—the interpersonal environment. The issue, then, is not the existence of inner states and feelings—almost no one says they don't exist—but the use of them as explanations.

In sum, other theorists feel that phenomenology and existentialism are probably best suited as descriptive systems of the inner world of people and as treatment or therapy strategies. They seem less suited for pure scientific enterprises. The phenomenologists themselves are often not concerned about the charge that they are subjective and unscientific. Both phenomenologists and existentialists hold that humans can best be understood by methods that investigate feelings, values, beliefs, consciousness, and other internal states.

THE LEARNING PERSPECTIVE (THE BEHAVIORAL MODEL)

The *learning perspective* is one that attempts to demonstrate that abnormal (as well as normal) behaviors are primarily learned. We should bear in mind that no single learning theory can account for all abnormal behaviors. What we shall discuss are several learning theories that account for the development of certain abnormal behaviors. These theories are *contiguity theory, reinforcement theory,* and *observational learning (modeling) theory*. The *behavioral model* of abnormality departs considerably from the other psychological perspectives discussed in this chapter. First, this model does not infer motives, needs, impulses, instincts, or other inner causes to explain behavior. Second, abnormal behavior is not seen as symptoms of some underlying disease, unconscious conflict, or feeling of incongruence (Bellack & Hersen 1977). That is, external behavior is not viewed as secondary or as less important than what goes on within a person. Rather, the behavioral model focuses directly on behavior; in fact, the word *symptoms* is really not consistent with the behavioral model since it implies an underlying disease process. The

focus is also on the environment of the individual exhibiting the abnormal behavior. Again, the behavioral model maintains that abnormal behavior is principally learned. Finally, abnormal behavior is not viewed as being distinct from normal behavior in the way it is developed and maintained (Kazdin 1975).

CONTIGUITY THEORY

Contiguity theory holds that a learned "connection" is made between two stimuli because they have occurred together at approximately the same time; or that a learned connection is made between a stimulus and a response because they have occurred contiguously. *Contiguity* in this sense means "occurring or happening at the same time." For example, if a person developed a phobic fear of automobiles, a contiguity position would suggest that the automobile, a stimulus, had somehow become "associated" or connected in time with

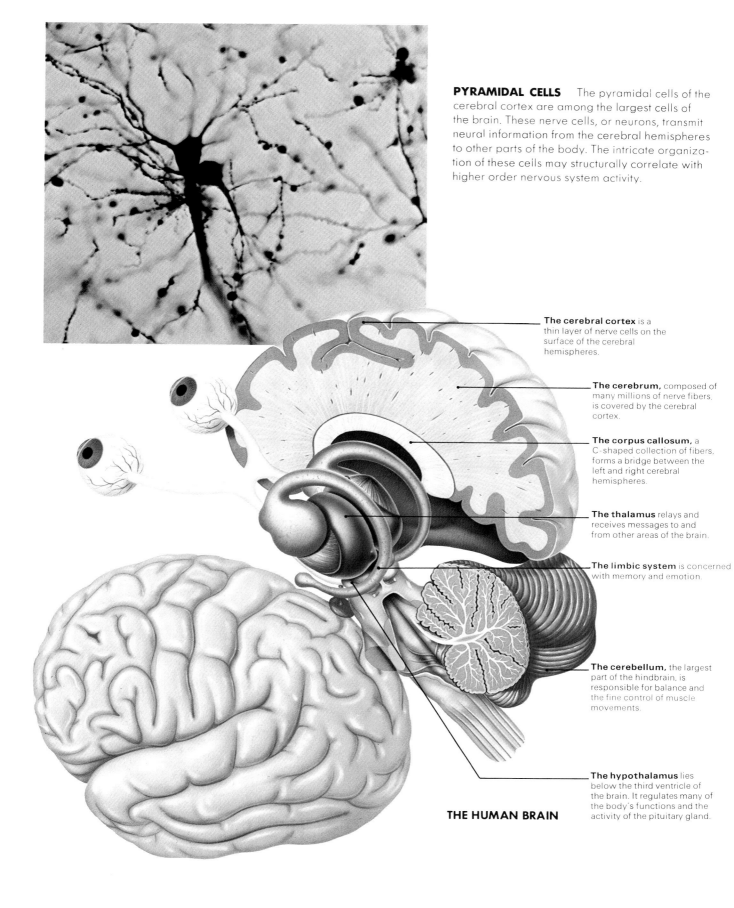

PYRAMIDAL CELLS The pyramidal cells of the cerebral cortex are among the largest cells of the brain. These nerve cells, or neurons, transmit neural information from the cerebral hemispheres to other parts of the body. The intricate organization of these cells may structurally correlate with higher order nervous system activity.

The cerebral cortex is a thin layer of nerve cells on the surface of the cerebral hemispheres.

The cerebrum, composed of many millions of nerve fibers, is covered by the cerebral cortex.

The corpus callosum, a C-shaped collection of fibers, forms a bridge between the left and right cerebral hemispheres.

The thalamus relays and receives messages to and from other areas of the brain.

The limbic system is concerned with memory and emotion.

The cerebellum, the largest part of the hindbrain, is responsible for balance and the fine control of muscle movements.

The hypothalamus lies below the third ventricle of the brain. It regulates many of the body's functions and the activity of the pituitary gland.

THE HUMAN BRAIN

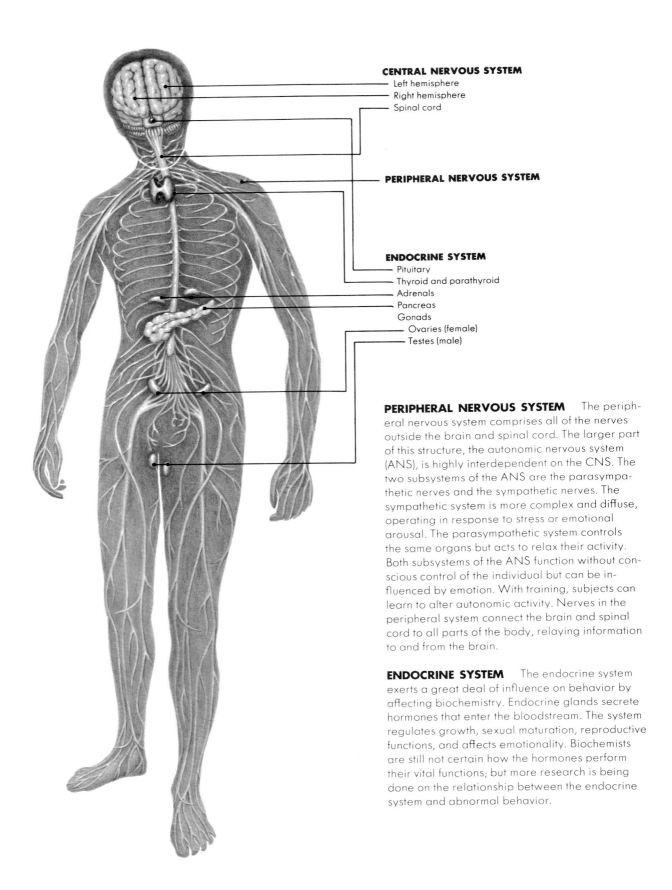

CENTRAL NERVOUS SYSTEM
— Left hemisphere
— Right hemisphere
— Spinal cord

PERIPHERAL NERVOUS SYSTEM

ENDOCRINE SYSTEM
— Pituitary
— Thyroid and parathyroid
— Adrenals
— Pancreas
Gonads
— Ovaries (female)
— Testes (male)

PERIPHERAL NERVOUS SYSTEM   The peripheral nervous system comprises all of the nerves outside the brain and spinal cord. The larger part of this structure, the autonomic nervous system (ANS), is highly interdependent on the CNS. The two subsystems of the ANS are the parasympathetic nerves and the sympathetic nerves. The sympathetic system is more complex and diffuse, operating in response to stress or emotional arousal. The parasympathetic system controls the same organs but acts to relax their activity. Both subsystems of the ANS function without conscious control of the individual but can be influenced by emotion. With training, subjects can learn to alter autonomic activity. Nerves in the peripheral system connect the brain and spinal cord to all parts of the body, relaying information to and from the brain.

ENDOCRINE SYSTEM   The endocrine system exerts a great deal of influence on behavior by affecting biochemistry. Endocrine glands secrete hormones that enter the bloodstream. The system regulates growth, sexual maturation, reproductive functions, and affects emotionality. Biochemists are still not certain how the hormones perform their vital functions; but more research is being done on the relationship between the endocrine system and abnormal behavior.

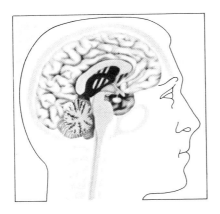

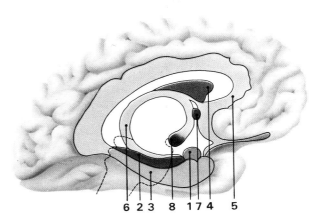

6 2 3 8 1 7 4 5

LIMBIC SYSTEM

The limbic system (red) is involved with memory, learning, emotionality, and sexuality. Emotions result from the interaction between the limbic system and the cerebral cortex.

The limbic system consists of a group of interconnected structures, all of which lie deep in the temporal lobes of the brain and in the region of the thalamus. The amygdala (**1**) is believed to be concerned with aggression. The hippo-campus (**2**), lying above the parahippocampal gyrus (**3**), is concerned with memory. The septum pelucidum (**4**) is thought to be associated with pleasure reactions. The cingulate gyrus (**5**), the fornix (**6**), and the anterior commissure (**7**) carry nerve fibers to and from other structures in the limbic system, as do the mammillary bodies (**8**), which are also vitally concerned with memory. These eight structures comprise the limbic system.

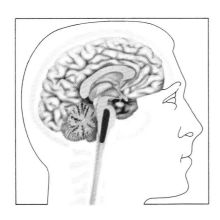

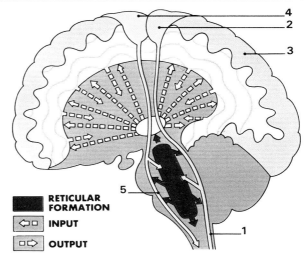

4
2
3

■ **RETICULAR FORMATION**

◁□ **INPUT**

□▷ **OUTPUT**

5

1

RETICULAR FORMATION

The reticular forma-tion (red) is located within the brain stem. It is composed of hundreds of short-axon neurons, which make up a dense and intricate nerve complex.

Information entering the brain along the sensory nerve pathway (**1**) passes to the sensory cortex (**2**). However, nerve branches from the path-way first send impulses to the ascending reticular formation, which stimulates activity and attentive-ness throughout the entire cortex (**3**). The resultant outgoing information leaves the brain from the motor cortex (**4**), through the motor pathway (**5**), and then into the spinal cord.

SEDATIVES AND BARBITURATES

Secobarbital

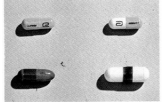

Pentobarbital

Phenobarbital

Miscellaneous barbiturates

STIMULANTS

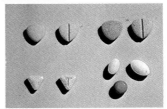

Amphetamines

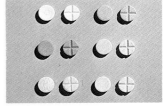

Amphetamines

Amphetamines

OPIUM

HEROIN

COCAINE

LSD

PEYOTE

MARIJUANA

Drugs may be classified in terms of their chemical composition or their effects on the user. Barbiturates, for example, depress the function of the central nervous system. They can yield such symptoms as euphoria, mania, hallucinations, or tranquility. Amphetamines are stimulants that increase feelings of optimism, alertness, or euphoria; they also increase physical energy.

Marijuana users experience a "high" characterized by euphoria and a pleasant "drifting" sensation. Cocaine, another stimulant, increases energy levels and sleeplessness; it produces extreme euphoria and reduces depression and tension. Hallucinogenic drugs result in hallucinations. Opium, a major illegal drug, produces physiological addiction. Feelings of euphoria, revery, relief from pain, and drowsiness are among the effects of opium derivatives like codeine, morphine, and heroin.

CULTURE AND BEHAVIOR

Human nature is amazingly flexible, and people learn an incredible array of behaviors. By inspecting various cultural practices concerning eating, sexuality, aggressive behaviors, child rearing, and so on, we can become convinced rather quickly that what characterizes our so-called "human nature" most precisely is our ability to learn almost any set of complex behaviors. We have listed diverse human activities recorded by various ethnographic studies. These rather bizarre examples make the point that human beings can do almost impossible things, develop what we consider bizarre desires and tastes, and value things that would repulse most of us. These data were adapted principally from Williams (1972).

1. Pain reflexes can be altered by learning. If the culture teaches voluntary control over certain pains, then its people may approach them with seeming indifference. For example, the Cheyenne practiced mutilation; the Fiji firewalkers practice their skills with stoic posture. In New Delhi, during 1970, Raman-and Yogi was locked in an airtight box where he cut his oxygen requirements to less than one-quarter of what was thought necessary to sustain life. This raj yogi stayed in the box for over three hours (Calder 1971). Apparently the yogi had learned to alter his metabolic requirements for oxygen.
2. Affection can be expressed in a variety of ways: the Masai of Africa spit on one another as a display of affection. Polynesian males greet each other by rubbing one another's back.
3. The degree of hardness or softness of the feces or excrement can be learned or culturally conditioned, even in instances of similar diet.
4. Ethnographic studies have shown that

"magical" deaths can be induced if the person is convinced that he or she is a victim of a curse or witchcraft.
5. All sorts of bizarre substances may be viewed as "delicious" or pleasing to the taste. For example, the Vedda of Ceylon delight in eating varieties of rotted wood mixed with honey; certain South American tribes (the Guiana) regularly eat pebbles —others also eat clay. In still other cultures the taste has been acquired for snakes, dogs, grubs, gibbons, monkeys or putrefied meat (with a side order of house rat and rice); all sorts of grotesque insects are regarded as culinary delights. One anthropologist, who lived for a short while with a group of worm-eating primitive people (they ate a particular large worm by removing its head and sucking out its "delicious" viscera) noted that nothing was more sickening to these people than the typical American breakfast: a scrambled unborn chicken embryo—an egg.

This vast array of learned behaviors is not the result of genetic endowment or other hidden inner forces. Powerful desires, views about "deliciousness," expressions of affection, expressions of masculinity and femininity, and literally countless other behaviors are a consequence of learning. Given these facts, it is not at all difficult to see that many abnormal behaviors, even of the most unusual type, could under certain environments be learned. The child who trembles and fears her school bus; the man who finds cadavers sexually arousing; the child who vomits, but only at certain times and only in the class of a particular teacher; the grown man who cringes at the sight of an open field or meadow—all these behaviors may be learned in special environments.

some aversive or fear-inducing stimulus. Because of the time connection between the automobile and some aversive stimulus, the automobile acquires fear-producing potential.

CLASSICALLY CONDITIONED FEAR Perhaps the most cited example of classically conditioned

abnormal behavior was reported by the behavioral psychologist John B. Watson (1878–1958). In a famous experiment, Watson was able to develop a learned phobic fear of rats in an 11-month-old child, Albert B.

In conditioning Albert, Watson selected the striking of a steel bar as the *unconditioned stimulus*

Culver Pictures

John Broadus Watson (1878–1958) is referred to as the founder of behaviorism.

because this sound produced strong emotional arousal—fear. No prior learning was required for this stimulus to produce fear in Albert. Watson next selected as a *neutral stimulus* a white rat, to which Albert had no particular reaction prior to the conditioning. To describe exactly what Watson accomplished (in particular the phenomenon of stimulus generalization) we quote Andrew Salter (1961):

> Watson found that the infant was not at all disturbed by a white rat, but showed fear only at the loud striking of a steel bar. After eight presentations of white rat and loud noise simultaneously, when the white rat was presented alone, the infant cried bitterly and tried to escape.
>
> Five days later the infant was again tested, to determine if the fear reaction had transferred to any previously emotionally neutral objects. Such was the case. The child was still afraid of the rat, but now he was also afraid of a hairy dog, a fur coat, and to a slight degree, of cotton. . . . The fear response conditioned to the white rat had become transferred to all furry objects. Everything else in the room when the condi-

CREATING PSYCHOPATHOLOGY BY CONDITIONING

The first major proponent of contiguity theory was the Russian physiologist and psychologist Ivan Pavlov (1849–1936). As most readers know, Pavlov observed that if a neutral stimulus, say, a bell, was presented to a dog immediately before the presentation of food (the unconditioned stimulus), after a number of such presentations, the bell alone (now a conditioned stimulus) would elicit a *learned response* of salivation (conditioned response).

By the same token, if a neutral stimulus, say, a tone, is presented just before another powerful unconditioned stimulus—say, an electric shock—after a few associations, the tone will take on shock-eliciting features. These two examples represent what is called *respondent* or *classical conditioning,* which is based on contiguity of two stimuli: the bell and the food in the first case, and the tone and the shock in the second.

Additional examples of classical conditioning have been reported over the years since Pavlov's initial work at the turn of the century. For example, Pavlov and Shenger-Krestovnikov were able to develop *experimental neurosis* in dogs by using the conditioning process. Pavlov began by teaching the dogs to discriminate between a circle and an ellipse. Then he progressively diminished the difference between the two. When the two forms became very similar, the dogs started to break down: they would urinate, howl, and show great agitation. Pavlov had succeeded in producing an acute neurotic reaction by manipulating the animals' environment. Since Pavlov's time, other researchers have also developed abnormal behavior in animals by exposing them to various conditions. W. H. Gantt was one of the first American researchers to develop neurotic reactions in dogs. Gantt, as well as Liddell some time later, noted that stressful conditions usually "condition" the cardiac muscles more readily

tioning took place was still emotionally neutral. (pp. 25–26)

Other researchers also were able to induce neurotic symptoms in humans or animals by employing Pavlov's conditioning methods. Liddell and his

Culver Pictures

Ivan Pavlov (1849–1936) was a Russian physiologist who developed an early learning procedure now often called **"classical conditioning" or "respondent conditioning."**

than the skeletal muscles—and so stress typically involves high heart rate and elevated blood pressure in the experimental animal. In the 1940s, Masserman demonstrated through a series of experiments that all sorts of abnormal behaviors could be learned or conditioned into dogs, monkeys, and cats. For example, he experimentally induced the following:

1. High heart rate, low startle thresholds, and raised blood pressure in animals exposed to certain environmental stressors.
2. Phobic responses to simple stimuli.
3. Sexual deviations, such as diminished heterosexual interests.

4. Psychophysiological reactions (asthmatic breathing, anorexia, genitourinary dysfunction, and so on).
5. Sensorial disturbances—apparent disorientation, confusion, and hallucinations. (Data cited in Shagass 1975, p. 431)

Finally (we will discuss this research more fully in later chapters) Seligman and his associates have shown that dogs exposed to inescapable shock subsequently fail to learn simple tasks such as escaping from shock.

associates (Anderson, Parmenter, & Liddell 1935) demonstrated, for instance, that *experimental neurosis* (experimentally induced) could be developed in sheep. Interestingly, these sheep also exhibited disturbed cardiac functioning; neurotic human patients often report heart complaints.

In connection with Liddell's observations concerning heart dysfunctions, we should mention that a major consequence of classical conditioning in which aversive stimuli are used (an electric shock, for example) is strong emotional arousal mediated by the *autonomic nervous system.* The emotions accompanying classical conditioning in which an aversive unconditioned stimulus is used are usually fear and rage. We should therefore expect that after conditioning, not only will the unconditioned aversive stimulus elicit strong emotional arousal, but so will any neutral stimuli that has been associated with the powerful unlearned event. That is, strong emotional arousal—fear in particular—can be conditioned to all sorts of neutral stimuli or settings if by accident such pairing has occurred.

REINFORCEMENT THEORY

> Nature has placed mankind under the governance of two sovereign masters, pain and pleasure. It is for them alone to point out what we ought to do, as well as to determine what we shall do.
>
> Jeremy Bentham (1789)

During the eighteenth century, as Jeremy Bentham's statement suggests, the influence of pleasure and pain—the environment—on behavior was keenly recognized. This particular trend in thinking could be observed especially in the field of criminology. Cesare Beccaria, for instance, published an essay on crime and punishment in 1764. One of the themes of his essay was that punishment could deter criminal behavior. More specifically, Beccaria believed that mild yet prompt punishment was more effective than severe punishment administered erratically. Within Beccaria's frame of reference, the English philosopher Jeremy Bentham announced what he believed to be a fundamental principle of human behavior: the principle of *psychological hedonism*. This principle states that human beings do those things that produce pleasure, but avoid doing those things that produce pain. Though against strong punishment, Bentham made this point:

> It is a great merit in a punishment to contribute to the reformation of the offender, not only through fear of being punished again, but by a change in his character and habits.

The writings of both Beccaria and Bentham, hinting strongly that behavior was guided by the avoidance of pain and the seeking of pleasure, influenced several nineteenth-century psychologists,

Christopher S. Johnson/Stock, Boston

B. F. Skinner is an American psychologist who developed operant conditioning. Skinner maintains that behavior is generally a function of its consequences.

most importantly, psychologist Edward Thorndike.

For Edward L. Thorndike (1874–1949), hedonism played a major role in his theory of learning. He further suggested that the simplest yet most characteristic form of learning for humans and animals was trial-and-error, based again on hedonism. Like Pavlov, Thorndike set out in his laboratory to make evident the conditions that determined the acquisition of a response. To find out how an animal learned, Thorndike developed puzzle boxes. He would place an animal in the box and then watch to see how it would escape. From many such observations, he concluded that responses that led to escape (he defined this as pleasurable) were retained, while those that did not lead to escape were not retained.

The work of Thorndike evolved into what is now called *operant conditioning*, developed more fully by B. F. Skinner. Unlike classical conditioning, operant conditioning develops new behaviors that bring about positive consequences or removes negative events. In classical conditioning a new stimulus—say, a bell—is conditioned to elicit the same response that has previously occurred, whereas in operant conditioning a new *response* is learned.

For humans, behavior that produces social approval, food, or other positive consequences, or that reduces damaging or aversive events, illustrates *operant behavior.* The behavior "operates" on the environment to bring about changes in it.

Applied to abnormal behavior, classically conditioned behavior problems typically involve learning to fear new stimuli—a phobic fear of planes, crowds, and the like. In operant conditioning, elaborate maladaptive behaviors may be acquired because they result in positive consequences or reduction of aversive events. In particular, many maladaptive behaviors are maintained or shaped into existence because *reinforcers,*either by accident or by intention, follow the problem behavior. For instance, almost all schoolchildren at one time or another get headaches or mild stomachaches and plead with their parents to stay away from school. It is certainly possible, however, for a child to discover that the parents can't be sure whether he or she is sick. In this instance the child may find that pretending to be sick produces the same positive consequences (staying home, watching television, getting attention) as real sickness does. Gradually, if the parents continue to make staying home pay off handsome dividends, the "staying-home response" will occur more and more often.

Building on the work of Thorndike and psychologist Clark Hull, Neal Miller (1909-   ) and John Dollard (1900-   ) developed a *drive-reduction theory* of abnormal behavior. Essentially, they suggested that responses that reduce the drives of fear, anxiety, or conflict will be strengthened. Stated differently, any behavior that terminates or avoids the fear situation or lessens the experiences of anxiety and conflict will occur again. Repression, then, would be an operant or drive-reduction action because it lessens painful thoughts.

Miller and Dollard then developed an experimental model of abnormal behavior employing *avoidance conditioning.* Avoidance conditioning can be illustrated with this case: If a rat is given a shock in a white compartment of its cage, but is allowed to escape from the shock by running into a black compartment, after several trials the rat will learn to avoid the shock by always running into the black compartment. Another colleague of Miller's, O. H. Mowrer, conducted similar investigations and further stated that avoidance conditioning is

actually a combination of both classical conditioning and operant conditioning: there is classical conditioning of fear of the white compartment, but instrumental avoidance (an operant behavior) of the compartment reduces the fear. Thus, it would seem that both operant and classical conditioning are at work in the formation of many maladaptive behaviors.

OBSERVATIONAL LEARNING (MODELING)

The third learning theory, *observational learning* (Bandura & Walters 1963), states that abnormal behavior can be acquired if an individual sees another person model or perform a particular behavior. Certain conditions seem to determine whether a particular person will copy an abnormal behavior. For instance, if the model(s) has status or prestige and resembles the viewer in age, sex, and other attributes, then the likelihood of the viewer's acquiring or adopting the behavior is enhanced.

Examples of behavior acquired by observational learning abound. Aggressive responses, fear of particular objects, and other complex unadaptive behaviors can be developed through modeling (Kazdin 1974; Bandura 1965). Observational learning also can be used to increase desired behaviors or lessen undesired behaviors by presenting a model that performs the appropriate responses (Bandura 1971; Rachman 1972; Kazdin 1974b). (One of the sociological perspectives discussed in the next section, Sutherland's disassociation hypothesis, bears much resemblance to the observational theory.)

CRITICISMS Like the other perspectives, the learning model has been criticized on several points. Because they deal with observed behavior, learning theories are generally based on "scientific" data. Learning theory terminology can accommodate the scientific method: reproducible observations, operational descriptions, hypothesis formation, and public verification (Dunham 1977). Nonetheless, it has been criticized on other grounds.

First, most of the evidence dealing with psychopathology comes from studies conducted with animals, not humans. For ethical reasons, we obviously cannot conduct similar experiments with people. But there are some problems with using data drawn from animal studies. Bachrach (1972) suggests that most experiments should not be unduly "artificial," but should be *representative models*. For the most part, animal research attempts to reveal and record "basic processes" (Skinner 1957). The problem, then, is extrapolating or generalizing basic animal processes to humans. The experiment provides controls that reveal causal factors that induce psychopathology. But, in the real world, can those same factors be assigned the status of "causal agents" simply because animal data "suggested" so? Are animals representative samples of people? As Sidman (1960, p. 15) wonders, ". . . why should we expect a rat's psychosis to bear any . . . resemblance to that of a human being?"

Second, learning theory and animal data concerning psychopathology tend to underplay or ignore biological components and individual differences. (Pavlov's early investigations, however, did acknowledge individual differences.) The rapidly developing *cognitive social learning* approach is, however, starting to take into account the importance of individual differences (see Mischel 1977).

A third area of criticism is that learning theory of the Skinnerian variety denies the importance of inner states or drives (Herrnstein 1977). Radical behavior theories, then, must look mainly to the immediate environment to account for behavior. If the environmental history of the organism is considered, the problem of verifying those past conditions emerge. However, some current social learning approaches do hypothesize certain internal states to explain various forms of behavior.

THE SOCIOLOGICAL PERSPECTIVE

The last psychosocial perspective we will consider is the *sociological perspective*. It has been included with the psychological perspectives because it shares many of the features of the other viewpoints. For one, the sociological perspective, like other views discussed in this chapter, is chiefly an environmental viewpoint. It gives virtually no weight to biological factors or individual differences as casual or determining agents. Behavior, for the most part, is viewed as emerging from social or cultural variables. Further, this perspective holds that the elimination or prevention of deviant or abnormal behavior is best achieved through changes in social factors. To highlight these social factors, we have selected four subcategories of sociological perspectives: the *ecological perspective*, the *value-conflict perspective*, the *anomie perspective*, and the *labeling perspective*.

Although all these viewpoints are very different, their common point is that abnormal behavior (or *deviance*) is a manifestation of social organizations.

THE ECOLOGY MODEL

Sociologists at the University of Chicago, between the early 1900s and the mid-1930s, conducted numerous investigations that attempted to show that deviance (crime, mental illness, etc.) was unequally distributed in various areas of Chicago. Faris and Dunham (1939) demonstrated specifically that mental illness was linked to particular areas in a city. A higher concentration of deviants was found in the inner city and a lower concentration in areas farther out. Mental disorders were found to be connected with poverty, social disorganization, and recent migration. Following the University of Chicago investigations, a classic ecological study, the *New Haven Study*, was conducted by Hollingshead and Redlich (1958). This investigation found the prevalence of mental illness to be much greater in the lower social classes. Schizophrenia, for example, was diagnosed much more frequently in the lower classes. It was subsequently found, however, that this statistic was in part a result of considerable time spent in the hospital; that is, lower-class patients remained hospitalized for longer periods of time than did other groups. It is unclear why this occurs.

Following the New Haven study, another project, called the *Midtown Manhattan Study*, was undertaken (Strole, Langner, Michael, Opier, & Tennie 1962). This investigation also documented that the frequency of psychophysiological reactions, neurosis, and the like was connected to social class. For instance, individuals who changed status and moved up socially had a decreased frequency of symptoms, while those who moved downward showed an increase. From this perspective it was held that those raised in or exposed to lower social

VALUE-CONFLICT PERSPECTIVE

The *value-conflict perspective* relates chiefly to problems of crime (Davis 1975). That is, this perspective deals more with explanations of criminal behavior than with mental illness or other behavior problems. Basically, this perspective holds that crime is a normal process, reflecting a different set of values that conflict with more acceptable ones. Stressors such as poverty, disease, physical surroundings—the things that ecological theorists used as causal agents—are not seen as the principal causes of deviance. Rather, values induce abnormal behavior.

But how are the values transmitted? That is, how does the person acquire the "wrong" values? Edwin Sutherland's theory of *differential association* represents the value-conflict perspective and suggests a means by which conflicting values are acquired. He proposes that crime and delinquency (to some extent this could apply also to drug use) are learned through *association* with those having criminal attitudes and deviant behaviors (Sutherland 1939). In many ways, Sutherland's differential association theory resembles the observational or modeling theory of learning proposed some time later by the psychologist Albert Bandura. In fact, a nineteenth-century criminologist, Gabriel Tarde, developed a theory of crime based on imitation or modeling, suggesting that a person becomes deviant because he or she has seen others perform the problem behaviors.

Sutherland and Cressey (1970) list nine assumptions about the acquisition of criminal behavior:

1. Criminal behavior is learned. (That is, it is not inherited.)
2. Criminal behavior is learned in interaction with other persons in a process of communication.
3. The principal part of the learning of criminal behavior occurs within intimate personal groups. (Movies, newspapers, and other impersonal sources of data play little role in the genesis of criminal behavior.)
4. When criminal behavior is learned, the learning includes (a) techniques of committing the crime, which are sometimes very complicated, sometimes very simple; and (b) the specific direction of motives, drives, rationalizations, and attitudes.
5. The specific direction of motives and drives is learned from definitions of the legal codes as favorable or unfavorable.
6. A person becomes delinquent because more definitions are favorable to violation of law than are unfavorable to violation of law.
7. Differential associations may vary in frequency, duration, priority, and intensity.
8. The process of learning criminal behavior by association with criminal and anticriminal patterns involves all the mechanisms that are involved in any other learning.
9. Although criminal behavior is an expression of general needs and values, it is not explained by them, since noncriminal behavior is an expression of the same needs and values.

In addition, Sutherland was one of the first to reject the idea that crime is restricted to members of the lower social classes. Indeed, he was perhaps the first social scientist to conduct research on the so-called white-collar criminal.

class conditions—poor physical surroundings, parents with poor mental health, economic deprivation, physical illness, and so on—had a higher risk of developing deviance.

Critics of these studies rely on the *drift hypothesis* to challenge the ecology model. The drift hypothesis simply states that those with psychopathologies or other disorders will "drift" downward socially. These critics say that social class is a symptom and not the cause of deviance.

ANOMIE PERSPECTIVE

Anomie is a social stressor implying a condition of being without rules or law—a state of normlessness. Émile Durkheim (1858–1917) was the first sociologist to popularize the term in sociological literature. He used *anomie* to refer to a breakdown in the social norms that regulate individual conduct. In particular, he used the concept to explain suicide. In general, because of anomie, a given individual would feel powerless, isolated, and alienated in a disintegrating culture. Deviance would ensue. *Anomie* has also been used to refer to a subjective feeling of *alienation*. MacIver (1950) states:

> [Anomie] signifies the state of mind of one who has been pulled up from his moral roots . . . who has no longer any sense of continuity, of folk, of obligation. (p. 84)

Robert Merton, unlike Durkheim, has attempted to explain the causes of anomie in more detail and to describe individual styles of adapting to this social stressor. We should note that Merton's formulation applies more to anomie as it induces crime and drug abuse than as it relates to mental illness.

Generally stated, Merton's thoughts concerning deviance are these:

1. Deviance is caused by anomie.
2. For some social groups there exists a *limited access* to culturally valued goals (money, power, status).
3. There exist individual modes for adapting within the culture.

Let us briefly examine Merton's second and third points. For Merton, "limited access" means that although our society emphasizes generally similar goals for everyone, everyone does not have equal opportunities for achieving those goals. Merton (1975) makes this important point in support of his thesis:

> A high frequency of deviant behavior is not generated merely by lack of opportunity. . . . It is when a system of cultural values extols, virtually above all else, certain *common* success-goals *for the population at large* while the social structure rigorously restricts or completely closes access to approved modes of reaching these goals *for a considerable part of the same population* that deviant behavior ensues on a large scale. (pp. 185–215)

Nonconformist or deviant behavior follows this discrepancy between different groups' access to goals. (This condition is anomie.) A corollary to this point is Merton's suggestion that our culture strongly emphasizes the goals but places little emphasis on how they are to be achieved. The third point introduces the notion that there are categories of individual adaptation. According to Merton (1968), people can be categorized on two dimen-

sions: whether they pursue the cultural goals and whether they employ culturally approved means to reach those goals. He lists five individual modes of adaptation and suggests that these adaptation styles are "role behaviors" that are more or less enduring:

The *conformist* internalizes societal rules and therefore strives for cultural goals, using institutionalized (acceptable) means to achieve them. Because this is the most common style, it represents the "normal" person. The *innovator* also pursues the cultural goals but he or she may use illegitimate (unacceptable) means to achieve those goals. For example, making money would be accepted as the cultural goal, but rather than use acceptable means (working at a job) this person would substitute criminal activity. The *ritualist* is a person who avoids the cultural goals but abides by the institutional norms. As Davis (1975) remarks:

> [The ritualist] will become a bureaucratic virtuoso. Lower middle-class respectables, caught up in lower-echelon organizational routines, are most likely to respond with ritualistic performances. (p. 111)

The ritualist, then, is one who gives up when unable to achieve the valued goals. In compensation, the ritualist may, for example, become a stiff, rule-abiding bureaucrat. The *retreatist* rejects both the cultural goals and the means sanctioned to achieve them. In short, the retreatist withdraws or disengages from the goals and means as much as possible. Alcoholics, drug abusers, psychotics, and certain aged persons seem to employ this coping tactic. Stereotypically, the "beatniks" of the 1950s and the "hippies" of the 1960s characterize certain features of retreatism. Finally there is the *rebel*. These persons may be viewed more clearly as political activists or people who attempt to initiate social change (Davis 1975).

In conclusion, anomie and limited access to goals induce deviance; the social conditions of normlessness and unequal opportunity foster rule-breaking.

THE LABELING PERSPECTIVE

The most recent sociological approach, and the one most relevant to abnormal psychology, is the *labeling perspective* (Scheff 1975; Schur 1971; Lemert 1967). Basically, *labeling* refers process of negatively classifying a person who

THE SOCIOLOGICAL APPROACH TO MENTAL HEALTH INTERVENTION

Considering the sociological approach to treatment or prevention, Korchin (1976) provides us with several contrasting models of intervention. For one, he describes the *clinical models,* including the custodial approach (state mental hospitals) and the therapeutic approach, exemplified by services provided by clinical psychologists and psychiatrists in private practice. In contrast to the clinical models are the *community models* and the *social action model* which employ the ecological frame of reference.

Concerning *community models,* Korchin writes: "The community models, . . . shift emphasis from the individual toward the social setting" (p. 110). He continues by noting that the community models assume that the determinants of human problems reside not within a person but within the social setting. *Public health* is one illustration of the community model.

As Korchin says, in the public health emphasis,

> the shift is from direct involvement with the human problems of particular people toward efforts to alter some of the social conditions which affect whole communities. (p. 114)

The ultimate extension of the sociological approach to intervention would probably be what Korchin calls the *social action model.* He writes:

> It rests on the fundamental assumption that society, not the patient, is disturbed and needs change. . . . Within this view, therapeutic and community approaches are both used to influence and control the individual in accordance with the dominant ideology of the state, industry, and other centers of power in our society. (p. 115)

performs a disapproved behavior. Labeling is therefore done by those other than the rule-violators: psychologists, police, teachers, psychiatrists, and so on.

The thesis of the labeling perspective is essentially this: Once a person is tagged, labeled, or defined as a deviant, he or she maintains the pathological role (defined socially). As Tittle (1975) states, officially classifying a behavior as deviant makes the "deviant" worse, inciting further rule-breaking.

In 1938, the sociologist Frank Tannenbaum sketched the prototype of labeling theory, especially as labeling related to crime. He made this noteworthy statement:

> The process of making the criminal . . . is a process of tagging, defining, identifying, segregating, describing, emphasizing, making conscious and self-conscious; it becomes a way of stimulating, suggesting, emphasizing, and evoking the very traits that are complained of. . . .
>
> The person becomes the thing he is described as being. . . . The way out is through a refusal to dramatize the evil. (pp. 19–20)

Another concept that labeling theorists have relied on is the distinction between what Lemert (1951) called *primary* and *secondary* deviance. Simply put, primary deviance is the initial rule-violation without the social reactions of labeling and condemnation. Secondary deviance is the deviance that follows labeling and the person's initial acceptance of the "deviant role" as his or her social definition. This distinction is the crux of labeling theory, for it is held, to some extent at least, that whatever the initial cause, abnormal behavior is maintained by societal reactions to it. As Hawkins and Tiedman (1975, p. 47) propose, societal reaction therefore becomes the new cause and displaces the original one.

Labeling theory, then, is a theory of deviant roles. Breaking rules is not really what matters, but rather detection and labeling of rule-breaking. Secret deviance — that is, abnormal behavior that is not detected and labeled — has a different effect on the performer than does the same deviance that is discovered and labeled. The discovered deviant becomes stigmatized, and this initiates the self-fulfilling prophecy.

While labeling theory may be a useful model for particular deviances, it is not very persuasive with certain psychopathologies, particularly those with an early onset. Early infantile autism, childhood schizophrenia, depression, and many other psychopathologies do not seem to lend themselves to explanation by the labeling perspective; whereas the approach may be relevant to crime, drug abuse, and detected sexual deviations. The most significant shortcoming of the labeling perspective is that mentioned by Akers (1968): "The label does not create the behavior in the first place." Another criticism leveled at the labeling theorists (one that they do not object to) is that the labeling perspective removes responsibility from the violator and initial causal agents (by treating the violator as a victim) and lays the responsibility on the diagnostician and others who detect and protest the initial deviance. In Hawkins and Tiedman's words, the labeling perspective is an "underdog ideology."

CRITICISMS

As we noted previously, especially for the labeling perspective, the sociological perspective has limitations. Without going into great detail, let us summarize a few of the chief limitations.

Much of the data presented in this last perspective is mainly descriptive. *Naturalistic research* characterizes much of the information provided by the sociological perspectives. In the naturalistic method, the researcher usually attempts to reveal an association or correlation between two variables; for example, schizophrenia and social class. It is important to recognize that the researcher has no control over these variables, since he or she is only observing how one interacts with the other. This is the limitation. A correlation between social class and mental illness simply describes the relationship between these variables; it does not allow one justifiably to state that schizophrenia, for example, is *caused* by membership in the lower social class.

Although the naturalistic research method has certain advantages over experimental or laboratory methods — one advantage is that the behavior in question occurs in a natural setting — there exist many psychopathologies that cannot be easily detected in naturalistic conditions. For example, the family is a highly important social unit, a place where behavior problems emerge; but psychopathology in the family is difficult to study through observation by an outsider (see chapter 18). Sociocultural causation might be studied most effectively through the experimental method, but ethical and practical considerations limit this approach.

SUMMARY

1. The first psychosocial perspective was the *psychodynamic* view, which generally includes a number of theoretical positions that suggest that past traumatic events are stored in consciousness and exert profound influences on current behavior. *Psychoanalysis, ego analysis* (neo-Freudian views), and *transactional analysis* are three examples of psychodynamic theories.

2. *Psychoanalysis* was the first psychodynamic theory of personality and psychopathology. Freud proposed three hypothetical structural components of personality: *id, ego,* and *superego*. The *id* is the inborn (genetic) personality structure out of which the other two agents emerge. The id represents all that is inherited; instinctual strivings such as sexual strivings and aggressive drives are its products. *Libido* is a particular component of the id, providing sexual energies that, according to Freudian theory, motivate much behavior. At birth, only the id exists; the *ego* evolves from it. This second personality structure is in contact with reality and so mediates between the demands of the id and external reality. Its chief function is to gratify the id, but in the context and limits of the real world (physical and social environment). The third and last personality component to develop is the *superego,* which, in simple language, represents conscience. The superego, like the id, exerts pressure on the ego, but to satisfy moral demands. The superego influences behavior mainly through self-criticism; it is

a product of parental injunctions. Often the ego must attempt to resolve conflict among the id, superego, and external reality.

4. *Psychoanalysis* was one of the first theories of abnormal behavior; early analysts considered mainly *neurosis.* They theorized that inner conflict among the three components, as well as frustration created by external reality, prompts deviant behavior. To protect itself from being overwhelmed, however, the ego sets up psychological strategies, called *ego defense mechanisms,* by which it can reduce the awareness of conflict and restore some equilibrium. Each defense mechanism has a slightly different purpose. *Repression,* one of the most common, tries to reduce anxiety and guilt by keeping unpleasant material out of awareness. This is only a temporary benefit, however; psychoanalytic theory maintains that repressed conflict cannot be resolved. Worse still, repressed material may be converted into more disturbing symptoms such as ulcers or headaches.

5. Psychoanalysis as a therapy suggests that *insight* is the chief goal. Insight or awareness about the unconscious conflict leads to recovery or eventual diminishing of symptoms. Freud thought that insight could be developed through *free association* or *dream interpretation.*

6. The neo-Freudians comprise a number of analysts who were not completely satisfied with Freud's emphasis on the importance of sexuality. Among the more famous neo-Freudians are Alfred Adler, Harry Stack Sullivan, and Carl Gustav Jung.

7. *Transactional analysis* (TA) is one of the newest psychodynamic views. It was proposed in the 1960s by Eric Berne. Transactional analysis is based on the idea that humans have a need to be recognized and appreciated; they must be "stroked," or disordered behavior will ensue. Social interaction is a transaction motivated by the desire for strokes.

8. Transactional analysis as a personality theory suggests that we have three ego states: Parent, Adult, and Child. (Unlike the id and superego, the transactional personality structures are all *ego* states.) The Parent structure represents internal states that resemble past messages from one's parents

(similar to Freud's superego). The Adult is the rational structure; unlike Freud's *ego,* which bargains and negotiates between the id and superego, the Adult is always straight and computerlike. The Child ego state represents the person's childlike feelings and behaviors. Each of the ego states dominates at various times.

9. *Scripts* and *injunctions* are psychodynamic forces acquired from parental commands and edicts about how we should live and who we will be. According to TA, various mental disorders are the result of scripts and injunctions made by parents years ago. Alcoholism, for example, is considered to be a type of "game" that is script-directed.

10. As a therapy, transactional analysis has several aims. The first is to analyze transactions and so determine the person's script decisions and motivations. Second, a contract is made between the client and therapist; this contract is an agreement by the client about which behaviors she or he would like to change. Third, some TA therapists have tried *reparenting,* in which the client regresses to an early developmental period, at which point the therapist "rescripts" or gives the client new Parent or Child ego states.

11. The *Phenomenological-Existential Perspective* is another major psychosocial perspective. *Phenomenology* is concerned with how things appear in consciousness. Unlike the psychodynamic positions, phenomenology places emphasis on the "here-and-now," not the past. Carl Rogers' *perceptual field,* for example, includes all of our present perceptions, feelings, and experiences. This field determines behavior. Disorganized behavior occurs when this field is *incongruent.*

12. *Client-centered therapy,* developed by Carl Rogers, is a humanistic, phenomenological therapy. It stresses the importance of consciousness (not the unconscious). Rogers and other phenomenologists maintain that, given support and the proper therapeutic environment, the individual's inherent potential can be unleashed and healthy behavior will emerge.

13. *Existentialism* is related to phenomenology in that it stresses the importance of "meaning and purpose." Existence is all that mat-

ters; choice and freedom are inescapable stressors that confront us. Uncertainty and limits of knowledge are also existential stresses that induce abnormal behavior. *Logotherapy*, developed by Victor Frankl, is one variety of existential therapy. The purpose of logotherapy is to assist the person in finding meaning and purpose for his or her existence.

14. The third major psychosocial perspective is the *learning perspective*, which holds that abnormal behavior is a learned response. The *behavioral model* is another name for the learning perspective; this model suggests that the focus should be on behavior, not on what we think goes on within a person. Symptoms should be dealt with, not inferred underlying causes. Three classes of learning theories are included in the behavioral model, each attempting to account for how abnormal behavior was learned. The classes are *contiguity theory*, *reinforcement theory*, and *observational learning* (modeling).

15. The *sociological perspective* resembles the learning perspective but does not draw from learning theories. It is based chiefly on sociological theories of deviance, which assume that cultural context, group factors, and even physical environment may play major roles in predisposing an individual to abnormal behavior. We discussed this perspective in the context of four subcategories: the *ecological* perspective, the *value-conflict* perspective, the *anomie* perspective, and the *labeling* perspective.

Ecology models, first made in the 1930s, found a strong association between conditions in the community — poor housing, lower socioeconomic status, poor health, poor schools—and increased rates of mental illness and crime. The *value-conflict* perspective contends that crime and other forms of deviant behavior are chiefly the consequence of learning a different set of values than those that govern normal behavior. The *anomie* perspective contends that normal behavior is regulated by a social structure in which the norms are clear-cut; when the norms governing behavior become vague and ambiguous, anomie (normlessness) prevails and deviance occurs. The *labeling perspective* contends that a deviant person's deviance increases once he or she is labeled and defined as being different. Labeling theory does not adequately account for the initial development of deviance (primary deviance), but only for secondary deviance, the abnormal behavior that follows labeling.

RECOMMENDED READINGS

Alexander, F. *Fundamentals of psychoanalysis.* New York: Norton, 1963.

Barrett, W. *Irrational man: A study in existential philosophy.* New York: Anchor Books, 1962.

Berne, E. *What do you say after you say hello?* New York: Grove Press, 1972.

Glasser, W. *The identity society.* New York: Harper & Row, 1972.

Sahakian, W. S. *Psychology of personality: Readings in theory.* Chicago: Rand McNally, 1977.

Scheff, T. J. *Labeling madness.* Englewood Cliffs, N. J.: Prentice-Hall, 1975.

Skinner, B. F. *Beyond freedom and dignity.* New York: Knopf, 1971.

THE CLASSIFICATION OF ABNORMAL BEHAVIOR

4

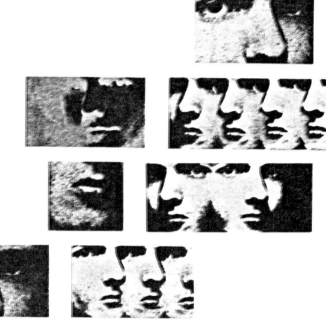

OVERVIEW In this chapter, we will examine issues involving the classification and criteria of abnormal behavior. An early classification system was developed in the 1880s by the German psychiatrist Emil Kraepelin. Although it still served as a broad framework, his schema was significantly modified when the classification system currently employed in the United States was initially developed—the *Diagnostic and Statistical Manual of Mental Disorders*, usually referred to as the DSM. In discussing the DSM, we will note a number of its major limitations and problems, in particular, its reliability and validity. Despite these problems, the DSM has been widely used because it provides clinicians with a method of broadly discussing major types of psychopathology. A newer version

of the DSM (DSM-III) is scheduled to be published sometime in 1980 and will, it is hoped, improve the reliability and validity of classification; a pre-publication version of the DSM-III has been used in this text. Our discussion of issues involved in classification will conclude by examining the assumptions of continuity versus discontinuity of various forms of psychopathology. Are there qualitative differences between the various types of disorders (discontinuity assumption)? Or are the various types essentially the same except for quantitative differences in severity, ranging from mild forms of anxiety to severe forms of psychotic behavior (continuity assumption)? We will review research evidence related to this issue.

Finally, in any discussion of abnormal behavior, an important and necessary first step is the precise definition of abnormality. On what basis do we decide whether or not an individual's behavior is abnormal? Unfortunately, there is at present no general consensus about its definition or about the criteria that should be used. This situation exists because there is no adequate definition of normal-

ity against which various forms of deviant behavior can be assessed. We will discuss certain criteria that can be used in attempting to define normality/abnormality. This discussion will provide the reader with an appreciation for the many complexities and difficult issues involved in defining psychological normality/abnormality.

CLASSIFICATION OF ABNORMAL BEHAVIOR

In classification, the various forms of abnormal behavior are arranged in specific categories. The descriptive categories developed are intended to help organize our thinking concerning the etiology, symptoms, and treatment of abnormal behavior. They are also intended to aid in communicating the various types of psychological problems that individuals may experience. To date, no completely satisfactory classification system has been developed for abnormal behavior. We will discuss an early classification system developed by Kraepelin as well as the current official classification system of the American Psychiatric Association. During this discussion, some of the inconsistencies and problems in the organization of psychopathology by these systems will become apparent, thus explaining why the systems are unsatisfactory in their present form.

KRAEPELIN'S CLASSIFICATION SYSTEM

The German psychiatrist Emil Kraepelin is credited with developing the first systematic and widely accepted classification scheme for mental disorders. The first edition of his classic textbook in psychiatry, entitled *Lehrbuch der Psychiatrie*, was published in 1883. This edition was called a *compendium*, that is, simply a brief outline. Through the years, Kraepelin constantly continued to work out new details and revise old ones, so that the ninth edition of the text, published in 1927, a year after Kraepelin's death, was a huge two-volume work consisting of 2,425 pages. In his textbooks, he painstakingly integrated a great deal of clinical data to delineate the symptoms associated with specific mental disorders. He noted that certain symptom patterns occurred with sufficient regularity to be used as a basis for identifying and

classifying mental disorders. The classification schema he developed is the basis of our present-day diagnostic system.

A guiding philosophy behind Kraepelin's works was the belief that once various forms of mental illness were successfully distinguished and classified, then one presumably would be able to predict the outcome of a specific type of disorder. Classification would also provide a framework within which medical research could begin to look for agents responsible for the disease and treatment methods for curing it. The *nosological* system he developed greatly influenced the field of psychiatry for many years, during which time great emphasis was put on the description and classification of disorders.

On the basis of detailed clinical data and documented statistical tables, Kraepelin defined and labeled the two major forms of severe mental illness or psychoses: *dementia praecox* and *manic-depressive psychosis*. Dementia praecox, which is now referred to as schizophrenia (a term introduced by Eugen Bleuler, a contemporary of Kraepelin), was viewed as having an onset early in life (*praecox*) and progressing to an incurable and apparently irreversible madness (*dementia*). Different subvarieties of the illness were noted—hebephrenic, paranoid, catatonic, simple—which were associated with various specific symptom patterns. Manic-depressive psychosis was viewed as consisting of extreme states of elated excitement (mania) and melancholia (depression) which often occurred cyclically, with patients moving from one extreme to the other. Both dementia praecox and manic-depressive psychosis were seen as biological-metabolical defects. Adhering primarily to an organic viewpoint or medical model, Kraepelin viewed mental disorders as diseases. This viewpoint, which did not emphasize the importance of psychological (psychogenic) factors in

The Bettmann Archive

Emil Kraepelin (1856–1926) developed the first systematic classification system of mental disorders.

many disorders, seriously limited the utility of the Kraepelinean system. Although still used as a broad framework, the system was significantly modified when the current classification scheme was developed.

THE AMERICAN PSYCHIATRIC ASSOCIATION DIAGNOSTIC SYSTEM

The *Diagnostic and Statistical Manual of Mental Disorders* (DSM) was adopted by the American Psychiatric Association in 1952 as its official classification schema of mental disorders. In 1968, a modified version (the DSM-II), developed in collaboration with the World Health Organization, was adopted. A newer and considerably revised version, the DSM-III, was scheduled for publication in 1980. Throughout this text, we will compare the DSM-II and DSM-III.

The intent of this international classification system is to allow mental health professionals throughout the world to compare types of disorders, incidence of occurrence, and other relevant

data concerning mental disorders. Table 4.1 outlines the clinical categories of the DSM-II. As can be seen, each condition has been assigned a three-digit number; when necessary, conditions are further qualified by additional digits following a decimal point. For example, the diagnosis of schizophrenia is 295; schizophrenia, schizo-affective type, is indicated by 295.7; schizophrenia, schizo-affective type, excited, is indicated by 295.73. It should be noted that when the DSM-II was published, homosexuality was classified as a mental disorder — sexual deviation. Since that time, however, it has been "declassified" and is no longer considered a mental disorder. This change is incorporated into the DSM-III listing in table 4.2.

The DSM-II was developed to provide mental health professionals with a diagnostic nomenclature to categorize the wide variety of psychological disorders seen in hospital and clinic settings. These disorders differ greatly in terms of severity, degree of impairment produced, and the causative factors that determine them.

PROBLEMS OF THE DSM-II Although the DSM-II has been widely used, it has certain serious limitations. Korchin (1976) has pointed out a number of these problems: (1) The construction of categories used in this classification system was not based on any one major theoretical orientation. The result was a system that was not logically derived and integrated and that failed to relate information concerning the possible etiology or treatment of various disorders. (2) The categories are of different "widths," so that some describe a loose grouping of problems (e.g., marital maladjustment), while others describe a relatively well-defined condition (e.g., anxiety neurosis). (3) The principles on which the classification system are based are mixed, so that some conditions are defined operationally on the basis of the presence of behavioral symptoms (e.g., I.Q. level, anxiety), while others are defined on the basis of originating conditions (e.g., brain damage). (4) The diagnostic categories fit hypothetical "textbook cases" well, but many times do not adequately describe "real life" individual cases in which there may be overlapping and unique patterns of symptoms. Related to this difficulty is the fact that the classification system focuses a great deal of attention on infrequent, severe, or bizarre forms of abnormal behavior, while mild personality patterns that occur with great frequency in everyday life are minimized. (5) The system uses only a few impre-

MENTAL RETARDATION

310.xx	Borderline
311.xx	Mild
312.xx	Moderate
313.xx	Severe
314.xx	Profound
315.xx	Unspecified

With each: Following or associated with

.00	Infection or intoxication
.10	Trauma or physical agent
.20	Disorders of metabolism, growth or nutrition
.30	Gross brain disease (postnatal)
.40	Unknown prenatal influence
.50	Chromosomal abnormality
.60	Prematurity
.70	Major psychiatric disorder
.80	Psycho-social (environmental) deprivation
.90	Other condition

ORGANIC BRAIN SYNDROMES (OBS)

A   Psychoses

SENILE AND PRE-SENILE DEMENTIA

290.00	Senile dementia
290.10	Pre-senile dementia

ALCOHOLIC PSYCHOSIS

291.00	Delirium tremens Korsakoff's psychosis
291.20	Other alcoholic hallucinosis
291.30	Alcohol paranoid state
291.40	Acute alcohol intoxication
291.50	Alcoholic deterioration
291.60	Pathological intoxication
291.90	Other alcoholic psychosis

PSYCHOSIS ASSOCIATED WITH INTRACRANIAL INFECTION

292.00	General paralysis
292.10	Syphilis of central nervous system
292.20	Epidemic encephalitis
292.30	Other and unspecified encephalitis
292.90	Other intracranial infection

PSYCHOSIS ASSOCIATED WITH OTHER CEREBRAL CONDITION

293.00	Cerebral arteriosclerosis
293.10	Other cerebrovascular disturbance
293.20	Epilepsy
293.30	Intracranial neoplasm
293.40	Degenerative disease of the CNS
293.50	Brain trauma
293.90	Other cerebral condition

PSYCHOSIS ASSOCIATED WITH OTHER PHYSICAL CONDITION

294.00	Endocrine disorder
294.10	Metabolic or nutritional disorder
294.20	Systemic infection
294.30	Drug or poison intoxication (other than alcohol)
294.40	Childbirth
294.80	Other and unspecified physical condition

B   Non-Psychotic OBS

309.00	Intracranial infection
309.13	Alcohol (simple drunkenness)
309.14	Other drug, poison, or systemic intoxication
309.20	Brain trauma
309.30	Circulatory disturbance
309.40	Epilepsy
309.50	Disturbance of metabolism, growth or nutrition
309.60	Senile or pre-senile brain disease
309.70	Intracranial neoplasm
309.80	Degenerative disease of the CNS
309.90	Other physical condition

PSYCHOSES NOT ATTRIBUTED TO PHYSICAL CONDITIONS LISTED PREVIOUSLY

SCHIZOPHRENIA

295.00	Simple
295.10	Hebephrenic
295.20	Catatonic
295.23	Catatonic type, excited
295.24	Catatonic type, withdrawn
295.30	Paranoid
295.40	Acute schizophrenic episode
295.50	Latent
295.60	Residual
295.70	Schizo-affective
295.73	Schizo-affective, excited
295.74	Schizo-affective, depressed
295.80	Childhood
295.90	Chronic undifferentiated
295.99	Other schizophrenic

MAJOR AFFECTIVE DISORDERS

296.00	Involutional melancholia
296.10	Manic-depressive illness, manic
296.20	Manic-depressive illness, depressed
296.30	Manic-depressive illness, circular
296.33	Manic-depressive, circular, manic
296.34	Manic-depressive, circular, depressed
296.80	Other major affective disorder

PARANOID STATES

297.00	Paranoia
297.10	Involutional paranoid state
297.90	Other paranoid state

OTHER PSYCHOSES

298.00	Psychotic depressive reaction

NEUROSES

300.00	Anxiety
300.10	Hysterical
300.13	Hysterical, conversion type
300.14	Hysterical, dissociative type
300.20	Phobic
300.30	Obsessive compulsive
300.40	Depressive
300.50	Neurasthenic
300.60	Depersonalization
300.70	Hypochondriacal
300.80	Other neurosis

PERSONALITY DISORDERS AND CERTAIN OTHER NON-PSYCHOTIC MENTAL DISORDERS

PERSONALITY DISORDERS
301.00   Paranoid
301.10   Cyclothymic
301.20   Schizoid
301.30   Explosive
301.40   Obsessive compulsive
301.50   Hysterical
301.60   Asthenic
301.70   Antisocial
301.81   Passive-aggressive
301.82   Inadequate
301.89   Other specified types

SEXUAL DEVIATION
302.00   Homosexuality
302.10   Fetishism
302.20   Pedophilia
302.30   Transvestism
302.40   Exhibitionism
302.50   Voyerusim
302.60   Sadism
302.70   Masochism
302.80   Other sexual deviation

ALCOHOLISM
303.00   Episodic excessive drinking
303.10   Habitual excessive drinking
303.20   Alcohol addiction
303.90   Other alcoholism

DRUG DEPENDENCE
304.00   Opium, opium alkaloids and their derivatives
304.10   Synthetic analgesics with morphine-like effects
304.20   Barbiturates
304.30   Other hypnotics and sedatives or "tranquilizers"
304.40   Cocaine
304.50   Cannabis sativa (hashish, marihuana)
304.60   Other psycho-stimulants
304.70   Hallucinogens
304.80   Other drug dependence

PSYCHOPHYSIOLOGIC DISORDERS
305.00   Skin
305.10   Musculoskeletal
305.20   Respiratory
305.30   Cardiovascular
305.40   Hemic and lymphatic
305.50   Gastro-intestinal
305.60   Genito-urinary
305.70   Endocrine
305.80   Organ of special sense
305.90   Other type

SPECIAL SYMPTOMS
306.00   Speech disturbance
306.10   Specific learning disturbance
306.20   Tic
306.30   Other psychomotor disorder
306.40   Disorders of sleep
306.50   Feeding disturbance
306.60   Enuresis
306.70   Encopresis
306.80   Cephalalgia
306.90   Other special symptom

TRANSIENT SITUATIONAL DISTURBANCES
307.00   Adjustment reaction of infancy
307.10   Adjustment reaction of childhood
307.20   Adjustment reaction of adolescence
307.30   Adjustment reaction of adult life
307.40   Adjustment reaction of late life

BEHAVIOR DISORDERS OF CHILDHOOD AND ADOLESCENCE
308.00   Hyperkinetic reaction
308.10   Withdrawing reaction
308.20   Overanxious reaction
308.30   Runaway reaction
308.40   Unsocialized aggressive reaction
308.50   Group delinquent reaction
308.90   Other reaction

CONDITIONS WITHOUT MANIFEST PSYCHIATRIC DISORDER AND NON-SPECIFIC CONDITIONS

SOCIAL MALADJUSTMENT WITHOUT MANIFEST PSYCHIATRIC DISORDER
316.00   Marital maladjustment
316.10   Social maladjustment
316.20   Occupational maladjustment
316.30   Dyssocial behavior
316.90   Other social maladjustment

NON-SPECIFIC CONDITIONS
317.00   Non-specific conditions

NO MENTAL DISORDER
318.00   No mental disorder

cise and gross categories to cover a wide range of problems that require more detailed and differentiated coverage. For example, the behavioral and emotional problems of children and adolescents are contained in only a small number of diagnostic categories. As a result of this limited coverage, clinicians working with children have had to develop diagnostic systems tailored for this age group.

There are a number of other problems with the DSM-II. One concerns the issue of reliability. *Reliability* in classification is determined by the degree to which different diagnosticians agree that a particular diagnostic label should be applied to a given individual. Obviously, high reliability is necessary and important in any classification system. Unfortunately, diagnosing patients using the DSM-II is not very reliable. A number of studies have empirically demonstrated this lack of reliability. For example, Schmidt and Fonda (1956) conducted a study in which pairs of psychiatrists independently diagnosed a sample of 426 recently hospitalized patients. When patients were classified into one of three broad major categories (organic, psychotic, characterological), there was 85 percent agreement among the psychiatrists. However, when they were asked to categorize specific diagnostic subtypes, such as the specific type of personality or neurotic syndrome, agreement among them decreased dramatically to well below the 50 percent level. Other studies have reported similar results (e.g., Mehlman 1952; Raines & Rohrer 1955). These findings indicate that reliability is relatively high in classifying according to major categories, but decreases significantly when attempts are made to diagnose more specific subcategories or subtypes.

Reliability is closely associated with the concept of validity in psychiatric diagnosis. Reliability gauges the principles by which categories are formed and the characteristics that define such categories. *Validity* gauges the correlates of category membership. It refers to the statements or predictions that can be made about a disorder once it is classified. There are different kinds of validity. In psychiatric diagnosis, three different types are important to consider: (1) *Predictive validity* refers to the finding that a member of a diagnostic category will respond in a particular way to a specific situation or treatment. (2) *Concurrent validity* refers to the finding that symptoms or behavior patterns, not used as diagnostic referents in the original classification of a disorder, are

found to be associated with a particular diagnosis. (3) *Etiological validity* refers to the finding that the same antecedent or precipitating factors are associated with a particular disorder in all individuals who make up a particular diagnostic group. Often the concepts of reliability and validity overlap. That is, the less reliable a diagnostic category is, the greater the difficulty in making a valid statement about that category. For example, suppose a person is diagnosed as a hysterical neurotic. If there is a low degree of agreement among clinicians in making this diagnosis and differentiating it from other types of neurotic behavior (i.e., low reliability), then one cannot expect the clinicians to be able to make valid and diagnostically meaningful statements about the antecedent conditions of the disorder (etiological validity), or about what other behaviors might be demonstrated by the patient (concurrent validity), or about how the patient might respond to treatment (predictive validity). Many of the diagnostic categories of the DSM-II suffer from a lack of validity.

Besides these problems of validity and reliability of classification, another problem associated with the DSM-II has been the frequent overlapping of symptoms demonstrated by patients in different diagnostic categories. Ziegler and Phillips (1961) examined the frequency of occurrence of 35 symptoms among a group of 793 patients who had been diagnosed as psychoneurotic, schizophrenic, manic-depressive, or having a character disorder. Of the 35 symptoms (e.g., depressed, tense, insomnia, lying, assaultive), 30 were found in the group diagnosed as manic-depressive, 34 in the character disorder group, and all 35 in both the schizophrenic and neurotic groups. The fact that the same symptoms occur in so many patients who have been assigned to different diagnostic categories limits the utility of the diagnostic system; clearly it fails to convey precise and discriminating data about individuals in each specific category. In defense of the DSM-II, it should be noted that many clinicians make their diagnoses on the basis of a pattern of a number of symptoms occurring together, rather than the absence or presence of a single symptom. The Ziegler and Phillips study examined only the presence or absence of single symptoms. It can be argued that the results of their study are necessarily limited because they did not truly reflect what occurs when a clinician engages in the task of diagnosis. There is still a problem, though, since the current classification system does not specify precisely the pattern and severity of symptoms that need to be present for a clinician to make a specific diagnosis. The new DSM-III delineates such factors more adequately.

Finally, it should be pointed out that DSM-II is based to a large extent on the medical or disease model of mental illness, with an emphasis on viewing psychologically disturbed behavior in disease terms. As we discussed in chapter 2, this model has been severely criticized by influential mental health professionals such as Szasz (1961) and Sarbin (1969).

Despite the criticisms and limitations of the DSM-II, it has still been widely used because it can be an aid to clinicians. However inexact and overlapping the diagnostic labels may be, they have provided a basis for discussing major forms of psychopathology and a starting point from which to investigate possible causal conditions and therapeutic techniques for specific disorders. Used simply as a way of broadly differentiating between major diagnostic categories, it has been of some value. Problems arise when any classification system becomes a way of labeling and stereotyping patients without attempting to understand each one individually. Often a simple descriptive label, such as "schizophrenia," becomes transformed into an explanation of the behavior it was simply meant to summarize. This circular reasoning can lead a clinician, after classifying a patient as schizophrenic on the basis of delusional and irrational thinking, to explain that the patient is engaging in this abnormal thinking pattern because he or she is suffering from schizophrenia. There is also the real danger of the lay person using such terms to label and stigmatize a person as "sick."

THE NEW DSM-III   A third edition of the DSM has been planned for publication in 1980. This new edition is significantly different from the DSM-II, and a number of changes are to be made in many of the major categories of psychopathology. Throughout this text, we will discuss these proposed category changes in the appropriate chapters and refer to the available parts of the new system. Table 4.2 presents the most recent draft of the proposed DSM-III.

A number of comprehensive and explicit diagnostic criteria are detailed in the new system. The hope is that these criteria will improve the reliability and validity of diagnosis, both of which were problems in the older DSM-II. For example, it is proposed that individuals be assessed on each of

five axes: (1) The psychiatric syndrome present, with a clear delineation of the major symptoms associated with the disorder. (2) The evaluation of personality and developmental disorders in the patient's history. This is an attempt to be sure that a clinician will assess the possible presence of long-term disturbances, which are sometimes overlooked when attention is directed at current symptoms of the disorder. (3) The assessment of possible nonmental medical disorders in an attempt to ensure as complete a diagnosis as possible. (4) The severity of psychosocial stressors. This will, it is hoped, lead to a careful assessment and isolation of possible precipitating or exacerbating situational factors. (5) The highest level of adaptive functioning in the past year. This will provide information about the degree and severity of impairment.

Besides a detailed description of "essential" and "associated" features of each disorder in this multiaxial classification framework, the new system also includes details from the research literature on factors such as average age of onset, time-course of the disorder, usual premorbid history of patient, degree of impairment usually produced, prevalence and sex ratio, and the possibility of genetic factors being involved. Specific criteria are delineated that will spell out precisely the number of symptoms that must be present in order to apply a diagnostic label.

These changes, with an emphasis on clear descriptions and delineation of specific criteria, should help increase the diagnostic reliability and validity of this classification system.

CONTINUITY VERSUS DISCONTINUITY ASSUMPTIONS

The DSM approach views mental disorders in separate and discrete categories, making the assumption that there are qualitative differences between the various types of disorders. For instance, neuroses and psychoses are viewed as qualitatively different kinds of psychopathology. In contrast to this position, some mental health professionals take a *continuity* position and assume that there is a linear continuum of psychopathology, from normal to personality disturbances to neuroses to psychoses. This model assumes that the disorders do not differ qualitatively, but only in terms of severity. Inherent in this position is the notion that a normal individual does not leap

ORGANIC MENTAL DISORDERS

Section 1.
SENILE AND PRESENILE DEMENTIAS
290.00 Progressive idiopathic dementia, senile onset
290.10 Progressive idiopathic dementia, presenile onset
290.40 Multi-infarct dementia

SUBSTANCE-INDUCED
Alcohol
303.00 Intoxication
291.40 Idiosyncratic intoxication (pathological intoxication)
291.80 Withdrawal
291.00 Withdrawal delirium (delirium tremens)
291.30 Hallucinosis
291.10 Amnestic syndrome (Korsakoff's syndrome)
291.20 Dementia associated with alcoholism
Barbiturate or similarly acting sedative or hypnotic
292.71 Intoxication
292.81 Withdrawal
292.01 Withdrawal delirium
292.21 Amnestic syndrome
Opioid
292.72 Intoxication
292.82 Withdrawal
Cocaine
292.73 Intoxication
Amphetamine or similarly acting sympathomimetic
292.74 Intoxication
292.04 Delirium
292.34 Delusional syndrome
292.84 Withdrawal
Hallucinogen
292.45 Hallucinosis
292.35 Delusional syndrome
292.55 Affective syndrome
Cannabis
292.76 Intoxication
292.36 Delusional syndrome
Tobacco
292.87 Withdrawal
Caffeine
292.78 Intoxication (caffeinism)
Other or unspecified substance
292.09 Delirium
292.19 Dementia
292.29 Amnestic syndrome
292.39 Delusional syndrome
292.49 Hallucinosis
292.59 Affective syndrome
292.69 Personality syndrome
292.79 Intoxication
292.89 Withdrawal
292.99 Other or mixed organic brain syndrome

Section 2. Syndromes accompanying specific physical disorders
293.00 Delirium
294.10 Dementia
294.00 Amnestic syndrome
293.81 Organic delusional syndrome
293.82 Organic hallucinosis
293.83 Organic affective syndrome
310.10 Organic personality syndrome
294.80 Other or mixed organic brain syndrome

SUBSTANCE USE DISORDERS
305.00 Alcohol abuse
303.90 Alcohol dependence (alcoholism)
305.40 Barbiturate or similarly acting sedative or hypnotic abuse
304.10 Barbiturate or similarly acting sedative or hypnotic dependence
305.50 Opioid abuse
304.00 Opioid dependence
305.60 Cocaine abuse
304.20 Cocaine dependence
305.70 Amphetamine or similarly acting sympathomimetic abuse
304.40 Amphetamine or similarly acting sympathomimetic dependence
305.30 Hallucinogen abuse
305.20 Cannabis abuse
304.30 Cannabis dependence
305.10 Tobacco use disorder
305.90 Other or unspecified substance abuse
304.60 Other specified substance dependence
304.90 Unspecified substance dependence

SCHIZOPHRENIC DISORDERS
295.10 Disorganized (hebephrenic)
295.20 Catatonic
295.30 Paranoid
295.90 Undifferentiated
295.60 Residual

PARANOID DISORDERS
297.10 Paranoia
297.30 Shared paranoid disorder (Folie à deux)
297.90 Paranoid state

SCHIZOAFFECTIVE DISORDERS
295.7x Schizoaffective disorder
Code phenomenology and course in fifth digit as:
1 = manic, episodic
2 = manic, chronic
3 = manic, in remission
4 = depressed, episodic
5 = depressed, chronic
6 = depressed, in remission
7 = mixed, episodic
8 = mixed, chronic
9 = mixed, in remission

AFFECTIVE DISORDERS

EPISODIC AFFECTIVE DISORDERS
Manic disorder
296.00 Single episode
296.10 Recurrent
Major depressive disorder
296.20 Single episode
296.30 Recurrent
Bipolar affective disorder
296.40 Manic
296.50 Depressed
296.60 Mixed

CHRONIC AFFECTIVE DISORDERS
301.11 Chronic hypomanic disorder (Hypomanic personality)
301.12 Chronic depressive disorder (Depressive personality)
301.13 Cyclothymic disorder (Cyclothymic personality)

ATYPICAL AFFECTIVE DISORDERS
296.81 Atypical affective disorder
296.82 Atypical depressive disorder
296.70 Atypical bipolar disorder

PSYCHOSES NOT ELSEWHERE CLASSIFIED
295.40 Schizophreniform disorder
298.80 Brief reactive psychosis
298.90 Atypical psychosis

ANXIETY DISORDERS
Phobic disorders
300.21 Agoraphobia with panic attacks
300.22 Agoraphobia without panic attacks
300.23 Social phobia
300.29 Simple phobia
300.01 Panic disorder
300.30 Obsessive compulsive disorder
300.02 Generalized anxiety disorder
300.00 Atytpical anxiety disorder

FACTITIOUS DISORDERS
300.16 Factitious illness with psychological symptoms
301.51 Chronic factitious illness with physical symptoms (Munchausen syndrome)
300.18 Other factitious illness with physical symptoms

SOMATOFORM DISORDERS
300.81 Somatization disorder (Briquet's syndrome)
300.11 Conversion disorder
307.80 Psychalgia
300.70 Atypical somatoform disorder

DISSOCIATIVE DISORDERS
300.12 Psychogenic amnesia
300.13 Psychogenic fugue
300.14 Multiple personality
300.60 Depersonalization disorder
300.15 Other

PERSONALITY DISORDERS

301.00 Paranoid
301.21 Introverted
301.22 Schizotypal
301.50 Histrionic
301.81 Narcissistic
301.70 Antisocial
301.83 Borderline
301.82 Avoidant
301.60 Dependent
301.40 Compulsive
301.84 Passive-Aggressive
301.89 Other or mixed

PSYCHOSEXUAL DISORDERS

GENDER IDENTITY DISORDERS
302.50 Transsexualism
302.60 Gender identity disorder of childhood
302.85 Other gender identity disorder of adolescence or adult life

PARAPHILIAS
302.81 Fetishism
302.30 Transvestism
302.10 Zoophilia
302.20 Pedophilia
302.40 Exhibitionism
302.82 Voyeurism
302.83 Sexual masochism
302.84 Sexual sadism
302.89 Other

PSYCHOSEXUAL DYSFUNCTIONS
302.71 With inhibited sexual desire
302.72 With inhibited sexual excitement (frigidity, impotence)
302.73 With inhibited female orgasm
302.74 With inhibited male orgasm
302.75 With premature ejaculation
302.76 With functional dyspareunia
306.51 With functional vaginismus
302.79 Other

OTHER PSYCHOSEXUAL DISORDERS
302.01 Ego-dystonic homosexuality
302.90 Psychosexual disorder not elsewhere classified

DISORDERS USUALLY ARISING IN CHILDHOOD OR ADOLESCENCE
This section lists conditions that usually first manifest themselves in childhood or adolescence. Any appropriate adult diagnosis can be used for diagnosing a child.

MENTAL RETARDATION
317.00 Mild mental retardation
318.00 Moderate mental retardation
318.10 Severe mental retardation
318.20 Profound mental retardation
319.00 Unspecified mental retardation

PERVASIVE DEVELOPMENTAL DISORDERS
299.00 Infantile autism
299.80 Atypical childhood psychosis

SPECIFIC DEVELOPMENTAL DISORDERS
315.60 Specific reading disorder
315.10 Specific arithmetical disorder
315.32 Developmental language disorder
315.39 Developmental articulation disorder
307.60 Enuresis
307.70 Encopresis
315.50 Mixed
315.80 Other

ATTENTION DEFICIT DISORDERS
314.00 With hyperactivity
314.10 Without hyperactivity

CONDUCT DISORDERS
312.00 Undersocialized conduct disorder aggressive type
312.10 Undersocialized conduct disorder, unaggressive type
312.20 Socialized conduct disorder

ANXIETY DISORDERS OF CHILDHOOD OR ADOLESCENCE
309.21 Separation anxiety disorder
313.21 Shyness disorder
313.00 Overanxious disorder

OTHER DISORDERS OF CHILDHOOD OR ADOLESCENCE
313.22 Introverted disorder of childhood
313.81 Oppositional disorder
313.23 Elective mutism
313.83 Academic underachievement disorder

DISORDERS CHARACTERISTIC OF LATE ADOLESCENCE
309.22 Emancipation disorder of adolescence or early adult life
313.82 Identity disorder
309.23 Specific academic or work inhibition

EATING DISORDERS
307.10 Anorexia nervosa
307.51 Bulimia
307.52 Pica
307.53 Rumination
307.59 Atypical

SPEECH DISORDERS
307.00 Stuttering

STEREOTYPED MOVEMENT DISORDERS
307.21 Transient tic disorder
307.22 Chronic motor tic disorder
307.23 Tourette's disorder
307.20 Atypical tic disorder
307.30 Other

REACTIVE DISORDERS NOT ELSEWHERE CLASSIFIED

POST-TRAUMATIC STRESS DISORDER
308.30 Acute
309.81 Chronic

ADJUSTMENT DISORDERS
309.00 With depressed mood
309.24 With anxious mood
309.28 With mixed emotional features
309.82 With physical symptoms
309.30 With disturbance of conduct
309.40 With mixed disturbance of emotions and conduct
309.83 With withdrawal
309.89 Other

DISORDERS OF IMPULSE CONTROL NOT ELSEWHERE CLASSIFIED
312.31 Pathological gambling
312.32 Kleptomania
312.33 Pyromania
312.34 Intermittent explosive disorder
312.35 Isolated explosive disorder
312.39 Other impulse control disorder

OTHER DISORDERS

UNSPECIFIED MENTAL DISORDER (NON-PSYCHOTIC)
V40.90 Unspecified mental disorder (non-psychotic)

Note: The traditional neurotic subtypes are included in the Affective, Anxiety, Somatoform, and Dissociative Disorders.

LEVELS OF PSYCHOLOGICAL DYSFUNCTION
Table 4.3

As proposed by Menninger, Mayman, and Pruyser 1963. From Korchin 1976, pp. 107–108

1. THE FIRST ORDER OF DYSFUNCTION.

When threat exceeds the coping capacity of everyday mechanisms, some degree of dyscontrol and dysorganization becomes evident. More extreme mechanisms come into play. At this level, the behavioral effectiveness and relative comfort are largely maintained, but at a cost. Most visible is "nervousness." With it are exaggerated evidence of inhibition, hyperemotionalism, restlessness, worry, some somatic and sexual dysfunctions, and conscious efforts at self-control.

2. THE SECOND ORDER OF DYSFUNCTION.

At this level there is some detachment from reality and distinct subjective discomfort. Such symptoms appear as fainting, dissociations, phobias, hysterical conversions, compulsions, sexual perversions, addictions, and "frozen emergency reactions" (i.e., personality deformities). In general, this level includes much of what has been described as the symptom neuroses and character neuroses in the past. However, Menninger sees them as at the same level of dysfunction in terms of their being alternate ways in which aggressive discharge is blocked from consciousness (e.g., fainting), or displaced to the body (e.g., somatic symptoms), or symbolically or magically averted (e.g., obsessive thoughts).

3. THE THIRD ORDER OF DYSFUNCTION.

This level is characterized by the escape of naked aggression, leading to repetitive or episodic acts of violence. These are manifestations of much more gross ego failures than at the second level. Included too would be the convulsions and seizures of epileptic patients and the catastrophic reactions of the brain-damaged. However, the functional episodic dyscontrol, whether acute or chronic, is viewed as adaptive since it averts the even more catastrophic disintegration of the person, ultimately represented at the fifth level.

4. THE FOURTH ORDER OF DYSFUNCTION.

Here are the extreme states of disorganization, repudiation of reality, and regression which have classically been identified as psychoses. Particular syndromes include despondency, disorganized excitement, self-absorption, mannerisms and bizarre delusions, persecutory preoccupations, disorientation, and confusion.

5. THE FIFTH ORDER OF DYSFUNCTION.

This involves the ultimate disintegration of the person, complete deterioration, "psychogenic death," out of despair or hopelessness, and suicide. All adaptive efforts, even those of a psychotic adjustment, have failed.

directly into psychosis, but first develops a personality disturbance or neurosis and then progresses to psychosis. It is assumed that the development of a neurosis represents the individual's failure to effectively handle or adapt to stress and anxiety. If neurotic individuals reach the point where they can no longer adapt or cope even using their neurotic mechanisms, it is assumed that they finally will give up all attempts, abandon reality, and become psychotic.

Menninger, Mayman, and Pruyser (1963) have developed a theoretical framework of psychopathology based on a continuity position. They assume that functioning in everyday life involves the use of a variety of coping mechanisms to deal with tension and threats. Psychopathology is viewed in terms of five levels of dysfunction in the ability to cope and adapt adequately. These five levels of dysfunction, as summarized by Korchin (1976), are presented in table 4.3. As can be seen, Menninger and his co-authors assume a continuum from normal functioning to severe forms of psychopathology. As they indicate:

> The various orders of dyscontrol which we have described and illustrated are not pigeon holes into which people may be fitted; they are only still photographs of a moving picture of human life. In every individual are potentialities for destructiveness and self-destructiveness and in every individual there are potentialities for salvage, concern, growth, and creativity. The ceaseless struggle between these opposing trends occupies all the energies of our lives. One could say these were all degrees of failure, but one could also see these as all degrees of success . . . if the phenomena of human life are looked at in this way, psychiatry passes from being a science of classifying and name-calling into a discipline of counsel for the maximizing of the potentialities of the individual and the improvement of social happiness. (Menninger, Mayman, & Pruyser 1963, p. 272)

In contrast to the above, professionals who adhere to a *discontinuity* position—that is, who assume there are qualitative differences between various types of disorders—argue that there are no data that clearly demonstrate a continuum extending from normal functioning to personality disturbance to neurosis and psychosis. Moreover, there is no direct evidence indicating that when psychotic patients improve, they go through a neurotic phase before complete recovery. A continuity position,

EYSENCK'S MODEL OF PSYCHOPATHOLOGY

Eysenck's (1960) model of psychopathology categorizes individuals on three different dimensions: neuroticism, psychoticism, and introversion-extroversion. The dimension of neuroticism refers to a person's emotionality, or how easily he or she becomes aroused. The psychoticism dimension refers to the individual's contact with reality (e.g., whether one's thought processes are impaired and whether one has delusions or hallucinations). The introversion-extroversion dimension refers to a person's sociability. It also reflects that person's conditionability. The extrovert is the sociable and lively person who acquires conditioned responses slowly; the introvert is the opposite type.

Eysenck has developed a variety of tests, such as personality questionnaires and laboratory tests, to measure these dimensions. He suggests that by determining an individual's ratings on each of these dimensions, one can assign him or her to a traditional descriptive diagnostic category. Those individuals rated extremely high or low on a particular dimension are considered to be abnormal.

The attractive feature of this model is that it provides specific guidelines for gauging abnormality. The ultimate value of this model will be determined by future research that assesses the ability of the three dimensions to yield valid and reliable diagnostic decisions.

Courtesy H. J. Eysenck

Hans Eysenck, a renowned British psychologist, developed a statistical model of psychopathology that categorizes individuals on three different dimensions: neuroticism, psychoticism, and introversion-extroversion.

however, would enable a professional to predict that this would occur.

On the other hand, there is some evidence that can be used to support a discontinuity position. Eysenck (1960) has presented a model of psychopathology that suggests there are separate, qualitatively different, factors of neuroticism and psychoticism. In one study, Eysenck (1955) administered a battery of perceptual, motor, and association tasks to a variety of psychiatric groups. A factor analysis (a statistical method by which one can isolate major factors accounting for performance differences between individuals) was done on these task performances. This analysis yielded two major factors: a neuroticism factor consisting of tasks that differentiated normals from neurotics; and a psychoticism factor consisting of tasks that differentiated normals from psychotics. Trouton and Maxwell (1956) also isolated these two independent factors of neuroticism and psychoticism when factor-analyzing a clinical checklist of patients' symptoms and histories.

These data do not definitely indicate that a discontinuity model is more valid than a continuity approach. However, considering the increase in evidence indicating the importance of genetic factors that may predispose an individual to schizophrenia, along with the fact that there is no comparable strong evidence for such factors' importance in neurotic conditions (Korchin 1976), such data do strengthen the discontinuity assumption. The fact that treatment provided to psychotics is usually quite different than that given to neurotics also implies that most treatment professionals assume there are qualitative differences between these major types of disorders. This, of course, does not unequivocally prove that the discontinuity model is more correct than the continuity model. A great deal of additional research is needed to assess which is the most valid approach. It may be that for some forms of neurotic and psychotic behaviors, there is continuity from normal to neurotic and psychotic behavior; for other forms, there may be discontinuity.

CRITERIA OF ABNORMAL BEHAVIOR

In any discussion of abnormal behavior, an important and necessary first step is to define *abnormality*. Unfortunately, there is no clear consensus about such a definition simply because there is no adequate definition of normality against which various forms of maladaptive or disordered behavior can be judged abnormal. A number of approaches have been proposed in an attempt to define normality/abnormality but, as we shall see, there are still no simple and uniform criteria that are universally used. A discussion of some of these criteria will provide an understanding of the many complexities and issues involved in attempts to define normality/abnormality.

SANITY OR INSANITY: CAN WE TELL THE DIFFERENCE?

Throughout this text, we discuss various forms of behavior that are labeled as "abnormal." It is therefore important to develop an understanding of what the word *abnormal* means and how it is used in the field of psychology. At first, this appears to be a relatively easy and straightforward task. After all, it is usually not very difficult to obtain a general consensus that a grossly and visibly deviant form of behavior is abnormal. Less grossly deviant characteristics, however, which make up the majority of behaviors defined as abnormal, are much more difficult to agree upon.

The word *abnormal* itself implies some deviation from a clearly defined norm. In physical medicine, normality is viewed as the physiological and functional integrity of the body. Abnormality or pathology, which is a deviation from this integrity, can usually be clearly delineated and generally agreed upon by physicians independently assessing a patient. In psychology, the definition and delineation process is less clear and precise because there is no generally accepted standard of psychological normality against which particular types of deviant or disturbed behavior can be evaluated and considered abnormal. As a consequence, the boundary line between normal/abnormal or sanity/insanity cannot be precisely delineated. This has created a basic problem for mental health practitioners, who are expected to be able to make such a distinction. A relatively dramatic demonstration of this inability to differentiate between these two states has been reported by Rosenhan (1973) in a study called "Being Sane in Insane Places." After a brief review of this study, we will consider a number of alternative views and criteria that have been suggested to provide a more precise definition of psychological normality/abnormality.

In Rosenhan's study, which was conducted over the course of three years, a number of normal persons were admitted individually to twelve different psychiatric hospitals across the United States. Rosenhan was careful to ensure that none of the participants had any past or present psychiatric problem. At the admissions desk of the hospital, the "pseudopatients" reported hearing a sometimes unclear voice that said "empty," "hollow," and "thud." The patients reported no other abnormal symptoms. They accurately reported their life histories except, of course, for the fact that they were participating in an experimental study and that their present employment was related to mental health. All twelve pseudopatients were hospitalized, and eleven of the twelve cases given a diagnosis of "schizophrenia."

Immediately after the pseudopatients were officially admitted to the hospital, they stopped talking about the hallucinations they had earlier reported and behaved in their usual manner. Rosenhan was interested in determining whether the sanity of these patients would be detected by the hospital staff. It was found that in no instance was it detected that the pseudopatients were quite sane, even though their behavior was completely noneventful and normal. The only instances of detection were made by some of the actual hospitalized patients!

In commenting on these findings, Rosenhan suggested that many mental health professionals working within a medical model framework interpret almost any type of behavior within an institutional setting as a presumed mental illness. There have, however, been some recent major criticisms of this study (Millon 1975; Spitzer 1975; Weiner 1975). For example, Spitzer (1975) states that the only valid finding of the Rosenhan study was that the pseudopatients were not detected by psychiatrists within the hospital setting as having simulated signs of a mental disorder. After all, at the time of their admission, the pseudopatients did report that they heard voices. Psychiatrists, like physicians diagnosing physical disorders, have to assume that patients are telling the truth. Moreover, all the pseudopatients were discharged in one to two months, even though in most cases they were given a label of "schizophrenia in remission." Spitzer therefore argues that Rosenhan's result is a "rather unremarkable finding" that is not directly relevant to the real problems associated with the reliability and validity of psychiatric diagnoses. Nevertheless, the Rosenhan study does provide a good example of how sanity/insanity distinctions are not readily apparent.

STATISTICAL CRITERIA

The statistical approach views normality as consisting of whatever characteristics or behaviors are most frequent in the population. Abnormality is simply defined as any behavior that deviates from the norm or average. Many characteristics of people in the overall population distribute themselves into a normal bell-shaped curve, with the majority of individuals in the middle range or center of this distribution curve. There are fewer people at both extremes of the distribution. For example, in measures of height, the great majority of adult males fall in the middle range with a height of about 5 feet 8 inches. Heights that deviate greatly from this middle range, such as a "dwarf" with a height of 4 feet or a "giant" with a height of 8 feet, would be considered abnormal with regard to the height characteristic. Similarly, abnormal behaviors would be considered as those that occur infrequently in the general population and are not like those of most people. If we consider anxiety, for instance, as a dimension of abnormality, then people who deviate from the average level of anxiety in the normal population—that is, either experience too much anxiety (a neurotic individual) or too little anxiety (a sociopathic individual)—would be considered abnormal.

A major appeal of the statistical model is that it provides an objective and easily quantifiable gauge of normality/abnormality. Indeed, the concept is frequently used in clinical research and practice. However, the approach has a number of shortcomings. First of all, it does not define the characteristics that should be measured in determining normality/abnormality. What characteristics (e.g., anxiety, depression, illogical reasoning, aggressiveness) are important to consider? Related

to this is the fact that the model does not, in itself, provide a basis for deciding whether abnormality is unidirectional or bidirectional for a given characteristic. For example, the presence of low intelligence is frequently used as an indicant of mental retardation, which is considered a form of abnormality. But, how should we describe an individual with an extremely high level of intelligence, which is equally infrequent in the general population? Is being an intellectual "genius" a form of psychological abnormality? Most would say it is not.

The model of psychopathology proposed by Eysenck is an example of a statistical model. In his model, however, the decision about what defines abnormality is made outside the statistical model, avoiding the problems just mentioned. Eysenck's theory of personality organization specifies these factors.

There are two additional problems with the general statistical approach. The first is that it does not provide a distribution curve cut-off point to use in defining normality/abnormality. For example, in considering anxiety as a dimension of abnormality, is "high anxiety" the level experienced by the upper 5 percent of the population distribution or the upper 10 percent? What cut-off point or dividing line should be used? Finally, this model equates "mental health" with the ordinary or the norm, that is, being like everyone else. Many would argue that one cannot assume a person is lacking in "mental health" merely because he or she is nonconforming or extraordinary, as are many innovative artists, inventors, and scholars.

CULTURAL CRITERIA

The cultural approach is related to the statistical model in that it views normality/abnormality relative to a norm or standard. It goes further, though, in defining what characteristics should be considered abnormal. This approach assumes that abnormal behavior can be defined simply as deviations from the acceptable behavior patterns and normative expectations of a given society. The concept of *cultural relativism*, introduced by anthropologists in the 1930s, is used in this approach to emphasize that "abnormal" is merely a label that society gives to behavior that deviates from social expectations. For instance, in our society, having feelings of persecution or delusions that people are plotting against you (symptoms of paranoia) or engaging in sexual relations with a child is labeled as abnormal behavior. In other societies, these same behaviors might not be considered abnormal.

One major problem inherent in this approach is that it can never provide a permanent and cross-culturally accepted group of criteria to use in defining abnormal behavior because of different and changing standards within various cultural groups (i.e., cultural relativism). A recent case in point in the United States is homosexuality. Historically, homosexuality has been considered abnormal in most Western societies, even though a certain percentage of nearly every society has been homosexual. In the days of the early Greeks, however, it was not only tolerated and publicly sanctioned, but also viewed as a positive form of behavior. Today in the United States, homosexuality is no longer classified as a form of abnormal behavior. Through persistent pressure exerted on the American Psychiatric Association by "gay liberation" groups, homosexuality was "declassified" in the 1970s. On the other hand, despite the APA decision, a fairly large segment of U.S. society continues to regard homosexuality as "abnormal" by their cultural criteria. This case serves as a good demonstration of how cultural relativism acts to define abnormality, suggesting that the search for absolute criteria for many forms of abnormal behavior may be a vain endeavor.

Another point to note about cultural criteria is that the acceptance of a model based on cultural relativism assumes that there can never be a "sick society," but only "sick people" in that society. That is, one form of behavior is considered as normal as any other form as long as society accepts it. For example, under certain conditions, such as war or self-defense, killing another human being is considered normal in our society. Taken to its extreme, however, if mass persecutions and the killing of other human beings are accepted and condoned by society as a major safeguard to that society, as they were in Nazi Germany and in many present-day authoritarian societies, then there is nothing "abnormal" about such behaviors. This general tenet is not readily acceptable.

LEGAL CRITERIA

The ability to define normality/abnormality or, more specifically, to determine sanity/insanity has always been an important legal concern. At present, there are three major areas of law in which the determination of an individual's "mental health status" is important: (1) The assessment of *competency*, which a court of law uses to determine whether an individual is, or was, psychologically capable of understanding and adhering to all the responsibilities of a legal contract entered into, such as purchasing property, completing a will, or agreeing to marriage. (2) Legal *commitment*, which is a procedure involving the mandatory placement of an individual in a mental institution. The primary basis for such commitment is the determination that an individual is "dangerous due to a mental disorder" and capable of hurting himself or herself or other people. (3) The assessment of *criminal responsibility*, which a court of law uses to determine whether a criminal act committed by an individual was the direct result of some type of "mental illness." If it is determined that some "mental illness" precipitated or was responsible for the criminal act, the individual is not held legally responsible for the act.

These criteria for determining sanity/insanity, and the great implications they have for the civil rights of individuals involved in the legal process, will be discussed in more detail in chapter 13. It is difficult to assess many forms of mental impairment and even more difficult to determine the past "mental state" of an individual at the time of the behavior in question. Moreover, the use of legal criteria is on extremely shaky grounds, since it erroneously assumes that there is a well-developed basis for determining and precisely defining normality/abnormality.

PERSONAL CRITERIA

An apparently straightforward approach to defining abnormality is to use the individual's own subjective self-report and self-appraisal of his or her mood and state of psychological discomfort. That is, if an individual reports an unusually high degree of anxiety or tension, and this affective state is viewed as a dimension of abnormality, he or she can be defined as having a psychological abnormality. Indeed, personal self-report is an extremely important consideration in defining abnormality. The exclusive use of such criteria clearly has certain major limitations. For instance, this approach depends totally on whether the individual can correctly and adequately describe the mood or psychological state. Many patients, because of the nature of their disorder, cannot do this. For example, the schizophrenic individual with a major thought disturbance and little contact with reality would probably provide inaccurate self-appraisals. Another limitation is that many individuals, because of everyday stresses and demands, are likely to report transitory states of psychological discomfort. These temporary states may not provide a meaningful basis on which to determine the presence of a significant and persistent form of abnormality.

MENTAL HEALTH CRITERIA

This approach attempts to define the state of an individual's mental health, with an emphasis on positive aspects of adjustment and functioning. Abnormality is viewed as the absence of mental health. In its extreme form, this approach attempts to describe an ideal state of mental health. The achievement of positive mental health (Jahoda 1958; Shoben 1957), the development of self-actualization (Maslow 1968), and becoming a "fully functioning person" (Rogers 1963) are examples of this orientation. Buss (1966) has provided a good summarization of this approach and has pointed out some difficulties associated with it. One difficulty concerns the criteria by which an ideal state of mental health is to be defined. Many times the criteria are unclear and vague and are difficult to establish and assess. For example, what is the precise meaning of "self-actualization," and how can it be objectively measured? These ideal states of mental health might also be ones that are represented in very few human beings. As Buss (1966) notes after examining the various criteria of ideal mental health:

> . . . It is obvious that very few individuals will meet all the criteria that describe an ideal person. If this ideal is normal, are the rest of us abnormal? The answer is no, because the concepts of normality and adjustment implicitly refer to most persons." (p. 5)

A less extreme form of the mental health approach attempts to describe a reasonable rather than an ideal state of mental health. It defines normality as simply the absence of gross psychopathology. In this approach, straightforward criteria can be developed and employed by comparing clinical

groups who are hospitalized or who are seeking treatment. Buss (1966) has provided an example of such an approach, with an emphasis on practical criteria of abnormality that are usually observed in clinical groups. He emphasizes three criteria—discomfort, bizarreness, and inefficiency—and describes them as follows:

Discomfort may take many forms. It may be physical discomfort which prompts an individual to take medicine or seek a physician to relieve aches, pains, fatigue, etc. If the physician determines that the discomfort is due to a disease process, the ailment will be labeled as a medical problem. If no disease or organ dysfunction is found, then the patient will be regarded as psychologically abnormal and probably referred to a psychiatrist. Often the distinction between medical and psychological symptoms involving physical complaints is difficult to make. That is, certain neurotic symptoms look similar to those found in organic diseases. Moreover, certain kinds of physical symptom patterns are caused by psychological factors. These are called psychophysiological disorders (see chapter 7). The second kind of discomfort described by Buss is *worry*. The worry or apprehensiveness may be about the present or the future and may be related to any aspect of life, from fear of social situations to fear of "going crazy." These anxieties produce a state of discomfort from which an individual seeks relief. Related to worry is *depression*, the third kind of discomfort discussed by Buss. He notes that changes in mood are part of normal everyday living, and a temporary depressed mood may be an entirely appropriate response to failure or disappointment. However, if the depression remains long after the occurrence of the event that initially elicited it, or if its occurrence is not related to any sorrow-producing event, then the depression is abnormal.

Bizarreness is defined by Buss as abnormal deviations from accepted social standards of behavior, or deviations from reality. This particular category includes such major deviations as delusions and hallucinations, as well as less severe forms of odd behavior such as motor tics, phobias, and compulsive rituals. This criterion also includes asocial acts such as the chronic breaking of the rules of society, including such behaviors as delinquency, chronic drunkenness, addiction to drugs, and sexual perversions. According to Buss, sexual perversions are the most difficult deviations to identify because of cultural relativism, with the standards of sexual normality varying not only among societies but also within different segments of a given society.

Inefficiency, according to Buss, may be assessed in two different ways. The first is to compare an individual's actual performance with his or her true potential. For example, a person with a high intelligence level would be expected to perform effectively in intellectual tasks and also to be able to hold a responsible vocational position. If this individual cannot rise any higher in vocational status than, say, the job of janitor, it would suggest a breakdown in efficiency. Such a striking differential between actual and potential performance is, according to Buss, indicative of abnormality. The second way to evaluate inefficiency is to compare an individual's performance with the requirements of his or her particular job or role. The more disorganized the performance, the less efficient the person is in performing the job or role. An example

is the corporate executive who no longer can efficiently manage all the details required in his or her job.

Buss (1966) readily admits the limitations of such criteria in providing a precise definition of abnormality. He suggests that the concept of abnormality should be regarded as a rough, everyday notion rather than a precise scientific construct. The criteria serve as broad clinical bases for labeling an individual as abnormal. Indeed, the limitations associated with the various criteria of abnormal behavior we have reviewed in this section suggest that it may be impossible to agree upon any precise and universally accepted definitions. Rather, the use of the criteria presented by Buss, which can be used as clinical bases for describing an individual as psychologically abnormal, may provide the most practical approach to the problem of defining abnormality.

SUMMARY

1. Classification involves arranging the various forms of abnormal behavior into specific categories. Emil Kraepelin is credited with developing the first systematic and widely accepted classification schema for mental disorders. Although his schema served as a broad framework, it was significantly modified when the currently employed classification system in this country was developed in 1952—the *Diagnostic and Statistical Manual of Mental Disorders* (DSM). A modified version (DSM-II), developed in collaboration with the World Health Organization, was adopted in 1968; a further revision (DSM-III) was scheduled for publication in 1980.

2. Although the DSM-II has been widely used, it has certain serious limitations and problems. Two such problems concern its reliability and validity. *Reliability* gauges the degree to which different diagnosticians using a classification schema agree that a particular diagnostic label should be applied to a given individual. *Validity* refers to the statements or predictions that can be made about a disorder once it is classified. Research has demonstrated that the DSM-II lacks a high degree of reliability and validity.

3. Despite the problems associated with the

DSM-II, it has been widely used because it has given mental health professionals a basis for discussing major forms of psychopathology. It also provided a starting point from which to investigate causal conditions and therapeutic techniques for specific disorders.

4. A newer version of the DSM, the DSM-III, was scheduled to be published sometime in 1980. In attempting to improve the reliability and validity of classification, the authors of the DSM-III have adopted a multiaxial framework in which individuals are assessed not only in terms of the psychiatric syndrome but also in regard to history, physical disorders, psychosocial stressors, and level of functioning. The new system emphasizes clear descriptions and specific criteria.

5. Both the DSM-III and DSM-II present a view of mental disorders as separate, discrete categories. They make the assumption that there are qualitative differences between the various types of disorders. In contrast to this *discontinuity* position, some take a *continuity* position in assuming that the disorders do not differ qualitatively, but only in terms of the severity of psychopathology. Although much additional research is

needed to assess which is the more valid position, the evidence to date seems to support a discontinuity position. The possibility also exists that in some forms of neurotic and psychotic behavior, there may be continuity from normal to neurotic to psychotic; while for some other forms, there may be discontinuity.

6. In attempting to define abnormality, it was pointed out that there is no clear consensus as to its definition simply because there is no adequate definition of normality against which various forms of maladaptive or disordered behavior can be judged and considered abnormal.

7. Various criteria have been proposed in an attempt to define normality/abnormality: statistical, cultural, legal, personal, and mental health criteria. After discussing the limitations of these criteria, we suggested that it may be impossible to agree on any precise and universally accepted definition. Buss (1966) argues that the concept of abnormality should be regarded simply as a rough, everyday notion rather than a precise scientific construct. He presents three criteria—discomfort, bizarreness, and inefficiency—that may provide a more practical clinical basis for describing an individual as psychologically abnormal.

Korchin, S. J. *Modern clinical psychology: Principles of intervention in the clinic and the community.* New York: Basic Books, 1976.

Rosenhan, D. L. On being sane in insane places. *Science,* 1973, *179,* 250–258.

Spitzer, R. L. On pseudoscience in science, logic in remission, and psychiatric diagnoses: A critique of Rosenhan's "On being sane in insane places." *Journal of Abnormal Psychology,* 1975, *84,* 442–452.

**RECOMMENDED
READINGS**

5

THE ASSESSMENT OF ABNORMAL BEHAVIOR

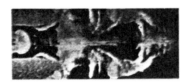

OVERVIEW The attempts to develop an effective classification system, which were reviewed in chapter 4, stimulated simultaneous efforts to construct effective and reliable techniques for the assessment of abnormal behavior. The techniques developed have been quite diverse. In this chapter, the reader will be introduced to projective and nonprojective psychometric assessment techniques, interviews, and other forms of self-report procedures, direct behavior sampling, physiological assessment, and medical evaluations. Projective techniques were developed by psychodynamically oriented theorists interested in the hidden or covert aspects of an individual's personality. Because of certain problems associated with these projective techniques, many personality theorists attempted to develop tests that were more psychometrically

sound and that could be objectively scored and quantified. Out of this tradition, structured psychometric tests were developed to measure factors such as personality characteristics, intelligence, and the presence of organic brain damage. Many mental health practitioners now are placing greater emphasis on the direct measurement of behavior and its situational determinants. Verbal self-report, overt behavioral actions, and physiological responding can be used in such assessment. During the review of these various assessment techniques, we will discuss the issues, advantages, and limitations of each. We will also point out the different theoretical assumptions on which these methods are based. To a great extent, these assumptions dictate the type of data that are collected and assessed.

PROJECTIVE TECHNIQUES

Projective techniques were developed by psychoanalytically oriented theorists interested in the hidden or covert aspects of an individual's personality. Such tests were viewed as providing clinicians with a "royal road to the unconscious," which presumably would allow them to identify the true "underlying causes" of that person's behavior. *Projective* techniques, a term coined by Frank (1939), were viewed as methods that present the subject with a situation for which there is little or no well-defined cultural pattern of responding, so that the individual must "project" upon that ambiguous situation his or her feelings, attitudes, motives, and ways of viewing life. These factors, many of which are assumed to be at the level of the unconscious, make up the individual's "core" personality structure, according to psychoanalytic theory, and determine the way in which he or she will behave. It is assumed that this "core" is most readily assessed through the types of responses elicited by the ambiguous, nonthreatening stimuli that projective tests present. Such stimuli give the individual freedom to respond in unique ways. Since subjects are not aware of the purpose of the test or how their specific responses will be interpreted, there is a greater chance that they will reveal certain facets of their personality that they may be unaware of or attempt to conceal. Because of the response variety such tests allow, and their relative resistance to conscious control, projective techniques may provide a clinician with an effective means for uncovering subtle and hidden aspects of personality.

Projective tests are often referred to as *unstructured* tests because the test respondents are told they are free to give any response they desire. This is in contrast to most nonprojective tests, (which will be discussed in the next section), in which the respondents have less freedom in the type of response they may give and are often limited to choosing among such responses as "true," "false," and "cannot say." Through the years, a number of different projective tests have been developed. Lindzey (1959) has described five classes or categories of projective techniques: (1) *Associative* techniques in which the subject is instructed to respond to the stimulus material presented with the first word, image, or thought that comes to mind. Examples of such techniques are the Rorschach Inkblot Test (Rorschach 1942) and the Word Association Technique (Kent & Rosanoff 1910). (2) *Construction* techniques in which an individual is required to create or construct something, such as a story or picture. Examples of such techniques are the Thematic Apperception Test (TAT) (Murray 1938) and the Blacky Pictures Test (Blum 1950). (3) *Completion* techniques in which the respondent is requested to complete an incomplete product, such as an incomplete sentence, in any manner he or she wishes. Examples of such techniques are the Rotter Incomplete Sentences Test (Rotter & Rafferty 1950) and the Picture-Frustration Study (Rosenzweig 1945). (4) *Choice* or *ordering* techniques in which the individual is instructed to choose from, or make order among, stimuli such as a set of inkblots or pictures, according to some specified criteria such as correctness or attractiveness. Examples of such techniques are the Szondi Test (Szondi 1944) and the Picture Arrangement Test (Tomkins 1952). (5) *Expressive* techniques in which the individual is asked to express himself or herself freely in some way, as in play or painting. Examples of such techniques are the Play Technique (e.g., Levy 1933) and the Draw-A-Person technique (Machover 1948).

These classes of projective techniques are not mutually exclusive. Many projective tests represent combinations of classes. Nevertheless, as Sarason (1972) indicates, this classification schema is useful in that it provides a general method of characterizing these various projective methods.

Two of the most frequently used projective techniques are the Rorschach and the TAT. We will briefly review these two tests in order to provide the reader with a better understanding of what is involved in the administration, scoring, and interpretation of projective techniques.

THE RORSCHACH INKBLOT TEST

The Rorschach Inkblot Test was developed by the Swiss psychiatrist Hermann Rorschach. His major work on this test was published in 1942 (Rorschach

The Rorschach projective test is a widely known diagnostic tool. It is a means of assessing internal conflicts and motivations of which an individual may not be aware. Responses may be scored according to several major systems.

1942). Since its introduction, it has become a widely used technique in the clinician's repertoire of diagnostic tests. The Rorschach test is administered by an examiner who presents a series of ten bilaterally symmetrical inkblots. The respondent is requested to describe what he or she sees or what the inkblot resembles or suggests. After responding to all ten inkblots, the subject is shown the inkblots once again, and the examiner asks what characteristics of the inkblot determined the response and interpretation. The subject's responses to the inkblots are then usually scored for location (the portion of the card included in the response), quality of the response, content of the response, and various determinants of the inkblot (such as color, shape, suggestion of movement, human or animal characteristics) that suggested the response given. These responses and scores are then used by the clinician as "signs" that reflect the individual's underlying personality dynamics. A number of major scoring systems have been developed (e.g., Beck 1961; Exner 1974; Klopfer, Ainsworth, Klopfer, & Holt 1954), although they all rely on Rorschach's initial insights into the relationship between perceptual characteristics of the blots and the mental life of the individual responding to them. Exner is especially noteworthy for his efforts toward standardizing and developing objective criteria and norms for both children and adults.

THE TAT

At about the same time that the Rorschach was introduced in the United States, a Harvard University psychologist, Henry Murray, developed the Thematic Apperception Test, or TAT (Murray 1938). This test consists of a series of 30 pictures and one blank card. Most of the pictures depict scenes with personal connotations. Different sets of pictures were developed for young males, young females (both under 14 years of age), adult males, and adult females. The cards are presented one at a time, and the individual is instructed to make up a story suggested by each picture. He or she is instructed to make up as complete a story as possible, with plot and characters, and to describe what the situation is, what has led up to the situation, what the characters are feeling and thinking, and what the outcome will be. The respondents are encouraged to give their first impressions and to give free rein to their imaginations.

In asking subjects to engage in fantasy in response to an ambiguous, unstructured stimulus, Murray's main goal was to have them interpret the stimulus according to their tendency or readiness to perceive in a certain way (thus the term *apperception*). The themes that recur in the fantasies are interpreted in terms of *needs* and *presses* and are used in assessing overt and covert aspects of personality. *Needs* are defined by Murray as internal motivators of behavior, such as need for achievement, aggression, abasement, etc. *Presses* are defined as environmental determinants of behavior, such as physical danger, rejection by a loved one, etc. It was assumed that assessment of these covert (needs) and overt (presses) factors would provide an understanding of the individual's core personality structure.

Although the scoring of the Rorschach has traditionally been far from objective, the scoring of the TAT is even less standardized and objective. Although special scoring keys have been developed to measure specific themes on the TAT, such as the need for achievement (McClelland, Atkinson, Clark, & Lowell 1953) and aggression (Mussen & Naylor 1954), comprehensive scoring techniques are rarely used. Unlike the Rorschach, the

TAT has no generally accepted systems of scoring and interpretation. Rather, the clinician uses a great deal of subjective interpretation of the possible meaning and significance of various aspects of the stories. The problem of using subjective clinical interpretation is one of several problems associated with projective techniques.

PROBLEMS ASSOCIATED WITH PROJECTIVE TESTS

The freedom that subjects have in responding to an unstructured, "situationless" stimulus, which is one of the major features and strengths of projective techniques, is at the same time a major weakness that creates a number of problems for such tests. One problem is the lack of reliable scoring of subjects' responses. Scoring often involves subjective judgments by the clinician, which can result in a low degree of agreement among judges (i.e., low interscorer reliability). Another related and more significant problem is the interpretation of the significance of a response once it is scored. Such interpretations usually are based predominantly on the clinical judgment of the test interpreter. The clinician has to organize and synthesize a great deal of diverse data and generate hypotheses that provide a coherent and consistent account of the patient.

The first problem, scoring, can be dealt with by providing judges with manuals that contain explicit instructions for scoring to help increase interscorer agreement and reliability. It has been demonstrated also that extensive training in a particular scoring system, with judges being trained with examples and sample scoring decisions, leads to satisfactory levels of agreement (Goldfried, Stricker, & Weiner 1971).

The second problem, interpretation, is more serious and can significantly affect the validity of projective techniques. Because of the subjectivity involved in interpreting the meaning of certain responses, it is not at all surprising that the interpretation of projective tests varies widely depending on the skill and the experience of the examiner. Indeed, Anastasi (1968) suggests that projective tests may be as much a projection of the examiner's biases, perceptions, and theoretical orientation as they are of the respondent's personality characteristics.

The validity of projective tests is generally

The Thematic Apperception Test is a projective test for personality measurement in which the subject is asked to make up a story about the picture.

unsubstantiated when they are used to generate a comprehensive personality description of an individual (e.g., Anastasi 1968; Kleinmuntz 1967; Nunnally 1967). In one type of study commonly used to assess the validity and utility of these techniques, experienced clinicians construct a personality description of an individual based upon that person's responses to a projective test such as the Rorschach. The clinicians are "blind" with respect to any other information about the individual. Usually, only a low degree of agreement is found between the clinicians' descriptions and classifications of the individuals (e.g., Little & Schneidman 1959). In addition, the descriptions often are so general that they are applicable to almost anyone (Liebert & Spiegler 1974). It is, of course, possible to measure the validity of projective tests in some instances. For example, if a patient is diagnosed as a shoe fetishist because of that person's responses on a projective test, there may be confirming evidence in the form of self-reports, etc.

In fairness to projective techniques, it should be pointed out that some clinicians have a great deal of skill in obtaining meaningful information about an individual through such tests. Unfortunately, however, a great many clinicians do not have such expertise.

NONPROJECTIVE TECHNIQUES

As a result of the problems associated with projective techniques, many personality theorists became dissatisfied and attempted to develop more psychometrically sound tests that could be objectively scored and quantified. Out of this tradition, a variety of *structured* tests were developed to measure personality characteristics. Tests of intelligence and tests for organic brain damage also were developed using a structured test format. Statistical norms for these tests are usually developed by administering the test to large groups of individuals at different times, so that the way one individual responds to test items can be compared with the way certain kinds of other people tend to respond.

PERSONALITY TESTS

Both unidimensional and multidimensional personality tests have been developed. *Unidimensional* tests are developed by investigators interested in one particular facet or dimension of personality. For example, the Taylor Manifest Anxiety Scale (Taylor 1953) was developed to assess an individual's general level of anxiety. One of the earliest developed unidimensional tests was the Personal Data Sheet, later known as the Psychoneurotic Inventory. It was devised by Woodworth (1919) during World War I as an attempt to gauge the level of adjustment of soldiers and thereby provide a method of screening out those who might break down emotionally on exposure to wartime stress. The test did prove of some benefit as a gross screening device, and was a simple and economical alternative to interviewing all recruits individually.

Unlike unidimensional tests, *multidimensional personality inventories* are directed at obtaining multifaceted personality descriptions. One of the most widely known and used multidimensional personality tests is the Minnesota Multiphasic Personality Inventory (MMPI), which was developed by Hathaway and McKinley (1943). These psychologists were interested in developing a testing instrument that would provide mental health professionals with a comprehensive method to use in the description and diagnosis of abnormal behavior. In developing the test, Hathaway and McKinley initially compiled a large set of items

from psychiatric textbooks, psychiatric examination forms, previously developed personality and attitude scales, and their own personal clinical experiences. From this large group of more than a thousand items, they decided on 550 items that ranged widely in content, including statements concerning current or past behaviors ("I have used alcohol excessively"; "I pray several times a week"), beliefs and attitudes ("I believe there is a God"), feelings ("I am happy most of the time"), symptoms ("I wake up fresh and rested most mornings"), and traits ("I am certainly lacking in self-confidence").

The test is scored for ten psychiatric-personality scales, as well as three "validity" scales used to check for the subjects' faking, misunderstanding, or sloppiness in taking the test. The ten "clinical" or psychiatric-personality scales are:

1. *Hs*: Hypochondriasis scale. Assesses whether subjects have an exaggerated concern about their physical health, often with somatic complaints that have a psychological basis.
2. *D*: Depression scale. Assesses intense unhappiness and depression.
3. *Hy*: Hysteria scale. Assesses psychologically caused physical symptoms in persons with an apparent unconcern or indifference about their condition.
4. *Pd*: Psychopathic Deviate scale. Assesses the degree of difficulty in social adjustment, the presence of delinquency and other antisocial behavior, and the tendency to "act out."
5. *Mf*: Masculinity-Femininity scale. Assesses the degree to which individuals engage in typical sex-role type behaviors and have feelings and attitudes traditionally ascribed to one or the other sex.
6. *Pa*: Paranoia scale. Assesses paranoid symptoms such as feelings of persecution, suspiciousness, worriedness, and interpersonal sensitivity.
7. *Pt*: Psychasthenia scale. Assesses whether individuals experience unreasonable fears, high anxiety levels, excessive doubts, and feelings of guilt.
8. *Sc*: Schizophrenia scale. Assesses whether individuals have characteristics indicative of the various subtypes of schizophrenia

such as hallucinations and social withdrawal/isolation. A high score on this scale may also indicate a somewhat artistic individual who engages in abstract thinking, or simply a socially withdrawn person.

9. *Ma*: Hypomania scale. Assesses impulsivity, excessive activity, and degree of manic excitement.
10. *Si*: Social Introversion-Extroversion scale. Assesses the degree of sociability.

The three "validity" scales are:

1. *L*: Lie scale. Assesses the subject's frankness or deception in answering the questions. It contains items that describe socially desirable but improbable behaviors; answering "false" to such questions as "I sometimes put off till tomorrow what I might do today," and "I get angry sometimes" would indicate deception.
2. *F*: Infrequency scale. Assesses the degree of carelessness, confusion, or effort to deceive by subjects in answering the questions. It contains items that are answered in the same direction by at least 90 percent of normal subjects, and is a measure of how similar the subject's responses are to those of the general population.
3. *K*: Defensiveness scale. Another method, although more subtle, for assessing test-taking attitudes that may cause defensiveness or "faking good."

All the clinical scales, except the Mf and Si scales, were developed by comparing the responses of nonpsychiatric normal subjects with those of patients in a particular psychiatric diagnostic group. For example, in developing the depression scale, the responses of normal subjects who appeared to have no major behavior abnormalities were compared with those of patients diagnosed as suffering from depression. Only patients who were unequivocally diagnosed as depressed by a group of psychiatrists were included in the tested patient group. Each of the 550 items was then examined to determine whether the persons diagnosed as depressed responded differently than the normal subjects. Those items on which the depressed and normal subjects' answers differed significantly were used to make up the Depression scale. A high score on this scale indicates that the individual has responded to those items in a manner like that of the depressed patient group originally used by

Hathaway and McKinley in diagnostic studies.

For the Mf scale, separate scales were developed for men and women based on those items for which the responses of men and women differed. A high score on this scale indicates that an individual has interests similar to those of members of the opposite sex. The Si scale was developed by comparing items of college students who scored low and high on a test of introversion-extroversion.

After the MMPI was developed, it soon became evident that the test could not be used successfully because individuals obtaining high scores on a scale often did not fit precisely into that particular diagnostic category. Moreover, it was found that many apparently normal individuals scored high on the clinical scales. Subsequently, though, it was found that useful diagnostic discriminations could be made by assessing combinations or patterns of scale scores. This is the manner in which the MMPI is currently used. For example, individuals with a high score on both the Pd and Ma scales (not just the Pd scale) were found to be associated with psychopathic and other antisocial forms of behavior. Several empirically based manuals containing profile patterns, along with case descriptions of patients with these profile patterns, have been developed for clinical and personality assessment (Dahlstrom, Welsh, & Dahlstrom 1972; Gilberstadt & Duker 1965; Marks & Seeman 1963). These manuals are "cookbook" interpretations of the MMPI that provide clinicians with standards against which to match their cases. These cookbook manuals have added to the popularity and widespread use of this personality inventory. There are now even computer services that score and provide a detailed printout of the cookbook interpretation of MMPI profiles.

PROBLEMS ASSOCIATED WITH STRUCTURED PERSONALITY TESTS Structured personality tests also present certain problems. One significant and well-demonstrated difficulty is the presence of response sets or biases. A *response set* or *bias* is a particular test-taking attitude that causes an individual not to answer items on a test in terms of their manifest content. That is, he or she has a characteristic and consistent way of responding to items on a test regardless of what the items actually say. Three major types of response sets have been shown to affect structured personality tests: response deviation or dissimulation, response acquiescence, and social desirability.

Response dissimulation. Response deviation or dissimulation is the tendency for an individual to answer items in an uncommon direction, with the goal of presenting an overly favorable or unfavorable picture of himself or herself. This is the most obvious response set, and the one that received the first attention of test constructors and users. For example, Grayson and Olinger (1957), using psychiatric patients as subjects, found that some of their patients who were given instructions to "fake good," that is, to look psychologically "healthy," could significantly change their MMPI profiles in that direction. Of course, this response set is not a serious problem if the respondent is motivated to answer honestly. If an individual is not so motivated, however, the possibility of faking is always present. The rationale for the development of the validity scales on the MMPI was to provide a means by which the examiner could determine whether a respondent was faking. However, these scales do not guarantee that such faking will be detected in an individual who is test-wise, has even a superficial working knowledge of abnormal psychology, and is careful not to give contradictory answers to similar questions that are worded slightly differently.

Acquiescence. The acquiescence response set is the tendency to agree with test items no matter what their content. On a personality inventory such as the MMPI, the questions are worded so that agreement increases the scale score. That is, the total score on a scale is a direct function of how often the respondent agrees with, or responds "yes" to, the items. The more often an individual answers "yes" to an item that is part of the MMPI depression scale, for example, the higher his or her depression score will be. If a nondepressed individual has an acquiescence response set and so answers "yes" to these items regardless of their content, then he or she will have a scale score that suggests the presence of depression.

Messick and Jackson (1961) have suggested that the acquiescence response set can be a significant influencing factor on tests such as the MMPI. Others, though, have indicated that this response bias plays only a minor and nonsignificant role (e.g., Block 1965; Rorer 1965). Nevertheless, a test administrator and interpreter must be aware of the possibility of this response set affecting test responses.

Social Desirability. Social desirability set is the tendency to answer items in the direction that is most socially acceptable, regardless of whether the answers are true. Edwards (1953) published the first significant research study that showed test subjects' tendency to respond to self-report questionnaire items on this basis. This study demonstrated a high correlation between the probability of an item's being endorsed and its independently determined value on the social desirability scale.

To control for social desirability, certain inventories use a *forced-choice* question format. In this format, pairs of self-reference statements are presented simultaneously to the respondent, who is to choose the statement that is the most self-descriptive. The alternatives in each pair of statements are made equivalent in terms of social desirability. An example of a forced-choice format inventory is the Edwards Personal Preference Schedule (Edwards 1959). The inventory contains 225 pairs of items, with the items of each pair being comparable in social desirability ratings. For example, a respondent would be asked to choose which of these two statements is more descriptive of him or her:

(A) I feel like blaming others when things go wrong for me.
(B) I feel that I am inferior to others in most respects.

Since these two items have been rated as equivalent in social desirability, then the item chosen is assumed more likely to describe the respondent. This type of format assures that the questionnaire responses will not merely reflect the degree to which a respondent wishes to appear socially conventional or likeable.

There has been some criticism of the forced-choice format on the grounds that it produces annoyance and conflict in individuals who are forced to choose between two strongly undesirable statements (Guilford 1959). Nonetheless, it is an interesting psychometric alternative to true-false inventories such as the MMPI, and allows the tester to rule out the possibility that responses to a test that is attempting to measure personality characteristics are being significantly affected by the social desirability response set.

INTELLIGENCE TESTS

Alfred Binet, a French psychologist, began trying to measure intelligence in the 1890s in response to the need of the Paris school board for a method by which they could predict which children would profit most from schooling and which children were "uneducable" or retarded. He empirically examined a variety of tasks to determine which ones

Alfred Binet (1857–1911), a Frenchman, developed the first widely used test of intelligence.

could be used to differentiate between bright and dull children. From the scales developed, which reflected performance on tasks that were found to differentiate successfully between these children (such as comprehension, memory, imagination, motor ability), a single overall score was determined that reflected a simple, general indication of mental status. This score was found to differentiate effectively and reliably between children with respect to scholastic standing.

In subsequent years, the scales developed by Binet were revised and extended a number of times. In 1916, Lewis Terman of Stanford University revised the scales and produced the now classic Stanford-Binet Intelligence Test. This test, along with the Wechsler Adult Intelligence Scale (WAIS) and the Wechsler Intelligence Scale for Children—Revised (WISC-R), developed by David Wechsler, has become extremely influential. Wechsler was prompted to develop his tests because he felt the Stanford-Binet to be deficient, since it provided only a single score of intelligence. He believed that intelligence could be measured more effectively as an aggregation of a number of separate abilities. The WAIS was constructed to consist of a total of 11 subtests, 6 of which were verbal (general information, comprehension, similarities, digit span vocabulary, arithmetic), and 5 nonverbal or performance-oriented (digit symbol, block design, picture arrangement, object assembly, picture completion). This variety allows an analysis of patterns of subtest scores, so that one can assess an individual's specific intellectual strengths and

weaknesses. Three intelligence quotients (IQs) are routinely obtained from the Wechsler test, instead of the one overall IQ of the Stanford-Binet: Verbal IQ, Performance IQ, and Full Scale IQ.

The Stanford-Binet and Wechsler scales are used to determine an individual's rank or standing relative to a large number of other people of the same age. In the area of abnormal psychology, they have become widely used procedures for diagnosing mental retardation. They also play a major role in the area of evaluating an individual's overall intellectual functioning, such as the quality of thinking and performance.

PROBLEMS ASSOCIATED WITH INTELLIGENCE TESTS Performance on an intelligence test cannot be assumed to provide a direct measure of a person's "native capacity." Unfortunately, many lay persons, as well as some mental health professionals who should know better, believe that intelligence tests do provide such a measure. An IQ score is the product of many factors, including the individual's motivation to do well on a test of intellectual skills, his or her current emotional state, past encouragement of intellectual competence, and familiarity with the language and tasks used in IQ tests. Davis (1948), for example, has suggested the presence of *cultural bias* in many items on IQ tests. He has shown that, in many instances, the items selected for inclusion on intelligence tests are likely to be more familiar to middle-class children than to their lower-class peers. One reason is that many such tests have been developed to predict the intellectual performance valued by middle-class persons, and many have been standardized on white middle-class subjects.

In response to the criticism of cultural bias, a number of so-called "culture-fair" or "culture-free" intelligence tests have been developed, such as the Culture-Free Intelligence Test developed by Cattell (1949). In such tests, an attempt is made to include content material that is not necessarily more familiar to individuals in one particular cultural or socioeconomic group. However, a completely satisfactory culture-fair test has not yet been developed. Even when the emphasis is on nonverbal material (which is assumed to be unaffected by the middle-class individual's relative advantage in verbal skills), the test still is not completely free from dependence on past experiences that may differ from group to group. Class differences found with these tests are often very similar to the differences found with more traditional intelligence tests (e.g., Marquart &

Performance on an intelligence test is the product of many factors, including the individual's motivation to do well, current emotional state, and familiarity with the language and tasks required in such tests.

Bailey 1955). Cleary, Humphreys, Kendrick, and Wesman (1975) have recently raised serious questions concerning such tests' actual validity and "culture-fair" nature.

Even if an intelligence test were developed that was "culture fair" in content, one would still have the potential problem of lower motivation among certain cultural or socioeconomic groups to do well in school and school-type tasks. This factor could significantly affect performance on the test.

One last point about intelligence tests con-

cerns the problem of labeling a person as mentally retarded or "slow" simply on the basis of performance on an intelligence test. Such labeling or "pigeonholing" often has significant implications for the way in which an individual is treated. A child may become viewed as "uneducable" and assumed not to have the capacity to learn. Obviously, this will significantly affect the way a teacher, for example, interacts with the child, and the amount of energy invested in providing him or her with learning experiences. Labeling can be a serious problem, but can be avoided if individuals realize the limitations of intelligence tests and the many factors that many affect performance on them. These issues are discussed more fully in chapter 15.

TESTS FOR ORGANIC BRAIN DAMAGE

In recent years, there has been a growing interest in clinical neuropsychology, an applied area of clinical psychology concerned with the diagnosis of brain dysfunction. As seen in chapter 4, one major diagnostic category of both the DSM-II and the DSM-III (DSM-III has proposed to use the label "Organic Mental Disorders") refers to abnormal behavioral patterns caused by organic brain pathology. *Neuropsychological assessment* involves the search for behavioral manifestations or patterns of performance aberrations that are associated with specific brain disorders. This is an important assessment method because many of the currently used medical-neurological tests—the angiogram X-ray technique to detect a brain tumor, the measurement of the electrical activity of the brain, the examination of the retina to detect blood vessel damage, and the evaluation of perception and motor coordination—can assess gross brain damage but cannot detect more subtle dysfunctions. Neuropsychological test results may provide clues about the nature of such subtle disturbances (Lezak 1976).

Halstead (1947) developed the first comprehensive neuropsychological test battery for the assessment of brain damage, which was later modified by Reitan (1955). Reitan (1964) has empirically demonstrated that this test battery can reliably identify the etiology and location of certain brain lesions with a high degree of accuracy. The norms used in such identification were developed by comparing test performance patterns of patients with known organic disorders in specific parts of the brain to those of normal individuals with no known brain disorder. The original Halstead-Reitan Battery consisted of the following tests:

- *Category Test*, which measures abstracting ability.
- *Critical Flicker Fusion Test (CFF)*, which measures visual perception.
- *Tactual Performance Test*, which measures tactile perception.
- *Rhythm Test*, which measures auditory perception.
- *Speech Sounds Perception Test*, which also measures auditory perception.
- *Finger Oscillation Test* or *Finger Tapping Test*, which measures manual dexterity.
- *Time Sense Test*, which measures visual-motor reaction time and the ability to estimate a just-elapsed time span.
- *Trail-Making Test,* which measures visual attention and visual-motor tracking coordination.
- *Aphasia Screening Test*, which tests for aphasia (the loss of ability to speak, read, write, or understand).
- *Sensory Examination*, which tests for finger agnosia, skin writing recognition, and sensory adaptation in the auditory, tactual, and visual modalities.
- *Wechsler-Bellevue Intelligence Scale I* or the *WAIS*, which measures a variety of cognitive-verbal and motor-performance tasks.
- *MMPI*, which measures personality factors.

It should be noted that "cookbook" interpretation manuals, similar to those discussed for the MMPI, are being developed for neuropsychological test interpretation. They will provide clinicians with standards against which to match their cases and make the interpretation of test-battery results much more objective.

PROBLEMS ASSOCIATED WITH TESTS FOR ORGANIC BRAIN DAMAGE   If there is a problem with neuropsychological techniques, it is that these tests are relatively new assessment procedures and are still undergoing modification and validation. Moreover, there is still not a full understanding of normal brain organization and functioning. Neuropsychological tests will need to be revised continually as more information is accrued about brain functioning.

LIMITATIONS AND ADVANTAGES OF TESTING

Psychological tests can be used to provide valuable information about individuals. Our review of neuropsychological techniques revealed how this assessment procedure can be an effective method for evaluating brain damage. Such information often can greatly aid a neurologist in diagnosing the type and location of a particular brain dysfunction, avoiding extensive exploratory neurosurgery to determine the possible presence of a brain lesion or other organic damage. In reviewing intelligence tests, we observed how such tests can provide an effective means of predicting academic performance and other skills related to academic-type tasks. We also pointed out the possible problems that can be caused by misinterpreting the meaning of an IQ score, and the stigma attached to an individual who has been labeled as having a "low IQ."

Various personality tests can give a general overall picture of individual personality characteristics. Such information may be important in planning and implementing an appropriate treatment program for an individual experiencing some form of disordered behavior. Unfortunately, these personality tests have certain major limitations.

The initial assumption upon which traditional projective and nonprojective personality tests were based was that abnormal behavior could be understood by evaluating the individual's underlying personality characteristics or predispositions. These predispositions were viewed as the motivating causes and determinants of behavior. It was assumed that the assessment of these inner characteristics would allow an examiner to fully understand and classify the problem behavior. But the attempt to assess these characteristics has met with certain significant problems. For example, the problems of reliability and validity in projective tests raise serious questions about the worth and continued use of projective assessment procedures in their present form. Even the more psychometrically sound and empirically constructed personality tests, such as the MMPI, suffer from the possibility of various individual response biases affecting test results. Another and more significant problem associated with structured tests is related to one of the basic assumptions about such tests. It was assumed that the underlying "constructs" exert causal effects on behavior, and so the task of assessment was seen as the search for *signs* that would be reliable indicants of these underlying dispositions. This is the same assumption and approach used by projective test users. Nonprojective test constructors who take a trait approach, however, make the additional assumption that behavior is consistent across situations, and that one can construct tests to tap general personality "traits" or dispositions that cause this consistency of behavior. That is, if a man has a major trait of aggression, it is assumed that his behavior will be largely determined by this trait and that it will most likely prompt him to behave in an aggressive manner no matter what the situation. This assumption of consistency of behavior, however, has been seriously questioned in recent years.

Mischel (1976) has reviewed a great deal of evidence that argues against any simple conception of consistency of behavior that does not specify the importance of situational determinants. For example, Bandura and Walters (1963) found that aggressive behavior in children was relatively situationally specific. That is, whether the children behaved aggressively or not depended on the situation. Such studies cogently argue for the position that specific stimulus situations can have important influences on the type of behavior an individual displays.

Because of the situational specificity of behavior, most comprehensive and large-scale efforts to predict behavior on the basis of personality tests usually have been shown to be unsuccessful (Mischel 1968). This fact, together with a general disenchantment with classification, has prompted numerous mental health practitioners to abandon the routine application of many traditional assessment procedures. Indeed, the worth and continued usage of any assessment procedure is ultimately tied to its practical utility in making treatment predictions in individual cases. It has been shown that most traditional assessment test procedures lack this utility. Meehl (1960) has suggested that most clinicians fail to utilize extensive traditional assessment tests in psychotherapy, but arrive at their own notions rapidly during the first few therapy sessions. Bannister, Salmon, and Lieberman (1964) reported, in a study with 1,000 psychiatric patients, that differential assessment classifications did not lead to different forms of

treatment. This suggests that there is usually a dichotomy between assessment and treatment.

In the next sections we will discuss other methods of assessment that are being used more and more to evaluate behavior disorders. In these procedures, greater emphasis is placed on evaluating an individual's behavior in specific environmental contexts. With the increased use of learning or social-behavioral approaches for the treatment of behavior disorders, such types of assessment procedures also increased. They do not attempt to assess and determine various underlying dispositions, since, from this viewpoint, these dispositions are not the major or only causes of maladaptive behavior. Instead, the emphasis is upon the direct measurement of behavior and its situational determinants.

Kanfer and Saslow (1969) have described this *functional behavioral analysis* approach as a means of collecting information that will relate directly to specific techniques of treatment intervention. They have developed a systematic format of procedures to aid clinicians in collecting and organizing their treatment-oriented data. The approach emphasizes the integration of assessment and treatment. Assessment is a vital procedure used to clearly define the focal problem behavior and also to allow quantifiable interpretation of therapy results. Goldfried and Kent (1972) emphasize that in various behavior therapy techniques, successful implementation and evaluation depend directly on the accurate assessment of the problem behavior one wishes to change and on the clear delineation of the variables maintaining these behaviors. The emphasis is on the situational determinants of behavior and calls for reliable determination of an individual's response to life situations and various aspects of his or her environment.

Users of traditional assessment procedures have criticized assessment techniques that emphasize situational factors for ignoring the importance of an individual's unique characteristics. Mischel (1973) has noted, however, the importance of evaluating "person" factors such as individual expectations, subjective values, personal constructs, etc., that interact with situational factors in determining behavior. Thus, instead of studying global traits or inner characteristics inferred from tests and behavioral signs, the emphasis is on the study of an individual's cognitive activities and behavior patterns in relation to the specific situational conditions that elicit, maintain, and modify them.

OTHER METHODS OF ASSESSMENT

DIRECT OBSERVATION OF BEHAVIOR

Behaviorally oriented therapists working within a learning theory paradigm emphasize the role of stimulus conditions in regulating and moderating behavior. As a result, they have been concerned with the direct assessment of behavior and the evaluation of changes in behavior caused by changing conditions. The assessment of aggression, for example, would involve the direct behavioral assessment or *sampling* of aggression responses produced by an individual in a specific situation. In contrast, therapists who take the trait and psychodynamic approaches to assessment would use responses on tests (e.g., the psychodynamically oriented assessors interpreting aggression themes on the TAT) as a *sign* of an underlying personality characteristic of aggression in an individual. The difference between these *sample* and *sign* approaches is highlighted by Mischel (1976):

> In one sense, all psychological approaches are based on behavioral observation: check marks on MMPI answer sheets and stories in response to inkblots obviously are behaviors just as much as crying or running or fighting . . . The difference between approaches depends on how these behaviors are used. As we saw, in the dynamic orientation the observed behaviors serve as highly indirect *signs* (symptoms) of the dispositions and motives that might underlie them. In contrast, in behavior assessments the observed behavior is treated as a *sample* and interest is focused on how the specific sampled behavior is affected by alterations and conditions. Behavioral approaches thus seek to directly assess stimulus-response covariations. (pp. 199–200)

Comprehensive and reliable methods for the direct observation and measurement of behavior have been developed for a wide variety of behaviors, including aggression, fear-produced avoidance behavior, psychotic behavior, and social withdrawal. The major goal of these methods is the careful and reliable measurement of specific behaviors that will allow one to determine whether systematic changes in stimulus conditions produce specific changes in behavior. To provide a test of measurement reliability, at least two observers are used to make the ratings. A comparison of the degree of agreement between observers provides an indication of whether the behavior in question has been clearly defined and can be easily interpreted and scored. The ratings used in behavioral assessments normally consist of counting the occurrences of the behavior during a specific time period in order to determine its frequency. Mischel (1976) presents an example of a behavioral assessment device and procedure developed by Lovaas, Freitag, Gold, and Kassorla (1965):

> Lovaas and his collaborators . . . devised an apparatus that consists of a panel of buttons that are depressed by the observer. Each button represents a category of behavior (for example, "talking," "running," "sitting alone") and is attached to an automatic pen-recorder. Whenever a button is depressed, the corresponding pen on the recorder is activated. A continuous record is thus provided . . . The observer depresses the button when the subject starts the specific behavior designated by the button and does not release the button until the particular behavior is discontinued. The observer after a little practice can devote his whole attention to watching what the subject is doing and yet record up to twelve different categories of behavior without looking at the button panel. The apparatus permits a record that is precise enough to include duration and the specific time of onset of each behavior. The method can then be applied to discover covariations among the individual's different behaviors and between his behavior and that of other people in the situation . . . Lovaas used the recording device primarily to record the behavior of severely disturbed children, but the procedure can be used to observe the behavior of any person in almost any setting. The categories of behavior selected can be as specific or broad as the purpose for which the observation in being made requires. The one necessity is that the category be such that independent observers show high agreement in their scoring of the behavior it represents. (p. 202)

Of course, a mechanical apparatus like that used by Lovaas and his colleagues is not essential in making behavioral assessments. Indeed, most are conducted by having observers simply count or check off on a checklist specific behaviors that occur during certain time periods. (An example of such an assessment will be presented later in this section.)

CLINICAL INTERVIEW AND SELF-REPORT MEASURES

A widely employed method of assessment which cuts across all theoretical orientations is the clinical interview. It is a major method for exploring and delineating specific concerns, feelings, and problems that an individual may be experiencing. The type of data or information collected in the interviews tends to differ depending on the interviewer's theoretical orientation. For example, a behaviorally oriented assessor might be concerned with determining the specific stimulus/environmental conditions associated with an abnormal piece of behavior. On the other hand, a psychodynamically oriented assessor would be interested in reconstructing the individual's early developmental history as a means of determining underlying personality characteristics that may be causing certain behaviors of clinical concern.

The degree to which an interview is structured may vary. The great majority of interviews are conducted in a very loose, unstructured format in which the interviewer determines the kinds of questions asked and the way in which they are asked. This format can present a problem if one is interested in comparing the content and material gathered from certain patients by different interviewers. The differing experience and clinical skills of the interviewers will make comparisons across interview data difficult, if not impossible.

An alternative is to impose more structure on the interview situation. One such structured interview system is the Current and Past Psychopathology Scales (Spitzer & Endicott 1969). It consists of an interview guide gauged to gather specific information. The clinician focuses attention on a uniform set of typical patient characteristics. The interviewee's responses to specific questions are scored on a six-point scale that measures the degree of certain behaviors and feelings present. With this format, the same questions are asked and phrased in an identical manner, and the responses

elicited can be scored and compared across patients.

Spitzer (1966) has also developed the Mental Status Examination Record, an automated, IBM-scored form for describing a patient's clinical characteristics. It is a standardized and quantitative procedure that allows a clinician to compare individuals over time and also to compare different patient groups, because they are assessed on the same items and rated in the same categories. This automated procedure allows the collection of objective and quantifiable interview data and produces a diagnostic statement about an individual.

Many have assumed that it is virtually impossible to score objectively or make order out of verbalizations elicited during unstructured interviews. However, a great deal of research has been conducted indicating that one can quantify the content of verbal self-reports collected in interview situations (e.g., Sarason 1954). A technique known as *content analysis* is employed. In a sense, content analysis of verbal behavior is analogous to the rating of overt behavior. Categories of verbal behavior are constructed that can be reliably rated by content analyzers or scorers. The categories may be simple and straightforward or quite complex. The content analysis system tells the rater what unit of speech to attend to and categorize and what criteria to follow in making categorizations. The frequency of certain categories of verbal behavior is used as an assessment measure.

Carl Rogers and his colleagues (e.g., Rogers 1942; Rogers & Dymond 1954) have used content analyses of clients' verbalizations extensively to document how verbalizations reflect self-concepts and how they change during the course of client-centered therapy. Since that time, the content analysis of interview data has become a widely used and systematic research method (Mischel 1976). An example of the use of content analysis is presented in a case study reported by Murray, Auld, and White (1954). This study assessed the progressions of a client's conflict statements during the course of psychotherapy sessions. This client was beset by marital problems. Two types of statements were assessed—statements about hostility conflicts and about sexual conflicts with her husband. Sexual conflicts were actually not discussed until later on in her psychotherapy. Sarason (1972) notes that these findings are consistent with the usual clinical observation that the type of conflicts expressed change during the course of psychotherapy, from relatively superficial ones to more significant ones (see figure 5.1).

A sample page from a structured interview guide devised by Spitzer and Endicott. (From The Schedule for Affective Disorders and Schizophrenia, Third Edition, 1978, developed by Robert L. Spitzer and Jean Endicott; used by permission)

SADS   6

DYSPHORIC MOOD AND RELATED SYMPTOMS

If the subject is currently manic or high, the following questions should be introduced with a statement such as: *I know you are feeling very good now; however, many people have other feelings mixed in or at different times, so it is important that I ask you about these feelings also.*

Subjective feelings of depression based on verbal complaints of feeling depressed, sad, blue, gloomy, down in the dumps, empty, ''don't care.'' Do not include such ideational aspects as discouragement, pessimism, or worthlessness; suicide attempts or depressed appearance (all of which are to be rated separately).

How have you been feeling? Describe your mood.

Have you felt depressed (sad, blue, moody, down, empty, as if you didn't care)? (Have you cried or been tearful?) (How often? Does it come and go?) (How long does it last?)

(How bad is the feeling? Can you stand it?)

		234
0	No information	
1	Not at all	
2	Slight, e.g., only occasionally feels ''sad'' or ''down''	
3	Mild, e.g., often feels somewhat ''depressed,'' ''blue'' or ''downhearted''	
4	Moderate, e.g., most of the time feels ''depressed''	
5	Severe, e.g., most of the time feels ''wretched''	
6	Extreme, e.g., most of the time feels extreme depression which ''I can't stand''	
7	Very extreme, e.g., constant unrelieved extremely painful feelings of depression	

(What about during the past week?)

PAST WEEK* 0 1 2 3 4 5 6 7   235

Distinct Quality of Mood. Extent to which the depressed feelings are felt by the subject to be qualitatively different from the kind of feeling he would have or has had following the death of a loved one (not just more severe, or mixed with other symptoms, such as loss of interest).

Is this feeling of (use patient's terms) different from the usual feelings that you would get, or have had after someone close died? (or from a sad movie or story?)

(How is the feeling different?)

		236
0	No information or unable to understand question	
1	No difference or just more severe	
2	Questionable or minimal difference	
3	Definitely different, but only mildly so	
4	Very different	

Describe: _____

Extent to which feelings of depression are associated with specific concerns.

When you feel this way, do you always know what you are (depressed) about or do you sometimes just feel bad and not know why?

		237
0	No information or unable to understand question	
1	Nearly always, e.g., ''It's all because of my business failing.''	
2	Most of the time	
3	Usually not	
4	Practically never, e.g., ''There is absolutely no reason for me to feel this way.''	

Skip to item on Worrying, page 7.

* Selected items scattered throughout the interview are also rated for the level of severity for the week prior to the interview. In many cases the level of severity during this week will be the same as when the symptom was at its most severe. This information may be obtained either during the course of the interview by asking whether it has been any different in the past week, or by skipping the past week's ratings and returning to them as a group at the end of Part I. The rating for the past week should never be more severe than that for the worst week.

Another method of collecting and assessing self-report data is the use of self-report questionnaires. For example, Geer (1965) developed the Fear Survey Schedule to measure the degree of anxiety experienced by individuals with certain situations or objects, such as speaking before a group of people, being in crowded places, driving a car, rats and mice, etc. This measure allows the assessor to define and quantify to some degree relevant stimuli and response patterns assumed to be important components of an individual's problematic or abnormal behavior. The structured interview scales developed by Spitzer and Endicott are a type of self-report survey that is verbally administered to clients.

Of course, the possibility of individuals falsifying their responses, a potential problem in psychometric personality tests, can also be a problem in interviews and other forms of self-report data. However, in most clinical settings it is assumed that a client seeking professional help would not want to falsify his or her responses.

PHYSIOLOGICAL ASSESSMENT

The measurement of physiological responses can also serve as an important assessment procedure. Numerous studies have investigated the physiological changes associated with emotional states such as anxiety, depression, and psychosomatic dis-

orders, as well as most other forms of psychopathology (see Greenfield and Sternbach 1972). Recently it has become possible to record numerous physiological responses or events in a human subject by attaching recording electrodes to the surface of the subject's skin and monitoring physiological activity on a polygraph as it occurs. Responses from nearly all the organ systems of the human body can be recorded indirectly with surface electrodes, including the cardiovascular and respiratory systems, the gastrointestinal system, the cortical system, and the activity of the sweat glands and the somatic muscles. All these systems generate bioelectric signals. A polygraph contains a number of electronic devices that allow one to amplify or increase the strength of a bioelectric signal so that it can be visually seen and measured. The polygraph provides a visual record, with pen deflections on a moving paper chart reflecting changes in the bioelectrical signals produced by a particular physiological response system.

A major attraction of using physiological measures in assessment is the possibility of obtaining an objective evaluation that is unaffected by factors such as subject response biases, interviewer bias, and unreliable clinical interpretation of test responses. However, there are a number of problems associated with this method. One is the presence of individual differences in physiological responding. Not all individuals show the same pattern of physiological response to a particular stimulus or situation. The response system that is "activated" most differs from subject to subject. That is, one individual may be a "heart rate responder" who shows a great increase in heart rate in a certain situation, but little accompanying increase in electromyogram (EMG) readings of muscular activity. Another individual, who is an "EMG responder" and who is exposed to the same situation, may respond with a great amount of EMG increase but little heart rate change. These individual differences account for the common finding that correlations among physiological measures have usually been found to be relatively low under conditions of rest or stress (Lang 1971). Thus, the same physiological measure may not be equally sensitive across all individuals.

Another problem is the interpretation or meaning of a particular physiological response. One reason for the great interest in using physiological measures in assessment was the possibility that they would directly reflect the individual's psychological state. However, contrary to popular

CONFLICT STATEMENTS
Figure 5.2

Statements about hostility conflicts and sexual conflicts by a client beset by marital problems. (From Murray, Auld, & White 1954)

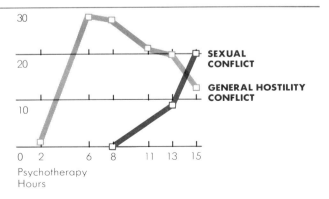

Percentage of Total Statements

SEXUAL CONFLICT

GENERAL HOSTILITY CONFLICT

Psychotherapy Hours

THE "LIE DETECTOR" TEST

The increasing use of the "lie detector" test has produced a rapidly growing and thriving industry in the United States. In this interrogation method, an individual is asked various questions while a number of his or her autonomic responses are monitored on a polygraph. The traditional polygraph test records three channels of physiological data. One channel records GSR or sweat gland activity; a second plethysmographic channel usually records changes in upper-arm blood volume, from which heart rate and pulse volume changes can be determined; the third channel records respiration, which is monitored from an expandable belt placed around the subject's chest. A recent development—the Psychological Stress Evaluator—can add a fourth channel of data. It records the presence of a low-frequency speech component that is present in normal speech sounds, but is assumed to decrease during conditions of emotional stress such as lying. The claims made by the developers of the Psychological Stress Evaluator that it is an effective "lie detector" device have not as yet been independently corroborated.

Lykken (1974) has presented a good summary of the usual procedure employed in the typical lie detector examination:

> The standard lie detector test is normally preceded by a pre-test interview in which the list of questions to be used is gone over with the subject to be sure that he understands wording and feels he can answer them truthfully and unambiguously with a simple yes or no. Another purpose of the pre-test interview is to indirectly convince the subject that the lie detector really works, that he has nothing to fear if he is innocent and truthful, but that any attempt at deception will be detected easily. After the preliminary conversation, the subject is seated in the examining room and the transducers are attached to his hand, arm, and chest. The agreed-upon list of questions is presented, usually two or three times, and the examiner may engage in some discussion with the subject between testings in order to insure that the questions are unambiguous and that for example, the subject is not responding to a critical question for some unsuspected but irrelevant reason. Although I have not seen it recommended in published manuals, one may suppose that professional examiners frequently suggest to subjects that their attempts to deceive have in fact been detected (whether they have or have not) with the intent of precipitating a confession from a guilty subject. It is a fact that the lie detector functions effectively as a "painless third degree" and that the confessions of guilt elicited in this situation might themselves provide sufficient economic justification for its use by the police, even if the technique were wholly invalid and the polygraph were merely a stage prop. . . . The question list used would consist of from 5 to 10 questions that can be answered yes or no. It would include one or more "critical" or "relevant" question of the form, "Did you fire the bullet that hit Jones?" and one or more "irrelevant" questions pertaining to unrelated and unexciting matters, for example, "Are you sitting down?" Most modern polygraphers also include

belief, physiological response measurement does not provide a totally objective measure or "direct road" to the individual's psychological state. As noted by Lang (1971):

> Investigators originally hoped that single measures of autonomic functioning would have a simple and direct relationship to the psychological constructs in vogue. However, it became apparent very soon that

skin conductance increase, for example, did not equal "anxiety" or "drive" nor was its relationship to these constructs simple or fixed. In point of fact, a great variety of situations and events will evoke skin conductance changes, ranging from the closing of a door or the sound of a friendly voice, through a whole gamut of emotional and physiological stressors. Nearly all physio-

several control questions which are intended to serve as emotional standards. The control question should be unrelated to the matter under investigation, and it is expected that the subject will answer it truthfully; however, the control question is chosen with the intention that it will elicit an emotional response from the subject, preferably a response involving an attitude of guilt, for example, "Can you remember ever stealing anything before you were 18 years old?" Finally, some examiners try to include a "guilt complex" question, for example, a question relating to some other real or imaginary crime of which the subject is innocent. (pp. 729–730)

In evaluating a lie detector test, the examiner usually assesses whether autonomic response disturbances associated with the answers given by an individual to critical questions are more magnified or persistent than responses associated with irrelevant and emotional control questions. A global evaluation is made, without any standard or specific measurement of the autonomic responses.

Because no specific measurements are usually made of autonomic responses, the lie detector test does not yield any objectively derived numerical score. As a consequence, the examiner must interpret the results. In many ways, this interpretative process is similar to that involved in the evaluation of projective test responses, with the examiner looking for physiological *signs* (instead of verbal signs such as responses given to particular Rorschach inkblots) of an individual's assumed internal state (awareness that one is guilty or not guilty).

Users of the "lie detector" test argue that it is an extremely valid and reliable assessment procedure. However, Lykken (1974), after reviewing the relevant literature, indicates that there is no well-replicated empirical evidence demonstrating the test's absolute validity. This lack of proven validity, unfortunately, has not prevented the widespread use of the procedure by individuals who "peddle" it commercially as though it were an entirely effective and error-free technique. Many of these persons, moreover, lack the basic training in psychology and physiology that is needed to critically evaluate the assumptions on which the test is based. An understanding of these assumptions would make one more cautious in its indiscriminate use.

One of the basic assumptions on which the test is based is that physiological measures can be used as a direct measure of some internal psychological state. However, as Lang (1971) has noted, this is an example of *indicant fallacy*. There is no evidence to indicate that there is a unique pattern of autonomic responses that emerges when an individual is deliberately lying, but does not when that person is answering truthfully. There are well-documented individual differences in physiological response tendencies that argue against the possibility of there being a specific "lying" response.

Autonomic responses are usually used in the lie detector test because they are viewed as "involuntary" responses that an individual cannot "fake" or control. However, it has been empirically demonstrated that individuals can learn *voluntarily* to control autonomic responses through the use of biofeedback training procedures. (This research is discussed in chapter 6.) It is therefore conceivable that an individual who has acquired voluntary control over physiological responses could "beat" the lie detector procedure.

logical responses can be generated by a great variety of internal and external stimuli, and it seems unlikely that any physiological event could be used in an exact substitutive way, as an index of psychological state. Thus, by observing the physiology of an organism, we are not able to go backwards and reconstruct the stimulus input or the psychological state that contributed to its generation. To assume this

kind of reciprocal relationship is the classic *indicant fallacy*. It is this fallacy that prompts the criminal to confess when faced with the lie detection apparatus. However, the polygraph does not detect lies. A lie is a complex psychosocial event that has no distinct physiology, and must be understood, in the main, within its own domain of expression. Thus, the polygraph has no special power to validate . . . suppositions

One relatively new issue in the use of "lie detector" tests concerns the civil rights of individuals who are made to undergo the test before being hired for a job. Employers have adopted this as a means of avoiding employee theft, since they are led to believe that it is a precise, quick, and economical method to weed out potential thieves. If an applicant fails this test—a test that we have indicated is not an unequivocally accurate index of guilt—or if he or she refuses to take the test, that person usually is not hired. That is, a person can be deprived of a job on this basis alone. Moreover, many times the type of control questions that are asked, such as the example provided by Lykken—"Can you remember ever stealing anything before you were 18 years old?"—are a gross invasion of privacy that one should not have to undergo as part of an employment selection procedure.

Lykken (1974) presents a dramatic real-life account of the potential serious consequences of a "false-positive" lie detector finding; that is, a test indicating an innocent individual is guilty:

> . . . An advertising agency in Minneapolis kept a $6,000 movie camera in a locked cabinet. The camera was stolen without forcible entry and a local private detective agency urged that the four employees who had keys to this cabinet should be asked to take a polygraph test. The employees, who felt of course that they could hardly claim to be innocent and yet refuse to take the test, agreed to these plans; one of two clearly "failed" the lie test. This apparent culprit happened to be a young, black, account executive who was doing so well with the company that they were reluctant to accept this verdict. The young man was sent back for a second test by a different examiner; again he "failed." A third test was conducted by the most experienced of the polygraphers and this one too resulted in a verdict of "probable deception." Just at the moment when the company president had regretfully determined to fire this apparent thief, a fortuitous set of circumstances led a fifth individual, who had never taken the lie test, to confess that he had stolen the camera, completely exonerating the other suspect. Except for this lucky accident, that first young man would not now be holding a well-paying job, making good use of his considerable talents, but instead he would be out on the street, saddled with a history of having been fired from his previous employment for having failed a lie detector test, and with negligible hope for ever again finding work in his chosen profession. (pp. 736–737)

In short, the "lie detector" test as currently used is not an infallible, totally objective, or direct method for assessing an individual's guilt or innocence. Much more basic research is needed to determine unequivocally the validity of this technique. Also, the development and evaluation of more objective and standardized procedures are needed. Podlesny and Raskin (1977) conducted a thorough review of the laboratory research on physiological measures used for detecting deception and pointed out some of the associated problems. They have made a number of suggestions for additional laboratory research that will generalize to field applications of *detection of deception* techniques. Until additional research is done, one should be aware of the potential misuse of this assessment technique, and its social consequences.

about the intentions or emotional state of human subjects. (p. 99)

RELATIONSHIPS AMONG ASSESSMENT MEASURES

We have reviewed a number of behavioral measures that can be used in assessment—verbal self-report, overt behavioral actions, and physiological responding. A great deal of interest and attention has been directed at the empirical fact that these three component measures of behavior are not always highly correlated with one another (Lang 1968). As a result, these three components should be considered as separate but interacting response groups, which may be separately influenced by different situational factors at different times. They may even obey different learning principles. At the same time, however, because of their potential interaction, change in one behavioral component may affect subsequent changes in responses of the other components. Moreover, individuals differ in their learning history associated with each response group, resulting in individual differences in the intensity and functional importance of the components in reaction to a particular feared stimulus. For example, one cannot automatically assume that if an individual verbally reports a high degree of anxiety, he or she will demonstrate the physiological response pattern usually associated with high anxiety (e.g., increase in heart rate and GSR). The reverse is also true. This can greatly complicate the assessment procedure, especially if one wants to compare different assessment procedures that use different

behavioral component measures. It has led many clinical researchers to assess all three behavioral components simultaneously in a particular evaluation situation, in order to delineate the specific patterns which emerge. In a study by Paul (1966), all three components were assessed to demonstrate this type of multicomponent assessment. This study also provides a good example of how therapy-evaluation research can and should be carried out.

PAUL'S STUDY OF THERAPY EFFECTIVENESS

Paul (1966) investigated the relative efficacy of various treatment techniques for modifying intense anxiety about public speaking. College students who reported having severe anxiety about speaking in public were assigned to one of four treatment groups. Subjects in one group received a behavioral treatment technique called *systematic desensitization*. (This technique will be discussed in detail in chapter 6.) Subjects in a second group received brief, traditional, insight-oriented psychotherapy. In a third group (attention-placebo), students served as control subjects and received only a placebo "tranquilizer" that was chemically inert or inactive, along with bogus training that they were told would help them handle stress. Thus, expectations were raised in these subjects that they would be helped with their speech anxiety. They were given attention, but no real treatment. Students in a fourth group were used as no-treatment control subjects. They received no specific or special treatment.

Before and after treatment, all subjects had to deliver a speech in front of an audience while the three behavioral components of their anxiety were measured (self-report, direct observation of behavior, and physiological). Overt behavior was measured using the Timed Behavioral Checklist for Performance Anxiety developed by Paul. This instrument lists 20 observable manifestations of anxiety: Paces, Sways, Shuffles Feet, Knees Tremble, Extraneous Arm and Hand Movement, Arms Rigid, Hands Restrained, Hand Tremors, No Eye Contact, Face Muscles Tense ("Drawn," "Tics," "Grimaces"), Face "Deadpan," Face Pale, Face Flushed, Moistens Lips, Swallows, Clears Throat, Breathes Heavily, Perspires, Voice Quivers, Speech Blocks or Stammers. The persistent and simultaneous occurrence of a great many of these behaviors is usually a sensitive measure of the presence of anxiety. Four trained observers in the audience recorded the presence or absence of these behaviors during successive 30-second periods of the first four minutes of speech presentation. Physio-

PAUL'S SPEECH ANXIETY STUDY
Figure 5.3

Percentage of subjects in each of the four experimental groups displaying decreases in anxiety (as measured by behavior ratings, self-report, and physiological measures) in the speech-anxiety study conducted by Paul (1966). (From Bandura 1969)

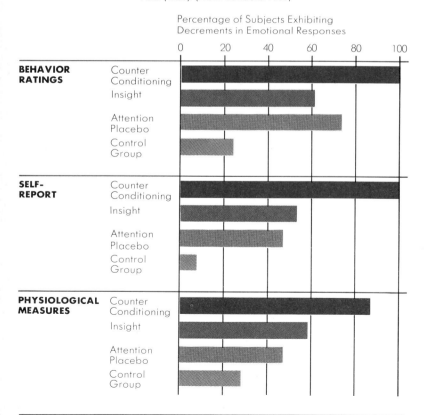

Percentage of Subjects Exhibiting Decrements in Emotional Responses

EVALUATING THERAPY EFFECTIVENESS

Reliable and objective assessment procedures are of critical importance in evaluating therapy effectiveness. If one claims that a particular form of treatment is therapeutically effective with a specific disorder, then it is important to be able to support that claim empirically. This can be done by conducting an objective and quantifiable assessment of change in the disorder that the particular treatment produces. Paul's (1966) therapy study of anxiety about speechmaking provides a good illustration of how such an assessment can be conducted.

Paul's study employed the *experimental method* to determine the causal relationship between a particular treatment and therapeutic improvement. An experiment involves the manipulation of *independent variables* (the various treatment procedures being evaluated) and the objective measurement of their effects on *dependent variables* (in the case of Paul's study, the self-report, overt behavioral, and physiological components of anxiety). In a therapy evaluation study such as this, it is also essential to include appropriate control groups that do not receive any known form of active treatment. Without appropriate control groups against which to compare the treatment groups, one cannot be absolutely sure that the changes were not simply due to the passage of time or the attention given to the patients by the therapist. In Paul's study, the no-treatment control group was included to control for passage of time and the subjects' knowledge that they were participating in a treatment evaluation study. The attention-placebo group

was included to control for the important effects that *placebo* and attention factors can have on the therapy process.

Although some have denied the importance of the placebo effect, it has been shown to produce significant and sometimes long-lasting therapeutic benefits. In a review of the placebo effect, Shapiro (1971) gives this definition:

> A *placebo* is defined as any therapy, or that component of any therapy, that is deliberately used for its nonspecific, psychologic, or psychophysiologic effect, or that is used for its presumed specific effect on a patient, symptom, or illness, but which, unknown to patient and therapist, is without specific activity for the condition being treated. . . . A placebo, when used as a control in experimental studies, is defined as a substance or procedures that is without specific activity for the condition being evaluated. . . . The *placebo effect* is defined as the nonspecific, psychologic or psychophysiologic effect produced by placebos. (p. 440)

In the area of drug therapy, Shapiro (1971) notes that for centuries the use of medication has been largely a placebo-effect process, with chemically inert or inactive drugs producing therapeutic improvement in people who believed that these drugs or "magic potions" would help them. Frank (1961) has presented evidence that improvement in various physical and psychological problems can occur after a patient ingests a pill that the

logical measures, including heart rate and sweat gland activity, were taken immediately before the speech. The self-report measure was a rating, on an Anxiety Differential Scale developed by Husek and Alexander (1963), of the degree of anxiety experienced just before the speech was delivered.

Paul compared the relative treatment effectiveness of the four groups by comparing pre- and post-treatment assessments of anxiety. As the graph shows, systematic desensitization (counterconditioning) was consistently the most effective treatment procedure. The insight-oriented and attention-placebo conditions were not significantly

different from one another, although on the self-report and overt behavior components, students in both these groups showed more reduction in anxiety than did the no-treatment control group subjects. They were not significantly different from the no-treatment control group on the physiological component. Thus, as mentioned earlier, a change in one behavioral component will not directly reflect changes in other components. The study, though, did show a relatively close relationship between the three component measures in terms of direction of change. One cannot assume that this will always be the case.

physician has suggested will help alleviate the problem. Frank also notes that placebo effects are similar to many faith-healing procedures in which the individual believes he or she will be helped. Because of the possibility of placebo effects, it is therefore essential to include a placebo control group to separate out such effects when testing the efficacy of a treatment technique.

Once a therapy evaluation study is completed, it is important to determine the *statistical significance* of any differences found between treatment and control groups. The concept of statistical significance refers to the probability that the differences obtained would occur on a chance basis alone. In psychological research, a difference is considered statistically significant if the likelihood is 5 or less in 100 that the differences observed are chance findings. This is called the .05 level of significance ($p < .05$). The .01 level of significance indicates that the likelihood is one in 100 that the differences found were due to chance.

Besides the type of experimental design employed by Paul (1966) to evaluate therapy effectiveness, there are a number of other experimental designs that can be used in evaluation research. (A review of some of these designs can be found in Campbell and Stanley 1970.) One particularly useful method of assessing therapy effects is the *time series* analysis. This method permits the study of a single subject over time, with the subject serving as his or her "own control." It allows one to assess statistically whether a causal relationship exists between a specific treatment and improvement in a patient undergoing that treatment. This method can be a valuable evaluation tool in many clinical settings where a clinical researcher may not have access to a large number of subjects to include in an extensive therapy evaluation experiment. Gottman (1973) has provided a detailed account of how time-series analysis methods can be applied to psychotherapy research.

Behaviorally oriented treatment approaches have emphasized the evaluation of therapeutic effectiveness by the experimental method. This approach has not, unfortunately, been applied to all clinical therapy approaches.

Because the effectiveness of many therapeutic approaches has not been documented, individuals seeking psychological help usually have no way of knowing what therapy technique would be most effective for their particular problem. This lack of information prompted Ralph Nader and his Health Research Group to publish *Through the Mental Health Maze* (1975) as a "consumer's guide" presenting information about fees, training, and experience, type of patients preferred and not preferred, type of therapy employed, evaluation procedures used, and other pertinent information about 348 mental health professionals in the Washington D.C., metropolitan area. It also provides a sample patient/therapist contract that specifies fees and treatment goals. Such a contract, the Nader group assumes, would make therapists more accountable, minimize the chance of a misunderstanding between therapist and client, and also force patients to be more explicit about what is bothering them. If this guide proves helpful, similar guides for other parts of the country may be developed.

MEDICAL EVALUATIONS

In discussing assessment procedures used to detect organic brain dysfunction, we briefly mentioned some medical/neurological tests commonly used in diagnosing these disorders. Whenever there are symptoms or a suspicion of organic brain dysfunction, a complete medical/neurological evaluation is an important and necessary first step. In fact, many treatment professionals make it a standard policy for all their clients to undergo a complete medical examination before starting therapy, regardless of the client's presenting problem. This is done to ensure that there are no organic underpinnings of the problem behavior they are attempting to modify. As will be discussed in chapter 14, various forms of pathology are caused by organic brain disorders. These disorders can be the result of rather dramatic events such as a serious head injury, as well as more subtle injury effects and factors such as vitamin deficiencies, hormonal imbalances, hypoglycemia, and the like.

Failure to assess the presence of organic

factors can obviously have serious consequences for a patient. Psychotherapy administered to an individual to alleviate anxiety or depression that is caused by an undetected hormonal imbalance cannot be expected to be effective. Similarly, an undiagnosed visual or auditory handicap in a child may cause him or her to have some learning difficulties in school. Unaware of this perceptual problem, a teacher may diagnose the presence of an assumed organically caused "learning disability," or even mental retardation if the handicap seriously interferes with learning. Frequently the child does not realize that he or she has a perceptual problem if it has been present since birth. After all, perceiving in this manner seems "normal."

These examples highlight the importance of adequate medical evaluation. However, it should be pointed out that there is a wide range in the degree of thoroughness of such evaluations. A relatively superficial evaluation that indicates no dysfunctions can mistakenly lead a clinician to rule out any possibility of organic involvement. The simple statement that a medical evaluation was performed and found no evidence for a somatic disorder cannot be accepted uncritically. One must be certain that such an evaluation is thorough.

SUMMARY

1. The interest and need for developing a classification system to categorize the various forms of psychopathology simultaneously prompted efforts to construct formal techniques for assessing abnormal human behavior.

2. Projective tests were developed by psychoanalytically oriented theorists interested in the hidden or covert aspects of an individual's personality. The validity and utility of these tests, however, are generally unsubstantiated when they are used to generate comprehensive personality descriptions of individuals. They do not differentiate effectively between various forms of psychopathology.

3. As a result of the problems associated with projective tests, many personality theorists attempted to develop more psychometrically sound tests that could be scored objectively and quantified. Out of this tradition, *structured* tests were developed to measure factors such as personality characteristics, intelligence, and the presence of organic brain damage.

4. One of the most widely known and used multidimensional personality tests is the MMPI. Such tests are associated with certain problems. The most significant is the possible presence of *response sets* or biases that may distort test results. A response set is a characteristic and consistent way of responding to items on a test regardless of what the items actually say. The three major forms of response bias are response acquiescence, social desirability, and response deviation or dissimulation.

5. Alfred Binet developed the first formal test of intelligence as a means of differentiating between scholastically bright and dull children. The Stanford-Binet Intelligence Test and the intelligence tests developed by Wechsler have become extremely influential and are widely used in the assessment of mental retardation. Performance on an intelligence test, however, cannot be assumed to provide a direct measure of an individual's "native capacity." An IQ score is the product of many factors, including the individual's motivation to do well on a test of intellectual skills, past encouragement of intellectual competence, and familiarity with the language and tasks used in IQ tests. The potential problem exists of a person being labeled as mentally retarded or "slow" simply on the basis of performance on an intelligence test.

6. Clinical neuropsychology is an applied area of psychology concerned with the diagnosis of brain dysfunction. The Halstead-Reitan Neuropsychological Battery can be used reliably to assess the presence of certain brain lesions. Tests such as this are relatively new assessment procedures that are still undergoing modification and validation.

7. Because behavior is apparently situationally

specific, comprehensive efforts to predict behavior solely on the basis of personality tests have been unsuccessful. This fact, together with a general disenchantment with classification, has prompted many mental health practitioners to abandon the routine use of traditional assessment procedures. Greater emphasis is placed on the direct measurement of behavior and its situational determinants. Such an approach also emphasizes the integration of assessment and treatment. Mischel (1976) has noted the difference between this *sample* approach and the traditional *sign* approach to assessment.

8. Verbal self-report, overt behavioral actions, and physiological responding are behaviors that can be used in assessment. These three component measures of behavior, however, cannot be assumed to be always highly correlated with one another. As a result, many clinical researchers assess all three behavior components simultaneously in order to delineate the specific patterns that emerge. The therapy evaluation study conducted by Paul (1966) demonstrates this type of multicomponent assessment.

9. In many cases, it is important to have a patient undergo a thorough medical examination to determine whether a particular behavior disorder is caused by some organic dysfunction.

RECOMMENDED READINGS

Anastasi, A. *Psychological testing* (3rd ed.). New York: Macmillan, 1968.

Goldfried, M. R., & Kent, R. N. Traditional versus behavioral assessment: A comparison of methodological and theoretical assumptions. *Psychological Bulletin*, 1972, *77*, 409-420.

Lezak, M. D. *Neuropsychological assessment.* New York: Oxford University Press, 1976.

Lykken, D. T. Psychology and the lie detector industry. *American Psychologist*, 1974, *29*, 725-739.

Megargee, E. I. (Ed.). *Research in clinical assessment.* New York: Harper & Row, 1966.

Mischel, W. Toward a cognitive social learning reconceptualization of personality. *Psychological Review*, 1973, *80*, 252-283.

Shapiro, A. K. Placebo effects in medicine, psychotherapy, and psychoanalysis. In A. E. Bergin & S. L. Garfield (Eds.), *Handbook of psychotherapy and behavior change.* New York: Wiley, 1971.

PART 2

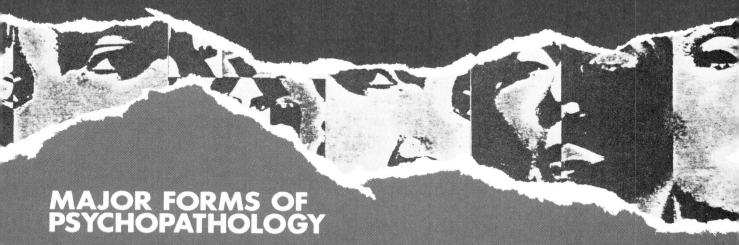

MAJOR FORMS OF
PSYCHOPATHOLOGY

6 NEUROSES

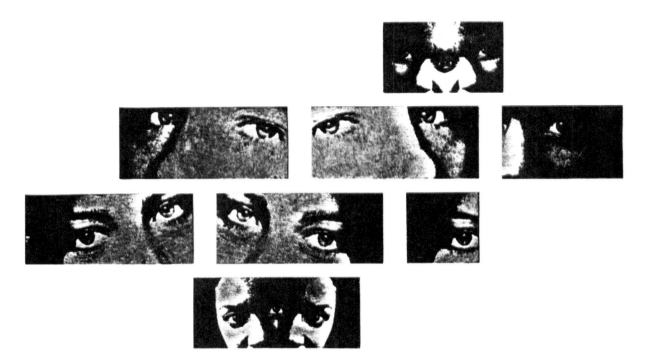

OVERVIEW In this chapter, we will discuss the major types of neurotic behavior. The DSM-II distinguished between eight separate types of neuroses: anxiety, phobic, obsessive-compulsive, hypochondriacal, neurasthenic, depressive, and depersonalization. The DSM-III, however, eliminates the general category of neurosis, replacing it with these four different categories: affective, anxiety, somatoform, and dissociative disorders. In many clinical cases of neurosis, symptoms often "overlap" from one category type to the next, so that reliability is somewhat low when one attempts to differentiate between the specific categories. The hallmark or chief characteristic of neurosis is the presence of anxiety. We will discuss two major theoretical accounts of this emotional state—psychoanalytic theory and learning theory—as well as

issues involved in its measurement. It will be pointed out that there exists no direct evidence unequivocally demonstrating which of these two approaches is the more valid. We will, however, review research that questions the effectiveness of psychoanalysis in treating neuroses. We will also discuss a number of recent behavior therapy techniques, based on learning theory, that have been shown to be therapeutically effective in modifying many forms of neurotic behavior. These include techniques such as systematic desensitization, behavioral rehearsal, cognitive "restructuring" methods, and biofeedback procedures.

We will also discuss the current trend toward a "prescriptive" approach to psychotherapy which, rather than applying the same general form of therapy to all disorders, as has been done in the past, attempts to individualize psychotherapy so that the type of treatment developed and employed is tailored to the specific disorder and characteristics of the patient. Using such an approach, the

prognosis or outlook for therapeutic improvement of the neurosis is good. Finally, we will discuss procedures used in the assessment of neurotic behavior.

SYMPTOM DESCRIPTION AND ETIOLOGY

Neurosis is an emotional disorder that is characterized primarily by the presence of anxiety. As noted in the DSM-II:

> Anxiety is the chief characteristic of the neuroses. It may be felt and expressed directly, or it may be controlled unconsciously and automatically by conversion, displacement, and various other psychological mechanisms. Generally, these mechanisms produce symptoms experienced as subjective distress from which the patient desires relief. (p. 39)

The neurotic individual experiences anxiety and distress in everyday situations that do not normally elicit such behavior from other persons. In response, these individuals develop various forms of coping techniques to try to avoid or lessen the emotional impact. Although such coping mechanisms may be partially effective in reducing anxiety, they may be as distressing as the anxiety itself. In this chapter, we will discuss various coping techniques as we review the major types of neurotic disorders.

Besides anxiety, which can be considered the hallmark of neurosis, additional feelings and behaviors usually are present in this emotional disorder. The neurotic individual is many times unhappy, guilt-ridden, and very rigid and restricted in the types of behaviors he or she will engage in to deal with various situations and problems. Moreover, the individual usually has limited insight into the cause or reason for this neurotic behavior. Although the symptoms can often be very handicapping and severe, neurotics can usually still function relatively well within the culture and typically do not require hospitalization. They are, though, usually in need of some form of therapy.

The following are the major forms of neurotic reactions as they were spelled out by the DSM-II:

- *Anxiety neurosis*, characterized by diffuse, and often severe, "free-floating" anxiety, which is not related to any one particular

situation, object, or threat.
- *Phobic neurosis*, characterized by an intense fear of an object or situation. The individual realizes that this fear is irrational and that the object or situation presents no real danger to him or her.
- *Obsessive-compulsive neurosis*, characterized by the persistent presence of unwanted thoughts, urges, or actions that the individual recognizes as irrational but cannot stop.
- *Hysterical neurosis*, characterized by complaints of some organic physical illness for which there is no actual underlying organic evidence to explain the symptoms. Rather, there is evidence that the symptoms are being caused by psychological factors. There are two additional specialized forms of this disorder: (1) *conversion type*, characterized by the presence of dramatic, debilitating physical symptoms, such as paralysis or blindness, without any underlying physiological dysfunction or cause; (2) *dissociative type*, characterized by reactions such as amnesia and multiple personality.
- *Hypochondriacal neurosis*, characterized by the individual's being preoccupied and engrossed with his or her body's functioning and various presumed diseases, even though there is no physical ailment.
- *Neurasthenic neurosis*, characterized by the presence of chronic fatigue and weakness and lack of enthusiasm.
- *Depressive neurosis*, characterized by abnormally prolonged periods of dejection and despondency, usually precipitated by some environmental setback or interpersonal loss. (We will discuss this form of neurosis in detail in our discussion of affective disorders in chapter 8.)
- *Depersonalization neurosis*, characterized by feelings of personal alienation and lack of meaning in life, which are accompanied

DEMOGRAPHICS	USUAL AGE AT ONSET	PREVALENCE	SEX RATIO
ANXIETY NEUROSIS	Usually in adolescence or young adulthood	About 2–5% of population	More frequently diagnosed in females
PHOBIC DISORDERS	Fairly evenly distributed throughout life	About 1% of population has a debilitating phobia. About 5% of population has mild phobias	More frequently diagnosed in females
OBSESSIVE-COMPULSIVE DISORDERS	Usually begins in pre-adolescence, but may start later in life	Severe form is rare. About 1–2% of population has mild form of this disorder	Unknown
HYPOCHONDRIASIS AND NEURASTHENIA	May occur at any stage of life, although it most frequently begins in adolescence and early adulthood	About 1% of population	More frequently diagnosed in females
HYSTERICAL NEUROSIS (BRIQUET'S SYNDROME)	Usually begins in adolescent years or, rarely, in the twenties	Relatively rare—less than 1% of population	More frequently diagnosed in females
CONVERSION DISORDERS	Usually in adolescence or early adulthood, but symptoms may first appear during middle years or even later	Widely differing estimates, although probably less than 1% of population	Unknown
DISSOCIATIVE DISORDERS			
AMNESIA	Usually young adults	Rare, although it becomes fairly common during a natural disaster or in wartime	Equal
FUGUE	Does not appear to be restricted to any one age group	Rare, although it becomes more common during a natural disaster or in wartime	Unknown
MULTIPLE PERSONALITY	Usually in late adolescence and young adults	Extremely rare	More frequently diagnosed in females

by apathy and little sense of purpose and control over one's life and destiny. We will not discuss this form of neurosis in any detail in this chapter because there is very little empirical data to indicate that it is a distinctively separate and important neu-

rotic pattern. This type of neurosis is similar to a relatively new form being described by an increasing number of clinicians—*existential neurosis*. This neurosis is characterized by an intense sense of emptiness and lack of fulfillment in life, even though the afflicted individual may have a well-paying job and be performing effectively in society with regard to material standards.

DSM-III CATEGORIES

The new DSM-III eliminates the general category of *neurosis* and includes these subtypes in four new categories:

- *Anxiety disorders*, which includes problem behaviors associated with a significant degree of subjective feelings of anxiety. This category will include DSM-II disorders such as generalized anxiety, phobias, and obsessive-compulsive behavior.
- *Somatoform disorders*, which includes disorders that suggest the presence of some organic physical illness (thus the term *somatoform*), but for which there are no organic findings to explain the symptoms. This category will include DSM-II disorders such as hysteria (to be referred to as *somatization disorder*) and hysterical conversion reactions (*conversion disorder*).
- *Dissociative disorders*, which includes disorders characterized by alterations in consciousness. This category will include DSM-II disorders such as hysterical dissociative reactions.

- *Affective disorders*, which includes disorders characterized by severe alterations in mood (mania or depression). This category includes the DSM-II subcategory of depressive neurosis.

The major rationale for the new categorization schema is the elimination of a single category (neurosis) that comprised a wide range of complaints, *all* of which the DSM-II assumed to reflect some degree of unconscious, repressed anxiety. Many clinicians and researchers have questioned this assumption. In its delineation of different categories associated with different arrays of behavioral symptoms, the new system is more behaviorally oriented.

In this chapter, we will present the neurotic disorders according to the DSM-II groupings and also list them under the appropriate category headings from the DSM-III. Table 6.1 shows the relationship between the two systems.

OVERLAPPING OF NEUROTIC SYMPTOMS

Reliability is relatively low when one attempts to diagnose specific subtypes of major forms of psychopathology such as neurosis, because of the frequent overlapping of symptoms from one sub-

*The final version of the DSM-III is not available at this writing and there is still some question where hypochondriasis and neurasthenia will be placed. Hypochondriasis may end up being listed as an anxiety disorder, while neurasthenia will probably be placed in the affective disorders category.

DSM-II	DSM-III
Anxiety neurosis Phobia Obsessive-compulsive	Anxiety Disorders
Hypochondriasis* Neurasthenia* Hysterical neurosis Hysterical neurosis, conversion type	Somatoform Disorders
Hysterical neurosis, dissociative type Depersonalization neurosis	Dissociative Disorders
Depressive neurosis	Affective Disorders

DSM-II AND DSM-III CATEGORIES OF NEUROSES
Table 6.1

category to another. The following brief case descriptions presented by Lewinsohn, Shaffer, and Liber (1969) illustrate how an individual can often display a variety of neurotic category symptoms. These cases are not unique or exceptional, but rather reflect a common occurrence of multiple symptoms displayed by many neurotics:

TWO CASES OF NEUROSIS

The client, Mary K., is an attractive, 24 year old female. She was referred to the Psychology clinic following a fainting spell. Prior to this she had been depressed for several months. In addition to feelings of dysphoria, she also complained of a stiff neck, a urinary infection, a constant preoccupation with having a brain tumor. Except for the urinary infection medical examinations had not revealed any physical basis for the other symptoms or complaints. . . . (p. 20)

Mrs. G. was born in 1930. For the intake interview, she reported herself to be on the brink of total despair, of finding it increasingly difficult to keep going, of spending large amounts of time in bed, generally appeared to be confused and very upset. She complained of having difficulty sleeping because of excessive ruminations about incidents in which she believed she had been rejected by other people. She also mentioned recurring fantasies in which she saw her children killed by wild animals or in an automobile accident or by drowning. She also complained about the absence of close friends. . . . She said that she no longer had any feeling for her husband and that she had neither the capacity nor desire to love him. She indicated an interest in discussing past experiences about which she felt a great deal of guilt. (pp. 21–22)

In both these cases, it was determined that the individuals were having significant marital problems that appeared to be causing their symptoms. Therapy was therefore directed, with success, at eliminating the marital discord and the concomitant symptoms.

In many cases of neurosis, the individual may display a variety of neurotic symptoms. This should be kept in mind when we review the major forms of neurosis in greater detail. Although we will review each form separately, the reader should realize that these neurotic subtypes often overlap.

Before reviewing the major forms of neurosis, it will be worthwhile to discuss the concept of anxiety at greater length because this emotional state forms the core of many neurotic reactions. We will discuss various theoretical accounts of anxiety as well as methods employed in its measurement.

THE CONCEPT OF ANXIETY

Two major theoretical accounts of anxiety have had the most significant impact in the area of abnormal psychology and in psychology in general—psychoanalytic theory and learning theory. We will first discuss psychoanalytic theory, which proposed the first comprehensive account of anxiety and its significance in personality development and psychopathology.

PSYCHOANALYTIC THEORY

As we discussed in chapter 3, Freud hypothesized the presence of three separate parts of the psychic structure—the id, ego, and superego. These three parts were viewed as being in perpetual conflict with one another and with the individual's external environment. The id is always seeking to gratify or fulfill basic instinctual impulses, and this drive for immediate satisfaction of impulse demands creates conflicts between the id and the external world, which may punish the direct expression of socially unacceptable impulsive behavior. The id also conflicts with the superego, which incorporates societal values and standards into the psychic structure. The ego attempts to mediate between the demands of the id, the superego, and the external world. The potential for conflict produced by this dynamic interplay was viewed as a major factor in the development of human personality.

According to Freud, the conflict between these components produces anxiety. He saw anxiety simply as a state of painful tension that an individual would seek to reduce or avoid. Three kinds of anxiety were differentiated: (1) Objective or reality anxiety refers to the fear produced by real dangers in the external world, such as the anxiety produced by being robbed at gunpoint. (2) Moral anxiety refers to the superego or conscience-produced guilt, which a person may experience when he or she thinks about socially unacceptable impulses or behaviors, either actual or contemplated. (3) Neurotic anxiety refers to an individual's fear that his or her instincts or impulses will get out of control and possibly prompt him or her to behave in a manner that society will punish. When this anxiety reaches the point where it cannot be dealt with effectively by realistic means, then the ego will employ defense mechanisms in an attempt to alleviate it. A number of such ego defense mechanisms were mentioned in chapter 3.

As an example of the psychoanalytic account of anxiety development, Mischel (1976) summarizes how neurotic anxiety might develop and be dealt with by the individual:

> The sequence . . . begins with the child's aggressive or sexual impulses that seek direct release. These expressions or efforts at discharge may be strongly punished and blocked by extreme external dangers or threats (e.g., intense parental punishment such as withdrawal of love) and hence lead to objective anxiety. The child may become especially afraid that his impulses will lead to loss of parental love; in time, therefore, he may come to fear his own impulses. Because this state is painful, he tries to repress his impulses (or defend against them with mechanisms). If the ego is weak, the repression is only partly successful and the instinctual impulses persist. Unless expressed in some acceptable form, these impulses become increasingly "pent up," gradually building up to the point where they become hard to repress. Consequently, there may be a partial breakdown of repression and components or derivatives of the impulses may break through, producing some neurotic anxiety. Anxiety, in this view, functions as a danger signal warning to the individual that repressed impulses are starting to break through the defense. Rather than emerging directly, however, the person's unacceptable impulses or motives express themselves indirectly and symbolically in disguised or transformed ways. (pp. 37–38)

Anxiety in this view, then, is a sign that the ego is not coping effectively with unacceptable impulses. What evidence exists that can be used to support the psychoanalytic account of anxiety? By their nature, many of its concepts and ideas are difficult to test or measure scientifically. For example, how can we objectively measure conflict between the id and the external world, or how can we measure repressed impulses? Even when attempts have been made to test this theoretical orientation directly, results have been discouraging (e.g., Mischel 1976). It should be pointed out, however, that Pribram and Gill (1976) have noted the similarity between Freudian theory and some of the recently developed neurophysiological models of perception and information processing. In the future, with the development of the appropriate research technology, some of the concepts proposed by Freud may be proven valid scientifically. Freud was trained as a neurologist and developed many "hunches" concerning the neurological underpinnings of conscious/unconscious processes.

LEARNING THEORY

One of the earliest learning theory accounts of anxiety was a model based on simple Pavlovian classical conditioning. The repeated pairing of a conditioned stimulus with an unconditioned stimulus eventually results in the elicitation of a conditioned response by the conditioned stimulus alone. In the typical *aversive conditioning* situation, in which anxiety is experimentally induced in laboratory animals, a neutral stimulus such as a bell accompanies a painful stimulus such as an electric shock. The electric shock alone naturally produces pain and anxiety in the animal. The neutral bell alone would not produce such a response. However, with continued presentation of the bell and the shock together, the conditioned stimulus (bell) alone eventually will elicit signs of anxiety in the animal, even though the unconditioned stimulus (shock) is no longer presented. Anxiety has become associated or conditioned to the once-neutral bell.

With this model in mind, Watson and Rayner (1920) demonstrated a classic example of human aversive classical conditioning, the study of young Albert in which a fear response was conditioned to a white rat (chapter 3). Another dramatic demonstration of aversive conditioning in human subjects was a study conducted by Campbell, Sanderson, and Laverty (1964). The unconditioned stimulus used was extremely traumatic: an injection of a drug called Scoline which produces momentary motor paralysis and temporarily interrupts breathing while the subject remains completely conscious. Although the drug injection produced no bodily damage or harm, it did produce momentary terror in subjects who could not breathe and felt they were dying. The conditioned stimulus used was a neutral tone. With only one pairing of the tone with the drug injection, a long-lasting conditioned fear response to the conditioned stimulus (tone) was produced in the subjects. This response was associated with physiological indicators of anxiety such as elevated heart rate, muscle tension, and respiration. This conditioned fear response was also found to be resistant to extinction; that is, it continued to persist through many repeated trials of the conditioned stimulus alone.

Although such studies dramatically demonstrate the presumed conditioning of fear, there are problems associated with them. For example, there have been a number of unsuccessful attempts to replicate the findings reported by Watson and Rayner. For one thing, attempts to demonstrate this effect and that of the Campbell et al. (1964) study are rare because of the possible hazards to human subjects. In addition, the simple classical conditioning model on which these demonstrations were based is no longer wholeheartedly embraced by all psychologists because it is viewed as incomplete.

Mowrer (1947), who has been the major critic of the simple classical conditioning model, has proposed a two-factor theory of learning to account more completely for conditioning anxiety. His model is credited with being the first widely accepted learning model to account for anxiety. Mowrer argues that two basic learning processes need to be taken into account: (1) The first is identical to the Pavlovian model, in which the emotional or anxiety response (conditioned response) to the neutral conditioned stimulus is acquired through classical conditioning. (2) In the second, the anxiety serves as an acquired drive, acting to motivate subsequent escape and avoidance behavior. It also serves to reinforce such behavior by its drive reduction consequences. The second process was hypothesized because of observations that animals would learn new responses, such as hurdling a high barrier (e.g., Miller 1948), in order to avoid the anxiety-producing conditioned stimulus. As soon as the conditioned stimulus was presented, the animal would flee the situation without waiting around to determine whether the painful unconditioned stimulus would be presented.

If you were a visitor to an animal research laboratory, unaware that fear and avoidance behaviors had been conditioned in an animal, its behavior might appear very "strange" to you, prompting you to label the animal as neurotic. After all, why would an apparently neutral and innocuous stimulus make an animal start to behave anxiously and attempt to flee the situation by hurdling a high barrier? Similar questions are frequently asked when viewing the behavior of a neurotic individual. A case study reported by Gatchel (1977) provides a good illustration of claustrophobia-type behavior that is analogous to the behavior demonstrated by the neurotic laboratory animal:

A CASE OF FEAR

The client was a 23-year-old married male university student. As a young child, the client had developed an extreme fear of receiving injections. Approximately two years ago, he developed an infection which required the attention of a physician. After making an appointment with the physician, he developed an extreme amount of anxiety in anticipation of possibly receiving an injection for the infection. At the physician's office, it was determined that an injection of medication was indeed needed, and a nurse proceeded to administer one. Immediately upon administration, the client reported that his ears began "ringing," his heart started to rapidly palpitate, and he then momentarily "blacked out" for a few seconds. The nurse apparently became panic-stricken because he remembered hearing her hysterically shouting for the doctor, who was with another patient. He reported that the experience was highly traumatic, with the feeling of being immobilized and trapped in the small examination room, with his ears ringing, heart palpitating, and a frantic nurse shouting for the doctor. He also reported being extremely embarrassed by the entire incident afterwards. . . . His physician assessed that the short blackout was not due to any allergic reaction caused by the medication because the client had no history of such an allergy, having received the medication in the past. There were also no physiological aftereffects. The physician suggested that the high degree of anxiety associated with receiving the injection most probably prompted the fainting spell. . . . Later that day, the client felt well enough to return to his part-time job. While working alone in a small enclosed area at his place of employment, the client started to re-experience the ringing sensation in his ears and heart palpitations which preceded the brief fainting spell earlier that day. He immediately exited from his working area for fear that he might black out once again. As soon as he did exit the symptoms subsided. Ever since that day, whenever in an enclosed area, he became hypersensitive to the emergence of these symptoms. Whenever he perceived the onset of the symptoms, he would immediately attempt to escape from the situation. The success in alleviating the symptoms apparently reinforced his escape behavior. He would also attempt to avoid situations which he thought would precipitate an attack. He subsequently quit his part-time job because he was experiencing an increasing number of anxiety attacks which seriously disrupted his work routine and created a great deal of discomfort. These attacks also disrupted his course work at the university. In all of his classes, he had to sit close to an exit in the event that he experienced the onset of an attack. He had frequent episodes during the course of a day, prompting him to leave the classroom with the resultant disruption of his class work. Even everyday activities such as going shopping with his wife were seriously curtailed due to his fear of having an anxiety attack in the middle of the store with no ready access to an exit. (pp. 689–690)

This patient developed an extreme fear (conditioned response) of enclosed places (conditioned stimulus) because of his traumatic experience in the physician's office (unconditioned stimulus). This fear generalized to other situations so that he became extremely anxious whenever in an enclosed area. He avoided such situations whenever possible. When he could not, his anxiety became so intense that he had to flee the situation. Each time he avoided or fled such situations, his fear and avoidance behavior were maintained because (according to Mowrer) flight brought relief and reduced anxiety. This behavior was very self-defeating and made this patient unhappy and dissatisfied. Yet he clung to his method of dealing with anxiety by avoiding enclosed areas, even though he was aware that it was self-defeating and was seriously limiting his life. This type of paradoxical situation is usually referred to as the *neurotic paradox*.

Although the learning model of anxiety proposed by Mowrer is widely embraced by psychologists, it cannot be accepted uncritically because of certain limitations associated with it. A major limitation is that although conditioned anxiety has been produced time and time again in laboratory animals, there have been few systematic and controlled experimental demonstrations of the effect with human subjects (Davison & Neale 1974). One reason is that, because of ethical considerations, the high-intensity aversive unconditioned stimuli that must be employed to produce such conditioning cannot be used in experimentation with human subjects. Moreover, there are no clear-cut, objective clinical data definitively showing a causal relationship between the development of anxiety and a specific aversive conditioning experience. Although the case study by Gatchel (1977) suggests such a relationship, alternative explanations could be given. A psychoanalytically oriented theorist could easily come up with a reasonable interpretation emphasizing unconscious conflicts as precipitating this anxiety.

Even though this learning model has certain limitations, many experimental and clinical researchers use it because it provides an effective theoretical framework to use in the further investigation and integration of research and clinical data on anxiety. Using this theoretical framework, a number of very effective treatment techniques have been developed for alleviating anxiety. For example, in the case study reported by Gatchel (1977), a biofeedback therapy technique was used successfully to treat the claustrophobia. This technique, as well as other behaviorally oriented techniques, will be discussed later in this chapter.

THE MEASUREMENT OF ANXIETY

Anxiety is an important concept not only in the area of neurosis, but also in considering most other forms of psychopathology and even in the study of the functioning of normal individuals. It is not surprising, therefore, that a great deal of research has been conducted to investigate this concept. Much of the research has been directed at evaluating how anxiety can be most reliably measured. As we shall see, this is not an easy task.

The term *anxiety* is used to label a feeling state that is available only to self-observation. Studying such an inner-experiential state poses a fundamental problem for investigators who seek to describe it in objective terms because, by definition, a human feeling can be observed directly only by the individual who is experiencing it. To study this phenomenon of human experience empirically, we ordinarily must infer its existence indirectly from some measurable form of behavior. In this perspective, anxiety, rather than being an actual observable entity or "thing," is treated as a *construct* that is inferred to account for some form of behavior. For example, we might observe that some people perform poorly on a particular task, which prompts our interest in determining what causes these individual differences in performance. We might develop a hunch that some internal characteristic such as anxiety is causing the differences, so that low-anxious persons do well and high-anxious persons do poorly on the task. We are viewing anxiety as a *mediator*, that is, an unobservable inferred concept that is being hypothesized to account for a certain behavior, i.e., task-performance differences. In order to test our hunch experimentally, we would need to define precisely (operationally) what we mean by anxiety and then develop a method for measuring it.

In our review of the study of speech-making anxiety by Paul (1966) in the preceding chapter, we saw how he operationally defined the construct of anxiety in terms of three components of behavior: self-report, observational, and physiological. He tied this construct to observable forms of behavior, which could be objectively and reliably measured. The process of developing an operational definition and using objective and quantifiable behavioral referents as measures is essential if one is using a construct to explain some form of behavior.

In discussing Paul's study, we also pointed out that one cannot always assume that the three behavior component measures will be highly correlated. An individual may verbally report that he or she is not anxious, but obviously be sweating and trembling, with a greatly accelerated heart rate. It is important to assess multiple responses in specific situations, with the expectation that there may be complex interactions between the measures that may differ from one type of anxiety situation to the next. It is important, too, to realize that many measures of anxiety are also indicators of other emotional states. For instance, a greatly accelerated heart rate is not associated only with anxiety, but also with sexual arousal. So, heart rate is not a unique discriminator of anxiety alone. However, if an individual says he or she is anxious, appears to be anxious because of the presence of behaviors such as trembling or sweating, and displays a greatly elevated heart rate, then we would be on

relatively solid ground to infer the presence of anxiety.

We should note that operantly oriented learning theorists such as Skinner (1953) argue that one does not need to hypothesize unobservable constructs-mediators to account for or predict behavior. Skinner asserts that since a construct (such as anxiety) needs to be tied to observable and quantifiable situations and behaviors, then one does not have to get involved with inferences about that construct. One should deal instead with only the observable behavior and skip the unnecessary process of making inferences. Skinner further argues that the consistent use of constructs to explain behavior may lead to their being accepted uncritically, and may generate the false impression that an adequate explanation of a certain behavior has been developed when it has not. The effect might be to decrease interest in a further search for methods to use in the prediction and control of that particular behavior. Indeed, many mental health professionals erroneously assume that we know precisely what anxiety is, how it affects behavior, and how we can reliably measure it in all situations. In our discussion of the phenomenon of anxiety as an explanatory construct for neurotic behavior, it is important to realize that this construct has a number of distinct referents, some easily observed and measured, others requiring a high degree of inference.

As a result of Skinner's strong arguments, some behaviorally oriented clinicians (for example, Ullmann & Krasner 1969) prefer not to use a construct such as anxiety to explain neurotic behavior. Indeed, an investigator or clinician must be very cautious in using such a construct, lest it become a way of explaining behavior that is not really understood. This can lead to the common trap of circular reasoning. That is, a clinician may indicate that a neurotic patient is behaving in a certain way because he is anxious. When asked how she knows the patient is anxious, the clinician replies by pointing out the behaviors the patient is demonstrating! Such circular reasoning is an easy trap to fall into when one employs constructs to explain behavior. However, even with these potential problems, a construct can be extremely useful in helping to conceptualize and organize relevant data and research on a particular phenomenon. It also helps to communicate information about this phenomenon to others. Throughout the text, we will be using a variety of constructs to help communicate information and facts about various forms of psychopathology.

MAJOR TYPES OF NEUROTIC BEHAVIOR

In discussing the major forms of neurotic behavior, we will focus on the various causes and stressors that psychoanalytic theory and learning theory have proposed to account for the specific neurotic disorders. These two approaches will be emphasized because they are the most widely used models for conceptualizing the etiology of the neuroses and because space does not allow us to review all the other approaches. (The recommended readings at the end of chapter 3 can provide those interested with a detailed account of how those other models view and deal with neurotic disorders.)

At present, no one model or classical theory of learning comprehensively explains the development and maintenance of the various forms of neurotic behavior. This is partly because there is still a great deal of disagreement among theorists about the basic principles governing learning. The learning theory conceptualizations that we discuss are not necessarily the only acceptable ones that have been proposed.

ANXIETY DISORDERS

ANXIETY NEUROSIS Anxiety neurosis is the most common form of neurotic behavior. It is characterized by diffuse and often severe "free-floating" anxiety that does not seem to be related to any one particular situation or object. Physiological symptoms, reflective of heightened autonomic arousal, include responses such as an elevated heart rate and blood pressure level, sweating, intestinal distress, and muscular tension and weakness. Anxious individuals also report symptoms such as insomnia, worry, forgetfulness, difficulty in concentrating, irritability, and, frequently, mild depression. Besides their chronically high level of anxiety, these individuals often experience acute episodes of panic. Such *anxiety attacks* usually last anywhere from a few seconds to well over an hour. They come on suddenly, climb quickly to a high intensity, and then gradually subside. The attacks are accompanied by intense feelings of panic over some presumed impending distress or catastrophe without the individual having any idea of the source of the threat. Acute symptoms include shortness of breath, profuse sweating, and dizziness. Anxiety attacks can be extremely painful psychological experiences for the individual while they last. The following case study illustrates the occurrence of anxiety attacks in an individual suffering from anxiety neurosis:

A CASE OF ANXIETY

John L., age 26, a laborer at the United States Steel Plant, came to the Veterans Administration outpatient clinic because he feared he was losing his mind. Even before going into the military he had been having what he called "panic attacks" where he would become dizzy and weak, and then completely immobile. During his two years of army duty he experienced these attacks, especially while lecturing the troops on the dismantling and assembling of weapons. Afterward he showed great concern about their opinions of a "goofball" like him "trying to tell them how to do something."

Following his military service, he accepted a laborer's job at the steel mill, and while acknowledging that he was not intellectually challenged by the work, he explained that he would attend college and then seek other employment as soon as he overcame his "insanity bit." However, he feared being unable to compete with the others even in the present job, and he frequently complained that his co-workers teased and harassed him.

One day, during lunch break, while being ridiculed by some of his associates, he had his first real anxiety attack at work. He reported that something seemed to snap in his ears, after which everything sounded louder than usual, and he held his hands over his ears until he fell to the ground. Once down, he became afraid that he might never get up again; but he jumped up suddenly and reassured everyone around him that he was all right. The first anxiety attack lasted about 60 seconds, but thereafter he had a constant fear of its recurrence, and he sought help because he was afraid that he was losing his mind.

Psychotherapy, conducted on a twice-a-week basis for about six months, disclosed that although his anxiety was of long duration, the immediate precipitants of his military and post-service attacks were related to his marriage just before entering the army. His wife was a vivacious young woman, who, in sharp contrast to John, was self-confident and outgoing. During therapy, he began to understand the relationship between his anxiety and his lack of self-confidence as a lover, provider, and person. He had to learn also that his apprehension about future attacks was very much related to their actual occurrence. (Kleinmuntz 1974, p. 164)

Causes and stressors. In Mischel's review of the psychoanalytic view of how anxiety neurosis may develop, the chief precipitating factor was hypothesized to be the ego's fear that socially unacceptable instinctual id impulses will express themselves and lead to punishment. It is assumed that the ego uses the defense mechanism of *repression* in an attempt to inhibit the expression of these impulses. The individual is not consciously aware of the inner turmoil between the id and the ego and therefore cannot pinpoint or verbalize what he or she actually fears. This is because the anxiety results from conflict between the id and ego that the ego is attempting to repress, that is, keep at the level of the unconscious. Anxiety is the high price an anxiety neurotic pays for not allowing unacceptable impulses to be expressed directly.

Acute anxiety attacks are viewed as the temporary "breakthrough" of the unacceptable impulses which are always striving for expression. The momentary loss of control by the ego creates a temporary sense of panic while the ego attempts to inhibit and prevent the further discharge and expression of these impulses. The anxiety attacks end when the ego once again temporarily reestablishes its fragile defense against the id impulses.

We noted in chapter 3 that the psychoanalytic interpretation has never been scientifically demonstrated to be valid. Many psychoanalytically oriented personality theorists, however, argue that appropriate research methodology has not yet been developed to provide an adequate test of the theory (Pribram and Gill 1976). These theorists also point out that learning theory accounts of anxiety neurosis development in humans have not been directly and experimentally demonstrated to be valid either. However, many others argue that an indirect test of the validity of a theory in clinical psychology is its usefulness in serving as a model for the development of treatment techniques to

SHYNESS: THE "PEOPLE PHOBIA"

A common type of phobia is shyness, or what Zimbardo (1977) refers to as "people phobia." In recent years Zimbardo has conducted much research, across age groups and cultures, on this problem behavior. A preliminary and somewhat surprising finding was that an estimated 40 percent of people surveyed considered themselves to be shy. More than 80 percent labeled themselves as being or having been shy in the past, at present, or always.

Shyness tends to be situationally specific. That is, different types of situations elicit shyness in different individuals. Most of the individuals who reported being shy indicated that their shyness appeared only occasionally, but that these specific occasions were sufficiently important to justify labeling themselves as shy. About 4 percent of the individuals sampled reported being shy all the time, in all situations. These individuals are extremely self-conscious, worry about what other people think of them, and view all social situations as unpleasant. Physiologically, they show such responses as an increased heart rate, "butterflies" in the stomach, blushing, and perspiration. They fear any novel or spontaneous interpersonal situation. Obviously the quality of their lives is significantly diminished by this inappropriate behavior.

A number of behavior therapy techniques have been developed to help people learn to cope more effectively with their shyness. They include systematic desensitization and social skills training.

successfully modify a particular form of psychopathology. Several recent studies have demonstrated some clinical effectiveness of short-term psychoanalytically oriented therapy in treating neurotic outpatients (Sloane, Staples, Yorkston, Cristol, & Whipple 1974; Staples, Sloane, Whipple, Cristol, & Yorkston 1976), but a number of other research surveys have questioned the effectiveness of psychoanalytically oriented treatment of the neuroses (Eysenck 1952; Malan 1973). Behaviorally oriented treatment techniques based upon learning theory have proven to be more effective therapeutically. It should be noted, however, that in proposing psychoanalytic theory to account for personality dynamics and their development, Freud was very clear in pointing out that the theory would not necessarily serve as a useful model for developing an effective psychotherapeutic technique.

We previously reviewed Mowrer's (1947) two-factor learning model of conditioned anxiety. This same general model often is used to explain the development of anxiety neurosis, although it is assumed that the anxiety is conditioned to a greater number and variety of situations or objects. Bandura (1969) has reviewed evidence indicating that emotional responses can generalize spontaneously to a wide range of stimuli. Such generalization, for example, was observed in Watson and Rayner's (1920) study of little Albert. The child's fear conditioned to the white rat was found to generalize to other "furry" objects that had not been originally paired with the unconditioned stimulus. Learning theorists cite this phenomenon of generalization to explain why an anxiety neurotic may experience anxiety in a wide range of situations, without seeing a direct relationship between the anxiety and a specific traumatic situation, so that it may appear extremely irrational. As Mischel (1976) indicates:

> Suppose . . . that the child becomes afraid of the room in which the dog bit him and of similar rooms. If the connections between his new fear of rooms and the dog's attack is not recognized, the fear of rooms now may seem especially bizarre. (pp. 338–339)

Modeling or imitation learning, which was neglected in early models proposed by learning theorists, has been shown to be an important form of learning (Bandura 1969). Research has demonstrated that we may learn a particular behavior by witnessing someone else perform it. *Vicarious emotional conditioning* is a term used to denote the learning of an anxiety response through modeling. As an example, in studies conducted by Berger (1962), it was arranged for individuals to view another person (the model) in an aversive conditioning situation. The model was connected to a shock apparatus. A buzzer was sounded, the lights were dimmed, and the model jerked his arm as though shock were being administered, feigning pain. Physiological responses of the individuals witnessing this behavior were recorded. After watching the model "suffering from the painful shocks" a number of times, these observers demonstrated an increase in their emotional responding

The Bettmann Archive

Psychoanalytic theory views acute anxiety attacks as temporary breakthroughs of impulses that are unacceptable to the individual.

whenever the buzzer sounded, even though they themselves had no direct contact with the noxious shock.

As with two-factor learning accounts of anxiety neurosis, direct evidence is lacking for the importance of vicarious emotional conditioning in the development of anxiety. Some studies appear to suggest its importance. Jenkins (1968), in an investigation of behavior disorders in children, found that overanxious children are frequently found to have neurotic mothers who display a great deal of anxiety. These data might be interpreted as suggesting that children may learn to behave anxiously because of the modeling of such behavior in their parents. Data such as these, however, are open to the alternative explanation of genetic involvement. This same issue will appear again and again in our discussion of the possible etiology of various forms of psychopathology: Is the disorder learned or is it genetically determined? For anxiety neurosis, current research suggests the involvement of both factors.

Rosenthal (1970), after reviewing a variety of studies that investigated the possible genetic transmission of neuroses, concluded that there is evidence to support this possibility. For anxiety neurosis specifically, Slater and Shields (1969) found evidence for the possible genetic transmission of this disorder. It should be noted, though, that the strength of the relationship found in these studies is not great enough to exclude the simulta-

Copyright 1977 by United Features Syndicate, Inc.

neous involvement of other nongenetic factors.

Eysenck (1957), in proposing a theory of the etiology of neurosis, suggests the interaction of both a genetic and a nongenetic factor: (1) An emotionality or autonomic lability factor, which is largely inherited and which accounts for the tendency of neurotic individuals to become easily aroused and physiologically overreactive. This tendency toward emotional overreaction is assumed to predispose an individual to develop a neurosis. (2) A socialization or learning influence with conditioned anxiety, such as discussed by Mowrer (1947), capable of "triggering" the development of a neurosis. Thus the theory takes both genetic and learning factors into account. Such a theory is usually referred to as a *diathesis-stress* theory because it assumes a genetic or constitutional predisposition toward a disorder (diathesis) that predisposes an individual to develop a psychopathological disorder after exposure to some stressful event. Such an approach shows the greatest promise of providing the most comprehensive understanding of the etiology of both anxiety neurosis and other forms of neurosis.

PHOBIC NEUROSIS A *phobia* is an intense irrational fear of some specific object or situation that presents no real danger to an individual, or a fear that is blown up out of proportion to the actual danger. Traditionally, the names given to phobias were formulated by using a Greek term for the feared object or situation followed by the suffix *-phobia*. Some of the common phobias include:

- Acrophobia—fear of high places.
- Agoraphobia—fear of open places.
- Claustrophobia—fear of closed places.
- Hematophobia—fear of blood.
- Monophobia—fear of being alone.
- Nyctophobia—fear of darkness.
- Pyrophobia—fear of fire.
- Zoophobia—fear of animals or some particular animal.

The intensity of these irrational fears differentiates a phobic neurotic from other people, who often have some minor irrational fears. For example, many people feel "queasy" about flying. However, individuals with a phobia about flying will avoid doing so at all costs, even if it is essential for them to do so. These phobic individuals are aware that there is no cause for this much fear, but cannot help themselves. If they are forced to fly, they will experience a great deal of incapacitating anxiety that will significantly disrupt their behavior.

Causes and stressors. The psychoanalytic view of phobias suggests that they represent the ego's use of the defense mechanism of *displacement*. Anxiety, generated by conflict between instinctual impulses and attempts by the ego to repress these instincts, is displaced to some external object or situation that may symbolize the conflict-initiating impulse. For example, as Buss (1966) suggests:

> Phobias involving considerable displacement have two advantages. First, the original impulse or idea is allowed to return from the repressed in such distorted form that it is not recognized as such and therefore cannot cause further anxiety. Second, the displaced object or situation may be such that it can be avoided. If an individual hates and fears his mother, it is to his advantage to displace the fear to a distant object. . . . (p. 88)

A small boy, for example, may displace his fear toward his mother to a schoolteacher. The schoolteacher may come to symbolize the mother, and the fear of the former becomes unconsciously equal to the fear of the latter. The child can consciously admit to fear of the teacher, but the fear of one's mother is not admissible. Besides protecting the individual from anxiety-arousing thoughts and impulses, the phobic reaction may provide *secondary gains*. That is, the fear developed may gain the individual attention and sympathy from family members, or may allow him or her to avoid responsibility or to control others through the disorder. For example, the child may develop a phobic reaction toward school in general that allows him to remain home and maintain his dependency toward family members (see school phobia in chapter 16).

The learning theory approach views phobias as conditioned fear responses. This approach also considers the possible importance of secondary gains in maintaining these disorders. For example, in the case of school phobia, behavior therapists such as Lazarus, Davison, and Polefka (1965) have suggested that such behavior can be a means of allowing a child to maintain dependency on the mother. If the mother wants to maintain the child's dependency, she, in turn, may reinforce the child's avoidance behavior.

OBSESSIVE-COMPULSIVE NEUROSIS In this form of neurosis, the individual has obsessive unwanted thoughts and/or compulsive ritualistic activity that he or she must carry out or else experience anxiety. Like phobic individuals, many of these neurotics realize that their behavior is irrational, but they cannot control it.

Many people at times have minor obsessive thoughts, such as persistently wondering about whether we have locked all the doors in the house before leaving for a dinner engagement, or constantly thinking about an important upcoming date. In the obsessive neurotic individual, however, such thoughts are unusually persistent and long-lasting, and seriously interfere with everyday functioning. The DSM-III notes that the most common forms of obsessions are repetitive thoughts of violence and of contamination.

In compulsive reactions, the individual feels compelled to engage in a behavior that he or she does not want to perform. Again, many people engage in minor forms of compulsive behavior such as stepping over cracks in sidewalks or putting on one's clothes in the same sequence every morning. A compulsive neurotic, though, demonstrates an excessive degree of compulsiveness that can interfere with everyday functioning. For example, the individual with a handwashing compulsion must interrupt his or her activities periodically during the day to run to the washroom and wash the hands. Performing this act usually brings about a temporary feeling of reduced tension and anxiety. If the individual cannot carry out the compulsion, he or she will be overcome with anxiety. The DSM-III lists

MACBETH When Shakespeare had Lady Macbeth compulsively wash her hands after murdering King Duncan, he captured a compulsive act. Such acts are usually attempts at undoing and are bound up with anxiety and guilt.

the most common forms of compulsion as handwashing, counting, checking, and touching.

Causes and stressors. Psychoanalysts view obsessions and compulsions as resulting from ego attempts to defend against socially unacceptable id impulses. An obsessive thought may result from the ego's use of the *reaction formation* defense mechanism. In this defense mechanism, the individual develops attitudes or behaviors that are diametrically opposed to his or her actual id impulses. For instance, persistent thoughts about one's child being harmed or killed may actually represent ambivalent and often destructive feelings toward the child. The ego, through this obsession, defuses the unacceptable feelings and impulses by making the parent feel overly concerned and worried about the child's fate and welfare.

Compulsive acts are viewed as resulting from the use of the ego defense mechanism of *undoing*: carrying out some ritualistic act, e.g., folding

ROBERT BURTON ON NERVOUS PEOPLE

[Nervous people] are not always sad and fearful, but usually so, and that without a cause; although not all alike, (saith Altomarus), yet all likely fear, some with an extraordinary and a mighty fear, Aretœus. Many fear death, and yet, in a contrary humour, make away themselves. Some are afraid that heaven will fall on their heads: some afraid they are damned, or shall be. They are troubled with scruples of Conscience, distrusting God's mercies, think they shall go certainly to Hell, the Devil will have them, & make great lamentation, Jason Pratensis. Fear of Devils, death, that they shall be sick of some such or such disease, ready to tremble at every object, they shall die themselves forthwith, or that some of their dear friends or near allies are certainly dead; imminent danger, loss, disgrace, still torment others, &c. that they are all glass, and therefore they will suffer no man to come near them; that they are all cork, as light as feathers; others as heavy as lead; some are afraid their heads will fall off their shoulders, that they have frogs in their bellies, &c. Montanus speaks of one that durst not walk alone from home, for fear he should swoon, or die. A second fears every man he meets will rob him, quarrel with him, or kill him. A third dares not venture to walk alone, for fear he should meet the Devil, a thief, be sick, fears all old women as witches, & every black dog or cat he sees he suspecteth to be a Devil, every person comes near him is maleficiated, every creature, all intend to hurt him, seek his ruin. Another dares not go over a bridge, come near a pool, rock, steep hill, lie in a chamber where cross beams are, for fear he be tempted to hang, drown, or precipitate himself. If he be in a silent auditory, as at a sermon, he is afraid he shall speak aloud at unawares, some thing undecent, unfit to be said. If he be locked in a close room, he is afraid of being stifled for want of air, and still carries biscuit, Aquavitœ, or some strong waters about him, for fear of fainting, or being sick; or if he be in a throng, middle of a Church, multitude, where he may not well get out, though he sit at ease, he is so misaffected. He will freely promise, undertake any business beforehand, but, when it comes to be performed, he dare not adventure, but fears an infinite number of dangers, disasters, &c. Some are afraid to be burned, or that the ground will sink under them, or swallow them quick, or that the King will call them in question for some fact they never did, & that they shall surely be executed. The terror of such a death troubles them, and they fear as much, & are equally tormented in mind, as they that have committed a murder, and are pensive without a cause, as if they were now presently to be put to death. They are afraid of some loss,

clothes or washing one's hands over and over again, may partially ease anxiety about some imaginary or actual wrongdoing. Specifically, compulsive handwashing is viewed as a ritualistic cleansing that "undoes" or makes right actual or fantasized transgressions. Anxiety is inhibited or removed by compulsive acts which are assumed symbolically to make things right again. Lady Macbeth's compulsive handwashing after the murder of King Duncan is often used as an example of an act of undoing.

An example of a compulsive behavior that Freud (1896) described in one of his early papers was that of a young boy:

An 11-year-old boy had instituted the following obsessive ceremonial before going to bed. He did not sleep until he had told his mother in the minutest detail all the events of the day; there must be no scraps of paper or other rubbish on the carpet of the bedroom; the bed must be pushed right to the wall; three chairs must stand by it and the pillows must be in a particular way. In order to get to sleep he must first kick out a certain number of times and then be on his side.

Many learning theorists view obsessive-compulsive behaviors as learned because of the reinforcing consequences. For example, engaging in compulsive handwashing is viewed as an escape-response from anxiety produced by a preoccupation with dirt and germs. Washing one's hands in the belief that this behavior will temporarily eliminate dirt is viewed as reinforcing. Another mechanism that may be involved is the learning of "superstitious

danger, that they shall surely lose their lives, goods, and all they have, but why they know not. Trincavellius had a patient that would needs make away himself, for fear of being hanged, and could not be persuaded, for three years together, but that he had killed a man. Plater hath two other examples of such as feared to be executed without a cause. If they come in a place where a robbery, theft, or any such offence, hath been done, they presently fear they are suspected, & many times betray themselves without a cause. Louis XI., the French King, suspected every man a traitor that came about him, durst trust no officer. Some fear all alike, some certain men, and cannot endure their companies, are sick in them, or if they be from home. Some suspect treason still, others are afraid of their dearest and nearest friends (Melanelius out of Galen, Ruffus &c.), & dare not be alone in the dark, for fear of Hobgoblins and Devils: he suspects everything he hears or sees to be a Devil, or enchanted; and imagineth a thousand chimeras and visions, which to his thinking he certainly sees.

From *The Anatomy of Melancholy*, by Robert Burton, 1651.

---

behavior'' through chance reinforcement. Skinner (1948) demonstrated that pigeons learned a number of unusual behaviors, such as turning counterclockwise in their cages, when they received reinforcement for such ''odd'' behavior. It is assumed that human beings might similarly learn unusual behaviors, such as compulsively putting one's clothes on in a particular sequence, through such chance reinforcement of certain thoughts or actions.

SOMATOFORM DISORDERS

The DSM-III defines somatoform disorders as a group of disorders in which the patient exhibits symptoms suggesting a physical disorder, hence ''somatoform.'' In DSM-III, the somatoform category is subdivided mainly into somatization disorder, conversion disorder, and psychalgia. Below we describe several classic somatoform disorders.

HYPOCHONDRIACAL AND NEURASTHENIC NEUROSES Hypochondriasis and neurasthenia commonly are viewed as resulting from similar causes. The major characteristic of hypochondriacal reactions is preoccupation with and frequent verbalization of supposed physical ailments. Neurasthenia is characterized by the presence of mental and physical fatigue, as well as complaints about various aches and pains.

The hypochondriac often declares that he or she is physically a wreck; this person dramatizes and magnifies all minor maladies and is preoccupied and engrossed with the functioning of the body even though there is no actual physical ailment. The presumed ailments are not usually related to any one particular symptom pattern or disorder, and the hypochondriac usually has difficulty giving a precise description of the symptoms. These individuals are constantly alert for any signs of a new illness. Again, it is common for people to have concerns about health and bodily functioning. In fact, many first-year medical students develop the ''medical student syndrome'' when they begin reading about various disorders for the first time and start to notice subtle bodily reactions that they interpret as possible symptoms of some particular disorder. With time, this ''syndrome'' usually passes, as students become more familiar with the disorder and realize that their training initially has made them oversensitive to their own bodily processes and reactions. But hypochondriacs demonstrate an exaggerated and chronic form of this ''syndrome.'' Many times, it appears that such persons have a phobia of dying or illness, since they feel they are suffering from any new disease they hear about. Hypochondriacs are very sincere in their concern about their health and the fact that they are ''suffering from a disease,'' although they usually demonstrate little of the anxiety about being ill that one would expect. Although the typical case does not involve the presence of an actual disorder, sometimes a hypochondriacal reaction is superimposed on some actual organic pathology, with the result that the symptoms are magnified out of all proportion to the disorder.

In neurasthenia, the chief presenting problem is excessive tiredness, which results in a lack of initiative and motivation to start or finish tasks. These individuals usually try to counteract this fatigue by spending a great deal of time sleeping. However, no matter how much sleep they get, they usually awaken unrefreshed and fatigued. This situation, combined with the fact that they do not have a history of being overworked, usually rules out the possibility of underlying muscular/ neurologial fatigue causing the disorder.

Causes and stressors. Traditional psychoanalytic theory provides only a sketchy account of these disorders. Neurasthenia is described by Fenichel (1945) as ''. . . an outcome of insufficient orgasm; it occurs if masturbation has become insufficient, that is, if anxiety and guilt feelings disturb the satisfactory character of the masturbation'' (p. 188). Fenichel thus views it as primarily the result of excessive sexual tension, the key factor involved being insufficient orgasm. Neurasthenic individuals are viewed as being in a state of tension caused by the conflict between urges to discharge their sexual excitement and forces defending against its expression. The hypochondriac is viewed as having unacceptable sexual and aggressive impulses that generate feelings of guilt. In order to deal with, say, unacceptable hostility impulses toward another person, the ''. . . original hostile attitude toward an object is turned against the ego, and hypochondriasis may serve as a gratification of guilt feelings'' (Fenichel 1945, p. 263). That is, the guilt-producing impulses are displaced to one's own self.

To deal with the conflicts generated, the defense mechanism of *repression* is also often employed. Buss (1966) states:

> . . . Being tired and playing the sick role both represent attempts to aid repression. The patient says in effect, ''I am not sufficiently energetic or healthy to act aggressively or sexually.'' This is an attempt to disarm not only potential punishing agents in the environment but also a potentially punishing superego. (p. 86)

It is assumed that secondary gains may be important factors in these disorders. Being ''sick'' or excessively fatigued may allow one to avoid demands of a possibly unpleasant life, while at the same time eliciting sympathy from others and perhaps acting to control their behavior. If an individual feels inadequate and views his or her life as a failure, then the sick role can provide a means of dealing with these feelings—no one would expect a ''sick'' or ''overly fatigued'' individual to be able to perform or achieve as much as other people.

As might be expected, learning theorists view these forms of behavior as learned because of reinforcing consequences such as these secondary gains. Also, it is assumed that such behavior can be learned through modeling. For example, early in life a child might observe his or her parents demonstrating an overconcern about health or other symptoms of hypochondria or neurasthenia. This might prompt the child to behave in a similar manner.

HYSTERICAL NEUROSIS The proposed DSM-III includes a category labeled *Briquet's syndrome* or *Somatization disorder* to describe a chronic disorder characterized by frequent and multiple somatic complaints, such as headaches, nausea, abdominal pain, bowel trouble, etc., that are not due to any real physical illness. This replaces the older DSM-II category of *hysteria*. These patients frequently seek out medical attention from a number of physicians and may be hospitalized and even operated on. In fact, there is a definite increased risk of surgery in hysteria because these patients usually report the presence of dramatic and persistent symptoms that may closely mimic a variety of medical conditions. A related disorder is the *Munchausen syndrome,* a chronic *factitious disorder* in which the patient exhibits factitious (not real) physical symptoms, and can obtain and sustain multiple hospitalizations. Often it is difficult to distinguish a factitious disorder, malingering, and hysterical neurosis from one another.

The DSM-II distinguished two other specialized forms of hysterical neuroses: conversion reactions and dissociative reactions. In the DSM-III, however, dissociative reactions are placed in a separate category.

HYSTERICAL CONVERSION REACTIONS Conversion hysteria is additionally characterized by the development of an apparent significant organic impairment even though the affected organ is sound. The DSM-III dropped the term ''hysterical'' and simply calls the reaction *conversion disorder*. Reports have been made of the impairment of sensory functions with symptoms such as blindness, anesthesia (loss of sensitivity), and analgesia (loss of sensitivity to pain); and the impairment of motor functions with symptoms such as muscular tremors and paralysis of a limb. The loss of motor function and the resultant paralysis often are selective in nature. For example, the student with ''writer's cramp'' may not be able to write an examination, but may be able to use the same muscles in shaking someone's hand or playing the guitar. In passing, it should be noted that conversion symptoms are also often found in nonhysterical patients, commonly in medically ill persons, psychiatric outpatients, and normal hospitalized postpartum women (Woodruff, Goodwin, & Guze 1974).

Two other points should be made in discussing conversion reactions. First, it has traditionally been assumed that these reactions are found primarily in women (hence the name *hysteria*); and they are, in fact, the vast majority of diagnosed cases. However, males also develop such reactions. During both world wars, for example, many males faced with stressful combat conditions developed conversion-type reactions, such as paralysis, that prevented them from going into battle (Ziegler, Imboden, & Meyer 1960). Indeed, Freud was one of the first clinicians to point out that hysteria is not found only in women. Second, although conversion reactions were once quite common, they constitute only about 5 percent of all neurotics treated today (Coleman 1976). This may be because physicians today can make more sophisticated diagnoses of true organic dysfunctions.

As delineated by Coleman (1976), there are a number of criteria commonly used in distinguishing between hysterical and organic disorders: (1) The presence of *la belle indifference* in hysterical disorders, so that the patient presents his or her problems in a matter-of-fact way, with little demonstration of the anxiety or panic one might expect in a person who has suddenly developed a symptom such as arm paralysis or loss of speech. (2) The

common failure of the hysterical disorder to clearly parallel the symptoms of a true physical dysfunction; for example, the absence of muscular atrophy or "wasting away" of a paralyzed limb in a hysterical paralysis, which would occur in a true organic paralysis. (3) The selective nature of the disorder, as in the case of "writer's cramp." (4) Under hypnosis or narcosis, the symptoms can often be removed or reduced by the suggestion of a therapist. Also, if a hysterical individual is suddenly awakened from sleep, a "paralyzed" limb may show some movement.

Kolb (1973) presents a case study of how a conversion reaction can alleviate the anxiety generated by an individual's conflicting desires and simultaneously yield a secondary gain that allows him or her to escape from an unpleasant situation.

A CASE OF HYSTERICAL CONVERSION

"M., a young man who had been a dancer and an acrobat in a circus, enlisted in the army during peace time. Here he found the discipline rigid, his duties irksome, and his experiences monotonous. He longed for travel, excitement, attention, and the opportunity for exhibition enjoyed in his former life. The situation became quite intolerable, but to leave meant that he would be treated as a deserter. A hysterical conversion reaction, induced by two conflicting mo-

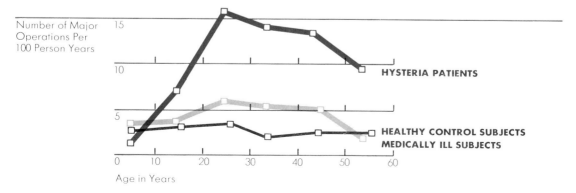

A comparison of the number of major surgical operations performed on hysteria patients, medically ill subjects, and healthy control subjects. (From Cohen et al. 1953)

**HYSTERIA
AND SURGERY**
Figure 6.1

tives, the one to conform to the requirements of military life, the other to secure escape from a hated situation, provided a solution that permitted him to gain his own end, i.e., to obtain immunity from unpleasant experiences and tasks, and at the same time alleviated his anxiety and enabled him to maintain his self-respect. On arrival at the mental hospital to which he was transfered, he could neither walk nor stand, and his legs were anesthetic to even vigorous prickings by a pin. At the same time, he displayed a significant attitude of unconcern (*la belle indifference*) as to his disabilities, although, as far as he was consciously aware, they were complete and incurable. His absence of concern is to be explained by the fact that the penalty was less than the gain, although one must not conclude that this weighing of advantages and disadvantages was at all a matter of conscious reflection. A few months later, the man was discharged from the army on a surgeon's certificate of disability. Soon the suspended motor and sensory functions began to return. Persistent efforts to walk met gradually with success, and in another three months he left the hospital practically well. (p. 418)

Causes and stressors. According to psychoanalytic theory, conversion hysteria involves the ego's use of the basic mechanism of *conversion*. Conflict-produced tension may temporarily overwhelm the ego and must be discharged in some manner. Conversion symptoms are viewed as the compromise between the id impulses seeking expression and the ego's defense attempts. Unacceptable impulses are converted into physical symptoms that may be symbolic representations of the repressed thought or impulses. The resultant compromise (the actual physical symptoms) allows the ego to isolate the conflict and engendered affect from awareness, thus leaving the hysteric relatively free of conflict (hence the presence of *la belle indifference*).

Learning theory approaches see conversion reactions as behaviors that are learned to avoid or reduce anxiety-producing stressful situations. Getting sick can be a face-saving way to avoid an emotional situation perceived as inescapable and intolerable. The maintenance of the reaction is usually reinforced by the reduction in anxiety that may occur and by the sympathy and interpersonal support that may be gained. It is assumed that a conversion hysteric behaves according to his or her idea of how an individual with a particular disease-precipitating loss of motor or sensory ability would act (Ullmann & Krasner 1969).

DISSOCIATIVE DISORDERS

HYSTERICAL DISSOCIATIVE REACTIONS The DSM-II distinguishes four different types of hysterical dissociative reactions: amnesia, fugue, somnambulism, and multiple personality. The DSM-III has a *dissociative disorders* category, which is composed of four subcategories: psychic amnesia, psychic fugue, multiple personality, and depersonalization disorder. In the main, these new categories parallel DSM-II. The essential feature of most dissociative disorders, according to DSM-III, is a sudden, temporary alteration in consciousness, memory, identity, or motor behavior. If changes in identity occur, for example, the person may temporarily forget his or her identity.

Amnesia is characterized by the partial or total loss of memory of past experiences. Hysterical amnesia differs from organic amnesia in that no known underlying organic brain dysfunction is involved. Memories of past experiences are not totally lost in this disorder, for they can be recalled under hypnosis or narcosis or in cases where the amnesia spontaneously disappears. In amnesia, individuals typically cannot remember their name, age, friends, or any details about themselves. Their learned behavior patterns (speaking, reading, etc.), though, are not disrupted. They appear quite normal except for the amnesia.

In the *fugue* state, individuals not only develop amnesia but also flee a situation; hours, days, weeks, or even years later, they may "wake up" and find themselves in some strange place without any idea of how they got there and with complete loss of memory for the fugue period. Behavior during the fugue period may range from going on a shopping excursion to moving to a new part of the country and starting a new life with a new identity. When the individual "wakes up," he or she is completely amnesic for the events that occurred during the fugue period.

Somnambulism, or sleepwalking, can occur during the day (diurnal somnambulism) as well as at night (nocturnal somnambulism). During a diurnal somnambulistic episode, an individual may stop whatever he or she is doing and start wandering

Wisconsin Center for Film and Theater Research

DR. JEKYLL AND MR. HYDE © **1932, Paramount Pictures. This is, of course, a fictional account of a scientist who chemically induced some dramatic physical and psychological changes in himself, alter-** nating between the "good" Dr. Jekyll and the "evil" Mr. Hyde. Often, in cases of multiple personality, a rare clinical syndrome, an individual develops opposite traits of this nature.

around in a daze or act out some event. The person then returns to the previous activity with no memory of the episode. In nocturnal somnambulism, the pattern is generally the same. The individual gets out of bed and starts walking around. He or she may even get dressed, leave home, and return later, with no memory of these wanderings on awakening in the morning. While in the somnambulist state, the person is only minimally responsive to the environment. For example, he or she may walk into the middle of a busy street with no realization of the danger involved. If awakened during the episode, the somnambulist will act confused and have no memory of how he or she got there. (DSM-III has dropped somnambulism from its list of dissociative disorders, placing it instead under the heading sleep disorders.)

An extreme and rare form of dissociative hysteria is the *multiple personality*. Robert Louis

Stevenson's classic story "The Strange Case of Dr. Jekyll and Mr. Hyde" presented an example of multiple personality that fascinated the public. The usual multiple personality consists of two or more completely distinctive and well-developed behavior-personality organizations. In what is referred to as the *alternating personality* (as in Jekyll and Hyde), there are two personalities or identities that alternate with one another. Each personality has amnesia for the thoughts and behavior of the other. Another type of multiple personality involves one or more dominant personalities and one or more subordinate ones. The dominant personality tends to control the person's behavior, while the subordinate personality operates subconsciously but is totally aware of the thoughts and behavior of the dominant personality. The subordinate personality is viewed as co-conscious with the dominant personality. If and when the co-conscious or subordinate personality surfaces, it can usually discuss in detail the problems and peculiarities of the dominant personality. One of the best-known cases of this type was described by Thigpen and Cleckley (1957) in their book *The Three Faces of Eve.*

Causes and stressors. Because of their rarity, dissociative reactions have received little attention from psychoanalytic theorists. What attention has been given has emphasized the use of massive repression in an attempt to defend against unacceptable impulses, principally sexual in nature. It is assumed that because of a sudden outburst or expression of these unacceptable impulses, the ordinary kind of repression cannot be employed. A more pervasive form of repression is used in order to place the entire event or outburst episode in the unconscious. The individual "splits off" from awareness an entire portion of his or her personality. He or she may become unaware of events that have transpired (amnesia), or behave in such a way

that unconscious impulses are expressed in isolation from the main core of the personality (split personality, fugue, or somnambulism). It is assumed that when the unacceptable response episode has been expressed completely, there is a return to the usual personality with no memory of what events have occurred.

Many learning theorists view dissociative reactions as similar in nature to conversion reactions. That is, they are assumed to be learned avoidance responses that serve to allow the individual to avoid a highly stressful situation. This conceptualization is very similar to the psychoanalytic formulation in its emphasis on using a behavior to avoid confronting a stressful event (unwanted expression of a socially unacceptable impulse). Again, as in psychoanalytic theory, not much attention has been directed at delineating the exact mechanisms involved in these disorders.

TREATMENT OF NEUROSES

One of the major forms of treatment for neurotic disorders is *chemotherapy.* Minor tranquilizers or anti-anxiety drugs, such as Librium, Miltown, and Valium, are commonly prescribed by psychiatrists as well as general practitioners for reducing anxiety and tension. These tranquilizers can be effective means for reducing high levels of anxiety in certain individuals in combination with certain forms of psychotherapy. However, the indiscriminate use of minor tranquilizers alone, without an attempt to deal with the situational-interpersonal factors involved, will not bring about any permanent long-term improvement in this behavior disorder. Besides the lack of long-term improvement, certain side effects such as drowsiness usually are associated with such drug usage. Further, individuals may develop tolerance for a particular dosage level, so that the amount of drug must be increased continuously to dangerously high levels to produce the same tranquilizing effects. If the medication is terminated after prolonged and heavy usage, severe withdrawal symptoms such as insomnia, tremors, and hallucinations may occur.

Why has the prescribing of tranquilizers become so widespread? First, they are seen as a cheaper alternative to the expense involved in traditional psychotherapy. Second, there is usually

less stigma attached to taking a drug for a "medical nervous disorder" than to seeking out clinical therapy for a psychological problem, which may, unfortunately, be viewed as an admission that one may be "crazy."

EFFECTIVENESS OF PSYCHOTHERAPY

Eysenck (1952) reported an influential survey study that assessed whether traditional forms of psychotherapy were any more effective in treating neurotic disorders than no treatment at all. He reported the therapy outcome data of 19 clinical groups consisting of more than 7,000 patients. Five of the groups received psychoanalysis and fourteen received "eclectic" psychotherapy. To obtain an estimate of "spontaneous improvement" among untreated cases (that is, patients who improved without receiving any treatment), Eysenck used the discharge rate of hospitalized neurotics from New York state hospitals and the improvement rate among life insurance claimants treated by medical general practitioners. Results of this survey study suggested that neurotic individuals who received psychotherapy fared no better than those who received no treatment. He found that among those neurotic patients who received no psychotherapy but only custodial or medical care, 72 percent were reported to have improved. In contrast, Eysenck reported, only 44 percent of psychoanalytic patients and 66 percent of eclectic psychotherapy patients improved. Eysenck later presented additional studies to support his position (Eysenck 1966).

Obviously, these results do not speak well for the effectiveness of traditional psychotherapeutic techniques, especially psychoanalysis, in treating neuroses. It should be pointed out, however, that this was not a controlled outcome evaluation experiment but merely a survey of already existing data. Nevertheless, the results were used by many to argue against the therapeutic effectiveness of traditional psychoanalytic treatment of the neuroses. At the same time, some strong objections were levied against Eysenck's criticism of psychotherapy. Bergin (1971) has summarized these objections.

Bergin points out that a survey of studies (such as Eysenck 1952) is associated with a number of difficulties that can significantly affect the conclusions made about therapeutic effectiveness. Such difficulties include (1) the lack of exactly similar therapy cases across the various clinical group studies surveyed; (2) the lack of equivalent outcome criteria used in the various studies; (3) the great range in the amount and quality of therapy received by patients in the various studies; (4) the great differences in the duration and thoroughness of therapy follow-up evaluations; (5) the great variability in the nature of onset and the duration of disturbances reported in the various studies; (6) the imprecise delineation of criteria employed to gauge therapeutic improvement. Bergin demonstrates how a number of arbitrary decisions concerning the handling of the criteria data can significantly affect outcome results. For example, he demonstrates how, with the same data, the improvement rate for psychoanalyses could be calculated at 83 percent rather than the 44 percent calculated by Eysenck. The way in which this discrepancy can arise has been effectively summarized by Korchin (1976):

> In order to put the published findings of all clinics on the same scale, Eysenck groups therapy results under four headings: (1) cured or much improved; (2) improved; (3) slightly improved; and (4) not improved, died, left treatment. His improvement rate

is based on the first two categories. Thus, "percent improved" is

$$\frac{(1) + (2)}{(1) + (2) + (3) + (4)}$$

> Those judged "slightly improved" and those who died or left therapy for any reason, as well as those who were not helped, were all on the side of failure. . . . In the particular case of the Berlin Psychoanalytic Institute Data (Fenichel 1930), the outcomes for completed cases were originally reported in these categories: (1) uncured; (2) improved; (3) very much improved; and (4) cured. For his analysis, Eysenck chose to include Fenichel's "improved" in his own "slightly improved," thus excluding them from the improved groups used in calculating successful treatment. On the basis of Fenichel's description of this group, however, Bergin believes that it is as or more reasonable to put them on the success side of the ledger. Moreover, including all those who died or terminated for whatever reason along with the genuinely unimproved farther deflates "percent improved." When Bergin recalculates the box score by (1) eliminating premature dropouts entirely, (2) counting Fenichel's "improved" as improved, and (3) eliminating nonneurotic cases which Eysenck included, he reaches a startling 91 percent improvement rate for the Berlin Psychoanalytic Institute rather than the 39 percent reported by Eysenck. He feels, correctly I believe, that his interpretation of the available information is logical and reasonable. At the very least, this numerical contretemps shows the essential difficulty in dealing with clinical survey statistics. It shows how readily they can be turned to make any point. (pp. 429–430)

Reassessment of the original Eysenck data, as well as examination of a number of more recent and better controlled studies by investigators such as Bergin (1971) and Meltzoff and Kornreich (1970), presents a more favorable judgment of psychotherapy. Bergin (1971) suggests that there may be a modestly positive average effect of psychotherapy, although he prefaces this statement with the assertion that:

> . . . the averaged group data on which this conclusion is based obscure the exis-

tence of a multiplicity of processes occurring in therapy, some of which are now known to be either unproductive or actually harmful. . . . The weakness of the average effects implies that only some methods or some therapists are especially effective. . . . Certainly, if we had the opportunity to impose our will upon the future, we would call a moratorium on classical psychotherapy outcome studies and upon a large proportion of the traditional therapy currently practiced . . . there is little point in further promoting the average, nonspecific, typical kind of therapy. (pp. 263-264)

In a more recent review of therapy outcome studies, Malan (1973) assesses various survey reviews from the perspective of dynamic psychotherapy. He reports that the traditional psychotherapy approach is effective with psychophysiological disorders, but that its effectiveness with neuroses is "weak in the extreme." This statement, too, needs to be tempered somewhat in light of the earlier mentioned therapy-evaluation studies conducted by Sloane and colleagues (Sloane et al. 1974; Staples et al. 1976) in which short-term psychoanalytically oriented therapy administered by well-trained and experienced therapists produced considerable therapeutic improvement in neurotic patients.

The issue of the effectiveness of traditional psychotherapy is far from resolved. A major problem associated with evaluating the effectiveness of psychotherapy (or any form of therapy) is, as Korchin indicates, one of interpretation. Just what constitutes improvement is open to debate, since the various therapeutic orientations usually employ different criteria for judging success. For example, behaviorally oriented therapists may define success specifically in terms of changes in some observable form of behavior (such as number of days of work lost due to anxiety). In contrast, psychoanalytically oriented therapists may require more overall improvement of their patients. Observable forms of behavioral change alone, unattended by a basic personality change, are less likely to be viewed as evidence of improvement by psychoanalysts. The use of different improvement criteria obviously makes comparisons between approaches difficult, if not impossible.

Korchin (1976) suggests that rather than attempting to make sense out of the past therapy

evaluation research, it may be worthwhile to assess carefully the specific factors (e.g., patient and therapeutic characteristics) involved in successful therapeutic outcomes.

SPECIFIC BEHAVIOR THERAPY TECHNIQUES

SYSTEMATIC DESENSITIZATION Systematic desensitization is a technique developed by Joseph Wolpe (1958) as a means of alleviating irrational anxiety. It is based on the principle of *counterconditioning*, where an attempt is made to substitute relaxation for anxiety in response to a particular situation or object. This technique, as typically employed, involves the pairing of deep muscle relaxation (taught by a relaxation procedure developed by Jacobson in 1938) with imagined scenes depicting situations associated with anxiety. Wolpe had his patients imagine the anxiety-producing situations or objects because many of the fears treated were abstract in nature (e.g., fear of rejection) and thus could not be easily presented *in vivo* (that is, in real life). However, when situations or objects can be practically presented in real life (e.g., a specific object such as a snake), behavior therapists often use *in vivo* systematic desensitization.

In this treatment procedure, a graded *hierarchy* of scenes is constructed that consists of items ranging from low anxiety to high anxiety-provoking situations. The client gradually works up the hierarchy, learning to tolerate increasingly more difficult scenes as he or she relaxes. Relaxation tends to inhibit anxiety from occurring in the imagined scenes. The ability to tolerate anxiety-related imagery of situations or objects is found to produce a significant reduction of anxiety in the related real-life situations. This treatment procedure has proved effective with a great many anxiety-related disorders such as phobias, insomnia, reactive depression, and psychophysiologic disorders such as ulcers, asthma, and hypertension (e.g., Rimm and Masters 1974).

Progressive muscle relaxation often can serve as a powerful therapeutic technique in its own right. Clinicians often use it by itself to treat a wide variety of disorders including generalized anxiety, insomnia, headaches, neck tension, and mild forms of agitated depression. Its use is based on the premise that muscle tension is closely related

Joseph Wolpe developed a widely used desensitization treatment for the alleviation of anxiety.

to anxiety, and that an individual will feel a significant reduction in experienced anxiety if tense muscles can be made to relax. Other techniques such as transcendental meditation (TM), yoga, autogenic training, and biofeedback are also commonly used to reduce physiological activation, which is assumed to be closely tied to anxiety.

Before using systematic desensitization or any other anxiety-reducing technique, clinicians must be careful to evaluate precisely which of two types of specific anxiety reactions they are dealing with. The first type involves situations or objects that are associated solely with irrational anxiety, with no evidence that the individual really lacks the appropriate skills to cope effectively with what he or she fears. For example, a client may have a severe degree of anxiety related to going out with a member of the opposite sex, which may have initially been produced by an embarrassing incident on a past date. Regardless of what initially produced the anxiety, however, the client does know how to act appropriately on a date; that is, he or she has the requisite skills. However, the high level of anxiety present may be sensed by the other person, interfering with the individual's "coming across" appropriately. If the individual's anxiety could be reduced, he or she would be able to

perform effectively. In this instance, systematic desensitization alone may be the only treatment needed to reduce the fear of dating.

In the second type of phobic reaction, the feared situation is associated with irrational anxiety and, in addition, the individual does lack appropriate skills to perform effectively. Such individuals may never have learned the appropriate dating skills expected by their peer group. So they may experience anxiety not only because of a past traumatic experience that produced anxiety, but also because they actually lack the appropriate interpersonal skills to behave effectively. The lack of interpersonal skills may "turn off" the dating partner. Such failures tend to further increase the already high level of anxiety associated with dating. In this case, not only is desensitization needed to reduce the irrational anxiety, but appropriate skills also must be taught to the client so that he or she will not continue to experience failure on subsequent dates simply because of a lack of appropriate interpersonal skills. Behavior rehearsal techniques, discussed in the next section, have been developed to teach such skills. Curran (1977) has recently reviewed a number of experimental investigations that strongly suggest the clinical effectiveness of social skills training approaches in the treatment of heterosexual social anxiety.

It should also be noted that there may be additional problems associated with ineffective dating behavior that these techniques do not deal with directly. For instance, the client may have unrealistic ideas, goals, or expectations about dating in general, about the kind of person he or she will be attractive to, or about what will happen on initial dates. The therapist needs to be sensitive to such possible contributing problems.

BEHAVIORAL REHEARSAL Allowing clients to "act out" or "role play" their interpersonal problems and usual manner of behaving is a method used in many different types of psychotherapy. Moreno (1947), for example, incorporated role playing into his psychodynamic approach to group therapy. Role playing one's past feelings and one's perceptions of how other people feel and behave is often used in insight-oriented therapy and other humanistic-existential approaches to psychotherapy. In behavior therapy, role playing or behavioral rehearsal procedures that attempt to simulate real-life situations have been developed and formalized to train individuals how to perform new behavior patterns. The therapist often "models" or

In different individuals, different types of situations elicit shyness. Most people report being shy on some occasions, but people who report being shy all the time view all social situations as unpleasant.

"coaches" the appropriate behavior that a client may be lacking. A client lacking appropriate dating behavior, for instance, would be taught appropriate skills through behavioral rehearsal. As Goldfried and Davison (1976) note, behavioral rehearsal is similar to the way in which an actor goes about learning a theatrical role. They cite a discussion by Sarbin and Allen (1968) that nicely illustrates this similarity:

> The actor has available some information which he must learn in the form of a script. He must learn not only the verbal responses, but also the actions and gestures appropriate to the part. . . . For the actor simply to study the requirements of the role is not enough: before the role is completely learned, the actor must *practice* in order to perfect his part. . . . Another feature of the dramaturgic model of role learning is the presence of a coach. . . . Because of his own special skills and prior training, the coach can guide and advise the novice. Often the coach has played the role that the actor is trying to learn or has observed frequent performances of the role by experts. He detects mistakes, he suggests a regime of training, and in a variety of other ways aids the actor in mastering his role. He is in a position to regulate the pace of learning, because he knows whether the actor's progress is rapid enough for him to

meet the expected standard within the time available; he may speed up or slow down the learner's pace as required. . . . An important function of the coach is to provide social reinforcement to the learner. Praise and criticism provide incentives for the learner, and at the same time furnish feedback which can be used to improve performance. After a scene the coach may give the actors an evaluation and critique of the performance, much in the manner of parents who praise their child for acting like a "big boy" all day. . . . The coach frequently serves as a model for the learner. Sometimes the coach enacts the role for the novice, explicitly instructing him to imitate. (Sarbin & Allen 1968, p. 548)

Behavioral rehearsal procedures are being used more and more in training social skills such as ways of behaving in interpersonal situations. Related to these procedures are *assertion training* techniques, which are used with individuals who experience a great deal of anxiety because of problems in asserting themselves. Salter (1949) was the first to give a great deal of attention to the fact that unassertive behavior often causes anxiety. Many individuals cannot stand up for their rights and greatly regret their inability to do so. This may create a great deal of interpersonal anxiety. Salter developed a method to teach such socially inhibited individuals how to express their feelings to others more effectively and assertively. More recently, McFall and colleagues (McFall & Lillesand 1971; McFall & Marston 1970; McFall & Twentyman 1973) have reported the therapeutic effectiveness of assertion training in reducing anxiety in various interpersonal situations.

COGNITIVE METHODS   Albert Ellis (1962) originally developed Rational-Emotive Therapy (RET) on the assumption that cognitions can produce emotions. He assumed that psychological disorders such as the neuroses are caused by faulty or irrational patterns of thinking. Accordingly, he indicates that the focus of therapy should be directed at changing the internal or covert sentences that people say to themselves and that produce negative emotional responses. There has been some experimental support for Ellis's suggestion that irrational beliefs are associated with anxiety. Newmark, Frerking, Cook, and Newmark (1973) conducted a study in which a questionnaire was administered to neurotics, patients with per-

In psychodrama therapy, the participants act out a variety of roles in order to explore an emotional problem.

sonality disorders, and normal controls. This questionnaire assessed an individual's endorsement of various beliefs, including many irrational ones that Ellis proposed as causes of anxiety. It was found that neurotic patients endorsed many more irrational beliefs (e.g., "one must be perfectly competent, adequate, and achieving to consider oneself worthwhile") than the other subject groups.

Ellis (1962) summarized the results of 172 case histories of clients he treated, with either RET or traditional psychoanalytic therapy, and found RET to be the more effective treatment. Although this was far from a controlled outcome evaluation study, it did suggest the potential effectiveness of his therapy technique. More and more behavior therapists are beginning to use his basic technique as a "cognitive restructuring" method in a variety

of behavioral disorders (Goldfried & Davison 1976).

Meichenbaum (1972), for instance, reported success in using cognitive restructuring techniques to modify anxiety. In this procedure, the therapist determines the specific thoughts or self-verbalizations that are presumed to give rise to the anxiety. The therapist then assists the client in modifying these negative self-verbalizations and replacing them with positive self-statements. As an example of this approach, Meichenbaum presents the following illustrations of persons with a high degree of anxiety:

> The following examples illustrate the relationship between the client's self-statements and his levels of anxiety. The first situation concerns the presentation of a public speech during which some members of the audience walk out of the room respectively, on two speakers, both of who possess essentially the same speaking skills. This exodus elicits different self-statements from high versus low speech-anxious speakers. The high speech-anxious individual is more likely to say to himself: "I must be boring. How much longer do I have to speak? I knew I never could give a speech," and so forth. These self-statements engender anxiety and become self-fulfilling prophecies. On the other hand, the low speech-anxious individual is more likely to view the audience's departure as a sign of their rudeness or to attribute their leaving to external considerations. He is more likely to say something like, "They must have a class to catch. Too bad they have to leave; they will miss a good talk." Similarly in our work with test anxiety we found that high versus low test-anxious individuals say different things to themselves during an examination. Consider the situation in which other students hand in their exams early. For the high test-anxious individual this event elicits worrying-type self-statements, namely, "I can't get this problem. I'll never finish, how can that guy be done?" etc. The result is an increase in anxiety and further task irrelevant and self-defeating thoughts. In comparison, the low test-anxious student readily dismisses the other student's performance by saying to himself, "That guy who handed in his paper early must know nothing. I hope they score this exam on a curve." The same stimulus event (viz., two

BIOFEEDBACK

Before Harry Houdini performed one of his famous escapes, a skeptical committee would search his clothes and body. When the members of the committee were satisfied that the Great Houdini was concealing no keys, they would put chains, padlocks and handcuffs on him. . . . Of course, not even Houdini could open a padlock without a key, and when he was safely behind the curtain he would cough one up. He could hold a key suspended in his throat and regurgitate it when he was unobserved. . . . The trick behind many of Houdini's escapes was in some ways just as amazing as the escape itself. Ordinarily when an object is stuck in a person's throat he will start to gag. He can't help it—it's an unlearned, automatic reflex. But Houdini had learned to control his gag reflex by practicing for hour after hour with a small piece of potato tied to a string. (Lang 1970)

Through the years, other unusual instances of voluntary control over physiological functions have been noted in the scientific literature. Lindsley and Sassaman (1938) reported the case of a middle-aged male who had the ability to control the erection of hairs over the entire surface of his body. McClure (1959) noted the case of an individual who could willfully produce complete cardiac arrest for periods of several seconds at a time. Numerous instances of voluntary acceleration of pulse rate were reported by Ogden and Shock (1939). The Russian psychologist Luria (1958) described a mnemonist who had attained remarkable control of his heart rate and skin temperature. This person could abruptly alter his heart rate 40 beats per minute. He could also raise the skin temperature of one hand while simultaneously lowering the temperature of the other hand. It has also been documented that many yogis and fakirs can control various physiological responses at will.

Such acts of bodily control have traditionally been viewed as rare feats that only certain extraordinarily gifted people could accomplish. However, in recent years behavioral scientists have demonstrated that the average person can learn a degree of control over physiological responses. The principal training method developed and utilized in this learning process has been labeled "biofeedback."

There has been a growing interest, in both the scientific community and the general public, in the area of biofeedback because of its many potentially important clinical applications. For example, it would be therapeutically valuable if we could teach patients with hypertension how to lower their blood pressure, or teach the patient with migraine headaches how to control the cranial artery dilation involved in the pain process. Already, biofeedback techniques (learned control of heart-rate deceleration) have shown promise of therapeutic effectiveness in reducing anxiety.

The biofeedback technique is based on the fundamental learning principle that we learn to perform a particular response when we receive feedback or information about the consequences

---

people walking out in the midst of a speech or students handing in their examinations early) elicits different perceptions, attributions, and self-statements in high versus low anxious individuals . . . Hence, the goal of intervention with "neurotics" is . . . to make the "neurotic" patient aware of the self-statements which mediate maladaptive behaviors and to train them to produce incompatible self-statements and behaviors. (Meichenbaum 1972, pp. 20–21)

Like systematic desensitization, this technique has been demonstrated in controlled therapy evaluation studies to be highly effective in reducing anxiety. In terms of the differential effectiveness of these two therapy techniques, Rimm and Masters (1974) have suggested that systematic desensitization may be most effective for clients who show a relatively small number of phobias or fears, whereas those persons who experience multiple fears in a great many interpersonal situations might profit most from cognitive restructuring techniques. Additional research is needed to test experimentally the validity of their suggestion.

Another cognitive method that has recently

of the response we have just made and then make appropriate adjustments. This is how we have learned to perform the wide variety of skills and behaviors we use in everyday life. For instance, we learn how to drive a car by receiving continuous feedback about how much we need to turn the steering wheel to turn the car a certain distance, or how much pressure we must apply to the accelerator in order to make the car move at a certain speed. If we are denied this feedback, as, for example, by being blindfolded, we would never receive information about the consequences of our driving responses. We would therefore never be able to learn the appropriate adjustments needed to perform a successful maneuver with the car. Information feedback is thus very important. Annent (1969) has reviewed numerous experimental studies demonstrating the importance of feedback in the learning and performance of a wide variety of motor skills.

Availability of feedback is also important in learning how to control internal physiological responses. Because we normally do not receive feedback of these internal events in day-to-day life, we cannot control them. But if a person is given biofeedback of, say, heart rate via a visual display monitor, he or she becomes aware of the consequences of heart rate change and how adjustments can be made to modify and eventually control it. Receiving feedback removes one's "blindfold," thus enabling one to learn how to voluntarily control a response. The recent development of sensitive physiological recording

devices and digital logic circuitry has made it possible to detect small changes in visceral events and provide subjects with immediate biofeedback of these events.

Since the initial pioneering experiments with animal subjects conducted in the late 1950s and early 1960s by Neal Miller (1969), there have been demonstrations of human subjects' learned control of a wide variety of what were once assumed to be "involuntary responses"—sweat gland activity, blood pressure, salivation, neuromuscular activity, skin temperature, various brain wave rhythms, and even penile tumescence. Much of the work that has been done in the field of biofeedback during the last decade has been collected and reprinted in several books (e.g., Barber, DiCara, Kamiya, Miller, Shapiro, & Stoyva 1976).

One important word of caution is necessary concerning the therapeutic effectiveness of biofeedback procedures. There is currently a lack of systematic, well-controlled studies that demonstrate conclusively the clinical effectiveness of these techniques. For the most part, claims of effectiveness are based on uncontrolled group or single case studies. A great deal of research is needed to determine whether biofeedback techniques are active therapeutic procedures or merely powerful placebo conditions. Some recent research reported by Gatchel (1978) has suggested that placebo factors play a significant role in clinical applications of biofeedback.

been developed is *thought stopping*. It is used with clients who experience distress because of obsessive thoughts they have difficulty controlling. The technique is relatively straightforward, and has been summarized by Rimm and Masters (1974):

> The client is asked to concentrate on the anxiety-inducing thoughts, and, after a short period of time, the therapist suddenly and emphatically says "stop" (any loud noice . . . may also suffice). After this procedure has been repeated several times (and the client reports that his thoughts were indeed interrupted or blocked), the locus of control is shifted from the therapist to the client. Specifically, the client is taught to emit a subvocal "stop" whenever he begins to engage in a self-defeating rumination. (p. 430)

As Rimm and Masters note, recent empirical evidence is very promising and shows that thought-stopping procedures are effective in dealing with obsessional thinking.

BIOFEEDBACK TRAINING In recent years, it has been shown that human subjects can learn to

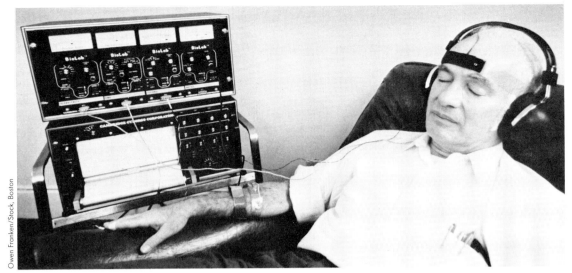

Owen Franken/Stock, Boston

**In biofeedback therapy, an individual
learns to control certain physiological
components of anxiety like muscle
tension.**

control their physiological responses through *bio-feedback* procedures. Clinical interest has been great because of the possibility that biofeedback training may prove to be an effective treatment for fear and anxiety. Learning theorists such as Mowrer (1947) have suggested that autonomic nervous system arousal is a basic component of an anxiety response. A variety of therapies have been designed to modify the psychological substrata of anxiety and tension states: progressive relaxation therapy (Jacobson 1938), autogenic training (Schultz & Luthe 1959), and transcendental meditation (Benson & Wallace 1972). The main goal of these therapies is to produce a low state of autonomic arousal that competes against the stress response and accompanying elevated arousal level. Gatchel and his colleagues (Gatchel 1977; Gatchel, Hatch, Watson, Smith, & Gaas 1978; Gatchel & Proctor 1976) have demonstrated the effectiveness of learned control of heart rate deceleration as a therapeutic technique for reducing anxiety. Since heart rate acceleration is strongly associated with fear (Lang, Rice, & Sternbach 1972), the use of learned control over this visceral response appears to be a direct and powerful tool for bringing about fear reduction. This is a relatively new technique, and a great deal of additional evaluation research is needed to test its effectiveness with a variety of behavior disorders. It does show promise as a general treatment technique.

BROAD-SPECTRUM BEHAVIOR THERAPY   Lazarus (1971) has coined the term *broad-spectrum behavior therapy* to emphasize the fact that most behavior therapists employ several different treatment procedures for a specific disorder in an attempt to deal effectively with all the important controlling or causal variables. For example, in the case of school phobia, it was suggested that not only the child's basic fear of going to school had to be treated and modified, but also the dependency relationship between the child and the mother, which might be helping to maintain the problem behavior. Just as traditional psychoanalytic therapy attempts to determine the underlying unconscious or "root" causes of a behavior disorder, behavior therapy also seeks to assess the major causes of such behavior. However, the search is not for underlying unconscious causes, which are difficult to assess, but for the learned and environmental determinants or causes. As Bandura (1969) suggests, if by "searching for the cause of a disorder" one means the search for the strongest and most significant causal and controlling variables, then the goal and task of all therapists, traditional psychotherapists as well as behavior therapists, is the same. The chief difference is that behavior therapists assume that the search for environmental determinants and the direct modification of behavior is heuristically the most feasible and effective approach, whereas traditional psychotherapists assume that it is more important to uncover and to attempt to treat unconscious motivations of behavior.

MATCHING DISORDER TYPE WITH THERAPY TYPE

A major problem in traditional forms of psychotherapy has been the attempt to apply the same general form of therapy to all disorders. This attempt has not been very successful in dealing with the various forms of neurotic behavior. Behavior therapy has taken a different approach, with the goal of developing specific treatment techniques to deal with particular disorders. In recent years there also has been more effort to individualize psychotherapy so that the type of treatment employed is tailored to the specific disorder and characteristics of the patient. Goldstein and Stein (1976) have published a text entitled *Prescriptive Psychotherapies* in which an attempt is made to outline the type of treatment that is most effective in dealing with particular disorders. Such an approach will help ensure the appropriate matching of patient-therapist-treatment variables to produce the most successful therapeutic outcomes.

DIAGNOSIS AND ASSESSMENT

INTERVIEW / REFERRAL

As with most forms of psychopathology, the clinical interview is the most frequently used procedure for assessment of the neuroses. As we pointed out earlier, the interview is an assessment method that cuts across all theoretical orientations. It is a major method for exploring and delineating specific concerns, feelings, and problems an individual may be experiencing. When an individual is referred to a mental health professional or voluntarily seeks out help for a neurotic disorder, the behavioral manifestations usually become quite evident during the course of the initial *intake* or diagnostic interviews. A well-trained clinician will be sensitive to the various neurotic manifestations discussed earlier in this chapter. Anxiety is usually the most significant of these, and it can often be assessed through the client's self-report and direct observation of the behavior and affect he or she demonstrates during the interview. Measurement of physiological responses usually reveals increased levels of arousal in neurotic individuals and, in the future, may become a valuable adjunctive assessment procedure in the clinic.

As we discussed earlier, problems in reliability of assessment can arise when one attempts to "pigeonhole" a neurotic individual into one of the traditional diagnostic subcategories, since symptoms often overlap from one category to the next. However, with the present trend toward individualizing psychotherapy, individuals usually are not put into a specific category. Rather, an attempt is made to assess the specific presenting problem(s) and the precipitating / situational factors that are maintaining the problem behavior. This detailed assessment is needed in order to decide which of the many therapeutic techniques will be most effective in treating the neurotic disorder. Without precise and accurate assessment, an effective treatment program cannot be developed.

TESTING

The most commonly used and influential test for differentiating among various psychiatric disorders, including the neuroses, is the MMPI (Minnesota Multiphasic Personality Inventory). This test generally produces a characteristic pattern for specific types of neurotic disorders that can be used to differentiate them from other clinical disorders and nonpsychiatric patterns of behavior. The MMPI pattern shown is typical for an individual suffering anxiety. The elevated psychasthenia (Pt) scale suggests the presence of unreasonable fears and a high level of general anxiety. Note that an elevation appears not only in the psychasthenia scale, but also in the depression (D) and hysteria (Hy) scales. This again highlights the fact that neurotic

128

categories often overlap. The so-called *neurotic triad* is commonly found in neurotics, with the hypochondriasis, depression, and hysteria scales standing the highest in the profile.

A word of caution is necessary about interpreting scores on the MMPI or any other single assessment test. The fact that an individual shows a profile pattern similar to that of an anxiety neurotic group does not necessarily mean that he or she is actually an anxiety neurotic. It indicates only that the individual is answering a series of questions on the inventory in a manner similar to the way in which a diagnosed anxiety neurotic might answer. Other causal factors can also cause this type of responding. Results of the test are only suggestive and should not be used as the sole basis for making a diagnosis. As we emphasized earlier, in using only a single source of data, such as self-report responses, one must be aware that it may not directly parallel other components of behavior, such as observational and physiological. A comprehensive evaluation including as many components as possible of behavior in specific situations should be used before one can expect to make an accurate assessment.

Because neurotic individuals usually have an elevated level of anxiety, they tend to be significantly different from non-neurotic individuals on inventories that assess anxiety, such as the Taylor Manifest Anxiety Scale (Taylor 1953). This test consists of items from the MMPI. It gauges *trait* anxiety, that is, a stable and characteristic high level of anxiety that would be expected in a chronic anxiety neurotic.

Note that a distinction is usually made between *trait* and *state* anxiety. *State* anxiety is viewed as an individual's momentary anxiety in response to a specific situation or object; it varies in intensity over time and across situations. Usually a person with high trait anxiety is more likely to show higher state anxiety than a person with low trait anxiety (Spielberger 1966). That is, individuals who report that they are anxious in general tend to show greater emotional arousal to specific stressors than individuals who report that they are generally non-anxious.

SAMPLE MMPI PROFILE
Figure 6.2

Note that this profile suggests the presence of anxiety and depression. (From Lanyon & Goodstein 1971)

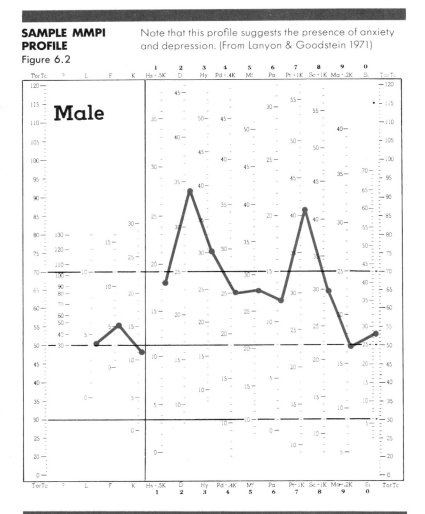

PROGNOSIS

With the appropriate type of treatment, the outlook for improvement in neurotic individuals is good. Some estimates have indicated that 90 percent or more of neurotic individuals can benefit significantly from appropriate types of treatment (Coleman 1976). Of course, the degree of improvement will depend on the clinical skills of the therapist and his or her ability to isolate and effectively deal with all the major contributing factors maintaining the behavior disorder. For example, if there is a great deal of secondary gain derived from a neurotic disorder that is generating significant anxiety, then simply treating the anxiety without dealing with the possible environmental/interpersonal variables maintaining the behavior will probably not lead to a total elimination of the disorder.

One additional point should be made concerning the prognosis for therapeutic improvement. When therapy is directed at changing a specific target or problem behavior and successfully accomplishes this goal, it often has many far-reaching generalization effects. For example, individuals who overcome a fear of a specific object or situation often develop an increased confidence in their ability to overcome other problems and so will be better able to cope with general environmental demands. Moreover, by overcoming specific fears, these individuals no longer have to avoid potentially rewarding experiences that in the past were associated with anxiety. This will often result in their general everyday functioning becoming more rewarding and satisfying.

SUMMARY

1. Neurosis is an emotional disorder that is characterized primarily by the presence of anxiety. The DSM-II distinguished between eight separate types of neurosis: anxiety, phobic, obsessive-compulsive, hypochrondriacal, neurasthenic, depressive, and depersonalization. In many clinical cases, however, symptoms overlap from one category type to the next, so that reliability is somewhat low when one attempts to differentiate between the specific categories. The new DSM-III eliminates the general category of neurosis and includes the subtypes in four new categories: *anxiety* disorders, *somatoform* disorders, *dissociative* disorders, and *affective* disorders.

2. Psychoanalytic theory views anxiety as a state of tension caused by intrapsychic conflict between the demands of the id, ego, and superego.

3. One of the earliest learning theory accounts of anxiety was a model based on simple Pavlovian classical conditioning. Mowrer (1947), a major critic of this model, proposed a two-factor theory of learning to account more completely for conditioned anxiety. It is credited with being the first widely accepted learning model of anxiety. However, as with the psychoanalytic model, there are no clear-cut, objective clinical data definitively demonstrating the validity of this theoretical orientation.

4. Even though the learning model has not been definitively shown to be valid, many experimental and clinical researchers use it because it provides a heuristic theoretical framework to use in the further investigation and integration of research and clinical data on anxiety. Using this theoretical framework, a number of effective behaviorally oriented treatment techniques have been developed for alleviating anxiety and neurotic disorders.

5. Anxiety, rather than being an actual observable entity or "thing," is usually treated as a *construct* that is inferred to account for some form of behavior or clinical phenomenon. In using a construct such as anxiety to explain behavior, it is necessary to define operationally what we mean by it and then develop a method for measuring it objectively. The study by Paul (1966) demonstrated how this can be done.

6. Anxiety neurosis is the most common form of neurotic behavior. It is characterized by diffuse, and often severe, "free-floating" anxiety that is not directly related to any one particular situation, object, or threat.

7. Eysenck (1957) has proposed a theory of the etiology of neurosis that suggests the interaction of both genetic and nongenetic learned factors. Such a theory is usually referred to as a *diathesis-stress* theory because it assumes a genetic or constitutional predisposition toward a disorder that predisposes an individual to develop a psychopathological disorder after exposure to some stressful event. Such an approach shows promise of providing the most comprehensive understanding of the etiology of anxiety neurosis, as well as other forms of neurosis.

8. A phobia is an intense irrational fear of some specific object or situation that pre-

sents no real danger to an individual, or a fear that is blown up out of proportion to the danger it actually poses.

9. In obsessive-compulsive neurosis, the individual has obsessive unwanted thoughts and/or compulsive ritualistic activity that he or she must carry out or else experience anxiety. Like phobic individuals, these neurotics realize that their behavior is irrational but still cannot control it.

10. The DSM-II distinguished between two major types of hysterical neurosis: conversion reactions and dissociative reactions. The DSM-III creates a separate category for dissociative disorders. Conversion reactions involve the presence of symptoms of some physical illness although there is no known underlying organic pathology. Four different types of dissociative reactions have traditionally been distinguished: (a) amnesia, in which the person suffers partial or total loss of memory; (b) fugue, in which the person loses his or her memory and in this condition flees from the usual environment to some new situation or geographical location; (c) somnambulism or sleepwalking; (d) multiple personality, in which different personalities are present within the same individual.

11. Hypochondriacal neurosis involves the overdramatization of one's physical ailments. Neurasthenic neurosis is characterized by the presence of mental and physical fatigue, as well as complaints of various aches and pains.

12. A popular form of treatment for neurotic disorders is chemotherapy, specifically the use of minor tranquilizers. However, the in-

discriminate use of minor tranquilizers alone, without an attempt to deal with the specific situational-interpersonal factors involved in the neurosis, will not result in any permanent improvement in this behavior disorder.

13. A number of recently developed behavior therapy techniques have been shown to be therapeutically effective in modifying many forms of neurotic behavior. These techniques include systematic desensitization, behavioral rehearsal, cognitive restructuring methods, and biofeedback procedures. The term *broad-spectrum behavior therapy* was coined by Lazarus (1971) to emphasize the fact that most behavior therapists employ several different treatment procedures for a specific disorder in order to deal effectively with all the important variables maintaining the disorder.

14. The current trend is toward a "prescriptive" approach to psychotherapy which, rather than applying the same general form of therapy to all disorders, as has been done in the past, attempts to individualize therapy so that the type of treatment is tailored to the specific disorder and characteristics of the patient. With such an approach, the prognosis for therapeutic improvement of the neuroses is good.

15. In the assessment/diagnosis of the neuroses, the clinical interview is the most frequently used procedure in all theoretical approaches. It is an effective method by which to delineate the situational-interpersonal factors that may be maintaining a problem behavior.

RECOMMENDED READINGS

Barber, T. X.; DiCara, L. V.; Kamiya, J.; Miller, N. E.; Shapiro, D.; & Stoyva, J. *Biofeedback and self control: An Aldine Annual on the regulation of bodily processes and consciousness.* Chicago: Aldine, 1976.

Bergin, A. E. The evaluation of therapeutic outcomes. In A. E. Bergin and S. L. Garfield (Eds.), *Handbook of psychotherapy and behavior change: An empirical analysis.* New York: Wiley, 1971.

Goldfried, M. R., & Davison, G. C. *Clinical behavior therapy.* New York: Holt, Rinehart, & Winston, 1976.

Goldstein, A. P., & Stein, N. *Prescriptive psychotherapies.* New York: Pergamon Press, 1976.

Gray, J. *The psychology of fear and stress.* New York: McGraw-Hill, 1974.

Masserman, J. H. *Behavior and neurosis.* Chicago: University of Chicago Press, 1943.

Pribram, K. H., & Gill, M. *Freud's project reassessed.* New York: Basic Books, 1976.

Skinner, B. F. *Science and human behavior.* New York: Macmillan, 1953.

PSYCHOPHYSIOLOGICAL DISORDERS

7

OVERVIEW The symptoms of psychophysiological disorders are similar to those of actual organic diseases. The distinction between the two is usually made on the basis of etiology: psychophysiological disorders have no known medical cause, but appear to be caused primarily by psychological or emotional factors. Moreover, recent research has indicated that almost all physical illnesses are either caused, exacerbated, or prolonged to some degree by psychological factors. We will review six of the most common psychophysiological disorders: asthma, dysmenorrhea, essential hypertension, migraine and muscle contraction headaches, neurodermatitis, and peptic ulcers. We will also discuss various theoretical accounts of these disorders. Learning theory views these disorders as it

does any other behavior—as learned responses. The most widely accepted psychoanalytic approach views each psychophysiological disorder as having its own specific psychodynamic constellation and personality characteristics. Numerous other attempts have been made to delineate personality trait characteristics that are associated with specific psychophysiological disorders. A variation of the personality trait conceptualization is a specific-attitudes theory which suggests that specific attitudes are associated with the occurrence of particular disorders. Finally, we will discuss a diathesis-stress model which takes into account genetic, physiological, and attitude/personality factors in the etiology of these disorders. We will also review the current treatment ap-

DEMOGRAPHICS	USUAL AGE AT ONSET	PREVALENCE	SEX RATIO
GENERAL	May occur at any stage of life	Relatively common. It has been estimated that more than half of all individuals seeking medical attention have some physical disorder directly related to psychological problems	Differs considerably for specific disorders
ASTHMA	Childhood and adolescence	About 4–5% of population	More common in males than females
DYSMENORRHEA	Puberty	Difficult to determine exact prevalence. Estimates have ranged all the way from 4% to 62% of female population	Occurs in females only
ESSENTIAL HYPERTENSION	May occur at any stage of life, although it becomes viewed as more serious during adulthood	About 10–14% of population	More common in females than males
HEADACHE:			
MIGRAINE	Late childhood and adolescence	About 8% of population	More common in females than males
TENSION	Adolescence	About 30% of population suffer at least occasional tension headaches	More common in females than males
NEURODERMATITIS	Childhood	About 2% of population	Equal in males and females
PEPTIC ULCER	May occur at any stage of life, although usually begins at adolescence and after	About 2% of population	Male-female ratio is 2 or 3 to 1

proaches used with these disorders; other than medical treatment required to deal with disturbing organic pathology that may be present, treatment approaches are similar to those employed with neurotic disorders.

SYMPTOM DESCRIPTION AND ETIOLOGY

Psychophysiological disorders were defined by the DSM-II as "physical symptoms that are caused by emotional factors and involve a single organ system, usually under the control of the autonomic nervous system" (p. 46). They are characterized by physical symptoms, involving organs of the body, that are intimately linked with psychological factors — thus the term *psychophysiological*. They have traditionally also been called *psychosomatic*. In chapter 6, we discussed certain neurotic disorders that appeared to involve some physical dysfunction or discomfort. Hysterical paralysis, for example, affects an aspect of bodily functioning. In such disorders, however, no actual underlying organic damage or defect can be isolated. In contrast, psychophysiological disorders are actual physical disorders with a clear organic involvement. A common misconception about these disorders is that the afflicted person is not suffering any actual physical defect or discomfort, but that it is merely "all in the mind." It is assumed that the person is not actually suffering from a "real disease" but is merely imagining it or malingering. This is an unfortunate myth. Individuals with psychophysiological disorders have a real organic defect, are suffering real discomfort, and are in need of some medical treatment.

The symptoms of psychophysiological disorders are similar, and often identical, to those present in a systemic disease. How are we then to distinguish a psychophysiological disorder from a purely systemic disease? This distinction is usually made on the basis of etiology. In the case of hypertension, for example, *renal hypertension* is a systemic disease caused by kidney malfunctioning. *Essential hypertension,* on the other hand, is classified as a psychophysiological disorder because there is no known medical cause; that is, it is *idiopathic.* But although psychological factors appear to cause the chronic elevation of blood pressure in this disorder, the physical problem is very real. In many disorders, the distinction between psychosomatic and nonpsychosomatic disorders is difficult to make. Buss (1966) has pointed out that psychological factors may be sufficient but not necessary causes of certain somatic disorders, so that the line between purely psychophysiological and systemic disorders is frequently blurred. For example, in the case of childhood asthma, Rees (1964) isolated three causal factors: allergic, infective, and psychological. These factors, either alone or in any combination, can trigger an asthmatic attack. Rees suggests that multiple causation is usually the rule, with various sequences and combinations of these factors culminating in the attack.

We do not yet know enough about the process by which psychological factors produce changes in somatic factors. Also, in the field of medicine the exact causes of many disorders are not totally understood. The general rule of assessment has traditionally been that a particular case of hypertension, asthma, and the like should not be diagnosed as psychophysiological until a complete medical evaluation has ruled out organic medical factors as the primary cause, and there is good

Jan Lukas, Rapho/Photo Researchers

It is assumed that hypertension is related to chronic stress produced by environmental and psychological factors.

evidence for emotional factors that are antecedent to the disorder.

THE MIND-BODY PROBLEM

The relationship between the mind and the body has long been a controversial topic among philosophers, physiologists, and psychologists. Are expe-

Rene Descartes (1596–1650) proposed a dualistic theory of mind and body.

riences purely mental, purely physical, or an interaction of both? Traditionally, in western culture, it has been hard to view the mind and body as one. A major reason for this has been the lack of an English word adequately denoting the union of mind and body. Moreover, with the rise of physical medicine during the Renaissance, the view of the mind influencing the body came to be regarded as unscientific. The understanding of the mind and soul was relegated to the areas of religion and philosophy, further perpetuating a dualistic viewpoint.

One of the earliest and most influential attempts to deal with the mind-body problem was proposed by the French philosopher Descartes in the seventeenth century. He took a dualistic viewpoint in assuming that the physical body and spiritual soul/mind were separate. However, he assumed that they could interact. He proposed that the pineal gland located in the midbrain was the vital connection between mind and body.

With the nineteenth-century discovery that microorganisms caused certain diseases, there came further acceptance of a dualistic viewpoint. This view began to change, however, about the mid-nineteenth century. Claude Bernard, a Frenchman, was the first influential physician to emphasize the contributions of psychological factors to bodily ailments. Subsequently, Freud was very influential in emphasizing the interaction of psychological and physical factors in various disorders.

During the twentieth century, psychosomatic medicine became a very important area of medical science, with an emphasis on treating patients as "whole" beings and on considering psychological factors as important in the course of most any disease. Lipowski (1977), in a comprehensive overview of the field of psychosomatic medicine during the 1970s, noted a great resurgence of interest in this field. Most professionals today take the position that mind and body are not separate entities, but a unity. A change in emotional state will be accompanied by a change in physiological responding; conversely, a change in physiological functioning will frequently be accompanied by alterations in emotional affect. In clinical treatment, a *holistic* approach is now advocated, with the view that to understand disease and health, it is important to study people as "individual mind-body complexes ceaselessly interacting with the social and physical environment in which they are embedded" (Lipowski 1977, p. 234).

There are psychological factors involved in all diseases. In fact, Graham (1972) suggests that the psychological and physical explanations of a disease or disorder are merely different ways of describing the same event. The modern view of these disorders is that they are the result of many causes—physical, psychological, and sociocultural. It is the search for the unique interaction of these factors that interests investigators of psychophysiological disorders. The mind and body are not separate entities.

MAJOR CATEGORIES OF PSYCHOPHYSIOLOGICAL DISORDERS

The DSM-II has delineated nine major categories of psychophysiological disorders, with the major categorizing factor being the affected part or system of the body. The DSM-III, as we will discuss shortly, takes a very different approach to the whole question of psychophysiological disorders. Table 7.1 lists these nine categories, along with a list of some of the disorders included in each. (It should be pointed out that some workers assume that many of the disorders listed can occur primarily as the result of organic causes, with no significant emotional factors involved.)

In addition to the major categories listed in the table, it has become increasingly recognized that psychological or emotional factors play an important role in the precipitation and/or exacerbation of most organic illnesses (a reflection of mind-body interaction). Indeed, research has indicated that a great many disorders may be partially precipitated by psychological factors, including neurological disorders such as multiple sclerosis, infectious diseases such as pulmonary tuberculosis, and even malignant diseases such as cancer and leukemia (Wittkower & Dudek 1973). The DSM-II did not take such disorders into account.

A NEW APPROACH TO CLASSIFICATION

Many professionals in the field of psychosomatic medicine now take a multicausal etiological view of disease. In describing psychosomatic disorders, the current trend is not to talk about any distinct group of disorders, but about any physical condition that is precipitated, exacerbated, or prolonged by psychological factors. The DSM-II, in contrast, listed a group of psychophysiological disorders that were assumed to be qualitatively different from all other types of organic illnesses.

Lipp, Looney, and Spitzer (1977) have pointed out that a classification system of psychophysiological disorders is needed that takes into account the degree to which psychosocial factors can influence any physical condition. They have proposed that the third edition of the DSM (DSM-III) delete the separate section on psychophysiological disorders and substitute a section entitled "Psychological Factors in Physical Conditions." This section would include not only the psychophysiological disorders listed by the DSM-II, but also any physical condition in which psychological factors are found to be significant in precipitating,

---

DSM-II CLASSIFICATION OF PSYCHO-PHYSIOLOGICAL DISORDERS
Table 7.1

1. **SKIN DISORDERS**
   Acne—Eruption of blemishes on skin, especially facial skin.
   Eczema—Inflammation, itching, and redness of the skin.
   Hives (Urticaria)—Raised edematous patches of skin usually associated with intense itching.
   Neurodermatitis—Skin eruptions, ranging from a chronic rash to running sores.
   Psoriasis—Circumscribed red patches on skin covered by white scales.

2. **MUSCULOSKELETAL DISORDERS**
   Backache—Pain in the muscles of the back produced by chronic tension.
   Muscle tension headache—Headache caused by chronic contraction of the head and neck muscles.

3. **RESPIRATORY DISORDERS**
   Bronchial asthma—Breathing difficulties including wheezing, gasping, and coughing.
   Hyperventilation—Extremely fast and deep breathing.

4. **CARDIOVASCULAR DISORDERS**
   Essential hypertension—Chronically elevated blood pressure.
   Migraine headache—Headache caused by dilation of cranial vasculature.
   Raynaud's disease—Cold hands and/or feet caused by decrease of blood supply to these limbs.

5. **HEMIC AND LYMPHATIC DISORDERS**

6. **GASTROINTESTINAL DISORDERS**
   Gastric ulcers—Lesion in the walls of stomach.
   Gastritis—Excessive amount of gas in the digestive tract.
   Mucous colitis—Inflammation of the colon which produces disturbances in bowel functioning.

7. **GENITOURINARY DISORDERS**
   Dysmenorrhea—Painful and/or irregular menstrual periods.
   Dyspareunia—Painful intercourse experienced by the female.
   Impotence—Inability of male to achieve or maintain a penile erection.
   Vaginismus—Irregular and involuntary contractions of the vaginal muscles prior to or during intercourse.

8. **ENDOCRINE DISORDERS**
   Goiter—Enlargement of thyroid gland that is not due to a neoplasm.
   Obesity—Excessive overweight.

9. **DISORDERS OF ORGANS OF SPECIAL SENSE**
   Ménière's disease—Disorder of the semicircular canals of inner ears, and progressive deafness.

10. **OTHER TYPES**

THE STRESS OF CHANGE

One popular area of psychosomatic medicine is the study of the relationship between changes in one's life and the occurrence of medical problems and illnesses. Recent research indicates that a variety of illnesses—not just psychophysiological disorders—appear to be precipitated by the stress associated with any changes in a person's life, whether they are pleasant or unpleasant. Holmes and Rahe (1967) developed the Social Readjustment Rating Scale to gauge the impact of different types of life changes. This scale rates each of these changes in terms of *life change units* (LCUs). The following is a list of the different types of changes in this scale.

As can be seen, certain changes are assumed to be more stress-producing than others and so are associated with greater LCUs. An individual who is administered this scale simply checks off life changes he or she has undergone during the previous year. The sum of the LCUs associated with these changes is then computed. In one study conducted by Holmes, it was found that 86 percent of those persons whose LCUs during a one-year period were over 300 experienced some significant health problem; only 48 percent of these individuals scoring between 150 and 300 had similarly significant health problems.

There have been a number of other life-change scales developed and found to be associated with the subsequent development of health changes (Cline & Chosey 1972; Cochrane & Robertson 1973). This research strongly suggests the importance of the stress associated with life changes in the development of medical problems. Future long-term studies will more clearly isolate the causal factor involved in this relationship.

LIFE EVENT	LCUs
Death of spouse	100
Divorce	73
Marital separation	65
Jail term	63
Death of close family member	63
Personal injury or illness	53
Marriage	50
Fired at work	47
Marital reconciliation	45
Retirement	45
Change in health of family member	44
Pregnancy	40
Sex difficulties	39
Gain of new family member	39
Business readjustment	39
Change in financial state	38
Death of close friend	37
Change to different line of work	36
Change in number of arguments with spouse	35
Mortgage over $10,000	31
Foreclosure of mortgage or loan	30
Change of responsibilities at work	29

LIFE EVENT	LCUs
Son or daughter leaving home	29
Trouble with in-laws	29
Outstanding personal achievement	28
Wife begins or stops work	26
Begin or end school	26
Change in living conditions	25
Revision of personal habits	24
Trouble with boss	23
Change in work hours or conditions	20
Change in residence	20
Change in schools	20
Change in recreation	19
Change in church activities	19
Change in social activities	18
Mortgage or loan less than $10,000	17
Change in sleeping habits	16
Change in number of family get-togethers	15
Change in eating habits	15
Vacation	13
Christmas	12
Minor violations of the law	11

exacerbating, or prolonging the disorder. These physical conditions would be listed according to the comprehensive classification system of the International Classification of Diseases (1968), which would delineate the actual physical condition from which the patient suffers. A code number from the DSM-III would then be attached to indicate that psychological factors are important in the etiology of the condition. This number would indicate the degree to which psychological factors play a role—either "probable," "prominent," or "unknown."

Such a classification system, likely to be adopted in the DSM-III, would provide clinicians with important information and allow them to avoid considering a given condition exclusively in psychological or organic terms. It should also help promote an integrated psychological-somatic approach to patient cure and medical research.

We will next discuss six of the most prevalent forms of psychophysiological disorders—asthma, dysmenorrhea, essential hypertension, headache, neurodermatitis, and peptic ulcers.

MAJOR FORMS OF PSYCHOPHYSIOLOGICAL DISORDERS

ASTHMA Asthma is a disorder of the respiratory system, characterized by shortness of breath, coughing, wheezing, and a sensation of choking, which is caused by a decrease in the diameter of the bronchi through which air passes to the lungs. These constrictions are produced by swelling of the bronchial mucosa and/or contraction of the bronchial muscles. Asthmatic attacks usually begin suddenly, with the symptoms lasting anywhere from less than an hour to several hours or even days. They vary in intensity from mild attacks of wheezing to intense attacks in which breathing becomes so difficult that the patient feels he or she is suffocating. Between these attacks, no abnormal symptoms are usually detected. Asthma is a common psychophysiological disorder, with an estimated occurrence of approximately 4–5 percent in the general population.

As noted earlier, Rees (1964) isolated three causal factors when examining the case histories of children with asthma: (1) Allergy factor, in which some substance (e.g., an allergen such as pollen or dust) causes a chemical reaction that constricts the bronchi. This factor was found to be the dominant cause in 17 percent of the cases examined. (2) Infection factor, which was found dominant in 42 percent of the cases. Rees noted that 35 percent of the children had their first asthmatic attacks during a respiratory infection. Moreover, 80 percent of the patients had a history of respiratory infection during the development of asthma, in contrast to only 30 percent of nonasthmatic control children. The most common type of respiratory infection was acute bronchitis. (3) Psychological factors such as anxiety, depression, and other emotional reactions

which may cause an asthmatic attack. This factor was found dominant in 30 percent of the cases.

These data indicate that infection and psychological factors are very important in the etiology of asthma. The fact that psychological factors were found dominant in only 30 percent of the cases indicates that, contrary to most common conceptions, asthma is not always a psychophysiological disorder. Multiple causations are most common, with the majority of cases involving two or all of these factors in various sequences and combinations.

DYSMENORRHEA Dysmenorrhea, classified as a psychophysiological disorder of the genitourinary system, is characterized by irregular or painful menstrual periods. An accurate estimate of the percentage of women who suffer from this disorder is difficult to determine because many women, because of cultural factors, accept menstruation as a bothersome and sometimes painful process that is simply "part of being a woman" and so do not seek medical help for menstruation-related problems. Moreover, many doctors still dismiss such problems as "purely emotional," merely recommend painkillers, and seldom thoroughly look for organic involvement. As a result of these difficulties in estimating its exact frequency of occurrence, estimates of the percentage of American women with dysmenorrhea range all the way from 4 to 62 percent (Santamaria 1969).

No systematic, large-scale studies have clearly delineated the impact of psychological factors in the development of dysmenorrhea. The bulk of evidence suggesting such a relationship has been obtained from uncontrolled clinical observations. For example, many women report that changes in their life situation (e.g., moving away from their family) and the concomitant emotional effects produce changes in the length and level of pain produced by menstruation. Also, many women report that their menstrual cycles have been delayed when they feared they might be pregnant. Thus, clinical accounts do suggest that emotional factors are involved in this disorder. Controlled research is needed that will help validate these speculations.

ESSENTIAL HYPERTENSION Essential hypertension is characterized by chronically elevated blood pressure for which no organic cause is known. Hambling (1952) has distinguished three major stages in the development of this disorder. The first, or *prehypertension*, stage is marked by

PSYCHOLOGICAL APPROACHES TO SEXUAL PROBLEMS

Sexual dysfunctions involve physical impairments that appear to be significantly influenced by psychological factors. Psychological stress can affect the genitourinary system, which includes the organs and muscles that control urination, defecation, erection potential, orgasmic potential, ejaculatory potential, and other functions. Two broad types of psychophysiological genitourinary disorders that are associated with a great deal of emotional discomfort are *male coital inadequacy* and *female coital inadequacy*. The heading of male coital inadequacy includes the problems of *ejaculatory dysfunction* (premature ejaculation) and *impotence* (erection failure).

Ejaculatory dysfunctions often take the form of *premature ejaculation*. Until rather recently, premature ejaculation was not viewed as extremely problematic. But since the sexual responsiveness and satisfaction of women have begun to be considered in our society, male inadequacy has become more important. In fact, the definition of premature ejaculation is often determined by considering the feelings of the female. Masters and Johnson (1970), for example, refer to a premature ejaculator as one who fails to satisfy his female partner during at least 50 percent of their coital connections. Other sex researchers specify a time; some state that orgasm or ejaculation within 60 seconds is a criterion. But there seems to be no absolute time. In simple terms, it is assumed that the longer the male postpones ejaculation, the greater will be his female partner's satisfaction.

Regarding the cause of premature ejaculation, Marmor (1976) suggests that many males are conditioned (perhaps through masturbation) to focus predominantly on achieving orgasm while playing down "the other sensual and interpersonal aspects of lovemaking." Masters and Johnson (1970) suggest the same thing: that some males have learned to produce rapid orgasms. For instance, as an adolescent, it might be necessary for a boy to masturbate to reach climax as rapidly as possible, thereby lessening his chances of getting caught. Probably other reasons, such as anxiety or fear of failure in performing also account for premature ejaculation.

Masters and Johnson's treatment for premature ejaculation involves deemphasizing performance, working with the female partner and instructing her in a method called the *squeeze method*: just prior to ejaculation, the male is told to signal her of the onset, at which time she removes and squeezes the penis for a few seconds before re-inserting it. Other techniques involve having the two people press their pubic bones together for a few seconds until his urge to ejaculate is reduced (Goldstein 1976).

Impotence is the second type of male coital inadequacy. The term refers to the inability of a male to achieve an erection sufficient to engage in intercourse (Marmor 1976). While premature ejaculation has probably always occurred with fairly consistent frequency, Liddick (1972) and other sex researchers argue that impotence is on the increase, in part because of the new demands placed on the male. The women's liberation movement, according to Liddick, has put more pressure on the male to perform well in the sex act. It should be noted also that erection difficulties increase with age (Kinsey et al. 1948). Reynolds (1977) has recently reviewed various techniques that have been used in the treatment of this problem behavior.

Problems of female coital inadequacy include *orgasmic dysfunction*, *frigidity*, *dyspareunia*,

the individual's reacting to psychological stress or pain with a diastolic blood pressure response of over 95 mm of mercury (the normal resting diastolic blood pressure level is about 80 mm of mercury). The second, or *benign hypertension*, stage is characterized by a labile or fluctuating blood pressure and a permanent diastolic blood pressure level of above 95. Also, in response to this chronically elevated blood pressure, the walls of the small arteries thicken slightly. Finally, in the third, or *malignant hypertension*, stage, diastolic blood pressure level is permanently above 130. This severe elevation of blood pressure can cause physical damage to the kidneys, the retinas of the eyes, and other bodily organs.

It is assumed that hypertension is related to chronic stress produced by environmental and psychological factors. Most individuals demon-

and *vaginismus*. Orgasmic dysfunctions, according to Masters and Johnson (1970), are of two essential forms: (1) women who have never experienced an orgasm; and (2) women who have experienced orgasms before, but are currently unable to do so. *Frigidity*, by contrast, involves repulsion of sexual contact with a male and almost invariably is accompanied by orgasmic dysfunction. The following case study describes frigidity in a 23-year-old female:

> I have a problem with my husband. I have not enjoyed sex since we got married. It was pretty good before, but now I can't stand for him to touch me. It's just getting unbearable! If he touches my breasts, I get cold shivers and my body tightens up all over. Sometimes I feel like screaming when he touches me! We do still have sex sometimes, but I don't enjoy it at all. In fact, it repulses me. I feel I have to go along with it sometimes, or he will wonder what is wrong with me. I don't think he is aware that if we had no sex relations, I'd be quite happy. (Loew, Grayson, & Loew 1975, p. 153)

The causes of orgasmic dysfunctions and frigidity are generally thought to be psychogenic, but the evidence is only sketchy. Factors that have been linked to both these reactions include disturbed interpersonal relationship between the woman and her partner (McDermott 1970); traumatic sexual experience with a male (Marmor 1976); guilt and shame induced by religious beliefs (Masters & Johnson 1970); heterosexual aversion or homosexual inclination (Ellis 1973). Treatments for orgasmic dysfunctions and frigidity are numerous, but in recent years the most popular have involved behavior therapy, in particular systematic desensitization (Lazarus 1975) and a technique developed by Masters and Johnson (1970). Sotile and Kilmann (1977) have reviewed the literature that indicates the success of these procedures. Although systematic desensitization involves learning to relax in the presence of anxiety-evoking stimuli (the male penis, for example), the behavior therapy technique advocated by Lazarus is complemented with role playing, thought-stopping techniques, group therapy, and marital counseling. The Masters and Johnson approach essentially involves the treatment of male and female as a unit, reeducating them in emotional and sexual responsiveness. Ellis (1973) also notes that the male partner should be involved in the therapy. Ellis emphasizes that the male should learn to be more gentle, but also instructs him on special areas of female sexual sensation. The woman, according to Ellis, should practice thinking about things that arouse her sexually.

Dyspareunia refers to painful intercourse experienced by the female; *vaginismus* refers to irregular and involuntary contractions of the vaginal muscles prior to or during intercourse. The two disorders tend to occur together (Marmor 1976). If these two reactions are emotionally or psychologically induced, the subject's history and background often will reveal etiological variables. Masters and Johnson list three contributing stressors: strong religious life, traumatic sexual experience; and heterosexual aversion. For these disorders too, Masters and Johnson emphasize treating male and female together. Behavioral approaches have been found to be effective in the treatment of these disorders.

strate a physiological response to stress characterized by, among other reactions, acceleration of the heart rate and constriction of the arterial walls. These reactions, especially the arterial constriction, lead to an elevation of blood pressure. Chronic hypertension, as Hambling indicates, can lead to serious consequences such as kidney damage or a heart attack or stroke due to the persistent stress on the heart. It is a serious disorder and is currently a critical health problem in the United States; the American Heart Association estimates that approximately one out of every nine Americans suffers from hypertension. Hypertension is an especially dangerous disorder because it is frequently present for many years without any serious symptoms or signs except the elevated blood pressure level. As a result, it may not be diagnosed and treated until it reaches a critical stage of

Vicki Lawrence/Stock, Boston

The incidence of headaches is high in the general population. Many headaches are psychological reactions to stressful situations.

development in which organ damage has already occurred or the person has suffered a heart attack or stroke.

HEADACHE Headaches can result from a wide variety of organic causes such as tumors, systemic infections, concussions, etc. The great majority of headaches, however, are psychophysiological in nature and can be divided into two major categories: (1) migraine headaches and (2) muscle contraction or tension headaches. These are common in the general population. The incidence of migraine headaches has been estimated to be about 8 percent of the population. There are no reliable statistics on the incidence of muscle contraction or tension headaches, but they are much more common than migraines, and about 30 percent of the population suffer at least occasional tension headaches.

Migraine headaches are cardiovascular disorders that are believed to result from severe dilation or stretching of the blood vessels in the brain, so that more blood is delivered to an area than it can adequately handle. Also, a pain threshold chemical (*bradykinin* or *neurokinin*) is thought

to be released at the site of the dilated vessels, causing an inflammatory reaction. *Edema* develops (i.e., the walls of the blood vessels become filled with fluid), resulting in a sharp, painful, and throbbing sensation in the head; the pain often is unilateral, that is, on only one side of the head. The headache is often preceded by an *aura*, a subjective sensation alerting the person that the headache is about to start. Other symptoms such as nausea, vomiting, and dizziness may accompany it. Migraine headaches usually do not occur during an immediate period of stress, but rather during the post-stress period. They can last anywhere from a few hours to several days.

Clinicians such as Dalessio (1972) have distinguished among at least three subcategories of migraine headaches: (1) *Classic migraine* occurs periodically, with a frequency ranging from a few times a week to a few times in an entire lifetime. The headache is preceded by *prodromal* visual symptoms such as zigzag lines in the visual field. The headache pain itself is unilateral, with a steady ache spreading to other parts of the head in the later stages. Nausea, vomiting, and loss of appetite usually accompany the migraine attacks. (2) *Common migraine*, sometimes called ''Monday'' or ''weekend'' headache, appears to be directly tied to some specific environmental stress. The headache usually involves a steady pain, which is not always unilateral as in classic migraine. There are usually no significant prodromal symptoms but, in classic migraine, nausea and vomiting can occur. (3) *Cluster headache* is characterized by a series of closely spaced attacks (e.g., several within a one-day period) followed by a remission of months or years. The pain is extremely severe and unilateral and is often accompanied by excessive sweating and flushing. Prodromal symptoms, nausea, and vomiting are usually not present.

Muscle contraction or tension headaches are quite different from migraine headaches. They are caused by sustained contraction of the head and neck muscles. They often last for days or weeks and usually begin during an immediate stress period. There are no significant prodromal symptoms, and the headache itself consists of a nonthrobbing ache, with a sensation of tightness frequently described as a feeling of a ''tight band'' around the head.

Clinical observation frequently reveals an association between emotionally stressful events and the emergence of symptoms in chronic headache sufferers. Wolff conducted a number of studies using an "emotional provocation technique" to precipitate headaches in patients (Dalessio 1972). The psychological stress produced by this technique, in which patients were criticized and rebuked for their behavior, was found to trigger headache attacks. Bakal (1975) thoroughly reviewed the literature on migraine and muscle contraction headaches and concluded that headache appears to be a psychological reaction to stressful stimulation.

NEURODERMATITIS   This common type of skin disorder is characterized by chronic, nonallergic reddening of the skin and by skin eruptions, ranging from rashes to running sores, accompanied by intense itching. These symptoms are similar to those of other psychophysiological skin disorders such as eczema, psoriasis, and hives. It is therefore often difficult for the untrained eye to differentiate one from another.

Emotional or psychological factors are assumed to be involved in skin disorders such as neurodermatitis because it is readily demonstrated that the skin responds to emotional situations (e.g., facial blushing when embarrassed). If chronic, such modification of the blood circulation beneath the skin can be damaging, because the health of the skin is dependent on proper blood circulation. Skin reactions associated with emotional stress usually clear up when the stress situation is alleviated, but may be resistant to medical treatment if the stress situation is not alleviated, both factors suggesting the psychosomatic nature of these disorders.

Although neurodermatitis usually clears up when stress is eliminated, it may leave some residual scars if the skin was especially itchy and continually scratched. It also may leave "psychological scars" since most cases are clearly visible and often unsightly, causing a poor self-concept and a disruption of interpersonal relationships because of extreme self-consciousness. Even though skin disorders are not of the life-threatening type of psychophysiological disorders such as hypertension, they can seriously disrupt an individual's life and level of self-esteem.

PEPTIC ULCERS   A peptic ulcer is a lesion or sore in the lining of the stomach or the upper part of the small intestine or duodenum which lies immediately below the stomach. Ulcers are quite common in the general population, and sometimes are "quiet," in the sense that they cause no pain or discomfort and remain unnoticed and therefore unreported. More

© 1976 by Ray Ellis, Rapho/Photo Researchers

Some clinicians claim that biofeedback therapy has been effectively employed in the treatment of migraine headaches. One particular technique, pictured here, involves training the subject to raise her hand temperature. The rationale for this technique is that hand temperature is inversely related to blood vessel dilation in the head, which is involved in the production of these headaches. Raising the temperature of the hands reduces the dilation of the vessels.

often than not, however, an individual feels discomfort, ranging from a "burning sensation" in the stomach, usually the first sign of an ulcer, to severe pain (caused by enlargement of the lesion) accompanied by nausea and vomiting. If the ulcer perforates (breaking blood vessels in the walls of the stomach), vomiting of blood will occur. If hemorrhaging and internal bleeding are severe, the person may die.

Peptic ulcers are thought to be produced by excessively high levels of gastric acid secretion (specifically, hydrochloric acid). The stomach produces acid to aid in the digestive process, but the walls of the stomach and duodenum have a protective mucous lining that normally is able to resist its mildly corrosive action. If the stomach continues to secrete acid even when food is no longer present, however, then the acid may begin to eat away the protective mucous lining in the stomach of individuals who cannot tolerate this excessive secretion. When the output of acid is excessive and a particular site is no longer resistant to the acid, an ulcer will develop.

The most popular theory to explain the excessive secretion of stomach acid in the absence of food is that psychological stress causes an increase in secretion. This theory is based on both animal and human research demonstrating a relationship between stress and gastric acid secretion activity. In one of the earliest demonstrations of the relationship between emotional stress and acid secretion in humans, Wolf and Wolff (1947) reported a case study of a patient called Tom. Tom underwent an operation to repair some severe gastrointestinal damage. During the course of the operation, a plastic window was inserted over Tom's stomach, allowing physicians to observe his gastric functioning. Whenever Tom was exposed to an emotionally stressful stimulus, his flow of gastric acid would increase.

In research with animals, it has been demonstrated that persistent exposure of rats to stress (unpredictable or uncontrollable electric shock) leads to a significant increase in the ulceration rate (e.g., Price 1972; Weiss 1968). A widely publicized earlier study by Brady, Porter, Conrad, and Mason (1958), which became known as the "executive monkey" study, reported that ulcers were not produced in all monkeys exposed to uncontrollable electric shock, but only in those who could actively control the occurrence of this stress and avoid it by pressing a bar. Brady and colleagues interpreted these results to suggest that the ulcers were due to the pressure and responsibility of actively responding and attempting to control stressful events. These data were used to support the popular, but unsubstantiated, notion that ulcers

are more frequent in persons in responsible, high-level, executive positions. However, there was a major methodological flaw in the design of the Brady study that put the interpretability of these results seriously in question.

The Brady results now appear to be an artifact of the manner in which the monkeys were assigned to the two experimental groups (four monkeys in each group). All monkeys were originally placed on the "executive" schedule, and the first four who started pressing the bar became the "executives"; the last four were assigned to the uncontrollable group. Since this study, it has been demonstrated that the more emotional a monkey is, the sooner it begins pressing the bar when it is shocked (e.g., Sines, Cleeland, & Adkins 1963). So in fact, the four most emotional animals, those possibly genetically predisposed to develop ulcers, were assigned to the "executive" group. The four least emotional became the uncontrollable group subjects. This created a major methodological problem in the study.

Weiss (1968, 1971) repeated this type of "executive" study, but with a truly random assignment of rats to experimental groups. The results of these studies showed unequivocally that the executive animals who could control shock got fewer ulcers than the nonexecutive rats. These latter animals demonstrated more anxiety in the form of ulcer severity.

Research to date therefore indicates that exposure to emotional stress is associated with an increase in gastric secretion and, therefore, an increased likelihood of stomach ulcerations. From the above results of Weiss, it also appears that lack of control is an emotional stress associated with ulceration.

CAUSES AND STRESSORS

PSYCHOANALYTIC THEORY

The first psychological formulation of psychosomatic disorders was Freud's elaboration of conversion hysteria. Although conversion hysteria was not considered a psychosomatic disorder because there was no actual organic dysfunction, the basic

psychological mechanisms in both were considered similar. As you will recall from earlier chapters, psychoanalytic theory assumes that when socially unacceptable and forbidden impulses cannot be expressed, they will be repressed and alternative channels for discharging them will be sought. If appropriate alternative channels cannot be found, more drastic methods will be employed, such as those that occur in hysterical conversion reactions. For example, if a child's wish to strike his or her parents is unacceptable because of the threat of severe punishment, and if repression cannot adequately defend against the expression of this impulse, then the child might develop paralysis of the arm. This is a compromise coping method that allows the simultaneous discharge of energy and a defense against the action. Repressed instinctual impulses, therefore, are expressed at a somatic level, through the production of a somatic symptom that has a meaningful symbolic relationship to the psychic event. Psychophysiological disorders were interpreted in a similar fashion.

This formulation was subsequently expanded to emphasize the importance of *regression* in accounting for which psychophysiological symptoms a person chooses to develop. It was assumed that the physical symptom is the result of regression to an earlier stage of development associated with an unresolved conflict that resulted in fixation at this stage. That is, the present complaint symbolizes the point in the patient's developmental life history that was associated with trauma. Whereas neuroses are viewed in terms of regression to earlier *psychological* periods, psychosomatic disorders are regressions to earlier *physiological* periods, reproducing a physiological response elicited at the time of the original conflict. For example, an individual who had a great deal of conflict associated with feeding during the oral stage of development, resulting in anxiety and fixation, may develop gastrointestinal symptoms such as ulcers. The disorder of the digestive system symbolizes the conflict associated with the feeding situation.

Even many psychoanalysts have regarded this psychodynamic formulation as highly speculative, and there has been little supportive evidence for it. A more widely accepted psychodynamic approach is that of Franz Alexander (1950), who suggested that each of the psychophysiological disorders has its own specific psychodynamic constellation and personality characteristics. His formulation was based to a large extent on clinical observation of patients undergoing psychoanalysis. He believed that repressed psychic energy could be discharged directly to the autonomic nervous system, leading to impairment of visceral functioning. He assumed that specific unconscious emotional conflicts were associated with specific psychosomatic disturbances; the following are some of the associations hypothesized:

- *Ulcer*: Alexander assumed that ulcer patients have significant dependency needs. The classical "ulcer personality," characterized by the desire to be cared for, is usually opposed by observable opposite tendencies toward independence, aggression, and achievement. It is assumed that a reaction formation against the childish needs for help and dependency takes the form of assuming an excessive amount of responsibility. Alexander suggests that the great need for parental love becomes repressed and produces the parasympathetic overactivity that can lead to ulcers. The physiological consequence is that the stomach is always "preparing to receive food, which is symbolically equated with parental love" (Buss 1966, p. 405).
- *Asthma*: According to Alexander, an unresolved, childish relationship with one's mother is the basic underlying conflict of this disorder. The basic unconscious wish is to be nurtured and protected by a maternal figure, and there is a great fear of being separated from the mother. Alexander suggests that the asthmatic, because of this fear, has a strong impulse to cry for the mother, but is prevented from displaying such behavior because of the shame and guilt it would produce. If the individual should start crying, it is extremely difficult to stop. The asthmatic attack is viewed as superficially resembling an attempt to stop crying or to hold back tears, with a similar breathing pattern of wheezing, sniffing, and shallow, irregular respiration.
- *Essential hypertension*: Alexander emphasizes the importance of rage as the major emotion underlying essential hypertension. It is assumed that the individual has a great many hostile impulses that cannot be discharged.

There has not been much research to support the validity of Alexander's formulations, except in the case of essential hypertension, where there has been some support for the presence of certain personality characteristics (Buss 1966). However, the evidence is far from conclusive, and the notion of repressed hostility and rage has been presented to account for many other psychological disorders. Moreover, some investigators have found clear-cut

NETWORK © 1976, United Artists. An individual who is chronically exposed to stressors that produce a great deal of **emotional strain has an increased probability of developing physiological and psychological problems.**

personality correlates of high blood pressure and others have not (e.g., McGinn, Harburg, Julius, & McLeod 1964). The evidence is still very much equivocal even for this aspect of Alexander's theory.

OTHER PERSONALITY-TRAIT APPROACHES

There have been numerous other attempts to delineate personality traits that are associated with specific psychophysiological disorders. Indeed, the view that a disorder such as peptic ulcers is typical of the ambitious, high-achieving, hard-working executive is engrained in popular folklore and language. This particular view, though, has not been substantiated. In fact, it has been reported that ulcers are more likely to develop in blue-collar workers who are chronically discontented with their jobs (Kahn 1969).

Coronary-prone personality characteristics. A more recent personality-trait approach suggesting the relationship between a particular constellation of personality traits and a psychophysiological disorder—hypertension and related cardiovascular disorders—has been presented by Friedman and Rosenman (1974). They suggest that the Type A personality is characterized by the aggressive, high-achieving individual who does everything rapidly—eats, talks, walks, etc. This person becomes easily frustrated and fidgety if he or she must wait at a traffic light or in a line, and is typically upset if

kept waiting in any situation. The Type A person feels very guilty if he or she is relaxing and not working. This personality type is assumed to be likely to develop hypertension and other cardiovascular disorders. In contrast, the Type B personality, who is associated with the opposite characteristics, is assumed to be less susceptible to cardiovascular disorders.

Research evidence is still being collected to test this formulation. However, even if the evidence demonstrates a relationship between Type A/Type B personality characteristics and hypertension, an important question that will remain is why some hard-driving Type A individuals develop hypertension while others do not. Other factors, such as biological/genetic predisposition, most likely will need to be taken into account. (Later in this chapter we will review a diathesis-stress model of psychophysiological disorders.)

Personality characteristics and cancer. Some interesting recent research has suggested a relationship between certain personality traits and cancer. Wittkower and Dudek (1973) suggested that malignant diseases such as cancer may be partially precipitated by psychological factors. Greer and Morris (1975) directly evaluated the relationship between personality characteristics and the incidence of breast cancer. In this study, a total of 160 women who were diagnosed as having a breast tumor were interviewed and given a battery of psychological tests on the day before undergoing an exploratory operation to determine whether the tumor was malignant (cancerous) or benign. Following the operation, it was found that 69 of the women had breast cancer and 91 had benign tumors. A major finding of the study was an association between the manner in which emotions, especially anger, were expressed or inhibited and the presence of breast cancer. Those women who were either extreme expressors of anger (e.g., had frequent temper outbursts) or extreme suppressors of anger (e.g., very rarely openly showed their anger) had a higher incidence of breast cancer than did those women who were normal expressors of anger.

An important feature of this study is that the psychological and interview data were collected before either the patient or the investigator knew whether the tumor was malignant. This feature in experimental design increases one's confidence in suggesting a cause-effect relationship. Of course, these results must be independently replicated by other investigators to ensure their reliability. If they are replicated, the implications are great for the area of disease prevention. For example, it may prove beneficial to teach individuals less extreme ways of handling emotions such as anger. Research on other forms of cancer may also reveal similar relationships.

SPECIFIC-ATTITUDES THEORY A variation of the personality-trait conceptualizations is the *specific-attitudes* theory proposed by Graham and colleagues (Graham 1962; Graham, Stern, & Winokur 1958). These investigators conducted a series of experiments examining the relationship between specific attitudes toward a distressing life situation and the occurrence of particular psychophysiological disorders. These attitudes, which related to what individuals felt was happening to them and what they wanted to do about it, were originally obtained in clinical interviews with patients suffering from various psychophysiological disorders.

The attitudes were assessed first in a study by Grace and Graham (1952) in which 128 patients with 12 different psychosomatic disorders or symptoms were evaluated. This evaluation indicated that patients with the same disorder showed similarities in describing their attitudes toward events that occurred just before the appearance or worsening of their symptoms. Subsequent and better-controlled studies further validated the presence of these attitudes (Graham, Lundy, Ben-

jamin, Kabler, Lewis, Kunish, & Graham 1962), leading these investigators to conclude that different psychophysiological disorders were indeed associated with different attitudes. Some of the associations found were:

- *Acne*: The individual feels he or she is being picked on and wants to be left alone.
- *Asthma*: The person feels left out in the cold, and wants to shut out another individual or the situation.
- *Hives*: The individual feels he or she is taking a beating and feels helpless to do anything about it.
- *Hypertension*: The person feels threatened with harm by an ever-present danger and, as a result, needs to be on guard, watchful, and prepared.
- *Migraine*: The person feels that something has to be achieved and then relaxes after the effort.
- *Raynaud's disease*: The individual wants to take hostile physical action but does not have any idea what the actual act should be.
- *Ulcers*: The person feels deprived of what is due him or her and wants to seek revenge and get even.

Graham and colleagues reasoned that if the specific-attitudes theory is correct, it would then follow that experimentally inducing a particular attitude should elicit the associated physiological reaction in normal subjects, since these reactions precede the actual development of psychophysiological disorders. For example, the feeling of being mistreated and taking a beating while believing that one is helpless to do anything about it (the attitude associated with hives) would be expected to elicit a rise in skin temperature. If this happened chronically, it would be expected to lead to the development of a skin disorder such as hives. To partially test this hypothesis, Graham, Stern, and Winokur (1958) hypnotized normal subjects and presented them with suggestions designed to produce the specific attitudes associated with either hives or Raynaud's disease (a disorder involving cold hands caused by poor blood circulation). These two disorders were selected by the investigators because the skin temperature responses are different. Each subject was tested twice, once with each attitude. Inducing the "hives attitude" produced an increase in skin temperature, while the "Raynaud's disease attitude" produced a decrease in skin temperature. Thus, the hypothesis was confirmed. In a subsequent study, Graham, Kabler, and Graham (1962) hypnotically induced the hypertension attitude and found that it produced an increase in diastolic blood pressure.

Although these results partially support the specific-attitudes theory, some conflicting results also have been reported (Buss 1966; Peters & Stern 1971). In the Peters and Stern (1971) study, the results for hives and Raynaud's disease could not be replicated. When subjects high in hypnotic susceptibility were hypnotized, the attitudes associated with hives and with Raynaud's disease both produced a decrease in skin temperature.

In addition to these conflicting results, Buss (1966) has indicated that it is highly doubtful that the large number of specific attitudes listed by Graham and colleagues (a dozen or more) will each be found to be associated with a specific physiological response pattern. So, although this theory shows some promise, more research is needed to validate it, with appropriate modifications of the theory itself depending on the results of this future research.

LEARNING THEORY

Learning theory views psychophysiological disorders, like other behaviors, as learned responses. It is assumed that both classical and instrumental (operant) conditioning, especially the latter, can play a role in these disorders. To date, however, no specific comprehensive learning model has been proposed to account for the development or exacerbation of the various psychophysiological disorders.

Since Pavlov's early work, it has been reliably demonstrated that physiological functioning can be classically conditioned (e.g., Cannon 1929; Lacey 1956). It is thus assumed that certain physiological response patterns can be classically conditioned to produce a psychophysiological disorder and that the disorder also can generalize to other situations. In one case study, Dekker, Pelse, and Groen (1957) demonstrated how, through classical conditioning, a neutral stimulus paired with pollen could come to elicit an asthmatic attack by itself in an individual who is allergic to pollen.

**GRAHAM'S
CARTOONS
Figure 7.1**

Graham showed these cartoons to hospitalized patients who had psychophysiological disorders. The patients were then asked to choose the cartoon that reminded them the most of a situation they had been in. The results of the study support the hypothesis that specific attitudes are related to specific physical symptoms. Pictured here are cartoons most often chosen by patients with the following disorders:
(a) Hives: This person feels he is taking a beating (being unfairly treated or mistreated), and is helpless to do anything about it.
(b) Raynaud's disease: This person wishes to take hostile action, such as hitting or strangling.
(c) Essential hypertension: This person feels that he is threatened with harm and has to be on guard.
(d) Duodenal ulcer: This person feels deprived of what is due him and wants to get even. (From Graham 1962. Courtesy of the author and University of Wisconsin Press and the Regents of the University of Wisconsin; Reprinted in Sternbach 1966)

A   B   C   D

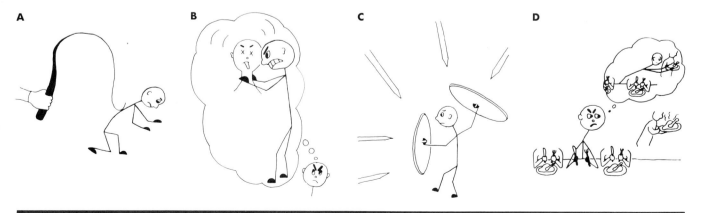

Two asthma patients inhaled allergens (unconditioned stimulus), to which they were very sensitive. Inhalations of a neutral substance served as the conditioned stimulus. After a series of trials pairing the allergens and the neutral substance, asthmatic attacks could be elicited by the once neutral substance alone. Thus, classical conditioning can significantly broaden the range of stimuli/situations that can precipitate an attack. This possibility has also been noted by Bandura (1969).

Instrumental or operant conditioning is viewed as the dominant form of conditioning or learning involved in the development of psychophysiological disorders. Lang (1970) notes that if a change in physiological functioning (for example, stomach contractions that produce indigestion) is consistently rewarded—by increased attention, for instance, or the availability of an excuse to avoid participating in an unpleasant situation or task—then it may come to be a learned mode of dealing with the environment to achieve some desired goal. The physiological change may be maintained for this secondary gain and may eventually produce tissue damage and disturbance of functioning.

It has been shown that a wide variety of physiological responses, including autonomic responses, can be instrumentally conditioned (e.g., Miller 1969). Turnbull (1962) has experimentally demonstrated that the reinforcement of certain breathing patterns can induce respiratory patterns that progressively come to approximate asthmatic breathing.

The behavioral/learning examination of psychophysiological disorders is still in the early stage of development. Future research will need to delineate more clearly the exact learning mechanisms involved and how they may interact with biological predispositions.

PHYSIOLOGICAL FACTORS

One of the simplest and earliest theories of psychophysiological disorders, proposed by the psychoanalyst Alfred Adler, is that they occur because of a bodily weakness, either a weak *organ* such as the stomach (ulcers) or a weak physiological *system* such as the cardiovascular system (essential hypertension). It is assumed that this bodily weakness can be inherited or can develop as a result of disease, such as a respiratory infection predisposing an individual to develop asthma. As we noted earlier, Rees (1964) found that 80 percent of the

Neal E. Miller has demonstrated that blood pressure, heart rate, and other autonomic responses can be operantly conditioned using biofeedback procedures.

asthmatics he examined had suffered from a previous respiratory infection.

An extension of the *weak organ/system* theory is that specific physiological response patterns to situations, including stressful ones, are inherited. This is known as the *specific-response pattern* approach. It has often been shown that individuals differ in physiological responding to situations (e.g., Lacey 1967). One person may demonstrate an increase in heart rate and blood pressure level, but little increase in muscle tension; another person in the same situation may display very little increase in heart rate and blood pressure, but a great increase in muscle tension. This difference in response patterns is known as *individual response specificity*. As an example of these individual differences in an actual clinical population, Malmo and Shagass (1949) demonstrated that under stress, patients with cardiovascular symptoms showed more cardiovascular response than increase in muscle tension, whereas patients with muscle tension headaches showed an opposite pattern.

The *specific-response pattern* approach assumes that individuals tend to respond to stressful situations in their own idiosyncratic ways. The particular physiological system or organ that is most constantly activated, and therefore more stressed, may be susceptible to a breakdown and the resultant development of a psychophysiological disorder. That is, the person who persistently responds to situations with a greatly elevated blood pressure level may sufficiently stress the cardiovascular system to cause a disruption of its homeostatic mechanism and, as a result, become susceptible to essential hypertension. There is some evidence to suggest that patterns of physiological reactivity are inherited, implying a possible genetic involvement in psychosomatic disorders.

GENETIC FACTORS

Richmond and Lustman (1955) recorded the autonomic responses of newborn babies (three to four days old) to a series of loud tones and found large, stable, individual differences. These data indicate that physiological response patterns are probably inherited, since there is little possibility that socialization/learning factors could have had any impact on their development in such young infants.

With reference to specific psychophysiological disorders, Mirsky (1958) demonstrated that *pepsinogen* levels of ulcer patients are significantly higher than those of patients without ulcers. Pepsinogen, a stomach secretion, is a good measure of gastric secretion activity. In the stomach, it is converted to the enzyme *pepsin* which digests proteins and which, together with hydrochloric acid, is the primary active agent in gastric digestive juices. Many investigators view an excess of pepsinogen as a cause of ulcers. In an initial study, Mirsky assessed significant individual differences in pepsinogen levels in newborn infants. Moreover, infants with high pepsinogen levels were likely to be members of families in which there was a high pepsinogen level. Thus, there is some evidence that pepsinogen level, which is seen as an important contributing factor in the development of ulcers, is genetically inherited.

In another study, Weiner, Thaler, Reiser, and Mirsky (1957) sought to evaluate whether oversecretors of pepsinogen were more prone to develop ulcers than undersecretors. From a group of newly inducted soldiers, a group of oversecretors and a group of undersecretors were selected on the basis of a gastrointestinal examination conducted before basic training. Only soldiers who did not have ulcers at the time were chosen for the study. At the end of basic training (approximately four months later), the men were reexamined. It was found that 14 percent of the oversecretors had developed ulcers, whereas none of the undersecretors had. A similar study by Mirsky (1958), conducted with a population of children and civilian adults, showed a similar tendency for ulcers to develop in those individuals with a high pepsinogen level.

Thus, the evidence indicates that individuals who develop ulcers may be genetically predisposed because of excessive secretion of gastric acid which, in turn, produces stomach lesions and ulcerations. Family studies have also suggested the importance of genetic factors. For example, Rosen and Gregory (1965) reported that brothers of ulcer patients are about twice as likely to develop ulcers as comparable members of the general population.

There has been little research systematically evaluating whether genetic influences are significant in the development of other psychosomatic disorders. Numerous family studies have shown that patients with various psychophysiological disorders come from families in which there is a high incidence of the same disorder, but such findings could be attributed to common factors in learning and experience rather than to a genetic factor. A number of studies, for example, have indicated that certain patterns of disturbed parent-child relationships are common in cases of childhood asthma (e.g., Purcell, Brady, Chai, Muser, Molk, Gordon, & Means 1969). Such common family relationship experiences could partially or totally explain the high family-incidence findings. A great deal of additional research, using better methodology such as twin studies, is needed to delineate the importance of genetic predispositions in the various psychophysiological disorders.

AN INTEGRATIVE DIATHESIS-STRESS MODEL

Sternbach (1966) has proposed a comprehensive model of psychophysiological disorders that takes into account many of the factors discussed so far. He presents these factors in an If-Then proposition, as reproduced in table 7.2.

Sternbach starts out with the concept of *individual response stereotypy*, which he sees as a constitutional predisposition to respond physiologically to a situation in a particular way, with consistent activation of certain physiological systems or organs. He next postulates the existence of *inadequate homeostatic restraints*. Inadequacy may be due to stress-induced breakdown, previous accident or infection, or genetic predisposition.

Finally, the *persistent exposure to activating situations* combines with the other two factors to produce a *psychosomatic episode*.

STRESS   Before reviewing Sternbach's model in further detail, we should briefly discuss the general concept of *stress*, which most workers view as one of the major activating situations in the production of psychophysiological disorders. Selye (1956) presented the first comprehensive and influential biological theory of stress, suggesting that the body reacts to a stressful/threatening situation by mobilizing its physiological resources. If the stress is too prolonged, these emergency resources become exhausted and a variety of physiological symptoms appear.

Selye refers to these symptoms as *diseases of adaptation*. The essential *alarm reaction* of a person to a stressful situation illustrates the initial onset of such symptoms, in which physiological responding is activated. Stress has long been considered important in psychophysiological disorders because of its significant impact on physiological responding. This case history illustrates the role that stress plays in a typical psychophysiological disorder, an ulcer-gastrointestinal reaction:

A CASE OF STRESS

Edward Polowski was examined by a specialist in internal medicine, and then referred to a clinical psychologist for further evaluation. The patient complained of a longstanding problem of severe cramps and diarrhea whenever he ate highly seasoned foods or encountered any type of stressful situation. This problem was diagnosed as an irritable colon when the patient was a child. Since that time, he had been treated by a series of physicians, all of whom confirmed this diagnosis. The patient reported the medications prescribed for him had varied in effectiveness, and he had recently been in severe discomfort.

Edward was 35 years old, married, and the father of a six-year-old boy and a two-year-old girl. He was a college graduate with a degree in library science and had been a librarian in the same city library since he graduated from college. Edward stated that he began having unusually severe gastrointestinal symptoms at the time that a new director was appointed to the library a number of months ago. . . .

Edward related that he had had numerous occurrences of intestinal difficulties ever since childhood. These episodes were associated with circumstances such as his mother or teacher insisting that he do something he did not want to do. He also became ill when he had to make a public appearance such as participating in his First Communion or in a play at school. His mother tended to be quite concerned about making him comfortable when he had intestinal symptoms, although she always told him that it was just a "nervous stomach." She said that she knew how he felt because she was also troubled with a "nervous stomach" when she was anxious or upset.

When Edward was nine years old, his mother took him to her physician because Edward was in severe discomfort. He was in the midst of an episode of cramps and diarrhea that lasted for about a week. The onset of the symptoms was associated with Edward's complaints that his new teacher was too strict and forced him to keep going over material he had already mastered. Edward stayed home from school during the latter part of that week, and the physician prescribed some medication which relieved a great deal of the discomfort. Mrs. Polowski pleaded with the doctor to call the school principal and explain the reason for Edward's symptoms. This was done and Edward reported that his teacher became somewhat more flexible in relation to his school activities. Edward had other occurrences of cramps during that school year, but none as severe as the earlier occasion.

Edward also had periodic intestinal problems while he was growing up, but these attacks usually lasted for just a few hours at a time. In high school, he experienced another prolonged occurrence of intestinal symptoms during a final examination period. Edward generally received good grades in school, but he was always quite

---

Sternbach 1966

	Individual response stereotypy		Inadequate homeostatic restraints		Exposure to activating situations
IF		**AND**		**AND**	

THEN
Psychosomatic
Episodes

anxious before a test because he was afraid that he would not do well. He was very anxious during these particular examinations because he had received lower grades than he had expected on some of his previous tests. He therefore studied a great deal and ignored his mother's assurances that he would do well on the exams.

Edward began having intestinal symptoms during the examination period, and the symptoms did not subside, even with medication, until ten days later when he went to a physician. He was given a complete medical examination, including a number of special tests of the gastrointestinal tract. These tests revealed no structural defects or damage, and the problem was again diagnosed as chronic irritable colon. Edward was given a new medication to take when he felt that the symptoms were about to recur. (Leon 1977, pp. 231-233)

Along with exposure to actual external activating/stressful situations, Sternbach also includes in his model the possibility that, in the absence of such objective real-life stressors, an individual may perceive ordinary situations or events as stressors and so react to them with heightened physiological responding. These misperceptions are due to the person's chronic attitudes (e.g., *specific attitudes*) or personality traits that significantly affect his or her perception and interpretation of stimuli. Sternbach (1966) summarizes his model as follows:

> . . . We begin with a person who has response-stereotypy to the extent that whatever the nature of the activating stimulus, one response system always or usually shows the greatest magnitudes of change as compared to his other response systems. This person also has a deficiency in feedback control so that either in initial responsiveness, or in rebound, some limit is exceeded by this maximally reactive system which results in some tissue damage or symptom appearance. This event will occur either when a stressful situation arises which is specifically stimulating to the response system in which the individual is also maximally reactive, or when any stressful situation occurs which is of sufficient intensity and/or frequency to result in maximum and/or frequent reactivity. In the absence of objective real-life stressors, this condition may be met by the individual whose set is such that he perceives ordinary events as if they were those stressors, and who will reveal the existence of that set both by the appearance of symptoms and by verbal expression of attitudes. . . . (p. 156)

Besides the factors proposed in Sternbach's model —genetic, physiological, attitude/personality—a host of variables obviously need to be taken into account in any comprehensive understanding of the various psychophysiological disorders. Clearly the investigation of psychophysiological disorders is complex. Treatment may have to be directed at a number of factors, such as the modification of stress-induced physiological overactivation and the individual's possible cognitive misperception of situations or events. A multimodal treatment approach will have to be taken.

There has been some recent animal research to support a diathesis-stress model of a particular psychosomatic disorder—hypertension. Friedman and Iwai (1976) demonstrated that when rats who were made genetically susceptible to hypertension through selective inbreeding were chronically exposed to psychological stress (an approach-avoidance conflict), they showed persistent elevation in systolic blood pressure. In contrast, rats who were genetically resistant to hypertension and who were exposed to the same psychological stress did not develop similar high blood pressure. These results indicate that psychic stress is selectively effective in producing hypertension-type effects depending on the animal's genetic predisposition. Such findings provide strong support for a diathesis-stress model of hypertension.

TREATMENT OF PSYCHOPHYSIOLOGICAL DISORDERS

Often the disturbing organic symptoms of some psychophysiological disorders (bleeding ulcers, coronary heart disease) demand immediate as well as long-range medical treatment. In such cases, medication and dietary patterns must be prescribed to deal effectively with the physical manifestations of the disorders. Simultaneously, treatment directed at modifying the psychological/behavioral causes and stressors should be administered.

Except for the fact that psychophysiological disorders may require medical treatment of organic pathology, the treatment of these disorders is similar to that of the neuroses. As with neurotic disorders, a major form of treatment is chemotherapy. Minor tranquilizers are commonly prescribed to reduce the anxiety and emotional tension usually associated with these disorders. As we emphasized in the last chapter, if tranquilizers are used in this way, they should be used in combination with some form of psychotherapy. Chemotherapy should not be used alone without a concomitant attempt to deal with the situational-interpersonal factors involved in the etiology and maintenance of the disorders. As we saw in the last chapter, a number of therapeutic techniques have been found to be effective in treating neurotic disorders. Many of these same techniques can also be used in the treatment of the anxiety component of psychophysiological disorders.

TRADITIONAL PSYCHOTHERAPY APPROACHES

We noted in chapter 6 that there is still a great deal of debate about whether traditional forms of psychotherapy are any more effective in treating psychopathology than no treatment at all. In the case of psychophysiological disorders, however, there appears to be little debate. Malan (1973), who assessed the various therapy-effectiveness survey review studies from the perspective of dynamic psychotherapy, found that the traditional psychotherapy approach is effective with psychophysiological disorders. One type of psychophysiological disorder that has been found to be especially responsive to this form of therapy is *ulcerative colitis* (ulceration and inflammation of the colon, often accompanied by disturbances in normal bowel functions). On the basis of research at the Psychoanalytic Clinic for Training and Research at Columbia University's College of Physicians and Surgeons, it has been shown that colitis patients can be effectively treated with psychoanalytically oriented psychotherapy (Karush, Daniels, O'Con-

BEHAVIOR THERAPY TECHNIQUES USED TO TREAT PSYCHOPHYSIOLOGICAL DISORDERS
Table 7.3

DISORDER	TREATMENT	INVESTIGATORS
Asthma	Systematic desensitization	Moore (1965)
	Respiratory resistance biofeedback	Feldman (1976)
Dysmenorrhea	Systematic desensitization	Mullen (1971)
Essential hypertension	Blood pressure biofeedback	Benson, Shapiro, Tursky, & Schwartz (1971); Elder, Ruiz, Deabler, & Dillenkoffer (1973)
Migraine headache	Systematic desensitization, assertive training	Mitchell & Mitchell (1971)
	Vasomotor biofeedback	Friar & Beatty (1976)
	Temperature biofeedback, autogenic training*	Sargent, Green, & Walters (1973)
Muscle contraction headache	EMG biofeedback†	Budzynski, Stoyva, Adler, & Mullaney (1973)
	EMG biofeedback, relaxation training	Chesney & Shelton (1976); Haynes, Griffin, Mooney, & Parise (1975)
Neurodermatitis	Relaxation training	Ratliff & Stein (1968)

*Autogenic training is a relaxation technique that uses simple imagery. It was developed by Schultz and Luthe (1959) for the treatment of a wide variety of psychological and somatic disorders.

†EMG biofeedback is a procedure that provides auditory and/or visual display of muscular activity. EMG means electromyography.

nor, and Stern 1969; O'Connor, Daniels, Karush, Moses, Flood, & Stein 1964). This research also demonstrated that ulcerative colitis patients who are characterized as being overly dependent and symbiotic in their interpersonal relationships (i.e., who see themselves as helpless victims of others, with a tendency to blame others for their frustrations and faults) are most responsive to insight-oriented psychotherapy. Weinstock (1962) has reported similar findings. Thus, there is evidence for the effectiveness of traditional psychotherapeutic techniques in the treatment of psychosomatic disorders.

BEHAVIORAL TREATMENT TECHNIQUES

Since most of the behaviorally oriented techniques were reviewed in the last chapter, we will only summarize the results demonstrating their effectiveness in treating various psychophysiological disorders.

Goldstein and Stein (1976) and Price (1974) have reviewed the application of behavior therapy to the treatment of various psychophysiological disorders. These procedures are directed at modifying the maladaptive psychosomatic disorders by teaching individuals new and more adaptive patterns of behavior and helping them develop more effective ways to cope with stress. Table 7.3 briefly summarizes the psychosomatic disorders found to be responsive to the various behavior therapy techniques and lists some of the relevant studies. However, a great deal of systematic research is still needed to validate unequivocally the clinical effectiveness of these techniques with the various psychosomatic disorders.

As has been noted, most behavior therapists use several different treatment procedures for a specific disorder, in order to deal effectively with all the important controlling or causal variables. For example, in training an individual with hypertension to relax and voluntarily lower his or her blood pressure levels, the therapist might also have to teach this person other methods for coping effectively with stressful situations. Blood pressure can be temporarily elevated as the result of inability to cope with perceived aggression or frustration (e.g., Hokanson & Burgess 1962). The individual may need to learn interpersonal social skills, such as assertion training, or cognitive restructuring techniques, in order to cope more effectively with such stressors.

The treatment of asthma. Price (1974) notes that asthmatics apparently can be divided into two groups according to the etiology of the disorder: those with a large somatic predisposition (e.g., an allergy) and those with a low somatic predisposition (i.e., psychological factors playing a predominant role). It would seem that psychological/behavioral techniques would be most effective with asthmatics having a low somatic predisposition. Indeed, Alexander (1972) found that asthmatics with low somatic predisposition respond better to relaxation training than do those with high somatic predisposition. Careful pre-treatment assessment of the etiology of this disorder is needed to differentiate between the two types of asthma, so that the most effective treatment (predominantly psychological or predominantly medical) can be administered. In the future, a similar differentiation may be found useful for other types of psychophysiological disorders.

DIAGNOSIS AND ASSESSMENT

INTERVIEW / REFERRAL

The symptoms of psychophysiological disorders are similar, and often identical, to those present in a systemic disease. The major initial goal of assessment, therefore, is to diagnose whether the array of symptoms presented by a patient are due

to some medical cause or whether emotional or psychological factors play the predominant role in the causation and exacerbation of the disorder. The general rule of assessment is that a particular disorder should not be diagnosed as psychophysiological until a complete and thorough physical evaluation has definitely ruled out medical factors as the prime cause, and unless there is also good evidence for the presence of psychological factors antecedent to the disorder. Most of the psychosomatic patients that a psychologist/psychiatrist sees are referral cases from physicians who, after being unable to find any major medical cause for the disorder, suspect that psychological factors may be playing an important role. Unfortunately, many physicians who are unable to isolate a specific medical cause for a disorder simply treat the symptoms by prescribing drugs that may produce temporary relief. However, as has been emphasized, such chemotherapy cannot be expected to produce long-term improvement in a disorder due primarily to psychological factors.

The first step in assessment is a complete physical examination to rule out specific medical problems. This examination may also be the basis for deciding whether to prescribe medication to control a disorder temporarily (e.g., drugs to control high blood pressure in hypertensive patients) and whether the patient needs to make dietary changes. If medical causes are ruled out, then clinical assessment is directed at isolating the specific psychological/situational factors that are causing or maintaining the problem behavior. Usually some emotional stressor or some difficult life situation that the person does not know how to cope with effectively is at the root of the problem behavior. Although there are exceptions, the clinical picture of psychophysiological disorders tends to be phasic, with the appearance or worsening of symptoms directly related to the amount of stress the individual is experiencing, and their disappearance related to a decrease in stress. A highly pressured and insecure business executive suffering from ulcers, for example, may find that they are quiescent and not bothersome during an extended vacation away from the pressures of the job. Once the specific causative factors are isolated, then a treatment program to deal effectively with the disorder can be constructed on the basis of this assessment.

TESTING

As in the psychometric assessment of other forms of psychopathology, the MMPI (Minnesota Multiphasic Personality Inventory) is often routinely used with psychophysiological disorders. Although there is no specific clinical scale in this test to diagnose

the presence of a psychosomatic disorder, there are a number of profile scale *patterns* that have proven to be reliable in their diagnosis. The most common of these profile patterns is the 1-2-3 type (simultaneously high scores on hysteria, depression, and hypochondriasis scales). As Gilberstadt and Duker (1965) note, the high-frequency symptoms associated with this profile type, which occur in various psychosomatic disorders, include

> . . . abdominal pain, anorexia, nausea, vomiting, anxiety, blindness — eye complaint, ear complaint, depression, dimness, headache, insomnia, irritability, nervousness, sexual difficulty, tension, weak — tired — fatigued, and worrying. (p. 25)

Psychophysiological disorders, however, are not limited to this profile pattern. Other pattern types have been found to diagnose specific forms of psychosomatic disorder. For example, specific profile patterns are associated with ulcer patients (Sullivan & Welsh 1952), headache patients (Dahlstrom & Welsh 1960), and neurodermatitis patients (Gilberstadt 1962).

Body image. In this discussion of testing, we should briefly review an approach developed by Fisher and Cleveland (1958). These investigators have proposed that psychosomatic disorders are related to *body image*. They are specifically interested in the *boundary* feature of body image; that is, whether the individual views his or her body as clearly and sharply bounded from external objects, or as lacking a clear demarcation from these external or "non-self" objects. They use the Rorschach Inkblot Test to assess this boundary feature. The more definite the boundary, the higher the *barrier* score and the lower the *penetration* score on the Rorschach. Examples of high barrier scores are test responses such as "man with armor," "turtle shell," etc.; high penetration scores are responses such as "broken body," "bleeding person." These scores are assumed to be related to the site of psychosomatic symptoms. High barrier scores have been found to be more frequent in patients with external surface symptoms such as arthritis and neurodermatitis, whereas high penetration scores are associated with patients suffering from internal symptoms such as stomach ulcers and ulcerative colitis.

There has been some experimental validation of the effectiveness of barrier/penetration Rorschach scores in differentiating between broad categories of psychophysiological disorders. Buss (1966) has provided a review of some of this research. Research to date, however, has not demonstrated this technique's effectiveness in reliably differentiating on a more specific basis, such as the delineation between ulcer patients and colitis patients, who both produce high penetration scores.

PROGNOSIS

As with the neuroses, the outlook for improvement in psychophysiological disorders is good if the appropriate type of treatment is administered. Of course, the degree of improvement still depends on the clinical skills of the therapist and his or her ability to isolate and effectively deal with all the major contributing factors maintaining the behavior disorder.

The major exception to the generally favorable prognosis for psychosomatic disorders is the instance in which some long-lasting dysfunction— such as severe ulceration of the stomach or chronic hypertension leading to coronary heart disease— has produced irreversible and clinically severe organic changes and damage. In such cases, the disappearance of symptoms cannot be expected, even if the stressors that originally caused the disorder are removed or the individual develops more effective coping skills. The only thing to be hoped for is that treatment will prevent the irreparable damage from becoming worse and will help the individual effectively adjust to the life changes produced by this permanent organic disease.

SUMMARY

1. Psychophysiological (or psychosomatic) disorders are characterized by physical symptoms that involve organs of the body and are caused by psychological factors.

2. Unlike certain neurotic disorders such as hysterical paralysis, in which there are physical symptoms but no actual underlying organic damage or defect, individuals with psychophysiological disorders have some real organic dysfunction.

3. The symptoms of psychophysiological disorders are similar, and often identical, to those present in a systemic disease. The distinction between the two is usually made on the basis of etiology: psychophysiological disorders have no known medical cause (they are idiopathic); they appear to be caused primarily by psychological or emotional factors.

4. The DSM-II included nine major categories of psychophysiological disorders. It has become increasingly recognized, however, that psychological or emotional factors play a very important role in the precipitation and/or exacerbation of most organic disorders. The classification system proposed in the DSM-III would take into account the degree to which psychological factors can influence any physical disorder.

5. We reviewed six of the most common types of psychophysiological disorders: (a) asthma, a disorder of the respiratory system characterized by shortness of breath, coughing, wheezing, and the sensation of choking; (b) dysmenorrhea, a disorder of the female genitourinary system characterized by irregular or painful menstrual periods; (c) essential hypertension, a cardiovascular disorder characterized by chronically elevated blood pressure; (d) headache, both the migraine type, believed to result from severe dilation or stretching

of the blood vessels in the brain, and the muscle-contraction type caused by sustained contraction of the head and neck muscles; (e) neurodermatitis, a common type of skin disorder characterized by chronic reddening of the skin and skin eruptions accompanied by intense itching; (f) peptic ulcers, lesions or sores in the lining of the stomach or upper part of the small intestine (duodenum).

6. An early psychoanalytic formulation of psychophysiological disorders was Freud's elaboration of his theory of conversion hysteria. This formulation was subsequently expanded to emphasize the defense mechanism of *regression* in accounting for the specific psychophysiological symptom a person develops. These psychoanalytic formulations, however, have been viewed as highly speculative even among psychoanalysts. A more widely accepted psychoanalytic approach is that of Franz Alexander, who suggested that each psychophysiological disorder has its own specific psychodynamic constellation and personality characteristics.

7. There have been numerous other attempts to delineate personality-trait characteristics that are associated with specific psychophysiological disorders. One such example is Friedman and Rosenman's hypothesis of Type A-Type B personality types and their relationship to cardiovascular disease.

8. A variation of personality trait conceptualizations is Graham's *specific-attitudes theory*. This theory suggests that there are specific attitudes that are associated with the occurrence of particular psychophysiological disorders. Although this approach shows promise, more controlled research is needed to validate it.

9. Learning theory views psychophysiological disorders as learned responses and assumes that both classical and instrumental conditioning can play a role in their etiology and maintenance. However, no comprehensive learning model has been proposed to account for the various psychophysiological disorders.

10. Some evidence indicates the importance of genetic factors in predisposing a person to develop a certain psychophysiological disorder. However, additional research is needed to delineate more clearly the importance of genetic predisposition in the various disorders.

11. One of the simplest physiological theories concerning psychophysiological disorders is that they occur because of weakness in an organ or system. An extension of this *weak organ / system theory* is the *specific-response pattern* approach, which assumes that individuals tend to respond to a stressful situation in their own idiosyncratic way. The particular system or organ that is most constantly activated in an individual is the one most susceptible to a breakdown and the subsequent development of psychophysiological symptoms.

12. A *diathesis-stress* model proposed by Sternbach takes into account the genetic, physiological, and attitude / personality factors. This model illustrates the complexity of investigating these disorders.

13. Although psychophysiological disorders often require immediate as well as long-range medical treatment for the organic pathology present, the treatment of these disorders otherwise is similar to that of the neurotic disorders. The prognosis for improvement is likewise good if the appropriate type of treatment is administered. Of course, if chronic dysfunction has produced irreversible and clinically severe organic changes and damage, the prognosis is less favorable.

14. The major initial goal of assessment of psychophysiological disorders is to determine whether there is any organic cause for the disorder. Generally, a particular disorder should not be diagnosed as psychophysiological until a thorough physical examination has definitely ruled out medical factors as the primary cause. Clinical assessment is then directed at isolating the specific psychological / situational factors that are causing or maintaining the problem behavior.

15. A number of MMPI profile patterns have been found to be associated with specific psychophysiological disorders. Barrier / penetration scores on the Rorschach test have also been found to differentiate between broad categories of psychosomatic disorders.

RECOMMENDED READINGS

Friedman, M., & Rosenman, R. H. *Type A behavior and your heart*. New York: Knopf, 1974.

Holmes, T. H., & Rahe, R. H. The social readjustment rating scale. *Journal of Psychosomatic Research*, 1967, *11*, 213–218.

Kahn, R. L. Stress: From 9 to 5. *Psychology Today*, 1969, *3*, 34–38.

Lachman, S. J. *Psychosomatic disorders: A behavioristic interpretation*. New York: Wiley, 1972.

Lipowski, Z. J. Psychosomatic medicine in the seventies: An overview. *American Journal of Psychiatry*, 1977, *134*, 233–243.

Masters, W. H. & Johnson, V. E. *Human sexual inadequacy*. Boston: Little, Brown, 1970.

Price, K. P. The application of behavior therapy to the treatment of psychosomatic disorders: Retrospect and prospect. *Psychotherapy: Theory, Research, and Practice*, *11* (summer 1974), 138-155.

Wittkower, E. D., & Dudek, S. Z. Psychosomatic medicine: the mind-body-society interaction. In B. Wolman (Ed.), *Handbook of general psychology*. Englewood Cliffs, N.J.: Prentice-Hall, 1973.

AFFECTIVE DISORDERS AND SUICIDE

8

OVERVIEW The affective disorders are characterized by a disturbance of mood, either extreme elation (mania) or depression. The main mood disturbances as categorized by the DSM-II are major affective disorders, which include the manic-depressive psychoses and involutional melancholia; psychotic depressive reaction; and depressive neurosis. The reliability or degree of agreement among clinicians using this classification schema of affective disorders, specifically the diagnosis of various types of depression, is low. This low reliability exists because patterns of symptoms vary greatly from person to person and may interact in a complex fashion with other forms of psychopathology, so that the ideal "textbook case" is not common. As a result, attempts have

been made to delineate specific symptom or behavior patterns that are associated with different forms of affective disorders. The DSM-III makes major changes in classification, as we shall see.

We will review a number of models proposed to account for depression. In so doing, we will note that the various learning, cognitive, and physiological/biochemical approaches are all reasonable, intuitively appealing, and supported by some experimental data. However, no one model appears broad enough to adequately explain the wide range of depressive phenomena. It will be emphasized that the integration of several orientations can lead to a more complete understanding of this disorder. Depression is often a self-limiting disorder that dissipates on its own with time. When

DEMOGRAPHICS	Usual Age at Onset	Prevalence	Sex Ratio
DEPRESSIVE DISORDERS	Fairly evenly distributed throughout adolescence and adult life	5–15% of population	Female-male ratio, 2 to 1
MANIC DISORDERS	Usually prior to age 30	Relatively rare. Usually, this diagnosis will be later changed to bipolar disorder after a depressive episode	Equal
BIPOLAR, MANIC-DEPRESSIVE DISORDERS	Usually prior to age 30	.5–1% of population	Equal
SUICIDE	Most usual age range is 25–45	Precise statistics are hard to determine. Widely differing estimates— 25,000–60,000 per year	Male-female ratio, 3 to 1

appropriate treatment is administered, then the prognosis for fairly rapid improvement is good. Electroconvulsive therapy, chemotherapy, and various psychotherapy/behavior therapy techniques will be discussed. We will also review methods used in the assessment of these affective disorders.

Suicide will be discussed in this chapter because depression plays a central role in this act. Various facts and myths about suicide will be reviewed, as well as the causes and stressors involved. Finally, suicide prevention techniques and attempts to predict high-risk suicidal persons will be discussed.

SYMPTOM DESCRIPTION AND ETIOLOGY

The term *affect*, which in clinical psychology is used interchangeably with the term *emotion*, is the key characteristic that dominates the clinical picture of the affective disorders. These disorders are marked by disturbances of mood in which extreme elation (mania) or depression cause a great deal of debilitating psychological distress for the afflicted person. Throughout history, depressive disorders have been noted in literature and described by authors such as Dostoevsky and Shakespeare, as well as by a number of famous historical figures. Both Lincoln and Churchill, for example, told of experiencing recurrent episodes of depression. Saul, King of Israel in the eleventh century B.C., apparently suffered from manic-depressive episodes. More recently, the astronaut Edwin Aldrin reported that after his return from the moon he experienced episodes of depression (Aldrin & Warga 1973). The widely publicized history of depressive episodes experienced by U.S. Senator Thomas Eagleton prevented him from being allowed to become the vice-presidential candidate when George McGovern was seeking the presidency in 1972. As we shall see, such disturbances of affect, especially depression, are not at all uncommon in our society. Most of this chapter will be devoted to a discussion of depression, by far the most prevalent type of affective disorder.

Depression is the common cold of psychopathology and has touched the lives of us all, yet it is probably the most dimly understood and most inadequately investigated of all the major forms of psychopathology. . . . The prevalence of depression in America today is staggering. Excluding the mild depressions we all occasionally suffer, the National Institute of Mental Health estimates that "four to eight million Americans may be in need of professional care for the depressive illness." Unlike most other forms of psychopathology, depression can be lethal. "One out of every 200 persons affected by a depressive illness will be a suicidal death." This estimate is probably on the low side. In addition to the unmeasurable cost in individual misery, the economic cost is large: treatment and loss of time at work alone cost between 1.3 and 4.0 billion dollars a year. (Seligman 1975, pp. 76–77)

All of us have experienced depression at various times in our lives. We can readily recall the dejected mood, loss of desire to do things, and general tiredness accompanying this psychological state. These states of depression are usually infrequent and pass in a short time. For some individuals, however, this mood state occurs frequently and severely, persisting for long periods of time. It becomes a significant psychological problem that seriously interferes with the afflicted person's everyday functioning. With the intensification of a dejected mood, the individual often loses interest in the world and lacks the motivation and desire to get involved in tasks. The future looks bleak, and he or she believes that nothing can be done to change this condition. As Mendels (1970) notes, the central symptoms of depression are "sadness, pessimism, and self-dislike, along with a loss of energy, motivation, and concentration." In addition, the depressed individual may often experience crying spells, loss of appetite, weight, sleep, and sexual desire, and a desire to avoid people.

Because of the prevalence of this disorder, and its association with suicide, there has been a recent increase in research directed at delineating its causes and possible treatment. This research, however, has been greatly handicapped because of the lack of a precise and clear definition of depression. As Wilcoxon, Schrader, and Nelson (1976) succinctly note:

. . . Everyone feels "down" at times, but is clinically severe depression merely an intensification of these feelings or is it something entirely different? Does clinical depression represent a psychological reaction to stress or is it a disease? Are low mood and crying spells the primary hallmarks of depression or are other behaviors the chief characteristics of the disorder? In his excellent book on the subject, Beck (1967, p.6) points out that the term *depression* has been used to describe many things: ". . . a particular feeling or symptom, a symptom-complex or syndrome, and a well-defined disease entity." Communication among researchers has been hampered because of this lack of consistency of definition. (p. 201)

These authors go on to indicate that the majority of experimental clinicians view depression as a group of related behaviors such as those just listed. Unfortunately, the extent to which these behaviors are present in any one clinical case, and the combinations in which they occur, vary. Moreover, they often occur along with other symptoms, such as generalized anxiety, which may dominate the clinical picture. It is therefore extremely difficult to provide a comprehensive stereotypic example of depression. This case of depression described by McNeil (1967) highlights many of the symptoms we have mentioned as being associated with this disorder.

A CASE OF DEPRESSION

Ralph was sinking swiftly into what he called a "blue funk." Nothing much had happened worth getting upset about but Ralph knew he was going to feel bad the moment he got out of bed. He woke up thinking, "Something is missing; something is wrong." He opened his eyes and sensed a great emptiness, but it was only what he deserved. He had made a mess of his life and had failed everyone who had ever had confidence in him. He had failed them miserably and it was all his own fault. . . . Ralph was both sad and ashamed because he knew it was happening again. He recognized how grim he was feeling and that it was worse today than yesterday. He had felt it coming and he dreaded it, but it was like the bad dreams he had regularly in which a building was toppling down on him while he was able to run only in slow, slow motion. . . . What Ralph hated most about these frequent nightmares was not just the fright and anxiety they caused him or, for that matter, the aftereffects of trying to work the next day while exhausted. It was his inability to get back to sleep. Alone in the early hours of the morning he always began to brood about his life, the kind of person he was, his weaknesses and many failures, and the generally miserable condition of the world. By the time he got to work he was deeply depressed and could barely manage the day's tasks. His biggest difficulty was concentrating. He would begin a task, knowing it had to be completed in a certain time, and with a sudden "start" realize that he had again become lost in

thought and had not even begun to work. Ralph's depressive episodes were not uncommon, so his fellow staff members had learned to recognize the symptoms and give him a wide berth for the day. . . . The details of the events leading to Ralph's hospitalization had repeated themselves year after year. As Ralph became increasingly depressed, his whole relationship to life, his work, and other people deteriorated rapidly. His energy would wane, and he would become obsessed with the idea he was a worthless, hopeless, useless person leading a meaningless life. . . . (pp. 154–155)

CLASSIFICATION OF MAJOR TYPES OF MOOD DISORDERS

The DSM-II attempted to differentiate between various forms of depression. However, as we shall discuss, it is difficult reliably to assign depressed individuals to one of the depression categories spelled out by the DSM-II. Because of these difficulties, the DSM-III will greatly change the classification format. The formal depression categories in the DSM-II classification system are (1) *major affective disorders*, which include manic-depressive illnesses and involutional melancholia; (2) *psychotic depressive reaction;* (3) *depressive neurosis.* We will briefly review these categories and point out the problems associated with them, and then discuss the changes proposed for the DSM-III.

MAJOR AFFECTIVE DISORDERS *Manic-depressive psychoses* are characterized by a disorder of mood—extremes of depression or elation (mania)—that does not appear to be associated with any particular precipitating environmental event. The lack of a clear precipitating event is used to distinguish this disorder from the psychotic depressive reaction and from depressive neurosis. Like the psychotic depressive reaction, these disorders are associated with a loss of contact with reality that may significantly interfere with the individual's functioning in his or her environment and can lead to hospitalization. In contrast to the manic-depressive psychoses and psychotic depressive reaction, depressive neurosis is a less severe form of depression that is not associated with any significant thought disorder or distortion of reality.

As mentioned in chapter 4, Kraepelin coined the term *manic-depressive illness* to characterize all cases in which there was an abnormally high degree of affect, either mania alone, depression alone, or the combination of the two. Thought process disturbances such as hallucinations and delusions often accompany these disorders. *Manic-depressive psychosis, manic type,* consists primarily of manic episodes characterized by extreme elation, irritability, flight of ideas, and a marked increase in speech and motor activity. *Manic-depressive psychosis, depressed type,* consists of episodes characterized primarily by an extremely depressed mood. Unlike the psychotic depressive reaction, there does not appear to be a clear precipitating stressor or event triggering this form of depression. It is viewed as a primary mood disorder that is *endogenous,* that is, internally caused, rather than *exogenous* or *reactive,* that is, externally caused by some precipitating environmental event. *Manic-depressive psychosis, circular type,* consists of at least one attack each of an episode of depression and an episode of mania, with a circular or cyclical alternation between these mood states. Brief periods of normality may also exist, serving as a transition between depression and mania. The duration of each episode may vary considerably from person to person. The characteristics of these mood states are the same as when they occur as separate disorders.

Besides these major forms of manic-depression, there is also a category termed *manic-de-*

pressive psychosis, mixed type, which is used in those cases where manic and depressive symptoms seem to appear almost simultaneously. An individual may manifest many of the usual signs of mania, such as a flight of ideas and an increase in speech and motor activity, but simultaneously, depression is present that impedes him or her from initiating and carrying out any meaningful sequence of behavior. Although the person may be tense and diffusely excited, the depressive retardation prevents him or her from initiating any significant and organized form of activity.

A CASE OF CIRCULAR MANIC-DEPRESSION

A deeply religious man in the late forties, married, with one child, had been diagnosed twelve years earlier by a psychiatrist as constitutionally manic-depressive, and told that there was nothing to be done but control the condition by means of drugs. This "control" proved in practice to be of little use to him and his life was a misery as he swung between periods of profound depression with sluggish inactivity and acute guilt over his uselessness, and periods of compulsive early rising and hectic overwork. He could at such times feel strong guilt over sexual fantasies and aggressive outbursts in real life which he found hard to control, especially with his wife and child. Apart from these extremes, in his general attitudes he was rigidly puritan, intolerant of many things "on principle," a strict disciplinarian, and extremely independent. He said, "I have St. Augustine's 'heart of steel towards myself.' "

Analysis of his guilt brought out ever more clearly that it was aimed mainly against his feelings of weakness, and guilt was mixed with contempt of himself. It was weak to be unable to control his temper and irritability, and also to need anyone's help. His "ego-ideal" was that of the strong and rather silent man who had iron self-control, which he could relax at times for the child's amusement in nonsense talk and joking; behind this he remained a deadly serious person. With his university training and gifts of leadership he was, when at his best, a successful and valuable obsessional personality, but this was always breaking down into the manic-depressive mood swing. . . .

His life had been one long struggle to keep going at all, since he had really always felt inadequate and apprehensive. He said, "It's hell, going through life having to screw yourself up all the time to face everything you have to do, even though you know you can do it." Gradually analysis focused less and less on guilt over sex and aggression, and more and more on his fears, timidities, shrinking from life, and the constant tension of forcing himself on, in the teeth of these drawbacks. His manic-depressive cycle appeared to him now as an oscillation between ruthless overdriving of his secretly frightened inner self, leading on to collapse into physical and mental exhaustion. He could see clearly enough how his parents had completely undermined or prevented the development of any natural, spontaneous self-confidence in him, and how seriously beset he had been in his teens by a crippling feeling of inadequacy and inability to "make good."

For practical purposes his treatment began to focus on his inability at that time to relax and rest. He was afraid to "let go" in sleep and could not still his overactive mind. The analysis of his hidden manic drive in terms of his dread that if he once stopped he would never get started again, enabled him to see its real significance. It was a desperate struggle to overcome the emotionally crippled and fear-ridden child inside, and to force himself to be adult—a well-intentioned but self-defeating method of working hard to keep his ego in being, to be alive, to be a real "person" while a weak infantile ego in which he felt he was a "nobody" was hidden in the depths of his unconsciousness. (Guntrip 1969, pp. 156–158)

Another affective disorder category sometimes used is *schizoaffective psychosis.* In certain cases, a major disturbance of affect may be present in addition to schizophrenic-type symptoms. This type of psychosis has prompted certain investigators to suggest that manic-depressive psychoses and schizophrenia are not separate and distinct forms of abnormal behavior but merely opposite ends of a continuum. At one end of the continuum are basically pure *mood* disturbances, while at the other end are relatively pure *thought process* disturbances. In between these two extremes are the disorders, such as schizoaffective psychosis, that include elements of both mood and thought process disturbances.

The other primary subtype of major affective disorders spelled out by the DSM-II is *involutional melancholia*. This form of depression is differentiated from other depressive reactions primarily by its time of initial onset—during the involution (change of life) period, usually viewed as occurring between the ages of 45 and 60 in women and 50 to 65 in men. Besides depression, this disorder is characterized by worry and anxiety about minor matters and severe insomnia. Also, it is frequently associated with feelings of guilt and somatic complaints. The initial onset is gradual, and the individual usually has not had previous depressive episodes. Characteristically, it lasts a long time if treatment is not administered. Distinguishing involutional melancholia from other forms of affective disorders, the DSM-II states:

> . . . This disorder is distinguished from *Manic-depressive illness* by the absence of previous episodes; it is distinguished from *Schizophrenia* in that impaired reality testing is due to a disorder of mood; and it is distinguished from *Psychotic depressive reaction* in that the disorder of mood is not due to some experience. Opinion is divided as to whether this psychosis can be distinguished from the other affective disorders. It is, therefore, recommended that involutional patients not be given this diagnosis unless all other affective disorders have been ruled out.

PSYCHOTIC DEPRESSIVE REACTION   This psychotic reaction, which is viewed as reactive in nature, is characterized by the occurrence of an extreme depressive mood precipitated by some event or experience in the individual's environment. There is also the presence of a thought process disturbance in which reality testing is impaired. For example, delusions and hallucinations related to guilt or worthlessness may be present. This impairment causes difficulty in functioning adequately in one's environment. These characteristic thought disturbances are used to distinguish this form of depression from depressive neurosis.

DEPRESSIVE NEUROSIS   In this form of reactive depression, the individual responds to an identifiable stressful event or internal conflict with a greater than normal amount of dysphoria and dejection that does not disappear after a reasonable period of time. As noted above, depressive neurosis is differentiated from the other form of reactive depression (psychotic depressive reaction) by the absence of disturbances in thought processes. Even though this form of depression may last for many months, it usually clears up or decreases in severity.

PROBLEMS ASSOCIATED WITH THE CLASSIFICATION OF DEPRESSION

As Mendels (1970) notes, the degree of agreement among clinicians when diagnosing patients according to this traditional classification schema of depression is poor, usually just over 50 percent accuracy. This unreliability exists because patterns of depressive symptoms vary greatly from person to person and may interact in a complex fashion with other forms of psychopathology, so that the ideal "textbook case" is not common. Indeed, a major obstacle to a more effective treatment of depression is the great heterogeneity of symptoms involved in this disorder (Becker 1977). Also, the diagnostician must make a great deal of subjective evaluation, which contributes to low reliability. For example, the clinician needs to determine how inappropriate are the depression and dejection that a patient is displaying, and whether they are directly related to some specific precipitating event. If an individual experiences depression in response to a specific event such as loss of a loved one, this mood state is considered a normal grief reaction; but how long must this mood persist—one month, two months?—before it is considered a form of depression? The clinician has to determine this, as well as what kind and how great a loss or environmental stress can be expected to cause a significant and extended depression of mood. Moreover, the clinician needs to determine whether the depression is definitely precipitated by some environmental stressor. Mendels (1970) has noted that many times this is more difficult than it appears to be. For example, a man may describe his depression as being caused by his recent loss of an important job. A careful assessment by the clinician, however, might reveal that the man had lost this position because of a recent decrease in his work efficiency. The work inefficiency, in turn, was associated with the earlier and more gradual onset of the depression. Thus, the depression was not directly precipitated by the specific situation suggested by the patient.

The lack of reliability in diagnosing different forms of depression, as well as other forms of psychopathology, has prompted many clinicians to

The Museum of Modern Art/Film Stills Archive

DEATH OF A SALESMAN © 1951, Columbia
Pictures. Often, a significant unwanted
change in one's life can produce rather
severe and persistent depression. Willy
Loman, having lost his job, and realizing
that he has grown old, is beset by unbearable feelings of helplessness, despair,
and depression that eventually drive him
to commit suicide.

suggest discarding attempts at formal classification. However, as we pointed out in chapter 4,
some form of classification is important because it
provides a basis for communicating information
about a certain disorder, delineating characteristics that certain patients have in common, and
integrating data related to the disorder's etiology
and treatment.

Better methods need to be developed for the
subclassification of depressed individuals. As with
other forms of psychopathology, recent attempts
have been made to delineate specific behavior
patterns that are distressing to an individual, and
then developing treatment methods to deal with the
specific behavior. The proposed DSM-III attempts
to avoid past problems by basing classification on
observed behavior rather than on an assumed
etiology.

Attempting to differentiate between types of
depression through presumed etiology (endogenous versus exogenous or reactive, which is a
major method employed by the DSM-II, has not
been very successful because of the problem of

determining whether depression is caused directly
by some environmental event. Recent research,
though, has indicated that the endogenous-exog-
enous distinction may be effectively used to distinguish between patterns of behavior. In reviewing
a series of studies concerned with the division of
depressed patients into endogenous and exogenous groups, Mendels and Cochrane (1970)
indicated that the following behavioral symptoms
were found more often in patients diagnosed as
endogenous depressives, and could be used to
differentiate them from **exogenous** depressives:
deeply depressed, lack of reactivity to environmental changes, a loss of interest in life, middle-
of-the-night insomnia, bodily symptoms, motoric
retardation, no self-pity, and the lack of a precipitating stress. In commenting on this distinction,
Mendels (1970) suggests that:

. . . in a large group of patients with depression there are a number who demonstrate a fairly pure depressive picture, and
that in others there are features of hysteria,
character disorder (inadequacy), anxiety,

and other nondepressive characteristics. Thus the so-called endogenous factor may represent the core of depressive symptomatology whereas the clinical features of the reactive factor may represent symptoms of psychiatric disorders other than depression, which, when present, contaminate the depression syndrome. When depression is present in association with these other features, it might be regarded as just one of several symptoms, anyone of which might dominate. (p. 46)

An analogous approach that shows promise in distinguishing between types of depression also avoids the exclusive use of etiology. The approach by Robins, Munoz, Martin, and Gentry (1972) attempts to distinguish between "primary" and "secondary" depression. Depression is defined as "primary" if it is associated with specified affect and behavioral symptoms, and has not been preceded by, or associated with, some other major personality disorder or a life-threatening physical illness. In contrast, "secondary depression" results from, or is secondary to, some more dominant form of psychological or physical disorder. As Becker (1977) notes, a thorough assessment of the utility of this approach has not yet been conducted, but initial results of its validity and reliability appear encouraging.

Apparently the most promising approach for subclassifying types of depression is to try to use specific behavioral patterns in combination with an assessment of whether there are any clear precipitating environmental stressors involved and, also, whether other forms of psychopathology are present. With this approach, a clinician could more readily decide on the appropriate treatment strategy. A "primary" or "endogenous" form of depression would be treated differently than a "secondary" or "reactive" type. In the latter type, a number of behavior disorders besides depression would probably have to be dealt with. In the former, depression would be the only major disorder requiring treatment. Also, knowledge of whether some precipitating event was involved would allow the therapist to structure therapy accordingly. If no specific event triggered the depression, then the possibility of biochemical/physiological underpinnings for the disorder is suggested, and a search can be made for a possible biological cause. As we shall see, there is

evidence accumulating that suggests the involvement of biochemical/physiological mechanisms in the etiology of certain forms of depression.

THE DSM-III CLASSIFICATION APPROACH

The proposed DSM-III has greatly modified the classification of affective disorders, eliminating the three main categories of major affective disorders, psychotic depressive reaction, and depressive neurosis. This significant change was prompted by the many problems we have just mentioned as associated with these classifications. The DSM-II attempted to differentiate between psychotic depression and manic-depression, depressed type, on the basis of the presence or absence of a precipitating event. However, it is often very difficult to determine whether there was any clear environmental event, and so differentiation on this basis is often not reliable. Research also suggests that the distinction between neurotic depression and psychotic depression may be based merely on severity of the disorder, thus making the two discrete categories unnecessary. Finally, it became apparent that involutional melancholia was being distinguished from the other disorders solely on the basis of age of onset. The revisors of the DSM viewed it unnecessary to base a discrete category solely on this age variable.

In the 1978 draft of DSM-III, these three major categories of affective disorders have been proposed: (1) *Episodic affective disorders,* in which there are periods of depression lasting for a short period of time (less than two years). Within this category, the main subclassifications can be viewed as "episodic," such as manic episodes (in which extreme elevated mood is the dominant behavioral symptom), depressive episodes (in which there are dominant behavioral symptoms of depression), and bipolar episodes (involving a full picture of both manic and depressive periods, intermixed or alternating every few days). (2) *Chronic affective disorders,* in which there exists a long-standing (at least two years) manifestation of manic, depressive, or bipolar symptoms. (3) *Atypical affective disorders,* a category used for classifying individuals who cannot be classified under the previous two broad categories.

The new categories, and the major subcategories to be listed in DSM-III, avoid many of the old problems associated with DSM-II. The main improvement in the DSM-III is that it assists the clinician in making a diagnosis by establishing objective behavioral criteria. Table 8.1 compares the two systems.

CAUSES AND STRESSORS

PSYCHOANALYTIC THEORY

One of Freud's students, Karl Abraham (1911), made the first systematic attempt to account for manic-depressive disorders in terms of psychoanalytic theory. Freud later expanded many of Abraham's ideas in a paper published in 1917 entitled *Mourning and Melancholia*. Abraham compared depression with normal grief reactions that occur following the loss of a real or fantasized love object. The major difference between the two was assumed to be that in a grief reaction, the mourner is consciously concerned with the lost person and has no significant ambivalent or guilt feelings surrounding the loss; by contrast, the depressed individual is dominated by feelings of personal loss, guilt, and self-blame. Abraham suggests that the depressed individual had ambivalent feelings of love and hate towards the lost person. This ambivalence prompts two major emotions: (1) anger and resentment toward the lost love object because of the perception of having been deserted or rejected; (2) feelings of guilt precipitated by the depressed person's belief that he or she in some way failed to respond appropriately and adequately to the lost loved one. These ambivalent feelings produce a self-centered sense of loss, rejection, and despair. It is this self-centered quality that basically differentiates depression from a normal grief reaction, which is realistic and directed outwardly towards the lost loved one.

According to Freud, the loss of a love object, although an essential factor in the development of depression, did not have to involve the actual death or loss of a person. Withdrawal of love and affection by an important figure during a critical period of development in a person's life was assumed to predispose that individual to develop depression later in life in response to similar situations involving a real or imagined withdrawal or loss of love. An especially critical period was assumed to be during the *oral stage* of development. If emotional difficulties occurred then, usually because of withdrawal of love from the infant, the person became *fixated* at the oral stage. A consequence of this fixation was the development of an *oral eroticism* personality characteristic. This characteristic is associated with great dependency on external sources, such as people or events, to provide emotional gratification. If this gratification is lost, by the death of a person or loss of an object providing this gratification, or by the withdrawal of love or affection, the loss is symbolic of the earlier infantile deprivation and resultant emotional difficulties. Since this individual is already "sensitized" by early infantile problems, the loss has a greater than normal emotional impact and leads to a depressive reaction.

A number of other psychoanalytically oriented approaches have been proposed to account for depression but will not be reviewed here. There has been little or no research assessing the validity of these approaches, or of the model presented by Abraham and Freud. Of the small amount of research that has been conducted, Mendels (1970) has found little evidence to support any of these approaches. Cohen, Baker, Cohen, Fromm-Reichman, and Weigart (1954), in exploring the family backgrounds of twelve individuals classified as manic-depressive, did find that these depressed individuals demonstrated excessive dependency, conformity, and need for social approval. These can be viewed as the *oral eroticism* personality characteristics hypothesized by Abraham and Freud as being present in depressives. However, these same basic characteristics are also found in nondepressed individuals and in other

Lawrence Frank/Black Star

Most of us have experienced periods of sadness such as follows the loss of a loved one. Unfortunately, for some individuals, this grief and depression is quite severe and long-lasting.

forms of psychopathology, and are therefore not very discriminating or illuminating with regard to the etiology of depression.

COGNITIVE THEORY

In contrast to approaches that consider the thought disorder present in many depressed patients to be the result of a basic disturbance of mood, cognitive approaches suggest that it is a disturbance in thinking that results in the disturbed mood state. The most widely known and comprehensive of these approaches is Beck's (1967, 1974) cognitive model of depression. This model views depression as being caused by certain kinds of illogical thinking. It is suggested that the depressed individual does not think illogically in general, but only with regard to himself or herself, resulting in a great deal of self-depreciation, guilt, and self-blame. Beck outlines four logical errors a depressive is assumed to engage in. (1) *Arbitrary inference* denotes the tendency to come to a conclusion from an experience or situation that is not supported by a sufficient amount of real evidence. For example, a person may feel uncomfortable in a social situation because she thinks the other people there think poorly of her. However, there is no factual basis for this notion, and the individual fails to realize that there are more plausible explanations for the situation. (2) *Selective abstraction* refers to the tendency to draw a conclusion on the basis of only one of several elements of a multifaceted situation, with that one element being taken out of context and exaggerated. For example, a person may receive some corrective criticism directed at a specific aspect of his work. He immediately jumps to the conclusion that *everything* he does is inadequate even though all other aspects of his work are very competent. The individual ignores the context of the entire work situation by fixating on one specific aspect of it. (3) *Overgeneralization* involves drawing erroneous conclusions about one's overall ability or worth solely on the basis of only a single, and often

COMPARISON OF DSM-II AND DSM-III SUB-CATEGORIES OF AFFECTIVE DISORDERS Table 8.1	DSM-II	DSM-III*
	Manic-depressive psychoses, depressed type Involutional melancholia Psychotic depressive reaction Depressive neurosis	Depressive disorder
	Manic-depressive psychoses, manic-type	Manic disorder
	Manic-depressive psychoses, circular type Manic-depressive psychoses, mixed type	Bipolar affective disorder

*For each of these DSM-III subcategories, the major classification category can be either *episodic affective disorder*, *chronic affective disorder*, or *atypical affective disorder*.

minor, incident. For example, a woman may conclude that she is a bad person because her children are not as well disciplined as those of her friends. She overly generalizes from a limited specific detail. (4) *Magnification and minimization* denote cases in which a person makes grossly inaccurate judgments about the significance of events and the effect of his or her behavior on them. Examples include those individuals who overly exaggerate their difficulties and shortcomings and minimize their achievements and capabilities. These individuals tend to exaggerate unduly the significance of information.

Illogical thought patterns are viewed by Beck as distorting the depressive's perception of reality, causing a negative view of one's self, one's present experiences, and the future. Such thought patterns are assumed by Beck to have been acquired during the developmental learning experiences of early childhood and adolescence, which involve interactions with the environment, other individuals' opinions of the person, and identification with significant others (such as parents) in one's environment.

Beck developed his formulation on the basis of an analysis of the primary thought pattern characteristics of depressed patients as compared with nondepressed psychiatric patients. The analysis was based primarily on observations made during psychotherapeutic interviews. It led him to suggest that depression, rather than being a primary mood disturbance, is a primary disorder of thought resulting in a disturbance of affect and behavior that coincides with the cognitive distortion. Similarly, Ellis (1962) suggests that the way an individual views and thinks about himself or herself may lead to disordered behavior such as depression. (We reviewed Ellis's RET approach in chapter 6 on the neuroses.) It should also be noted that experimental research has demonstrated that negative affect such as depression can be induced in subjects who are required to make self-referent depressive mood statements (e.g., Velton 1968). Such research supports the notion that mood states are affected by thought patterns.

LEARNING THEORY

Among learning theorists, Ferster (1965) was the first to note that the loss of a close friend or loved one causes a sudden change or reduction in the schedule of positive reinforcement that normally maintains much of a person's behavior. Behaviors are reduced if they are no longer being positively rewarded. Ferster also pointed out that many depressed persons are extremely restricted in the number of people with whom they normally interact, in some cases there being only one person. Such restricted interaction makes the depressive extremely vulnerable, since the loss of that individual, or the withdrawal of his or her attention, will cause a significant reduction in positive reinforcement and, hence, a drastic change in the depressed person's behavior. In agreement with Ferster, Lazarus (1974) also views depression as a "function of inadequate or insufficient reinforcers." Once positive reinforcement is withdrawn, it is assumed that an individual will stop emitting behavior and will become inactive and withdrawn, all of which are symptoms of depression.

Spitz (1946) observed a syndrome of extreme depression in hospitalized infants, which he labeled *anaclitic depression*. This depression developed after the child was abruptly separated from his or her mother, who had previously been the primary "reinforcer" and responder to the infant's needs. Spitz noted that after an initial period of distress highlighted by crying and protesting, the children became depressed and showed apathy, unresponsiveness, and general sadness. On the basis of a reduced-reinforcement conceptualization, then, one would predict this depression.

In studies with laboratory animals, it has also been demonstrated that the loss of a significant figure (i.e., a significant source of positive reinforcement) in an animal's environment produces depression-type behavior. For example, Harlow and Suomi (1974) report that when young rhesus monkeys are separated from their mothers and placed in isolation from other monkeys, they display depressed behavior marked by reduced rates of locomotion, play, and exploratory behavior. Many of these behaviors persisted as long as eight months after the isolation and separation ended.

THE LEWINSOHN MODEL In recent years, Lewinsohn (1974) has been actively involved in empirically testing and extending the reduced-reinforcement conceptualization of depression. Lewinsohn also points to the importance of a lack of appropriate social skills in the development of depression. He defines social skills as the "emission of behaviors which are positively reinforced by others" and notes that if an individual lacks social skills, it will significantly limit the availability of positive reinforcers in his or her immediate environment. Lewinsohn's model of depression is shown schematically in the chart. The major assumptions underlying this model are these: (1) Depressive behaviors such as verbal statements of dysphoria, decreased activity, and somatic symptoms can be produced when behavior receives low positive reinforcement. (2) A number of different environmental events—a loss through death, separation, or rejection, some form of misfortune, or a deficit such as inappropriate social skills—are presumed to be causally related to a low rate of positive reinforcement. (3) The low rate of positive reinforcement tends to reduce the activity level of the individual even more which, in turn, may decrease even more the availability of positive reinforcements. Lewinsohn views the depressed person as being on a prolonged extinction schedule. (4) A small part of the social environment— close family and friends—may initially provide some reinforcement in the form of sympathy and concern from others, which reinforces and maintains the depressive behaviors. However, eventually even these individuals will begin finding the depressive behaviors aversive and annoying, and they will begin to avoid the depressed person. Their avoidance decreases the individual's rate of receiving positive reinforcement even more and so further accentuates his or her depression.

Lewinsohn, Shaffer, and Libet (1969) conducted a number of studies assessing specific features of this model. The major dependent measure employed was the rating (by trained raters) of observable behaviors of depressed persons in specific situations such as a family interaction or some other social interaction/situation. An attempt was made to document carefully the frequency and types of behaviors engaged in, and the number of reinforcements (e.g., attention, praise, etc.) received. Although these studies confirmed certain features of this model of depression, a great deal of additional research is needed to substantiate the notion that a low rate of positive reinforcement leads directly to a depressed mood. Also, it should be noted that there has been some recent research in which an increase in positively reinforcing activity did not alleviate depressed moods in mildly depressed college students (Hammen & Glass 1975), thus not confirming a major feature of Lewinsohn's model. Again, more research with a wide range of depressive behaviors is needed to test this model further. At this stage in its development, though, it holds promise for explaining and treating certain forms of depression.

THE LEARNED HELPLESSNESS MODEL Another learning formulation of depression has been proposed by Seligman (1975), who argues that the

**MODEL OF
DEPRESSION**
Figure 8.1

Schematic representation of Lewinsohn's model of depression. (From Lewinsohn, Shaffer, & Libert 1969)

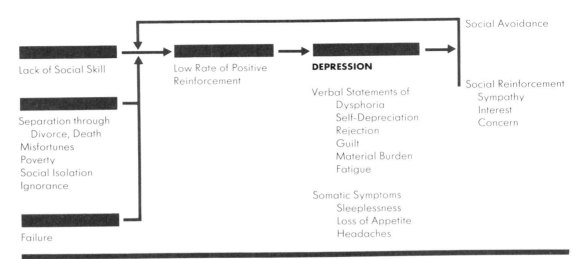

Social Avoidance

Lack of Social Skill

Low Rate of Positive
Reinforcement

DEPRESSION

Social Reinforcement
Sympathy
Interest
Concern

Separation through
　Divorce, Death
Misfortunes
Poverty
Social Isolation
Ignorance

Verbal Statements of
　Dysphoria
　Self-Depreciation
　Rejection
　Guilt
　Material Burden
　Fatigue

Somatic Symptoms
　Sleeplessness
　Loss of Appetite
　Headaches

Failure

concept of *learned helplessness* may serve as a model for reactive depression in humans. The concept of learned helplessness was initially developed from a series of studies on traumatic avoidance learning in dogs (e.g., Seligman & Maier 1967). In these studies, it was found that inescapable and uncontrollable aversive events presented to animals, such as the administration of electric shock by the experimenter, significantly affected their behavior and resulted in their inability to learn to escape the shocks when they were subsequently given the chance to do so. These dogs began to demonstrate a helpless, "giving-up" form of behavior in which they stopped moving around the experimental chamber, lay down, and quietly whined. Even if they were then placed in a situation in which they could escape the electric shock by performing some behavior, they failed to try to do so. Their past experience of "learned helplessness" apparently eliminated their motivation to initiate any behavior.

Learned helplessness was interpreted as a phenomenon that develops when an organism learns that responding and reinforcement (e.g., escape from shock) are independent; that is, it is perceived that one's behavior cannot control environmental events. Seligman uses this concept to explain reactive depression that develops as a reaction to environmental stress and is characterized by apathy and inertia. He has noted a number of parallels between the symptoms produced by learned helplessness and those symptoms found in depression. Table 8.2 summarizes the features common to learned helplessness and depression.

More recently, the same type of learned helplessness effect has been shown in human subjects. In one such study, Gatchel and Proctor (1976) employed three groups of subjects. One group (escapable group) heard a series of loud aversive tones that they could turn off by pushing a button a certain number of times. A second group (inescapable group) heard the same series of loud tones and were given the same understanding that they could learn to turn them off. But no matter what they did, they could not turn the tones off. A third group (control group) listened passively to the tones with the understanding that they could not be turned off. After the subjects had been "pretreated" in these ways, the degree of impairment (learned helplessness) was measured by assessing their performance on a cognitive task requiring them to solve a series of anagrams. (Anagrams are words with the letters scrambled, the task being to unscramble the letters and form a word.) Successful performance requires the subject's active attention and motivation. Results indicated that, relative

	LEARNED HELPLESSNESS	DEPRESSION	
SYMPTOMS	Passivity	Passivity	SUMMARY OF FEATURES COMMON TO LEARNED HELPLESSNESS AND DEPRESSION Table 8.2
	Difficulty learning that responses produce relief	Negative cognitive set	
	Dissipates in time	Time course	
	Lack of aggression	Introjected hostility	
	Weight loss, appetite loss, social and sexual deficits	Weight loss, appetite loss, social and sexual deficits	
	Norepinephrine depletion and cholinergic activity	Norepinephrine depletion and cholinergic activity	
	Ulcers and stress	Ulcers (?) and stress	
		Feelings of helplessness	
CAUSE	Learning that responding and reinforcement are independent.	Belief that responding is useless.	
CURE	Directive therapy: forced exposure to responses that produce reinforcement	Recovery of belief that responding produces reinforcement	
	Electroconvulsive shock	Electroconvulsive shock	
	Time	Time	
	Anticholinergics; norepinephrine, stimulants (?)	Norepinephrine, stimulants; anticholinergics (?)	
PREVENTION	Immunization by mastery over reinforcement	(?)	

HELPLESSNESS, HOPELESSNESS, AND DEATH

Seligman (1975) has contended that *learned help-lessness* may cause reactive depression in humans. He also suggested that this phenomenon can actually cause death in some individuals who, after learning that their lives and behaviors are futile, totally give up hope and the will to live. Seligman presents a number of examples of deaths that apparently were caused by helplessness. One rather dramatic example is that of an American soldier held captive during the Vietnam War:

> When, in early 1973, medical army officer Major F. Harold Kushner returned from five and a half years as a prisoner of war in South Vietnam, he told a stark and chilling tale. His story represents one of the few cases on record in which a trained medical observer witnessed from start to finish what I can only call death from helplessness.
>
> Major Kushner was shot down in a helicopter in North Vietnam in November 1967. He was captured, seriously wounded, by the Viet Cong. He spent the next three years in a hell called First Camp. Through the camp passed 27 Americans: 5 were released by the Viet Cong, 10 died in the camp, and 12 survived to be released from Hanoi in 1973. The camp's conditions beggar description. At any one time there were about eleven men who lived in a bamboo hut, sleeping on one crowded bamboo bed about sixteen feet across. The basic diet was three small cups of red, rotten, vermin-infested rice a day. Within the

first year the average prisoner lost 40 to 50 percent of his body weight, and acquired running sores and atrophied muscles. There were two prominent killers: malnutrition and helplessness. When Kushner was first captured, he was asked to make antiwar statements. He said that he would rather die, and his captor responded with words Kushner remembered every day of his captivity: "Dying is easy; it's living that's hard." The will to live, and the catastrophic consequences of the loss of hope, are the theme of Kushner's story.

> When Major Kushner arrived at First Camp in January 1968, Robert had already been captive for two years. He was a rugged and intelligent corporal from a crack marine unit, austere, stoic, and oblivious to pain and suffering. He was 24 years old and had been trained as a parachutist and a scuba diver. Like the rest of the men, he was down to a weight of ninety pounds and was forced to make long, shoeless treks daily with ninety pounds of manioc root on his back. He never griped. "Grit your teeth and tighten your belt," he used to repeat. Despite malnutrition and terrible skin disease, he remained in very good physical and mental health. The cause of his relatively fine shape was clear to Kushner. Robert was convinced that he would soon be released. The Viet Cong had made it a practice to release, as examples, a few men who had co-operated

to the other groups, the "inescapable" pretreatment group showed greatly impaired performance at solving the anagrams. As did the animal studies, these data suggest that learned helplessness, which develops when an organism learns that responding does not influence the possibility of escaping an aversive event, undermines the motivation for initiating any behavior, even solving anagrams.

Seligman assumes that, as in learned helplessness, the critical feature in depression is the depressed person's perception of his or her inability to control environmental events. Miller and

Seligman (1973) provide some evidence to support this notion. These investigators found that when depressed persons were required to work on a task in which the amount of reinforcement they received was directly contingent on their behavior (performance of a motor task), they perceived that they had less control over the degree of reinforcement received than did a group of nondepressed individuals who worked on the identical task. These results indicate that, compared with nondepressed individuals, depressives have the perception that their behavior does not adequately control environmen-

with them and adopted the correct attitudes. Robert had done so, and the camp commander had indicated that he was next in line for release, to come in six months.

As expected, six months later, the event occurred that had preceded these token releases in the past. A very high-ranking Viet Cong cadre appeared to give the prisoners a political course; it was understood that the outstanding pupil would be released. Robert was chosen as leader of the thought-reform group. He made the statements required and was told to expect release within the month.

The month came and went, and he began to sense a change in the guards' attitude toward him. Finally it dawned on him that he had been deceived—that he had already served his captors' purpose, and he wasn't going to be released. He stopped working and showed signs of severe depression: he refused food and lay on his bed in a fetal position, sucking his thumb. His fellow prisoners tried to bring him around. They hugged him, babied him, and, when this didn't work, tried to bring him out of his stupor with their fists. He defecated and urinated in the bed. After a few weeks, it was apparent to Kushner that Robert was moribund: although otherwise his gross physical shape was still better than most of the others, he was dusky and cyanotic. In the early hours of a November morning he lay dying in Kushner's arms.

For the first time in days his eyes focused and he spoke: "Doc, Post Office Box 161, Texarkana, Texas. Mom, Dad, I love you very much. Barbara, I forgive you." Within seconds, he was dead.

Robert's was typical of a number of such deaths that Major Kushner saw. What killed him? Kushner could not perform an autopsy, since the Viet Cong allowed him no surgical tools. To Kushner's eyes the immediate cause was "gross electrolyte imbalance." But given Robert's relatively good physical state, psychological precursors rather than physiological state seem a more specifiable cause of death. Hope of release sustained Robert. When he gave up hope, when he believed that all his efforts had failed and would continue to fail, he died.

Can a psychological state be lethal? I believe it can. When animals and men learn that their actions are futile and that there is no hope, they become more susceptible to death. Conversely, the belief in control over the environment can prolong life. . . . The psychological state of helplessness increases the risk of death. . . . Instances of death from helplessness are by no means rare, and they are often only slightly less dramatic than the ones Kushner saw. (pp. 166-169)

tal events. In effect, they have learned to be helpless.

Seligman (1975) has presented additional data to support his view that learned helplessness may serve as a valid model of reactive depression in humans. However, other investigators have questioned the learning principles on which the learned helplessness phenomenon is assumed to be based (Levis 1976) and have presented evidence indicating that there is not a direct parallel between learned helplessness and naturally occurring depression with respect to physiological responding (Gatchel, McKinney, & Koebernick 1977). In the study by Gatchel and colleagues, learned helplessness was associated with a lower level of GSR, while depression was associated with a greater level of GSR in response to uncontrollable aversive events. These data suggest that there may be different underlying physiological deficits involved in learned helplessness and depression. Nevertheless, despite these disconforming data, the significant amount of evidence Seligman has presented to support his model demands that the learned helplessness concept be taken into account when evaluating the etiology of reactive depression.

There is a major difference between Seligman's learned helplessness model and Lewinsohn's (1974) learning model, which emphasizes a reduced positive reinforcement concept of depression. The latter model is essentially noncognitive in nature and assumes that mood is directly related to how overt behavior is reinforced. In contrast, Seligman's model is more cognitive because it emphasizes the person's perception of the controllability of events in the environment. Research is needed that directly compares the validity of these two models. Blaney (1977) has contrasted and compared Beck's cognitive view, Seligman's learned helplessnes model, and Lewinsohn's approach, evaluating each of them in terms of empirical support and adequacy as a theory. This paper offers a more in-depth review of these models.

An apparent paradox. Abramson and Sackeim (1977) have noted a paradox in the way in which depression is viewed in Beck's (1974) cognitive self-blame conceptualization and Seligman's (1975) learned helplessness formulation. They astutely point out that the view of depressives as both helpless *and* self-blaming is theoretically paradoxical. The cognitive theory assumes that because of a basic disturbance in thinking, depressed patients have a tendency to assume personal responsibility and blame themselves for failures in their lives. On the other hand, the learned helplessness model proposes that depression is the result of learning and the subsequent belief that behavior and outcomes are independent of one another (i.e., situations are uncontrollable). Inherent in the proposition is that if outcomes are uncontrollable, then to take personal responsibility or self-blame for them is theoretically illogical.

> In this respect the formulations of Beck and Seligman are incompatible. . . . The merging of Beck's model and Seligman's model of depression would result in the paradoxical situation of individuals blaming themselves for outcomes that they believe they neither caused nor controlled. (Abramson & Sackeim 1977, p. 843)

There have been clinical observation and experimental data to support both views of depression. This paradox is, then, manifested on an empirical level. Of course, both models need to be tested further. This additional research may lead to a necessary revision of the models that would eliminate the paradox. However, if both models are

subsequently shown to be valid, an important question that needs to be examined is how this paradox—individuals assuming responsibility and self-blame for outcomes that they perceive they neither cause nor control—operates in depression. Is the presence of these two contradictory beliefs an inherent critical feature of depression, or are there two different types of depression, each associated with a different belief? Abramson, Seligman, and Teasdale (1978) have recently addressed this issue. The final resolution of this question, however, awaits future research.

BIOLOGICAL/CONSTITUTIONAL THEORIES

The view that depression is due to biological/constitutional causes has a long history starting with the ancient Greeks. The Greek physician Hippocrates developed a system by which persons were assigned to one of four temperamental categories, attributed to a predominance of one of the bodily humors (blood, phlegm, choler, black bile). The *melancholic* or depressive temperament was viewed as the result of an overabundance of black bile in the body fluids. Although this system was subsequently disregarded, there is still a search underway for genetic and physiological/biochemical factors that may underlie affective disorders. We will briefly review some of the research investigating such factors.

GENETIC FACTORS There have been a number of studies that strongly suggest the presence of genetic factors in affective disorders, especially in the manic-depressive psychoses. Winokur (1969) found that affective disorders occurred with greater frequency in the first-degree relatives (parents, children, siblings) of a group of patients with affective disorders than they did in a control group. Similarly, Rosenthal (1970) reviewed a series of studies in which it was found that first-degree relatives were approximately ten times more likely than members of the general population to be diagnosed as manic-depressive. Also, in a review of the genetic research on manic-depressive psychosis in twins, Price (1972) reported that 66 out of 97 monozygotic (identical) twin pairs were concordant for this disorder, while only 27 out of 119 dizygotic (fraternal) twin pairs were concordant for the disorder.

Although these findings are not conclusive

evidence, they do strongly suggest that some genetic factor may play a role in the development of affective disorders, especially in the manic-depressive psychoses. Of course, as Mendels (1970) notes, this factor may neither be "a necessary or sufficient cause in itself." That is, certain forms of depression may not involve a genetic predisposition, or genetic and environmental factors may interact.

Evidence indicating possible genetic factors in depression implies that organic variables may be involved, and disturbed physiological/biochemical processes have been found in depression.

PHYSIOLOGICAL/BIOCHEMICAL FACTORS

A number of investigators suggest that a basic disturbance in the central nervous system is a major cause of depression. Kraines (1966), for example, hypothesized that depression is caused by a disturbance of functioning in the hypothalamus. An important regulating center in the brain, the hypothalamus is known to regulate mood. A number of studies have shown that hypothalamic functioning is disturbed in depressed patients, along with the functioning of the pituitary, adrenal, and thyroid glands, which all are affected by the hypothalamus. After reviewing such research, Kraines concluded that depression results from an inhibition of hypothalamic functioning. However, it must be noted that a great deal of his supporting evidence consists of preliminary and uncontrolled findings that are far from conclusive. Although the hypothesis shows promise, a great deal of additional research is required. Nonetheless, other biochemical research also points to the possible importance of the hypothalamus in depression.

There is an increasing amount of data indicating biochemical disturbances may play an important role in depression. Schildkraut (1965) proposed a *catecholamine hypothesis* of depression that suggests the involvement of one of the catecholamines, *norepinephrine,* in this disorder. Norepinephrine is an important neurotransmitter involved in the carrying of nerve impulses from one neural fiber to another within the sympathetic nervous system. Schildkraut contends that too much norepinephrine results in overstimulation of nerve fibers, producing the overexcitability of mania. In contrast, too little norepinephrine produces an understimulation of nerve fibers and thus the underexcitability of depression. Schildkraut in fact suggests that electroconvulsive therapy (ECT), which will be discussed later in this chapter, is an effective treatment for relieving depression be-

cause it acts to increase the norepinephrine supply available in the brain. Although there is as yet no direct evidence supporting a causal relationship between norepinephrine and depression, there are data, reviewed by Kety (1970), that highlight its possible importance.

Weiss and colleagues have recently reported a series of studies demonstrating that in animals exposed to uncontrollable aversive events (such as those in which Seligman produced learned helplessness), there is a significant depletion of brain norepinephrine levels (Glazer, Weiss, Pohorecky, & Miller 1975; Weiss, Glazer, Pohorecky, Brick, & Miller 1975). These researchers suggest that exposure to uncontrollable events causes a depletion of norepinephrine that, in turn, produces the behavioral symptoms of learned helplessness/depression. It should be noted that norepinephrine is the primary transmitter substance in the hypothalamus; Kraines (1966) hypothesized that a hypothalamic disturbance was the underlying cause of depression. This hypothesis, obviously, might be compatible with the research on norepinephrine if one assumes a direct relationship between hypothalamic dysfunction and norepinephrine level disturbances. This is a very promising area of research that is currently receiving a great deal of attention by investigators.

Directly related to the research on the importance of norepinephrine in depression are some experiments by Thomas and Balter, cited by Seligman (1975). These results also point to the possible importance of underlying physiological/biochemical causes of depression. The study by Thomas and

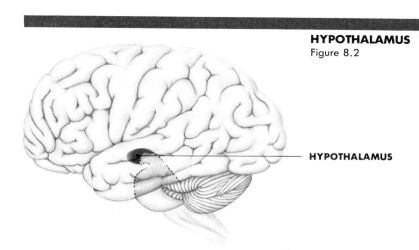

HYPOTHALAMUS
Figure 8.2

HYPOTHALAMUS

Balter involved the stimulation of two structures in the hypothalamus—the *medial forebrain bundle* (MFB) and the *septum*. Stimulation of the medial forebrain bundle is thought by many to be the physiological basis for pleasure. Norepinephrine is the primary transmitter substance in the MFB. The septum, a neighboring structure, inhibits the activity of the MFB when stimulated. Thomas and Balter observed that when the septum of cats was stimulated directly with electricity, the cats became passive and lethargic. Positive reinforcement did not seem as rewarding as usual, and punishment was less disturbing and disruptive. These findings prompted the investigators to propose that septal excitation or stimulation, which inhibits MFB activity, was a primary cause of helplessness.

To test this proposal more systematically, Thomas produced learned helplessness in cats by exposing them to inescapable electric shock. A cannula (a small hypodermic needle that allows the injection of chemicals into the body) was implanted in the septum of the cats. Atropine, a drug that dramatically "shuts off" the activity of the septum, was then injected into the septa of cats that had been exposed to inescapable shock. These cats were not helpless in the shuttle box and would learn to escape from it to avoid shock; but the cats who did not receive atropine and who also had experienced inescapable shock were helpless. They did not attempt to escape.

In the final step, all the cats were administered more inescapable shock. The cats who had been helpless now were also given atropine; this eliminated their helplessness. The cats who previously had been given atropine (and who had escaped normally) got no atropine this time. They became helpless. These data tend to support nicely the view that helplessness can be explained by the relative activity of the septum, since blocking it with atropine eliminated helplessness. Such research on norepinephrine depletion and hypothalamic activity may aid in uncovering the physiological basis of helplessness and also, possibly, of human depression.

Another theory implicating biochemical causes in depression suggests that the disorder is the result of an imbalance in sodium and potassium chloride levels. Sodium and potassium are two *electrolytes,* which play an important role in the transmission of nerve impulses. (Electrolytes are the electrically charged particles that carry an electrical current from one nerve fiber to the next.) The effective transmission of electrical impulses

from one neuron to the next depends on the precise balance in distribution of sodium and potassium electrolytes inside and outside the nerve cells. The functioning of the nervous system will become disturbed if the balance of these electrolytes is disturbed.

A number of studies have indicated that psychotically depressed persons have an abnormally high level of sodium chloride, but that these levels tend to return to normal after the patient recovers from depression (Coppen 1967; Shaw 1966). One drug that reduces mania and sometimes depression is lithium carbonate. Coppen (1967) has demonstrated that this lithium salt may achieve its therapeutic effect by reducing the patient's sodium level. This also suggests the possible importance of electrolytic imbalance in depression.

There are a number of other physiological/biochemical theories proposed to account for depression that we will not review here. The reader is referred to a review by Dupue and Evans (1975) for a comprehensive survey of these various models.

AN INTEGRATIVE MODEL OF DEPRESSION

We have reviewed a number of models of depression that are based on quite different assumptions. The learning approaches advocated by Lewinsohn and Seligman, the cognitive model proposed by Beck, and the various physiological/biochemical approaches all are reasonable, intuitively appealing, and supported by some experimental data. However, although each model appears to do an adequate job of explaining certain types of depressive disorders, no one theory appears broad enough to explain adequately the wide range of depressive phenomena. The fact that evidence supports one particular model does not rule out the possible credibility of other models emphasizing different factors. Probably it will be shown eventually that different variables are associated with different forms of depression, and/or unique interactions between various factors are associated with specific forms of depression.

Noting the complexity of depressive disorders, a number of investigators have recently suggested that an approach emphasizing the integration of several orientations needs to be taken, rather than a one-dimensional approach, in order to understand and treat this disorder (e.g., Akiskal & McKinney 1973; Wilcoxon, Schrader, & Nelson 1976). Akiskal and McKinney, for example, emphasize that affective disorders are a complex interaction between genetic, biochemical/physiological, developmental, and situational/learning variables. These investigators argue that it is not worthwhile to consider any one cause in isolation from others.

In a relatively short period of time there have been a number of significant findings (only a sample of which we have reviewed) indicating the possible importance of various factors in the etiology of depression. This has become an exciting and very promising line of research that, with the development of more sophisticated experimental technology, should eventually lead to a better understanding and treatment of these affective disorders.

TREATMENT OF AFFECTIVE DISORDERS

EFFECTIVENESS OF TREATMENT VERSUS NO-TREATMENT

Depression often is a self-limiting disorder that dissipates on its own with time. Mildly-moderately depressed persons will usually improve spontaneously within a few weeks or a few months if no treatment is administered. The great majority of more severe cases recover within less than one year. Because depression is often a self-limiting disorder, precise statistics on the success rates for various treatment procedures are often not very reliable. Moreover, as Mendels (1970) indicates, depressed patients often respond favorably to nonspecific placebo procedures. Although most clinicians would claim that treatment will facilitate therapeutic improvement and help prevent a relapse, there is currently no well-controlled investigation definitively demonstrating that treatment leads to greater and more prolonged improvement than that produced by spontaneous improvement or by nonspecific placebo factors. Such claims need to be substantiated in future research studies.

SPECIFIC TREATMENT TECHNIQUES

ELECTROCONVULSIVE THERAPY Electroconvulsive therapy (ECT) was first introduced in 1938 by Cerletti and Bini primarily for use in schizophrenia. It soon became apparent that although ECT was not effective in treating schizophrenia, it was very effective in the treatment of depression. The

basic ECT procedures are summarized by Mendels (1970):

> The basic procedure of applying an electrode to each side of the forehead and passing a current of about 70 to 130 volts through the frontal lobes of the brain for a period of less than half a second still applies, but there have been certain significant modifications. Today most patients receive an intravenous barbiturate (such as Pentothal or Brevital) that rapidly induces anesthesia, together with an intravenous injection of a muscle relaxant (such as succinyl choline). The use of these or similar drugs has made the administration of ECT a much simpler procedure than in the past. The patient experiences little physical discomfort and the risk of complications is considerably reduced. . . . The majority of depressed patients who respond to ECT do so after six to eight treatments given at the rate of three a week. (pp. 105–106)

There has been a great deal of debate over the continued use of ECT. It is argued that some of the side effects, such as loss of memory, difficulty in concentration, confusion, and the possible destruction of a great number of brain cells, make ECT too risky to use, especially considering the availability of recently developed antidepressant drugs that are suitable and effective alternatives. This argument is countered by those who point to the effectiveness of ECT in producing a remission of depressive symptoms. Some estimates suggest that it is 90 percent effective in producing improvement

WHY DOES ECT WORK?

"Shock" techniques have been used throughout history as a means of "knocking a patient back into his senses." Valenstein (1973) reported some rather gruesome medieval procedures such as dropping a patient into a pit of snakes or a vat of cold water, or deliberately causing some infection. The notion behind such crude techniques was that they would traumatize the patient sufficiently to mobilize his or her bodily strength to offset the stress and come out of the stupor. Electroconvulsive therapy (ECT) is viewed by many as another example of this "shock" method.

ECT has an interesting history. In 1933, Sakel used large doses of insulin to produce comas in psychotic patients. The treatment was prompted by his speculation that psychotic behavior was a result of too much adrenalin, which could be offset by insulin. In 1935, a Budapest psychiatrist, Meduna, observed that there appeared to be a lower incidence of epilepsy in schizophrenic patients relative to the general population. He also observed that in those schizophrenics who also suffered from epilepsy, the schizophrenic symptoms temporarily disappeared after a seizure. Meduna therefore attempted to produce epileptic-type convulsions in schizophrenics in an attempt to reduce their bizarre symptoms and behavior. He first tried chemical methods, but encountered a number of problems—the main one being a high fatality rate. In 1938, two Italians, Cerletti and Bini, introduced electroshock for the artificial production of convulsive seizures in mental patients, which proved to be a safer procedure. Electroshock has not proved to be effective in the treatment of schizophrenia, but has been found to be highly effective in the treatment of certain forms of depression.

Why ECT works is still very much a matter of conjecture. Some investigators have suggested that it lowers the brain cellular barriers to chemicals such as norepinephrine and allows more to enter the brain (e.g., Essman 1972). In one study, Kety, Javoy, Thierry, Julou, and Glowinski (1967) subjected a group of rats to electroconvulsive shock and examined norepinephrine level changes. One group of rats received electroconvulsive shock twice a day for a week. A second group of controls was treated in exactly the same manner, even having electrodes attached, except that the shock current was not turned on. Twenty-four hours after the last shock, changes in norepinephrine metabolism were examined in both groups of rats. There was a significant increased turnover and absolute level of norepinephrine in the brains of the shocked animals. On the basis of these results, Kety and colleagues suggest that an electroconvulsive shock regimen stimulates the synthesis of norepinephrine in the brain. Such data also suggest that norepinephrine depletion

in certain forms of depression, specifically manic-depressive psychosis and involutional melancholia (Coleman 1976). It should be noted, though, that the use of ECT has been reduced by recent developments in chemotherapy. The treatment still is used to bring about rapid alleviation of severe depression, especially in suicidal patients. What is currently needed is a method of selecting those depressed subjects who will respond most favorably to this form of treatment.

Some preliminary data reported by Mendels (1967) suggest that factors used in distinguishing between endogenous and reactive depression may be used in predicting response to treatment. Symptoms indicating endogenous depression appear to be associated with a favorable reaction to ECT. Additional research is needed to delineate more clearly behaviors and symptoms that can be used in objectively determining who will respond best to this treatment or to other forms of therapy. Often, this decision is based on subjective clinical impressions rather than careful, systematic determination.

CHEMOTHERAPY Antidepressant drugs are being used increasingly with success in treating depression. Trade-name drugs such as *Tofranil* and *Elavil* have been demonstrated to be effective in the treatment and prevention of this disorder (e.g., Raskin 1974). *Lithium carbonate* has been proven to be highly effective for treating manic reactions, as well as preventing the reoccurrence of manic-depressive reactions (Schou 1968). (We earlier indicated that this lithium salt may achieve its therapeutic effect by reducing an abnormally high

may underline depression, and that ECT that stimulates the metabolism of norepinephrine is a way of overcoming this depletion. The *catecholamine hypothesis* of depression proposed by Kety and colleagues (1967) and the research by Weiss and colleagues (1975) on learned helplessness both point to the important role that norepinephrine may play in affective states and behavior.

Of course, these data are only suggestive and do not clearly elucidate the mechanism involved in ECT. To date, because of the poor research methodology employed in studies attempting to assess ECT effectiveness in humans, there is still not even conclusive evidence that the introduction of current into the brain is the only major factor responsible for improvement of a patient (Costello & Belton 1970). Some investigators have suggested that it may work simply because a patient becomes sufficiently afraid of being shocked and so recovers. Others have even speculated that ECT may be viewed as a form of punishment that a depressed patient with severe guilt feelings believes he or she deserves. These guilt feelings are alleviated after the patient receives this "just punishment," and he or she then gets better. None of the speculations, however, is supported by hard facts. Obviously, some systematic and methodologically sound research is needed before the mechanisms involved in ECT are clearly understood.

level of sodium chloride.) Table 8.3 is a summary of the generic and trade names of two classes of antidepressant drugs.

Because anxiety is often present along with depression, many times tranquilizers and anti-anxiety drugs are prescribed in combination with antidepressants. The use of a drug regimen can be an effective means of reducing high levels of depression and anxiety and can also be used to maintain the treatment improvement achieved by ECT. However, as pointed out in earlier chapters, the indiscriminant use of chemotherapy alone, without an attempt to deal with possible situational/interpersonal factors involved, may not lead to any permanent long-term improvement in most forms of this behavior disorder. This is also true for ECT. Chemotherapy or ECT usually needs to be employed in combination with psychological treatment techniques to be sure of dealing adequately with factors that may prompt a reoccurrence of the depressive reaction. This is especially true in cases of depression where there has been a significant personal loss resulting in a lingering feeling of hopelessness and helplessness, or in cases where there has been a lowering of self-esteem. A number of innovative psychotherapeutic techniques have been developed that show promise for the treatment of such cases.

PSYCHOTHERAPY / BEHAVIOR THERAPY

There have not been any systematic attempts to document objectively the effectiveness of traditional psychoanalytical approaches to the treatment of depression. Some recent attempts have been made, however, to assess the effectiveness of a number of behaviorally oriented and cognitively oriented treatment procedures. One such behaviorally oriented approach attempts directly to increase the frequency of adaptive, nondepressive behavior while simultaneously decreasing depres-

ANTIDEPRESSANT DRUGS
Table 8.3

GENERIC NAME	TRADE NAME
I. Tricyclic drugs (imipramine-type drugs)	
Imipramine	Tofranil
Amitriptyline	Elavil
Desipramine	Norpramin
	Pertofran
Trimipramine	Surmontil
Opipramol	Insidon
Nortriptyline	Aventyl
Protriptyline	Vivactyl
II. MAO Inhibitors	
Pheniprazine	Catron
Phenelzine	Nardil
Etryptamine	Monase
Pargyline	Eutonyl
Iproniazid	Marsilid
Isocarboxazid	Marplan
Nialamide	Niamid
Tranylcypromine	Parnate
Chlorpromazine	Thorazine
Chlorprothixene	Taractan
Thioridazine	Mellaril

*Note: Tricyclic drugs have no substantial effect on normal or nondepressed persons. Tricyclic are usually preferred over MAO inhibitors.

sive behavior and feelings of helplessness and hopelessness. Liberman and Raskin (1971), for example, have reported some favorable results with a method in which contingent therapist attention is used as reinforcement. The therapist systematically ignores the client's complaints and other depressive verbalizations but verbally reinforces and attends carefully to nondepressive verbalizations and reports of effective coping with problematic situations.

A similar behaviorally oriented treatment technique was developed and employed by Lewinsohn (1974). As we noted earlier, Lewinsohn views depression as caused by a low rate of response-contingent positive reinforcement. His treatment approach is therefore directed at increasing the patient's participation in pleasant, positively reinforcing activities. In one study, Lewinsohn and Graf (1973) assessed the effectiveness of this technique in modifying depressed moods in ten depressed college students. For each patient, these investigators determined the ten activities that were most highly associated with a nondepressed mood over a 30-day period. The therapist reinforced these ''target'' behaviors by increasing therapy time (reflective nondirective listening) whenever the patient increased the frequency of these behaviors. It was found that such reinforcement increased the frequency of these behaviors (e.g., going to a party with friends), which, in turn, were associated with a significantly positive change in mood.

Seligman's (1975) learned-helplessness formulation also has direct implications for the treatment of depression. Since in this approach, depression is the result of the individual's perception that he or she cannot control environmental events, it follows that increasing the individual's perception of control should lead to a significant reduction in depression. There has not yet been much work directly testing the treatment implications of this formulation. However, a therapy study reported by Burgess (1969) provides some support. In the treatment program she developed, a ''graded-task'' approach was utilized in which events were constructed for patients to perform that were ordered so as to maximize successes and minimize failures. For example, patients began with some minimal form of behavior, such as making a telephone call. Burgess indicates that it is essential for patients to succeed in these attempts rather than merely starting and then giving up. The task requirements are then increased, and the patient is reinforced for successful completion by the attention and interest of the therapist. Results indicate

that this treatment approach was effective in relieving depression. Seligman (1975) also reported some preliminary data that indicate the success of such a graded-task approach in increasing positive mood level.

An approach that emphasizes the modification of covert behaviors, such as self-statements and attitudes, rather than the overt behaviors emphasized in these behavioral approaches, is the cognitive therapy technique developed by Beck (1967). This technique is very similar to the rational emotive therapy (RET) approach developed by Ellis (1970). As discussed earlier, Beck views depression as caused by maladaptive or irrational cognitions or beliefs. The major goal of therapy is to modify these negative cognitive patterns and to replace them with more realistic and positive ones. Beck reports that this approach effectively relieves depression. Shaw (1977) has compared this form of cognitive therapy and Lewinsohn's behavioral treatment of depression in terms of clinical effectiveness. Results of a study treating depressed college students indicated that both treatment techniques alleviated depression more, as measured by self-report and objective clinical ratings, than did no treatment of a control group. However, the cognitive modification therapy group improved significantly more than the behavior therapy group. Additional therapy-comparison research of this type is needed to assess the reliability of these findings of differences.

It should also be noted that Beck (1974) has pointed out the relation of cognitive therapy to behavior therapy. Cognitive therapy, like behavior therapy, is designed to modify a person's idiosyncratic maladaptive behavior. The behavior in this case is the maladaptive ideation or cognition that causes the depressed mood. Beck draws a number of parallels between cognitive and behavior therapy. First, in both, the therapy is more structured and the therapist is more active in directing change than in other psychotherapies. Second, both cognitive and behavior therapists direct their therapeutic techniques at overt symptoms or behavior problems. They also typically take their patients' self-reports at face value. Third, neither therapy technique relies a great deal upon recollections or reconstructions of early childhood experiences. Finally, both behavior and cognitive therapists assume that patients' maladaptive behavior patterns can be unlearned, and that insight into the origin of the problem behavior is not necessarily required. A number of clinicians have been active in developing cognitive techniques in conjunction with behavior therapy procedures as a means of modifying what clients say to themselves (e.g., Meichenbaum 1972).

Fuchs and Rehm (1977) assessed the effectiveness of a treatment program directed at the simultaneous modification of both overt and covert behaviors. The program consisted of a self-control training procedure constructed explicitly to train depressed individuals to (1) modify inaccurate and negative cognitive thoughts about personal behavior and situations; (2) modify any unrealistic and unattainable goals the persons have set for themselves which may lead to failure and a resultant lowering of self-esteem; (3) teach clients appropriate self-reinforcement techniques so that positive, nondepressed behaviors are rewarded. This self-control behavior therapy technique was significantly more effective in reducing self-report and behavioral measures of depression than were a nonspecific group therapy technique and a no-treatment control condition. The approach thus appears promising and seems to warrant further examination.

In chapter 6 we discussed the broad-spectrum behavior therapy approach advocated by Lazarus (1971) for treating neurotic behavior.

Using the approach, Lazarus (1974) has outlined a multimodal behavioral technique for treating depression in which overt behavior, cognition, and interpersonal relationships are some of the components modified. Instead of concentrating on only one aspect of behavior and functioning, he attempts to deal with all the relevant aspects of the depression demonstrated by a patient. When needed, medication also is prescribed as part of the treatment program. Lazarus reports that 22 of the 26 clients with chronic depression whom he treated with this approach showed significant improvement within an average of three months of therapy. This approach, too, shows great promise for the treatment of depression. Wilcoxon, Schrader, and Nelson (1976) provide a more detailed review of all these approaches.

We should again point out that a high level of anxiety commonly is associated with the state of depression. In such cases, cognitive behavioral techniques for the treatment of anxiety could be employed as part of the therapy program. Such a comprehensive program, with the use of other adjunctive treatment methods such as chemotherapy, will ensure a more stable and long-term adjustment.

DIAGNOSIS AND ASSESSMENT

INTERVIEW / REFERRAL

Because of the difficulty associated with conceptualizing depression, defining its major features, and deciding what is to be measured, it is not surprising that the diagnosis of the various forms of depression can be problematic. As indicated earlier, better methods need to be developed for the subclassification of depressed individuals. An increasing number of clinicians are focusing on delineation of the specific behavior patterns that are distressing to an individual. On the basis of this assessment, they attempt to develop a treatment program to deal with this disordered behavior. Most of these assessment data can be collected in a clinical interview. Beck (1967) indicates that four categories of behavior should be evaluated: (1) Emotional difficulties—Is the individual unhappy? Does he or she feel guilty? (2) Cognitive difficul-

ties—Is the patient delusional? Does the patient have an unrealistically low self-image? (3) Motivational and behavioral difficulties—Does the person engage in very low pleasurable activities? Does he or she lack appropriate social skills to interact effectively? (4) Physical difficulties—Does the individual complain of sleeplessness, headaches and other somatic complaints, and loss of interest in sex?

As Wilcoxon, Schrader, and Nelson (1976) point out, when such information has been collected, the clinician has a clearer picture of what the client is calling "depression." This provides a more accurate determination of the disorder than assessment attempts that try to determine which of the traditional classification subtypes (neurotic depression, psychotic depression, etc.) the patient appears to represent. This information also will be more valuable in allowing the clinician to construct a treatment program tailored for the individual.

To aid in the collection of data related to depression, the Hamilton Rating Scale for Depression (Hamilton 1960) was developed as a structured interview procedure. It consists of a 17-item list of symptoms that are rated by a clinician during the course of an interview. Symptoms (such as depressed mood, guilt, somatic complaints) are rated for severity on a 0 to 4 point scale. The major purpose of this scale is to quantify the information concerning the frequency and intensity of depression symptomatology assessed during an interview. The reliability for this scale is relatively high, with an estimate of .87 from several studies (Mendels 1970).

Another method for assessing depression is the direct measurement of specific overt behaviors. Williams, Barlow, and Agras (1972) developed a behavioral checklist for use by paraprofessionals, such as ward attendants, in a hospital setting to rate the frequency, timing, and intensity of an individual's overt depressive behaviors. It can provide a relatively reliable index of the degree of a patient's depression.

TESTING

A number of psychological tests and rating scales have been developed for the clinical assessment of depression and its differential diagnosis. However, the problems associated with the definition of depression also significantly limit the utility of psychological tests and scales. It is not surprising that the reliability of these methods is usually poor. As we have indicated a number of times, test results should never be used as the sole basis for a diagnosis. They should be viewed merely as an adjunct to more thorough assessment procedures based on social history and interview/behavioral evaluation.

The MMPI is the most widely used psychological test for assessing the various forms of psychopathology, including depression. The Depression (D) scale on the MMPI measures the degree of clinical depression, which is defined as "pessimism of outlook on life and the future, feelings of hopelessness or worthlessness, slowing of thought and action, and frequently preoccupation with death and suicide." The problem with the use of this scale is that it does not solely suggest the presence of depression. Patients with other forms of psychopathology may also be depressed and have elevated D scores.

A number of self-rating scales are used for the assessment of depression and are popular because of their ease of administration. The Multiple Affect Adjective Check List (Zuckerman & Lubin 1965) and the Depression Adjective Check List (Lubin 1965) consist of a number of adjectives suggesting unhappiness, dissatisfaction, and apathy, which the testee is asked to check if they describe his or her feelings and behaviors. The number of depression-related adjectives checked is assumed to provide a quantitative measure of the individual's level of depression. Another self-rating scale, the Beck Depression Inventory (Beck 1967), consists of 21 sets of statements from which the individual is asked to choose the one statement that he or she feels is most self-descriptive. For example, one set of statements is:

I do not feel sad.
I feel blue or sad.
I am blue or sad all the time and
   I cannot snap out of it.
I am so sad or unhappy
   that it is quite painful.
I am so sad or unhappy
   that I cannot stand it.

Beck (1967) reports that this Inventory reliably discriminates depression from other psychological disorders. Finally, the Zung Self-Rating Depression Scale (Zung 1965) consists of 20 items that individuals are requested to score as "a little of the time," "some of the time," "part of the time," and "most of the time." The items are statements such as "I feel downhearted and blue," "I get tired for no reason," and "My life is pretty full." Zung indicates that scores on this scale are significantly correlated with MMPI D scale scores.

PROGNOSIS

As we have noted earlier, depression is often a self-limiting disorder that usually dissipates on its own with time. Even severe cases usually recover within less than one year. The chief exception is involutional melancholia; Rosenthal (1970) has estimated that the spontaneous recovery rate in this disorder is one to four years in approximately 30–60 percent of the cases. The rest become chronic hospitalized cases if no treatment is provided for them.

When an appropriate treatment is administered to mild-moderate forms of depression that do not require hospitalization, then the prognosis for fairly rapid improvement is good. In more pronounced forms of depression where hospitalization is needed, patients can be discharged within a few weeks if given the appropriate treatment. For involutional melancholia, the hospital stay may be slightly longer (about one month). The relapse rate for depression can also be kept low with the appropriate supportive and follow-up therapy.

One of the serious consequences of depression is the increased probability that the afflicted person will attempt suicide. There is, in fact, a greater incidence of suicide in this patient group than in the general population (Schanche 1974). Conservative estimates are that one out of every 200 persons suffering from depression ends up attempting suicide. Thus, even though the general prognosis for improvement from depression is good, there is still a great need for even more effective treatment techniques. Some of the recent techniques discussed earlier show great promise. Research also is needed to develop a method that will enable a therapist to decide objectively what treatment is best suited and most effective for a particular depressed individual. Methods also need to be developed that will allow mental health professionals to determine which depressed patients are "high risks" for suicide, so that appropriate prevention/intervention techniques can be developed and used.

SUICIDAL BEHAVIOR

Although a variety of factors contribute to suicidal behavior, depression plays a central role. In retrospective studies examining the available clinical records of individuals who committed suicide, it has been reported that approximately 75 percent of the sample of patients had been depressed to some degree prior to their suicide (e.g., Barraclough, Nelson, Bunch, & Sainsbury, 1969; Leonard 1974).

Exact statistics on the incidence of suicide are difficult to determine. One reason is that many individuals who commit suicide attempt to make their deaths appear accidental so that their survivors can collect insurance, or their families will escape the stigma and shame associated with suicide. There have been some estimates that at least 15 percent of all fatal automobile accidents are actually suicides (Finch, Smith, & Pokorny 1970).

Even though precise statistics on suicide are difficult to determine, estimates of suicides committed in the United States each year range from 25,000 to 60,000 (Epstein 1974). In addition, another 200,000 individuals attempt to commit suicide but fail. The overall national rate of suicide has increased in recent years, so that it now ranks about eleventh among causes of death. For the 15–24-year-old age group, for which the suicide rate has doubled in recent years, it is the second most common cause of death. (Although the suicide rate in the United States may seem high—approximately 12 individuals per 100,000 population—a number of countries have higher rates: the rates in Czechoslovakia and Sweden are twice that of the U.S., while Hungary's suicide rate is the highest in the world and about three times that of the U.S.)

Other facts about suicide in our country, as summarized by Coleman (1976), include the following: The peak age for suicide attempts is between 24 and 44 years of age (it should be noted, however, that other data, as we shall review in Part III, suggest that suicide is more probable after 50). The rate of successful suicides is three times greater for males than females; however, more females than males attempt suicide. The most common method of suicide for women is drugs, most frequently barbiturates. Men usually employ more violent and lethal techniques, particularly guns. This is probably why men are usually more successful than women in actually committing suicide. In chapter 17, we shall again discuss suicide and life-threatening behavior as it relates especially to adolescents.

MYTHS ABOUT SUICIDE

Through the years, a number of popular misconceptions have evolved concerning suicide. Investigators such as Pokorny (1968) and Shneidman (1973) have noted a number of these. One myth is that the individual who discusses suicide or threatens suicide will not actually carry out the act. The fact is that in roughly three-quarters of all successful suicides, the person communicated his or her intent beforehand, within a few months of the fatal attempt. People seldom commit suicide without some warning, such as stating that it would be better for everyone if they were dead and then proceeding to give away their valuable possessions. Most persons contemplating suicide are ambivalent about taking their lives and will usually try to express in some way this ambivalence and the psychological stress they are experiencing. Such clear warnings and signals should be taken seriously.

Another prevalent misconception is that when an individual has unsuccessfully attempted suicide, then that person was not actually serious about ending his or her life. Again, studies have shown that in about 75 percent of completed suicides, attempts or threats had been made earlier. These may represent one last warning or attempted communication to others by an individual who is ambivalent about taking his or her life, or a "trial run" to allow the individual to prepare for a more effective future attempt.

Some of the many other myths about suicide: (1) *To commit suicide is a sign of insanity.* Even though most individuals who commit suicide are extremely unhappy, the majority of these individuals are in touch with reality, are rational, and are not psychotic. (2) *Suicide is influenced by such factors as the season, weather, temperature, day of the week, etc.* There is no conclusive evidence to substantiate such claims. (3) *An individual with a terminal physical illness is unlikely to commit suicide.* The awareness that one is going to die soon does not preclude the possibility of suicide. In one study of patients with malignant tumors, Farberow, Shneidman, and Leonard (1963) found that suicides are committed by patients who may have only a few hours or days to live. (4) *When an individual's emotional state improves, the risk of suicide decreases.* A great many people, especially deeply depressed patients, attempt suicide after their mood appears to be getting better. A sudden rise in spirits is frequently the "calm before the storm," a danger signal that should not be misinterpreted as a sign of improvement and decreased suicidal risk.

SUICIDAL TYPES

It is generally recognized that there is no single suicidal personality type. There are a multitude of factors that can prompt an individual to think about or to commit suicide. Shneidman and Farberow (1970), on the basis of extensive investigations of suicide, developed a system of suicidal categories based on the type of reasoning that may lead an individual to attempt suicide. Table 8.4 summarizes their four hypothesized categories: catalogic, logical, contaminated, and paleologic. As the table shows, a number of thought processes and mood characteristics are involved, making it impossible to delineate one major suicidal type.

CAUSES AND STRESSORS

Most attempts at suicide occur as a result of some severe life stress. Factors discussed earlier in our review of affective disorders, such as serious interpersonal conflict, failure experiences, loss of a sense of meaning of life, and the development of feelings of helplessness/hopelessness are similarly involved in suicidal behavior. Of these factors, it has been pointed out that a feeling of hopelessness is the most dominant feeling associated with suicide (Kovacs, Beck, & Weissman 1975). Lester and Beck (1975), in a study of 254 attempted suicide cases, found that a sense of hopelessness was a better predictor of suicidal intent than any other aspects of depression. Besides these general stressors, various theoretical orientations have emphasized specific causes underlying suicidal behavior. Chapter 17 will also present a few causes and stressors related to adolescent suicide.

SOCIOLOGICAL ORIENTATION The French sociologist Emile Durkheim (1897) made one of the first extensive assessments of suicide. He suggested that suicide should not be viewed as the act of an isolated individual, but as an act of an individual within a social context. He analyzed the records of suicide from various countries and during different historical periods. On the basis of this analysis, he categorized three different types of self-destructive behavior. *Anomic suicide* occurs when there is a sudden change in the normal functioning of an individual's society. For example, following the Wall Street stock market crash in 1929, many persons affected by this financial disaster committed suicide because they believed they would no longer be able to continue the lives they had grown accustomed to. *Egoistic suicide* is committed by an individual who is not integrated into the society. For example, the "loner" who has no ties with others in society lacks social support during periods of stress that might precede a

suicidal attempt. Feeling alone and isolated, this individual sees no other alternative but to take his or her own life. *Altruistic suicide* is committed in response to an accepted value system of the individual's culture. The practice of *hara-kiri* in Japan and the suicide missions of Japanese Kamikaze pilots during World War II belong to this category. More recently, the self-immolations of Buddhist monks during the Vietnam War also fit this category.

Durkheim's sociological framework, while providing a useful descriptive and categorization system, is limited because it does not adequately explain the different reactions of individuals who are exposed to the same demands and stressors

FOUR TYPES OF SUICIDE (FROM SHNEIDMAN & FARBEROW 1970)
Table 8.4

TYPE	LOGIC PROCESS	PERSONAL CHARACTERISTICS	SUGGESTED TREATMENT
Catalogic	The logic is destructive, with the person unable to think rationally.	An individual who is lonely, feels helpless and fearful, and feels pessimistic about making meaningful personal relationships.	Dynamic psychotherapy, with the goal of providing the individual with a meaningful, rewarding relationship, so that his/her search for identification is stabilized.
Logical	The reasoning is acceptable, with the person making a rational decision that life is no longer worth living.	An individual who is older, or widowed, or in physical pain, and who wishes to end the psychological or physical pain through suicide because of no other perceivable alternative.	Treatment directed at eliminating physical pain (through analgesics and sedatives) and providing support and companionship by means of active milieu therapy.
Contaminated	The reasoning is based upon a religious/cultural concept of death.	An individual whose beliefs permit him/her to view suicide as a transition to another life or as a means of saving reputation.	Treatment necessarily has to do with deeply entrenched cultural or religious beliefs and would have to deal with and clarify the semantic implications of the concept of death.
Paleologic	The person's reasoning is due to psychological disturbances such as psychosis.	Individuals who are delusional and/or hallucinating.	Treatment must deal primarily with the psychosis or other disorder, and should include protecting the individual from his/her own impulses. Only subsequently could suicidal tendencies be dealt with.

Emile Durkheim (1858–1917), a French
sociologist, was among the first to systematically evaluate the causes of suicide.

Yukio Mishima, the celebrated Japanese
novelist, committed hara-kiri shortly
after this picture was taken.

within a given society. Not all the people who were financially ruined by the Wall Street crash committed anomic suicide. Likewise, not all Buddhist monks committed altruistic suicide during the Vietnam War. Durkheim did recognize the importance of taking into account individual differences, and proposed that the temperament or emotional state of a person would interact with social factors to produce suicide. However, he did not make a systematic attempt to delineate those individual temperament factors proposed to be important. As a result, the sociological orientation cannot be used to predict which of many individuals will commit suicide in response to the same social situation.

BEHAVIORAL ORIENTATION The behavioral orientation is similar to the sociological approach in its emphasis on the importance of social factors in suicide. However, behaviorally oriented theorists

such as Ullmann and Krasner (1975) view self-destructive behavior as resulting directly from a change in an individual's schedule of reinforcement. The suicidal individual may feel that, because of some real or imagined loss of a positive reinforcer such as a job, family, health, etc., his or her current life situation is no longer very satisfying or reinforcing. Concomitant with the loss of positive reinforcement in the current life situation, the individual may begin to view the thought of death as positively rewarding because it seems that it will produce a number of desired reactions, such as attention and pity from others who will feel sorry for him or her. Also, in some cases, it is a form of revenge, because the person anticipates that those who have hurt him or her will be punished by feelings of guilt and remorse for possibly causing the suicide.

The behavioral approach views suicidal behavior as it does any other form of maladaptive behavior—as primarily the result of certain reinforcement contingencies operating in an individual's environment. The treatment of a suicidal patient, therefore, would be similar to the treatment of any maladaptive behavior, particularly depression, with the goal of modifying the individual's pattern of reinforcement. However, there has been no comprehensive study to evaluate whether this behavioral orientation is effective in dealing with suicidal behavior.

PSYCHOANALYTIC ORIENTATION Psychoanalysts employ an extension of the psychoanalytic theory of depression to account for suicide. It is assumed that when an individual loses someone for whom he or she had ambivalent love-hate feelings, and with whom he or she has partially identified, the hate feelings and resultant aggression may be directed inward. If these hate feelings are strong enough, the resulting ''anger-in'' may prompt an individual to commit suicide. The individual is not so much killing himself or herself as killing the other person. The ambivalence of many suicidal individuals about taking their own lives is assumed to be the result of the ambivalent love-hate feelings toward the lost person and, as a result of introjection, toward themselves. Such hostility-aggressive impulses were believed to be produced by the *thanatos*, or death instinct, which, if directed inward, would prompt an individual to take his or her own life.

This psychoanalytic view of suicide has not, however, been demonstrated to be valid, and has not led to the development of an effective treatment procedure for dealing with suicide.

MENNINGER'S VIEW OF SUICIDE The influential and highly regarded psychiatrist Karl Menninger wrote a book in the 1930s entitled *Man Against Himself*, which, among other things, describes how the act of suicide is on a continuum with lesser self-destructive behaviors such as self-mutilation, persistent abuse of alcohol and dangerous drugs, and disregard of personal health requirements. With this viewpoint, the concept of suicide is not confined to self-murder. Ending one's life is simply the ultimate and quickest form of self-destructive behavior. There are degrees or levels of self-destructive behavior, with a variety of life-threatening acts that are less lethal, and slower-acting, than suicide.

Dave Harvey/Black Star

Karl Menninger is a highly regarded psychiatrist who has contributed significantly to the field of mental health. The Menninger Clinic in Kansas is a well-known and prestigious mental health treatment center.

Menninger (1963) later elaborated on the psychological motives for suicide. Regarding the kinds of suicide, he wrote:

There are accidental suicides, there are suicides which are substitutes for murder, there are suicides which are a cry for help, and suicides which are miscarriages of an attempt to get oneself rescued. But some suicides are also expressions of total despair and ruthlessly directed at one's own self-annihilation. The essence of this ultimate form of suicide is the disintegration of the ego and the overwhelming of the organism with self-directed destructiveness. . . . (pp. 268-269)

Menninger indicates that suicides are frequently

acts of revenge. He suggests that the suicidal individual may wish to make the survivor feel guilty and remorseful over the suicide (e.g., "Now you'll be sorry that you weren't kinder to me"). Suicide may also be a response to anticipated rejection, a flight from humiliation and feelings of inadequacies. Finally, Menninger indicates that there are certain suicides motivated by the belief that death will result in a "magic revival" or a rebirth.

These views are based on clinical impressions. It will be necessary to determine whether they are empirically supported and can lead to the development of a comprehensive model to use for the prediction, prevention, and/or treatment of suicidal behavior.

SUICIDE PREVENTION

In recent years, many suicide prevention centers have been established throughout the United States to attempt to aid an individual during a suicidal crisis. The main goal of these centers is to help the individual who is contemplating suicide to cope with the immediate life situation triggering these thoughts and wishes. As noted earlier, the great majority of suicidal persons are ambivalent about taking their own lives. Attempts are therefore made to try to convince these persons that they have some reason for staying alive, and to persuade them to postpone the act until the immediate crisis passes and the decision can be evaluated more objectively. The hope is that the person can be dissuaded from committing suicide and convinced to get involved in some form of therapy or assistance so that he or she can work through the problems that are causing this desire to die.

Most suicide prevention centers operate a 24-hour-a-day "hot line," staffed by psychiatrists, psychologists, social workers, or other trained personnel and volunteers, available for telephone contact. These centers also provide therapy for suicidal individuals or a referral service to direct these individuals to other mental health organizations that will provide more intensive and long-term assistance. Although it is difficult to assess precisely the success of these centers in reducing suicides, there have been some preliminary data suggesting that they are having an effective impact (Coleman 1976).

SYLVIA PLATH ON SUICIDE

Doesn't your work interest you, Esther?

You know, Esther, you've got the perfect setup of a true neurotic.

You'll never get anywhere like that, you'll never get anywhere like that, you'll never get anywhere like that.

Once on a hot summer night, I had spent an hour kissing a hairy, ape-shaped law student from Yale because I felt sorry for him, he was so ugly. When I had finished, he said, "I have you typed, baby. You'll be a prude at forty."

"Factitious!" my creative writing professor at college scrawled on a story of mine called "The Big Weekend."

I hadn't known what factitious meant, so I looked it up in a dictionary.

Factitious, artificial, sham.

You'll never get anywhere like that.

I hadn't slept for twenty-one nights.

I thought the most beautiful thing in the world must be shadow, the million moving shapes and cul-de-sacs of shadow. There was shadow in bureau drawers and closets and suitcases, and shadow under houses and trees and stones, and shadow at the back of people's eyes and smiles, and shadow, miles and miles and miles of it, on the night side of the earth. . . .

"Say, lady, you better not sit out here, the tide's coming in."

In many suicide prevention centers, the staffs use *demographic* factors in determining how great the suicidal risk is for a particular individual. Usually a checklist is employed to help guide the staff member's questioning of each hot-line caller. For example, characteristic factors associated with *high-risk* suicidal persons point to middle-aged or older males who are divorced or separated and living alone and who have a previous history of suicidal attempts. These demographic variables, in combination with the suicidal person's expression of an intense sense of hopelessness, are usually quite predictive of actual suicide attempts.

Investigators are continuing to search for factors that will allow them to better predict

The small boy squatted a few feet away. He picked up a round purple stone and lobbed it into the water. The water swallowed it with a resonant plop. Then he scrabbled around, and I heard the dry stones clank together like money.

He skimmed a flat stone over the dull green surface, and it skipped seven times before it sliced out of sight.

"Why don't you go home?" I said.

The boy skipped another, heavier stone. It sank after the second bounce.

"Don't want to."

"Your mother's looking for you."

"She is not." He sounded worried.

"If you go home, I'll give you some candy."

The boy hitched closer. "What kind?"

But I knew without looking into my pocketbook that all I had was peanut shells.

"I'll give you some money to buy some candy."

"Ar-thur!"

A woman was indeed coming out on the sandbar, slipping and no doubt cursing to herself, for her lips went up and down between her clear, peremptory calls.

"Ar-thur!"

She shaded her eyes with one hand, as if this helped her discern us through the thickening sea dusk.

I could sense the boy's interest dwindle as the pull of his mother increased. He began to pretend he didn't know me. He kicked over a few stones, as if searching for something, and edged off.

I shivered.

The stones lay lumpish and cold under my bare feet. I thought longingly of the black shoes on the beach. A wave drew back, like a hand, then advanced and touched my foot.

The drench seemed to come off the sea floor itself, where blind white fish ferried themselves by their own light through the great polar cold. I saw sharks' teeth and whales' earbones littered about down there like gravestones.

I waited, as if the sea could make my decision for me.

A second wave collapsed over my feet, lipped with white froth, and the chill gripped my ankles with a mortal ache.

My flesh winced, in cowardice, from such a death.

I picked up my pocketbook and started back over the cold stones to where my shoes kept their vigil in the violet light.

From *The Bell Jar*, by Sylvia Plath. Copyright © 1971 by Harper & Row Publishers, Inc.

suicide. In a recent investigation, Kiev (1974) analyzed the clinical and social data collected from 300 individuals at the time of a suicide attempt and one year later. The results of the one-year follow-up data revealed that three factors had prognostic significance in predicting subsequent and more serious suicide attempts: (1) degree of interpersonal conflict; (2) presence of symptom distress; and (3) the social setting of the suicide attempt (e.g., proximity of others and the individual's inclination not to seek help afterward). These results indicate that an assessment of a patient's social environment following one suicide attempt can help predict future attempts.

One relatively recent investigative tool being employed in this search is the *psychological autopsy*. This method analyzes as many sources of information as possible about a person who did commit suicide. Information such as the individual's personality makeup, life situation, and state of mind at the time of the suicide, obtained from crisis telephone calls, suicide notes, and interviews with close friends, family members, and work associates, are carefully assessed to determine sources of information that are useful in predicting suicide. The original purpose of these psychological autopsies was to determine whether a death was accidental or suicidal. However, they have produced a great deal of useful information that may aid in better predicting suicide.

SUMMARY

1. *Affective disorders* are marked by disturbances of mood in which extreme elation (mania) or depression cause a great deal of debilitating psychological distress for the afflicted person.

2. Currently, there is no precise and clear definition of depression. The DSM-II attempted to differentiate between various forms of depression in proposing the following categories: (1) major affective disorders, which include manic-depressive disturbances and involutional melancholia; (2) psychotic depressive reaction; (3) depressive neurosis. Research has indicated, however, that it is difficult reliably to assign depressed individuals to one of these categories.

3. The lack of reliability in diagnosing different forms of depression has prompted many clinicians to discard the traditional DSM-II classification system and attempt to delineate specific behavior patterns associated with different types of depression. Because of these difficulties, the proposed DSM-III will greatly change the classification format of the affective disorders. Three categories are proposed: depressive disorder, manic disorder, and bipolar disorder.

4. Psychoanalytic theory views depression as similar to a normal grief reaction caused by the real or imagined loss of a loved one or object. The major difference between the two is assumed to be that in a grief reaction the mourner is consciously concerned with the lost person or object and has no significant ambivalent or guilt feelings surrounding the loss; the depressive, however, is dominated by feelings of personal loss, guilt, and self-blame.

5. Beck's cognitive theory of depression views this disorder as caused by certain kinds of illogical thinking. Rather than viewing depression as a primary mood disturbance, Beck views it as a primary disorder of thought that results in a disturbance of mood.

6. Some learning theorists such as Ferster (1965) view depression as the result of sudden change or reduction in the schedule of positive reinforcement that normally maintains much of a person's behavior. Lewinsohn (1974) has been actively involved in empirically testing and extending this reduced-reinforcement conceptualization of depression. Another learning formulation of this disorder was proposed by Seligman (1975), who views reactive depression as a result of learned helplessness. There have been some empirical data supporting both these learning formulations.

7. A number of studies strongly suggest the presence of genetic factors in affective disorders, especially in the manic-depressive psychoses. These data imply that organic factors are involved in this disorder. There is evidence that disturbed physiological/biochemical processes are found in depression.

8. Kraines (1966) has suggested that depression is caused by a disturbance of functioning in the hypothalamus. There is also an increasing amount of data to indicate that biochemical disturbances play an important role in depression. For example, Schildkraut (1965) proposed a *catecholamine hypothesis* that suggests the involvement of one of the catecholamines, *norepinephrine*, in depression. Finally, research has also indicated the possible importance of electrolytic imbalances in depression.

9. Noting the complexity of depressive disorders, a number of investigators have recently suggested that rather than assuming any one single-dimensional approach, an *integrative approach* emphasizing the interaction between genetic, biochemical/physiological, developmental, and situational/learning variables needs to be taken in order to understand and treat depression more completely.

10. Depression often is a self-limiting disorder that dissipates on its own with time. When an appropriate form of treatment is administered to mild-moderate forms of depression that do not require hospitalization, the prognosis for fairly rapid improvement is good. In more pronounced forms of depres-

sion where hospitalization is needed, patients can be discharged within a couple of weeks if administered the appropriate treatment. Treatment techniques such as ECT, chemotherapy, and psychotherapy are usually effective.

11. Although there are a variety of factors that contribute to suicidal behavior, depression plays a central role.

12. Exact statistics on the incidence of suicide are difficult to determine. Estimates indicate that the overall national rate of suicide has increased in recent years, so that it now ranks about eleventh among causes of death in the United States.

13. It is generally recognized that there is no single suicidal personality type. Most suicidal attempts usually occur as a result of some severe life stress.

14. In recent years, there has been an increase in the number of suicide prevention centers established throughout the country to attempt to aid individuals during a suicidal crisis. Recent attempts have been made to isolate factors that will aid in predicting *high-risk* suicidal persons. The *psychological autopsy* is one investigative method used to isolate such factors.

RECOMMENDED READINGS

Akiskal, H. S., & McKinney, W. T. Depressive disorder: Towards a unified hypothesis. *Science,* 1973, *182,* 20–29.

Beck, A. T. *Depression: Clinical, experimental and theoretical aspects.* New York: Harper & Row, 1967.

Becker, J. *Affective disorders.* Morristown, N.J.: General Learning Press, 1977.

Dupue, R. A., & Evans, R. The psychobiology of depressive disorders. In B. A. Maher (Ed.), *Progress in experimental personality research.* New York: Academic Press, 1975.

Mendels, J. *Concepts of depression.* New York: Wiley, 1970.

Seligman, M. E. P. *Helplessness.* San Francisco: W. H. Freeman, 1975.

Shneidman, E. S., Farberow, N. L., & Litman, R. E. (Eds.), *The logic of suicide.* New York: Science House, 1970.

Wilcoxon, L. A., Schrader, S. L., & Nelson, R. E. Behavioral formulations of depression. In W. E. Craighead, A. E. Kazdin, & M. J. Mahoney (Eds.), *Behavior modification: Principles, issues, and applications.* Boston: Houghton Mifflin, 1976.

9

SCHIZOPHRENIC AND PARANOID DISORDERS

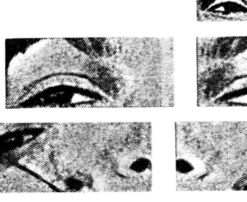

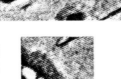

OVERVIEW In this chapter, we will discuss schizophrenic and paranoid disorders. Besides the presence of thought disorders, schizophrenia is characterized by disorders of attention, affect, motor behavior, and social behavior. As will be discussed, paranoid schizophrenia is one of the eleven subtypes of schizophrenia included in the DSM-II. (Along with hebephrenic, catatonic, and undifferentiated schizophrenia, this category is retained in the DSM-III.) Besides paranoid schizophrenia, the DSM-II also includes two other types of paranoid psychoses—paranoia and the paranoid state or reaction. At present, there is no conclusive evidence to indicate whether these three forms of paranoid states are sufficiently different to be labeled as separate categories of psychoses, or

are merely variants of the same basic schizophrenic disorder. The reliability of diagnosing the various DSM-II subtypes of schizophrenia has not been very high, because there is considerable overlap between subtypes, and also because patients may shift symptom patterns from one type to another over time. As a result of this lack of reliability, a number of dimensions have been proposed to account for the heterogeneity of patients diagnosed as schizophrenic. We will discuss four such dimensions that have been found to be effective in differentiating between types of schizophrenia.

We will review psychoanalytic, phenomenological-existential, and learning models proposed to account for schizophrenia. It will become apparent that there is a paucity of evidence to support any of these models. However, investigations of developmental and environmental factors have delineated certain important variables associated with schizophrenia, and considerable evidence indicates a genetic involvement. Currently, a diathesis-stress model of schizophrenia is popular.

Before the development of modern antipsychotic drugs and other recent treatment techniques, the prognosis for improvement of schizophrenia was generally poor. However, even though the outlook for improvement today is much better, schizophrenic patients still constitute approximately one-half of the total resident population in mental hospitals. This indicates that even more effective treatment techniques are still needed for this disorder.

SCHIZOPHRENIA: SYMPTOM DESCRIPTION AND ETIOLOGY

Imagine that you are given the following task: you are to describe the unicorn, explain where it comes from, and specify how to capture it. If you know anything about unicorns you will immediately go to the library and start looking under Mythology. There you will find descriptions of a fabulous animal with one horn and, in the more expensive books, you will discover colored illustrations. The pictures and verbal descriptions will show that the unicorn comes in assorted colors and sizes, and that it has a single horn in the middle of its forehead. If you stop at that point you will arrive at a satisfactory description, but if you delve further you will find that the unicorn cannot be captured except by a virgin, and even then only rarely. What's more, the essential conditions are not very well specified. You will soon realize that the descriptions differ depending on the particular mythology book you are reading. Thus, although the heraldic unicorn most often consists of a horse's body, a lion's tail, and a spirally twisted long horn, not all representations of the unicorn are the same. The Old Testament, to take but one example of peculiar practice, uses the word, unicorn, to refer to a two-horned animal. . . . How does this relate to schizophrenia? Let me state the relation in as simple and as straightforward way as I can: Schizophrenia is a unicorn. In neither case do we have definitive information about the cause for its appearance. In both cases a voluminous literature is available, and in both cases various authors have written about the phenomenon lacking the knowledge of what others proposed. Schizophrenia, like the unicorn, is described in various ways by various people. And its elimination, like the capture of the unicorn, appears to require some special conditions, not all of which have yet been specified. (Salzinger 1973, pp. 1–2)

This passage nicely communicates the problem of the many uncertainties about the description, etiology, and treatment of schizophrenia. Rather than being a single disorder, schizophrenia is more appropriately viewed as a group of disorders or, as Rosenthal (1968) suggests, "the schizophrenic spectrum." An array of characteristics and symptoms are present in schizophrenia, with the unique interaction and combination differing from patient to patient, so that the precise description and investigation of this disorder are problematic. This will become readily apparent when we review the major symptoms of schizophrenia.

SYMPTOMS OF SCHIZOPHRENIA

No psychological disorder has received more attention than schizophrenia, with its bizarre and unusual behavior. Although the DSM-II specifies that thought disorders are the primary characteristic of schizophrenia, a number of other major symptoms also are associated with this form of psychotic behavior: disorders of attention and perception, disorders of affect, disorders of motor behavior, and disorders of social behavior. As we briefly review these various symptoms, it will become obvious that schizophrenics display a great heterogeneity of symptoms. It is exceedingly rare for a schizophrenic patient to display the whole range of symptoms all the time. Most patients display only some of the symptoms some of the

DEMOGRAPHICS	USUAL AGE AT ONSET	PREVALENCE	SEX RATIO
SCHIZOPHRENIC DISORDERS	Most often during adolescence or early adult life	Approximately 1% of population	Equal
PARANOID DISORDERS	Generally somewhat later than schizophrenic disorders	Relatively rare	Not known

time. The various combinations of symptoms displayed by any one patient, which may change from time to time, frequently make it difficult to diagnose specific DSM-II subtypes of this disorder. This has created major problems for the DSM-II, which has tried to differentiate between the various subtypes on the basis of specific symptomatology.

DISORDERS OF THOUGHT The primary symptom of schizophrenia emphasized by the traditional classification system is the presence of *thought disorder*. Indeed, disturbed thinking is the most typical and readily observable characteristic. This disturbed thinking can take many forms, the primary types being *incoherence* and *delusions*.

The verbalizations of schizophrenics frequently are totally incoherent. The sentence structure used may be appropriate, with the proper use of nouns, verbs, and the like, but the meanings of the words themselves have a bizarre flavor and are difficult to comprehend. There may be *loose association* or *overinclusion,* which refers to the schizophrenic's difficulty in sticking to one topic when speaking. The patient often skips from one topic to another with no transition or coherence connecting the thoughts expressed. The schizophrenic's mind appears to wander aimlessly from one topic to the next with no attempt to tie together associations. McGhie and Chapman (1961) relate how a schizophrenic patient described this disorder of thinking:

> My thoughts get all jumbled up. I start thinking or talking about something but I never get there. Instead, I wander off in the wrong direction and get caught up with all sorts of different things that may be connected with things I want to say but in a way I can't explain. . . . Half the time I am talking about one thing and thinking

about half a dozen other things at the same time. It must look queer to people when I laugh about something that has got nothing to do with what I am talking about, but they don't know what's going on inside and how much of it is running round in my head. (pp. 108-109)

Many times, the schizophrenic will make up a new word, a *neologism*, that has no meaning to the listener. Another common type of incoherence is the *clang association*. This is a sentence or statement that consists of a series of rhyming words chained together not on the basis of any logic, but simply because they rhyme. When there is a complete breakdown of coherence, so that there are no associative links between words or thoughts, not even clang associations, then the schizophrenic's speech loses all communicative value. This total disorganization of speech is referred to as a *word salad*. This speech by a schizophrenic patient shows the breakdown of coherence:

> The players and boundaries have been of different colors in terms of black and white and I do not intend that the futuramos of supersonic fixtures will ever be in my life again because I believe that all known factors that would have its effect on me even the chemical reaction of ameno [sic] acids as they are in the process of combustionability are known to me. (From Maher 1966, p. 395)

The most common form of thought disorder present in schizophrenia is *delusional thinking*. Studies have found that more than two-thirds of hospitalized schizophrenics are delusional (Lucas, Sainsbury, & Collins 1962). Delusions are irrational beliefs that a person will defend even though the rest of society regards them as distortions of reality. There are different types of delusional thinking. *Delusions of persecution* involve the individual's belief that he or she is being plotted against by others, followed, listened to, or subjected to other forms of mistreatment. *Delusions of grandeur* refer to a belief that one is some powerful or famous person such as Jesus Christ or Napoleon. *Delusions of control* involve the patient's feeling that he or she is being controlled by some alien force, such as "cosmic energy" or extraterrestrial beings. The DSM-III, for example, mentions a type of delusion of control called "thought broadcasting," in which the individual believes his or her thoughts are being broadcast into the external world for others to hear. *Hypochondriacal delusions* are distortions of reality in which the individual believes that he or she is afflicted by some bizarre somatic disorder in which the "insides are rotting away" or the "brain is slowly dissolving and shrinking."

Delusions differ in quality and degree of bizarreness. For some schizophrenics, delusional thinking may be simply limited to fleeting references that do not dominate their thinking. For others, the delusions may be extremely *systematized* and dominate the clinical picture. A striking example of such systematized delusions has been presented by Rokeach (1964) in his book entitled "The Three Christs of Ypsilanti." In this book, he reviewed the cases of three men, each of whom was convinced he was Jesus Christ. This conviction dominated most of their daily behaviors. Each continued to maintain his belief even in the face of conflicting and disconfirming evidence. They were even unshaken after confronting one another! The following case includes excerpts from a conversation among the three men—Clyde, Joseph, and Leon:

A CASE OF DELUSIONAL THINKING

JOSEPH: My name is Joseph Cassel.

PSYCHOLOGIST: Joseph, is there anything else you want to tell us?

JOSEPH: Yes, I'm God.

PSYCHOLOGIST: Uh-huh. (turns to Clyde)

CLYDE: My name is Clyde Benson. That's my name straight.

PSYCHOLOGIST: Do you have any other names?

CLYDE: Well, I have other names, but that's my vital side and I made God five and Jesus six.

PSYCHOLOGIST: Does that mean you're God?

CLYDE: I made God, yes. I made it 70 years old a year ago. Hell! I passed 70 years old.

PSYCHOLOGIST: (turns to Leon)

LEON: It also states on my birth certificate that I am the reincarnation of Jesus Christ of Nazareth, and I also salute, and I want to add this. I do salute the manliness in Jesus Christ also, because the vine is Jesus and the rock is Christ, pertaining to the penis and testicles; and it so happens that I was railroaded into this place because of prejudice and jealousy and duping that started before I was born, and that is the main issue why I am here. I want to be myself. I do not consent to their misuse of the frequency of my life.

PSYCHOLOGIST: Who are "they" that you are talking about?

LEON: Those unsound individuals who practice the electronic imposition and duping. I am working for my redemption. And I am waiting patiently and peacefully sir, because what has been promised to me I know is going to come true. I want to be myself. I don't want this electronic imposition and duping to abuse me and misuse me, make a robot out of me. I don't care for it.

PSYCHOLOGIST: Did you want to say something, Joseph?

JOSEPH: He says he is the reincarnation of Jesus Christ. I can't get it. I know who I am. I'm God, Christ, the Holy Ghost, and if I wasn't, by gosh, I wouldn't lay claim to anything of the sort. I'm Christ. I don't want to say I'm Christ, God, the Holy Ghost, Spirit because I know this is an insane house and you have to be very careful. I know what I've done! I've engineered the affairs of the stronghold in a new world here, the British province. I've done my work. I was way down, way down. I was way, way up. I've engineered, by God! I've taken psychiatrics. And nobody came to me and kissed my ass or kissed me or shook hands with me and told me about my work. No sir! I don't tell anybody that I'm God, or that I'm Christ, the Holy Spirit, the Holy Ghost. I know what I am now and I know what I'm going to be. This is an insane house.

LEON: Don't generalize.

JOSEPH: I know who I am and I haven't got a hell of a lot of power right now. Christ! I do my work. The only thing I can do is carry on. I know what I am.

LEON: Mr. Cassel, please! I didn't agree with the fact that you were generalizing and calling all people insane in this place. There are people here who are not insane. Each person is a house. Remember that.

JOSEPH: This is an insane hospital, nevertheless.

ATTENTION AND PERCEPTION IN SCHIZOPHRENIA
Table 9.1

From McGhie & Chapman 1961

1. DISTURBANCES IN THE PROCESS OF ATTENTION
"I can't concentrate. It's diversions of attention that trouble me. I am picking up different conversations. It's like being a transmitter. The sounds are coming through to me but I feel my mind cannot cope with everything. It's difficult to concentrate on any one sound. It's like trying to do two or three things at the same time."

2. DISTURBANCES IN THE PROCESS OF PERCEPTION
a. Changes in Sensory Quality
"Sometimes I feel all right, then the next minute I feel that everything is coming towards me. I see things more than what they really are. Everything's brighter and louder and noisier."
b. Perception of Speech
"When people are talking I just get scraps out of it. If it is just one person who is speaking that's not so bad, but if others join in, then I can't pick it up at all. I just can't get into tune with that conversation. It makes me feel open—as if things are closing in on me and I have lost control."
c. Perception and Movement
"My responses are too slow. Things happen too quickly. There's too much to take in and I try to take in everything. Things happen but I don't respond. When something happens quickly or unexpectedly it stuns me like a shock. I just get stuck. I've got to be prepared and ready for such things. Nothing must come upon me too quickly."

3. CHANGES IN MOBILITY AND BODILY AWARENESS
"If I am doing something then I start thinking of what I am doing, that locks me up in a sense. For example, if I drop something and stop to pick it up, if I start to think of myself in that position and what I am doing, that locks me up in that position. If you keep thinking of where your body is it gets locked up."

LEON: My belief is my belief and I don't want your belief, and I'm just stating what I believe.

JOSEPH: I know who I am!

LEON: I don't want to take it away from you. You can have it. I don't want it.

PSYCHOLOGIST: Clyde, what do you think?

CLYDE: I represent the resurrection. Yeh! I'm the same as Jesus. To represent the resurrection (mumbles, pauses). I am clear . . . as a saint . . . convert . . . you ever see. The first standing took me ten years to make it. Ah, forty cars a month. I made 40 Christs, 40 trucks.

PSYCHOLOGIST: What did you make them out of?

CLYDE: I think that means 40 sermons. I think that's what it means.

PSYCHOLOGIST: Well, now, I'm having a little trouble understanding you, Mr. Benson.

CLYDE: Well, you would because you're probably a Catholic and I'm Protestant up to a saint.

PSYCHOLOGIST: Did you say you are God?

CLYDE: That's right. God, Christ, and the Holy Spirit.

JOSEPH: I don't know why the old man is saying that. He has it on his mind. He's trying to discharge his mind. It's all right, it's all right as far as I'm concerned. He's trying to take it out of his mind.

PSYCHOLOGIST: Take what out of his mind?

JOSEPH: What he just said. He made God and he said he was God and that he was Jesus Christ. He has made so many Jesus Christs.

CLYDE: Don't try to pull that on me because I will prove it to you!

JOSEPH: I'm telling you I'm God.

CLYDE: You're not!

JOSEPH: I'm God, Jesus Christ and the Holy Ghost! I know what I am and I'm going to be what I am!

CLYDE: You're going to stay and do just what I want you to do!

JOSEPH: Oh, no! Oh, no! You and everybody else will not refrain me from being God because I'm God. And I'm going to be God! I was the first in the world and I created the world. No one made me!

LEON: I don't like this whole meeting. This is mental torture and I'm not coming back.

In passing, we should note that the pathological nature of an individual's delusional thinking often is not as obvious as it was in this case. It may sometimes be difficult for a clinician to decide whether a patient's thinking is delusional or actually tied to reality. For example, a patient who has been recently hospitalized by family members may report that he or she is being mistreated by them. This may not necessarily be a distortion of reality, but may actually reflect the fact that the patient has been abused and mistreated.

DISORDERS OF ATTENTION AND PERCEPTION Considerable research indicates that schizophrenics perceive the world differently than normal individuals do. Indeed, patients frequently report that the world appears strange to them. Many have difficulties in attending to aspects of their environment. One of the most dramatic types of perceptual disorders is the *hallucination*. An hallucination is a sensory experience reported by a person in the absence of any external stimulation from the environment. Auditory hallucinations (e.g., hearing voices) are the most common type, with visual experiences less frequent. The voices heard in auditory hallucinations may be of one person or a group of people. Usually, the voices evaluate or comment on the individual's ongoing behavior. Somatic hallucinations (e.g., sensations of a snake crawling inside the abdomen), tactile hallucinations, and other perceptual distortions are also experienced by some schizophrenics.

McGhie and Chapman (1961) have categorized various disorders of attention and perception in schizophrenia, including patients' descriptions of these disorders. Some of these descriptions are presented in table 9.1.

DISORDERS OF AFFECT Although disordered affect is the main characteristic of the major affective disorders discussed in chapter 8, disturbances of affect also are present in schizophrenia. The DSM-II delineated three major forms of affective disturbance found in schizophrenia: flat affect, inappropriate affect, and ambivalent affect.

Flat affect denotes the state in which no situation or person can elicit an emotional response in the schizophrenic. No matter what is occurring around this person, he or she remains totally unemotional and apathetic. In *inappropriate affect,* the patient shows an emotional response that is out of context and not suited to the situation. For example, a schizophrenic may begin to giggle

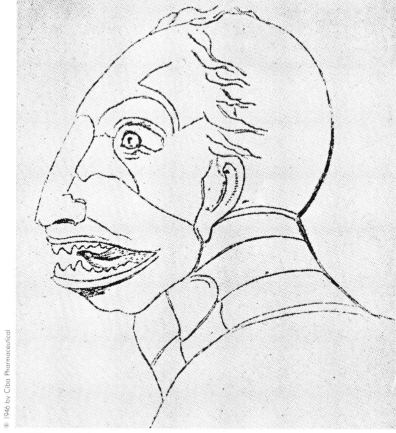

William Blake sketched this picture of a "Ghost of a Flea," which he said he saw hulking in the corner of his room and which told him that fleas contained the damned souls of bloodthirsty men.

uncontrollably on hearing about the death of a close friend. *Ambivalent affect* refers to an emotional state in which the patient simultaneously expresses positive and negative emotions toward a single person or event. For example, a woman may display both strong love and intense hatred toward her parents.

DISORDERS OF MOTOR BEHAVIOR The motor activity of schizophrenics also is often bizarre. Some display a significant increase in their overall level of activity, similar to the hyperexcitability found in mania. They often exhibit bizarre facial expressions and may gesture with unusual body movements. At the opposite extreme of the activity level, some schizophrenics display an unusual absence of motor behavior. In *catatonic immobility,* the patient adopts unusual postures for long periods of time. For example, the patient may

Schizophrenic patients often engage in a form of isolation behavior, which is at times accentuated by the barrenness of many large hospitals.

assume a fetal-type position and remain in it virtually all day. During such a catatonic state, the limbs of the patient may have what is referred to as *waxy flexibility*. Another person can manipulate the limbs and put them in odd positions that will then be maintained during the catatonic state.

DISORDERS OF SOCIAL BEHAVIOR Many schizophrenics withdraw from contact with individuals and contact with the external world. They begin to become involved in their own internal thoughts and fantasies to the neglect of external reality. This withdrawal and overemphasis on one's own fantasies is termed *autism*. Concomitant with their withdrawal behavior, they usually display a lack of interpersonal interaction.

TRADITIONAL CLASSIFICATION TYPES

In the DSM-II classification system, eleven different types of schizophrenia were named. Of these, four are most commonly delineated: simple, hebephrenic, catatonic, and paranoid. The proposed new DSM-III will retain the latter three subcat-

egories. We will briefly review these four subtypes, giving representative case examples from Salzinger (1973) to demonstrate their major characteristics.

Simple schizophrenia is characterized by the reduction of an individual's attachment to and interest in external objects and individuals. Basically, in this reaction we have a seclusive, colorless person who has broken away from reality by withdrawing. He or she shows great indifference to a job, to physical appearance, and to social involvement. Rather than creating bizarre hallucinations and delusions, the simple schizophrenic adapts to the stressors of his or her world with an incredible lack of commitment to anything. This person may appear to be an emotional void, though he or she may be able to work at some tasks and communicate on a very superficial level with others. This case is an example of a patient diagnosed as a simple schizophrenic:

A CASE OF SIMPLE SCHIZOPHRENIA

A patient, diagnosed as a schizophrenic, simple type . . . was hospitalized at the age of 21

NEW DSM-III CLASSIFICATION OF SUBTYPES OF SCHIZOPHRENIA

The proposed DSM-III lists five subtypes of schizophrenia. They include:

1. Disorganized (hebrephrenia), marked by fragmented delusions and hallucinations,
2. Catatonic, marked by psychomotor disturbances such as rigidity, posturing, and stupor
3. Paranoid, marked by preoccupation with persecutory or grandiose delusions.
4. Undifferentiated, marked by symptoms that cannot be classified in any of the other DSM-III Subtypes.
5. Residual, marked by the individual currently displaying no prominent symptoms (in partial remission), but at one time displaying episodes of bizarre psychotic behavior.

It is noteworthy that "simple" or "borderline" schizophrenia has been deleted from the new DSM-III. Instead, *simple, borderline,* or *latent* schizophrenia is included in a new diagnostic category — *Schizotypal personality disorder.*

after being caught peeping into someone's window. His childhood was described as quiet, but people around him had some difficulty in understanding his behavior even then. At age 19, after working for two years, he suddenly decided to stop, pointing out that since his father and sister were working there was no need for him to work too. At about this time he was first caught peeping into a woman's bedroom. He became careless of his appearance and did only occasional work. A year later he was again arrested for peeping. He spoke less and less and became antagonistic to his father and sister. After his third arrest he was committed to a mental hospital. He showed no concern over his predicament, laughing about it in a silly manner. While in the hospital, he was apathetic, inactive, and preoccupied, but he never expressed delusions or hallucinations. (Salzinger 1973, p.3)

Hebephrenic schizophrenia is perhaps the most fragmented of all the schizophrenic reactions.

Besides social withdrawal, the clinical picture is one in which there is usually a total collapse of reality-testing ability. These patients' behavior consists of laughing on inappropriate occasions, silliness, and basically childish acts. They engage in incoherent and illogical speech involving bizarre associations and neologisms. This case typifies hebephrenic characteristics:

A CASE OF HEBEPHRENIC SCHIZOPHRENIA

. . . The patient was hopitalized at age 25. She was characterized as having been very seclusive and reserved from childhood. The onset of her illness came after a visit to a dentist's office where she said the dentist had exerted some influence over her and loved her. She became careless of her appearance after the visit to the dentist, talked irrelevantly, began hearing voices, had long periods of laughing and smiling to herself, and was depressed at other times. At the examination, her speech was extremely irrelevant and she said that people had been talking about her for years. The voices accused her of self-abuse and told her that she was under the control of electricity and influenced by telepathy and thought waves. In the hospital she showed progressive deterioration, became more and more sloppy in her habits and appearance. She became more delusional and claimed that the doctors caused her to masturbate day and night. She continued to laugh and smile to herself. (Salzinger 1973, p. 4)

Catatonic schizophrenia may take one of two general forms — *catatonic stupor* and *catatonic excitement.* Physical pain and stressors in general seem to have little effect when a person is catatonic. In catatonic stupor, the person takes on a "mask-like" face and becomes rigid and motionless, standing or sitting inflexibly fixed like a mannequin. When the person is moved, however, he or she may behave like a compliant zombie, maintaining the position the "master" chooses. (This is the phenomenon known as *waxy flexibility.*) By contrast, in catatonic excitement, the individual seems to be "possessed" by some super-energizing force. He or she explodes violently and strikes out at anyone, may resist sleep, assail any physical restraint, or do battle with any unseen enemy. In some cases, this exhaustive pace can push the catatonic toward an "exhaustion death." When

MARGARET ATWOOD ON A WAY OF LOOKING AT THINGS

I go back to the cabin, enter it. The fire I made for breakfast is still smoldering: I add another stick of wood and open the draft.

I snap the catches on my case and take out the drawings and the typescript, *Quebec Folk Tales*, it's easily replaceable for them in the city, and my bungled princesses, the Golden Phoenix awkward and dead as a mummified parrot. The pages bunch in my hands; I add them one by one so the fire will not be smothered, then the paint tubes and brushes, this is no longer my future. There must be some way of canceling the Samsonite case, it can't be burned. I draw the big knife across it, X-ing it out. . . .

When the paper things are burned I smash the glasses and plates and the chimney of the lamp. I rip one page from each of the books, Boswell and *The Mystery at Sturbridge,* the Bible and the common mushrooms and *Log Cabin Construction,* to burn through all the words would take too long. Everything I can't break, frying pan, enamel bowl, spoons and forks, I throw on the floor. After that I use the big knife to slash once through the blankets, the sheets and the beds and the tents and at the end my own clothes and my mother's gray leather jacket, my father's gray felt hat, the raincoats: these husks are not needed any longer, I abolish them, I have to clear a space.

When nothing is left intact and the fire is only smoldering I leave, carrying one of the wounded blankets with me, I will need it until the fur grows. The house shuts with a click behind me.

I untie my feet from the shoes and walk down to the shore; the earth is damp, cold, pock-marked with raindrops. I pile the blanket on the rock and step into the water and lie down. When every part of me is wet I take off my clothes, peeling them away from my flesh like wallpaper. They sway beside me, inflated, the sleeves bladders of air.

My back is on the sand, my head rests against the rock, innocent as plankton; my hair spreads out, moving and fluid in the water. The earth rotates, holding my body down to it as it holds the moon; the sun pounds in the sky, red flames and rays pulsing from it, searing away the wrong form that encases me, dry rain soaking through me, warming the blood egg I carry. I dip my head beneath the water washing my eyes.

Inshore a loon; it lowers its head, then lifts it again and calls. It sees me but it ignores me, accepts me as part of the land.

When I am clean I come up out of the lake, leaving my false body floated on the surface, a cloth decoy; it jiggles in the waves I make, nudges gently against the dock.

They offered clothing as a token, formerly; that was partial but the gods are demanding, absolute, they want all.

The sun is three-quarters, I have become hungry. The food in the cabin is forbidden, I'm not allowed to go back into that cage, wooden

---

extreme hyperactivity is maintained for several days at a time, hyperthermia, vascular collapse, and then death can occur.

A CASE OF CATATONIC SCHIZOPHRENIA

. . . The patient was a 27-year-old laborer who had a relatively normal life. Three weeks before he was admitted to the mental hospital he started to show peculiar behavior; he became seclusive, had difficulty sleeping, and became sloppy about his person. At a bar he accused a person he had known for many years of "talking behind his back." He became very excited, so much so that even after he had been brought home he still stood at the window shouting and spitting at people who ostensibly were trying to "get" him. In the hospital, at first he was monosyllabic and slow. In the next few days he became completely mute and refused to eat. After five weeks of severe symptoms, including incontinence and standing in peculiar positions, he became somewhat more cooperative, but even after one year of hospitalization he rarely answered questions, still

rectangle. Also tin cans and jars are forbidden; they are glass and metal. I head for the garden and prowl through it, then squat, wrapped in my blanket. I eat the green peas out of their shells and the raw yellow beans, I scrape the carrots from the earth with my fingers, I will wash them in the lake first. There is one late strawberry, I find it among the matted weeds and suckers. Red foods, heart color, they are the best kind, they are sacred; then yellow, then blue; green foods are mixed from blue and yellow. I pull up one of the beets and scratch the dirt from it and gnaw at it but the rind is tough, I'm not strong enough yet.

At sunset I devour the washed carrots, taking them from the grass where I've concealed them, and part of a cabbage. The outhouse is forbidden so I leave my dung, droppings, on the ground and kick earth over. All animals with dens do that.

I hollow a lair near the woodpile, dry leaves underneath and dead branches leaned over, with fresh needle branches woven to cover. Inside it I curl with the blanket over my head. There are mosquitoes, they bite through; it's best not to slap them, the blood smell brings others. I sleep in relays like a cat, my stomach hurts. Around me the space rustles; owl sound, across the lake or inside me, distance contracts. A light wind, the small waves talking against the shore, multilingual water.

From *Surfacing*, by Margaret Atwood. Copyright ©1972 by Margaret Atwood.

mented by genuine adversaries. These imagined adversaries may be charged with sexual assaults; they may be blamed for making food taste as if it were poisoned, or accused of spraying deadly vapors. The paranoid schizophrenic's great assuredness about such false beliefs, despite all sorts of objective evidence that they are faulty, illustrates what some label *paranoid certainty*. That is, they assume their beliefs are correct beyond question. That the paranoid schizophrenic can convince himself or herself of the truth of these absurd convictions is proof that this person has broken with reality and has fragmented his or her relationships with others. Of all the traditional subtypes of schizophrenia, paranoid schizophrenia is the most common classification.

A CASE OF PARANOID SCHIZOPHRENIA

. . . This patient entered a psychiatric hospital after having failed to obtain a body for his "experiments in restoring life." He had been in the army for 16½ months without being hospitalized, despite the fact that he had been psychotic during the entire period. The patient had a number of delusions, including one that people had been trying to kill him for about eight years. According to him, he had been changing into a woman for the last five years and would soon be able to bear children. Of interest is the fact that this patient existed in society for quite awhile before his paranoid ideas came to be known, resulting in his hospitalization. (Salzinger 1973, p. 4)

showing himself to be disoriented. Through his limited conversation, it became clear that he had auditory hallucinations, occasionally becoming assaultive. (Salzinger 1973, p.4).)

Paranoid schizophrenia involves not only withdrawal from social contact and involvement, but also a delusional system composed of great suspicion such as believing that others are distrustful, sexually seductive, or after the power which the person believes he or she possesses. These patients behave as if they were being harassed and tor-

BORDERLINE SCHIZOID PERSONALITY

The DSM-II included a subcategory called *schizoid personality* under the *personality disorder* category. This subcategory is used for individuals who demonstrate certain aspects of the schizophrenic reaction, but only to a mild degree. These individuals show characteristics such as shyness, oversensitivity to social criticism, seclusiveness, detachment, and avoidance of close interpersonal relationships. They are usually "loners," not disturbed by their social distance and lack of "touch" with others, and not interested in greater social involvement. Although they may display some eccentric or bizarre behavior, oddities of thinking, delusions, and some paranoid ideation, they normally do not demonstrate the extreme schizophrenic symptomatology, such as debilitating thought disturbances, that would require hospitalization. Their symptoms are not severe enough to prevent them from adequately functioning in the community.

The proposed DSM-III categorization has distinguished two separate personality syndromes: *asocial personality (schizoid) disorder* and *schizotypal personality (latent, borderline schizophrenia) disorder*. The essential features of the first type is social isolation and inability to form interpersonal relationships. The second type involves not only the characteristic social isolation, but also various eccentric, odd behaviors and thinking. Again, the symptoms are usually not severe enough to meet the criteria of schizophrenia, and they do not significantly interfere with social or occupational functioning. Some individuals with this personality disorder, however, may eventually develop more severe symptoms, in which case the diagnosis of schizophrenia will likely be made.

DIMENSIONS OF SCHIZOPHRENIA

As with other forms of psychopathology, the reliability of diagnosing various subtypes of this disorder as spelled out by the DSM-II is not very high. Patterns of schizophrenic symptoms vary greatly from person to person, as well as within one person over time, and may interact in a complex fashion with other forms of psychopathology, so that the symptoms displayed are not as clear-cut as in the cases we have given. The result of this heterogeneity of symptoms, within and across patients, is low reliability when attempts are made to diagnose and classify specific subtypes of schizophrenia. Zubin (1967) summarized the results of six studies examining the reliability of classification of schizophrenia and found that, on the basis of overall agreement, the consistency of diagnosis between any two psychiatrists was exceedingly low and variable. Moreover, the reliability and utility of such classification are further affected by the variations in *base-rate* data at different hospitals. For example, Boisen (1938) reported that hebephrenic schizophrenia was diagnosed 76 percent of the time in one Illinois hospital, but in only 11 percent of the cases in a second hospital in the same state. The great deal of

IS SCHIZOPHRENIA CHRONIC?

Zubin and Spring (1977) note that there is little evidence for the traditional view that schizophrenia is a permanent psychiatric condition leading to chronic deterioration and lasting impairment. They suggest that it may be more heuristic to view this disorder as an episodic type of illness. They base their suggestion on several findings. For example, Bleuler (1974), in a lifetime follow-up of 208 schizophrenics, found that only 10 percent of these patients demonstrated the chronic unremitting type of disorder, requiring constant hospitalization, that most mental health professionals view schizophrenia to be. About 40 percent lived most of their lives functioning in the community, with occasional relapses requiring hospitalization. The remaining half of the patients achieved an effective adjustment in the community after an episode of the disorder. These investigators also point out that the 10 percent of unremitted cases may have been products of the pre-1950s ''custodial-care hospital period,'' in which attempts were seldom made to rehabilitate patients back into the community. Hospital statistics indicate that the average length of hospitalization for schizophrenia has decreased from several years in the custodial-care hospital period (before 1956) to only 37 days in 1975. This indicates a marked decline in the prevalence of chronic hospitalization. There now appears to be

subjective evaluation that the diagnostician must make undoubtedly contributes to these variable base-rate data from one hospital to the next. As Mischel (1968) notes in viewing these findings, reliability of classification based solely on the base-rate diagnosis of a particular disorder in a given hospital would probably be much higher than the individual clinical diagnosis based on the DSM-II. The DSM-III, on the other hand, explicitly spells out a number of signs that must be present to justify the diagnosis of a certain subcategory of schizophrenia, and so should increase the reliability of classification.

An interesting illustration of how different diagnostic practices can influence the diagnosis of schizophrenia can be found in two recent major studies—the United States-United Kingdom (USa characteristic pattern of brief episodes of illness, possibly requiring hospitalization, followed by recovery, relapse, and recovery. Zubin and Spring suggest that the relapse pattern occurs when adjustment back into the community is associated with stress and the absence of adequate supportive resources.

Zubin and Spring conclude that schizophrenia may be an episodic disorder:

> When episodes develop they are not lifelong. They terminate sooner or later with or without therapeutic intervention. . . . At the outset of an episode, the patient's competence and ability to cope adequately with life's exigencies appear to go underground. At the end of the episode, these attributes tend to reappear at their premorbid levels, and the patient can resume his former place in society. In general, the good premorbid patient returns to his formerly good adjustment and the poor premorbid to his poor adjustment. (pp. 122–123)

This view of schizophrenia, the authors point out, is contrary to the traditional view found in most textbooks. It requires further validation by independent researchers.

UK) Diagnostic Project (Cooper, Kendell, Gurland, Sharpe, Copeland, & Simon 1972) and the WHO Pilot Study in Schizophrenia (World Health Organization 1973). The US-UK study was conducted to assess why national statistics show such a disproportionate frequency of schizophrenia in the United States and of affective disorders in the United Kingdom. When a standard, structured diagnostic interview procedure developed by Gurland (cited in Zubin, Salzinger, Fleiss, Gurland, Spitzer, Endicott, & Sutton 1975) was used with samples of patients admitted to hospitals in the two countries, these differences did not emerge. Such results indicate that the national differences reflect differences in the diagnostic practices of psychiatrists in the two countries, rather than differing characteristics of patients. Psychiatrists in the United Kingdom

tend to apply the label of "affective disorder" to patients who demonstrate any mood disturbance, even if schizophrenic symptomatology is present; the reverse is true in the United States. The WHO study used a standard diagnostic procedure to assess the distribution of various subcategories of schizophrenia in nine different cultures. It was found that specific types of schizophrenia were distributed similarly when advanced cultures such as Washington, D.C., were compared with developing cultures such as Ibadan, Nigeria.

The lack of diagnostic reliability in using the DSM-II prompted many clinicians and researchers to look for better ways of subclassifying schizophrenia. This search has led to the use of dimensions along which schizophrenic subtypes could be differentiated. Four dimensions of schizophrenia have been proposed that have proved to be useful: the *process-reaction* dimension, the *chronic-acute* dimension, the *nonparanoid-paranoid* dimension, and the *withdrawal-activity* dimension. Before reviewing these dimensions, we should consider an interesting study by Morrison (1974). Morrison reviewed the admissions to a general psychiatric hospital in Iowa City over a 47-year period (1920–1966) and found that, while the overall percentage of schizophrenia remained relatively constant, there were dramatic changes in subcategory diagnoses over the years. Diagnoses of catatonic and hebephrenic schizophrenia significantly decreased, paranoid schizophrenia remained approximately the same, and the subcategory of chronic undifferentiated schizophrenia (a subcategory used when the psychotic episodes cannot be classified in any of the other major subcategories or when there are symptoms indicative of more than one subcategory) greatly increased. Hebephrenia and catatonia therefore seem to have been replaced in recent years by the undifferentiated schizophrenia subcategory. These results suggest that diagnosticians may have changed their definitions of the subtypes of schizophrenia over time. Today there is a greater tendency to categorize schizophrenics as either "paranoid" or "undifferentiated." This latter category may primarily reflect the absence of paranoid ideation in patients. As we shall see, the paranoid-nonparanoid dimension is being used more today because it appears to relate to prognosis for improvement.

PROCESS-REACTIVE DIMENSION   In the late nineteenth century, Kraepelin referred to this par-

DOCUMENT OF A SCHIZOPHRENIC
Figure 9.1

Document of a schizophrenic, as represented in
Rosen, Fox, and Gregory (1972). (Copyright 1972 by
W. B. Saunders Company. Used by permission.)

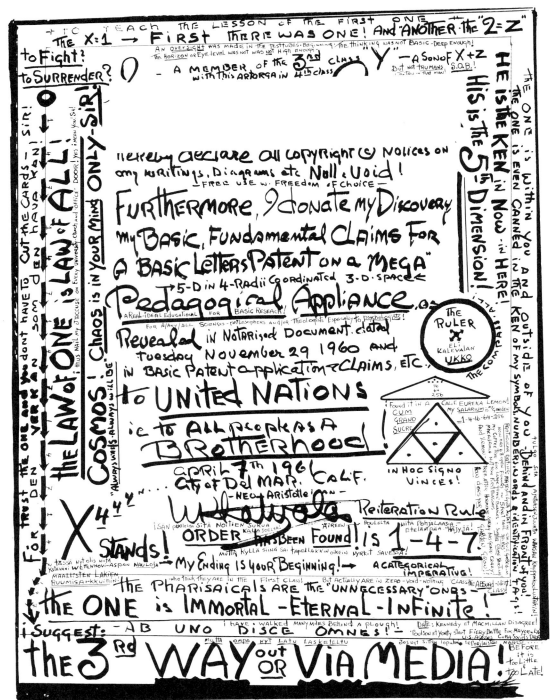

ticular dimension when developing his classification system to denote the presumed etiology of the psychoses. He divided the psychoses into two major groups—those that were organic in nature and the result of an abnormal biochemical/physiological *process*, and those psychoses that were psychological in origin and the result of a *reaction* to a life stressor. Although some proponents of this system view it as dichotomous—with only two different types of schizophrenia based on etiology—an increasing number of investigators are viewing it as a continuum. A patient might fall

anywhere between the two extremes. Despite these differing interpretations, there is fairly general agreement concerning the characteristics displayed by these two extreme types of schizophrenia:

. . . In general, the process schizophrenic has been sick for a long period of time, having had a history of insideous onset (slow and inconspicuous process of becoming abnormal) and social inadequacy and who has little chance of recovery, while the reactive schizophrenic has experienced sudden onset of the disorder, has a history of

From Kantor, Wallner, & Winder, 1953.

**DIFFERENCES IN
SOCIAL
HISTORY
BETWEEN
PROCESS AND
REACTIVE
SCHIZOPHRENICS**
Table 9.2

	PROCESS SCHIZOPHRENIA	REACTIVE SCHIZOPHRENIA
BIRTH TO THE FIFTH YEAR	a. Early psychological trauma b. Physical illness—severe or long c. Odd member of family	a. Good psychological history b. Good physical health c. Normal member of family
FIFTH YEAR TO ADOLESCENCE	a. Difficulties at school b. Family troubles paralleled with sudden changes in patient's behavior c. Introverted behavior trends and interests d. History of breakdown of social, physical, mental functioning e. Pathological siblings f. Overprotective or rejecting mother. "Momism" g. Rejecting father	a. Well adjusted at school b. Domestic troubles unaccompanied by behavior disruptions. Patient "had what it took." c. Extroverted behavior trends and interests d. History of adequate social, physical, mental functioning e. Normal siblings f. Normally protective, accepting mother g. Accepting father
ADOLESCENCE TO ADULTHOOD	a. Lack of heterosexuality b. Insidious, gradual onset of psychosis without pertinent stress c. Physical aggression d. Poor response to treatment e. Lengthy stay in hospital	a. Heterosexual behavior b. Sudden onset of psychosis; stress present and pertinent. Later onset c. Verbal aggression d. Good response to treatment e. Short course in hospital
ADULTHOOD	a. Massive paranoia b. Little capacity for alcohol c. No manic-depressive component d. Failure under adversity e. Discrepancy between ability and achievement f. Awareness of change in self g. Somatic delusions h. Clash between culture and environment i. Loss of decency (nudity, public masturbation, etc.)	a. Minor paranoid trends b. Much capacity for alcohol c. Presence of manic-depressive component d. Success despite adversity e. Harmony between ability and achievement f. No sensation of change g. Absence of somatic delusions h. Harmony between culture and environment i. Retention of decency

social adequacy, and has a favorable prognosis. (Salzinger 1973, p.18)

Kantor, Wallner, and Winder (1953) delineated various social history criteria that differentiate between process schizophrenia and reactive schizophrenia. These criteria are presented in table 9.2.

In viewing the table, one can readily observe that there are great differences between process and reactive schizophrenics in the degree of social and sexual adjustment before hospitalization. This level of adjustment is referred to as *premorbid adjustment*; that is, the style of coping prior to the onset of the major symptoms. Process schizophrenics typically have poor premorbid adjustments, while reactive schizophrenics have good premorbid adjustments. In fact, the terms *process* and *reactive* are used interchangeably with ''poor premorbid adjustment'' and ''good premorbid adjustment,'' respectively. In terms of prognosis for improvement, reactive schizophrenics generally have a better chance of improving than do those categorized as process schizophrenics.

CHRONIC-ACUTE DIMENSION   The DSM-II includes a category termed *acute schizophrenia* to refer to those patients who show a very rapid onset of symptoms and bizarre behavior that seem to be precipitated by some specific emotionally stressful experience. In contrast, *chronic schizophrenia* is used to characterize those patients who display a more gradual onset of abnormal symptoms that do not appear to be triggered by any particular event. This differential rate of onset is analogous to one of the criteria employed in the process (poor premorbid)-reactive (good premorbid) dimension.

In current research, the chronic-acute distinction is used somewhat differently, referring to the patient's length of hospitalization. As a general rule, *chronic* patients are defined as those who have been hospitalized for more than two years, whereas *acute* patients are those who have had a shorter period of hospitalization. The two-year cutoff point is used because the probability of being discharged generally is extremely low if one has been hospitalized for more than two years (Brown 1960). These types usually show quite different symptoms: Those schizophrenics with shorter periods of hospitalization usually display clear-cut bizarre behaviors. They also have a better chance of being released from the hospital. In contrast, patients hospitalized for longer periods of

time usually display more apathetic and withdrawn behavior, which would be expected as a result of prolonged institutionalization. The prognosis for their improvement and release is very poor. These differences in symptoms are very similar to those made in the use of the DSM-II clinical distinction between acute and chronic schizophrenia.

NONPARANOID-PARANOID DIMENSION
The paranoid-nonparanoid distinction is based on the presence (paranoid) or absence (nonparanoid) of delusions of persecution/grandeur. Paranoid schizophrenics, like reactive and acute schizophrenics, usually have a better prognosis for improvement, briefer hospitalization, and fewer rehospitalizations.

WITHDRAWAL-ACTIVITY DIMENSION   Venables (1957) was the first investigator to introduce the activity-withdrawal distinction of schizophrenia. He also developed an activity rating scale to help researchers studying this dimension. Until recently, however, this dimension has been almost completely neglected in the research on schizophrenia. Depue (1976), though, has demonstrated that it is of potential value, since it appears to be related to a number of behavioral, clinical, brain damage, and neurophysiological factors. The activity-withdrawal distinction appears to represent two different forms of schizophrenia. Patients on the ''activity'' end of the dimension are associated with excessive and impulsive motor and verbal behavior, greater degree of interpersonal contacts, less flat emotional effect, and lower incidence of delusions and hallucinations than ''withdrawal'' schizophrenics. They also have shorter institutionalization stays and faster recovery rates. Although there is currently no research comparing this dimension with others, the ''activity'' schizophrenics have many similarities to the reactive, acute, and paranoid schizophrenics. As we shall see in chapter 16 on childhood psychopathology, autistic infants may also be characterized as either hypoactive or hyperactive; a dimension that parallels the withdrawal-activity dichotomy.

RELATIONSHIPS BETWEEN DIMENSIONS
These four dimensions are not unrelated, but interdependent. As discussed earlier, patients with a poor premorbid adjustment (process schizophrenics) usually have less bizarre symptoms and a poorer prognosis for improvement than good premorbid schizophrenics. This is also true for schizo-

Edvard Munch (1863–1944) said he painted *The Scream* after watching a sunset that looked to him like clotted blood. Many of his works deal with vital emotional forces such as desire, jealousy, and death. In his mid-forties the artist spent several months in Copenhagen recovering from a nervous crisis. A psychotic, Munch used to whip those paintings that displeased him.

Louis Wain (1860–1939) was well known for the fanciful pictures he painted of cats. Typically, these cats assumed human poses and engaged in conventional human social activities such as tea parties. Wain was a popular and successful illustrator in the early years of this century.

When he reached his fifties, however, the artist began to show symptoms of schizophrenia. He continued to paint, and signs of his mental condition are evident in his work, which gradually progressed to more and more bizarre forms.

The artist, unable to shake his belief that his enemies were using electrical forces to control his mind against his will, was confined to mental institutions for the last fifteen years of his life.

The paintings shown here are vivid evidence of the artist's internal struggle and his strained mental state.

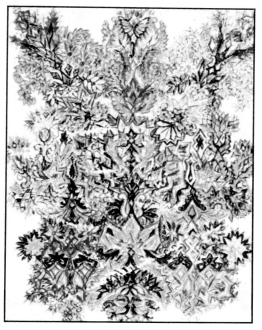

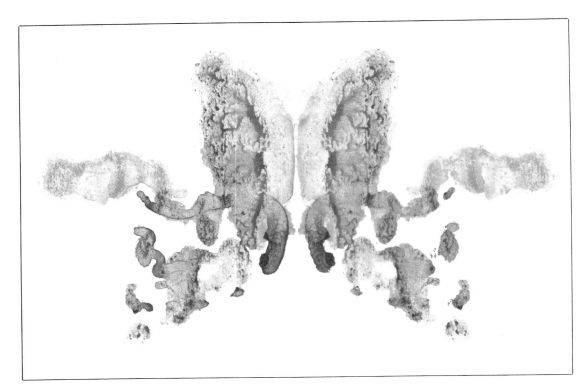

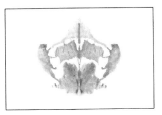 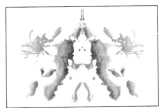 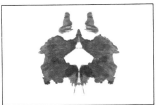 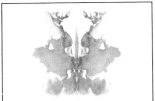

In the Rorschach Inkblot Test, introduced to the field in 1942, a subject is asked to describe what he or she sees in various inkblots. The inkblots themselves are ambiguous or vague stimuli, and hence what a subject sees in any one of them originates to a certain extent in the subject's mind.

The picture shown here is one of a series in the Thematic Apperception Test (TAT). In this projective test, the subject is asked to describe the events he or she thinks are taking place in the picture, as well as the thoughts and emotions of those involved. In so doing, the subject often reveals inner feelings and fears.

phrenics classified as *chronic* on the basis of length of hospitalization. Because of this relationship, we cannot be sure whether differences between process and reactive schizophrenics are due to differences in earlier social and sexual adjustment, or to the effects of differing amounts of time spent in the hospital.

Although some studies suggest that the process-reactive dimension is independent of the nonparanoid-paranoid dimension (e.g., Zigler & Levine 1961), numerous other studies show a correlation between these two dimensions (e.g., Buss 1966). It has been found that patients with poor premorbid adjustments generally do not have paranoid delusions, whereas, good premorbid schizophrenics are almost equally divided with regard to the presence or absence of paranoid delusions (Neale, Kopfstein, & Levine 1972). This strongly suggests a relationship. Moreover, at least in terms of prognosis for improvement, there is apparently a close relationship; paranoid schizophrenics, like reactive or acute schizophrenics, have a better prognosis.

Again, because of the relationships between dimensions, we cannot be absolutely certain whether differences betwen process and reactive schizophrenics are due to differences in premorbid adjustment, or to some other factors such as susceptibility to the presence of delusions. Nevertheless, regardless of the problem in interpretation caused by their interrelationships, these dimensions (summarized in table 9.3) have proved to be effective in differentiating between major forms of schizophrenia. Future research may lead to the development of criteria that will allow the detection of more subtle schizophrenia subtype differences. Subclassification on the basis of *combinations* of dimensions also may prove to be a worthwhile method.

EXPERIMENTAL LABORATORY RESEARCH WITH SCHIZOPHRENICS

For the past forty or so years, much experimental research has attempted to understand some fundamental perceptual and thought disturbances associated with schizophrenia. Rather than reviewing this vast array of research here, we will give a sampling of some of the representative work on the presence of attentional and cognitive deficits in schizophrenia. The reader is referred to compre-

hensive works by Broen (1968) and Chapman and Chapman (1973) for full reviews.

ATTENTIONAL DEFICITS Beginning in the 1930s, Shakow and colleagues conducted some of the basic research on attentional deficits in schizophrenia (Shakow 1963). They found that schizophrenics performed significantly slower on a simple reaction-time task than normals. Moreover, the slower speed of reactions was more marked in chronic or nonparanoid patients than in acute or paranoid patients. The reaction-time task in these studies required subjects to lift a finger from a telegraph key as soon as a light came on. Of course, one could argue that the schizophrenics' slower response was due to their difficulty in making a motor response rather than to any attentional deficit. However, there are other data against this argument.

DIMENSIONS OF SCHIZOPHRENIA
Table 9.3

PROCESS VS. REACTIVE	History of slow onset with no precipitating event, and poor premorbid adjustment. *vs.* Sudden onset with precipitating event, and good premorbid adjustment.
CHRONIC VS. ACUTE	Gradual onset and hospitalization for more than two years. *vs.* Sudden onset and shorter period of hospitalization.
NONPARANOID VS. PARANOID	Absence of delusions of persecution/grandeur *vs.* Presence of such delusions.
WITHDRAWAL VS. ACTIVITY	Few interpersonal contacts and decrease in behavior *vs.* Greater degree of interpersonal contacts and excessive and impulsive behavior.

Here, a researcher monitors a reaction time test. A subject in a darkened room out of the picture is asked to move a switch as quickly as possible after seeing a light or hearing a tone. Schizophrenics usually respond more slowly on such time tests than do normal subjects.

In a variation of the simple reaction-time task, subjects are given a preparatory interval. A warning stimulus such as a tone comes on, followed after a certain time interval by the actual reaction-time stimulus. Shakow found that when this preparatory interval is long (eight or more seconds), the performance of schizophrenics, especially chronic schizophrenics, becomes markedly slower. Such findings indicate that schizophrenics cannot maintain close attention required for a task for more than a few seconds. The most plausible explanation for this failure appears to be the schizophrenics' distraction by irrelevant stimuli, either internally generated by their own thoughts or externally generated by the environment.

Numerous studies indicate that schizophren-ics do have difficulty maintaining attention and not being distracted by irrelevant stimuli. For example, Rappaport (1967) assessed the performance of schizophrenic and normal subjects on a competing-message task. A number of auditory messages were presented simultaneously to subjects who were required to listen to only one of them and repeat it back. The performance of schizophrenics was always poorer than normal subjects whenever more than one message was presented. It appears that schizophrenics have difficulty ''filtering out'' irrelevant stimuli. They may be bombarded by a great deal of irrelevant stimuli, much of which they cannot block out. This deficit, along with the inability to maintain attention to relevant stimuli, is used to explain why schizophrenics have difficulty in ordering their thoughts logically and in communicating thoughts without the intrusion of loose associations and incoherence. Numerous major reviews of attentional research with schizophrenics have pointed out a possible breakdown of filtering mechanisms in schizophrenia that causes the flooding of sensory input and the subsequent disruption of cognition (e.g., Lang & Buss 1965; Neale & Cromwell 1970).

COGNITIVE DEFICITS Schizophrenics commonly give unusual associations in response to common words. Broen (1968) used the concept of *response hierarchy* to explain the presence of these unusual associations. Any stimulus, such as a word, can elicit a hierarchy of responses that vary in the probability of occurrence. For example, in normal subjects the word *table* can evoke high-probability responses (the word *chair* or *top*), low-probability responses (the word *tennis*), or rare-probability responses (the word *run* or *shoe*). Broen suggests that the word-response hierarchies of schizophrenics have ''collapsed'' so that formerly dominant responses (such as *chair*) and subordinate responses (such as *shoe*) became equal in probability of occurrence. This assumption is used to explain why schizophrenics sometimes give strange responses and word associations. Normal subjects, however, also sometimes give unusual low-probability responses. Some recent research suggests that the chief difference between schizophrenics and normals is not that normal subjects never make ''errors'' (low-probability responses) in thinking, but that schizophrenics make many more of these same types of errors. The differences, then, appear to be *quantitative* and not *qualitative*. Chapman and Chapman (1973) have conducted some of the most systematic research in this area.

Chapman and Chapman point out that words often have more than one meaning, and that the context in which they are presented is important. Schizophrenics often fail to pick up appropriate contextual cues, especially if they are not clear-cut. In one study reported by these investigators, a multiple-choice test was given in which words with double meanings (homonyms) were presented in two different contexts. In one context, the strong meaning response was correct; in the other context, the weak meaning response was correct. This is an item from this multiple-choice test:

When the farmer bought a herd of cattle, he needed a new pen. This means:

a. He needed a new writing implement.
b. He needed a new fenced enclosure.
c. He needed a new pick-up truck.

The weak meaning response (b) is the correct answer in this question. The incorrect answer in a is associated with the stronger meaning response to the word *pen* as it is more commonly used. More schizophrenics incorrectly choose the a alternative

than do normal subjects. They do not appear to pay attention to the appropriate contextual cues in the sentence.

The professor loaned his pen to Barbara. This means:

a. He loaned her a pick-up truck.
b. He loaned her a writing implement.
c. He loaned her a fenced enclosure.

The correct response to this question is b, which is associated with the stronger meaning response. In this instance, where contextual cues are not important, there are no differences in error rate between schizophrenics and normals.

These results indicate that schizophrenics make more errors than normals only under certain circumstances: when there are associative distractors in a sentence context that is not clear-cut. They appear to be distracted by dominant response tendencies (strong meaning responses) and they ignore subsidiary meanings. Such findings can be interpreted to reflect the schizophrenics' tendency to use inappropriate contextual cues, possibly leading to their misinterpretation and distortion of reality.

CAUSES AND STRESSORS

PSYCHOANALYTIC THEORY

The psychoanalytic explanation of schizophrenia emphasizes the importance of the defense mechanism of *regression* in this disorder. Regression refers to the reversal of the normal course of development and a return to behaviors or characteristics associated with an earlier period of development. The schizophrenic individual is assumed to have regressed back to the early part of the *oral* stage of development. In this early oral development stage, psychoanalytic theorists suggest, the young child is not yet aware that the self or id is a separate entity from external reality. The ego, which develops from the id and whose major function is reality testing, has not yet been sufficiently developed to make this distinction. Because the ego has not yet become differentiated from the id, it cannot effectively engage in reality testing.

Schizophrenia is viewed as a regression or return to this stage of development in which external reality is not taken into account. The rejection of external reality and the resultant inability to engage in reality testing are seen as the fundamental deficit in schizophrenia.

Psychoanalytic theory assumes that there are two major causes for the schizophrenic's regression and resultant break with reality. The first is an increase in the strength of id impulses, especially infantile sexual impulses seeking erotic gratification. The second is a concomitant increase in anxiety and guilt brought on by these socially unacceptable and forbidden impulses. To alleviate the anxiety and guilt, the ego attempts to defend against the expression of the forbidden impulses. When everything else fails, and the ego perceives that it can no longer effectively inhibit the expression of these undesirable impulses, the defense mechanism of regression is employed to return the

R. D. Laing rejects the notion that schizophrenia should be viewed as abnormal behavior; rather, he asserts that schizophrenics have merely adopted a different way of looking at things.

individual to an earlier developmental stage. By regressing back to the early oral stage before the ego (and thus reality) has been differentiated from the id, the individual can in effect reject reality. By rejecting reality, the individual can avoid the anxiety and guilt associated with the temptation to express infantile sexual and aggressive impulses. It was assumed that individuals who were *fixated* at the early oral stage of development were predisposed to demonstrate this regression and the resultant break with reality.

Because traditional Freudian psychoanalytic theory was developed primarily for describing the etiology of neurotic disorders, Freud gave very little attention to schizophrenia. As a result, the traditional psychoanalytic model of schizophrenia is not as fully developed as its model of the neuroses. Little research has been done to evaluate the validity of the theory.

PHENOMENOLOGICAL-EXISTENTIAL THEORY

R. D. Laing (1967) has been the most influential advocate of a phenomenological-existential model of schizophrenia. In this approach, schizophrenia is construed as resulting from society's imposing unreasonable restrictions on an individual, blocking attempts for personal growth and autonomy, and demanding conformity. Laing (1967) notes:

> . . . it seems . . . that *without exception* the experience and behavior that gets labeled schizophrenic is a *special strategy that a person invents in order to live in an unlivable situation.* In his life situation the person has come to feel he is in an untenable position. He cannot make a move, or make no move, without being beset by contradictory and paradoxical pressures and demands, pushes and pulls, both internally from himself, and externally from those around him. He is, as it were, in a position of checkmate. (pp. 114–115)

The schizophrenic individual is seen here as one who attempts to escape from a stressful, unbearable world by changing his or her inner representation and interpretation of reality. Laing also insists that schizophrenia is not "insanity," but merely a reflection of an individual who cannot suppress his or her instincts and emotions to conform to an abnormal society. He views schizophrenia as a retreat from the painful, mad reality of the external world, and as an existential search for meaning and personal autonomy. The "mad reality," according to Laing, is usually a stressful and distorted family system. Rather than trying to eliminate the patient's schizophrenic behavior, Laing suggests that the experience should be viewed as potentially meaningful and beneficial for personal growth. Therapy should therefore be directed at helping the client make the "trip" from the external world to inner reality as a means of developing greater personal enlightenment, much as an individual helps another through a psychedelic drug trip. Also, Laing uses family therapy (see chapter 18) with schizophrenics.

Laing's approach to schizophrenia assumes that it is not necessarily a serious psychological disorder, but merely a disruption of social relations that results in the search for the real meaning of one's life. In certain ways, this view is similar to aspects of Ullmann and Krasner's learning theory approach (discussed in the next section). Schizophrenia is viewed as a form of behavior learned in order to deal with unacceptable environmental demands. However, inherent in Laing's early writings is the idea that the schizophrenic experience is a potentially good, positive, growth process. There is little evidence, though, to indicate that individuals who have undergone schizophrenic episodes are any better off or more "enlightened" than before.

LEARNING THEORY

Ullmann and Krasner (1969) presented one of the earliest and most widely known behavioral accounts of schizophrenia. These theorists view this disorder, like other forms of maladaptive behavior, as learned. It is assumed that because of a lack of appropriate positive reinforcement, the schizophrenic individual has learned not to attend to the common social stimuli that most people respond to. Instead, they begin attending to internally generated cues, such as their own fantasies, and to socially irrelevant cues that do not facilitate appropriate social behavior and interaction. As a consequence, their behavior may appear abnormal or bizarre to the rest of society. Ullmann and Krasner suggest that once this social inattention is learned, it may lead to negative social consequences such as social rejection and the labeling of the individual as "bizarre" or "strange." These negative social consequences, in turn, may initiate a vicious cycle: The negative social reactions lead to an even greater reduction of reinforcement, so that the individual attends even less to social stimuli. The deviant social withdrawal may itself be reinforced by the social attention it receives and the possible benefits initially associated with being "sick" in our society — the ability to avoid accepting responsibility, and the possibility of withdrawing from a stressful world.

Braginsky, Braginsky, and Ring (1969), in fact, indicate that many individuals act "crazily" as a means of gaining admission to a mental hospital and so shielding themselves from the stresses of everyday living. These investigators present some convincing data to indicate that schizophrenics do not necessarily demonstrate a complete break with reality, as has been assumed. Indeed, many exert active control over their behavior, acting "crazily" when necessary, and have the ability to manipulate others so as to gain entrance into the comfortable, nondemanding confines of the mental hospital. They view this as a better alternative than living in the "cold, cruel world." This resembles the previously mentioned *Munchausen Syndrome* (chapter 6), the main fea-

tures being the need and ability to seek and sustain hospitalization.

Ullmann and Krasner also suggest how various behaviors associated with schizophrenia, such as hallucinations, delusions, and disordered affect, can develop as a result of lack of attention. However, as Ullmann and Krasner themselves admit, although an operant-behavioral etiology of schizophrenia is plausible, there is no conclusive proof for the hypothesis that schizophrenia is a learned thought disorder.

DEVELOPMENTAL ASPECTS OF SCHIZOPHRENIA

Numerous studies have attempted to evaluate the developmental histories of schizophrenics to discover whether there are specific factors that trigger this disorder. Such research has generally shown that persons who become schizophrenic usually have childhood histories indicating some behavioral problem even before they became schizophrenic. For example, Berry (1967) found that the preschizophrenic social behavior of these individuals was described as withdrawn and delinquent. Such developmental research has not been very illuminating, however, because these traits are also found in the childhood histories of many individuals who later do not become schizophrenic. Moreover, the data in these studies are primarily retrospective in nature, with the information usually collected by interviewing individuals who knew the person as a child. Their present recollections may be biased by their knowledge of the person's present emotional state, and may be unreliable because of an inability to remember past details clearly. The fallibility of recall seriously limits the general scientific usefulness of retrospective studies.

A desirable alternative to such retrospective studies is a *longitudinal study* in which a large sample of subjects is selected early in life and followed carefully over a long period of time. If certain of these children later become schizophrenic, one has a detailed and objective record of their developmental histories to evaluate and select out important contributing factors associated with the development of the disorder. The expense of such longitudinal studies of schizophrenia, however, is prohibitive. Since less than 1 percent of the general population becomes schizophrenic, one

DAVID AND LISA © 1962, Continental Distributing, Inc. Schizophrenics are often depicted in books and movies as persistently withdrawn from reality, without any desire or ability to develop meaningful relationships. In this film, such a misleading stereotype is abandoned, with the portrayal of two hospitalized patients who help each other to begin to overcome their problems and fears.

would need to use an extremely large sample of subjects to assure an adequate number of pre-schizophrenics. A method of investigation that partly overcomes this problem is the *high-risk study* of schizophrenia, in which only persons with a greater than average risk of becoming schizophrenic in adulthood are selected.

The first systematic high-risk study of schizophrenia was started in Denmark in the early 1960s by Mednick and Schulsinger. High-risk subjects were defined as those whose mothers were diagnosed as schizophrenic. This selection criterion was used because a number of earlier studies had indicated that approximately 15 percent of such children would be expected to develop schizophrenia later in life. Low-risk subjects (children born of nonschizophrenic mothers) were matched to the high-risk subjects on a wide range of variables: age, sex, socioeconomic level, educational level, just to name a few. There were 200 high-risk and 100 low-risk subjects used in this study, with the average age of both groups approximately 15

years. At the start of this longitudinal study, each individual was given a battery of psychological and physiological tests, and information was collected about their social histories and details surrounding their birth/delivery. All subjects were tested at regular intervals during the course of the study.

Although this high-risk project is still in an early stage, some preliminary findings have been reported on the basis of those high-risk subjects who developed psychiatric problems requiring professional help (Mednick 1970; Mednick & Schulsinger 1968,1973). The major findings to date are as follows:

1. Mothers of the psychiatrically disturbed high-risk children were committed to mental hospitals earlier and more permanently than those of the high-risk children who remained undisturbed. They were also rated as being more severely disturbed. Mednick indicates that these findings may mean one of two things: that the severity of the mother's disorder implies a strong genetic

predisposition that is passed on to the child; or that being separated from one's mother, who is permanently hospitalized, is sufficiently stressful to trigger disturbed behavior in the child.

2. On the basis of teachers' reports, it was found that a greater number of persons in the disturbed high-risk group remained upset and emotionally excited longer, once aroused, than did the undisturbed high-risk children. They were also rated as engaging in more socially disruptive behaviors, such as aggression and causing trouble in class.

3. The psychiatrically disturbed high-risk subjects demonstrated a significantly different pattern of physiological responding to stimuli than the other subjects, suggesting that they physiologically overreact when stimulated and take longer to adapt to such stimulation.

4. There was an unusually high incidence of complications during pregnancy or childbirth (e.g., prematurity, illness of mother during pregnancy, delivery complications, etc.) among the disturbed high-risk subjects. Also, it was found that the deviant physiological response patterns reported in (3) above were found only in those children with pregnancy or birth complications in their histories. These findings suggest that such complications in the birth process may contribute to the "triggering" of the schizophrenia developmental process in genetically predisposed persons.

This high-risk longitudinal study should continue to produce illuminating results for years to come, and a number of other high-risk studies have also been initiated. They will be valuable in furthering our understanding of schizophrenia, as well as possibly leading to the development of effective preventive-intervention treatment programs once the important developmental variables have been delineated and sufficiently validated.

FAMILY DYNAMICS AND SCHIZOPHRENIA

Many investigators who view environmental factors as important in the etiology of schizophrenia have looked at the history and mode of interpersonal relationships as possibly important causative agents. Since the family usually has the most significant impact on an individual, especially during the critical psychosocial developmental years, it is not surprising that investigators have extensively examined the importance of family dynamics in the development of schizophrenia.

Many theorists have suggested that there are problems in communication patterns in the families of schizophrenics, and that these patterns differ significantly from those found in the families of normal or neurotic children. In describing the parents of schizophrenic children, Wynne (1968) employs the concepts of *schizophrenicness* (signs of schizophrenia) and *schizophrenogenicness* (behavior that has a tendency to create schizophrenia in others because of faulty communication patterns that make it difficult for the listener to fully comprehend what is being said). He indicated that the parent's degree of schizophrenogenicness, that is, faulty communication patterns, is a much better predictor of whether a child will become schizophrenic than the parent's schizophrenicness.

There have been virtually hundreds of studies examining family dynamics and schizophrenia. However, the great majority of these have significant methodological flaws in experimental design that make the results impossible to interpret meaningfully. Fontana (1966) reviewed a great number of these family studies and found only five that met the methodological criteria he deemed necessary for interpreting results with any degree of certainty. On the basis of these five studies, he felt that only two broad conclusions could be made concerning the family patterns of schizophrenics: (1) There is much more conflict present between the parents of schizophrenic individuals than between the parents of normals. (2) Communication between the parents of schizophrenics is less clear than that between parents of normal individuals. That is, according to Fontana, conflict and lack of communication between parents of schizophrenics seem to be more closely associated with the occurrence of this disorder than any other family interaction pattern.

For many years, a popular family-communication pattern theory of schizophrenia was the *double-bind theory*, originally proposed by Bateson, Jackson, Haley, and Weakland (1956). This theory suggests that an important factor in the development of schizophrenia is an individual's constant exposure to a double-bind situation, resulting in that person's developing difficulty in

SOCIAL CLASS AND SCHIZOPHRENIA

Through the years, a number of studies have examined the role of social factors in psychopathology. These *epidemiological* survey studies have been based on clinical case history statistics and on direct assessment of psychopathology in the general population. One of the earliest such studies was conducted in Chicago by Faris and Dunham (1939). These investigators sought out the addresses of all Chicago residents who were admitted to public and private hospitals between the years 1922 and 1934. They then calculated the rates of various forms of psychopathology for each area of the city. It was found that hospital admission rates for patients diagnosed as schizophrenic were highest for residents of the inner city. Then, as now, this part of the city was marked by the greatest population density and the lowest socioeconomic level. Hospitalization rates decreased as one moved out toward the affluent neighborhoods in the outskirts of the city.

A similar study was conducted by Hollingshead and Redlich (1958), who examined social class differences in the incidence of mental disorders in New Haven, Conn. They used psychiatric hospitals and clinic statistics, as well as information from private practitioners. Results indicated that the prevalence of schizophrenia was higher in the lowest social class. In a follow-up study ten years later, Myers and Bean (1968) found basically the same relationship between social class and psychopathology.

Another study was the well-publicized Midtown Manhattan survey undertaken in 1950 by Srole, Langner, Michael, Opler, and Rennie

(1962). These investigators selected a representative sample of 1,700 persons living in the midtown Manhattan area of New York City. Each of these individuals was interviewed by a mental health professional, and information was collected concerning the individual's background and history, past and present psychological disorders, and family, social, and work adjustment. Each interviewee was later rated on a psychological health-impairment scale that had six categories: well, mild symptom formation, moderate symptom formation, marked symptom formation, severe symptom formation, and incapacitated. Individuals falling into the latter three categories were classified as "impaired." Results indicated a strong relation between social status and this index of mental health. In the lowest social group, 47.3 percent were rated as "impaired," while only 12.5 percent of the highest group were so classified.

Thus, a consistent relationship has been found between social class and psychopathology. Dohrenwend and Dohrenwend (1969) reviewed 44 such studies and found this consistent relationship. The lowest social class is associated with a greater incidence of schizophrenia than the other social classes. Such findings, however, do not necessarily indicate cause and effect. There has been a great deal of controversy about whether they indicate that the harsh conditions of inner-city life experienced by the lower social class produces mental illness, or whether they simply reflect a "drifting" of people already schizophrenic into the inner-city areas. That is,

communicating with himself or herself and others. In the double-bind situation, the individual receives mutually contradictory messages (for example, affection and rejection). To point out the contradiction is implicitly forbidden, so that no matter which alternative message the individual acts upon, he or she is a loser. For example, a mother may constantly complain to her son about his lack of affection toward her; however, when he tries to demonstrate his affection (e.g., putting his arm around her), she stiffens up and shows strong disapproval. No matter what he does, he loses.

Along with the popularity of the double-bind theory, the concept of the *schizophrenogenic mother*, as introduced by the psychoanalyst Fromm-Reichman (1948), was also widely accepted. This type of mother possessed personality characteristics that could produce schizophrenia in her children. She was characterized as cold, dominating, and conflict-inducing, simultaneously overprotective and rejecting of the child.

Although both the double-bind theory and the schizophrenogenic-mother concept of schizophrenia were popular and widely accepted, re-many have argued that schizophrenia, and its associated cognitive and motivational problems, results in a deteriorated life-style and an inability to work and follow a productive social life. A schizophrenic is likely to drift downward socially.

One possible method of resolving this controversy is to examine the social downward drift of schizophrenics. Such studies have been conducted. However, direct evidence of downward social drift from these studies has been equivocal. Some investigations have found that schizophrenics are downwardly mobile (e.g., Turner & Wagonfeld 1967), while others have not (e.g., Hollingshead & Redlich 1958). Another method for examining this relationship has been suggested by Kohn (1968). According to Kohn, if it could be demonstrated that fathers of schizophrenics are also from the lower social class, this would support the notion that lower social class is conducive to schizophrenia. On the other hand, if the fathers of schizophrenics were from higher social strata, then the downward social drift hypothesis would be supported. Studies conducted to date have found that the socioeconomic-occupational levels of schizophrenics are in fact generally lower than those of their fathers (e.g., Goldberg & Morrison 1963; Turner & Wagonfeld 1967). These data therefore tend to support the social drift hypothesis. However, more definitive epidemiological studies are still badly needed before a final determination can be made of the role of social class in producing schizophrenia.

search has *not* supported either of them as valid explanations for the development of schizophrenia. Jacob (1975) conducted a careful review of this family dynamics literature and concludes that it has not been shown that such patterns occur any more frequently in the families of disturbed children. As indicated previously, the only family dynamics factors found by Fontana to be associated with schizophrenia in methodologically sound and well-controlled studies were conflict and lack of communication between parents of schizophrenic children. These same family dynamics can be found in some other forms of psychopathology.

Even when family influences such as Fontana described are found, one is still not completely certain that the family interaction problems *caused* the psychopathology in one of the family members. One alternative explanation is that the schizophrenia present in a family member caused family problems that did not exist before the onset of the disorder. A third variable involved might be that both the child's disturbance and the faulty family interactions are due to a common genetic defect in the child and parent.

Obviously, family studies of schizophrenia are difficult to conduct because of the great many variables that need to be controlled. As a result, the question of whether certain types of family interaction patterns cause schizophrenia is still unresolved. There have been some relatively recent innovations in family interaction research methodology that may eventually allow one to determine the correct causality factor (e.g., Mishler & Waxler 1968). Moreover, *high-risk* family studies of schizophrenia, which we discussed in the last section, may also aid in determining whether certain family patterns are significant causative agents. In chapter 18, we will also discuss family pathologies and the family as a causal agent in abnormal behavior.

GENETIC FACTORS

There is considerable evidence to indicate a genetic involvement in schizophrenia. Such evidence comes from three major types of studies: family studies, twin studies, and studies of adopted children.

A number of family studies have demonstrated that the more closely one is related to a schizophrenic, the higher the probability that one will develop schizophrenia. Rosenthal (1970) has summarized the available studies that used the family study method of examining schizophrenia. Although the results varied considerably, with the *morbidity* risk factor reported ranging from 0.2 to 12.0 percent, twelve of the fourteen studies Rosenthal reviewed demonstrated a risk factor for developing schizophrenia higher than the 1 percent expected in the general population.

Family studies are generally the weakest kind of evidence to support the presence of genetic predisposition to a disorder. As family members have not only the same genes but also the same environment, is is impossible in such studies to determine whether the relationships found are due to genetic or environmental factors. It could be argued that the effects of a schizophrenic parent's disturbing and bizarre behavior on a young child during the developmental years may be sufficiently traumatic to cause disordered behavior in the child. Twin studies can provide a somewhat stronger test of the possible presence of genetic factors because they compare individuals raised in a highly similar environment who are either genetically identical (monozygotic twins) or similar but not identical (dizygotic twins). Differences in concordance rates between monozygotic and dizygotic twins raised in the same environment would be stronger evidence for possible genetic involvement. Such evidence has been found.

In the United States, Kallman (1946) performed one of the earliest large-scale twin studies and demonstrated a greater concordance rate of schizophrenia in identical twins than in fraternal twins. Rosenthal (1970) and Ban (1973) have summarized the findings of twin studies. These studies indicate that the concordance rate for monozygotic twins is approximately five times as great as the concordance rate for dizygotic twins. There is, however, a great deal of disparity in the concordance rates reported in the various studies, as shown in table 9.4, which summarizes the results presented by Rosenthal (1970). Despite this disparity, it can be seen that the concordance rate is usually much greater for identical than for fraternal

twins. Such data strongly suggest a genetic involvement. In no instance, however, has any study found a 100 pecent concordance rate. This indicates that, although there may be a genetic factor in schizophrenia, it is not the whole story.

The twin-study results are strongly suggestive, but must be interpreted with some caution. One can argue that monozygotic twins are not only alike genetically, but also share a more nearly identical environment than dizygotic twins. They are of the same sex and commonly tend to be dressed alike, treated alike, and usually confused with each other by other people. One way of overcoming this potential argument is to examine monozygotic twins who were separated from one another very early in life and reared apart. However, only a small number of such cases have been studied. Even though the majority of these cases demonstrated a high concordance rate suggesting genetic predisposition, the small number of cases prevents any definitive conclusion (Rosenthal 1970).

Another type of study—the adopted child study—attempts to eliminate the possible developmental effect of being raised in a similar environment. Such studies examine children who were adopted away from their original biological families at birth and raised by another family. These individuals have the genetic endowment of one family but the environmental learning experiences of another family. If it could be shown that children who are born to schizophrenic mothers, but avoid

TWIN STUDIES OF SCHIZOPHRENIA
Table 9.4

From Rosenthal, 1970

STUDY	MONOZYGOTIC (IDENTICAL) TWINS		DIZYGOTIC (FRATERNAL) TWINS	
	NUMBER OF PAIRS	% CON-CORDANT	NUMBER OF PAIRS	% CON-CORDANT
Luxemburger, 1928a, 1934 (Germany)	17–27	33–76.5	48	2.1
Rosanoff et al., 1934–35 (U.S. and Canada)	41	61.0	101	10.0
Essen-Möller, 1941 (Sweden)	7–11	14–71	24	8.3–17
Kallmann, 1946 (New York)	174	69–86.2	517	10–14.5
Slater, 1953 (England)	37	65–74.7	115	11.3–14.4
Inouye, 1961 (Japan)	55	36–60	17	6–12
Tienari, 1963, 1968 (Finland)	16	0–6	21	4.8
Gottesman and Shields, 1966 (England)	24	41.7	33	9.1
Kringlen, 1967 (Norway)	55	25–38	172	10
Fischer, 1968 (Denmark)	16	19–56	34	6–15
Hoffer et al. (U. S. veterans)	80	15.5	145	4.4

the potentially traumatic experiences of being raised in a schizophrenic family, still develop schizophrenia at the same rate as those children who were born to schizophrenic mothers but not adopted, it would be especially strong evidence for the presence of genetic predisposition.

Such an adoptee study was conducted by Heston (1966), who studied 58 adoptees born to hospitalized schizophrenic mothers. He simultaneously examined a control group of persons who were also adopted, but who did not have schizophrenic mothers, and who were matched for age, sex, duration of time in child-care institutions, and type of placement. Independent diagnoses of these individuals, made by several psychiatrists and based on a large variety of information, indicated that schizophrenia was found only in those children who had schizophrenic mothers. Heston also reported that approximately half of the children of schizophrenic mothers demonstrated major forms of psychopathology such as neuroses, sociopathy, and mental retardation.

A much larger-scale adoptee study was conducted in Denmark by Rosenthal, Wender, Kety, Welner, and Schulsinger (1971). The Danish government keeps much detailed demographic and other information about its citizens, going back as far as fifty years. Using these records, Rosenthal and colleagues were able to identify 5,500 adoptees and 10,000 of their 11,000 biological parents. Of this group of parents, they selected those who had at some time been hospitalized in a psychiatric institution with a diagnosis of either schizophrenia or manic-depressive psychosis. Using this criterion, they were able to identify 76 children of these parents who had been adopted by other families. These children were compared with a matched control group of adopted children whose biological parents had no history of psychiatric hospitalization. To date, results of this still ongoing study have indicated that about twice as many of the schizophrenic-parent children as control children were assessed to have schizophrenic characteristics.

Kety, Rosenthal, Wender, and Schulsinger (1971), using these same Danish records, reported results of a study that selected, from the group of 5,500 adoptees, 33 who were diagnosed as having psychiatric histories indicative of schizophrenia. These individuals were compared with a matched control group of adopted children selected from the same records. The investigators then identified the adoptive and biological parents, and the siblings and half-siblings, of these two

groups and determined which of them had psychiatric records. The biological relatives of the schizophrenic individuals were more often found to have schizophrenia than the control group.

DIATHESIS-STRESS MODEL OF SCHIZOPHRENIA

Looking at the results found in family studies, twin studies, and adoptee studies as a whole, one is led to conclude that genetic factors play an important role in the etiology of schizophrenia. However, as indicated earlier, the fact that there is never an exact relationship (e.g., less than a 100 percent concordance rate in twin studies) suggests the involvement of additional factors in this disorder. Currently, a widely held position proposes a *diathesis-stress* formulation of schizophrenia. That is, some individuals genetically inherit a diathesis (or predisposition) toward the development of schizophrenia, but schizophrenia will only actually develop in those predisposed individuals who are exposed to particular stressful experiences for which they have not developed effective coping behaviors. Meehl (1962) has proposed such a model. He suggests that the genetic predisposition that potential schizophrenics inherit is a neural defect which he calls *schizotaxia*. In schizotaxic individuals, Meehl assumes, the common everday stresses and strains of living produce a slightly peculiar personality structure or makeup that he labels *schizotypy*. If this schizotype happens to be raised in a positive, nonstressful environment, he or she will remain relatively normal, although possibly demonstrating certain slightly eccentric behaviors. But if by bad fortune, this individual is raised in a highly stressful environment, then he or she will develop schizophrenia.

A more comprehensive diathesis-stress model has recently been proposed by Zubin and Spring (1977). They introduce the concept of *vulnerability* as a "common denominator" that takes into account genetic, physiological, developmental, learning, and stress factors in the etiology of schizophrenia. This vulnerability model suggests that everyone is endowed with some degree of vulnerability for developing schizophrenia which, under suitable circumstances, can trigger an episode of the disorder. Numerous factors, ranging from inborn genetic characteristics to acquired learned propensities, contribute to a person's degree of vulnerability. The highly vulnerable person is one who encounters a great many factors, which are sufficient to produce a schizophrenic episode. Others, because of their genetic makeup and lack of other risk factors, have a low degree of vulnerability and in all likelihood will not develop the disorder. The attractive feature of this model is that it proposes means of measuring vulnerability. Such diathesis-stress models show great promise for better understanding this disorder.

THE BIOLOGICAL EVIDENCE

As pointed out in previous chapters, the existence of a genetic basis for a disorder implies that organic variables are involved. Numerous studies have indeed examined the possibility of disturbed biochemical and physiological processes in schizophrenia.

BIOCHEMICAL FACTORS The discovery that certain drugs (*psychotomimetic* drugs) can produce schizophrenic-type behavior prompted a great deal of interest in evaluating biochemical disturbances in schizophrenia. This biochemical research is still at an elementary stage of development, with the majority of results inconclusive and/or associated with methodological problems in research design. Salzinger (1973) has provided a good review of a number of these problems. Indeed, through the years there have been numerous reports in scientific journals as well as popular magazines and newspapers announcing the latest discovery of a "biochemical cause" for schizophrenia. To date, none have held up as valid under careful scientific scrutiny. There are commonly many factors, such as dietary habits, current health and medication history, alcohol and tobacco use, etc., that have significant effects on biochemical levels but that were not controlled for in past studies. Lang (1971) discovered the "grapefruit" phenomenon, for instance, when he thought he had found reliable biochemical differences between patients and normals. These differences turned out to be due to the fact that all the patients had grapefruit for breakfast the day of testing, while the normal subjects did not! The grapefruit affected the patients' biochemical levels. The point to keep in mind is that one must be careful to avoid prematurely accepting biochemical findings before all possible contributing factors have been controlled for.

Taraxein. Some investigators have suggested that certain unusual biochemical substances in the blood of schizophrenics may cause the disorder. Indirect support for this suggestion has come from some preliminary findings that schizophrenic patients undergoing kidney dialysis treatment (in which impurities of the blood are removed) demonstrate a marked reduction in schizophrenic symptomatology. Heath (1960) has long argued that a substance in the blood serum called *taraxein* is the cause of schizophrenia. He states that this protein substance is found only in the blood of schizophrenics and is genetically based; it interacts with other substances in the body to produce a toxic compound. This toxic compound causes disturbances in particular areas of the brain, particularly the septal region which controls pain and pleasure responses. To indicate the importance of this region, Heath points out that abnormal EEG recordings are sometimes found in the septal area of schizophrenics. He assumes that because of this disturbance, schizophrenics have a deficit in pain-pleasure responses, a disturbance of affect that is assumed to underlie schizophrenia.

Heath provided some experimental support of his theory. He was able to isolate taraxein in the blood. In a study conducted by Heath, Martens, Leach, Cohen, and Angel (1957), the administration of taraxein in nonschizophrenic prison volunteers produced schizophrenic-type symptoms and also altered the brain-wave activity recorded from the septal area. However, a number of investigators have questioned this biochemical theory because of the inability to replicate these findings (e.g., Kety 1960). Needless to say, additional research is required to unequivocally confirm or disconfirm this biochemical model of schizophrenia.

Psychotomimetic drugs. One chemical known to simulate schizophrenic-like behavior is the hallucinogenic drug *mescaline*. It resembles adrenalin, a chemical occurring naturally in the body. Osmond and Smythies (1952) and Hoffer (1964) suggested that an adrenalin-like substance, *adrenochrome*, and one of its metabolites, *adrenolutin*, are responsible for psychotic behavior. Research has shown that in schizophrenics a greater amount of adrenolutin was metabolized (manufactured) from adrenochrome, while in normal individuals adrenochrome was metabolized into another substance called *dihydroxy-N-methyl indole*. It is assumed that adrenolutin, which acts like mescaline, is responsible for symptoms of schizophrenia. Some studies, however, have failed to find such differences between schizophrenics and normals (Holland, Cohen, Goldenberg, Sha, & Leifer 1958), making this biochemical hypothesis inconclusive.

Another well-known psychotomimetic drug that has been investigated is LSD (lysergic acid diethylamide). The chemical cell structure of LSD closely resembles that of *serotonin*, a neurotransmitter substance found in the brain. Wooley (1962) has reported that an excessive amount of serotonin causes agitation like that produced by LSD, while an insufficient supply of serotonin causes suppression of activity like that in catatonic states. It is assumed that serotonin and another similar chemical, known as *tryptamine* (both of which are classified as *indolamines*), are chemically altered in an abnormal manner to form hallucinogenic compounds. Again, however, this biochemical model has not yet been adequately tested.

The similarities between symptoms of schizophrenia and those produced by drugs such as mescaline and LSD initially prompted many investigators to suggest that the biochemical underpinnings might be the same. However, schizophrenia and the so-called "model psychoses" produced by such drugs differ significantly from one another, not only in particular symptoms but in overall symptom patterning as well.

Dopamine hypothesis. The *dopamine hypothesis* of schizophrenia has received a great deal of attention during recent years. Dopamine is an important neurotransmitter substance in the brain that is involved in the chemical transmission of nerve impulses. This chemical neurotransmitter occurs only in certain areas of the brain, primarily in the "dopamine tract" leading from an area in the brainstem to an area in the limbic system. Several pieces of evidence suggest a dopamine abnormality in schizophrenia. First, one of the effects of amphetamines is to release dopamine in the brain. "Speed freaks" using amphetamines over long periods of time often act like schizophrenics. Griffith, Cavanaugh, Held, and Oates (1972) have demonstrated that when large doses of amphetamines were administered to individuals who had no evidence of schizophrenia, a psychotic reaction occurred in these individuals a few days later. In addition, small amounts of amphetamines appear to exacerbate certain symptoms of schizophrenic patients. This suggests an excessive amount of dopamine may be involved in the disorder.

Another piece of evidence is that patients who take the drug *L-dopa* (a chemical the body converts to dopamine when ingested) for the tremors and muscle rigidity caused by Parkinson's disease sometimes develop schizophrenic-like symptoms. The "dopamine tract" degenerates in Parkinson's disease, and the L-dopa treatment appears to compensate for this dysfunction.

Finally, *phenothiazine* drugs are highly effective in alleviating the symptoms of schizophrenia. Animal research has strongly suggested that these drugs block dopamine receptors in the "dopamine tract" (e.g., Nyback, Borzecki, & Sedvall 1968). They appear to block dopamine specifically but not other neurotransmitter substances.

Even though much of this evidence is indirect, it strongly suggests the involvement of some dopamine dysfunction in schizophrenia. The original dopamine hypothesis assumed that schizophrenics have an excessive amount of dopamine relative to normal subjects. More recent views suggest that schizophrenics may have more than twice the normal number of dopamine *receptors* in the brain. This excess of receptors may abnormally speed up the brain's transmission process, resulting in a flood of unrelated, illogical thoughts, along with the hallucinations and delusions that characterize a schizophrenic episode. Much additional research is needed to determine the precise mechanism that may be involved. It is a very promising area and, if supported by further research, could be a major breakthrough in finding a possible biochemical basis for schizophrenia.

PHYSIOLOGICAL FACTORS A number of investigations have demonstrated that levels of physiological activity differ between schizophrenics and normals (e.g., Buss 1966). Many investigators have interpreted these results as suggesting the possible presence of a biochemical disturbance in the neural transmission in the brain. Although differences have been found, there is still controversy as to whether schizophrenics' levels of physiological activity are higher or lower than normals'. Gruzelier and Venables (1975) note that while schizophrenics differ widely on measures of physiological activity, there appear to be two extreme and homogeneous groups, one demonstrating a high degree of physiological responding and another demonstrating a low degree. This differential rate of responding may prove to be an effective method for distinguishing between different forms of schizophrenia. Future research should more clearly elucidate these physiological response pattern differences and the possible underlying causative mechanisms producing them.

PARANOID DISORDERS

Besides paranoid schizophrenia, the DSM-II includes two other types of paranoid psychoses— *paranoia* and *paranoid state*. The DSM-III retains these two subcategories, plus the shared paranoid disorder, *folie a deux*. Paranoia is characterized by a well-systematized, logical delusional system that consists of delusions of grandeur and/or persecution. Except for this delusional system, though, the individual's overall personality structure is basically intact. There are usually not the significant thought disorganization and hallucinations typical of paranoid schizophrenia. Except for the delusions, the paranoiac often appears quite normal in his or her behavior. In fact, the delusions themselves often are expressed in such a way that the basic premises appear quite reasonable and may initially be accepted by the listener.

Paranoia usually develops gradually. Individuals may be confronted with a number of significant failures, both interpersonally and occupationally, that raise questions about their personal adequacy. They may begin to use the strategy of blaming others for wronging them, rather than accepting the possibility that their failures are due to their own inadequacies, along with resultant shame and humiliation this admission would produce. Colby (1977) has reviewed a number of psychological theories of paranoid phenomena and suggests that this particular viewpoint, which he labels the "shame-humiliation theory," seems to best explain the disorder.

Paranoiacs, in blaming others for wronging them, usually become overly vigilant and sensitive to anything in the environment that may provide "evidence" that others are working against them. They may come to believe that they are being singled out by "others" who are plotting against them. For example, they may blame their inability to rise up the corporate ladder not on lack of personal qualificatons, but on other people who are jealous of them and who want to get rid of them. They begin to further detect and falsify facts to fit their delusional system. Cameron (1959) refers to this process as the development of a "paranoid pseudo-community." They single out a group of people, both real and imaginary, who they believe are plotting against them. This pseudo-community, however, is not all-inclusive. It is limited to those situations in which the individual feels most threatened by inadequacy and failure.

The *paranoid state* is characterized by transient paranoid delusions, usually precipitated by some specific stress, that do not have the logical and systematic features of paranoia. Like paranoia, it is not accompanied by the bizarreness and thought-process deterioration of paranoid schizophrenia. This form is usually seen in persons who have recently changed their work or living situation, such as refugees, immigrants, prisoners of war, or young adults leaving home for the first time. Its onset is relatively sudden and it rarely becomes chronic. Finally, as we previously noted, the DSM-III also lists a subtype called *shared paranoid* disorder (*folie a deux* or double insanity). In this relatively rare form of paranoia, two people (e.g., husband and wife or two sisters) develop similar paranoid delusions.

Through the years, there has been a great deal of debate about whether the various forms of paranoid disorders are sufficiently different to be labeled as categories of psychoses, or are merely variants of the same basic schizophrenic disorder. In fact, these paranoid disorders by themselves are rarely observed in the clinic. One reason is that they are often accompanied by other forms of psychopathology. Another is that the "pure" paranoiac, except for isolated delusions such as those of the individual who feels exploited, the overly jealous spouse, or the fanatically religious person, is usually in contact with reality and can function effectively in society.

Research is needed to determine whether paranoid disorders are distinctively separate from one another. Because there is no definitive evidence to indicate that they are fundamentally different from schizophrenia, we will not spend any time separately discussing questions of etiology, treatment, prognosis, or assessment of the various paranoid disorders. We will simply assume that our

discussion in reviewing schizophrenia is applicable to the various types of paranoid disorders.

TREATMENT

EFFECTIVENESS OF TREATMENT VERSUS NO TREATMENT

Chemotherapy has been found to be an effective treatment modality with schizophrenic patients. Before the development of modern antipsychotic drugs, the outlook for improvement of schizophrenia was poor. However, even though there is ample evidence of significant clinical benefits produced by chemotherapy, Cawley (1967) has noted that nonspecific placebo factors may also contribute to this improvement. Expectations of improvement on the part of the clinical staff and the patients themselves may contribute to the therapeutic improvement. Also, as noted by Salzinger (1973), since drug therapy may calm down the patient temporarily, it may make it possible to offer patients other forms of therapy that they could not previously respond to. What is currently needed is a systematic evaluation of whether chemotherapy achieves its effect solely on the basis of the chemicals themselves, or whether nonspecific placebo factors in fact contribute to the therapeutic improvement.

Some behavior modification programs have been carefully evaluated and found to produce desirable behavior change in schizophrenic patients. In the majority of these program evaluation studies, there was no comparison-control group against which to compare the treatment group. It was shown that when the reinforcement contingencies that had been used to eliminate maladaptive behavior by replacing it with an incompatible adaptive behavior (e.g., administering a token whenever a schizophrenic patient speaks in a nonpsychotic "healthy" way) were removed, and the pretreatment behavior-reinforcement contingencies were restored, the patient returned to the previous maladaptive behavior (e.g., psychotic talk). Such an evaluation method demonstrates that the treatment technique had produced positive

behavior change. Designs such as these are usually referred to as *reversal* or *ABAB designs*.

SPECIFIC TREATMENT TECHNIQUES

CHEMOTHERAPY   Beginning in the late 1950s, antipsychotic drugs for use with schizophrenic patients were developed rapidly. *Phenothiazines* such as *chlorpromazine* (*Thorazine* is its trade name) are major tranquilizers that help control the symptoms of agitation and thought disturbances commonly found in schizophrenia. When necessary, a drug regimen that includes antidepressant drugs and/or minor tranquilizers is used if symptoms of depression and/or anxiety are also present. In his review of the effectiveness of chemotherapy, Lehmann (1966) concludes that drugs are usually the treatment of choice for schizophrenia because they are by far superior to any other treatment procedure in rapid effectiveness, sustained action over a period of time, and ease of administration with both acute and chronic schizophrenic patients.

Even though Lehmann points out the effectiveness of chemotherapy in alleviating major symptoms, he at the same time indicates that it does not provide a *cure* for this disorder. As we have pointed out for other disorders, the use of chemotherapy alone without an attempt to deal with possible situation/interpersonal factors involved may not lead to any permanent long-term improvement of most behavior disorders. Chemotherapy usually needs to be used in combination with psychological treatment techniques to ensure that one adequately deals with factors that might prompt a possible reoccurrence of the schizophrenic breakdown.

PSYCHOTHERAPY/BEHAVIOR THERAPY
Traditional psychoanalysts, including Freud, did

not assume that psychoanalysis would be very helpful for schizophrenic patients, because of their extreme withdrawal and resultant inability to enter into an appropriate therapeutic relationship. However, some psychoanalysts such as Harry Stack Sullivan and Frieda Fromm-Reichmann did suggest that psychoanalytic therapy could be used with schizophrenics if it was structured to aid patients in redeveloping contact with reality. The emphasis is not on increasing awareness of possible internal conflicts, as in treating neurotic patients, but rather on focusing on the "here and now" in dealing with present reality. This is similar to the therapy approach used by phenomenological psychotherapists such as Carl Rogers. A trusting therapeutic environment is developed in which an essential initial goal is the patient's realization that the therapist cares about him or her. This approach is based on the assumption (discussed earlier) that one of the basic contributing factors in the development of schizophrenia is faulty interpersonal relationships with significant others, especially with parents. It is assumed that an early history of traumatic interpersonal experiences produces subsequent withdrawal from any intimate relationships and general social isolation. The first step in treatment is, therefore, directed at redeveloping a trusting interpersonal relationship between patient and therapist. Obviously, a therapist using such an approach must have a great deal of patience and sensitivity to the schizophrenic's subjective troubled and confusing world. Not all therapists have the skill and experience to work effectively with this type of patient.

Although psychotherapists such as Fromm-Reichmann, Laing, and Sullivan have reported success in using such a treatment approach with schizophrenic patients, there have been no controlled studies documenting its effectiveness. Probably a few gifted therapists can work effectively with this type of patient, but a great many cannot. Such an approach also requires that patients be able to verbalize their thoughts and feelings coherently. Many schizophrenics, because of the presence of a significant thought-process disorder, are not able to do this. They would not be good candidates for this type of therapy.

PSYCHOTHERAPY EVALUATION RESEARCH

Grinspoon, Ewalt, and Shader (1968) conducted a study in which 20 male schizophrenics, hospitalized for three or more years, were assigned to one of two treatment groups: (1) An intensive psycho-

analytic therapy group that received 83 weeks of individual therapy from psychoanalysts experienced in working with schizophrenics, as well as in milieu therapy. Patients in this group also received placebo medication. (2) A group that received the above psychotherapy *plus* phenothiazene medication. Results of this study indicated that patients in the first treatment group showed little therapeutic improvement. Patients in the second group, however, demonstrated significant improvement.

Another feature of this study was that after 60 weeks of drug treatment, patients in the second group received placebo medication instead of the phenothiazene drugs. These patients were maintained on the placebos for three months, then put back on the phenothiazene medication. They continued to receive psychotherapy the entire time. With placebo medication, these patients reverted back to pretreatment levels of schizophrenic symptoms. They improved once again when the phenothiazenes were reintroduced. The point could be argued that the drug therapy allowed the patients to respond to the psychotherapy. However, the results do not support the effectiveness of psychoanalytic therapy alone with schizophrenic patients. A similar conclusion was made on the basis of a treatment-evaluation study conducted by May (1968).

MILIEU THERAPY In place of individual psychotherapy, group/social therapy techniques have been used with some success in treating schizophrenia. Within the institutional setting, *milieu therapy* is used, in which the entire clinical facility is used as a therapeutic community, with as few restraints as possible placed on the freedom of patients. Patients are urged to regulate their own activities, take part in a wide variety of activities, and develop socially appropriate interpersonal relationships. An attempt is made to develop a constructive environment in which an individual can learn more about herself or himself and more effective ways of responding to individuals, situations, and stress.

In chapter 4, we discussed Rosenhan's (1973) study entitled "Being Sane in Insane Places" as it related to the question of reliability of classification. In that same study, the pseudopatients observed that staff and patients were often segregated from one another. Except for caretaking duties such as administering medication, conducting a therapy session, or providing instructions to patients, the staff spent very little time interact-

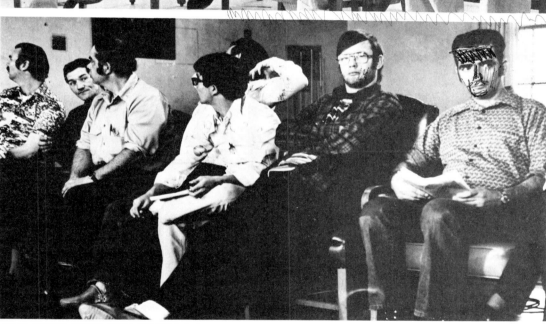

ONE FLEW OVER THE CUCKOO'S NEST © 1975, United Artists. A security ward council meeting as depicted in the film (top) and an actual ward council meeting at the Oregon State Hospital (bottom). The majority of mental hospitals today are not as inhumane as the one depicted in the film; however, the impersonal and often dehumanizing treatment of patients is a constant problem in many large institutions.

ing with patients as human beings. The staff seemed to view patients more as "sick" objects than responsible human beings. The patients therefore remained quite isolated from the hospital staff. Patients had very little personal privacy; for example, the staff could search their rooms at any time. The pseudopatients observed that such conditions increased patients' feelings of powerlessness and dehumanization, both of which are obviously very antitherapeutic. One of the significant advantages of milieu therapy is that patients are treated by the staff as responsible human beings who are capable of, and expected to, produce behavior change. It is a more humanistic approach than traditional custodial approaches (which are, unfortunately, still used in many hospitals today).

A slightly different type of milieu therapy is a form of residential community initially developed by R. D. Laing in London in 1965. This community, called Kingsley Hall, is one in which little distinction is made between patients and staff. The residence is set up as a group of people helping one another. In keeping with Laing's (1967) theory of schizophrenia, the schizophrenic reaction that a person is going through is not viewed as a breakdown, but merely as an experience that the person is going through which is both valid and meaningful for him or her. The goal of the staff is to emotionally support and work with the patient as he or she goes through this experience. In the United States, Soteria House in San Jose, California, is an example of a residential community patterned after Kingsley Hall.

An adequate evaluation of milieu-therapy type programs has not yet been made, so that their clinical effectiveness has not been objectively demonstrated (Mosher 1974). However, they show promise in helping schizophrenics to progress through their schizophrenic experiences in a nonthreatening environment.

BEHAVIOR THERAPY   A much more structured form of therapy is behavior modification. *Token economy* programs have been developed and shown to be effective in modifying and controlling the bizarre behavior patterns and problems of chronic schizophrenics in institutional settings (e.g., Ayllon & Azrin 1968; Krasner 1968). They are among the most successful rehabilitation programs for hospitalized patients. In such programs, an individual's undesirable behaviors are identified, and more desirable response patterns incompatible with the problem behavior are defined (e.g., eliminating psychotic talk with normal nonpsychotic talk). Patients are systematically reinforced with tokens whenever they engage in the socially desirable behavior. These tokens can be exchanged for special goods, such as candy or cigarettes, or special privileges such as a private room or community visits.

Token economy programs have been shown to be effective in increasing the frequency of socially adaptive behaviors even in severely regressed hospital patients. They are also effective in

improving the patient's sense of responsibility and self-reliance, and in decreasing feelings of helplessness and over-dependence. The shaping of these behaviors is valuable in preparing the patient for possible reintroduction into the community after discharge.

Behavioral rehabilitation programs emphasize a comprehensive approach to both in-hospital and post-hospital treatment. Atthowe (1976) has reviewed examples of such comprehensive programs. As he has indicated, these programs have been modeled after Paul's (1969) suggestion of the importance of dealing with the following target areas in rehabilitation:

1. *Resocialization* — includes areas such as the development of self-reliance, social skills, and communication skills.
2. *Instrumental role performance* — includes the development of appropriate vocational and "housekeeping" skills.
3. *Reduction or elimination of extreme bizarre behavior* — involves the modification of individual behavior or mannerisms identified as socially maladaptive and distressing.
4. *Provisions of at least one supportive "roommate" in the community.*   An understanding spouse, parent, or friend will ensure some degree of support for the patient when he or she returns to the community. Atthowe (1976) reported that a survey of discharged patients indicates that loneliness is a major factor that causes individuals to return to the hospital. Also, Leff (1976) found that the relapse rate for patients who return to a hostile, conflict-laden home environment is much greater than for patients who return to a more benign home environment. It is therefore important to provide some form of individual or group support in the community.

Atthowe (1976) has reported that the use of such a comprehensive behavioral rehabilitation approach in a Veteran's Administration hospital in California resulted in a recidivism rate of less than 12 percent over one year. This is much better than the 60–70 percent usual for most Veteran's Administration hospitals, and the 50 percent for general hospitals. These results are encouraging, especially considering that past attempts to rehabilitate psychiatric patients back into the community have not been very effective (Anthony 1977).

One special type of behavioral program that has been found to be very effective is the therapeutic community method developed by Fairweather and colleagues (Fairweather 1967; Fairweather, Sanders, Cressler, & Maynard, 1969). Mischel (1968) summarized the basic features of this program:

> This program, based on social learning principles, consists of a series of clear steps and contingencies that mark every phase of the patients' progress through the hospital and then out into a specially designed patient lodge located in the larger community. The therapeutic lodge was developed in response to the fact that many psychotic patients who have experienced more than two years of hospitalization continue to remain in the hospital enduringly and, if discharged, are returned to the hospital within a few months. . . . As a first step a patient group was organized in the hospital and lived and worked together in a special ward to encourage group responsibility and to approximate the conditions of a realistic society, the patients were given maximal autonomy over their own lives and daily activities throughout the program. They themselves had to make increasingly complex and difficult decisions about their collective behavior, the entire group being held responsible for the behavior of all its members at each stage. Progress to the next step was always made contingent upon success at the prerequisite step. While still in the hospital this group was presented with problems of the kind they would later have to confront in the community. These challenges involved, for example, organizing the lodge itself, caring for each other, planning and securing job employment, and so on. After a few weeks it was possible to move the group to the lodge, and after another month there they began to function as a basically autonomous, self-sufficient subsystem. For example, they organized and maintained a janitorial and yard service employing their own members, kept their own records, arranged their transportation, and assumed responsibility for their own living and working arrangements. Staff help, in the form of professional consultants to the lodge, gradually was replaced by lay volunteers, and then slowly was withdrawn completely. The patients themselves learned and assumed fully such responsible roles as nurse and work manager; within three years it was possible to withdraw all external help to the lodge, ex-patients now remaining together freely as a completely autonomous, self-sufficient group absorbed into the community. . . . The only remaining contacts with the hospital were follow-up visits from a member of the research staff at six-month intervals, and even that visit depended upon the approval of the ex-patients. (pp. 220–221)

The therapeutic lodge program was found to be very effective when lodge members were compared with a group of matched control patients simply released into society. The lodge patients remained in the community much longer and were employed much longer. Fairweather also noted the economic benefits of such a program. The cost per patient for the community lodge was less than five dollars per day; in contrast, the cost of hospitalization was about three to ten times more expensive, depending on the type of hospital. Moreover, when one takes into account the income earned by the employed members of the lodge, then the economic advantages of such a therapeutic community become even more significant.

FOLLOW-UP TREATMENT

As in the treatment of all disorders, appropriate follow-up treatment is important in dealing adequately with schizophrenia. For example, where a pathogenic family situation has contributed to the development of the disorder, a treatment program for the entire family may be needed. Outpatient care is helpful in aiding the patient adjust effectively back into the community. Indeed, Caffey, Galbrecht, and Klett (1971) reported a study which suggests that hospital treatment followed by a comprehensive outpatient aftercare program may be more effective than extended hospitalization. Comprehensive behavioral rehabilitation programs emphasize the importance of both in-hospital and post-hospital treatment. This will help to significantly reduce the readmission rate.

DIAGNOSIS AND ASSESSMENT

INTERVIEW / REFERRAL

A well-trained clinician usually has no great difficulty assessing the presence of symptoms associated with schizophrenia. The major symptoms of schizophrenia reviewed earlier—disorders of thought, attention and perception, affect, motor behavior, and social behavior—can be readily assessed on the basis of a clinical interview and observation of the patient's behavior. It should be mentioned, though, that many individuals going through an acute schizophrenic episode for the first time may also display symptoms of anxiety and depression that make diagnosis much more difficult. In acute episodes, individuals frequently become extremely fearful when they realize for the first time that they are experiencing bizarre cognitive and attentional symptoms. This anxiety, coupled with a morbid fear that they are ''going crazy'' and may be hospitalized, can create symptoms of anxiety and depression that can easily be confused with affective disorders. After a period of time, though, these patients gradually begin to lose their intense anxiety and depression, and the more usual schizophrenic cognitive disorders manifest themselves and dominate the clinical picture, making diagnosis much easier. Thus, certain schizophrenic patients may be diagnosed as suffering from an affective disorder when they are first hospitalized, and then only later be correctly rediagnosed.

As we discussed earlier, attempts to differentiate between various subtypes of schizophrenia on the basis of the DSM-II classification system have not been successful. Not only do the various subtypes overlap considerably in their definition and symptoms displayed, but patients may also shift symptom patterns from one type to another over time. Because of the overlap and change in symptoms over time, most clinicians acknowledge that the various subtypes cannot be clearly and reliably diagnosed. However, as noted earlier, a number of dimensions have been proposed as better ways of classifying the heterogeneous patients who are diagnosed as schizophrenic. A number of scales have been developed to measure some of these dimensions. Also, standard, structured diagnostic interview procedures have replaced the unstructured interviews used in the past with schizophrenics. They have been shown to lead to reliable diagnosis. We earlier mentioned the interview procedure developed by Gurland (cited in Zubin et al. 1975) which was effectively used in the United States-United Kingdom Diagnostic Project.

TESTING

Several methods have been developed to assess reactive-process (good-poor premorbid adjustment) schizophrenia. The Elgin Prognostic Scale (Wittman 1941) was one early diagnostic scale, but because of the vagueness in wording of many items and other problems related to rating these items, it has not been widely used. The Phillips Scale (Phillips 1953) is a more widely used measure of the premorbid adjustment status of schizophrenics. It was initially developed to predict those patients who would respond favorably to electroconvulsive therapy. However, it proved to be more predictive of the prognosis for schizophrenics, regardless of the treatment they received. This scale is filled out by a clinician from the patient's case history material related to his or her premorbid social and sexual adjustment in adolescence and early adulthood. There are six major categories: (1) recent sexual adjustment; (2) social aspects of sexual life during adolescence and immediately beyond; (3) social aspects of recent sexual life: 30 years +, (4) social aspects of recent sexual life: below 30; (5) personal relations: history; and (6) recent premorbid adjustment in personal relations.

Physiological measures also may prove to be effective in differentiating between various types of schizophrenia. Although there is not yet conclusive evidence to demonstrate the value of such measures in distinguishing between types of schizophrenia, Venables (1975) has reported that certain measures, such as GSR, show promise on the basis of a review of the existing literature.

BIOLOGICAL MARKERS OF SCHIZOPHRENIA

Electrical activity in the brain can be detected on a polygraph if surface recording electrodes are attached to the scalp. One type of electrical activity, called the *Cortical Evoked Potential* (CEP) is evoked by incoming sensory signals such as a flash of light or tone. The higher the intensity of the incoming stimulus, the larger the characteristic CEP response. Buchsbaum (1975) has found that some people tend to *augment* or increase responding and others tend to *reduce* responding to incoming sensory stimuli as reflected in measures of their CEPs. *Augmenters* show an increase in the size of the CEP as stimulus intensity increases, while *reducers* do not show an increase in the CEP as intensity increases.

In a series of clinical studies, Buchsbaum compared a group of acute schizophrenics, normal subjects, and manic-depressive patients. All patients were off medication. Schizophrenics typically showed CEP-reducer characteristics, while manic-depressives typically showed CEP-augmenter characteristics. The normal subjects fell in between these two groups. Moreover, within the schizophrenic group, those patients who showed the greatest reducer characteristics (i.e., greater CEP reduction to high intensity stimuli) went on to improve spontaneously without medication. This finding suggests that reducer characteristics may be an adaptive mechanism of the central nervous system to decrease or reduce the bombardment of incoming stimuli, especially high-intensity stimuli. The occurrence of an acute schizophrenic episode may reflect an attempt by an individual's CNS to temporarily filter out external stimuli. Those individuals who are able to do this most effectively (the extreme reducer group) may improve quickest because the filtering or shut-off of external stimulation allows their nervous systems to recover more readily from the stress that might have precipitated the disorder. Regardless of how one wishes to interpret these data, though, they clearly indicate that the CEP may be a biological marker that can differentiate among schizophrenia, depressive disorders, and normal psychological functioning. It may also provide a useful prognostic indicator of clinical improvment.

The MMPI is, again, a widely used psychological test for the various forms of psychopathology including schizophrenia and paranoia. The schizophrenia (Sc) scale measures confused, schizoid, bizarre thinking. The paranoia (Pa) scale measures paranoid thinking, sensitivity, and hostility. The elevation of these scales, or certain patterns of scales that are assumed to reflect specific subtypes of schizophrenia, are often interpreted to suggest the presence of a psychotic disturbance. Again, however, we must emphasize that test results should never be used as the sole basis for a diagnosis. They should be viewed merely as an adjunct to more thorough assessment procedures based on social history and interview/behavioral evaluation.

PROGNOSIS

Before the advent of effective antipsychotic drugs and modern treatment techniques in the late 1950s and early 1960s, the prognosis for improvement of schizophrenics was generally poor. The "treatment" of choice was usually simple custodial care in a mental institution. Today the outlook for improvement is much better. Coleman (1976) estimates that the discharge rate for first-time hospitalization cases is about 80–90 percent after a few weeks or months of hospitalization. The rate of rehospitalization, however, is still high—about 45 percent of the patients are readmitted to the hospital within the first year following their initial discharge. In general, approximately one-third of these patients recover, one-third show partial recovery, and the remaining one-third remain almost totally disabled psychologically (Coleman 1976). Although the number of schizophrenics hospitalized in mental institutions has declined steadily since the middle 1960s, schizophrenics still constitute approximately one-half the total resident population in mental hospitals in the United States today (Taube & Redick 1973). Clearly, although there have been advances in treatment in recent years, more effective methods are still needed.

As mentioned earlier in reviewing the various dimensions of schizophrenia, prognosis for improvement is better for one of the poles of a cluster of dimensions—reactive, paranoid, acute, good-premorbid, activity—than for the opposite poles—

process, chronic, poor-premorbid, withdrawal. Based on a composite of several studies, Coleman (1976) lists several conditions that are associated with favorable treatment outcomes of schizophrenia. These conditions are similar to those associated with the favorable poles of the dimensions: (1) reactive versus process; (2) a clear precipitating stress; (3) adequate heterosexual, social, and work adjustment prior to the onset of schizophrenia; (4) low incidence of schizophrenia and other forms of psychopathology in family background; (5) a favorable family/life situation to return to after release from the hospital, and appropriate aftercare in the community; (6) the presence of depression or other schizoaffective patterns along with the schizophrenia.

SUMMARY

1. The DSM-II classification system distinguished between eleven subtypes of schizophrenia. However, as with other forms of psychopathology, the reliability of diagnosing these various subtypes is not very high. This is because symptoms overlap across the various subtypes and patients may shift symptom patterns from one type to another over time. It is hoped that the DSM-III, with its use of more objective classification criteria, will remedy this reliability problem.

2. In the search for better ways of subclassifying different forms of schizophrenia, a number of dimensions have been proposed as more effective means of classifying the heterogeneous patients diagnosed as schizophrenic. Four dimensions have proven to be useful: *process-reactive* (poor premorbid-good premorbid) dimension, *chronic-acute* dimension, *nonparanoid-paranoid* dimension, and *withdrawal-activity* dimension. These four dimensions are interdependent.

3. A number of major symptoms are associated with schizophrenia: thought disorders (incoherence and delusions), disorders of

attention (e.g., hallucinations), disorders of motor behavior (hyperexcitability or catatonia), and disorders of social behavior (social withdrawal). It is exceedingly rare for a schizophrenic to display the whole range of symptoms all the time. Most display only some of the symptoms some of the time.

4. A number of theoretical models have been proposed to account for schizophrenia. Psychoanalytic theory suggests that regression to the early part of the oral stage of development is responsible for this disorder. The phenomenological-existential model, as advocated by Laing, views schizophrenia as a coping strategy a person develops to live in a stressful, insane world. Learning theorists such as Ullmann and Krasner view the disorder as a learned response of inattention to social stimuli. There is a paucity of evidence to support any of these models.

5. Numerous studies have attempted to evaluate the developmental histories of schizophrenia in order to determine whether there are specific factors that trigger this disorder. One type of developmental study that shows great promise for delineating

such factors is the high-risk developmental study. The first systematic high-risk study of schizophrenia was started in Denmark in the early 1960s by Mednick and Schulsinger. Preliminary results of this study have been illuminating. One of the findings suggests that complications in the birth process may contribute to "triggering" the schizophrenia developmental process in genetically predisposed persons.

6. Investigators who view environmental factors as important in the etiology of schizophrenia look at the history and mode of interpersonal relationships, especially within the family, as possible important causative agents in this disorder. The only consistent findings to date concerning the family patterns of schizophrenics are: (a) there is more conflict present between the parents of schizophrenics than between parents of normals; (b) communication between the parents of schizophrenics is less clear than that between parents of normal individuals. However, these same family dynamics can be found in other forms of psychopathology. There is no evidence to support the double-bind theory or the schizophrenogenic mother concept of schizophrenia.

7. There is considerable evidence for a genetic involvement in schizophrenia. Such evidence comes from three major types of studies: family studies, twin studies, and studies of adopted children. However, there is not an exact 100 percent relationship, which suggests the involvement of other factors also. Currently, a *diathesis-stress* model of schizophrenia, such as the one proposed by Meehl, is popular. This model assumes that some individuals who are genetically predisposed toward the development of schizophrenia will develop this disorder only if they are exposed to particular stressful experiences. The *vulnerability* model proposed by Zubin and Spring shows great promise for better understanding this disorder.

8. The existence of a genetic basis for schizophrenia implies that organic variables may be involved. Numerous studies have examined the possibility of disturbed biochemical and physiological processes in schizophrenia. The *dopamine hypothesis* of schizophrenia has received a great amount of indirect support in recent years. However, much additional research is needed before any one biochemical process can be implicated in this disorder.

9. Besides paranoid schizophrenia, the DSM-II and DSM-III include two other types of paranoid psychoses—*paranoia* and *paranoid state* or *reaction*. Paranoia is characterized by a well-systemized and logical delusional system consisting of delusions of grandeur and/or persecution. The paranoid state is characterized by transient paranoid delusions, usually precipitated by some specific stress, that do not have the logical and systematic features of paranoia. Neither of these disorders is associated with the bizarre behavior and thought-process deterioration of paranoid schizophrenia. At present, there is no conclusive evidence to indicate whether the various forms of paranoid states are sufficiently different to be labeled as different categories of psychosis, or are merely variants of the same basic schizophrenic disorder.

10. With the development of modern antipsychotic drugs, chemotherapy has been found to be effective with schizophrenic patients. Milieu therapy and behavior modification programs have also been found to produce desirable bahavior change. Before the advent of these techniques, the prognosis for improvement of schizophrenia was generally poor. Even though the outlook for improvement today is much better, schizophrenics still constitute approximately one-half the total resident population in mental hospitals. Even more effective treatment methods are still needed.

11. A well-trained clinician usually has no great difficulty assessing the presence of symptoms of schizophrenia. An individual going through an acute schizophrenic episode for the first time, however, may frequently display symptoms of an affective disorder, making diagnosis more difficult. With time, the affective disorder symptoms of anxiety and depression gradually disappear, and the more usual schizophrenic cognitive disorders manifest themselves and dominate the clinical picture.

RECOMMENDED READINGS

Ban, T. *Recent advances in the biology of schizophrenia*. Springfield, Ill.: Charles C. Thomas, 1973.

Broen, W. E. *Schizophrenia: Research and theory*. New York: Acadmic Press, 1968.

Chapman, L. J., & Chapman, J. D. *Disordered thought in schizophrenia*. Englewood Cliffs, N.J.: Prentice-Hall, 1973.

Dohrenwend, B.P., & Dohrenwend, B. S. *Social status and psychological disorder*. New York: Wiley, 1969.

Laing, R. D. *The divided self*. New York: Pantheon, 1969.

Mendel, W. M. *Schizophrenia: The experience and its treatment*. San Francisco: Jossey-Bass, 1976.

Mishler, E., & Waxler, N. *Interaction in families: An experimental study of family processes and schizophrenia*. New York: Wiley, 1968.

Salzinger, K. *Schizophrenia: Behavioral aspects*. New York: Wiley, 1973.

Zubin, J., & Spring, B. Vulnerability—A new view of schizophrenia. *Journal of Abnormal Psychology*, 1977, 86, 103–126.

ALCOHOLISM AND OTHER DRUG USE DISORDERS

10

OVERVIEW In this chapter, we will discuss the problem of alcoholism and other forms of drug abuse. Drug abuse can lead to psychological and/or physiological dependence that can pose serious problems for the individual and for society as a whole. Alcohol is a physiologically addicting drug; chronic and heavy use can also lead to serious nutritional deficiencies resulting in physical damage such as cirrhosis of the liver. We will review the stages of alcoholism and also the different types of alcoholism that have been described in an effort to understand problem drinking behavior. In so doing, it will become apparent that there is no single definition of alcoholism. A variety of different drinking patterns and a complex of determinants—psychological, sociocultural, and physiological—need to be considered in any attempt to define alcoholism precisely.

We will review psychological theories of alcoholism and conclude that there is at present none that satisfactorily explains this disorder. Sociocultural theories, which emphasize the importance of a society's drinking practices, customs, and attitudes towards alcohol, appear promising in the explanation of some forms of alcohol abuse. Finally, we will indicate that the treatment of alcoholism has traditionally been ineffective. Recently developed behavior therapy techniques, however, show promise for more successfully dealing with it.

We will also review other drugs that are abused—opium and its derivatives (morphine and

DEMOGRAPHICS		USUAL AGE AT ONSET	PREVALENCE	SEX RATIO
ALCOHOL ABUSE		Adolescence and early adulthood	Serious problem for about 5% of population. For 15% of population, there are some problems associated with alcohol use	Traditionally, male-female ratio has been 4 or 5 to 1. These differences are starting to diminish
HEROIN ABUSE		Adolescence and early adulthood	Currently, about 300,000 heroin addicts in this country	Males far outnumber females
BARBITURATE ABUSE		Late adolescence and adulthood	Exact statistics not known, although some have estimated approximately 1 million people abuse such drugs	Female-male ratio is approximately 2 to 1
AMPHETAMINE ABUSE		Late adolescence and early adulthood	Unknown	Males outnumber females
COCAINE ABUSE		Late adolescence and early adulthood	Unknown	Males outnumber females
HALLUCINOGEN ABUSE		Late adolescence and early adulthood	Rare	Exact ratio is not known
CANNABIS ABUSE		Adolescence and early adulthood	Not accurately known, though not thought to be great	Males outnumber females, though exact ratio is not known

heroin), amphetamines, sedatives (barbiturates and tranquilizers), cocaine, hallucinogens (LSD and mescaline), and cannabis (marijuana and hashish). As with alcoholism, there is no single definition of these forms of drug abuse. There are also no psychological theories that adequately explain such abuse. Certain sociocultural factors appear to be associated with drug use and abuse, although the exact cause-effect nature of this association is not yet known. Finally, we shall see that as with alcoholism, the treatment of these drug dependencies has traditionally been ineffective.

SYMPTOM DESCRIPTION AND ETIOLOGY

Alcohol and other drugs can serve useful personal and social functions. There are certain prescribed and acceptable medicinal, religious, and social uses for many drugs in our society. For example, minor tranquilizers can be beneficial for the temporary relief of anxiety. Moderate amounts of alcohol can reduce tension and facilitate social interaction. However, there are potentially harmful effects when they are overused. The excessive use of drugs can lead to physiological or psychological dependence that poses serious problems for the individual and for society as a whole. *Physiological dependence* or *addiction* is characterized by these features: (1) The experience of physiological *with-*

drawal symptoms, such as nausea, vomiting, and "the shakes," which occur after the sudden discontinuation of drug use. The exact pattern of withdrawal symptoms varies with the drug. Evidence that these are actual withdrawal symptoms, and not simply a "hangover," is the fact that they can be suppressed by resuming drug intake. (2) *Tolerance* develops, and increasing amounts of the drug must be ingested to produce the same desired physiological and psychological effects.

Physiological addiction usually occurs with chronic alcohol, barbiturate, and heroin usage. Other drugs, although not physiologically addicting, can produce *psychological dependence*. They may produce a strong and overwhelming desire for the pleasant state created by the drug. Without the drug, the individual experiences psychological tension and feels emotionally unable to cope with life.

Such psychological dependence can interfere with a satisfying life-style.

When physiological addiction is not present, the differentiation between drug *use* and *abuse* can be difficult. It is difficult to define abuse merely in terms of amount consumed, since some people can tolerate large quantities of a drug over a period of time with no significant detrimental effects. Other individuals are significantly affected by a very small amount. The simplest way to define abuse appears to be in terms of the effects of drug intake and the person's ability to function effectively in his or her environment. An abuse problem exists if ingestion of a drug, or abstention from a drug, interferes with the individual's effective emotional, physical, or social functioning in day-to-day living. As we shall discuss in this chapter, a number of drugs are seriously abused in our society.

ALCOHOLISM

Approximately 100 million Americans use alcoholic beverages moderately and without harmful effects. Another approximately 5–10 million abuse the use of alcohol and are labelled *alcoholics* or *problem drinkers* because of the harm they do to themselves, others, and/or society. The National Institute on Drug Abuse and Alcoholism has recently estimated that excessive problem drinking on and off the job is costing American industry approximately 15 billion dollars a year. Besides these significant economic consequences, it also presents a significant health hazard. It is second only to heroin as an addiction that can cause death. Finally, it has been estimated by the National Institute that 68 percent of the nation's highway fatalities are alcohol-related.

As we shall see, the precise statistics on the incidence of alcoholism vary depending on one's definition of alcoholism. There is as yet no one clear, precise, and totally accepted definition of alcoholism. There are several classes of alcoholism that often overlap. That is, there is a variety of excessive and deviant drinking behaviors that cause varying degrees of personal, interpersonal, and social harm. One relatively broad definition of alcoholism is that of the DSM-II:

This category is for patients whose alcohol intake is great enough to damage their physical health, or their personal or social functioning, or when it has become a prerequisite for normal functioning. (p. 45)

EFFECTS OF ALCOHOL

Alcohol is a central nervous system depressant drug that inhibits both the higher and lower brain centers. Results of this inhibition for some may be feelings of relaxation, warmth, freedom from tension, and a sense of well-being. The perception of discomforts such as minor aches and pains is also dulled. These "mellowing" effects, coupled with the fact that the consumption of alcohol often occurs in social situations associated with "good times," account for alcohol's popularity. Alcohol also makes one's behavior less inhibited, and the individual is more likely to try certain actions, such as asserting oneself in a particular group or speaking to an attractive person one has never met before.

Blood alcohol level refers to the amount of alcohol in the bloodstream. It is expressed as the amount of alcohol per specific volume of blood. The precise effects of alcohol blood level on behavior vary from one individual to another.

Factors such as the drinker's personality and present attitude, his or her physical and nutritional condition, physical size, and the history and duration of drinking all affect the type of behavior shown. As a general rule for the average nonabusive drinker, however, there are certain consistent patterns. When the blood alcohol level is .05 percent (achieved, for example, when a normal adult male drinks 2 or 3 cans of beer in one hour), the individual usually begins "feeling good," becomes less inhibited, and may start being the "life of the party." When the alcohol level reaches .10 percent (4–6 cans of beer in one hour), the person is usually considered to be intoxicated. Difficulties in motor coordination and impairment of speech, vision, and thought processes emerge. The individual also becomes less socially pleasant company. When the alcohol level reaches approximately 4–5 times this amount, the individual will be so intoxicated that he or she will pass out. Levels even higher than this can be lethal.

Besides the possibilities of unpleasant public scenes and socially unacceptable actions that may be regretted later, a number of other negative factors are associated with alcohol intoxication. One well-known and widely experienced negative after-effect is the unpleasant *hangover*, which includes symptoms of fatigue, headache, and nausea. Also, many experience a *blackout*, in which there is a short-term lapse of memory during moderate drinking, with an inability later to recall events during the drinking period. These two phenomena are not fully understood physiologically.

With frequent and chronic abuse of alcohol, a number of more significant negative consequences can occur. If a person consistently uses a drug such as alcohol to aid in coping with stress and anxiety, psychological dependency can develop. These individuals will develop a strong and overwhelming need for alcohol. Without it, they will feel psychologically tense and emotionally unable to cope with life. Physiological dependency can also occur, in which painful withdrawal symptoms occur if alcohol is not ingested. The alcoholic learns that only more alcohol will alleviate these symptoms, and so begins to drink continuously in order to avoid them. This physiological dependency is often a sign of alcohol addiction. Along with this addiction, alcohol tolerance occurs. Greater and greater amounts of alcohol need to be consumed to produce the same desired physiological and psychological effects.

Chronic heavy drinking can also produce serious nutritional deficiencies. Alcohol is a high-calorie drink that reduces the drinker's appetite for food; the alcohol itself, however, has little or no nutritional value. The individual may therefore begin to suffer from serious malnutrition and vitamin deficiencies. Heavy drinking also puts extra stress on the liver, which must work especially hard to assimilate the alcohol into the body. Cirrhosis of the liver may develop, in which liver cells are irreversibly damaged. This disorder can, and often does, cause death.

Psychotic types of reactions can also be precipitated by heavy drinking. One of the most widely known is *delirium tremens* (DTs). This reaction can occur in the excessive drinker either during a period of abstinence or withdrawal from alcohol or during periods of extensive drinking. Symptoms include *disorientation* in place and time, so that the individual may not know where he or she is or who other people are; *hallucinations*, especially of small animals such as bugs, rats, and snakes, which may appear to be attacking; these hallucinations can create intense fear in the individual, who may attempt to flee the situation or fight off the animals; *tremors* of the hands and legs; other physiological symptoms such as a change in regular heart rate, sweating, and fear. These episodes usually last between three to six days if no treatment is administered. Their severity can be greatly alleviated with certain tranquilizing drugs such as chlordiazepoxide (Librium).

This case study by Millon and Millon (1974) describes the typical experiences and behavior of a patient with delirium tremens:

**ALCOHOL AND
BEHAVIOR**
Table 10.1

From Ray 1974

BLOOD ALCOHOL LEVEL	BEHAVIOR
.05%	Lowered alertness; usually good feeling.
.10%	Slowed reaction times; less caution.
.15%	Large, consistent increases in reaction time.
.20%	Marked depression in sensory and motor capability; decidedly intoxicated.
.25%	Severe motor disturbance, staggering; sensory perceptions greatly impaired; smashed!
.30%	Semistupor.
.35%	Surgical anesthesia; minimal lethal dose.
.40%	Probable lethal dose.

A CASE OF DTs

Jim is a moderately successful lawyer, despite his chronic alcoholism. He "goes off on a bender" about once a month, disappearing for several days to a week. In the past ten years, Jim has been briefly hospitalized more than 20 times in conjunction either with delirium tremens or some other alcohol-related difficulty.

In a recent episode, his "girl-friend" called the emergency ward at the local hospital because Jim was jabbing himself with a fork "to get those miserable gnats off" his body. He was screaming and delirious upon admission to the hospital, terrified not only of the hallucinated gnats, but of the "crazy shapes" and "smelly queeries" that were "coming after" him. Nothing could be done to comfort Jim for several hours; he continued to have tremors, sweated profusely, cowered in a corner, drew his blankets over his head, twisted and turned anxiously, vomited several times and kept screaming about hallucinated images which "attacked" him and "ate up his skin."

After three days of delirium, with intermittent periods of fitful sleep, Jim began to regain his normal senses. He was remorseful, apologized to all for his misbehavior and assured them of his "absolute resolution never to hit the bottle again." Unfortunately, as was expected, he again was hospitalized three months later as a consequence of a similar debauch that was followed by delirium tremens. (p. 398)

Another form of psychosis that can develop as a result of heavy drinking is *Korsakoff's psychosis*. This reaction was first described by the Russian psychiatrist Korsakoff in the late 1800s. Its chief characteristic is a serious memory disturbance, including memory gaps and the inability to recognize and recall individuals or situations recently exposed to. This results in a partial inability to learn new associations. The individual attempts to conceal this memory deficit by *falsification* in which he or she tries to fill in memory gaps by making up stories or misapplying old reminiscences. As a result, the person appears disoriented and cognitively confused. This particular reaction, which is thought to be caused by Vitamin B deficiencies, other dietary deficiencies, and perhaps some neural degeneration, usually occurs in older alcoholics who have been chronic drinkers for years.

TEENAGE ALCOHOLISM   Alcoholism is not only an adult problem. It is increasingly becoming a significant problem among adolescents. The rate of alcoholism is increasing in this country, especially among teenagers. By the time that most adolescents graduate from high school, they have established a pattern of light to moderate drinking. The percentage of teenagers who drink varies between 30–40 percent and 60–80 percent, depending on regional, ethnic, and social differences (Maddox 1970). Approximately 2 to 6 percent of the adolescent population are problem drinkers for whom alcohol has become a significant factor in their lives (Braucht, Brakarsh, Follingstad, & Berry 1973).

Most adolescents view drinking as a sign of "adulthood" and sophistication. Unfortunately, for this age group there are a number of possible immediate negative consequences associated with drinking, including the increased likelihood of automobile accidents while intoxicated, as well as the possibility of this drinking intensifying and leading to alcoholism. Adolescent problem drinkers appear to come from homes in which parents are frequent and high users of alcohol; they belong to peer groups in which alcohol abuse is also encouraged (Braucht et al. 1973). Such data indicate the important influence that social factors such as parental modeling and peer pressure play in the development of deviant drinking patterns.

STAGES OF ALCOHOLISM

As we stated previously, approximately 100 million Americans use alcoholic beverages moderately without any harmful effects. A much smaller number become problem drinkers who abuse the use of alcohol, develop psychological, physiological, and social problems and, as a consequence, are labeled "alcoholics." Jellinek (1952, 1960) has delineated four stages in the progression from nonproblematic "social drinking" to alcoholism. On the basis of a study of over 2,000 alcoholics, he found a consistency in the stages of development of alcohol dependency:

1. *Prealcoholic symptomatic phase,* which is characterized by periodic drinking as a method of avoiding problems and dealing with stress. Initially, alcohol may be taken only occasionally to relieve tension produced by problematic, stressful situations. However, these causative situations become

more frequent, and the individual's tolerance for them gradually decreases so that he or she resorts to alcohol more and more. Eventually, drinking becomes constant. Jellinek indicates that it can take from several months to several years for the transition from occasional to constant drinking.

2. *Prodromal phase,* which is marked by heavy drinking that can produce blackouts or amnesic episodes. The individual remains conscious and can perform typical behaviors, but the next day will have no memory of the events that transpired during these blackouts. In this phase, alcohol becomes more of a drug than a simple beverage; the individual becomes preoccupied with alcohol and worries about whether there will be enough to drink during the course of the day. Guilt feelings about drinking behavior usually appear at this point.

3. *Crucial period,* in which the main characteristic is *loss of control*—once the individual takes the first drink, he or she cannot stop drinking until too sick or disoriented to drink any more. The first drink precipitates continual drinking until complete intoxication is achieved. During this period, these drinkers' social adjustment begins to suffer. They begin to drink in places and at times that are not appropriate. They start drinking during the day, which impairs their work effectiveness. The drinking problem becomes apparent to employers, family, and friends. These individuals also begin to suffer nutritional deficiencies because they neglect to eat properly. They go on periodic *benders* which may result in hospitalization because of physical ailments caused by the prolonged drinking. Finally, there are *withdrawal symptoms* if drinking is stopped, and these can only be relieved by consuming alcohol. The person begins drinking in the morning so as to avoid these withdrawal symptoms. He or she also develops an elaborate rationalization system to explain and defend the drinking behavior.

4. *Chronic phase,* in which drinking has become constant. Tissue tolerance for alcohol decreases so that it now requires *less* alcohol to produce intoxication. The alcoholic now shows little concern for job, family, or personal hygiene. He or she has lost all self-esteem, and shows little concern about

his or her behavior and its consequences. The person's entire life centers on the consumption of alcohol. He or she is no longer selective about drinking companions or the type of alcohol consumed, but will drink almost anything, including rubbing alcohol and hair tonic. Because of prolonged use of alcohol and neglect of diet, the person begins to develop physical symptoms to go along with the great many psychological problems that are present. These symptoms may become serious and lead to organ damage and death.

Jellinek indicated that it took between 12 and 18 years for this chronic alcoholism to develop. For some people, this period may be much shorter. We should also point out that many alcoholics do not precisely follow this course of development as outlined by Jellinek. For example, not all alcoholics experience blackouts (Goodwin, Crane, & Guze 1969), and in some individuals, these amnesic episodes occur in later rather than earlier stages. Moreover, in some instances, an individual appears to skip the social drinking phase and become an "instant alcoholic." Finally, some recent evidence questions the *loss of control* notion assumed to be present in alcoholism (Marlatt, Demming, & Reid 1973).

TYPES OF ALCOHOLISM

Jellinek (1960) has also described different patterns or categories of problem drinking and alcoholism. He realized that there are a variety of problems connected with the use of alcohol that may differ from one society to the next. Starting with the simple working definition of the term *alcoholism* as meaning the use of alcohol that causes damage to the individual or to society, he delineated four different patterns of problem drinking. These four categories are as follows:

1. *Alpha alcoholism* involves reliance on alcohol as the primary means of relieving bodily or emotional stress and discomfort. The individual uses drinking as an escape and coping mechanism. Although there is psychological dependence, there is no loss of control involved, and the individual is able to control the amount consumed. Usually there is no progression to greater

and more frequent drinking. The drinking pattern, however, does interfere with interpersonal relationships and work efficiency, and is viewed as socially maladaptive. This person is often referred to as the "problem drinker."

2. *Beta alcoholism* is the type in which physical complaints and complications, such as cirrhosis of the liver or gastritis, are associated with the drinking. Because of these symptoms, the individual should not be drinking. This individual, however, does not have a strong physiological or psychological dependence on alcohol.

3. *Gamma alcoholism* involves the development of increased tissue tolerance to alcohol, so that the individual must consume greater and greater amounts to produce the same desired affects. If the individual stops drinking, he or she will experience physiological withdrawal symptoms. These drinkers are also psychologically dependent upon alcohol and have completely lost control of their drinking. The typical "skid row" alcoholic is an example of this form of alcoholism. This person shows a total lack of concern for interpersonal relations and acceptable social behavior. Also, he or she suffers physical complaints and complications caused by prolonged drinking and insufficient nutrition and diet.

4. *Delta alcoholism* refers to individuals who cannot abstain from drinking but can regulate the amount they drink. An example of this drinking pattern is the Frenchman who normally consumes several bottles of wine a day, but whose work efficiency does not seriously suffer because of it. He has adapted to this high alcohol intake and does not lose control. Yet without alcohol, he would experience physical and psychological withdrawal symptoms. In contrast to gamma alcoholics, who lose control of their drinking after taking the first drink but who are capable of periods of sobriety for weeks or months, delta alcoholics continually ingest and maintain a high level of alcohol in their systems. Buss (1960) notes that this type of alcoholism is typical of Latin countries where wine consumption is high, while gamma alcoholism is more typical of Anglo-Saxon countries where whiskey consumption is high.

In addition to Jellinek's classification system, the DSM-II also has categorized different forms of alcoholism. In the DSM-II classification system (chapter 4), three separate categories are proposed. The first is referred to as *alcoholic psychosis;* it is caused by heavy and prolonged drinking that leads to brain damage and appearance of psychotic-type behavior. This type of alcoholism is included in the category known as *organic psychoses,* which will be discussed in chapter 14. A second type of alcoholism is listed in the DSM-II under *nonpsychoses of physical origin.* This is simple drunkenness of organic origin which does not involve psychotic-type behavior. The third form, in which the greatest proportion of alcohol-related problems are listed, are included in the DSM-II within the *personality disorder* category. In this category, four subgroups of alcoholism are included: episodic excessive drinking (defined as being intoxicated at least four times a year), habitual excessive drinking (defined as being intoxicated 12 or more times a year), alcoholic addiction (physiological dependence), and "other" alcoholism. The new DSM-III classification will use separate categories: (1) *Substance-induced* (alcohol, barbiturates, cocaine, and so on) *organic mental disorders,* which basically incorporates the first two DSM-II categories; (2) *Substance use disorders,* including the greatest proportion of alcohol-related problems. The first category includes organic brain syndromes such as Korsakoff's psychosis and alcohol amnesic syndrome. Other forms of alcoholism, minus the organic symptoms, are listed under the second category. Thus, DSM-III classifies alcoholism into two broad categories based on whether or not organic brain symptoms are present.

Both Jellinek's system and the DSM-II system of classification of alcoholism have significant limitations. Research has demonstrated that the various categories of alcoholism are not discrete, but often overlap. There is a wide variety of deviant and excessive drinking patterns. Also, the drinking pattern of alcoholics often changes as time and situations change. Reliability of classification can therefore be low. We should also point out that these classification systems also have a major shortcoming in that once an alcoholic is assigned a diagnostic label, the systems fail to suggest the type of treatment that should be administered or the prognosis for improvement. It is hoped that DSM-III will provide a more reliable and valid classification approach to alcoholism.

THOMAS DE QUINCEY ON TAKING OPIUM

I was necessarily ignorant of the whole art and mystery of opium-taking: and, what I took, I took under every disadvantage. But I took it:—and in an hour, oh! heavens! what a revulsion! what an upheaving, from its lowest depths, of the inner spirit! what an apocalypse of the world within me! That my pains had vanished, was now a trifle in my eyes:—this negative was swallowed up in the immensity of those positive effects which had opened before me—in the abyss of divine enjoyment thus suddenly revealed. Here was a panacea for all human woes: here was the secret of happiness, about which philosophers had disputed for so many ages, at once discovered: happiness might now be bought for a penny, and carried in the waistcoat pocket: portable ecstasies might be had corked up in a pint bottle: and peace of mind could be sent down in gallons by the mail coach. But, if I talk in this way, the reader will think I am laughing: and I can assure him, that nobody will laugh long who deals much with opium: its pleasures even are of a grave and solemn complexion, But crude opium, I affirm peremptorily, is incapable of producing any state of body at all resembling that which is produced by alcohol: and not in *degree* only incapable, but even in *kind:* it is not in the quantity of its effects merely, but in the quality, that it differs altogether. The pleasure given by wine is always mounting, and tending to a crisis, after which it declines: that from opium, when once generated, is stationary for eight or ten hours: the first, to borrow a technical distinction from medicine, is a case of acute—the second, of chronic pleasure: the one is a flame, the other a steady and equable glow. But the main distinc-

tion lies in this, that whereas wine disorders the mental faculties, opium, on the contrary (if taken in a proper manner), introduces amongst them the most exquisite order, legislation, and harmony. Wine robs a man of his self-possession: opium greatly invigorates it. Wine unsettles and clouds the judgment, and gives a preternatural brightness, and a vivid exaltation to the contempts and the admirations, the loves and the hatreds, of the drinker: opium, on the contrary, communicates serenity and equipoise to all the faculties, active or passive: and with respect to the temper and moral feelings in general, it gives simply that sort of vital warmth which is approved by the judgment, and which would probably always accompany a bodily constitution of primeval or antediluvian health. Thus, for instance, opium, like wine, gives an expansion to the heart and the benevolent affections: but then, with this remarkable difference, that in the sudden development of kindheartedness which accompanies inebriation, there is always more or less of a maudlin character, which exposes it to the contempt of the bystander. Men shake hands, swear eternal friendship, and shed tears—no mortal knows why: and the sensual creature is clearly uppermost. But the expansion of the benigner feelings, incident to opium, is no febrile access, but a healthy restoration to that state which the mind would naturally recover upon the removal of any deep-seated irritation of pain that had disturbed and quarrelled with the impulses of a heart originally just and good.

From Confessions of an English Opium-Eater, by Thomas De Quincey, 1822.

If a classification system is to be useful and effective, it must be able to distinguish between various broad classes of alcoholism, as well as account for the variety of patterns or pattern combinations of drinking behavior due to the overlapping of these broad classes. A recent report of a Scientific Advisory Council on Alcoholism (DISCUS 1976) distinguishes among three broad classes:

One class of alcoholism represents a psychological reliance upon the effect of alcohol to relieve bodily, emotional, or social discomforts. When such use of alcohol repeatedly violates the rules of society as to the time, occasion, and amount of drinking, it is disruptive. The damage caused by this type of alcoholism is restricted mainly to disturbance of personal relations. It usually

does not involve symptoms of withdrawal. This kind of drinking may be regarded as a symptom of the condition it relieves.
. . . Another type of alcoholism presents medical complications such as polyneuropathy, gastritis, cirrhosis of the liver, and other pathologies which may result from substantive excessive drinking. Physical or psychological dependence is not necessarily present in this class. The incentive for heavy drinking is often the custom of the social group with which the drinker identifies. Resulting damage in this instance is chiefly physiological. . . . A closely related type of alcoholism includes physical dependence on alcohol. This involves withdrawal symptoms, craving, and loss of drinking control. In such alcoholism there is a progression to extreme psychological, physical, and behavioral deterioration. (pp. 13–14)

In any consideration of alcoholism, one must be aware of the variety of possible drinking patterns and the possible complex of determinants—physiological, psychological, and cultural/situational—of maladaptive drinking behavior. There is no single definition of alcoholism. More and more mental health professionals are using patterns of behavioral criteria that occur together in making judgments concerning the severity of the problem drinking. Nathan and Harris (1975) have noted several such behavioral criteria:

(1) The person reports a loss of control of his drinking behavior. (2) He needs a drink to get going in the morning, to keep going during the day, or to prepare himself for stressful events—he has become psychologically dependent upon alcohol. (3) He has lost jobs or alienated his family or friends because of his drinking. (4) He has experienced blackouts, increasing tolerance for alcohol, or both. (5) He reports withdrawal symptoms when he stops drinking; he is physically dependent upon alcohol. (p. 329)

CAUSES AND STRESSORS

PSYCHOANALYTIC THEORY Traditional psychoanalytic theory views the alcoholic as a narcissistic individual who is *fixated* at the oral stage of development (Fenichel 1945). Various versions of this basic theory emphasize concomitant factors in the genesis of alcoholism. For example, Fenichel (1945) assumes that the male alcoholic has homosexual tendencies developed originally as a result of early childhood experiences with a frustrating mother. In response to being frustrated by his mother, the male child is assumed to become attached to his father who is perceived as more warm and accepting. This developmental course of events produces unconscious homosexual impulses towards the father. Alcohol is seen as a substance that can decrease or inhibit the anxiety, guilt, and shame precipitated by these unacceptable homosexual impulses. It is also viewed as providing oral gratification for individuals who are fixated at the oral stage. Fenichel also suggests that the initial drinking in bars with others provides the alcoholic with some degree of emotional satisfaction and comfort he has not received from his mother and other women.

There have been a number of other, broader versions of this psychoanalytic approach to alcoholism. Emphasis is placed on orality, homosexuality, disturbed parent-child relationships, and dependency problems. However, these same types of problems are also found in other forms of psychopathology, and therefore provide no discriminative value. There have been some attempts to delineate variables that occur in alcoholics but not in other psychological disorders (e.g., Button 1956). To date, though, there has been little empirical support for any of these approaches.

Alcoholism and the need for power. A relatively new psychodynamic formulation of alcoholism has been proposed by McClelland, David, Kalin, and Wanner (1972). They have suggested that a need for power is linked to both social and excessive drinking. They propose that men drink in order to increase their sense of power, especially the perception of their sexual and aggressive conquests. These investigators have conducted a number of studies that seem to support their hypothesis. For example, alcoholics have been found to have intense and excessive needs for personal power that are expressed after they drink alcohol (this "need for power" is measured by scoring power-related stories elicited by TAT cards). Also, it was demonstrated that when concerns about power were experimentally induced, alcoholics increased their drinking. McClelland and associates assume that, instead of prompting adaptive behavior that might lead to an increase in *actual* power, the alcoholics' need for power appears to impel them to choose drinking as an alternative path to this goal. This is an interesting theory that warrants additional investigation. In particular, it would be important to examine how this excessive need for power develops and why it prompts some people to drink excessively.

LEARNING THEORY Although attempts have been made to explain alcoholism in learning theory terms, there is currently no one widely accepted and comprehensive model. A common feature of most of these approaches is the assumption that alcohol consumption is positively reinforcing because of its ability to decrease anxiety. This *anxiety-reduction hypothesis* assumes that alcohol is a tension reducer and that it reduces anxiety in alcoholics. A variety of evidence has been accumulated to support this hypothesis. First, it has been demonstrated that alcoholics have high levels of anxiety (e.g., Jellinek 1960). It has also been shown that increased anxiety and increased alcohol intake are associated (e.g., McNamee, Mello, & Mendelson 1968). In animal studies, moreover, it has been demonstrated that alcohol consumption helps to decrease fear and conflict (e.g., Freed 1971), thus lending credence to the contention that alcohol reduces anxiety. Anxiety reduction due to alcohol consumption by human subjects has also been demonstrated in numerous studies (e.g., Coopersmith 1964).

Marlatt and Higgins have conducted a number of studies that assessed how stressful situations can increase drinking. In these studies, subjects were required to make "taste ratings" of wines. They were not told that the *amount* of wine consumed was of primary interest to the experimenters. In the first study, Higgins and Marlatt (1973) used 20 nonabstinent alcoholics and 20 social drinkers. They found that the alcoholics consumed more alcohol than the social drinkers in the tasting task. More importantly, however, anxiety due to a threatened shock did *not* increase wine drinking in either group. In a second study, Higgins and Marlatt (1975) used individuals classified as heavy social drinkers. They informed male subjects that they would be required to talk to a group of women about interpersonal attractiveness and then, after the taste test, be evaluated by these women on a number of personal qualities. These subjects consumed significantly more alcohol than subjects who were in nonevaluational control conditions. These studies show that some individuals

may learn to drink heavily as a means of coping with social anxieties and tension, though not with physical-threat anxiety situations such as shock.

These studies suggest a rather simple model of alcoholism development: Some individuals may learn to cope with tension-producing life situations by drinking alcohol. But despite the array of research tending to support the anxiety-reduction hypothesis, numerous research studies apparently contradict it. In a study by Nathan and O'Brien (1971), a group of male alcoholics and a matched group of nonalcoholics were compared on a variety of behavior dimensions. It was found that after an initial 12–24-hour period of drinking during which anxiety level does decrease, there is a period during which both anxiety and depression levels *increase*. These investigators conclude that alcoholism is much more complex than a simple anxiety-reduction model would assume. Similar results have been found by other investigators (e.g., McNamee et al. 1968).

In another study, Steffen, Nathan, and Taylor (1974) examined the relationship between self-report measures of tension and physiological measures of tension (muscle tension level) in alcoholics over a period of 12 days in which they had free access to alcohol. Although subjects became physiologically relaxed (reflecting a pharmacological effect of the drug) as they drank more, they became subjectively less comfortable. Similar results have been found for light social drinkers by Polivy, Scheuneman, and Carlson (1976). Despite the physiological tension-reducing properties of alcohol use, there seems to be a concomitant *increase* in the cognitive or self-report component of anxiety. It therefore appears that although the tension-reduction model may partly explain why the alcoholic initiates a new episode of drinking, it cannot explain why self-reported anxiety increases after a period of time following alcohol ingestion. A more comprehensive learning theory model needs to be developed that takes into account results such as these.

Before leaving this discussion, the results of one additional study should be cited. Tracey and Nathan (1976) systematically examined the drinking behavior of four female alcoholics to determine whether they differ from male alcoholics on certain important dimensions. Although numerous anecdotal reports suggest that female alcoholics differ from male alcoholics, there has been little empirical research examining these differences. In this study, it was found that the female alcoholics behaved more like male social drinkers than like male alcoholics. They demonstrated more controlled drinking (e.g., less "spree" drinking and no early morning drinking). They also showed *improved* affect while drinking. This finding is, of course, contrary to the studies discussed earlier, in which male alcoholics demonstrated an increase in anxiety while drinking. These results suggest that heavy but controlled drinking (female alcoholics) may lead to an improved affective state that uncontrolled heavy drinking (male alcoholics) prohibits. Most likely, these drinking pattern differences between sexes are learned and reflect different social sanctions.

This study was only a preliminary investigation employing a small number of subjects. If these results are replicated in future controlled studies, then any model of alcoholism will need to take such sex differences into account.

SOCIOCULTURAL THEORIES Drinking is a behavior that is often performed in the company of others. Patterns of drinking behavior are therefore often governed by social and cultural custom. Sociocultural theories assume that a society's drinking practices, customs, and attitudes towards alcohol and alcoholism contribute significantly to the development and maintenance of deviant drinking behavior within that society. A number of studies of sociocultural patterns of drinking tend to support this assumption. For example, in Jellinek's (1952) formulation of different types of alcoholism, *gamma* alcoholism is the most commonly found pattern in Anglo-Saxon countries such as England, while *delta* alcoholism is most common in Latin countries such as France. Drinking in France is characterized by moderate alcohol intake throughout the day, with the level of alcohol in the blood usually not reaching a point to cause extensive debilitating effects on behavior and loss of control.

It is interesting to compare the drinking patterns of France and Italy, neighboring countries that both have high rates of wine consumption. The rate of alcoholism in France is extremely high, while Italy's is extremely low. The reason for these differing rates appears to be different cultural patterns of drinking and different attitudes and moral sanctions toward drinking and drunkenness. In Italy, as in France, wine is a normal part of the daily diet. The Italians, however, drink almost exclusively with meals and easily accept an individual's decision not to drink. There are also strict moral sanctions against drunkenness. In contrast, the French are much more tolerant toward drunkenness than are the Italians.

In popular belief, the Irish have long been known for their high consumption of alcohol and frequent drunkenness (beer and whiskey, not wine). Bales (1946), in a study of Irish culture, presented evidence to support this belief. He indicates that the family patterns, religious traditions, and economic conditions of Ireland have long dictated late marriages and the strict separation of the sexes. Men spend a great deal of their time together, with aggression and sexuality apparently finding their outlet in drinking. Most drinking takes place outside the home in uncontrolled settings such as the local pub, where drunkenness is good-humoredly tolerated and even encouraged.

When one examines certain of these same ethnic groups in this country, some interesting patterns are observed. First-generation Italian-Americans, like their relatives in Italy, drink frequently but have a low rate of alcoholism. This is also true of Jewish-Americans, who seem to have similar moral sanctions against drunkenness and limit drinking to family and religious-festive contexts (Nathan & Harris 1975). However, recent research has indicated that second- and third-generation Irish-Americans have *lower* rates of alcoholism than first-generation Irish-Americans; in contrast, second- and third-generation American Jews have a much *higher* rate of alcoholism than first-generation Jews (Nathan & Harris 1975). These data indicate that as the various cultural groups become assimilated into the American culture, their rates of alcoholism become similar, changing to fit the American pattern. Thus, sociocultural factors appear to play a significant role in drinking patterns and alcoholism. In a longitudinal study of individuals from childhood to adulthood, McCord, McCord, and Guderman (1959) found that differences between those who became alcoholic and those who did not were primarily cultural rather than biological or psychological. Although a great deal of systematic research is still needed to definitely confirm the role of sociocultural influences, most investigators in this field do not doubt their impact. Even subcultural influences, such as the peer pressure that influences excessive and deviant drinking patterns among teenagers, can have a significant impact.

DEVELOPMENTAL PERSONALITY FACTORS A widely cited longitudinal research study called the Oakland Growth Study was started in the 1930s in

Oakland, California. In this study, a group of children were extensively studied and carefully followed through life. Information was collected concerning family behavior patterns, school behavior, and personality characteristics as assessed on personality tests and in interviews. In the 1960s, many of the individuals in the initial sample, who were now in their mid-30s, were contacted and interviewed to determine their alcohol drinking patterns (Jones 1968, 1971). On the basis of the interview, these persons were classified into one of five categories according to their drinking behavior: (1) problem drinking, (2) heavy drinking, (3) moderate drinking, (4) light drinking, (5) nondrinking/abstinence. The association between their current drinking behavior and the developmental information collected earlier in their lives was then examined. The adult male problem drinkers had been characterized in adolescence as impulsive, extroverted, and concerned about displaying masculine-type behavior. They had also shown certain characteristics not associated with the males without drinking problems: less calm and more sensitive to social criticism, less productive and industrious, and less socially perceptive. The associations found for females were less clear-cut. However, although certain male characteristics, which during adolescence may index social difficulties that serve as a source of stress, do appear related to future problem drinking, these same characteristics are found in other forms of psychopathology. That is, they appear to predict future psychopathology in general, not specifically alcoholism. Indeed, research has consistently failed to find "alcoholic personality" characteristics that differentiate between alcoholics and nonalcoholics (Bandura 1969; Miller 1976).

GENETIC FACTORS Evidence from family studies indicates that the incidence of alcoholism is higher in the children of alcoholic parents and the relatives of alcoholics than in the general population (Goodwin 1971). As with other disorders, such results do not necessarily imply the presence of genetic factors, since similar learning/environmental factors may be the causative agents. A more sensitive method for assessing this relationship is the adoptee study, in which children were separated from their alcoholic parents early in life and reared by another family. In an early study of this type, Roe, Burks, and Mittelmann (1945) found little evidence for possible genetic factors, since the adopted children were not found more likely to become alcoholic later in life than adopted children of nonalcoholic parents. Later, however, Goodwin, Schulsinger, Hermansen, Guze, and Winokur (1973) reported that adopted children whose biological parents were alcoholic grew up to have a greater drinking-problem rate and to seek out psychiatric treatment much more than adopted children of nonalcoholic parents. In a subsequent study, Goodwin, Schulsinger, Moller, Hermansen, Winokur, and Guze (1974) compared the alcoholism rates for sons of alcoholic parents who were adopted in infancy with those for their brothers who had stayed with the alcoholic parents. Both groups had high rates of alcoholism, suggesting a genetic involvement. The discrepant results of these studies may be due to the way in which the investigators defined "alcoholism/problem drinking." A broader definition would increase the number of drinking patterns defined as problematic and, therefore, increase the likelihood of defining any form of moderate-excessive drinking as "alcoholism/problem drinking." Obviously, additional research is needed to resolve the discrepant results.

A number of twin studies have been made to assess the possibility of a genetic predisposition in alcoholism. Kaij (1960), in summarizing a number of human twin studies, found that monozygotic twins have a higher concordance rate for alcoholism than dizygotic twins. In addition, animal research has produced, through selective inbreeding, a strain of mice that prefer alcohol (Rodgers & McClearn 1962). These data suggest the possible importance of genetic factors in the etiology of alcoholism. Again, much more systematic research is needed.

PHYSIOLOGICAL FACTORS If, in the future, genetic factors are found to be significant in the predisposition to certain types of alcoholism, then it will be important to determine the physiological/biochemical mechanisms these factors affect. One currently popular physiological theory of alcoholism is that alcoholics and nonalcoholics differ in the rate at which alcohol is metabolized by the body. As Miller and Eisler (1976) indicate:

> It may be that . . . there are physiological predispositions which affect abuse of a substance. For example, an individual with low gastrointestinal tolerance for alcohol may be less likely to abuse it. After one or two drinks he may experience slight discomfort or nausea and thus terminate

Alcoholics Anonymous is a well-known organization that concerns itself with the treatment of alcoholism. During AA meetings, individuals can gain insight into their problems.

drinking. The person who becomes an alcoholic may be able to tolerate more, and hence obtain less negative physiological feedback . . . Similarly, due to biochemical differences, some individuals may experience greater pleasant effects (highs) from a particular drug than others, and thus be more likely to use it repeatedly. (pp. 379–380)

Other studies, however, have found no evidence for physiological predispositional factors such as differential rates of ethanol metabolism between alcoholics and nonalcoholics (Mendelson 1968). To date, a specific physiological basis for alcoholism has not been isolated.

TREATMENT

An initial step in the treatment of alcoholism usually is a medical procedure called *detoxification*. Its purpose is to get the alcohol out of the alcoholic's system while helping the individual through the withdrawal symptoms. The alcoholic is hospitalized and drugs, such as chlordiazepoxide, are substituted for the alcohol. The drug regimen functions to overcome some of the distressing withdrawal symptoms such as nausea, vomiting, tension, and

anxiety, and to prevent delirium tremens and convulsions. High dosages of vitamins are also usually prescribed to counter any nutritional deficiences that the alcoholism may have produced.

After detoxification is completed, usually in about a week, some form of psychosocial treatment is administered to aid the alcoholic's social readjustment and to keep him or her from returning to the misuse of alcohol. The treatment of alcoholism is difficult. Traditional forms of psychotherapy such as psychoanalysis have not proven to be effective in the treatment of alcoholism (Hill & Blane 1967). A number of other techniques, however, have demonstrated some positive therapeutic effects.

ALCOHOLICS ANONYMOUS The best-known organization for treating alcoholism, Alcoholics Anonymous (AA), was started during the 1930s. Since that time it has spread around the world and now has more than 10,000 groups. There are usually AA groups in most hospitals and clinics. AA functions as a therapeutic program whose basic philosophy is that the alcoholic is not a "weak-willed," irresponsible person, but merely an individual who is afflicted with a "disease" — the physiological inability to tolerate alcohol. Just as some individuals cannot tolerate certain drugs, the alcoholic's system cannot tolerate alcohol. This is seen as a life-long problem from which the individual can never actually recover. The viewpoint is "once an alcoholic, always an alcoholic," and the goal is total abstinence.

AA provides a great deal of support and comradeship through group AA meetings attended by other alcoholics who have had similar experiences. It is assumed that an alcoholic needs help and reassurance from others to stop drinking. During these meetings, individuals can gain insight into their drinking problems and learn more effective methods of coping with everyday stresses. There is also a "spiritual" feature in this method, with many members professing to have gone through a "spiritual change" regarding their perceptions of themselves and the rest of the world. In addition to the AA group meetings, there is also a "buddy system," in which an alcoholic can call one or two members, who are on 24-hour call, if he or she feels it is impossible to keep from drinking. These "buddies" will come and help the individual to get over the urge and deal with any problems that may be causing him or her to want to drink again.

Unfortunately, there are no exact figures on

the success rate of AA, and few objective, long-term evaluation studies. AA is not effective with all alcoholics and reaches only a small percentage of them. The consensus, however, is that it can be an extremely beneficial supportive group for certain individuals. As a result, it is usually routinely recommended that alcoholics try AA to aid them in eliminating their problem drinking behavior.

An affiliated organization—*Al-Anon* Family Groups—has been established for the relatives of alcoholics. These group meetings provide support for the relatives of alcoholics and also allow them to gain insight into the possible motives behind the problem drinking. The meetings also aid in reducing some of the guilt and shame family members may be experiencing as a result of the alcoholism of a loved one. Such meetings provide a valuable means for relatives of alcoholics to deal with the emotional tensions and stress and other problems they are undergoing as the result of the alcoholic behavior.

BEHAVIOR THERAPY   The main goal of behavior therapy is to eliminate maladaptive behavior and, when necessary, replace it with more adaptive behavior. One behavioral technique used in the treatment of alcoholism is *aversion therapy*. Before reviewing these methods, we should emphasize that aversion therapy procedures are susceptible to misuse. They should be used only by trained professionals who, after careful evaluation of the characteristics of the patient and of the drinking behavior, determine that aversion therapy procedures will serve as valuable adjunctive techniques for eliminating abusive drinking. Patients should also be totally informed about the details of the procedure and the possible dangers involved, before they are given the option of receiving such treatment.

There are three basic varieties of aversion therapy methods which use different aversive stimuli: (1) chemical, including chemical nausea agents such as Antabuse, Apomorphine, and Emetine, and drugs that produce muscular paralysis such as Scoline; (2) electric shock; (3) verbal descriptions of nauseating scenes. As an example of an early chemical aversion procedure which was reported to be successful, Thimann (1949) gave patients an injection and oral dosage of Emetine. Immediately prior to the expected emesis, the alcoholic was exposed to the sight, smell, and taste of a favorite alcoholic beverage. The unpleasant negative reaction produced by the chemical was in this way classically conditioned to alcohol. Conditioning

sessions lasted from 20 to 30 minutes each day, and were repeated daily for five to six days. *Booster treatment sessions* of one day each at intervals ranging from 4 to 12 weeks were also given. In one of the most comprehensive and long-term follow-ups on this type of treatment, Lemere and Voegtlin (1950) assessed the follow-up data on over 4,000 patients. They found that one year after the completion of treatment, 60 percent of this group remained abstinent from alcohol. They also found that periodic booster treatments administered on an outpatient basis were essential for treatment success.

A more widely known form of chemical aversion treatment uses Antabuse. Antabuse (disulfiram) is a chemical that is taken in pill form by alcoholics each day, and two days after ingestion interferes with the metabolic processing of alcohol by the body. If the Antabuse patient drinks alcohol, an extremely unpleasant reaction occurs, including nausea and other physiological discomforts. One of the problems with this type of treatment is that the patient can discontinue the use of Antabuse after leaving the hospital. Also, as with other forms of aversion therapy, it cannot be used for patients with certain physical disorders because of the stressful nature of the chemical aversive treatment. As Bandura (1969) notes, there is a need for a well-controlled outcome study comparing the effects of Antabuse treatment with other forms of alcoholism treatment.

The drug *succinylcholine* (Scoline) has been used to induce muscular paralysis in aversion therapy. The usual procedure is to inform the patient about the method and the effects of the drug. A saline drug apparatus is then attached to a vein in the patient's arm. The patient is then given a glass of his or her favorite alcoholic beverage and told to grasp it, look at it, smell it, and then taste it. The patient then gives it back to the clinician. After a number of such "familiarization" trials, the succinylcholine is put into the patient's bloodstream via the drug apparatus. The patient is then handed the glass of beverage again to smell and sip, at which time the paralysis occurs. The patient becomes totally paralyzed, with the paralysis lasting from 60 to 90 seconds. During this time the patient is not able to move or breathe. If he or she starts to suffocate, or if the paralysis lasts for more than about a minute, then the patient is treated with a respirator. After a number of such trials, many patients develop a conditioned aversion to alcohol. It is assumed that the very powerful aversive sensation of respiratory paralysis makes this type

One aversive conditioning technique employed with alcoholics involves the pairing of an unpleasant event, such as an electric shock, with the act of drinking. The treatment setting is made to appear as much like an actual bar as possible.

of conditioning procedure especially effective in reducing drinking. However, research has shown that this technique is no more effective than less drastic procedures for reducing drinking in alcoholics (Miller & Eisler 1976).

Aversion therapy employing electrical stimuli typically involves instructing the patient to sip a sample of his or her favorite drink, but not to swallow it, at which time an electric shock is administered that can be terminated by spitting out the drink. This technique has been used with some success with alcoholics (e.g., Blake 1967; Miller & Hersen 1972).

Finally, verbally induced aversion (*covert sensitization*), first developed by Cautela (1970), involves inducing aversive stimuli in the patient's own thoughts. The alcoholic may be asked to imagine a scene such as follows:

> You are walking into a bar. You decide to have a glass of beer. You are now walking toward the bar. As you are approaching the bar you have a funny feeling in the pit of your stomach. Your stomach feels all queasy and nauseous. Some liquid comes

FROM ALCOHOLIC TO SOCIAL DRINKER

Through the years, a controversial question has been whether alcoholics can be treated and retrained to become controlled social drinkers. A common viewpoint, that of Alcoholics Anonymous, is that alcoholism is an irreversible "disease" and so the alcoholic must totally abstain from drinking. If not, he or she will "lose control" and not be able to stem the "craving" or stop drinking until totally intoxicated. Some recent research questions the notion that total abstinence is needed in the treatment of alcoholism; techniques have been developed that show great promise for teaching alcoholics to become controlled social drinkers. Lloyd and Salzberg (1975) have reviewed this evidence.

In one of the first studies of controlled drinking, Lovibond and Caddy (1970) trained alcoholics how to estimate their blood-alcohol levels on the basis of subjective feelings of intoxication. Patients then were requested to drink an alcoholic beverage to produce moderate blood-alcohol levels. When they drank and reached blood alcohol levels above a predetermined cutoff point, electric shocks were administered to the chin, face, and neck. A control group of alcoholics were selected and treated in an identical manner *except* that they were administered random electric shock instead of shocks contingent on their blood-alcohol levels. The first group demonstrated significant changes in drinking behavior, in addition to reporting dramatic improve-

up your throat and it is very sour. You try to swallow it back down, but as you do this, food particles start coming up your throat to your mouth. You are now reaching the bar and you order a beer. As the bartender is pouring the beer, vomit comes to your mouth. . . . As you run out of the barroom, you start to feel better and better. When you get out into the clean, fresh air you feel wonderful. You go home and clean yourself up. (Cautela 1970, p. 87)

The goal of this procedure is to pair unpleasant associations with drinking and pleasant associations with the absence of drinking.

ments in overall health and well-being. An evaluation study conducted by Sobell and Sobell (1973) also clearly showed the possiblity of producing controlled social drinking. Although much more systematic long-term evaluation research is needed, results such as these show promise for the possiblity for retraining some alcoholics to become controlled social drinkers.

A study published in 1975 by the Rand Corporation, a West Coast "think tank," also suggested the possibility of "controlled" drinking and questioned the dogma of complete abstinence for some alcoholics. The Rand Corporation report has generated a great deal of public controversy. Opponents of the controlled drinking approach, primarily the AA, argue that public acceptance of this position may give reformed alcoholics an "excuse" to take a few drinks in an attempt to become controlled drinkers. This might start them on the road back to alcoholism. These opponents have generated a great deal of public and political pressure against this report. Attempts are being made to force a retraction of the Rand report suggestion. This is unfortunate since the report did not advocate "controlled" drinking as a possibility for all alcoholics, but suggested that this goal *might* be possible with certain alcoholics. The report emphasized that much additional research is needed to determine whether this is a viable approach.

The systematic evaluation of the various aversion therapy techniques has only recently begun. In recent reviews of such techniques, Davidson (1974) and Miller and Eisler (1976) note that they appear to effectively reduce the immediate reinforcing properties of drug intake. However, there is still insufficient evidence to evaluate the long-term effectiveness of aversion therapy. Although a number of different aversive stimuli have been used, the most effective aversive stimulus has not been conclusively identified. Lamon, Wilson, and Leaf (1977) have demonstrated that a chemical-induced nausea technique (called the *pseudo-Coriolis effect*) is superior to electric shock in producing classical aversion conditioning to beverage consumption in normal subjects. An evaluation

of this technique with alcoholics is needed. It should also be noted that recent data suggest that the combined use of chemical and verbal aversion may produce the best results (Blanchard, Libet, & Young 1973). More such evaluation data are needed.

Multimodal treatment. Aversion therapy techniques show promise for eliminating maladaptive drinking, the *consummatory response*. However, treating only the consummatory behavior, without simultaneously dealing with the situational variables that may be contributing to the maintenance of this drinking behavior, lessens the probability of producing long-lasting improvement. For example, if alcohol is being used to help cope with a stressful life, then the alcoholic needs to learn alternative means of dealing with this stress. If not, he or she may start to misuse other drugs, such as tranquilizers, or eventually return to the use of alcohol. Miller and Eisler (1976) indicate that a comprehensive behavioral treatment program should have three major objectives: (1) To decrease the immediate reinforcing properties of the drug. This can be accomplished through the use of aversion therapy techniques. (2) To teach the person to perform new behaviors that are incompatible with drug abuse. For example, if the individual is drinking in order to reduce stress, then he or she can be taught more appropriate ways of dealing with this stress, for example, through relaxation training or learning more effective social skills to handle stressful situations. (3) To modify the person's social environment so that he or she receives maximum reinforcement for activities that do not include the use of drugs; for example, by providing positive reinforcement such as praise, attention, or other pleasurable responses during periods of sobriety and not during periods of intoxication. Such a comprehensive treatment program shows the greatest promise for bringing about long-term improvement, but needs to be individualized for each patient. "Individualized behavior therapy" has been shown to produce significant therapeutic improvement (Sobell & Sobell 1973).

In the treatment program developed by Sobell and Sobell, four procedures were used with patients: (1) Aversion therapy to modify the excessive drinking behavior. (2) Videotaped feedback to patients of their behavior while drunk. This procedure was intended to motivate change by showing patients the embarrassing and negative features of their behavior. (3) Helping patients to identify the specific situations and circumstances that tend to prompt their heavy drinking. (4) Training patients in new and more appropriate means of responding to those situations (e.g., relaxation, assertion training, etc.). These investigators conducted a comparison study between a group of alcoholics who wished to become "controlled" social drinkers (rather than total abstainers) and received this multimodal program, and a control group of alcoholics who received conventional forms of treatment (e.g., AA, drug therapy). The aversion therapy employed with the first group consisted of allowing them to drink at a specially devised hospital bar that was made to appear like a typical neighborhood bar. They were administered electric shock for any behavior that indicated heavy,

loss-of-control drinking, such as ordering straight whiskey rather than a mixed drink, ordering more than three drinks, or not sipping the drink in small amounts.

Results of this comparison study, which consisted of 17 treatment sessions, indicated that the alcoholics in the experimental group subsequently spent a smaller percentage of time either drunk or incarcerated/hospitalized for drunk-related behavior (10 percent versus 55 percent for the control group). Moreover, these experimental group subjects were rated as better adjusted, both interpersonally and vocationally.

OTHER FORMS OF DRUG ABUSE

Besides alcohol, a number of other chemicals are frequently abused in contemporary society. Of the chemicals listed by the DSM-II under the heading of "drug dependence," the following groups are significant: (1) opium, opium alkaloids such as morphine, and their derivatives such as heroin; (2) sedatives such as barbiturates and other tranquilizers; (3) psychostimulants such as amphetamines; (4) cocaine; (5) hallucinogens such as LSD and mescaline; (6) derivatives of the Indian hemp plant (*Cannabis sativa*) such as hashish and marijuana.

OPIUM, OPIUM ALKALOIDS, AND THEIR DERIVATIVES

This is the most significant category of physiologically addictive illegal drugs. Opium is derived from the sap of the poppyseed. Through history, it has been grown in great quantities in Asia and Turkey and used widely as both a medicine and an intoxicant. Today, opium itself is not commonly used because its derivatives produce more potent and predictable effects. Codeine, morphine, and heroin are the major opium derivatives, or *opiates*, that are used. Codeine and morphine are widely used and powerful pain killers in medical treatment. Indeed, many patients may first get "hooked" on these drugs as a result of their prescription to relieve pain. The drugs act to depress the functions of the central nervous system, and their immediate effects include feelings of

euphoria and reverie, relief from pain, and drowsiness. These pleasant effects last for about 3 or 4 hours. Many addicts describe the "rush," or feeling of well-being, that occurs during the first minute or so as comparable to a sexual orgasm.

American narcotic addicts most commonly use and prefer heroin (Ball & Chambers 1970), with an estimated 300,000 addicts in the United States (Bazell 1973). On the street, it is popularly referred to by slang terms such as "horse," "H," "junk," and "snow." It is illegally sold in the form of a white powder that is cut or mixed with milk sugar and other chemically inert substances, so that rarely does an addict take pure heroin. The drug addict usually began by sniffing it or by popping it, that is, injecting it under the skin. However, after physiological addiction occurs, the addict usually switches to intravenous injection or mainlining because it produces more rapid "rushes" and more predictable effects. The addict will experience painful physiological withdrawal symptoms if he or she does not take the heroin on a regular basis. Also, addicts develop a tolerance for the drug so that increasing amounts have to be taken to produce the same pleasant effects. Eventually, the "high" disappears regardless of how much heroin is taken. In order to reexperience this "high," the addict has to go through withdrawal symptoms in order to lower his or her tolerance. Many addicts continue to increase their dosages to harmfully high levels in order to experience the high. The result may be death from an overdose, a common occurrence in the drug community.

Because of the increasing tolerance, which necessitates greater amounts of the drug, heroin addiction is a very expensive habit to maintain. The need to maintain this expensive habit and avoid the pain of withdrawal symptoms is the reason many addicts turn to crime to finance their habit. As a result, the individual's life may focus on obtaining drugs by stealing and associating with undesirable criminal companions, who may be their "connection." Besides the development of these socially maladaptive behaviors, a number of negative physiological effects are produced by chronic heroin usage: malnutrition and vitamin deficiencies produced by loss of appetite, increased susceptibility to many physical ailments, and the danger of hepatitis or tetanus from unsterile needles.

SEDATIVES

The major types of sedatives or "downers" are the barbiturates, such as phenobarbital, Seconal, and Nembutal. These are the second most common category of illegal drugs that cause physiological addiction. Addiction appears to be the result of compensatory adaptation of the nervous system to the chemical. Barbiturates are commonly prescribed by physicians, and on the street are known as "barbs," "blue heavens," and other slang terms. Addiction may start in a tense person who takes a barbiturate as a sleeping pill at night to help get to sleep. The drug acts as a depressant, producing a feeling of relaxation and decreased mental alertness. High dosages are dangerous and can cause death; barbiturates taken along with alcohol are particularly dangerous. Indeed, over 1,500 suicides a year are attributed to barbiturate overdoses (Ullmann & Krasner 1969). Physiological addiction is common with chronic usage, as increased tolerance develops. If usage is stopped, the withdrawal symptoms are sometimes more severe than those of alcohol and opiate withdrawal. Death from convulsions can occur if withdrawal is too rapid.

This case of death caused by barbiturate abuse received a great deal of publicity in New York City in 1975:

A CASE OF BARBITURATE WITHDRAWAL

On July 17, 1975, a pair of 45-year-old identical

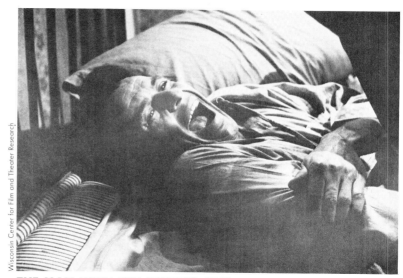

THE MAN WITH THE GOLDEN ARM © 1955, United Artists. Heroin is an extremely addicting drug. An addict who suddenly stops using it may suffer severe withdrawal symptoms, as pictured in this film. However, gradual withdrawal with careful medical supervision can eliminate many of the unpleasant effects.

twins, Stewart and Cyril Marcus—both eminent and well-to-do gynecologists, both known for their correct, conventional, and highly meticulous behavior—were found dead and partially decomposed in the apartment that they shared in New York City. Cyril, dressed only in his socks, was lying on the floor. Stewart, with only his shorts on, was sprawled on his bed. Both showed signs that advanced malnutrition had preceded their death. The floors of the apartment were strewn with layer upon layer of litter and garbage, a foot and a half deep: fast-food packages, old newspapers, chicken bones, paper bags, feces, and, notably, over a hundred empty barbiturate bottles.

The immediate conclusion of the police was that the brothers had killed themselves with barbiturate overdoses, in fulfillment of a suicide pact. But the Medical Examiner's office later revealed that Stewart had died several days before Cyril and furthermore that there was no trace of barbiturates in their systems. Thus the hypothesis was revised: the Marcuses had died not from barbiturate overdoses but rather from severe withdrawal symptoms associated with the drug. But soon this theory too came into question, as later evidence from the Medical Examiner's office revealed that one of the brothers (it was not specified which) did have substantial amounts of barbiturates in his brain—further support for the suicidal-overdose hypothesis.

A survey of the Marcuses' past history does little to help solve the mystery. What it does reveal is that the brothers were so similar and led such similar lives that somehow, in spite of the law of probabilities, it seems natural that they should have died together. Indeed, they did almost everything together. . . . And in the end, they went downhill together, with Cyril apparently leading the way. Whereas previously both had been known for their fastidious habits— Cyril, according to a former nurse of the Marcuses, could not bear the sight of a used Kleenex in a wastebasket—now their office became filthy; urine specimens, never analyzed, filled the refrigerator. The brothers began missing appointments, stopped sending out bills and filling out insurance forms, and admitted fewer and fewer patients to the hospital. When they did appear at the hospital, their behavior was increasingly bizarre. Once during surgery one of the brothers ripped the anesthesia mask from the patient's face and put it over his own face. Excused from the operating room, he was replaced by his brother, who appeared equally "out of it." Finally, after more than a year of such behavior, the Marcuses were dismissed from the New York Hospital. Then, apparently, they virtually barricaded themselves in their apartment until a month later a strange smell in the hallway of the apartment building alerted the building handyman that something was amiss. The door of the apartment was broken down by the police. By that time the Marcuses' struggle had been over for about a week. (CRM 1976, p. 256)

Minor tranquilizers are the most frequently abused nonbarbiturate sedatives. These include meprobamate (Equanil, Miltown), chlordiazepoxide (Librium), and diazepam (Valium). Unfortunately, many physicians routinely prescribe sedatives to patients without pointing out the potential problems associated with the chronic use of such medication. Addiction to these drugs is usually less serious and less frequent than barbiturate addiction. However, chronic usage can create serious physiological and psychological dependence and can have serious side-effects such as depression. Like the barbiturates, they are dangerous when combined with alcohol.

PSYCHOSTIMULANTS

The major amphetamines, which include Benzedrine, Dexedrine, and Methedrine, are stimulant drugs that increase feelings of euphoria, optimism, alertness, and physical energy. Popularly, they are called "uppers," "bennies," "pep pills," and "speed" (methamphetamine). In the past, these drugs were widely prescribed by physicians as mood elevators for depressed persons and as appetite suppressants in weight reduction programs. This was before physicans realized their great potential for abuse. Although these drugs do not appear to produce addiction, a great degree of psychological dependence usually develops. After the drug wears off, the positive feelings are followed by a mild "down." The user then takes more of the drug to restore the alert, positive feelings. Many times, the daily dosage of the chronic user will increase to several hundred times the initial level. Chronic users ("speed freaks") experience more pronounced "downs" or "crashes" if the drug is stopped, causing significant psychological depression for long periods of time.

Long-term use of amphetamines can also cause physical damage and exhaustion due to the loss of appetite and overstimulated activity. Overdoses are common and may produce psychotic episodes marked by hallucinations and/or paranoid delusions (amphetamine psychosis). Although these drugs do not cause physiological withdrawal symptoms if not taken, they can cause a great deal of psychological problems if chronically ingested.

COCAINE

Cocaine, or "coke," is a stimulant that is extracted from the leaves of the coca plant. It can be ingested by sniffing, swallowing, or injecting. The drug produces a state of extreme euphoria, increases energy level and sleeplessness, and has significant depression-reducing and tension-reducing properties. Cocaine is often viewed as the "darling of the drug culture" because of its powerful and initially pleasant effects. Its popularity has recently grown among middle- and upper-class persons.

Although it did not reach the attention of Europeans until the late nineteenth century, cocaine was widely used by Peruvian Indians long before Europeans reached America. The Indians chewed coca leaves for their stimulant effects. Cocaine was isolated from coca leaves by the German chemist Niemann in the 1850s. Its potential was first noticed when it was observed that it lifted the spirits and restored the energy of German soldiers worn out by arduous training exercises. Sigmund Freud was the first person to recognize its potential value in dealing with psychological disorders, especially depression and excessive tension. Many of his observations concerning the therapeutic effects of the drug were based on his own experiences after taking small doses of it. He came to view cocaine as a "wonder drug" and publicized its therapeutic effects. Soon, doctors throughout Europe were prescribing it for all kinds of conditions and disorders. Unfortunately, it was not until its usage spread that Freud and others realized that, although the drug is usually not physiologically addicting and produces no withdrawal effects, it can produce significant psychological dependence. Chronic cocaine usage can also produce a toxic psychosis, with symptoms similar to acute paranoid schizophrenia.

HALLUCINOGENS

Hallucinogenic drugs, commonly referred to as *psychedelics*, have the ability to produce potent hallucinatory effects and profound subjective experiences. LSD (lysergic acid diethylamide), the most widely known hallucinogen, was first synthesized from ergot by Albert Hofmann in Switzerland in 1938. A great deal of research on LSD was conducted by investigators who viewed it as a means of studying hallucinatory states and "model psychoses" thought to be related to schizophrenia. However, it was found that the "model psychoses" produced by LSD are not similar to the hallucinatory states that occur in schizophrenia. "Acid" was popularized in this country by Timothy Leary and others as part of the "hippie" movement of the 1960s. The LSD "trip" is produced by a very small dosage of the drug (100–200 micrograms, which is smaller than a grain of salt) and typically lasts about eight hours, although individual reactions vary greatly. Snyder (1974) describes a "trip":

> . . . Everything perceived—colors, textures, lines—attain a beauty and richness never seen before. Perception seems to be so incisive that the individual pores in your skin almost stand out and clamor for recognition. You may feel that your visual powers penetrate other people to plumb their secret lives. Contours of objects may become distorted . . . For example, if you look at your hand and focus upon the thumb, the thumb may proceed to swell, undulate, and even begin moving toward you . . . The sense of time changes dramatically. A minute may seem like an hour, a week like all eternity . . . the very concept of "future" loses any meaning. The time changes result from a speeding up of mental processes . . . one's perceptions and feelings are so heightened that they are intensively recording every instant. . . Closing one's eyes often produces remarkable visions filled with vivid and persistent eidetic imagery. . . . (pp. 42–43)

LSD experiences are not always enjoyable. "Bad trips" can cause a great deal of anxiety and fear, and even acute psychotic episodes in emotionally unstable individuals. McWilliams and Tuttle (1973) found that long-lasting psychological damage can occur in persons with unstable personalities or psychiatric disturbance, or who are experiencing some current crisis. This description of a "bad trip" was presented by Kolb (1973):

> A 21-year-old woman was admitted to the hospital along with her lover. He had had a number of LSD experiences and convinced her to take LSD to make her less constrained sexually. About half an hour after ingestion of approximately 200 μg, she noticed that the bricks in the wall began to move in and out and that light affected her strangely. She became frightened when she realized that she was unable to distinguish her body from the chair she was sitting on or from her lover's body. Her fear became more marked after she thought she would not get back into herself. At the time of admission she was hyperactive and laughed inappropriately. Stream of talk was illogical and affect labile. Two days later, this reaction had ceased. However, she was still afraid of the drug and convinced that she would not take it again because of her frightening experience." (p. 525)

Chronic use of LSD does not produce physiological

Marijuana is usually smoked in pipes or cigarettes.

dependence, and no withdrawal symptoms appear after one stops using it. Again, the probability of long-lasting psychological problems appears to exist only for emotionally unstable individuals. No significant psychological dependence usually occurs except in those who center their lives on "tripping out" as a way of avoiding the stresses of everyday life. Some investigators have claimed that chronic usage can produce chromosomal damage, but this claim has been questioned (McGlothlin, Sparkes, & Arnold 1970). Finally, one unusual result may be "flashbacks," the recurrence of perceptual hallucinations and other subjective experiences days or weeks after last taking the drug. Although such flashbacks can occur in the first-time LSD user, they are most common in chronic users or "acidheads." Horowitz (1969) reported that one in twenty chronic users experiences flashbacks.

Although most people assume that psychedelic drugs are modern-day discoveries, they have a long history of usage. For centuries, the Indians of Mexico and Central and South America have used two psychedelic drugs as part of their reli-

gious ceremonies—*mescaline,* derived from the "mescal buttons" on the top of the peyote cactus, and *psilocybin,* derived from certain Mexican mushrooms known as *psilocybe mexicana.* Ingestion of mescaline produces somewhat longer lasting hallucinogenic effects than LSD (about 12 hours). It also tends to be "smoother" in effect and produces less anxiety. The user tends to focus on sensual and perceptual effects which are experienced in unaccustomed ways. Psilocybin produces similar effects but usually lasts for a shorter period of time (4 hours). Like LSD, these drugs do not produce physiological dependence, but can be psychologically harmful to emotionally unstable individuals.

CANNABIS SATIVA

From the flowers and leaves of the hemp plant, a resin is produced containing the substance *tetrahydrocannabinol* (THC) which is the active chemical component in both hashish ("hash") and marijuana ("grass," "pot"). These drugs are usually smoked in pipes or cigarettes ("joints," "reefers"), although they may be swallowed or sniffed. Although the effects vary from one individual to the next, depending on factors such as past experiences with the drug and the user's personality and mood, the "high" is usually characterized by mild euphoria and a pleasant relaxation marked by the sensation of "drifting" or "floating away." There is currently no evidence that chronic usage of these drugs will cause physiological dependence since there are no withdrawal symptoms associated with its discontinued usage. Although the issue is still very controversial, some slight psychological dependence can perhaps develop with prolonged use. Many chronic users may develop signs of anxiety, agitation, or depression if they suddenly stop taking it. Marijuana use is viewed by many as preceding the use of other illicit drugs, but this notion is still unsubstantiated.

CAUSES AND STRESSORS

PSYCHOLOGICAL THEORIES The psychoanalytic and behavioral conceptualizations of alcoholism have been similarly applied to the abuse of other drugs. Psychoanalytic theory views the factors of orality, dependency, and disturbed parent-child relationships as important in the development of this form of drug abuse. Behavioral theory views drug abuse as learned because of its reinforcing properties. Wikler (1965), for example, has proposed an operant model in which it is assumed that each ingestion of a drug reinforces drug-taking behavior because of its immediate and extremely powerful reinforcing qualities. As with alcoholism, to date there has been no conclusive evidence supporting the validity of either of these approaches as a means of explaining drug abuse.

There is also very little conclusive evidence concerning personality factors involved in drug addiction. Braucht and colleagues (1973) found no clear personality factors common to adolescent users of psychedelic drugs. Adolescent narcotic users were found to be immature, insecure, irresponsible, and egocentric. However, these characteristics are not unique to narcotic addicts, being found in many psychopathological states.

SOCIOCULTURAL FACTORS Some sociocultural factors seem to be clearly associated with drug abuse. Braucht and colleagues found that the adolescent hard drug user is usually a member of an ethnic minority, from an improverished urban environment, and often from a broken home (Braucht et al. 1973). Indeed, heroin addiction is a significant problem in city ghetto areas. In contrast, psychedelic drug abuse is more common among middle- and upper-class adolescents. Marijuana and hashish usage appears to be equally prevalent among all socioeconomic groups and also to span a wide range of age groups.

The exact cause-effect nature of the relationship between sociocultural factors and drug abuse is not yet known. Why, for example, do persons in urban ghetto areas abuse narcotic drugs? Is it to escape the stress associated with living in the ghetto? If this is so, why do not all individuals who experience such stress take narcotics? Why do middle-class college students use psychedelic drugs? Is this usage also in response to some kind of stress? Gorsuch and Butler (1976) suggest that factors such as disruption of normal child-parent relationships, lack of involvement in organized groups, and few effective peer relationships may be predisposing factors in some individuals, while factors such as socialization to nontraditional norms, parental and peer modeling of drug use, and positive experiences with drugs may be impor-

tant for other individuals. There does not appear to be any single etiological factor that can totally account for the initial usage and subsequent abuse of drugs.

Gorsuch and Butler (1976) have suggested that a multiple-model approach may prove more worthwhile in the search for causes of drug abuse. They indicate that at least three paths exist that lead to initial drug abuse. The first is *iatrogenic,* or medically induced, abuse in which an individual first takes a drug prescribed by a physician for some legitimate medical purpose and then gets "hooked" on it. Gorsuch and Butler suggest that for this type of drug user, the usual expectations of the influences of parental background, peer group pressure, personality characteristics and attitudes are less likely to hold true. That is, this type warrants investigation as a separate group. A second type of abuser is the *unsocialized person.* This type of individual has received no specific socialization concerning drugs or of the norms of society regulating their usage. According to Gorsuch and Butler, the bulk of drug abusers belong to this type. They tend to be less socialized, both in terms of social conformity and of low involvement with others or with organized groups such as religious groups. Finally, the third type consists of those *socialized into a pro-drug culture.* Most commonly, friends teach or persuade their friends to use drugs, or older and admired individuals are seen as drug users. Gorsuch and Butler suggest that for this type of user, factors such as parental and peer modeling of drug use would be predictive of initial drug usage.

Gorsuch and Butler also suggest that all these models interact with the availability of the drug. For example, if a certain drug is not available at all, then none of these models can operate, simply because no one has access to the drug. If the drug becomes accessible, then the models may be predictive of what individuals become involved in drug usage. Also, if drugs become widely used throughout a particular culture, then the high base rate of usage may decrease the correlations. Thus, these authors espouse a multiple-model approach rather than assuming that one array of characteristics will identify those who do or do not abuse drugs. As they indicate:

> . . . it appears better conceptually to attempt to separate the different types and to determine the relationships of variables *within each type.* The role of peer influence, for example, must be examined differently

LONG DAY'S JOURNEY INTO NIGHT
© 1962, Embassy Pictures. In Eugene O'Neill's classic drama, drug dependence and alcoholism are viewed as symptoms of family disharmony. The characters here portrayed by Katherine Hepburn and Jason Robards use narcotics and alcohol to deal with the stresses that arise from their relationships.

for unsocialized persons than for those individuals socialized to the prodrug culture. Even though peer influence may have the identical definition in both instances, its impact may be considerably different. (p. 134)

There probably are other categories or types of users not delineated by Gorsuch and Butler. For those individuals who do not fall into one of the three categories, new categories would be sought to describe their drug usage. This multiple-model

approach, which recognizes the presence of several paths leading to initial drug use, appears promising in developing an understanding of the causative factors underlying drug abuse.

GENETIC AND PHYSIOLOGICAL FACTORS

Little systematic research has been done to evaluate whether there are genetic bases for the various forms of drug dependencies. Similarly, little evidence has been found for physiological factors underlying drug dependency. As in the area of alcoholism, some investigators have sought to isolate factors, such as differential rates or methods of metabolism, which might differentiate drug abusers from others. No such factors have been found, and there is still no adequate physiological theory of drug dependence.

As a first step in the search for physiological factors in drug dependence, certain investigators are attempting to identify specific sites of action in the brains of drug addicts (e.g., Snyder & Pert 1973). It is hoped that once these sites are identified, then the precise biochemical effects and mechanisms involved in the usage of specific drugs will be delineated, and any abnormalities that occur in drug addiction identified.

TREATMENT

As in the treatment of alcoholism, an initial step in the treatment of drug dependencies is detoxification. Complete and immediate withdrawal from the physiologically addicting drugs (heroin and barbiturates) can be extremely unpleasant. In fact, for barbiturates, such a sudden "cold turkey" method of withdrawal can be fatal. Detoxification from drugs is best accomplished in a medical setting by gradually decreasing the dosage level of the drug so that withdrawal symptoms do not occur. Gradual detoxification usually takes about one week in the moderately addicted individual. For those individuals who have become psychologically dependent on "hard" drugs, tranquilizers are usually prescribed to alleviate the anxiety and tension associated with their withdrawal from the drug. Once detoxification is completed, some form of psychosocial treatment needs to be administered in order to aid the individual's social readjustment and to keep him or her from returning to the abuse of the drug.

In recent years, *methadone* (Dolophine), a

DRUG USE IN
THE UNITED STATES

In 1977, the National Institute on Drug Abuse reported findings of three nationwide surveys on drug use in the U.S. It was found that, after cigarettes and alcohol, Americans use marijuana more than any other psychoactive drug: 53 percent of those between the ages of 18 and 25 have used marijuana, and 25 percent are current users; 22 percent of those between the ages of 12 and 17 have used marijuana, and 15 percent are regular or occasional users.

Cocaine is also circulating widely among the young: 3 percent of those between the ages of 12 and 17 have experimented with it; 13 percent of those 18 to 25 have used it at least once, 2 percent in the past month.

The studies also indicate that drug use is related to sex, education, and geographical location: Men use drugs more than women, and college students and graduates demonstrate the highest rate of experimenting with drugs. Geographically, the West, Northeast, and North Central states have the most regular drug users, and the South has the fewest.

Finally, with respect to tobacco and alcohol use, about one-quarter of all those aged 12–17, along with four out of ten adults, are smokers. Roughly one-third of young people and six out of ten adults drink.

Leo Chaplin/Black Star

Methadone maintenance programs have been developed both as a means of treatment and as a means of reducing the crime associated with a narcotics habit.

synthetic drug which has a heroin-like effect on pain, but does not produce euphoria, has become widely used in the treatment of heroin addicts. This drug was initially advocated by Dole and Nyswander (1965) for suppressing "narcotic hunger" or the craving for heroin. Methadone itself, however, is also physically addicting, and so there is a transfer of dependence from heroin to methadone. However, this is viewed as a more tolerable form of dependence. Methadone can later be withdrawn gradually with less unpleasant withdrawal symptoms than heroin, or it can be administered on a permanent basis.

Although methadone maintenance is viewed by some as the treatment of choice for hard-core addicts (e.g., Dole, Nyswander, & Warner 1968),

many drug specialists concur that abstinence from heroin through methadone treatment is far from a totally satisfactory treatment (e.g., Conner & Kremer 1971). Programs that merely supply methadone, without attempting to improve the individual's social and emotional well-being, are not likely to produce any long-term abstention in the great majority of addicts.

Many view methadone maintenance programs not simply as a means of treatment but as a means of reducing the crime and illegal activity associated with the high cost of maintaining a narcotics habit (Dupont & Katon 1971). It would allow the government to oversee the administration of the drug and perhaps decrease the involvement of organized crime in drug distribution. However, since success rates of methadone maintenance programs vary (Miller & Eisler 1976), a certain percentage of heroin addicts reject the methadone program because of the drug's inability to produce the desired euphoric "high" that they have come to enjoy, and return to heroin addiction and the accompanying life of crime that the expensive habit necessitates. Some have suggested that in order to reduce the crime associated with illegal abuse of heroin, heroin itself should be made available through public clinics (Stachnick 1972). This would not only reduce crime by making it inexpensive to support a heroin habit, but it would also decrease deaths due to overdoses and impure heroin, and medical problems such as hepatitis and tetanus caused by nonsterile needle injection methods. Such public clinics are available in England and appear to be a more effective alternative to attempting to control the illegal use of drugs. As attempts at control have not been successful in this country, the possibility of such public clinics deserves further study and consideration.

PSYCHOSOCIAL TREATMENT TECHNIQUES

As is true in the treatment of alcoholism, traditional forms of psychotherapy have not proven to be effective in the treatment of drug dependencies (Neuman & Tamerin 1971). Certain other techniques, however, show some promise for producing positive therapeutic effects.

SYNANON Synanon, which was originally founded in 1958 by a member of Alcoholics Anonymous who had experimented heavily with hard drugs, is a highly structured therapeutic-type community administered by former drug addicts. Although Synanon was initially modelled after AA, it has evolved into a quite different approach. The addict is not treated as being "sick," but rather as a rational human being who is responsible for his or her present behavior and adjustment. Self-reliance is stressed within a structured, family-oriented community. A type of group therapy or "synanon" is held several times a week, during which group pressure is exerted to "stay clean." An emphasis is placed on confrontation, in which ridicule and sarcasm are used to confront members with the self-deceptions they may be using to justify their use of drugs. They are continually pressured to accept personal responsibility and shed rationalization systems they employ to continue using drugs. Not all members can tolerate this confron-

tation, and many drop out because they find it extremely aversive.

As with AA, there are currently no precise, objective data on the success rate of Synanon. Volkmann and Cressey (1963) did study a group of 52 Synanon members, and found that 8 percent of the original group returned to the community and were free from drugs, 44 percent remained in Synanon residences, presumably drug-free, and 48 percent had left and were "unaccounted for." More recent research data are not available. Also, it should be noted that Synanon has been undergoing some major changes in orientation during the past few years. Thus, even though in the past it appeared to have some impact for a certain percentage of addicts, its overall effectiveness has never been determined, either before or after the changes in its orientation.

BEHAVIOR THERAPY Chemical, electrical, and verbal aversion therapy techniques, which are used in the treatment of alcoholism, can also be employed in the treatment of other drug dependencies. Their use with other drug abuse problems, however, is still relatively unexplored. Thompson and Rathod (1968) used a chemical aversion technique with a group of young heroin addicts in which the muscle-paralyzing drug *Anectine* was injected into the arm of the addict while he was preparing a "fix." Just before the paralysis occurred (in about 10 seconds), the addict was instructed to inject the heroin. Injection of heroin was thus paired with the momentary paralysis. Using this technique, Thompson and Rathod reported (on the basis of urine analyses) that eight of the ten addicts who completed five such treatment sessions remained drug-free for periods up to five months. These are just preliminary case study findings. Controlled studies are greatly needed to further evaluate the effectiveness of such a procedure.

There have been some case studies showing the effectiveness of electrical aversion techniques (Lesser 1967; Wolpe 1965) and verbal aversion techniques such as covert sensitization (Wisocki 1973) in the treatment of heroin addiction. One interesting use of electrical aversion therapy is in treating the "needle ritual" observed in many ex-addicts. Because of the strong association developed between "shooting up" and the pleasurable sensation subsequently produced by the heroin, many addicts who no longer use drugs actually continue to inject themselves with solutions, such as water or saline, for the pleasure of this act itself. Blachly (1971) developed a procedure that produced a decrease in the frequency of this "ritual." The patient injected himself with saline in front of a group of addicts, and received an electric shock from a specially devised needle whenever he attempted to press the syringe. A number of such trials decreased the frequency of the needle injection ritual. Such studies demonstrate the potential of aversion procedures in the treatment of drug addiction and related behaviors. Again, though, controlled evaluation outcome studies are needed.

As in the case of alcoholism, any comprehensive treatment program for drug abuse must not only try to decrease the immediate reinforcing properties of the drug through techniques such as aversion therapy, but must also teach the individual new behaviors that are incompatible with drug abuse and modify the social environment so that the person receives maximum reinforcement for activities that do not involve the use of drugs. Boudin (1972) reported a clever use of a reinforcement-contingency program in the treatment of a black woman graduate student who was an amphetamine abuser. A joint bank account was set up between the therapist and the client into which the client deposited almost all of her savings— about $500. A "contract" was made by which, if the client took drugs the therapist would send $50 of this money to the Ku Klux Klan. To a black woman student, losing $50 in this way was extremely aversive. At one point in therapy, $50 was actually sent to the Ku Klux Klan. Results of this program were very successful. Even though the "contract" was in effect for only three months, the client reported remaining drug-free during a 15-month follow-up.

CAFFEINE AND NICOTINE: TWO POPULAR FORMS OF DRUG DEPENDENCE

Caffeine, which is contained in coffee, cola drinks, and chocolate, and nicotine, which is contained in tobacco, are two commonly used stimulants that increase the general activity level of the central nervous system (CNS). These psychoactive drugs are usually not included in discussions of drug abuse because they are popular, legal, and widely

Leon R. Lewandowski

Tobacco addiction is the most common type of drug dependency in this country.

used, and have traditionally been viewed as causing no physiological damage. They usually do not distort one's perceptions, decrease mental functioning efficiency, or cloud one's memory. These two drugs, however, have brought about two of the most potent drug habits in the United States. If these stimulants are suddenly discontinued, a period of depression may result. This period of depression in part accounts for the difficult time many individuals encounter when attempting to "kick the habit."

CAFFEINE Caffeine is the most widely used stimulant. For many people, the morning cup of coffee seems absolutely necessary to prepare them to meet the new day. Coffee drinking alone in the United States accounts for an annual consumption of 15 million pounds of caffeine. The caffeine contained in colas and chocolate contributes (along with sugar) to the "quick energy release" associated with drinking a cola beverage or eating a candy bar. Caffeine stimulates cellular activity, with the effect concentrated to a large extent on nerve cells. Low doses of this drug result in mental alertness and increased efficiency. Higher doses can result in hyper-responsiveness and the motor tremors known as "coffee nerves."

NICOTINE Nicotine is also a widely used CNS stimulant which produces effects similar to those of caffeine. Although, like caffeine, it produces no apparent psychological damage, the means by which it is ingested—smoking—creates a physiological danger. It is accepted today that chronic smoking is a major contributor to a variety of medical diseases: lung cancer, a number of other cancers, as of the larynx and esophagus, bronchitis, emphysema, and coronary artery disease. Indeed, it has been estimated that approximately 15 percent of the annual mortality rate in the United States is due to diseases directly caused or exacerbated by tobacco consumption. As a result of this documented health hazard, legislation was passed banning tobacco advertisements from television and radio. Also, each pack of cigarettes sold in this country is required to include an advertisement indicating its potentially lethal effects. However, even though these dangers are widely known and advertised, the annual consumption rate is still high—over 200 packs of cigarettes per person over 18 years of age (Standard & Poor 1975). Despite growing social disapproval of smoking, widely advertised medical dangers of smoking, and the rising cost of cigarettes, as many people are smoking today as ever. This attests to the potent habit-forming effects of this stimulant.

Because of the addicting qualities of tobacco and its hazard to health, the DSM-III has a separate subcategory entitled "tobacco use disorders" under the general category of *substance use disorders*. Chronic tobacco use is now considered a mental disorder when there is either (1) psychological distress (e.g., anxiety or guilt over its use) associated with the need to repeatedly use tobacco, or (2) a serious tobacco-associated medical disorder in a person diagnosed to be physiologically dependent on tobacco.

Through the years, a variety of approaches ranging from hypnosis to traditional group therapy has been used in an attempt to treat chronic smoking behavior. Such approaches usually show an initial period of abstention followed by relapse. They have produced an estimated long-term abstinence rate (greater than one year) of less than

15 percent (Pomerleau & Pomerleau 1977). Recently developed behavior therapy techniques show greater promise for producing lasting change. For example, an aversive conditioning procedure involving the smoking of cigarettes at an extremely rapid rate until no additional smoking can be tolerated has been used with some success by Lichtenstein and colleagues. These *rapid smoking* treatment sessions are repeated until the smokers indicate no additional desire to smoke. "Booster" sessions are subsequently administered if the desire should return. Lichtenstein and Penner (1977) reported an outcome evaluation study that found that 34 percent of all subjects who entered this type of therapy were still abstinent two to six years after treatment.

Even though the rapid smoking technique appears to have some relative degree of long-term success, it is associated with some problems that limit its broad use. For example, smokers with cardiovascular and pulmonary disease (obviously an important target population requiring treatment) are not likely to be able to tolerate such intense rapid smoking without demonstrating some ill effect (McAlister 1975). Even in healthy individuals, rapid smoking may be dangerous (Hauser 1974). The use of other aversive stimuli, such as electric shock, has not been found to be as effective in reducing smoking (Pomerleau & Pomerleau 1977).

Some multimodal behavior therapy techniques have been developed to treat smoking. These involve procedures such as the identification of situations that precipitate smoking, the training of new habits incompatible with smoking, group support, and extensive follow-up. Such an approach has shown some preliminary favorable results (Bernstein & McAlister 1976). Additional evaluative research to resolve many of these questions conclusively is sorely needed.

Finally, as Pomerleau and Pomerleau (1977) point out:

A word of caution—quit rates for scientifically evaluated programs may seem low compared with the sometimes extravagant claims made by commercial programs. Outcome evaluations that do not account for all smokers who enter therapy and are based on follow-up data obtained less than a year after the start of treatment are inadequate for drawing conclusions about program effectiveness. (p. 94)

DIAGNOSIS AND ASSESSMENT

INTERVIEW/REFERRAL

The clinical interview is a valuable and frequently used method for the assessment of alcoholism and other drug dependencies, as it is with other psychopathologies. Because it is important to individualize psychotherapy, an attempt needs to be made to assess the specific features of the client's presenting problem and the precipitating/situational factors that are maintaining the problem behavior. Without precise and accurate assessment, an effective treatment program cannot be developed. Miller and Eisler (1976) note that it is often important to differentiate between *precipitating causes* and *maintaining causes*:

. . . Let us suppose that a middle-aged housewife is experiencing marital difficulties and begins to drink excessively in order to relieve tension and worry regarding her marriage. She and her husband eventually obtain a divorce and her drinking increases. She has established a pattern whereby excessive drinking becomes contingent upon any emotionally stressful event. Being intoxicated relieves her anxiety and allows her to escape temporarily from stressful circumstances. Once drinking has increased to a daily frequency, she finds that early morning drinking is reinforcing since it relieves agitation and hangover from the previous evening's drinking. She may associate with others who drink to excess through contacts made in bars. At this point the *precipitating factor* (stress of marital problems) is no longer present. Her drinking continues for other *maintaining reasons* such as peer approval, encouragement, recognition, and/or avoidance of withdrawal symptoms. Treatment must be geared toward the most currently potent maintaining factors, since the initial cause may have little relevance to her present drinking pattern. Once drinking is brought under control through treatment, intervention effects aimed at teaching her how to deal more appropriately with stressful events would

certainly decrease the chance of relapse. (p. 380)

This same type of differentiation may also need to be made when assessing the abuse of other drugs, and in planning an appropriate treatment program.

A number of instruments have been developed to aid in gathering drug-taking information during an interview. The Marlatt Drinking Profile (Marlatt, 1977), for example, is a structured, behaviorally oriented interview. Information is collected about drinking patterns and behavior, antecedents and consequences of drinking, and other facts useful for clinical purposes. Along with the self-report information gathered in such diagnostic interviews, physiological indices such as physiological dependence, increased tolerance, and the occurrence of withdrawal symptoms can be used to further validate the presence of addiction. When possible, direct behavioral measures of drug abuse should be used as part of the assessment procedure. For example, in alcoholism research Miller (1973) has described three general types of behavioral assessment techniques: (1) *experimental bars* in which patients are seated in a simulated bar situation while their drinking behavior is carefully observed and recorded; (2) *choice situations* in which patients are presented with a variety of alcoholic and nonalcoholic beverages and asked to choose; (3) *operant analysis* in which the patient must perform some response in order to obtain alcohol. The frequency and intensity of this responding is used to suggest the need for alcohol. Such direct behavioral measures may not be available in many diagnostic/assessment situations.

Many times a drug abuser first comes to the attention of his or her family doctor. This person may visit a physician for treatment of physiological disturbances caused by the abuse. If the physician is astute and concerned enough, he or she can make an early diagnosis and suggest that the patient needs professional help for the problem. This early diagnosis can be extremely valuable for the patient's welfare since the earlier the patient is aware that there is a problem, the earlier he or she is likely to seek help for it, and the better the prognosis for change.

TESTING

One of the earliest scales developed for the diagnosis of alcoholism was the Manson Evaluation (Manson 1948), a 72-item personality test. It was developed to differentiate between self-admitted alcoholics and nonalcoholics. In recent years, it has fallen into almost total disuse, and alcoholism scales derived from the MMPI are used. One such scale frequently used is one of 49 items developed by MacAndrew (1965). MMPI-derived profile patterns have also been used in the diagnosis of other drug addiction (e.g., Berzins, Ross, & Monroe 1971).

A problem associated with diagnosing alcoholism on the basis of personality profile patterns is that the same pattern many times occurs in the population of nonaddicts with histories of other kinds of antisocial behavior. Because of this problem, alternatives to the sole use of the personality profile pattern method have been developed. For example, the Addiction Research Center (ARC) at the Lexington (Kentucky) Federal Narcotics Center designed the ARC Inventory to diagnose drug addiction (Haertzen 1965). The Inventory consists of 550 items from the MMPI and a number of objective behavioral checklists. Studies have demonstrated that this Inventory may be better than the MMPI to differentiate between drug addicts, alcoholics, and sociopaths (Haertzen & Hooks 1969).

Tests that inquire directly about drug-taking behavior are viewed by many as a better alternative to personality profile pattern methods. The Alcadd Test (Manson 1949) represents the first such direct alcoholism scale. The Michigan Alcoholism Screening Test (MAST) was developed more recently (Selzer 1971). It is a 25-item scale inquiring about drinking habits, with questions such as "Do you feel you are a normal drinker?" These items have high *face validity*; that is, it is easy to understand what the items are trying to measure. Some have argued that high face validity creates a problem in that it opens the items to possible falsification by the subject. Of course, as we have emphasized, one should not assess or diagnose solely on the basis of one test. Such tests should only be used in combination with other sources of data. In a recent review of procedures used in the assessment of alcoholism, Miller (1976) indicated that multimodal assessment, using alcoholism self-report scales, behavioral assessment techniques, and physiological methods, should be employed rather than one single method of assessment.

PROGNOSIS

The treatment of alcoholism and other drug dependencies has traditionally been ineffective. As yet, there has been no comprehensive treatment technique developed that has produced long-term change greater than would be expected to occur without treatment. This is especially true in the area of narcotics abuse, where therapy recommendations are especially vague. A number of behavioral techniques show some promise for effective treatment, especially with alcoholism. Even if these comprehensive behavioral programs do not produce complete rehabilitation, they may keep drug abusers functioning effectively in the community for a longer period of time.

Of course, the critical feature involved in the success of any treatment is the patient's motivation to want to change. One of the reasons why drug addiction may be so resistant to treatment is that the patient may not want to give up the euphoric effects produced by the drug, which are possibly the only means of escaping a stressful life situation. Also, the life-style associated with drug taking may become highly attractive. Addicts rarely become abstinent voluntarily. Thus, even if effective comprehensive treatment programs are developed in the future, a certain number of individuals will continue to abuse drugs because they do not want to change. It is hoped that studies in the psychology of drug and alcohol abuse and dependence can be designed that will produce more conclusive findings regarding these dependencies.

SUMMARY

1. The abuse of drugs can lead to physiological and/or psychological dependence that can pose serious problems for the individual and for society as a whole. Physiological dependence or addiction can occur, in which withdrawal symptoms such as nausea and vomiting appear when drug use is suddenly stopped. Along with addiction, tolerance develops, and greater and greater amounts of the drug need to be ingested to produce the same desired physiological and psychological effects. Psychological dependence can also occur, causing an overwhelming desire for the psychological state produced by the drug.

2. Approximately 5–10 million Americans abuse the use of alcohol and are labeled alcoholics or problem drinkers. Such statistics, however, are not precise since there is no totally accepted definition of alcoholism.

3. Alcohol acts as a central nervous system depressant. *Blood alcohol level,* which refers to the percentage of alcohol in the bloodstream, has specific direct effects on behavior.

4. With frequent and chronic abuse of alcohol, a number of negative consequences can occur—physiological and psychological dependency, nutritional deficiencies, psychotic-type reactions such as delirium tremens and Korsakoff's psychosis, as well as a general disruption of social/interpersonal functioning.

5. Alcoholism is not only an adult problem. It is increasingly becoming a significant problem among adolescents.

6. Jellinek has delineated four stages in the progression from nonproblematic "social drinking" to alcoholism: (1) prealcoholic symptomatic phase; (2) prodromal stage; (3) crucial period; (4) chronic phase. Many alcoholics, however, do not precisely follow this course of development.

7. Jellinek also described four different patterns or categories of alcoholism, labeling them *alpha, beta, gamma, delta.* The DSM-II has also categorized different forms of alcoholism. However, both systems have significant limitations.

8. There is no single definition of alcoholism. More and more mental health professionals are using behavioral criteria that occur together to make judgments concerning the severity of problem drinking.

9. No completely satisfactory psychological theory for explaining alcoholism has yet been developed. Research has also consistently failed to find an "alcoholic personality." Sociocultural theories, which emphasize the importance of a society's drinking practices, customs, and attitudes towards alcohol as contributing to the development and maintenance of deviant drinking behavior, appear promising in the explanation of some forms of alcohol abuse.

10. Much more research is needed to determine genetic and physiological factors are important in the development of alcoholism.

11. An initial step in the treatment of alcoholism is usually a medical procedure called *detoxification.* After detoxification is completed, some form of psychosocial treatment needs to be administered. Traditional forms of psychotherapy have not proven effective. Other techniques, such as Alcoholics Anonymous and behavior therapy, have shown some positive therapeutic effects.

12. Besides alcohol, a number of other drugs frequently are used and abused in contemporary society: opium and its derivatives (morphine, codeine, heroin), amphetamines, sedatives (barbiturates and tranquilizers), cocaine, hallucinogens (LSD and mescaline), and cannabis (marijuana and hashish). Of these drugs, opium and its derivatives and the barbiturates are physiologically addicting.

13. As with alcoholism, there are no psychological theories that adequately explain the development of drug abuse. There are also no personality characteristics associated with drug abusers that can be used to differentiate them from individuals with other forms of psychopathology.

14. There do appear to be some clear sociocultural factors associated with drug abuse, but the exact cause-effect nature of this relationship is not yet known. Gorsuch and Butler (1976) have recently suggested that a multi-model approach may prove more worthwhile in the search for the exact cause-effect relationship than any single model.

15. There has been little systematic research evaluating whether there are genetic and physiological bases for the various forms of drug dependencies.

16. As in the treatment of alcoholism, an initial step in the treatment of other drug addictions is detoxification. Traditional forms of psychotherapy have not proven to be effective in the treatment of these problem behaviors. Synanon and some behavior therapy techniques show some promise for producing positive therapeutic effects. Also, in recent years, the synthetic drug methadone has become widely used in the maintenance-treatment of heroin addicts.

17. As it is with other forms of psychopathology, the clinical interview is a valuable and frequently used method for the assessment of alcoholism and other forms of drug dependency. There have been a number of instruments developed to aid in the gathering of drug-taking data during an interview; a number of tests have also been developed.

18. As suggested by Miller (1976), multimodal assessment using self-report, behavioral, and physiological measures needs to be employed rather than any one single method of assessment.

**RECOMMENDED
READINGS**

Gibbons, R., Israel, Y, Kalant, H., Popham, R., Schmidt, W., & Smart, R. (Eds.) *Research advances in alcohol and drug problems.* New York: Wiley. Volume 1: 1975; Volume 2: 1975; Volume 3: 1976.

Jellinek, E. M. *The disease concept of alcoholism.* Highland Park, N.J.: Hillhouse Press, 1960.

Lloyd, R. W., & Salzberg H. C. Controlled social drinking: An alternative to abstinence as a treatment goal for some alcohol abusers. *Psychological Bulletin,* 1975, 82, 815–842.

Miller, P. M., & Eisler, R. M. Alcohol and drug abuse. In W. E. Craighead, A. E. Kazdin, & M. J. Mahoney (Eds.), *Behavior modification: Principles, issues, and applications.* Boston: Houghton Mifflin, 1976.

Stachnik, T. J. The case against criminal penalties for illicit drug use. *American Psychologist,* 1972, 27, 637–642.

Westermeyer, J. A primer on chemical dependency: A clinical guide to alcohol and drug related problems. Baltimore: Williams & Wilkins, 1976.

PSYCHOSEXUAL DEVIATIONS

11

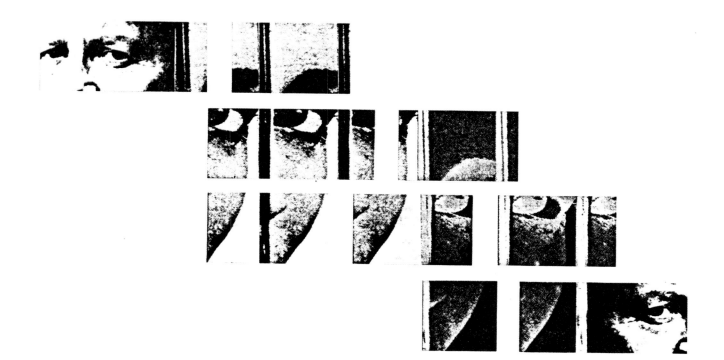

OVERVIEW   In this chapter we will examine the major types of sexually deviant behaviors, behaviors in which the individual's sexual interest is directed toward objects other than another human being, toward sexual acts not usually associated with intercourse, and toward coitus under unusual or bizarre circumstances. These include fetishism, transvestism, exhibitionism, voyeurism and peeping, sadomasochism, transsexualism, rape, and incest.

Before examining these deviations, we will introduce the reader to the typical research procedures used in sex research—questionnaires and interviews. Methodological problems associated with these procedures will be noted, as they affect the reliability and accuracy of much of the existing data on human sexual behavior. A separate discussion will look at the early sex researchers Richard von Krafft-Ebing and Havelock Ellis.

Individuals with psychosexual disorders do not make up a homogeneous group. For each disorder we will examine the symptoms and frequency, the causes and stressors as they are hypothesized, and treatment methods. Much of this information is speculative, as further research is needed in all areas of human sexual behavior. Most of the treatment methods, too, still require more research to determine their effectiveness. Case studies of some of these disorders are included, as is a separate featured discussion on sexual motivation and what influences it.

DEMOGRAPHICS	USUAL AGE AT ONSET	PREVALENCE	SEX RATIO
FETISHISM	Adolescence	Unknown	Virtually all cases reported have involved males
TRANSVESTISM	Cross-dressing usually begins in childhood and early adolescence	Unknown	Occurs almost exclusively in males
EXHIBITIONISM	Adolescence to middle age	Unknown	Has only been described in males
VOYEURISM & PEEPING	Varies, although usually in early adulthood	Unknown	Voyeurism occurs most often in males. Peeping has only been described in males
PEDOPHILIA	May begin at any time over range of adolescence and adulthood years	Unknown, although sexual offenses against children are currently a major criminal problem behavior	Occurs most often in males
SADOMASOCHISM	Varies, although usually by early adolescence	Rare	Appears to be more common in males than females
TRANSSEXUALISM	Usually have demonstrated identity or role problems as children. Full symptoms usually appear in late adolescence or early adulthood	Rare	Appears to be more common in males than females
RAPE	Adolescence and early adulthood	Usually underreported. More than 55,000 forcible rapes per year in U.S.	Exclusively in males
INCEST	May occur at any time over range of adolescence and adulthood years	Exact statistics not available, but some have estimated that it occurs in about 10% of population*	About 2:1 male-female ratio

*This figure involves incestuous behavior between any persons related by either blood or marriage. Thus, for example, sexual relations between distant cousins or stepfather and daughter are included along with those incidents involving sister-brother and father-daughter.

RESEARCH IN HUMAN SEXUAL BEHAVIOR

The subject of human sexuality, in particular abnormal sexual behavior, has always held a fascination for people. Such topics as transsexualism, fetishism, incest, or exhibitionism often stimulate people's curiosity to explore and read more about these subjects. Most readers probably have some preconceptions about deviant sexual behavior.

But we must be critical about the sources of the information forming our conceptions about abnormal sexual behavior for one main reason: the literature on human sexuality, as a whole, has been filled with misinformation and myths. For example, we noted in chapter 1 that less than a hundred years ago much of the medical profession, and the psychiatric community in particular, believed that masturbation was a cause of insanity. Indeed, the literature on the evils of masturbation was widely read and most certainly spilled over into contemporary writing and thought. Even in the twentieth century, scientific information about human sexuality (deviations included) has not kept pace with other areas of behavior research. In fact, only within the last ten or so years have issues dealing with sexual deviations been openly discussed. For a time, sex research was all but impossible to fund, and difficult to publish.

Not only has empirical evidence been sparse in this area, but also the dissemination of the factual information that did exist. Courses in sex education were difficult to initiate; when they were taught, controversy and dissension prevailed. Curiously, by 1960, only three medical schools in the United States offered programs in human sexuality.

Another important point is that much of the information we have about abnormal sexual behavior has been provided by a particular type of research precedure: the *controlled observation.* Controlled observation is best exemplified by the structured interview (with specific questions asked) or by the survey. Many of the classic studies on human sexuality and abnormal sexual behavior have employed controlled observation. Kinsey, Pomeroy, and Martin (1948) provided us with much data on sexual deviations and homosexuality during the late 1940s. More recently, studies have surveyed large numbers of people, questioning them about such things as homosexuality, incest, sadomasochism, and so on (Hunt 1974; Hite

1974, 1976). Although these studies do provide information describing sexual deviations (in particular the frequency), we should be very careful about accepting these findings. It has been suggested, for instance, that in the Kinsey study there was poor reliability between interviewers because each interviewer was permitted to restate or explore beyond the limits of the standardized interview. Kinsey referred to this freedom of the interviewer to depart somewhat from the structure as "flexibility in form of question." It is thus possible that different interviewers, because of their special rapport with the interviewee, could elicit more information. These methodological problems do raise questions about the Kinsey data. In new studies on women's sexual behavior, sampling problems are definitely possible. For example, in her early survey, Hite (1974) reported on a number of women who had read and answered her questionnaires as they appeared in newspapers and magazines—*Ms Magazine, Mademoiselle, Oui* (a magazine for men), *Village Voice,* and so forth. Although these publications gave Hite access to many women readers, those who filled out and returned the questionnaires would be from a rather select population. Were the responses of those women who returned the questionnaires representative of the entire population of women? Hite's sampling in this case is nonrandom sampling because not all women have an equal chance of being questioned. Another serious defect of the Hite survey is the low returns of the questionnaires. (She notes that in her early study 80,000 questionnaires were distributed but only 2,000 were returned.) With low returns on questionnaires, valid generalizations about sexual behavior cannot be made.

Thus we must be cautious in reviewing the data of controlled observations (interviews and questionnaires in particular) because serious problems of reliability and sampling bias exist. Further, data provided by the controlled observation are essentially descriptive and do not deal with explanations. Nevertheless, in this chapter we will review survey studies, and some purely speculative data. The speculative and some clinical data are included in certain sections where we lack any empirical evidence, so that the readers will be able to gain some insight into the problem.

THE EARLY SEX RESEARCHERS

Perhaps the first recognized "sexologist" was the German psychiatrist Richard von Krafft-Ebing, (1840–1902). In 1886 he published a volume on sexual perversions—*Psychopathia Sexualis.* Although this text is replete with inaccuracies, Krafft-Ebing is often credited with being the first to classify sexual deviations. To some extent Krafft-Ebing's text gave a degree of authority and respectability to the study of "sexual perversions," as they were then called. The book was widely read by lay people as well as the medical profession, and as Karlen (1971) notes, its great strength was "its exhaustiveness and authoritative tone." The book covered such behaviors as fetishism, sadism, homosexuality, nymphomania, satyriasis, zoophilia, and many more. Yet there were serious problems with *Psychopathia Sexualis.* For one, Krafft-Ebing presented numerous "perversions" in a negative and horrifying manner, claiming that many disorders were the result of hereditary predisposition. For another, he stated that masturbation was at the basis of many problems, including homosexuality. If the reader were to believe Krafft-Ebing's descriptions, it is conceivable that he or she would finish the book with a feeling of disgust and hatred for those described.

The Englishman Havelock Ellis (1859–1939) was, in a sense, a proponent of sexual amorality. In contrast to Krafft-Ebing, Ellis insisted that all sexual deviations were basically harmless, and that some deviates (homosexuals, for example) were actually superior to and more creative than normals (Karlen 1971). In his best and most voluminous effort, *Studies in the Psychology of Sex* (1897–1928), Ellis not only described many deviations but also the experience of what it was like to be deviant. Based on numerous case histories, selected from friends, associates, and patients around the world, Ellis devoted some space to the cause of sexual deviations. For example, Ellis, as well as many clinicians of his time, believed that homosexuality was in large measure a constitutional defect. While most of Ellis's notions about the cause of homosexuality have no empirical support, he did push forward our descriptive view of abnormal sexual behavior. Perhaps of greater importance, he helped establish a more humane and less critical attitude toward those with deviations. He was indeed a counselor by letter to many around the world who wrote to him for guidance and advice about their problems. His mission was "to bring peace and a feeling of worth" to those with sexual deviations (Karlen 1971).

SYMPTOM DESCRIPTION AND ETIOLOGY

Historically, most nonprocreative sexual activities have been viewed as pathological in Western cultures (Morin 1977). For instance, masturbation, sodomy, homosexuality, and other sexual activities were in the past often viewed as illnesses. Even today, in a more general sense, sexual activities that are not associated with coitus may be looked on as distasteful or strange. The truth is that we know very little about the mental health or pathology of those engaging in unusual sexual activities. Not only are data lacking to show that choice of sexual activities is related to mental health, but also the incidence or frequency of various sexual activities is not known.

Like many abnormal behaviors described earlier, sexual deviation has no single definition. A few sources, however, have offered to define sexual deviations. Lazarus and Rosen (1976) state simply that sexual deviations are sexual behaviors that are socially unacceptable. With somewhat more clarity, the DSM-II defined the category of sexual deviation in this way:

> This category is for individuals whose sexual interests are directed primarily toward objects other than people of the opposite sex, toward sexual acts not usually associated with coitus, or toward coitus performed under bizarre circumstances as in

necrophilia, pedophilia, sexual sadism, and fetishism. (p. 44)

As has been mentioned, the DSM-II once classified homosexuality as a sexual deviation, but this classification was removed in the 1970s. (Homosexuality is discussed separately in chapter 12.)

The newer DSM-III classifies abnormal sexual behaviors in three sections under the broad category heading *psychosexual disorders:*

1. *Gender identity disorders* — includes such problems as transsexualism and other disorders related to confusion of gender identity or role.
2. *Paraphilias* (sexual deviations) — includes such behaviors as fetishism, transvestism, zoophilia, pedophilia, exhibitionism, voyeurism, sexual masochism, sexual sadism, and a few others.
3. *Psychosexual dysfunctions* — includes inhibited sexual desire, inhibited sexual excitement (frigidity, impotence), inhibited female and male orgasms, premature ejaculation, and dyspareunia.

In this section we will examine the behaviors classified as *paraphilias* (sexual deviations). Later in the chapter we will discuss transsexualism as well as two other forms of sexually deviant behavior — rape and incest. We must recognize that not all these deviations engender the same degree of societal disapproval. Rape and pedophilia, for example, generate much disapproval for they are forms of criminal assault as well as unusual and bizarre behaviors; incest, too, is a crime in most places. Some sexual deviations considered here violate the rights of individuals more than do others that are practiced privately or between consenting adults.

Finally, as we have noted, little empirical evidence is available to suggest that most sexual deviants are less healthy than those with conventional sexual preferences. However, few people would disagree that rape, for instance, is more pathological than transvestism.

FETISHISM

The term *fetishism,* to describe a sexual aberration, was coined by the French psychologist Alfred Binet in 1880. Behaviorally defined, fetishism involves being aroused sexually by holding, tasting, smell-

The Bettmann Archive

Richard von Krafft-Ebing (1840–1902) was a German psychiatrist and neurologist who wrote a book describing sexual deviations. He maintained that many deviations were inherited.

ing, or viewing the fetish item, usually while masturbating. Although fetishism represents a distinct deviation, in many ways it bears close resemblance to transvestism, voyeurism, and other reactions.

Gebhard (1976) states that fetishisms can be divided into two categories: (1) fetish items that are inanimate, such as shoes, lingerie, or gloves; and (2) fetish items that are part of the female body, such as the legs or breasts. In an earlier work, Gebhard, Gagnon, Pomeroy, and Christenson (1965) preferred to think of fetishisms as occurring only with inanimate objects. Gebhard also suggests that fetishists can- be placed on a four-point continuum depending on how exclusively they employ the fetish item for sexual gratification. At the low end of the continuum might be a man who has slight sexual arousal toward some particular object worn by a female. The next step is stronger arousal toward the object, but this man may still be able to perform-sexually with a female partner. At the third point on this continuum, no sexual activity or orgasm can occur without the

BERNARD MALAMUD ON VOYEURISM

. . . Helen was with her mother as Ida counted the cash. Frank stood behind the counter, cleaning his fingernails with his jackknife blade, waiting for them to leave so he could close up.

"I think I'll take a hot shower before I go to bed," Helen said to her mother. "I've felt chilled all night."

"Good night," Ida said to Frank. "I left five dollars change for the morning."

They left by the rear door and he heard them go up the stairs. Frank closed the store and went into the back. He thumbed through tomorrow's *News*, then got restless.

After a while he went into the store and listened at the side door; he unlatched the lock, snapped on the cellar light, closed the cellar door behind him so no light would leak out into the hall, then quietly descended the stairs.

He found the air shaft where an old unused dumb-waiter stood, pushed the dusty box back and gazed up the vertical shaft. It was pitch-dark. Neither the Bobers bathroom window nor the Fusos' showed any light.

Frank struggled against himself but not for long. Shoving the dumb-waiter back as far as it would go, he squeezed into the shaft and then boosted himself up on the top of the box. His heart shook him with its beating.

When his eyes got used to the dark he saw that her bathroom window was only a couple of feet above his head. He felt along the wall as high as he could reach and touched a narrow ledge around the air shaft. He thought he could anchor himself on it and see into the bathroom.

But if you do it, he told himself, you will suffer.

Though his throat hurt and his clothes were drenched in sweat, the excitement of what he might see forced him to go up.

Crossing himself, Frank grabbed both of the dumb-waiter ropes and slowly pulled himself up, praying the pulley at the skylight wouldn't squeak too much.

A light went on over his head.

Holding his breath, he crouched motionless, clinging to the swaying ropes. Then the bathroom window was shut with a bang. For a while he couldn't move, the strength gone out of him. He thought he might lose his grip and fall, and he thought of her opening the bathroom window and seeing him lying at the bottom of the shaft in a broken, filthy heap.

It was a mistake to do it, he thought.

But she might be in the shower before he could get a look at her, so, trembling, he began again to pull himself up. In a few minutes he was straddling the ledge, holding onto the ropes to steady himself yet keep his full weight off the wood.

Leaning forward, though not too far, he could see through the uncurtained crossed sash window into the old-fashioned bathroom. Helen was there looking with sad eyes at herself in the mirror. He thought she would stand there forever, but at last she unzipped her housecoat, stepping out of it.

He felt a throb of pain at her nakedness, an overwhelming desire to love her, at the

---

fetish item; for example, his female partner may be required to wear high-heeled shoes to bed. At the ultimate end of the continuum, the exclusive fetishist substitutes the fetish item completely for his "living sexual partner."

Gebhard et al. (1965) were concerned about this question: "At what point on this continuum should a person be labeled as a fetishist?" They suggest that if a dividing line between normal fetishistic interests (which most males have) and more maladaptive interests is to be made, three criteria would suffice in categorizing a person as a fetishist in need of treatment: (1) He obtains definite and reasonably strong sexual arousal [i.e., enough to cause erection] from the fetish item alone. (2) He disregards an otherwise attractive sexual partner who lacks the fetish item and chooses an otherwise unattractive partner who possesses the item. (3) He begins collecting the fetish item (p. 414).

These investigators note, however, that all three of these criteria typically exist together in the more extreme fetishist, as in the case study following.

same time an awareness of loss, of never having had what he wanted most, and other such memories he didn't care to recall.

Her body was young, soft, lovely, the breasts like small birds in flight, her ass like a flower. Yet it was a lonely body in spite of its lovely form, lonelier. Bodies are lonely, he thought, but in bed she wouldn't be. She seemed realer to him now than she had been, revealed without clothes, personal, possible. He felt greedy as he gazed, all eyes at a banquet, hungry so long as he must look. But in looking he was forcing her out of reach, making her into a thing only of his seeing, her eyes reflecting his sins, rotten past, spoiled ideals, his passion poisoned by his shame.

Frank's eyes grew moist and he wiped them with one hand. When he gazed up again she seemed, to his horror, to be staring at him through the window, a mocking smile on her lips, her eyes filled with scorn, pitiless. He thought wildly of jumping, bolting, broken-boned, out of the house; but she turned on the shower and stepped into the tub, drawing the flowered plastic curtain around her.

The window was quickly covered with steam. For this he was relieved, grateful. He let himself down silently. In the cellar, instead of the grinding remorse he had expected to suffer, he felt a moving joy.

From *The Assistant*, by Bernard Malamud. Reprinted by permission of Farrar, Straus & Giroux. Copyright © 1957 by Bernard Malamud.

A CASE OF FETISHISM

[This male] recalls that at age six he was greatly impressed by a motion picture in which a male and female were tied back-to-back. The female was able to escape by getting her feet out of her high-heeled shoes. . . . In the following days he often re-enacted this scene with a baby sitter: here we have physical contact with a female, some exertion, and shoes involved. Then around puberty he saw a partially undressed adult female neighbor whose high-heeled shoes he then stole and used for masturbation. A full-fledged shoe fetish developed. (Gebhard et al. 1965, p. 418)

In acquiring the fetish item many fetishists become "fetish thieves." They may steal the preferred objects from clotheslines or burglarize a woman's house. It is interesting that fetish items usually must have been worn by a female in order to become eroticized. In this connection, Gebhard remarks that rarely does the fetishist, if married, use his wife's garments. If the wife wears the item, rather than a strange woman, it appears to de-eroticize the clothing.

CAUSES AND STRESSORS Theories about the cause of fetishism emerge chiefly from three areas: the cultural view, the learning view, and the psychoanalytic view. Although little empirical evidence exists to support any particular cause, these viewpoints may reveal clues about this deviation.

In connection with the *cultural view*, Gebhard (1976) points out that fetishisms occur only in well-developed civilizations. If this assertion is correct, it leads us to speculate that certain societies somehow eroticize various types of clothing. Female clothing, in particular, often becomes sexual stimuli. This statement seems very reasonable in our society—rarely is the attire of a male (shoes, underwear, and so forth) regarded as "sexy." One way of confirming the view that female attire is a sexual stimulus is to consider the strict ban on the wearing of women's clothes by men. (This point also is relevant to *transvestism*.) While women encounter little problem at all in dressing in "asexual" or "unisexual" male attire or even in, say, borrowing a man's shirt or sweater, it is generally taboo for males to wear female clothing. In this way, female clothing (or part of the female body) may take on erotic value. In the case of fetishism, the fetishistic object becomes more than something that is a cue to sexual arousal—contact with the object becomes a *substitute* for coitus. Just why certain males develop complete fetishistic interests and others only use fetishistic objects as cues to sexual activity is not explained by the cultural view.

The *learning view* offers another explanation for the development of fetishism. Ellis and Abarbanel (1973) suggest that this sexual deviation probably begins in childhood or adolescence when, by accident, the child "becomes sexually aroused by contact with some object belonging to or associated with his mother, sister, aunt, grandmother, or some other women" (p. 43). This notion was in fact proposed by Alfred Binet about ninety years ago. Binet believed that some trivial occasion might form a conditioned sexual stimulus. For example, a small boy might be bathed by a red-headed nurse who, while washing the child, touched his genitals. When the child matured, he might find the sight of red-headed women sexually arousing (Chesser 1971).

Finally, according to the *psychoanalytic view*, the fetishistic object represents or symbolizes the female genitals. Freud, in fact, went so far as to say that the fetishistic object is not just a substitute for the female genitals but rather a symbolic representation of a penis the boy imagines women should possess. Like the cultural view, psychoanalysis does not explain why one child develops a fetish and not another. To date, all these etiological notions represent little more than speculation.

TREATMENT METHODS Some preliminary data suggest that a fetish may be reduced through the use of certain behavior therapy methods. In particular, an *aversion therapy* technique called *covert sensitization* has been reported to be a useful technique (Kolvin 1967). In this technique, the patient is to imagine himself holding the fetish item, while at the same time thinking of a noxious or aversive scene (Marks 1976). For example, the subject might imagine the fetish item and then also imagine that it is giving off a nauseating stench. Another technique that has been tried with the subject's consent is *electric aversive shock* (not the same as electroconvulsive shock). In aversive shock, the aversive stimulus is not in the patient's fantasies but is a painful, but not tissue-damaging, shock to the forearm or finger. The shock is delivered when the subject imagines the fetishistic item or actually holds it. In one reported case, Marks and Gelder (1967) treated a subject who had a panty fetish. He received the shock while viewing the panties. After some 20 pairings of shock and viewing the panties, this subject no longer showed sexual arousal to the fetishistic item but, importantly, did respond to other appropriate sexual stimuli.

Although behavior therapy methods appear promising with fetishisms, much research involving larger samples of subjects needs to be conducted before any conclusive statements can be made.

TRANSVESTISM

Transvestism, as a term, was first introduced by the German sex researcher Mangus Hirschfeld in 1910. The literal meaning of transvestism is "cross-dressing;" that is, wearing clothes of the opposite sex. But the clinical definition is more complex than the literal meaning, stating that a male who receives sexual gratification from wearing female clothes or other items is a transvestite. This deviation resembles fetishism, and in fact is often referred to as "fetishistic cross-dressing." But Feinbloom (1976) notes that transvestites may just get "relief" from gender discomfort by dressing, with or without the sexual arousal that accompanies fetishism.

The male who cross-dresses may be a heterosexual, or he may be a homosexual. A homosexual who cross-dresses (the "drag queen") does not do so to experience sexual gratification, but to attract other men (Feinbloom 1976). Thus, according to the clinical definition of transvestism, a homosexual who cross-dresses is not a transvestite unless he is erotically aroused by the act of cross-dressing. For the heterosexual male, on the other hand, cross-dressing is a goal in itself.

The DSM-III lists four operational criteria for transvestism: (1) recurrent and persistent cross-dressing by a male, with or without sexual arousal; (2) interference with cross-dressing results in intense frustration; (3) heterosexual arousal pattern; homosexual acts may occur but are not the preferred pattern; and (4) does not fulfill the criteria for transsexualism.

What do transvestites do sexually? Generally, these men, because of the taboo on wearing female clothing, cross-dress secretly (Stoller 1975). Often, for example, a man will go alone to a motel where he can dress in privacy. While dressed, he may or may not masturbate. Invariably he needs a mirror to view himself. On occasion, and after "the initial thrills of solitary dressing are past, the transvestite wants to be seen [in public]" (Feinbloom 1976). In other instances, the transvestite may join a very private transvestite club that provides a place for members to meet and cross-dress. As Feinbloom notes, some men come dressed in female attire while others bring suitcases containing their wardrobe and dress after arriving.

Feinbloom conducted what she called a "participant observation" study of transvestites. Representing herself as a social scientist and clinician, she was admitted to numerous transvestite groups where she interviewed the men in detail concerning their feelings, desires, motivations, and problems encountered. She concludes that almost all transvestites view themselves as men. In a related study it was reported that most transvestites are married (Prince & Bentler 1972). Additionally, Feinbloom's personal impressions suggest that transvestites are not deeply disturbed. Another survey study of transvestites also supports her suggestion that these men are not typically disturbed (Bentler, Shearman, & Prince 1970).

CAUSES AND STRESSORS Many clinicians and sex researchers contend that transvestism is an acquired or learned behavior pattern. Ellis and Abarbanel (1973), for example, state that an invariable event in the early childhood of a transvestite is having been acidentally or intentionally dressed in female clothing. Another clinician, Stoller (1975) also maintains that many transvestites report that as children they were forced to wear girls' clothes. Unfortunately for this perspective, no one has shown what percentage of other males — not transvestites — were cross-dressed as children. Further, these clinical impressions do not reveal how many episodes of cross-dressing were necessary to sensitize or eroticize a child to clothing. Most important, these accounts do not explain why females are not transvestites — that is, eroticized to male clothing.

From a cultural viewpoint, it would appear that the development of transvestism requires more than just early cross-dressing. It would also seem necessary that the culture assign symbolic erotic value to female clothing. Indeed, Feinbloom contends that transvestism might disappear completely if our "stereotyped" clothing norms for males and females were to disappear.

From another perspective, psychoanalysts have in the past suggested that transvestism was a manifestation of the person's dual gender — male and female. This view is an extension of Freud's notion that we are all bisexual. Another related analytic argument proposes that transvestism is a symptom of an underlying emotional problem, that is, transvestism results from an underlying personality conflict about one's maleness.

TREATMENT METHODS The treatments of fetishism and transvestism are similiar, and so we shall briefly touch on therapy methods used with the latter deviation. So far, more research support exists for the effectiveness of behavior therapy (aversion therapy methods seem to be the treat-

The New York Historical Society

Edward Hyde (1609–1674), colonial governor of New York and New Jersey. It is claimed he often displayed himself publicly in female attire.

ment of choice) than for other methods (Marks and Gelder 1967). Psychotherapy in general, and psychoanalysis in particular, have offered few encouraging results in which specific symptoms were removed.

EXHIBITIONISM

The term *exhibitionism* was coined in 1877 by Lasègue, and its description and clinical symptoms have changed little since that time. Exhibitionism (known in slang as "flashing") refers to deliberate exposure of the genitals to females in situations where such exposure is inappropriate (Gebhard et al. 1965). The chief characteristic of the exhibitionist, in contrast to the normal desire to be admired sexually, is that exposure "represents the final sexual gratification without any intention of further sexual contact" (Mohr, Turner, & Jerry 1964).

Typically, the exhibitionist is a male between the ages of about 15 and 30. The majority of exhibitionists seem to be in their mid-twenties. In fact, this deviation is rarely committed by those over forty (Mohr et al. 1964).

Most clinicians report this typical picture: the exhibitionist exposes himself to a strange female, then may ejaculate at the scene, masturbate later, or simply enjoy the "psychic" release (Katchadourian & Lunde 1972). However, while the exhibitionist may feel great relief following the exposure, this may often be followed by a sense of shame and guilt (Chesser 1971).

A CASE OF EXHIBITIONISM

GEOFF

~~Larry~~ M is a 23-year-old white male who has been repeatedly arrested for indecent exposure. Typically, Larry cruises in his car near elementary or junior high schools. Upon seeing a group of girls playing near the street, he drives close by and stops, then asks them for directions. Usually one or two girls will come close to the auto. Larry keeps his penis covered with a city map; as soon as the girls are close enough to see him clearly, he opens the door of his car and removes the map, thus exposing himself. He experiences "psychic relief" and later masturbates in his home, thinking of his exposure and the girls' shock and alarm. He has been treated for four years with psychoanalysis, but his exposure incidents have not abated. Larry now faces a ten-year prison sentence if caught again.

CAUSES AND STRESSORS Although numerous accounts of exhibitionism have been written, here we shall briefly review only three etiological notions: the cultural view, the emotional stress view, and the psychoanalytic view. As with the etiological views of other sexual deviations, these are not substantiated by empirical data. In the main, most of the information about exhibitionism comes from anecdotal reports supplied by clinicians.

The *cultural view* suggests that factors in

certain cultures enhance the development of exhibitionism. Support for this suggestion comes from the observation that exhibitionism is much more common in certain countries. In the United States and in certain Western nations, for example, exhibitionism is a very common sexual offense; in fact, approximately one-third of all sexual offenses in Europe, the United States, and Canada involve indecent exposure (Rooth 1974). By contrast, exhibitionism is exceedingly rare in underdeveloped countries.

The discrepancy in the incidence of exhibitionism from country to country suggests that certain cultures such as ours eroticize nudity. Chesser (1971) notes that in many primitive cultures both sexes are scantily clothed, yet no one thinks anything about this form of "indecent exposure." Clearly, sexual motivation and orientation are strongly influenced by cultural pressures.

The *emotional stress view* suggests exhibitionism is a reaction to conflict or inadequacy experienced within the person's interpersonal environment. Witzig (1968), in a study of exhibitionist males, noted that many of his subjects were shy, had poor interpersonal skills in general, and often had poor sexual relationships with their wives. Exhibitionism would then be seen as a reaction to frustration caused by failures in interpersonal behaviors, fears about potency, and doubts about masculinity. Exposure is therefore a compensatory tactic.

The notion of compensation bears much resemblance to the etiology of exhibitionism as viewed by some psychoanalysts. For example, the psychoanalyst Otto Fenichel (1898–1946) stated that indecent exposure was a "reassurance against castration." According to orthodox analytic thought, exhibitionism is induced by the fear of castration and feeling of inadequacy to perform sexually.

TREATMENT METHODS The most common methods of treating exhibitionism involve three modes: psychotherapy, drug therapy, and behavior therapy. No data are available to demonstrate that psychotherapy effectively reduces exhibitionism, and so we shall focus on drug therapy and behavior therapy.

It is well documented that sex drive can be altered through drug therapy, specifically with hormones. Laschet (1973) reported cures of exhibitionists (27 cases) with the use of *cyproterone acetate*. This chemical acts essentially as an anti-androgen compound, thereby mimicking the female

hormone estrogen. The male injected with cyproterone acetate experiences a general diminution of
sexual arousal. Of course, major side-effects are to
be expected when chemicals or hormones are used
to control a specific sexual response. For example,
cyproterone would also markedly lessen appropriate sexual responses.

Behavior therapy has shown some promising
results in the treatment of exhibitionism, without
the risks evident in drug therapy (Serber 1970;
Wickramasekera 1972). Two types of behavior
therapy typically used are *systematic desensitization* and *aversion therapy*.

When applied to exhibitionism, systematic
desensitization involves three basic steps. First, the
subject is given training in deep skeletal musculature relaxation. This learned relaxation response is
believed reciprocally to inhibit anxiety and sexual
arousal. Second, the subject, with guidance from
the therapist, establishes a hierarchy of stimulus
situations that provoke genital exposure. The hierarchy ranges from the most exposure-provoking
situations to the least exposure-provoking stimuli,
with gradations of exposure-provoking settings
between the extremes. For example, in the case of
the exhibitionist Larry M., the most exposure-provoking situation was to encounter a group of
nonconsenting girls as they played together. By
contrast, the least exposure-provoking scene was
to stand before a group of adult males and females
whom Larry knew quite well. The final step is for the
subject to relax and imagine the least exposure-
provoking scene in his hierarchy. This procedure is
continued until he has imagined all exposure-
provoking settings while relaxed.

Numerous aversion therapy methods also
have been used to treat exhibitionists. One interesting and purportedly very effective aversion
technique is the *provoked anxiety method* developed by Jones and Frei (1977). As space limits a
complete description of this method, we will briefly
outline what they did. Working with 15 male
exhibitionists who had previously been resistant to
change, Jones and Frei followed this strategy,
which apparently induced great anxiety and subsequently led to cognitive changes and abatement
of genital exposure:

1. Each subject was undressed before a
   mixed-sex audience—the audience was
   composed of 5 to 12 people.
2. Each subject, while undressed, described
   his past exposure episodes and how he felt
   about them (there were a number of therapy sessions following this pattern).
3. Each subject was videotaped, and his undressing was played back at each subsequent session.
4. Each subject, while undressed, was asked
   questions about his exposure—how he felt,
   how his victim felt, and so on; an effort was
   made so that the questions were not critical
   and condemning.
5. Each subject was required to stand very
   close to the audience (4 to 5 feet) while
   actually exposing himself—most subjects
   reported that during actual exposure they
   stood at a much greater distance from the
   victims (about 12 feet).

Jones and Frei submit that they are unsure exactly
why their method has been effective. From self-
reports of the treated exhibitionists, however, the
procedure induced tension, shame, and disgust.
The role of provoked anxiety and its influence on
the abatement of exhibitionism needs to be further
explored before any rationale for the effectiveness
of this procedure can be offered.

VOYEURISM AND PEEPING

Voyeurism (scoptophilia) in general involves the act
of looking at a particular person to attain some
level of sexual gratification. Voyeurism is thus a
very broad term, including such things as watching
a stripper perform, looking at pornographic literature or films, and secretly watching a person
(peeping).

Peeping is a special case of voyeurism in
which a male, using Gebhard's words, "has no
legal right to be at the location from whence he
observes [her]" (p. 358). Almost all males are
voyeuristic to some extent, but since peeping
involves more risk, there are fewer peepers than
voyeurs. In this connection, another difference
between voyeurism and peeping is that peepers as
a group are highly delinquent in other ways
(Gebhard et al. 1965). Some females may indeed
be voyeuristic, but as yet no evidence suggests that
females engage in peeping.

CAUSES AND STRESSORS   Less has been written about voyeurism than about any other sexual
deviation we have discussed. Possibly one of the
reasons is that in certain settings voyeurism is
socially acceptable. Nevertheless, a few clinicians
have discussed conceivable causes of voyeurism

WHAT INFLUENCES OUR SEXUAL MOTIVATIONS?

Sexual motivation, to some extent, and sexual orientation, almost totally, are determined by learning. Since learning governs the object-choice of sexual behavior (the *orientation*), human beings are vulnerable to many idiosyncratic sexual deviations.

Sexual motivation, as Goldstein (1976) defines it, is the urge for sexual activity, such as masturbation and coitus. The term is often used interchangeably with *sex drive* or *sexual desire*. Since sexual motivation is conceived of as a drive, not a particular activity, it is generally thought to be more biologically determined than sexual orientation (Whalen 1966). Goldstein (1976) lists a number of variables that influence sexual motivation. We have added several studies to his list.

1. *Genotype*. It is possible that sexual arousal can be genetically manipulated in higher mammals. For instance, it is possible to breed rats that are apparently potent or frigid. Regarding humans, Chilton (1972) demonstrated that identical twins usually begin to masturbate at very similar ages, and engage in heterosexual activities at

similar periods in their life span. This is not the case for fraternal twins, suggesting that sexual motivation does have some genetic basis.

2. *Hormonal level*. Goldstein cites several investigations showing that hormones influence sexual motivation. Many researchers have argued that levels of androgen (a male hormone) are highly related to sex drive (Money 1961; Whalen 1966; Waxenberg et al. 1959).

3. *Hypothalamus and limbic system*. Evidence from animal studies suggests that the hypothalamus and limbic system are involved significantly with sexual motivation. In humans, an area or structure near the hypothalamus, the *amygdaloid nuclei*, also appear to be involved in sexuality. In 1939 Klüver and Bucy noted that, in animals, surgical removal of both temporal lobes of the brain—which are connected to the amygdaloid nuclei—causes heightened but indiscriminate sexual behavior, changes in sexual orientation (homosexuality), mouthing of objects, docility, etc. This bilateral lobec-

(Karpman 1963; Chesser 1971). Karpman, for example, suggests that voyeurism is a symptom of psychosexual infantilism. That is, achieving sexual gratification principally from peeping at a woman and then masturbating represents a very rudimentary level of sexuality. Voyeurism is therefore seen as an overcompensation for sexual immaturity.

The obscene phone caller or letter writer may share some of the same problems as the voyeur. Chesser (1971) proposes that these deviations are also compensatory sexual activities, representing the efforts of a man who has sexual desires, but no confidence in his interpersonal skills or sexual skills. (All these etiological notions are at best expressions of clinical opinion.)

TREATMENT METHODS Few systematic treatment studies dealing with voyeurism or peeping have been reported in the literature. Whaley and Malott (1971), however, cite one case in which *response cost* (a procedure in which a positive reinforcer is removed) was used with a voyeur. In

this instance, the reinforcer to be removed was a five-dollar bill. Whenever the thought of peeping emerged, the patient was to burn the money immediately. He made this remark to his therapist: "[That] was the most painful thing I ever did in my life. I burned up two five-dollar bills and that was enough. From then on, I stayed home and watched television" (p. 352). Beyond this single subject study, no systematic treatment procedures have been reported.

PEDOPHILIA

Pedophilia is a sexual aberration in which a child or young adolescent is selected as the sexual object. (The popular term is *child molesting*. If the child is a blood relative, the sexual deviation is called *incest*.) The child usually is between 8 and 11 years of age and is frequently acquainted with the pedophile (Mohr, Turner, & Jerry 1964). Although the child

tomy produces what is often called the *Klüver-Bucy syndrome.*

4. *Sight, hearing, smell, taste, and touch.* Goldstein (1976) cites studies noting the importance of sensory perceptions in sexual motivation. Many sensory events can indeed become associated with sexual arousal, and in some cases, as with fetishism or transvestism, may be substituted for a sexual partner.

5. *Previous sexual or erotic experiences.* If previous sexual experiences were reinforcing, that is, if they were pleasurable, these experiences will be attempted again. Some theorists insist that homosexuality and various sexual inadequacies are linked to negative sexual experiences or to guilt associated with sexual expression with the opposite sex. In this case, both sexual motivation and orientation might be affected.

6. *Age.* One elderly man commented on his and his wife's sex life now that they have reached old age: "It takes us all night to do what we used to do all night." Generally, sexual motivation and arousal in-

crease during puberty but then gradually decline after 30 or 35. Masters and Johnson (1966) note than in the older female (postmenopausal), vaginal lubrication decreases, and some pain may be experienced during coitus. In the older male, penile erection is slower, and erection may be sustained for a longer period without ejaculation.

7. *Cultural influences.* Goldstein states that laws and moral attitudes can affect sexual motivation. He mentions Winnick's *Godiva principle* (Winnick 1969), which states that we often become sexually attracted to activities and objects that are viewed as illicit, illegal, or immoral. Similarly, Strother Purdy (1972) refers to the phenomenon of being attracted to that which is forbidden as the "joys of iconoclasm." Purdy contends that in some cultures practices that hold great sexual interest and appeal are often taboo: incest, homosexuality, fellatio, cunnilingus, and others. In sum, the culture can program us to enjoy certain activities or it can taboo an act, which may increase its appeal.

victim usually is female, non-coital sex play occurs much more often than coitus, especially with children under 13. The pedophile may fondle, masturbate, or have oral-genital contact with the child.

CAUSES AND STRESSORS Gebhard and his colleagues at the Institute for Sex Research (Indiana University) noted that approximately two-thirds of the men they studied with this deviation were married. The pedophile, if there is a characteristic type, tends to be socially ineffectual and has a rather low frequency of sexual activity (Schofield 1965). Possibly he perceives children as less threatening and demanding than an adult partner. Gebhard also states that those men who choose very young children often are older men (50 to 60 years of age), who are unable to defer gratification until a more suitable partner comes along. Despite the gravity of his actions, the pedophile is often extremely guilt-ridden and moralistic. (Gebhard and his colleagues used the interview to collect most of their data and, as we

pointed out earlier, this technique has its weaknesses.)

In one of the rare experimental studies dealing with sexual arousal toward children Freund, McKnight, Langevin and Cibiri (1972) reported that normal males show some arousal to female children. When normal male adults were shown slides of isolated specific female body parts (the females ranging in age from 5 to 26), the researchers noted that greatest penile erection occurred when the subjects were observing body areas of the adult women. Yet Freund and colleagues also stated that there was significant penile erection even to very young girls. (It is unclear whether this study relates more to pedophilia or to voyeurism.) Beyond the investigation described above, meager research has been conducted in the area of pedophilia, and no single causal factor can be specified for this sexual deviation.

TREATMENT METHODS *Aversion therapy,* in particular covert sensitization, has shown encouraging results in the treatment of pedophiles (Marks 1976). Marks gives as an example of covert sensitization: "[A] pedophile might be asked to imagine himself masturbating a little boy who then proceeds to vomit all over both of them" (p. 276). While other investigators have also stated that covert sensitization may be helpful in diminishing pedophilia, there is yet no conclusive evidence that aversion therapy cures this deviation.

In other cases, *group therapy* and individual psychotherapy have been used with pedophiles. A few therapists report that group psychotherapy is the treatment of choice for pedophiles because through this method they learn to relate better to other people and to share their problems with those who can sympathize with their plight (Glover 1960; Kopp 1962; Mohr 1962).

SADOMASOCHISM

Sadomasochism is the broad term used to refer to a sexual deviation in which the individual derives sexual pleasure from inflicting or receiving pain. The terms *sadism* and *masochism* are joined together because many theorists contend that these sexual behaviors are always fused.

Sexual sadism refers to arousal by controlling or inflicting mild aversive stimuli on someone, typically a lover. Sexual masochism involves the opposite—receiving some gratification from being controlled or mildly hurt. Fantasy plays a significant part in mild sadomasochism. Thus, erotic excitement may be elicited by pretending to be tortured (or torturing), being bound or tied, or being somehow humiliated. These erotic scenarios are virtually always performed with consenting partners.

Sadism and masochism may best be understood if we think of these behaviors as falling on a continuum. For example, degrees of sadism range from gently scratching or biting one's lover prior to intercourse all the way to mutilation and torture. Most sadists and masochists, to be sure, deal principally in fantasy and do not engage in torturing people or receiving great pain.

Mild sadism and masochism are part of pre-coital rituals in many cultures. Choroti women spit in the faces of their lovers; Ponapean men bite off the eyebrow of their partner before intercourse; Trobriand Islanders bite each other till the blood runs; and Mbuti girls often severely beat their male partner prior to coitus. As Tripp (1975) remarks, these illustrations of sadomasochism represent "zesty" forms of the dominance-submissive theme often seen in pre-coital ritual.

At the extreme of sadism, however, is what we shall refer to as the *mutilation fetishist*. Chesser (1971) calls these persons *pathological sadists*. These individuals are clearly the most pathological of all persons discussed in this chapter, and should not be confused with sadomasochists. Typically the mutilation fetishist not only kills the victim, but also derives sexual pleasure from torturing him or her—actually carrying out the sadistic fantasy. Although mutilation fetishism is exceedingly rare, grisly mutilation crimes are occasionally reported. Virtually every large city has in its files cases of men, women, and children who have been brutally murdered. Several well-publicized mutilation killings have raised the question of how a person could develop such heinous motives.

CAUSES AND STRESSORS Neither the development of mild sadomasochism nor that of the more pathological sadism is understood. Information about sadomasochism has come mainly from clinical impressions and, in some cases, from anthropological studies. Evidence from other cultures tell us only that sadistic play may occur prior to lovemaking; we do not understand how or why it develops. Concerning pathological sadism (mutilations and sexual assaults), even less information is available. The new DSM-III lists "predisposing factors" of sexual sadism but the factors are not revealing. For example, it states that the sexual sadist, as a child, was exposed to an interpersonal environment that "stimulated" both aggressive and sexual feelings. More concretely, however, other clinical impressions have noted that the pathological sadist was, more likely than not, exposed to familial brutality and violence. If we examine the backgrounds of notorious sexual sadists, such as Ian Brady, we find that they had childhoods of unusual violence. (Brady was the sexual psychopath who tortured and killed a number of persons in the sensational "Moors murders.") Similarly, Albert De Salvo, the "Boston strangler," had a childhood filled with violence. As a child, De Salvo watched on many occasions as his mother was severely beaten by his father. Albert himself was severely whipped and recalls vividly the occasion on which his father knocked out his mother's teeth (Chesser 1971). Several members of the Manson cult, who engaged in mutilation rites, recall physically brutalizing childhoods. As one member stated, it became "exciting" finally to have a chance to control and brutalize someone else.

To further complicate this etiological picture, the proposed DSM-III states that sadism may coexist with other psychopathologies, such as sociopathy or schizophrenia. To conclude, we must again stress that the data dealing with sadomasochism are essentially retrospective. Although childhoods of familial brutality and severe rejection have been recounted by sadists, it seems likely that many individuals who are not sadists also had this sort of stressful environment.

TREATMENT METHODS Because mild sadism and masochism are usually engaged in privately between consenting adults, treatment is rarely sought. Pathological sadism, on the other hand, is not only a sexual deviation but, more importantly, a serious and violent crime. Incarceration without specific psychological treatment is the rule.

GENDER IDENTITY DISORDERS

The new DSM-III proposes a separate classification for psychosexual disorders involving questions of gender identity or role. Three specific disorders are gender identity disorder of childhood, gender identity disorders of adolescence or adulthood, and transsexualism. We will focus on the specific disorder of transsexualism—literally, crossing from one sex to the other.

TRANSSEXUALISM

Transsexualism is a disorder in which an individual persistently feels discomfort with his or her own anatomical sex. Such an individual may wish to undergo sex reassignment, often involving surgery and hormone therapy. Unlike the transvestite, who may have a blending of *gender identities* (male/female), the transsexual has a gender identity that is contrary to his or her anatomy (Money & Tucker 1975). The transsexual James/Jan Morris states:

> I was born with the wrong body, being feminine by gender but male by sex, and I could achieve completeness only when the one was adjusted to the other. (Money and Tucker 1975, p. 31)

The DSM-III suggests that transsexuals typically complain of being uncomfortable wearing clothes that correspond to their anatomical sex. The gender discomfort is often so extensive that the individual may have marked social and occupational problems. Furthermore, serious depression and suicide attempts may occur. Money and Tucker

(1975) relate the case of Robert Cowell who, because of his gender discomfort, later had surgery and became Roberta Cowell, a female. Cowell recounts that before the decision was made to undergo sex reassignment, he experienced profound depression:

> . . . the two possible solutions seemed to be either continuing with life in the certain knowledge that I was going to go on being desperately unhappy, or putting an end to it all. I envied the insane, who had at least escaped from reality. (p. 34)

CAUSES AND STRESSORS The etiological theories about transsexualism fall into the perspectives of psychology and biology. According to the DSM-III, transsexualism often develops in the context of a disturbed parent-child relationship. The absence of the father, coupled with close mother-son physical contact, has been suggested as a predisposing stressor for males who later assume a female gender identity. In a more common view, it is speculated that parents can condition their child in a gender role that is inconsistent with the child's anatomy. Finally, it has been suggested that the transsexual may have hormonal or biochemical dysfunctions. None of these theories is yet supported by firm evidence. Transsexuality has not been causally linked to central nervous system defects. Furthermore, no consistent parent-child relationship has been deduced.

On the other hand, there is some rather dramatic support for the role of learning in the establishment of gender, gained from the study of hermaphroditic babies (Money & Tucker 1975) and

Wide World Photos; UPI Photo

Dr. Renée Richards before and after sex reassignment.

sexual reassignment case studies. Regardless of the child's genitalia, chromosomes, hormones, etc., it appears that it is how the hermaphroditic child is brought up that matters. A child who is chromosomally a girl but who is raised and treated as a boy may develop a male *gender identity,* and "his" sexual orientation will be toward females. From this perspective, then, feelings of being a male or female can be learned.

Not all cases of sexual reassignment involve transsexuals, however. In the following case, described by Money and Tucker (1975), a surgical accident made sexual reassignment necessary for one of a set of identical boy twins. The case highlights the powerful role of learning.

A CASE OF SEX REASSIGNMENT WITHOUT TRANSSEXUALISM

A young farm couple took their sturdy, normal, identical twin boys to a physician in a nearby hospital to be circumcised when the boys were seven months old. The physician elected to use an electric cauterizing needle instead of a scalpel to remove the foreskin of the twin who chanced to be brought into the operating room first. When this baby's foreskin didn't give on the first try, or on the second, the doctor stepped up

the current. On the third try, the surge of heat from the electricity literally cooked the baby's penis. Unable to heal, the penis dried up, and in a few days sloughed off completely, like the stub of an umbilical cord.

[After the parents partly recovered from this horrendous event and the local doctors did not know where to turn next] . . . a plastic surgeon who knew of the Johns Hopkins program for helping hermaphroditic babies finally was called in as a consultant. He suggested the possibility of reassigning the baby as a girl.

[A] medical psychologist described the alternative to the parents. . . . [and explained that if] the child grew up as a boy, a plastic surgeon could graft skin from the child's belly to fashion a penis. [But] after this kind of operation the tissue of the artificial penis often breaks down, allowing leakage during urination, [and there is] danger of urinary and bladder infections. Another problem is that, since a skin graft penis has no touch or pain feelings, continuous care must be exercised to make sure that it does not become ulcerated by rubbing against clothing, or being bruised or squeezed. The most serious drawback, however, is that it has no sexual feeling and cannot erect.

On the other hand, if the parents stood by their decision to reassign the child as a girl, surgeons could remove the testicles and construct feminine external genitals immediately. When she was eleven or twelve years old, she could be given the female hormones that would normally feminize her body for the rest of her life. Later a vaginal canal could be surgically constructed so that her genitals would be adequate for sexual intercourse and for sexual pleasure, including orgasm. She would become as good a mother as any other woman, but only by adoption. (Money and Tucker 1975, pp. 93–94)

As it turned out, the child was sexually reassigned and raised as a girl. The case was followed closely by investigators, who noted that the child did indeed adopt a female gender identity. Thus, despite the child's biological maleness, the parents' commitment to raise her as a girl succeeded. This single case suggests strongly that behavior that is "feminine" and "masculine" is learned behavior.

TREATMENT METHODS   On the basis of available data, changing the gender identity of transsexual adolescents or adults is apparently very difficult. In fact, it may not be possible in most cases (Barlow, Reynolds, & Agras 1973). For the most part, sex reassignment seems to provide the most promising treatment; however, a longitudinal follow-up of those receiving reassignment has not been adequately investigated. Until these data have been collected and interpreted, it is too soon to evaluate sex reassignment as compared with counseling or behavior modification techniques. Possibly psychotherapy also may be required before and after sex reassignment.

Too little data are available to determine whether sex reassignment alleviates the psychological and social problems the person faced before surgery. After the sex reassignment, there are additional social problems of dealing with family, of telling others, or of others finding out. To be sure, professional guidance often is sought prior to and after sex reassignment. Although it may not be possible to alter gender identity, supportive therapy concerning self-acceptance is often undertaken.

SEXUALLY ABUSIVE BEHAVIORS

Under this category, we will discuss rape and incest, two major types of sexually deviant behaviors that involve sexual activity and often criminal assault. Rape, like the mutilation fetish, is a form of violent criminal assault expressed in a sexual way. Incest, which may or may not involve violence, is sexual behavior that violates deep cultural taboos. Although neither of these behaviors is listed in the DSM-III, they are nevertheless part of the overall picture of psychosexual deviation.

RAPE

Forcible rape is an assault on a woman in which physical force is used to accomplish coitus. (*Statutory rape* is the legal term for sexual relations with a minor, with or without force. If force is involved, then it, too, is forcible rape.)

The number of forcible rapes increased dramatically in the period between 1969 and 1974, and this trend is continuing. The increase over that five-year period approached 50 percent. The FBI in 1974 estimated that 55,210 women were forcibly raped, and yet this violent act is one of the most underreported crimes, primarily because of the victim's fear and/or embarrassment. Many rape victims also hesitate to report this crime for fear of unsympathetic handling of the case by police.

CAUSES AND STRESSORS   Many causes and motivational factors have been proposed as explanations for rape. Hatred of women, defense against homosexuality, admission into a subgroup of antisocials, desire for power, sadistic strivings, exaggerated masculine protest, and a reaction to sexual trauma during childhood or adolescence are just a few of the motivational or causal factors that have been offered. But none of these factors consistently turn up in the background of all rapists. What seems to be most clear is that rapists form a rather diverse group. If consistent or uniform statistics do exist for rapists, they really do not provide us with insight into the possible causes of this antisocial action. For example, two rather obvious uniform statistical generalities are that rapists are male and that they tend to be between 16 and 24 years of age. This tells us little. On the other hand, a few clinical studies and a few research investigations have attempted to reveal the backgrounds of rapists and suggest a sort of "rapist personality." Let us below briefly examine several of the pertinent studies.

The research of Abel, Barlow, Blanchard,

SUMMARY OF RAPISTS' CLINICAL HISTORIES
Table 11.1

Cited in Abel et al., *Archives of General Psychiatry*, 1977, 34.

RAPIST	AGE (YRS.)	NO. OF RAPES	EXTENT OF INJURY TO VICTIMS	OTHER INFORMATION
R1	23	1	Attempted to rape mother while extremely intoxicated, moderate injury to her	Denied having attempted rape of mother or other victim
R2	16	1	Threatened victim with knife, but no actual injury; mild force applied	Raped 1 year prior to measurements; 1 year of residential psychological treatment prior to measurements
R3	19	2	Mild force used; slapped victim's face & told her he would kill if she did not comply	Alcohol associated with 1 rape; IQ of 67
R4	14	2	Mild force only; attempted rape of 11- and 16-year-old girls	History of voyeurism; attempted rapes easily deterred
R5	25	2	Threatened 1 victim with gun; mild force used	Extensive history of exhibitionism; forced fellatio sometimes with girlfriend; history of head injury
R6	18	2 or more	Forced oral sex with 4- and 6-year-old girl and boy; mild force used	Male and female pedophiliac (victim either male or female); adult heterosexual arousal, history of voyeurism and exhibitionism; reported being "on drugs" at time of assaults; history of possible brain injury, extensive history of drug abuse
R7	51	2 or more	Extensive history of arousal to girls 12 years old or younger; mild to moderate force usually applied; attempted to kill 3-year-old child for fear of getting caught after sexually assaulting her	Transvestism, adult heterosexual and homosexual contact; reported his control of urges to force sex with young girls was extremely poor; psychiatric hospitalization 23 years before measures taken

Guild (1977) has provided us with a summary of the background and related behaviors of a sample of rapists. From inspecting Table 11–1, you can see that this sample of rapists varies widely in the extent of injury inflicted upon the victim. Some rapists, as Abel and his group suggest, are much more sadistic than other rapists.

From clinical observations, Cohen, Garofalo,

RAPIST	AGE (YRS.)	NO. OF RAPES	EXTENT OF INJURY TO VICTIMS	OTHER INFORMATION
R8	20	10 or more	Mild to moderate force used; forced anal intercourse and fellatio especially when intoxicated with alcohol	Extensive history of stealing, vandalism, poor social and work histories
R9	16	12	Moderate force used; only raped younger children, sometimes beat them before actual rape, extensive threats used	Raped boys or girls; IQ of 84, stole, poor social interactions, very aggressive in nonsexual areas as well
R10	17	20	Moderate-severe force; definitely preferred forced intercourse to mutually acceptable intercourse	Raped family members, males, females, young or old, many antisocial traits; IQ of 74
R11	25	30	Since 1972, extensive history of forced anal intercourse with women, definitely preferred forcing anal intercourse as compared with mutually enjoyable vaginal intercourse, moderate force used	History of voyeurism, adult heterosexual, rape always associated with patient's being intoxicated with alcohol; extensive fantasy life of raping women
R12	27	100 or more	Preferred teenage virgins; 4-year history of extensive contact with willing or unwilling teenagers; while intoxicated (alcohol) extensive harm to one victim, mild to moderate force used	History of exhibitionism; attempted to rape even when released on bond from rape charges within the month; extensive fantasies of raping
R13	35	100 or more	Severe force used, last victim spent 2 weeks in hospital recovering from injuries, bit victim's breasts, burned her with cigarettes, beat her with belts, switches, pulled out pubic hair; shoved poles into vagina; forced anal intercourse	Denied arousal to women without addition of sadistic cues; victims 20 to 50 years old; alcohol usually associated with forced sex; voyeurism by history

The Museum of Modern Art/Film Stills Archive

RASHOMON © 1950, Daiei. A traditional defense against a charge of rape, and one that today angers a good many people, is that the person accused of rape had in fact been seduced. Such a defense is explored in this film. Of course, there is no evidence that rape is a result of a victim's seductive efforts. It is a dangerous fantasy when men believe that women are aroused by sexual assault.

AGGRESSION AND AROUSAL
Figure 11.1

The gray line refers to aggression; the straight line refers to mutual intercourse. Note that sadists find aggression and sex erotic; rapists are in the middle, finding sex with aggression (rape) about as erotic as mutual intercourse; non-rapists, however, find mutual intercourse more erotic and report aversion to forcing themselves on their partners.

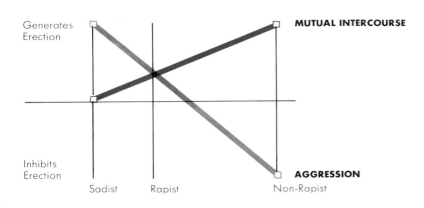

Boucher, & Seghorn (1975) suggest that there is a "history of prepubertal or postpubertal sexual traumata with older women" in the rapist's background. However, data gathered by means of retrospective reports are often biased and unreliable. Individuals are often unwilling or unable to remember the precise facts of events that happened many years ago. Notwithstanding, the clinical case history of Bill suggests that early sexual traumas may in some cases play a role in the development of the rapist.

A CASE OF RAPE

Bill was seen at age 14½. He was a large, well-built young boy, physically much bigger than his peers. In the summer following his tenth birthday, an attractive, married 20-year-old aunt took him into a picnic area, parked the car, and disrobed. He recalled being in a state of panic as she took his hands and placed them on her breasts and her genitals. He remembers that the feeling of fear was accompanied by excitement and sexual curiosity. That evening he lay awake until midnight at which time he arose, dressed, and walked to her house feeling once again both apprehensive and sexually excited. Although he knew she was home, she did not answer his knocking at the door, and, disappointed and angry, he went home. Following this, he found himself preoccupied with memories of the sexual experience. He became intensely aware of older women, mentally comparing their covered bodies with the memory of the nude body of his aunt. At this time he began to have sexually sadistic fantasies involving a female teacher and his mother. In the fantasy, he would steal into a house and find the teacher or his mother fully clothed. He would assault and undress them, make love to them, and then stab or shoot them. This fantasy, with little change in content, became a nightly masturbatory ritual at puberty, and at the age of 14½ he acted out the fantasy with a neighbor. She had offered him money to help her move furniture and as he followed her up the stairs to her home which was relatively isolated, he had the thought that she was sexually provoking him. He became angry and when they entered the home he put his arm about her throat and throttled her until she lost consciousness. He undressed her and had intercourse with her during which he recalls giving vent to a steady stream of obscenities and feelings of increased anger. He wanted to stab and cut her but instead reached for a metal lamp and beat her until he thought he had killed her. Bill did not recapture the memory of the early sexual experience with his aunt until the third year of his therapy, at which point there was a dream in which this aunt appeared. (Cohen et al. 1975, pp. 121–122)

Other theorists suggest that it is not sexual trauma (seduction) per se that plays a role in the development of a rapist, but rather defective parenting styles in general (Cohen et al. 1975; Goldstein 1976). For example, Cohen and colleagues note that this parenting style is common in the background of rapists: the father is weak, and the mother tends to be cold and a harsh but inconsistent disciplinarian. On the other hand, this parenting style (dominant mother/passive father) has been implicated in the development of numerous other abnormal behaviors, and so cannot be singled out as the sole causal factor. Finally, Amir

(1971) suggests a *social role theory* of rape. Amir believes that rape is often a means for confirming one's membership in a group that expects antisocial behavior from its members. It appears, then, that no single cause exists for rape.

TREATMENT METHODS Because most rapists are not repeaters, that is, they are not chronic rapists (Goldstein 1976; Schiff 1972), treatment effects of drug therapy, psychotherapy, and behavior therapy have not been thoroughly researched. However, particular drug compounds have been found to induce temporary impotency, as mentioned for exhibitionism. And a few researchers in Denmark have even resorted to castration for chronic rapists (Sturup 1961).

Psychotherapy and group therapy have also been attempted with rapists, but with inconsistent results. According to some clinicians, certain types of rapists are not suited for particular rehabilitative procedures. For example, rapists with strong sadistic components do not respond to therapy in general (Cohen et al. 1975).

INCEST

Incest has been taboo in virtually every society, and a number of explanations for this fact have been put forth. First, it has been held that the taboo results from religious beliefs about the wickedness of this behavior. Second, it has been held that incest could create deformed offspring, and thus the taboo resulted. Third, it has more recently been held (by Sigmund Freud, for one) that the incest taboo was an outgrowth of a natural proclivity toward this activity. For example, Freud stated that the incest taboo would be unnecessary if people did not wish to engage in this sort of sexual behavior. Freud pointed to the taboo as proof that all people had this desire. Recently, Summit and Kryso (1978) make a point similar to Freud's:

> The taboo has evolved . . . as a practical defense against a very natural experience. People who live together, who depend on each other for love and support, and who have intimate daily contact with each other will tend to develop sexual relationships with each other. (p. 239)

But if sexual feelings toward our own children are not extraordinary, why then is incest not more

LOLITA © 1962, Metro-Goldwyn-Mayer.
**James Mason here portrays a middle-
aged man who has a strong sexual
desire for his adolescent stepdaughter.**

widespread? In the following section we will attempt to answer this question.

Broadly defined, *incest* refers to the occurrence of sexual activity between blood relatives.
These activities can range from petting and fon-
dling to coitus and perverse sexual activities.
Additionally, incest may occur between a variety of
relatives: brothers and sisters, mothers and sons,
grandfathers and granddaughters, uncles and
nieces, and so on.

Estimates of the prevalence of incest are
contradictory. For example, surveys such as the
one by Morton Hunt (1974) suggests that father-
daughter incest is rare. Conversely, Henderson
(1975) proposes that this is one of the more
common varieties. These inconsistencies may arise
from the nature of questionnaires and interviews
and from people's unwillingness to disclose their
sexual behaviors. It is probably accurate to say
that Hunt's survey underestimated father-daughter

incest. This sort of incest would appear to be even
more underreported than rape, especially when a
very young child is involved. (The American Humane Associates estimate that at least 5,000 cases
of father-daughter incest occur each year, while
Summit and Kryso (1978) say the figure is more
like 36,000 cases a year.) What is a small child to
do if she is sexually abused? Whom does she tell or
confide in? Indeed, for the victim, this must certainly be a grave and stressful dilemma.

Apart from actual incest, fantasies about it
may be common. Werman (1977) suggests that
normals (as contrasted with adult psychotics) may
also have conscious incest fantasies. In part,
Werman proposed that excessive sexual stimulation in early childhood may predispose a person to
later have these sorts of fantasies.

CAUSES AND STRESSORS If sexual feelings
and fantasies concerning incest do exist in some

so-called normals, why then is incest not more widespread? First, most clinicians see incest not as normal, but as a reaction to particular stressors. For example, Summit and Kryso (1978) believe there are two basic characteristics of most incestual parents. The first characteristic is *lack of impulse control*. Summit and Kryso suggest that this characteristic may be either a result of transient stress or a trait of the individual. Lukianowicz (1972) reported that a sizable portion of incestuous fathers were alcoholic or antisocial. The second characteristic is *confusion of roles*—both the parent's and the child's. For example, Summit and Kryso note that many incestuous fathers relate to their daughters as if they were something other than their child:

> [He] relates to her more as if she were his wife: not the adult woman to whom he is married, but an imagined reincarnation of his bride-to-be. (p. 243)

The daughter too may accept a new role and respond to him in a more erotic manner (Summit and Kryso, 1978).

Other clinicians view the incestuous bond as a result of some family pathology (Gutheil and Avery, 1977). For example, overt incest between father and daughter has been suggested as a defense against the family's potential collapse (Gutheil and Avery, 1977). The sexual bond, it is speculated, somehow keeps the family together. Henderson (1975) claims that the wife often promotes the incestuous bond between husband and daughter to free herself from sexual obligations. The mother, according to Henderson's notions, subtly encourages the child to assume the role of sexual partner for the father.

Finally, we should bring out one other important point mentioned by Summit and Kryso: incest may have levels or degrees of expression. That is, a continuum of incest has been proposed. This continuum ranges from *incidental sexual contact* ("several mothers have told us of their erotic or orgasmic response to breast feeding . . . ") to *perverse* or *pornographic incest* that goes well beyond coitus with a child and that may include exploitation of the child by the parent (e.g., photographing the child or having the child act as an enticer to secure the parent additional sexual activities from other individuals).

TREATMENT METHODS Since incest is a criminal offense in most states, its discovery by the authorities may mean imprisonment, not therapy. When therapy is tried, it often is individual psychotherapy focusing on the father's alcoholism or other secondary problems that are thought to trigger incest. In other cases, treatment is directed toward the entire family. Unfortunately, the victims seldom receive the therapeutic support that the father is given. It was once common practice to remove the child (not the father!) from the home. For some unfathomable reason, it was held that her absence from the home would help the father and stop the incest. Although this relatively common procedure may well stop the incest, it treats the victim as culprit. More recently, efforts have been made to remove the father from the home instead. Finally, very little is known about the therapeutic consequences with an incestuous parent.

PSYCHOSEXUAL DISORDERS AND SOCIETAL REACTIONS

Several important points should be made about the psychosexual disorders and behaviors we have covered in this chapter. First, they engender differing degrees of societal disapproval and sanctions. Rape, pedophilia, and father-daughter incest, as well as pathological sadism, are not only sexual deviations but serious criminal offenses whose victims may suffer lasting psychological and physiological consequences. Second, persons with the same sexual deviation do not form a homogenous group. That is, a person's sexuality appears to be only one segment of his or her personality and behavior repertory; two exhibitionists, for example, apart from that deviation, may have little in common. Clinical data suggest also that sexual deviants differ in the amount of guilt or subjective distress they experience concerning their deviation. All told, sexual deviations do not represent a unitary condition with a particular type of underlying personality pattern. Furthermore, some individuals with sexual deviations feel satisfied with their particular sexual behaviors. Only additional research will reveal other important features of these people: How do their deviations affect their capacity to work? Their ability to love someone? How do these persons compare emotionally with those with conventional sexual behaviors?

SUMMARY

1. Much of the data available on the frequency of various sexual deviations have been collected through *controlled observations,* in particular, questionnaires and structured interviews. Methodological problems surround both these types of observations. With questionnaires, there are possibilities of both *sampling bias* (the sample is not representative of the population you wish to assess) and *low returns*. With interviews, several interviewers may be better than one in getting an individual to admit that he or she has engaged in an activity. This may create problems of reliability.

   Two of the earliest and most important sex researchers were Richard von Krafft-Ebing and Havelock Ellis. Krafft-Ebing compiled the first encyclopedia of sexual deviations, asserting that most ''perversions'' were a result of hereditary defects and presenting sexual deviations in their worse possible light. In contrast, Havelock Ellis was more tolerant of sexual deviations and advocated a more accepting and supportive attitude toward the sexual deviant.

2. Sexual deviations were defined by the DSM-II as those behaviors in which an individual's sexual interests are directed toward objects other than people of the opposite sex, toward sexual acts not usually associated with coitus, and toward coitus performed under bizarre circumstances. Homosexuality, however, was removed from the DSM lists of sexual deviations in the 1970s. The DSM-III lists three broad categories of *psychosexual disorders*: gender identity disorders, paraphilias (sexual deviations), and psychosexual dysfunctions.

3. *Fetishism* refers to a condition in which a person uses various objects (usually women's clothing) for sexual arousal or even in place of coitus. Various degrees of fetishistic behavior exist: some individuals use an object exclusively for arousal and orgasm; others incorporate their fetishistic item with coitus. It is likely that fetishistic behaviors are learned. The culture provides many possible objects that can be eroticized. Behavior modification methods appear promising as a treatment strategy.

4. *Transvestism* involves cross-dressing for the purpose of sexual arousal, relief of anxiety, or reduction of gender discomfort. Transvestites are almost always males. The specific cause of transvestism is unknown, but most clinicians believe that it is a learned reaction. Early cross-dressing in childhood is suggested as a precipitating event, perhaps tied in with the erotic associations of female clothing. Regarding treatment, behavior modification (*aversion therapy*) has been tried with some success. Generally, transvestites are not viewed as suffering from severe emotional disorders.

5. *Exhibitionists* expose their genitals to an unsuspecting individual, for the purpose of their own sexual arousal and gratification. The age of onset is between 15 and 30, with the middle twenties representing the peak age. Indecent exposure almost always is directed at a stranger. The etiological notions about exhibitionism are highly speculative and incomplete. Nevertheless, several notions have been offered. (a) The *cultural view* suggests that cultural factors enhance the development of exhibitionism. Particular nations do have higher rates than other nations, which suggests some cultural basis. Further, no explanation or discussion has been offered as to why there are cultural differences. Chesser suggests that the prohibition on nudity may have some bearing on exhibitionism. (b) *Emotional stress* may play a role in the development of exhibitionism. Individuals with poor interpersonal skills or other inadequacies, according to Witzig (1968), may be inclined to this reaction. Nevertheless, this emotional or frustration model of exhibitionism does not account for those who are frustrated or disturbed but do not expose themselves. Behavior modification may reduce exhibitionism. In particular, the *provoked anxiety method* appears promising.

6. *Voyeurism* refers to the act of looking at a person (usually a woman) to attain some level of sexual arousal or gratification. Peeping is illegal voyeurism—that is, the peeper has no legal right to be in the place where he is viewing the unsuspecting female. We noted that voyeurism has been said to represent a type of psychosexual infantilism. Other speculations state that the voyeur is shy and lacks appropriate heterosexual skills. Treatment methods for voyeurism and peeping have not been extensively investigated. In one instance, a behavior modification procedure called *response cost* was employed. Too little data are available to offer any interpretations of this treatment method.

7. The *pedophile* is a person who prefers children as sexual partners or uses children in various sexual activities. If the relationship exists between a child and an adult relative, the deviation is called *incest*. A few investigations have suggested that pedophiles are psychosocially immature, that they may have difficulties in normal heterosexual encounters and so turn to children. This notion is still unconfirmed, however. One investigation has suggested promising results in treating pedophiles with *aversion therapy*—covert sensitization in particular. This procedure involves imagining the sexual stimulus (a child), while at the same time imagining this stimulus in an aversive or repulsive situation. Group therapy has also been used with pedophiles.

8. *Sadomasochism* involves the connection between pain and sexual arousal. Sexual sadism can be mild or it can be severe and highly pathological, as expressed in the criminal behavior of the *mutilation fetishist* or *pathological sadist*. Sexual masochism is almost always mild. Fantasy plays a large part in mild sexual sadomasochism. This behavior is a part of pre-coital ritual in many societies. It is usually practiced between consenting partners. By contrast, the mutilation fetishist or pathological sadist is exceedingly disturbed and dangerous. These individuals may derive sexual pleasure by actually carrying out their sadistic fantasies. Speculation from clinical investigations suggests that these people, who resemble sociopaths, develop from a childhood of rejection and brutality. No systematic treatment was offered.

9. *Transsexualism* is a syndrome in which the person involved has a persistent sense of gender discomfort, a feeling that he or she is in the wrong body. Considerable anxiety and depression are related to the person's view of his or her anatomical sex. Often sex reassignment is sought, a very different motivation than that of transvestites. The causes are unknown. Speculation ranges from disturbed parent-child relations and false gender role treatment, to biochemical or hormonal dysfunctions. Evidence has confirmed none of these notions. Treatment effects are unclear. Sex reassignment is often the treatment of choice from the therapists' and client's view, but there are thus far no conclusive data on the adjustment of transsexuals after reassignment.

10. *Rape* is a violent crime in which force is used to have coitus with a woman. Rapists have been grouped into four categories: alcoholic type, assaultive type, amoral type, and explosive type. It is quite possible, however, that rapists do not form a homogenous group. The cause of rape is unknown, but some researchers and clinicians have offered these possibilities: rapists have deep-seated hatred for women; rape is a defense against homosexuality; and rape is a reaction to sexual seduction and trauma (by an older woman). Unfortunately, all these notions are unsupported by evidence other than a few case histories. Treatment for rapists has involved many methods—drug therapy, psychotherapy, behavior modification. Since the majority of rapists are not repeaters, the effectiveness of treatment strategies has not been extensively examined.

11. Incest is defined as sexual activity between blood relatives. Numerous varieties of incest exist, ranging from father-daughter incest to male cousin-female cousin incest. Little is known about the prevalence of incest between an adult (father) and a small child (daughter). Because of underreporting of this phenomenon, only a few questionnaire studies have attempted to provide us with estimates. Regarding the cause of in-

Major Forms of
Psychopathology
PART 2

cest, several speculative notions have been forwarded: the father may have lowered impulse control; the father as well as the daughter may experience role confusions; incest may be a pathological effort to bring stability to the family system.

RECOMMENDED READINGS

Barker-Benfield, G. J. *The horrors of the half-known life: Male attitudes toward women and sexuality in nineteenth-century America.* New York: Harper & Row, 1976.

Chesser, E. *Strange loves: The human aspects of sexual deviation.* New York: William Morrow, 1971.

Goldstein, B. *Human sexuality.* New York: McGraw-Hill, 1976.

McDermott, S. *Female sexuality: Its nature and conflicts.* New York: Simon and Schuster, 1970.

Meyer, J. *Clinical management of sexual disorders.* Baltimore: Williams & Wilkins, 1976.

Money, J., & Tucker, P. *Sexual signatures: On being a man or a woman.* Boston, Little, Brown, 1975.

HOMOSEXUALITY: ALTERNATIVE SEXUAL ORIENTATION

12

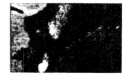

OVERVIEW In this chapter we will examine homosexuality, an alternative sexual orientation in which men and women are sexually attracted to members of their own sex. Until recently, homosexuality was considered a mental disorder and was classified by the DSM-II along with the sexual deviations discussed in chapter 11. However, because of new attitudes among mental health professionals, homosexuality has now been removed from the DSM classification of disorders. Only dyshomophilia—distress or unhappiness because of being homosexual—is now considered a disorder in the proposed DSM-III.

In the first part of this chapter we will look at the problems involved in classifying and defining homosexuality, variations in its occurrence, and other questions of background. The next two sections look separately at female homosexuality (lesbianism) and male homosexuality, in terms of incidence, individual characteristics, and suggested causes and stressors, both biogenic and psychogenic.

In the concluding section, various therapy methods for treating homosexuals who wish to change their orientation and those who wish supportive therapy will be discussed.

DEMOGRAPHICS		USUAL AGE AT ONSET	PREVALENCE	SEX RATIO
HOMOSEXUALITY		Early adolescence	Estimated at 2–5% of the population	Probably more common in males

SYMPTOM DESCRIPTION AND ETIOLOGY

In recent years, there has been pressure on the mental health profession to declassify homosexuality from its lists of mental disorders. Until the early 1970s, the DSM-II classified homosexuality as a mental disorder. Then in 1974, the American Psychiatric Association deleted homosexuality from the DSM-II. At that time, a new and more puzzling term was proposed in place of homosexuality: *sexual orientation disorder*. This term proved to be unsatisfactory, mainly because of the word "disorder." The result of pressure by professionals and gay rights proponents is that "homosexuality" and "sexual orientation disorder" are to be dropped from the new DSM-III. A late draft of the DSM-III states that the main reason for deleting homosexuality from its lists of mental disorders is that no scientific evidence has yet to emerge showing that homosexuals are impaired in their capacity to adapt. Moreover, the DSM-III suggests that homosexuality per se is not a psychopathology if the person accepts or is satisfied with his or her alternative sexual orientation, and exhibits no accompanying symptoms. A new term offered by the DSM-III in this connection is *dyshomophilia*.

DYSHOMOPHILIA

Accepting and being satisfied with one's homosexuality is critical, according to the new DSM-III. In fact, homosexuality may be considered pathological if the person experiences distress over his or her sexual orientation. *Dyshomophilia*, then, refers to a condition in which the person experiences distress and feels guilty or depressed because of his or her homosexuality. The clinical picture of dyshomophilia may be highlighted by anxiety, suicide attempts, and abuse of drugs and alcohol; these feelings and behaviors emerge after the person experiences homosexual urges or fantasies, or actually becomes involved in homosexual activity. Dyshomophilia, as the following case study illustrates, usually has its onset during early adolescence.

A CASE OF DYSHOMOPHILIA

Rob L. was 14 years old and was in the 8th grade at a private school when he was finally referred to a private clinical psychologist following his third suicide attempt. Prior to the suicide attempt, Rob had been very depressed and had mentioned that he might kill himself. After a short time in therapy, Rob acknowledged that he frequently had homosexual thoughts but later felt very depressed and guilty about these fantasies. He had engaged in mutual masturbation with one of his friends subsequent to the first fantasies, and the physical contact prompted his overwhelming feelings of shame.

The psychologist spent over five months with Rob and reported marked improvements in Rob's feelings of self-acceptance. This particular psychologist did not attempt to change Rob's sexual orientation, but rather made successful efforts to build up Rob's self-esteem. At last report, three years following the therapy, Rob says he no longer feels that his thoughts are dirty and perverted. His school record has improved dramatically, although he admits that a few of the students still ridicule him.

DEFINITIONS OF HOMOSEXUALITY

Homosexuality is difficult to define in mental health terms. Depending on the definition one employs, it is possible to contend that homosexuality is not statistically either very abnormal or deviant. If a definition of homosexuality is based not on physical contact but "intense emotional relations," then according to one of the earliest studies, half of all women would be considered homosexual (Davis 1929). Another question concerns the psychological health of homosexuals. Are homosexuals less emotionally stable than heterosexuals? There are some who assert that, regardless of the homosexual considered, all are emotionally disturbed. On the other hand, there are some who claim that homosexuals are healthier than heterosexuals. There is, of course, a middle position contending that psychopathology or emotional instability is independent of sexual orientation, whether heterosexual or homosexual. This middle position assumes that both homosexuals and heterosexuals can be emotionally healthy or emotionally disturbed. The new DSM-III, along with many psychologists, seems to take this middle position. The American Psychological Association stated in a recent meeting:

> Homosexuality per se implies no impairment in judgment, stability, reliability, or general social or vocational capabilities; Further, the American Psychological Association urges all mental health professionals to take the lead in removing the stigma of mental illness that has long been associated with homosexual orientation. (Conger 1975, p. 633)

The critical question remains: How is homosexuality to be defined? In an effort to avoid placing those interviewed into one of only two categories, Kinsey, Pomeroy, and Martin (1948) devised for their interviews a 6-point heterosexual-homosexual rating scale. A score of 1 indicated exclusive heterosexuality while a score of 6 indicated exclusive homosexuality. Kinsey's definition of homosexuality was based on those who scored 4 to 6 on the self-report scale. The assumption Kinsey made, and it still seems to be a useful one, is that some individuals are more homosexual or heterosexual than others. That is, he did not see homosexuality as an all-or-none phenomenon.

In contrast with Kinsey's self-report definitions of homosexuality, there exist conceptual definitions of homosexuality. In the conceptual definition, a clinician typically gives a few of the major characteristics he or she thinks represents this phenomenon. Here are four rather diverse definitions. As you will note, some definitions deal with more than sexual preference; some are judgmental rather than objective.

> . . . homosexuality may express fear of the opposite sex, fear of adult responsibility, a need to defy authority, or an attempt to cope with hatred or competitive attitudes to members of one's own sex; it may represent a flight from reality. . . . (Thompson 1964)

Marmor (1975) writes:
> [It] is restricted to persons with a strong preferential erotic attraction to members of their own sex. It implies the same spontaneous capacity to be aroused by members of one's own sex as heterosexuality implies in regard to members of the opposite sex. It is the preferential arousal pattern that is crucial in this definition, not the manifest behavior. (p. 1511)

And Tripp (1975) states:
> Homosexuality in all its variation always means that same-sex attributes have become eroticized, have taken on erotic significance.

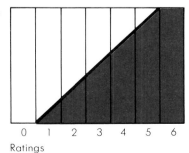

Based on by psychological reactions and overt experience, individuals rate as follows:
0. Exclusively heterosexual
1. Predominately heterosexual, only incidentally homosexual
2. Predominately heterosexual, but more than incidentally homosexual
3. Equally heterosexual and homosexual
4. Predominately homosexual, but more than incidentally heterosexual
5. Predominately homosexual, but incidentally heterosexual
6. Exclusively homosexual
(From Kinsey et al. 1948)

HETEROSEXUAL

HOMOSEXUAL

0 1 2 3 4 5 6
Ratings

Homosexuality represents such a broad spectrum of behaviors that it may be impractical to give a one- or two-sentence definition. The following section on variations of homosexuality supplies more evidence of this. Finally, let us note that homosexuality may be defined as a perception of the self as a homosexual. In a sense, this is what Kinsey did. As one clinician has said, "Anyone who says he or she is a homosexual, is."

VARIATIONS OF HOMOSEXUALITY   One of the major problems with defining homosexuality, or separating it from heterosexuality, involves the issue of *exclusiveness of sexual orientation*. Kinsey's research as well as several other investigations point out that there exist *exclusive homosexuals* and *inclusive homosexuals*. An exclusive homosexual is one who restricts sexual and erotic experiences to the same sex. Rarely will this person become involved with a member of the opposite sex. By contrast, the inclusive homosexual may have periodic encounters with both sexes. The inclusive homosexual is often given the controversial name *bisexual*. The name is controversial because some clinicians say we are all bisexual, so the name has no meaning: other clinicians say that it makes no difference if one has occasional encounters with the opposite sex: as long as the person has strong emotional or sexual experiences with the same sex, he or she is homosexual. In a sense, from this viewpoint, the notion of "bisexuality" is a euphemism. Nevertheless, there is no empirical evidence to suggest that we are all bisexual, or that those who have encounters with both sexes are any more or less homosexual than those who do not.

Another variable in homosexuality concerns the frequency or time one engages in homosexual activities. For example, *transitory homosexuality* (sporadic homosexuality) refers to one who for a short period of time engages in exclusive homosexuality, but later returns to heterosexual relationships. In other instances, transitory homosexuality may last for a considerable period. Those separated from the opposite sex, in prisons or boarding schools, for example, may engage in homosexuality. Later, when the opposite sex is available, heterosexuality usually emerges.

Thus, because there are levels or degrees of homosexual behavior, and because people may engage in both homosexual and heterosexual experiences at various times in their lives, no simple definition exists.

ONSET AND FREQUENCY OF OCCURRENCE

No firm evidence is available about the onset of homosexual orientation. Much of the information about the time of onset comes from clinical cases, which may be a poor source because many people may not seek help with sexual orientation problems. If we relied on clinical evidence, we would assume that homosexuality had its onset or became a problem to the individual during adolescence or early adulthood, simply because children virtually never seek help for homosexuality. Nevertheless, two types of onset patterns have been suggested. First, there are individuals who believe that they were homosexual from very early childhood. For example, as an adult, the person may recall that he or she had erotic feelings for someone of the same sex. Further, some adults recall that as children they had a different *gender identity*—a feeling that they shared the behaviors, attitudes, and values of the opposite sex. Jan Morris, the transsexual, recalls that as a child (then a young boy), he would have preferred to be a little girl. Of course, we have emphasized that such retrospective accounts may be highly unreliable.

The second type reports that he or she did not have homosexual feelings until late adolescence or adulthood (although they may recall feeling in childhood as if they were members of the opposite sex). The "late onset" variety seems to be much more common in female homosexuals than in males. Although many lesbians report that they felt they were homosexual from early childhood, the lesbian more often discovers her sexual orientation in late adolescence. (Another distinction should be made between *late onset* homosexuality and *transitory* homosexuality. As we mentioned earlier, transitory homosexuality often occurs under stress or when the opposite sex is not available. Transitory female homosexuality is very high among adult female prisoners, for instance, yet it would not be classified as late onset homosexuality.)

Significant problems exist in attempting to specify the number of people who have this alternative sexual orientation. Determining the frequency is a problem because of the varying definitions of homosexuality, the varying age of onset, and certainly, the reluctance of many people to admit their alternative sexual orientation to a researcher. We will never know exactly. But estimates are another matter, for surveys abound.

Summarizing various surveys (Kinsey et al. 1948, 1953; Hunt 1974), it can be estimated that approximately 25 percent of males and 15 percent of females have had *some* homosexual contact. But only 3 percent of the males and 2 percent of the females older than 15 have been categorized as exclusive homosexuals. British studies have reported similar results. Schofield (1965) claimed that approximately 5 percent of men and 2 percent of women were homosexual.

Another important point about homosexuality was raised by Feinbloom (1976). She observes that the definition and incidence of homosexuality rarely takes into account, "those people who desire and prefer those of the same sex but for some reason are unable to act upon those desires" (p. 11). In this connection, Marmor (1975) suggests that mature women are permitted by society to be "asexual," as evidenced by the higher rate of unmarried women. He concludes from this unequal rate that

> . . . large numbers of women who might otherwise be driven by their heterosexual aversions into homosexual patterns are able, instead, to take refuge in lives of no sexual involvement at all. (p. 1516)

Finally, the statistics on the incidence or frequency of homosexuality cannot take into account those who, although engaging in heterosexual activities (coitus), fantasize about homosexual involvement.

PSYCHOPATHOLOGY AND HOMOSEXUALITY

One of the most debated features of homosexuality is its association, if any, with mental illness. Are homosexuals as a group, inferior, no different, or superior to normals on certain mental health criteria such as neuroticism, depression, happiness, or psychophysiological disorders? We will cite a few studies that attempt to deal with this question, but we must be extremely careful in evaluating the data that will provide answers. For one, the differences found between homosexuals and heterosexuals in a given sample may not be representative of all homosexuals or all heterosexuals because of sampling bias. For another, the psychometric tests used to detect "mental illness" or mental health are not highly valid. Finally, homosexuals may report psychiatric problems that originate because of the

Homosexuals are becoming more open about their orientation.

rejection by a heterosexual society of the homosexual life style, not because of some inherent defect in their personalities.

Early sex research involved mainly descriptions and case histories. During the 1940s, pioneering empirical survey studies of sexual behavior were conducted by Kinsey, Pomeroy, and Martin (1948). The Kinsey studies were the most elabo-

Lee Trail/Black Star

Cary Wolinsky/Stock, Boston

rate surveys conducted on the incidence of homo-sexuality, yet these investigations did not attempt to assess the mental health or psychopathology of those with alternative sexual orientations. One of the first studies that did attempt to assess the problems and stresses of being a homosexual was conducted by psychologist Evelyn Hooker at the University of California at Los Angeles. During the 1950s, funded by a grant from the National Institutes of Mental Health, Hooker interviewed in depth hundreds of homosexual males. Her inter-views reveal that many were highly troubled and tormented by others' reactions to their homosexu-ality. Mainly, these homosexuals were distressed by the fact that they could find no one to talk to about their problem. Later, Hooker (1958) under-took to show that on the basis of projective techniques, clinicians could not differentiate be-tween the responses of homosexuals and hetero-sexuals. In another landmark study on homosexu-ality, Irving Bieber (Bieber et al. 1962), a psychoanalyst, headed up a project to examine the background and emotional stability of homosex-uals, as well as the causes of homosexuality. This project was funded by the Society of Medical Psychoanalysts, which provided the services of 77 New York psychoanalysts. From the information gathered by these analysts in interviews with more than 100 homosexual males, the basic conclusion was that male homosexuals had a profound fear of heterosexuality. In particular, they feared female genitals and coitus. Bieber's group also claimed that disturbed parent-child relationships were seen in the background of almost all the homosexuals studied. In a similar investigation conducted by Harvey Kaye, another New York psychoanalyst, female homosexuals were also said to have had disturbed early childhood experiences (cited in Wyden & Wyden 1968). Several criticisms of the Bieber study, however, were listed by Wyden and Wyden (1968):

1. Those homosexuals studied did not repre-sent most homosexuals—e.g., all were New Yorkers, and all were under treatment by a psychoanalyst (most homosexuals do not seek treatment).
2. Many families conform to the stereotype homosexuality-inducing family, but do not produce homosexuals. That is, many chil-dren have "close-binding, intimate" mothers as well as detached fathers, yet become heterosexual.
3. The Bieber study relied on retrospective memories of childhood.

RADCLYFFE HALL ON LESBIANISM

Pacing restlessly up and down her bedroom, Ste-phen would be thinking of Angela Crossby—haunted, tormented by Angela's words that day in the garden: 'Could you marry me, Stephen?' and then by those other pitiless words: 'Can I help it if you're—what you obviously are?'

She would think with a kind of despair: 'What am I in God's name—some kind of abomi-nation?' And this thought would fill her with very great anguish, because, loving much, her love seemed to be sacred. She could not endure that the slur of those words should come anywhere near her love. So now night after night she must pace up and down, beating her mind against a blind problem, beating her spirit against a blank wall—the impregnable wall of non-comprehen-sion: 'Why am I as I am—and what am I?' Her mind would recoil while her spirit grew faint. A great darkness would seem to descend on her spirit—there would be no light wherewith to lighten that darkness.

She would think of Martin, for now surely she loved just as he had loved—it seemed like madness. She would think of her father, of his

In a more recent replication of the Bieber study, Evans (1969) developed a 27-item questionnaire, adapted from the questions originally used by Bieber; Evans questioned a group of 143 male homosexuals (from a homosexual organization in Los Angeles) and 142 male heterosexuals. On the basis of their responses to the items, Evans con-firmed most of Bieber's findings. These were a few of the most prominent conclusions:

1. Homosexuals more often described them-selves as being frail and clumsy as chil-dren—less athletic.
2. Homosexuals more often reported being afraid of physical injury.
3. Homosexuals more often reported their mothers as being "puritanical, cold toward men . . . " and seductive.
4. Homosexuals more often reported (retro-spectively) that their fathers spent little time with them, discouraged masculine attitudes and activities; they were more aware of hating their fathers. (Evans 1969, pp. 130, 133)

comfortable words: 'Don't be foolish, there's nothing strange about you.' Oh, but he must have been pitifully mistaken—he had died still very pitifully mistaken. She would think yet again of her curious childhood, going over each detail in an effort to remember. But after a little her thoughts must plunge forward once more, right into her grievous present. With a shock she would realize how completely this coming of love had blinded her vision; she had stared at the glory of it so long that not until now had she seen its black shadow. Then would come the most poignant suffering of all, the deepest, the final humiliation. Protection—she could never offer protection to the creature she loved: 'Could you marry me, Stephen?' She could neither protect nor defend nor honour by loving; her hands were completely empty. She who would gladly have given her life, must go empty-handed to love, like a beggar. She could only debase what she longed to exalt, defile what she longed to keep pure and untarnished.

The night would gradually change to dawn; and the dawn would shine in at the open win-dows, bringing with it the intolerable singing of birds: 'Stephen, look at us, look at us, we're happy!' Away in the distance there would be a harsh crying, the wild, harsh crying of swans by the lakes—the swan called Peter protecting, defending his mate against some unwelcome intruder. From the chimneys of Williams' comfortable cottage smoke would rise—very dark—the first smoke of the morning. Home, that meant home and two people together, respected because of their honourable living. Two people who had had the right to love in their youth, and whom old age had not divided. Two poor and yet infinitely enviable people, without stain, without shame in the eyes of their fellows. Proud people who could face the world unafraid, having no need to fear that world's execration.

Stephen would fling herself down on the bed, completely exhausted by the night's bitter vigil.

From the Well of Loneliness, by Radclyffe Hall. Copyright © 1928 by Radclyffe Hall. Copyright renewed 1956 by Una Lady Troubridge, Executrix of the author.

The major conclusions of both Bieber and Evans' research were that homosexuality represents *pathological heterophobia,* or fear of the opposite sex. However, neither study shows that homosexuals are more pathological than heterosexuals on dimensions other than sexual orientation. Weinberg and Williams (1974), using a large sample of 1,057 homosexuals, found that on a questionnaire, male homosexuals reported being less happy and having less faith in others, compared with a large sample of heterosexual males. But on more psychiatrically related criteria, self-acceptance, and psychophysiological reactions, there was little difference between the homosexual group and the heterosexual group. In a study of 57 lesbians (not in therapy) and matched controls, Saghir and Robins (1973) also found little if any difference between female homosexuals and female heterosexuals. The Saghir and Robins study did find more evidence of depression and suicide attempts among the lesbian group. But Wilson and Greene (1971) found that heterosexuals scored higher on neuroticism than did a matched group of homosex-uals. Still another study noted that 84 nonpatient female homosexuals, when compared with matched heterosexuals, had lower scores on depression, submission, and anxiety. Moreover, the lesbians were more tender-minded than their heterosexual counterparts (Siegelman 1972).

To conclude this section let us try to resolve these conflicting results, or at least give a possible reason why different researchers produce conflicting evidence. First, as we noted at the outset, there is no agreed-on definition of homosexuality. Similarly, researchers cannot agree on sample definitions—how do we select a representative group of homosexuals (Morin 1977)? In fact, according to Morin, those who identify themselves as ''gay'' do not consider themselves ''homosexual.'' Morin writes:

> The term *gay,* like the terms *black, Chicano,* and *woman,* connotes a value system as well as designates group membership. *Gay* is proud, angry, open, visible, political, healthy, and all the positive things that *homosexual* is not. (p. 633)

Until problems of definition and sampling are resolved, conflicting findings will continue to be common. Based on these conflicting data, no absolute statements can be made about a relationship between homosexuality and psychopathology.

LESBIANISM (FEMALE HOMOSEXUALITY)

A *lesbian,* as Rosen (1974) defines the term, is a woman who is motivated in adult life by a primary erotic, psychological, emotional, and social attraction to and interest in women. This particular definition, a rather broad one, would indeed swell the incidence of lesbianism beyond what Kinsey reported. Charlotte Wolff is also committed to the view that lesbianism is more than just sexual contact between women (Wolff 1971). She asserts that lesbianism is prompted by an "emotional disposition" that results in intimate physical contact between females.

A CASE OF LESBIANISM

I was never told anything about sex. I heard other girls talking about it. When I was thirteen my mother came to me and told me about menstruation and I was horrified and thought that it wouldn't happen to me. I remember crying my eyes out. I didn't want to think that I was going to be the same as everybody else. When it did happen I kept it dark for as long as I could. I was terribly sensitive over it and most embarrassed in case anyone noticed that anything was wrong. The other girls at school would get themselves excused from games and gymnastics when they had their periods, but I would never admit to it. I was disgusted by it. I don't know why, but I have never liked babies, and the way people speak about having children, it has always seemed distasteful to me. My mother made me feel rather guilty about sex, because she would never talk about it. She would never say anything at all risqué in front of me. She was very much obsessed with me. I couldn't have a letter without her wanting to know who it was from, and what was in it. She was always very possessive.

I never went out with boys at all. I have never felt the need—it's just my makeup, I can't help it. I didn't have any kind of sexual experience, apart from the incident at school, until I was about twenty-three, when I met a girl and started an affair. Her mother was dying of cancer and I was sympathetic and that's how it started. We went away on a holiday together. Eventually we lived together, then after five years she got married. I was totally disgusted and very upset at the time, as I had no idea that she was bisexual. I didn't realize for a long time that she was going out with a man. (Wolff 1971, p. 104)

INCIDENCE OF LESBIANISM

The literature on female homosexuality, including case or clinical studies, national surveys, and a few anthropological investigations, has one glaring inconsistency: some investigators suggest that there are more lesbians than male homosexuals; others report the opposite. One long-time critic of the Kinsey studies, the psychiatrist Edmund Bergler, asserted that the lower incidence of lesbianism reported by Kinsey was a consequence of one major but subtle error: male homosexuals habitually overplay their sexual orientation. In other words, according to Bergler (1967), male homosexuals are more open and overt about their preferences, whereas lesbians habitually underplay and almost never flaunt their sexual orientation. Also in contrast to Kinsey, Hite (1976) reported a greater incidence of female homosexuality than did Kinsey. Yet anthropological and cross-cultural studies, in the main, suggest that lesbianism in most societies still is much rarer than male homosexuality.

But as we noted earlier, homosexuality in general is difficult to assess and define because researchers use different assessment procedures. Also, researchers select different samples of women. A particular researcher may question or test college women. Another may print a questionnaire, for women to fill out and return, in a magazine designed principally for men (a so-called "stroke" publication). Still another may conduct

Wisconsin Center for Film and Theater Research

THE CHILDREN'S HOUR © **1962, United Artists. This film, taken from a 1934 play by Lillian Hellman, concerns itself with** the social treatment received by two women who are perceived as being lesbians.

interviews based on a random sample of females. Certainly, the results of any questionnaire or test concerning incidence of lesbianism would be in part a function of the sample one was using. The exact frequency of lesbianism, therefore, cannot be known, given the problems of definition, levels of homosexuality, failure to disclose one's feeling, and so forth. At best we can say that its frequency is roughly equal to that of male homosexuality, between 2 and 5 percent.

CHARACTERISTICS OF FEMALE HOMOSEXUALS

There is no characteristic lesbian just as there is no characteristic heterosexual woman. Some common behaviors are often reported, and some false notions still persist about lesbians.

Female homosexuals, just like female heterosexuals, vary widely in physical appearance and mannerisms. The stereotype of a lesbian, a "butch" female who is grossly masculine, has short hair, and dresses in men's clothing, is very exaggerated and outdated. The background of lesbians is diverse, suggesting that there are many ways in which a person can develop her alternate sexual orientation. But aside from the diversities, several studies have examined the attitudes and feelings of *samples* of lesbians. When these are contrasted with heterosexual comparison groups, a few differences emerge.

Rosen (1974) studied a sample of 26 lesbians not in therapy. Three interesting attitudes were revealed about how these women perceived their mothers and fathers, how they saw men and women in general, and how they felt about homosexuality. This group viewed their fathers, mothers, and women as dominant, warm, kind, and loving, but they viewed men as being dominant, cold, punitive, and not loving. Concerning their feelings about homosexuality, approximately 20 stated that it was morally good, psychologically healthy, and physically statisfying. In this connection, it is interesting that the frequency of orgasm for female homosexuals is greater than for heterosexual females (Kinsey, 1953).

Karlen (1971) also gives us a rather general

DIFFERING ATTITUDES AND EXPERIENCES OF WOMEN

A study by Gundlach and Riess (1968) contrasted 226 self-identified lesbians with 234 heterosexual females. The results reveal some interesting differences in the feelings, attitudes, and experience of these two groups of women.

ITEMS	FEMALE HOMOSEXUALS (N = 226)	COMPARISON GROUP (N = 234)
ATTITUDES ABOUT MENSTRUATION		
1. Subject felt resigned about first menstruation	29%	13%
2. Subject felt grown up about first menstruation	23	42
3. Subject felt more attractive in body after first menstruation	10	30
4. Subject felt resentful or ashamed about body after first menstruation	23	7
TEEN-AGE SOCIAL BEHAVIOR		
1. How did you spend your time during your teens? —Socializing in mixed groups	18%	41%
2. —With boys	10	22
3. There was no or hardly any dating	56	25
4. Did you hug and kiss during high school dating with many boys or with a steady boyfriend?	37	54
5. Subject went beyond hugging and kissing in high school dating	36	47
6 Subject had intercourse during high school dating	12	14*
ADULT SEXUAL ATTITUDES AND RELATIONSHIPS		
1. What are your feelings about your femininity as an adult?		
a. decidedly feminine	12%	43%
b. more feminine than masculine	25	41
c. a little of both	40	16
d. more masculine than feminine	27	1
e. decidedly masculine	2	0*
2. Capacity to have orgasms:		
—easily	58	42
—sometimes or rarely	33	45
3. a. You can have sex without love	27	27*
b. You can have sex only with person you love	64	64*
c. You can love without much sex	31	19
4. Defloration is a promotion into womanhood	6	25
5. How did you feel when the lover relationship ended?		
a. as if a piece of me were torn off	44	17
b. suicidal	16	4

but accurate description of a lesbian pattern:
> A significant number of women have heterosexual marriages, get divorced, and then begin homosexual involvements. Lesbianism remains primarily an activity of single women, and to a lesser degree of the divorced and widowed. (p. 544)

It is also widely held that lesbians are less promiscuous and have more lasting relationships than do

	ITEMS	FEMALE HOMOSEXUALS (N = 226)	COMPARISON GROUP (N = 234)
ADULT SEXUAL ATTITUDES AND RELATIONSHIPS (cont.)	6. a. Subject had intercourse with a male	75%	94%
	b. But without climax	42	9
	7. Subject was		
	a. object of rape or attempted rape	31	21
	b. at age 11 or under	13	3
	8. Subject had sexual contact or caresses with a female	98	51
	9. Subject was married at one time	29	79
	10. Time with male partner		
	—1 to 9 years	21	48
	—10 or more years	12	40
	11. Time with female partner		
	—1 to 9 years	66	2
	—10 or more years	17	0
	12. Subject had children of her own	20	64
SOCIAL RELATIONS BEFORE PUBERTY	1. Before C.A. 12, played mostly with girls	25%	42%
	2. Before C.A. 12, played mostly with boys	31	9
	3. Who were your *real* friends?—Girls	57	75
	4. Who were your *real* friends?—Neither boys nor girls	18	7
	5. a. Subject was found in sex play before C.A. 12	36	27*
	b. A big fuss was made over the discovery	19	12*
	c. Subject's sex partner was male	27	19*
	6. Subject was known as a tomboy	78	48
	7. Before menstruation, subject wanted to be a boy	48	15
	8. Subject excelled in athletics	54	29
	9. Subject idealized or wanted to be like a female teacher	35	16
	10. Subject did not want to be like father	26	15
	11. Don't remember or didn't have sexual attraction to a male before menstruation	69	45
	12. Don't remember or didn't have sexual attraction to a female before menstruation	38	84

*All differences except those marked with * are significant at least at the .01 level

their male counterparts. Kinsey noted that 71 percent of the female homosexuals interviewed reported that they had restricted their sexual contact to a single partner. This is clearly not the case for male homosexuals.

CAUSES AND STRESSORS

There are two broad categories of theories about the development of lesbianism. (1) *Biogenic theories* include all the viewpoints arguing that female homosexuality is induced by biological factors such as hormonal imbalances, genetic error, or other unspecified constitutional influences. (2) *Psychogenic theories* include all the viewpoints arguing that female homosexuality is induced by special environmental circumstances.

BIOGENIC THEORIES The early sex researchers believed that sexual deviations, including female homosexuality, were biologically caused. Mangus Hirschfeld, Krafft-Ebing, Havelock Ellis, and most other pioneering sex researchers of the late 1800s and early 1900s considered lesbianism a biological defect. In recent years, various research efforts have attempted to show a link between biological factors and lesbianism. Most of these biological studies have focused on showing a correlation between hormones and sexual orientation, in particular, the presence and excess of male hormones. Margolese (1970), for example, states that a component of the male hormone testosterone (androsterone) found in high concentrations in either sex will cause those persons to have a sexual preference for females. Loraine and colleagues (1971) suggest that testosterone is found in higher

concentrations in female homosexuals than in female heterosexuals. Other studies also have found higher concentrations of testosterone in the urine of lesbians compared with heterosexual females (Griffiths et al. 1974; Loraine et al. 1970). Later, plasma testosterone levels also were linked to lesbianism (Gartrell et al. 1977). For example, Gartrell and associates selected samples of 21 homosexual females referred by a local homophile organization and 19 heterosexuals (matched by age, general health, nutrition, external genitalia, menstrual functioning, etc.). Gartrell then measured the concentration of plasma testosterone in each group. The essential findings were these: testosterone concentrations averaged 38 percent higher in the homosexual group than in the heterosexual group. Further, the homosexual women tended to show higher levels of testosterone if they were older, while the older heterosexual women showed lower levels of this hormone.

Interpretations of hormonal studies must be evaluated with great prudence because of the interaction between hormones and behavior: (1) Lesbianism may cause changes in plasma testosterone concentrations. (2) Factors such as stress, sleep problems, various life styles, etc., might

**TESTOSTERONE
LEVELS**
Figure 12.2

Plasma testosterone and age in homosexual and heterosexual women (From Gartrell et al. 1977)

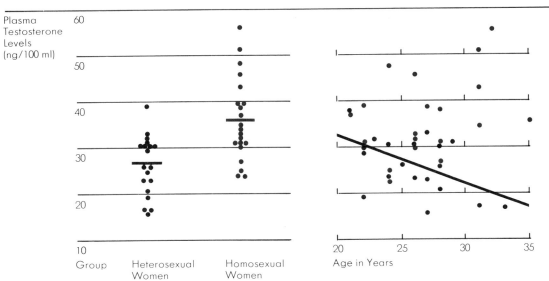

affect this hormone (Kreuz & Rose 1972). That is, plasma testosterone alterations may be a result of certain behaviors or stressful encounters: or heterosexuality may be stressful and result in lowered levels of plasma testosterone. For example, in male rhesus monkeys, stress or loss of status results in a significant drop in testosterone levels. Yet if these monkeys are placed near a seductive female rhesus, testosterone levels increase (Rossi 1978). This example, as well as many others in behavioral endocrinology, shatters the old model that hormones only affect behavior, not the other way around. Behavior can, to be sure, affect hormonal secretions. These findings do not permit the conclusion that plasma testosterone abnormalities cause lesbianism. It is hoped that further research will throw more light on the complex interaction of behavior and hormones.

PSYCHOGENIC THEORIES   The evidence so far fails to support the biogenic explanation of either female or male homosexuality. Apparently more important are such factors as *gender assignment*—how the child is reared, as a girl or boy—parental expectations, and possibly special environmental stressors. The three psychogenic or environmental positions we will examine are *psychoanalytic theory*, *pathogenic family theory*, and *learning theory*. There is, however, much overlap within these positions.

Psychoanalytic Theory. Psychoanalytic theory has dealt more with male homosexuality than with lesbianism. It is generally acknowledged that Freud reflected the attitudes of his society and times especially regarding women and human sexuality in general. His conception of sexuality—of sex drives—was tied directly to maleness; Freud held that to be "sexual" was essentially to be masculine. Posthumously, Freud has been criticized for his neglect of female sexuality and his phallicentric notions. But he did admit his shortcomings in this respect; in 1920, he wrote that he was mystified about lesbianism and how it was caused. Nevertheless, since Freud's time, but based essentially on his model of male sexual identity and male homosexuality, a few analysts have attempted to fit lesbianism into psychoanalytic theory. Rather than discussing fully how analytic theory would account for female homosexuality, we will rely on the analytic thought of Bieber (1962). As we mentioned, Bieber believed that homosexuality is a defense against fear of heterosexuality. Male homosexuals fear and hate women (*heterophobia*),

Ellis Herwig/Stock, Boston

Homosexual men and women are becoming politically active in an effort to counter the social disapproval.

and so they eroticize other males. Bieber concluded that male homosexuality is a result of disturbed parents: the mother was "close-binding" and seductive, the father detached and somewhat hostile. The development of lesbianism would represent the exact inverse of the male constellation: the father "close-binding" and seductive, and the mother rejecting and hostile (Riess 1974). The psychoanalytic position, then, sees the female child as becoming fixated on the mother because of a lack of warmth and affection from her. In a sense, this *mother-deficit* creates in the female child an overcompensated desire for a mother; in adulthood, this woman now seeks another woman who is, perhaps at an unconscious level, a sort of mother-substitute. Psychoanalytic investigators have yet to confirm these suppositions. Although Bieber and Evans' studies do lend some support to the notion that male homosexuality may be pathological heterophobia, investigations that deal specifically with lesbianism and psychoanalytic accounts have yet to be conducted.

Pathogenic Family Theory. The pathogenic family viewpoint is an outgrowth of psychoanalytic writing. Under this viewpoint fall various theories

FAMILY STYLES AND HOMOSEXUALITY

Wyden and Wyden (1968) found some interesting correlations between family types and the incidence of homosexuality.

1. Homosexuality is rare in large families.
2. Jewish families are the most unlikely ethnic group to produce homosexuals.
3. Parents of homosexuals, when their pre-homosexual children were young, tended to characterize sex play with little boys as disgusting.
4. Mothers of pre-homosexual daughters were often described as cool and unloving. (Note: this is in conflict with Rosen's 1974 study.)
5. Fathers of homosexual daughters, unlike fathers of homosexual sons, tend to be crude and autocratic, but also passive and docile toward their wives.
6. Affectionate and masculine fathers, and those who are strong figures in their family, rarely raise lesbians.

Heilbrun (1965) also has stated that gender identity for both females and males is best established when the father is nurturant and strong. Fathers who are highly masculine, yet nurturant, would thus appear to produce the fewest homosexual offspring. Finally, the Wydens' data are chiefly derived from interviews with clinicians and are not consistently confirmed by other investigators.

and notions suggesting that both female and male homosexuality develops out of disturbed family relationships. The pre-homosexual girl, therefore, is thought to have received special treatment by her mother and father that ultimately leads her to an alternative sexual preference (as well as the possibility of a cross-sexed gender identity). Several subareas fall within this position. First, there are notions that lesbianism develops because of a general disturbed family atmosphere. In this sense, female homosexuality is viewed as a product of emotional and psychological trauma within the family. Incest may represent the kind of pathological family setting that could trigger homosexuality in the female child. The behaviors of the parents toward the pre-homosexual daughter, and the relationship between the husband and wife, are believed to be important components in the development of the child's sexual orientation. For instance, fathers of some lesbians have been described as being cold, punitive, unloving, and alcoholic. A few lesbians have revealed that as young girls they were raped or seduced by their father or stepfather, and this experience generated fear and distrust of men in general (Rosen 1974; Lukianowicz 1972). Regarding seduction and sexual overstimulation, Wyden and Wyden (1968) state:

> Excessive sexual stimulation [e.g., a young child seeing his or her parents have intercourse, being seduced by a parent, or having parents undress in front of him or her] can arouse great fear—fears that some young people may find impossible to cope with. (p. 76)

Although it seems clear that such experiences do not always produce homosexuality, clinical data do suggest that a *seduction-trauma model* may be at the base of some homosexuality.

Learning Theory. The learning view shares much with other perspectives, but simply uses different terms to account for how homosexuality develops. The learning view states, however, that homosexuality can be acquired at any time. Lesbianism can be learned if heterosexual experiences have been repeatedly associated with something unpleasant or distasteful. Indeed, it is often held that the major determinant of lesbianism is heterosexual aversion (Feldman and MacCulloch 1971). Many lesbians state, "Only another woman can give me the tenderness I need." Being raped, of course, traumatizes many women and develops in some of them a heterosexual aversion. This does not mean that they will automatically become homosexual, but it does show that painful experiences can generalize to males as a group. Finally, if a woman is traumatized too often by men, or if her emotional needs are not fulfilled, the potential for avoiding heterosexuality increases. These possibilities involve the women who in the beginning of their sexual orientation are heterosexual but because of repeated exposure to negative situations with males gradually find emotional, then sexual, involvement with women more reinforcing. Rather than labeling these women as "nonexclusive lesbians," or "latent homosexuals," if we are involved in the labeling game, it would be more accurate to view them as *latent heterosexuals*.

Prostitutes quite often fit into this category. Some of these women have abandoned heterosexuality emotionally (though not physically), yet still retain a female gender identity. This suggests the possibility that homosexuality can be induced by aversive heterosexual experiences after childhood.

Perhaps the most common variant learning position states simply that parents can raise a child (biologically a female) to be a boy; by reinforcing certain male-like behaviors, and extinguishing or not reinforcing female-like behaviors, the parents develop in the child a cross-sexed gender identity. The discussion of transsexualism in chapter 11

indicated that evidence does exist for the view that how a child is reared, as a girl or boy, determines his or her gender identity and subsequent sexual preference. Recall from chapter 11 the clinical case reported by Money and Tucker where a biological male child was accidentally castrated and then, when reared as a female, the child succeeded in establishing a female gender identity.

All the evidence available so far indicates no particular events or stressors that unquestionably induce lesbianism. Rosen (1974), Marmor (1965), and many other therorists have argued that lesbianism has many possible causes.

MALE HOMOSEXUALITY

Male homosexuality is no easier to define than lesbianism. Hundreds of conceptual definitions exist, some very lengthy and abstract, some short and simple. In one of the shortest, Tripp (1975) says simply that males are homosexual if they find the ''same-sex attributes'' erotic. Other definitions state that these people ''prefer to achieve sexual gratification with members of the same sex'' (Hettlinger 1975). We must also consider Kinsey's concept of the homosexual-heterosexual continuum; that is, that some males are more homosexual than others. That is, a man cannot be identified or labeled as a homosexual because of one or several isolated homosexual experiences. As Kinsey would have said, it is the exclusive, long-term, sexual intimacy and the emotional attachment to men that suggest an alternative sexual orientation.

The dialogue in this case study, recorded in the apartment of two male homosexuals, was part of an interview with Arno Karlen (1971), who was writing a text, *Sexuality and Homosexuality*. In this conversation are three men, Don, Dick, and a neighborhood friend, Edward. Karlen has asked them to tell about the distinctions within the gay subculture in New York.

A CASE OF HOMOSEXUALITY

DON: The area around Broadway and 71st Street has swishy Spanish [Puerto Rican] fags, some Negroes—very effeminate guys, real trash, very badly educated.

DICK: No, you don't get the point! Those are leather boys hanging around up there, a different bunch from the ones on Christopher Street. Now, the East Fifties bars are another story. Homos and heteros both cruise there in the early evening. Gay executives go if they know it's safe. They aren't really part of gay life. Half the time in those places you can't be sure who's gay and who isn't. A lot of the discothèques have mixed crowds, too. But there aren't any real gay dancing bars left now.

DON: The West Village has people who are younger and more open. Up to about twenty-four, I'd say.

DICK: And prettier. Much prettier boys there. But there are some slightly older professional people there.

DON: Yes, lots of the artsy, full-time homosexuals in their early twenties and late teens, and future professional people. It's a kind of coming-out area for young people, some of whom graduate to uptown lives.

[KARLEN:] *What about ethnic groups? Are they different?*

DON: Very different. Most of the Negroes I meet who are gay just toady to whites, want to mix with them.

DICK: They'll fuck anything. But they don't look down on being gay the way whites do. They have their queens—I mean, there are straight men who have women but also have queens they fuck on the side, and they aren't considered homosexual by themselves or other people. Now, the Puerto Ricans aren't like that at all. Their queens are real queens.

DON: Yes, with them you're either *muy macho* or swishy. Just compare the Spanish queens with a gay bar in Oklahoma or the deep Midwest.

EDWARD: A gay bar there looks like a college bar. It's open and friendly, and not swishy at all. People wear very conservative clothes.

DON: It isn't tense and scared, like gay bars in New York. And that's true to a lesser degree of gay bars in, say, Philly or D.C. But look who go to the bars in New York—people who have to dress up in public. But Holland is really the place to be.

DICK: God, yes! It's really like paradise. Very quiet, very free. Now by comparison, let me tell you. I got arrested in the West Village a few months ago. I looked as straight as could be, and there was a girl with us, but the other guys were very swishy types. We were picked up and treated with all sorts of verbal abuse at the station. When we came in, the cop yelled. "Here's another six!" It sounded as though they had a quota to meet. But let me tell you, as soon as I gave my lawyer's name, it changed from "All right, Mary, move your ass!" to "Excuse me, sir!" But you know, it isn't the cops who make life tough, it's the latents.

DON: Yes, and the ones who come to work in your office can reveal you no matter what you do. There was one at mine who kept looking and looking at me. I was sure someone would notice. Finally I sat down across from him at lunch one day and stared back into his eyes. He got good and scared, and he hasn't even looked at me since.

DICK: The real trouble is that the latents are afraid of being revealed to themselves. My boss at my last job was a real hunk, a real football-player type. He was always asking me questions, like why I didn't go out with girls. I was afraid he'd keep asking questions, and then one day he'd discover his own latent homosexuality. . . .

INCIDENCE OF MALE HOMOSEXUALITY

As we have discussed, estimates suggest that approximately 3 percent of all American males are exclusive homosexuals. Estimates for nonexclusive homosexuality for males are approximately 25 percent, including younger males who have had a few homosexual experiences but later develop heterosexual orientations. All told, including both males and females, at least 10 million people in the United States are or will become exclusive homosexuals (Karlen 1971).

CHARACTERISTICS OF MALE HOMOSEXUALS

Virtually all sex researchers agree that the limpwristed, effeminate male does not represent the typical male homosexual's expressive behavior. Evans (1969) points out that approximately 95 percent of the male homosexuals surveyed thought of themselves as being very masculine. However, there exists some evidence suggesting that many male homosexuals have adopted a feminine gender identity. During erotic interaction, for instance, male homosexuals often imagine themselves to be female.

An interesting feature of male homosexuality is its contrast with lesbianism. Clinical studies have documented that male homosexuals are much more promiscuous and have less stable love affairs than do lesbians. In general, long-lasting male homosexual relationships or long-lasting homosexual marriages are quite rare (West 1968; Giese 1969). Karlen (1971), in his voluminous study on homosexuality, says that while male homosexuals may say they are looking for lasting relationships with other men, the reality is that that they are "quick to shack up," but have a "series of brittle, stormy, short-lived relationships." Karlen also notes that between homosexuals, "one-year" affairs are often considered to be an accomplishment and a criterion of healthy adjustment. (There are doubtless many cases of long-lasting male homosexual bonds.) Weinberg and Williams (1974) characterize the male homosexual as one who is typically single, but may live together with a roommate for varying periods of time in a type of marriage. Other homosexual males, of course, are married to women yet still engage in furtive homosexual cruising. Although many of these married men are termed "bisexual," Weinberg and Williams suggest that marriage between a homosexual male and a heterosexual female is a tactic to conceal his sexual orientation. Bergler called these unions "alibi-marriages."

CAUSES AND STRESSORS

Since we have presented the rationales for the biogenic and psychogenic theories of female homosexuality, we shall briefly discuss a few of the major findings about male homosexuality from these positions.

BIOGENIC THEORIES The biogenic research on male homosexuality typically attempts to demonstrate a link between hormones and sexual orientation. As did the studies on female homosexuality, many of these research projects assess small amounts of sex hormones found in the body fluid. These investigations are based on the work of John Money and Anke Ehrhardt, who showed that females exposed *in utero* to androgens developed many male-like behaviors (tomboyishness, aggressiveness, and so on). Loraine et al. (1971) and Margolese (1970) posit that testosterone levels are lower in male homosexuals than heterosexuals. Other investigators have stated that *androsterone* (a metabolite of testosterone) is related to sexual preference for either sex. According to this view, low levels of this substance in either sex induce a sexual preference for males, and high levels induce a preference for females. In a more widely cited study, Kolodny et al. (1971) sampled exclusive male homosexuals and normals to see if they could detect differences in plasma testosterone. They stated that male homosexuals had lower levels of this substance; an attempt to confirm these findings by another research team was unsuccessful (Tourney, Petrilli, and Hatfield 1975). As we noted previously, however, hormones affect sexual behavior, and sexual behavior, stress, and other activities affect the endocrine system. It is thus difficult if not impossible to determine which is cause and which is effect.

PSYCHOGENIC THEORIES As we indicated previously, the psychogenic position includes psychoanalytic theories of homosexuality, pathogenic family theories, and learning theories. All these viewpoints assume that male homosexuality, as well as lesbianism, is acquired from special environmental circumstances.

Psychoanalytic Theory. Psychoanalytic theorists have commented extensively on male homosexuality, its origins and symptoms. But no unified etiological theory of male homosexuality has emerged from this viewpoint. Freud, however, stated that all children pass through a homosexual stage of psychosexual development, and that because of various conflicts, a particular child might become *fixated* at the homosexual stage. Harry Stack Sullivan, an early psychoanalyst, considered homosexuality to be a coping device. In part, this orientation was an effort to deal with defective interpersonal relationships. Franz Alexander (1963) stated that the boy's failure to receive love from his mother promoted his identification with her. Alexander (1963) writes:

> [This] prompts him to give to [men] the kind of love he wished to receive from his mother and thus to enjoy vicarious satisfaction. (p. 263)

Also offered as a possible precipitating stressor is the child's fear of castration. Somehow the male child concludes that he might be castrated by his mother (women) and so he develops a phobia of sex with women. A few psychoanalysts have gone so far as to propose that male homosexuals have delusions that the female's vagina is fitted with teeth (Tripp 1975); this notion of the *vagina dentata* is, in fact, a religious belief in some cultures. Just why some males fear castration and become homosexual, and others resolve this so-called fear, is not spelled out clearly in analytic writing.

Pathogenic Family Theory. We have discussed the rationale behind the pathogenic family hypothesis in connection with lesbianism. Again, this hypothesis suggests that disturbances in the family induce homosexuality. The classic theory under this hypothesis is that of the *dominant (seductive) mother*. Irving Bieber has been the main proponent of this theory and, along with many other theorists, he asserts that the pre-homosexual boy has a mother who is highly seductive, overprotective, and close-binding. She may even have incestuous wishes that are never quite fulfilled. Apparently her close-binding seductive behavior toward her son causes him to think of sex with women as an incestuous act. To an extent, the psychoanalytic theories and the dominant mother theory are similar, for both hold that fear of heterosexuality (and the opposite-sexed parent) is at the root of homosexuality.

Learning Theory. Several observations concerning male homosexuality can be added to the learning theory approach discussed for lesbianism. For one, some evidence suggests that homosexuality can be learned by *modeling*. That is, homosexu-

ality can be induced in some individuals if a model
or leader initiates the practice. Tripp (1975) makes
this interesting point:

> . . . there are a number of . . . societies
> in which homosexuality is (or was) known
> to be relatively rare, sometimes very rare,
> and yet if an adroit homosexual foreigner
> should come along and introduce "the
> practice" to a few men in their teens and
> twenties, it may catch on like wildfire.

Tripp notes that many men [women?] drawn to

exotic travel—explorers, anthropologists, etc.—
were not only homosexual "but quite adept at
making their approaches. . . .")

Up until now, our knowledge of homosexuality has relied on data collected by retrospective
reports of childhood experiences. Until we longitudinally study the development of heterosexuality,
and the variables influencing its emergence, our
understanding of the conditions under which homosexuality develops will be limited. It is hoped
that future studies will yield more complete understanding.

TREATMENT OF HOMOSEXUALITY

A homosexual may seek therapy for several widely
different reasons: (1) to change his or her sexual
orientation; (2) to develop self-acceptance as a
homosexual; or (3) for the same reasons that
heterosexuals seek therapy—for depression, unhappiness, anxiety, and so on.

ALTERING SEXUAL ORIENTATION

A few behavior therapy techniques have been used
to decrease homosexual responses or to increase
heterosexual responses. But it is important to note
that a critical ingredient in sexual reorientation is a
strong desire to change. Tripp (1975) indicates,
however, that surveys over the years have shown
that from 90 to 96 percent of homosexuals do not
wish to become heterosexuals. Thus, assuming that
a desire for change is an important prerequisite for
therapy, and further assuming that few homosexuals want to change, we must conclude that only a
small number of homosexuals will be successfully
treated.

AVERSION THERAPY Under the heading of
aversion therapy are two techniques used to treat
homosexuality. (1) In *electric aversive shock,* the
homosexual is to imagine an erotic homosexual
scene while he or she is being given a shock
(Barlow et al. 1973). (2) In *aversive relief therapy,*
a heterosexual stimulus—a nude picture of the
opposite sex, for example—is presented as an
electric shock is terminated (Barlow 1973; Feldman
& MacCulloch 1971). For example, a male client is

shown a slide of a nude male that is attractive to
him. He is told that he may receive a shock while
viewing the slide. But he can achieve "relief" from
the shock by pressing a button that removes the
slide. In a variant of this procedure, a heterosexual
slide (a female nude in this case) would be seen as
the subject pressed the button and terminated the
shock. In essence, the female slide would take on
reinforcing qualities because it is associated with
termination of an aversive event.

The goal of both electric aversive shock and
aversive relief therapy is to decrease homosexual
responsiveness, which may be measured by a
penile erection meter or a clitoral erection meter. It
is also suggested that it may increase heterosexual
responsiveness. Although these methods fit well
into the learning view of homosexuality (heterosexual aversion), Barlow (1973) contends that no
evidence supports their effectiveness. Feldman and
MacCulloch, however, report therapeutic benefits
from aversion methods. McConaghy and Barr
(1973) found that after a one-year follow-up of
aversion therapy sessions, half the treated subjects
reported decreases in homosexual responsiveness
and half showed an increase in heterosexual
responsiveness. In some cases, homosexuals
treated by aversion therapy have shown significantly more penile erection to female slides than
did a matched control group of untreated homosexuals. Other approaches suggest that rather than
attempting to eliminate various homosexual responses (arousal, for example), the emphasis
should be on shifting gender role or identity. As
yet, however, no conclusive evidence demonstrates
that gender role or identity can be altered in
homosexuals.

MASTURBATORY CONDITIONING/FADING

Limited success in increasing heterosexual arousal has also been accomplished with two similar behavior therapy techniques: *masturbatory conditioning* and *fading*.

In *masturbatory conditioning*, the subject is instructed to masturbate to a series of pictures or erotic images. When masturbation is underway and high arousal is detected, the series of pictures are progressively changed to resemble an erotic heterosexual image (Barlow 1973). In *fading*, a slide of a nude male may be presented until the subject has a complete erection. Gradually, a female slide is "faded in" or superimposed over the male slide.

The theory behind both these techniques is that erotic arousal will become associated with the female slide and will increase the potential for heterosexual arousal. In fact, learning theory suggests that the male may become more aroused to the female slide, but not that he will be less aroused to the male slide. To a degree, then, these techniques are not training in heterosexuality, but rather training in bisexuality.

SELF-ACCEPTANCE THERAPY

Most male and female homosexuals who seek therapy do not wish to alter their sexual orientation or identity but rather to get relief from guilt, anxiety, or depression, or to elevate their feelings toward themselves as human beings. Such motivation to seek therapy to bolster self-esteem will increase if clinicians continue to view homosexuality as an alternative sexual orientation and not as a psychopathology to be eradicated.

Self-acceptance is often the biggest problem for homosexuals, primarily because of society's reactions toward this orientation. A national homophile publication, *Queen's Quarterly*, has as its slogan: "Self-acceptance is the first step to happiness." Clinicians and researchers also concur that the lack of self-acceptance is a stressor.

Weinberg and Williams (1974) maintain that a major source of insecurity for homosexuals is the contempt that heterosexuals feel or show toward them. Therapy, then, is often focused on helping these individuals increase their self-acceptance and lower their depression and guilt, and on aiding them in developing better social skills if they are needed. Many clinicians see group therapy as one vehicle by which a homosexual can learn to relate better to heterosexuals. Many therapy approaches probably could be employed to support the person and increase his or her feelings of adequacy and self-respect.

Finally, in view of the new attitudes toward homosexuality, particularly among mental health professionals, therapy will probably be aimed mainly at those who are *dyshomophilic;* that is, those who experience distress because of their homosexuality.

SUMMARY

1. Homosexuality is no longer considered to be a mental disorder by the major classification system, DSM-III. *Dyshomophilia*—distress or unhappiness because of being homosexual—is, however, listed as a mental disorder or pathological reaction.

2. There is no agreed-upon definition of homosexuality. A few theorists suggest that homosexuality can be defined by conceptual definitions; others prefer to develop behavioral scales (as Kinsey did, for example). Homosexuality may also be defined by self-definition; that is, one who states his or her alternate preference.

3. Homosexuality appears not to be a discrete, all-or-none, phenomenon. There are degrees and various styles of homosexuality. First, there are exclusive homosexuals; those who restrict sexual or erotic and emotional experience to the same sex. Second, there are inclusive or nonexclusive homosexuals. These individuals may have periodic sexual or emotional encounters with both sexes. A third variant is called transitory homosexuality. It does not apply necessarily to exclusive or inclusive patterns, but rather it refers to how often one engages in homosexuality: these individuals

"sporadically" engage in alternate sexual preferences.

4. The onset of homosexuality typically emerges during adolescence, but obviously there may be symptoms of erotic interest in the same sex during childhood. In other cases, individuals may not recognize their sexual and emotional needs until early adulthood.

5. The prevalence or frequency of homosexuality has been estimated by numerous researchers. Often there is a wide discrepancy among the figures reported. This discrepancy seems to be a function of the definition of homosexuality used by the researcher, or, in some cases, a function of the sample interviewed. Nonetheless, a general figure is that approximately 2 to 5 percent of individuals are exclusively homosexuals. These figures, however, represent only those who were willing to acknowledge their orientation.

6. An often debated issue in homosexuality revolves around the issue of psychopathology or the emotional health of homosexuals. Many studies have attempted to evaluate the mental health of homosexuals, as contrasted with heterosexuals. For the most part, the diagnostic tools used to assess mental health have not found significant differences between the two groups. A few investigations have revealed differences in attitudes toward parents of homosexual and heterosexual subjects, but methodological shortcomings abound in virtually all of these investigations. The Bieber investigations did suggest that homosexuals were quite often "heterophobic," that is, they feared or mistrusted the opposite sex. However to this point no investigation has revealed that homosexuals are more mentally disturbed and pathological than heterosexuals. If differences do exist, the methodology of assessment has yet to be developed that would reveal the differences.

7. *Lesbianism* has been defined in several different ways. Broadly, it has been defined as an erotic, emotional, and psychological attraction or attachment of one woman to another woman. Various theorists such as Wolff minimize the importance of sexual attraction and erotic activity, but stress instead the importance of emotional involvement in defining lesbianism.

8. The incidence or prevalence of lesbianism is estimated to be somewhere between 2 to 5 percent. Hite, however, claims that female homosexuality is much more prevalent than the traditional statistics revealed by Kinsey suggest.

9. The etiological theories of lesbianism are divided into two views—biogenic theories and psychogenic theories. The biogenic viewpoints suggest that alternate sexual orientation in women is strongly influenced by biochemical factors such as hormones. Elevated plasma testosterone concentrations have been reported in some samples of lesbians. It is not clear, however, whether lesbianism caused the increases, or vice versa. The psychogenic views argue that emotional disturbances between the parents and child may contribute or induce homosexuality. The psychoanalytic position posits that homosexuality is actually a fear of heterosexuality—heterophobia. The close-binding parent of the opposite sex, who is also seductive, is viewed as a homosexual-inducing feature.

10. Male homosexuality has been defined in a similar manner. Same-sex attributes have become eroticized.

11. The prevalance of male homosexuality is thought to be slightly higher than that of lesbianism, but this may be because males are often more open about revealing alternate sexual orientations. Exclusive male homosexuals are estimated to comprise approximately 3 percent of the male population; others claim they, like lesbians, comprise between 2 and 5 percent.

12. The etiological theories of male homosexuality are also divided into two views: biogenic theories and psychogenic theories. The biogenic positions propose that biochemicals or hormones, testosterone in particular, differ between heterosexual and homosexual samples. Testosterone levels have been found to be lower in male homosexuals when contrasted with heterosexual controls. The psychogenic theories essentially state that childhood traumas alter the child's sexual orientation. The psychoanalytic view holds that male homosexuality is a symptom of phobic fear of women. The *dominant mother theory* is a psychogenic position arguing that mothers who are dominant, seductive, overprotecting, and close-

binding often produce homosexual males. The learning view suggests that for both male and female homosexuals the parents have selectively reinforced cross-sexed behaviors.

13. Therapy may be sought by a homosexual for several reasons: (a) to change sexual orientation; (b) to develop or bolster self-esteem; or (c) to alleviate emotional problems apart from the homosexuality.

14. Various clinical methods have been used to change sexual orientation from homosexual to heterosexual. Aversion therapies of various sorts have been used. Generally, in aversion therapy a homosexual stimuli, a nude picture of the same sex, for example, is presented with an aversive event such as a shock. The pairing of these two stimuli is thought to weaken homosexual strivings. In another aversion therapy, aversion relief, a heterosexual stimulus is presented as an electric shock is terminated. The heterosexual slide is thought to take on reinforcing properties because it is associated with shock termination. The effectiveness of these procedures in producing heterosexual orientation has yet to be established. Some studies do show, however, that physiological responses—erection, for example—can be increased by showing heterosexual slides subsequent to aversion therapy. Last, many clinicians decline to try to alter sexual orientation and instead attempt to elevate the homosexual's feelings about herself or himself. Many clinicians believe that group therapy is one method by which self-esteem can be raised. Therapy, therefore, often focuses on helping the person overcome guilt and distress about homosexuality.

RECOMMENDED READINGS

Bergler, E. *Homosexuality. Disease or way of life?* New York: Collier Books, 1967.

Green, R., and Money, J. (Eds.). *Transsexualism and sex reassignment.* Baltimore: Johns Hopkins Press, 1969.

Hooker, E. Male homosexuality in the Rorschach. *Journal of Projective Techniques*, 1958, 22, 33–54.

Karlen, A. *Sexuality and homosexuality.* New York: Norton, 1971.

Loraine, J. A., Adamopoulos, D. A., Kirkham, E. E., Ismael, A. A., & Dove, G. A. Patterns of hormone excretion in male and female homosexuals. *Human Nature*, 1971, 234, 552–555.

McConaghy, N., & Barr, R. F. Classical, avoidance, and backward conditioning treatment of homosexuality. *British Journal of Psychiatry*, 1973, 122, 156–162.

Rossi, A. S. The biosocial side of parenthood. *Human Nature*, 1978, 1, 72–79.

Saghir, M. & Robins, E. *Male and female homosexuality.* Baltimore: Williams and Wilkins, 1973.

Stoller, R. J. *Sex and gender: On the development of masculinity and femininity.* New York: Science House, 1968.

Tripp, C. A. *The homosexual matrix.* New York: McGraw-Hill, 1975.

13

ANTISOCIAL BEHAVIOR

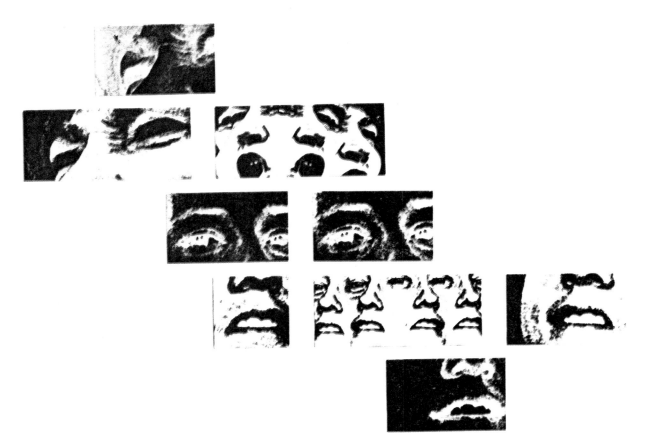

OVERVIEW In this chapter, we will discuss several kinds of antisocial behavior. The terms "antisocial personality," "psychopathy," and "sociopathy" are used interchangeably to describe individuals who engage in chronic antisocial behavior. We will also discuss two other types of antisocial behavior—secondary antisocial behavior and dyssocial or subcultural delinquency/criminality. In discussing research on sociopathy, it will be pointed out that sociopaths show a deficit in learning to avoid punishment and that possibly this is due to physiological underarousal. They can, however, learn to avoid punishment under certain conditions, particularly when the punishment is sufficiently meaningful and has an impact on them. We will discuss the fact that traditional psycho-

therapeutic procedures have not been found to be effective in changing the behavior of sociopaths. Operant behavior modification and therapeutic community programs have had some success. It will also be pointed out that differential treatment/rehabilitation programs are necessary to take into account the different causes of antisocial behavior. The high rate of recidivism indicates that the current common practice of "lumping together" the various types of offenders is not effective. As will be seen, the prognosis for the successful modification of maladaptive antisocial behavior can at present be described as pessimistic. Finally, assessment procedures that are commonly used to differentiate among the various types of antisocial behavior will be discussed.

SYMPTOM DESCRIPTION AND ETIOLOGY

The terms *antisocial personality, psychopathy,* and *sociopathy* are used interchangeably to describe individuals who, according to the DSM-II, are:

> . . . basically unsocialized and whose behavior pattern brings them repeatedly into conflicts with society. They are incapable of significant loyalty to individuals, groups, or social values. They are grossly selfish, callous, irresponsible, impulsive, and unable to feel guilt or to learn from experience and punishment. Frustration tolerance is low. They tend to blame others or offer plausible rationalizations for their behavior. A mere history of repeated legal or social offences is not sufficient to justify this diagnosis. (p. 43)

Hare (1970), in a review of the literature on sociopathy, cites numerous clinical and experimental reports that substantially agree with the clinical features of this personality characteristic. These reports support the contention that there are a group of traits that, when combined with chronic antisocial behavior, can be used in diagnosing an antisocial personality. The major behavioral manifestations are immaturity and inability to control impulses or delay gratification, lack of anxiety and guilt, lack of socialization, rejection of authority and discipline, failure to alter punished behavior, and inability to maintain meaningful interpersonal relationships.

The proposed DSM-III uses the term "antisocial personality," rather than sociopathy. The proposal lists a number of associated features, such as complaints of tension, inability to tolerate boredom, depression, and the conviction that other people are hostile towards them. Excessive drinking, functional illiteracy, illicit drug use, persistent lying, and a marked inability to sustain lasting, close, warm relationships with sexual partners, friends, and family are other features mentioned by DSM-III. It also notes that the usual age at onset for this reaction (for diagnosis) is about 18, although prodromal patterns may be exhibited in childhood.

The mere fact that a person engages in chronic antisocial behavior does not automatically label him or her as a sociopath. Rather, it has become common to classify criminal/delinquent individuals into one of three categories:

1. *Primary sociopathy,* which was described in the above DSM-II definition and list of behavioral manifestations.
2. *Secondary antisocial behavior,* a category including individuals who can experience guilt and remorse for their behavior, and whose antisocial behavior is motivated primarily by neurotic or psychotic emotional disturbances. These individuals' antisocial behavior is a symptom of a more basic underlying emotional problem. It should be noted that in the literature these individuals are often referred to as "neurotic sociopaths." We do not advocate the use of this confusing term because, by definition of behavioral characteristics, a sociopath lacks neurotic attributes.
3. *Dyssocial* or *subcultural delinquency/criminality,* which describes individuals who exhibit antisocial behavior because they were raised or are living in a delinquent subculture/environment that fosters and reinforces such behavior. They are not truly psychopathic or emotionally disturbed, but merely behave like others in their own gang, group, or family. As Hare (1970) notes, unlike the "true" primary sociopath, these individuals are capable of developing strong loyalities and emotional relationships with other human beings.

A number of studies support the existence of these three clinical subdivisions. For example, Jenkins (1964, 1966), using case history data, isolated three common clusters of personality characteristics found in delinquent children and those referred to guidance clinics. He labeled these three common clusters: (1) the *unsocialized-aggressive* syndrome, in which the individual displayed primary psychopathic behaviors such as assaultive tendencies, starting fights, cruelty, defiance of authority, malicious mischief, and inadequate guilt feelings; (2) the *overanxious* syndrome, in which the individual displayed neurotic behaviors such as seclusiveness, shyness, apathy, worrying, sensitiveness, and submissiveness; (3) the *socialized delinquent* syndrome, in which the individual displayed subcultural delinquent behavior such as associating with bad companions, engaging in gang activities, co-

DEMOGRAPHICS	USUAL AGE AT ONSET	PREVALENCE	SEX RATIO
SOCIOPATHY	Childhood and adolescence	Unknown	Much greater in males than females
SECONDARY ANTISOCIAL BEHAVIOR	Childhood	Common, though exact statistics not known	Much greater in males than females, with ratio estimates ranging from 4 to 1 to 12 to 1
DYSSOCIAL DELINQUENCY / CRIMINALITY	Childhood and adolescence	Prevalence varies greatly, and typically is related to low socioeconomic, urban individuals living in a disorganized community	Male-female ratio is 6 to 1

operative stealing, and habitual truancy from school and home. Hare (1970) reviews some other statistical studies of case history data, behavior ratings, and questionnaire response data that have obtained similar results.

In this chapter we shall consider all three of these subdivisions. The major focus, however, will be a detailed examination of the primary sociopath or psychopath. The main reason for this focus is that the majority of experimental and clinical psychological research has been done on this form of antisocial personality. There has been very little systematic study of the other two subcategories. The little research that does exist has been sociological-correlational, which does not allow a precise delineation of the possible etiological bases of the behavior.

SOCIOPATHY

Adhering to Cleckley's (1974) early formulations in his classic book on psychopathy, *The Mask of Sanity*, most view the psychopath as a person who exists within a severely restricted range of emotional arousal. This alteration in affect results in an inability to profit from past experience. This viewpoint, which stems from clinical observations, has generated considerable speculation regarding possible "cortical immaturity" and "autonomic underarousal" in the sociopath. Research has been directed at investigating physiological and learning correlates of psychopathy in order to test this speculation and to define characteristics of this personality type. A clear picture of the behavioral manifestations and developmental aspects of the sociopathic personality is given by this case history (Hare 1970) of a diagnosed sociopath.

A CASE OF SOCIOPATHY

Donald S., 30 years old, has just completed a three-year prison term for fraud, bigamy, false pretenses, and escaping lawful custody. The circumstances leading up to these offenses are interesting and consistent with his past behavior. With less than a month left to serve on an earlier 18-month term for fraud, he faked illness and escaped from the prison hospital. During the ten months of freedom that followed he engaged in a variety of illegal enterprises; the activity that resulted in his recapture was typical of his method of operation. By passing himself off as the "field executive" of an international philanthropic foundation, he was able to enlist the aid of several religious organizations in a fund-raising campaign. The campaign moved slowly at first, and in an attempt to speed things up, he arranged an interview with the local TV station. His performance during the interview was so impressive that funds started to pour in. However, unfortunately for Donald, the interview was also carried on a national news network. He was recognized and quickly arrested. During the ensuing trial it became evident he experienced no sense of wrongdoing for his activities. He maintained, for example, that his passionate plea for funds "primed the pump"—that is, induced people to give to other charities as well as to the one he professed to represent. At the same time, he stated that most donations to charity are made by those who feel guilty about something and who therefore deserve to be bilked. This ability to rationalize his behavior and his lack of self-criticism were also evident in his attempts to solicit aid from the very people he has misled. Perhaps it is a tribute to his persuasiveness that a number of individuals actually did come to his support. During his three-year prison term, Donald spent much time searching for legal loopholes and writing to outside authorities, including local lawyers, the Prime Minister of Canada, and a Canadian representative to the United Nations. In each case he verbally attacked them for representing the authority and injustice responsible for his predicament. At the same time he requested them to intercede on his behalf and in the name of the justice they professed to represent.

While in prison he was used as a subject in some of the author's research. On his release he applied for admission to a university and, by way of reference, told the registrar that he had been one of the author's research colleagues! Several months later the author received a letter from him requesting a letter of recommendation on behalf of Donald's application for a job.

Donald was the youngest of three boys born to middle-class parents. Both of his brothers led normal, productive lives. His father spent a great deal of time with his business; when he was home he tended to be moody and to drink heavily when things were not going right. Donald's mother was a gentle, timid woman who tried to please her husband and to maintain a semblance of family harmony. When she discovered her children engaged in some mischief, she would threaten to tell their father. However, she

Courtesy H. Cleckley

H. Cleckley's book, *The Mask of Sanity*, has become a classic work describing the characteristics of psychopathy.

seldom carried out these threats because she did not want to disturb her husband and because his reactions were likely to be dependent on his mood at the time; on some occasions he would fly into a rage and beat the children and on others he would administer a verbal reprimand, sometimes mild and sometimes severe.

By all accounts Donald was considered a willful and difficult child. When his desire for candy or toys was frustrated he would begin with a show of affection, and if this failed he would throw a temper tantrum; the latter was seldom necessary because his angelic appearance and artful ways usually got him what he wanted. Similar tactics were used to avoid punishment for his numerous misdeeds. At first he would attempt to cover up with an elaborate facade of lies, often shifting the blame to his brothers. If this did not work, he would give a convincing display of remorse and contrition. When punishment was unavoidable he would become sullenly defiant, regarding it as an unjustifiable tax on his pleasures.

Although he was obviously very intelligent, his school years were academically undistinguished. He was restless, easily bored, and frequently truant. His behavior in the presence of the teacher or some other authority was usually quite good, but when he was on his own he generally got himself or others into trouble. Although he was often suspected of being the culprit, he was adept at talking his way out of difficulty.

Donald's misbehavior as a child took many forms including lying, cheating, petty theft, and the bullying of smaller children. As he grew older he became more and more interested in sex, gambling, and alcohol. When he was 14 he made crude sexual advances toward a younger girl, and when she threatened to tell her parents he locked her in a shed. It was about 16 hours before she was found. Donald at first denied knowledge of the incident, later stating that she had seduced him and that the door must have locked itself. He expressed no concern for the anguish experienced by the girl and her parents, nor did he give any indication that he felt morally culpable for what he had done. His parents were able to prevent charges being brought against him. Nevertheless, incidents of this sort were becoming more frequent and, in an attempt to prevent further embarrassment to the family, he was sent away to a private boarding school. His academic work there was of uneven quality, being dependent on his momentary interests. Nevertheless, he did well at individual competitive sports and public debating. He was a source of excitement for many of the other boys, and was able to think up interesting and unusual things to do. Rules and regulations were considered a meaningless hindrance to his self-expression, but he violated them so skillfully that it was often difficult to prove that he had actually done so. The teachers described him as an "operator" whose behavior was determined entirely by the possibility of attaining what he wanted— in most cases something that was concrete, immediate, and personally relevant.

When he was 17, Donald left the boarding school, forged his father's name to a large check, and spent about a year traveling around the world. He apparently lived well, using a combination of charm, physical attractiveness, and false pretenses to finance his way. During subsequent years he held a succession of jobs, never staying at any one for more than a few months. Throughout this period he was charged with a variety of crimes, including theft, drunkenness in a public place, assault, and many traffic violations. In most cases he was either fined or given a light sentence.

His sexual experiences were frequent, casual, and callous. When he was 22 he married a 41-year-old woman whom he had met in a bar. Several other marriages followed, all bigamous. In each case the pattern was the same: he would marry someone on impulse, let her support him for several months, and then leave. One marriage was particularly interesting. After being charged with fraud Donald was sent to a psychiatric institution for a period of observation. While there he came to the attention of a female member of the professional staff. His charm, physical attractiveness, and convincing promises to reform led her to intervene on his behalf. He was given a suspended sentence and they were married a week later. At first things went reasonably well, but when she refused to pay some of his gambling debts he forged her name to a check and left. He was soon caught and given an 18-month prison term. As mentioned earlier, he escaped with less than a month left to serve.

It is interesting to note that Donald sees nothing particularly wrong with his behavior, nor does he express remorse or guilt for using others and causing them grief. Although his behavior is self-defeating in the long run, he considers it to be practical and possessed of good sense. Periodic punishments do nothing to decrease his egotism and confidence in his own abilities, nor do they offset the often considerable short-term gains of which he is capable. However, these short-term gains are invariably obtained at the expense of someone else. In this respect his behavior is entirely egocentric and his needs are satisfied without any concern for the feelings and welfare of others. (Hare 1970, pp. 1–4)

Donald's case history illustrates clearly some of the major behavioral concomitants of sociopathy: antisocial behavior without any apparent regret, anxiety, or guilt; inability to learn from experience; impulsive, thrill-seeking behavior; general poverty of affect; inability to maintain meaningful interpersonal relationships; little response to consideration or kindness; no sense of responsibility. The research on sociopathy that we shall discuss in this chapter has been based predominantly on sociopaths such as Donald, who were diagnosed while serving a prison term for performing some criminal antisocial behavior. Traditionally, when an investigator has wanted to do research on sociopathy, the penal institution was the logical environment in which to expect to find a large number of sociopaths. The controlled, structured nature of these institutions also provided a relatively attractive environment in which to conduct this research.

However, an important question in interpreting the data obtained from this population is whether these incarcerated sociopaths are truly representative of the sociopathic personality type or are a special case or type of sociopathy. One might well argue that the "unsuccessful" sociopath, who is caught by society and put in prison, may not be the same type of individual as a "successful" sociopath, who has developed the requisite skills to be "good at his trade" and is making it quite successfully in society. Although the distinction between "successful" and "unsuccessful" sociopaths may be insignificant, and although no experimental investigations have examined whether there are differences between the two, it is important to keep in mind that the research we review on sociopathy has been conducted primarily on the "unsuccessful," incarcerated sociopath. Whether the results can be generalized to "successful" sociopaths is a question that to date, has not been experimentally investigated.

To provide an illustration of what we are describing as a "successful" sociopath, this case study examines an individual who, by material standards, is doing quite well in society as a successful disc jockey and actor (McNeil 1967).

A CASE OF A "CON MAN"

Dan F. was not a patient of mine but he probably told me more about himself and was less defensive than most of the patients I had treated. He was a well-known actor, a "personality" who had appeared on national television a number of times but had never really made it big on what he called the "boob tube." He made a lot of money, had a handsome wife, a big house in an exclusive suburb, drove a beautifully appointed Mercedes, and couldn't care less that there were other people in the world. He was as close as I ever got to what I conceived a psychopath ought to be.

During the time I knew him he unfolded a hair-raising tale of life as he lived it, and it amused him to talk about himself. Most of the details of his conduct had to be taken at face value since I had no way to check their accuracy. Some of the stories were certainly untrue and I was convinced many others were greatly exag-

gerated. He seemed fascinated by the chance to talk to a "head-shrinker" in a social rather than therapeutic setting, and he, in turn, fascinated me. He was urbane, charming, knowledgeable about a variety of subjects, a seeming friend of every nightclub owner and entertainer in the city.

Physically, he was commanding—six feet tall, with curly hair and regular features that were enhanced and somewhat glamorized by his personal fastidiousness in dress and grooming. But it was his bearing that added the finishing touch. He wore arrogance and *noblesse oblige* like a handtailored garment. He was not just bluff and appearance. For ten years he was a disc jockey with a wide following, and he knew popular music so well that every singer, musician, and entertainer in town would drop over to pour out all the current frustrations he or she was undergoing at the moment and to get his advice. He played the therapist with such grace and smoothness that it was embarrassing. There was a faint air of the cool and distant in his interactions with other show business types, but it became clear that this restrained quality was exactly what the situation demanded. It was a *very* nervous game to be an entertainer, and he always played the part of the relaxed and understanding person who was both part of it while removed from its strain. He was sensitive to the needs of others when it was profitable and insensitive and callous about those who could not do him any good. . . .

Dan F. was brutally frank with his colleagues, and in a business so fraught with deception, insincerity, and mutual hustling, this was interpreted as refreshing honesty and an absence of guile. In an odd sort of way, his emotional quicksand looked like the Rock of Gibraltar to those more nervous than he. It was a startling state of affairs but, as I said, it was a nervous kind of business. . . .

The list of incidents I witnessed and the long succession of stories he related painted a grisly picture of life-long abuse of people for Dan's amusement and profit. He was adept at office politics and told me casually of an unbelievable set of deceptive ways to deal with the opposition. Character assassination, rumormongering, modest blackmail, seduction, and barefaced lying were the least of his talents. He was jackal in the entertainment jungle, a jackal who feasted on the bodies of those he had slaughtered professionally. He was, for example, the master of the blind copy memo. The maneuver took several forms. He would, for example, write a letter highly critical of a colleague, and send it to the station manager, indicating that a copy had been sent to the victim. The copy was, of course, never sent. The consternation and misunderstanding this caused was considerable, and the outcome often was exactly what he had in mind. Sometimes, the victim got the letter in copy form but the original was not sent to the station manager. His most spectacular device was to enlist the help of A to "get" B and, as the plot progressed, to implicate A to the station manager in a subtle fashion as the culprit: "I don't like to mention this, Mr. Manager, but lately A has been complaining about B behind his back, and I wouldn't put it past him to try to make trouble for B. If they can't get along with each other there may be trouble for you." It always worked since station managers seemed to spend their lives uncovering plots and counterplots on the part of the talent. Managing so many prima donnas without getting injured while an innocent bystander was an ability every station manager had to possess. . . .

As we discussed his early life he told me he could not recall a time when he was not "doing everybody I could and the easy ones twice." He remembered that when he was 12 years old he had read a pocket book about "con men." It was then he decided it would be his life's work. They were heroes to him and he "fell down laughing" when they took some "mark" for his "bundle." As he said, "There's a sucker born every minute, and I'm glad the birth rate's so high."

When Dan was a teenager he was a model of recklessness and revolt against authority. He pressed for those illicit experiences denied the young and became what every parent feared was the shape his own child would assume. Even at that age he knew in his bones what behavior would comfort the anxieties of "old folks" and lead them to believe that their half-remembered impulses were not typical of the newer generations they now had to confront. He assumed that parents preferred a lie to the truth, so he was careful to be what they hoped him to be rather than reveal himself for what he really was. He became a skilled small-tale conversationalist as he submitted himself to the critical scrutiny that regularly took place in the dead time that existed before his date made her dramatic entrance into the living room.

He was shy, he was humble, he was self-effacing. He was whatever he sensed they needed him to be to pull the teeth of the fears that chewed at them. He was declared "safe" by one parent couple after another, but he knew this contrived ease was never communicated between them in an open fashion. He played nice but this seldom interfered with his real thoughts and expectations. He became, in fact, what he described as a "Mom's Apple Pie" favorite for many parents. It must have been an incredible sight to watch him ingratiate his way into the hearts of his elders. He mentioned that he remained tense until that moment when he knew the planned, casual slip of addressing his date's mother as "Mom" would penetrate directly to her anxious and guilt-ridden heart. . . .

As he said, "I could con them the same as I fooled my own folks. When I got caught by the cops I always blamed the other guys. I would admit to just enough to make me appear to be a slightly imperfect but earnest kid who deserved another chance. They went for it time after time, not because they believed it but because they couldn't stand the idea that I was really a rotten kid. Mostly they didn't want to be bothered by it all. When I figured that out I didn't have to lie so much. They believed anything I told them because they didn't want to hear anything else and that way they got out of the whole messy deal quicker."

Dan F.'s youthful escapades were of the kind that some stable and reliable citizens brag about with a feeling of nostalgia for the lost vigor and juices of their youth. But for Dan F., nothing had changed. He had aged without maturing and his adolescent depredations against the "square" populace had become only more sophisticated and slick. Dan F. was a teenager trapped in his own lack of development. As a teenager among grown men, little else could be expected of him and he expected little else of himself since he was convinced he had figured out a magic formula by which to lead his life. . . .

What is the most likely fate of Dan F? It would be pleasing and comforting to most of us if we could believe that one day he will be punished for his behavior. There is very little likelihood that this will happen. Dan is successful in a material sense and doing very well for himself professionally. Canny and jungle-wise, he is firmly ensconced in a business in which being

SHAKESPEARE ON SOCIOPATHY

GLOUCESTER: Now is the winter of our discontent
    Made glorious summer by this sun of York;
    And all the clouds that lour'd upon our house
    In the deep bosom of the ocean buried.
    Now are our brows bound with victorious
        wreaths
    Our bruised arms hung up for monuments;
    Our stern alarums changed to merry meetings;
    Our dreadful marches to delightful measures.
    Grim-visag'd war hath smooth'd his wrinkled
        front;
    And now,—instead of mounting barbed steeds,
    To fright the souls of fearful adversaries,—
    He capers nimbly in a lady's chamber
    To the lascivious pleasing of a lute.
    But I, that am not shap'd for sportive tricks,
    Nor made to court an amorous looking-glass;
    I, that am rudely stamp'd, and want love's
        majesty

    To strut before a wanton ambling nymph;
    I, that am curtail'd of this fair proportion,
    Cheated of feature by dissembling nature,
    Deform'd, unfinish'd, sent before my time
    Into this breathing world, scarce half made up,
    And that so lamely and unfashionable
    That dogs bark at me, as I halt by them;
    Why, I, in this weak piping time of peace,
    Have no delight to pass away the time,
    Unless to see my shadow in the sun
    And descant on mine own deformity:
    And therefore, since I cannot prove a lover,
    To entertain these fair well-spoken days,
    I am determined to prove a villain,
    And hate the idle pleasures of these days.

From *Richard III,* by William Shakespeare.

cool produces a profit. He will continue to get fan-mail in great quantity, he will rise to new and greater heights, he will live his life as he always has but will expand its scope and the elegance of its design. He will be divorced again, but it will hardly matter to him. He will continue to see me socially because this is the one flaw in his armor—he feels compelled to parade his personal values before me to demonstrate that good guys finish last. I am certain that I cannot alter his way of life in any meaningful way. I suppose that change will occur only if he gets into serious trouble, and I doubt that he will be sufficiently insightful even then to recognize it when it happens. Dan will always make out one way or another and will get his share even if others go without. Dan F. is a psychopath par excellence. He will always be amusing and charming but one must be cautious. (McNeil 1967, pp. 83-89)

It is readily apparent that Dan is very similar to Donald in terms of certain basic behavioral concomitants of sociopathy. The major difference between the two is that Dan is successful in his sociopathic lifestyle—so successful, in fact, that one may seriously conjecture whether his lifestyle might not be a very adaptive one to have in our present-day society. Indeed, Harrington (1972) argues that sociopathy may not be limited any longer to a strictly clinical definition, but that the "psychopath lives among us and has been accepted as normal—he may be your neighbor, your enemy, or your friend. . . ." Harrington indicates that the early psychiatric literature on sociopathy depicted the sociopath as a rational, but dangerously unstable, impulsive, and erratic individual who inevitably would come in conflict with society and was bound to lose to society sooner or later. In Cleckley's classic book, case study after case study is presented of sociopaths who did "lose out" to society. These, however, were case reports of unsuccessful sociopaths. Harrington suggests that a successful sociopath may be more effective than many normal people:

> In the late 1940s and early 1950s, the conception of the part-psychopath began to emerge more clearly in psychiatric studies. . . . There was a sense of menacing strangers in our midst, brilliant, remorseless people with icy intelligence, incapable of

love or guilt, with aggressive designs on the rest of the world. . . . The successful psychopath, it was said, could dominate people as he damaged them precisely because of his lack of feelings. Uninvolved in others, he coolly saw into their fears and desires, and maneuvered them as he wished. Such a man might not, after all, be doomed to a life of scrapes and escapades ending ignominiously in the jailhouse. Instead of murdering others, he might become a corporate raider and murder companies, firing people instead of killing them, and chopping up their functions rather than their bodies. . . . We now have disquieting awareness of people among us who may at the same time be profoundly ill and yet, in many ways, far more capable than we are. (Harrington 1972, p. 18)

Harrington's suggestion is a very provocative and interesting formulation of psychopathy. At this time, however, it is still highly speculative.

One additional point should be noted before discussing the proposed causes and stressors of sociopathy. We have reviewed case studies only of male sociopaths, but this is not to suggest that sociopathy is an exclusively male disorder. Although it tends to be more prevalent in males, this may simply reflect society's tendency not to apply criminal-type characteristics as freely to females. Whatever the reasons for this sex-ratio difference, the basic core sociopathic characteristics are the same for males and females. This is evident in some of the classic case studies of sociopaths presented by Cleckley (1964).

CAUSES AND STRESSORS

Traditional psychoanalytic theory has provided very little in the way of a detailed explanation of psychopathy. Basically, it assumes that a faulty superego underlies this disorder. Because of inadequate identification with parents, the psychopathic individual does not develop appropriate superego controls. Psychoanalytic theory assumes that normal development of the superego depends on the child's identification with the same-sex parent. If appropriate superego controls are lacking, and the possibility of superego-produced

moral anxiety thereby decreased, the antisocial personality has little means of resisting the id's strive for immediate gratification of amoral needs. This accounts for such an individual's impulsiveness, inability to delay gratification, and lack of anxiety.

There has been little attempt to validate this psychoanalytic formulation. More speculation and research has been prompted by the physiological and learning orientations, which will be discussed next.

AVOIDANCE LEARNING AND PHYSIOLOGICAL UNDERAROUSAL Clinical observations have prompted the notion that the sociopath is emotionally underaroused and lacks the ability to develop anxiety. Such underarousal might have a physiological basis.

Sympathetic nervous system arousal. To test the assumption of underarousal in a controlled laboratory setting, Lykken (1957) conducted an investigation comparing sociopaths, neurotic criminals, and normal college students on an electric-shock avoidance learning task and on a task measuring GSR (galvanic skin response) conditioning to electric shock. Lykken hypothesized that if sociopaths are truly defective in their ability to develop anxiety, then they should demonstrate little anxiety in situations that normally elicit this response. They would also be expected to be deficient in avoidance learning under circumstances in which some anxiety is needed for learning to occur. It is also assumed that the higher the anxiety level, the faster the GSR conditioning.

The results of Lykken's experiment supported his general hypotheses. Compared with college students and neurotic criminals, sociopaths demonstrated reduced avoidance learning of punished (shocked) responses, and less GSR conditioning to electric shock. In GSR-conditioning experiments, the conditioned GSRs that occur using an aversive unconditioned stimulus, such as shock, index the extent to which anxiety/fear has been conditioned. Sociopaths showed less conditioned fear. They also reported less anxiety on a number of standard psychological tests measuring anxiety level. Thus, these data indicate that sociopaths do not develop conditioned anxiety/fear responses to aversive stimuli as readily as normal subjects and, in demonstrating reduced avoidance learning, operate at generally lower levels of anxiety than normals. Lykken's experimental demonstration co-

PUBLIC ENEMY © 1932, Warner Brothers. In many films, James Cagney depicted an individual who had definite sociopathic characteristics. The general disregard for the feelings and welfare of others were hallmarks of characters he portrayed in a number of memorable performances.

incides with the clinical observational data indicating an apparent absence of anxiety in these individuals.

If sociopaths' deficit in learning to avoid aversive stimuli is truly due to their low levels of anxiety, then one might predict that if the anxiety level could in some way be increased, they should no longer show this deficit in avoidance learning. An experiment testing this prediction was conducted by Schachter and Latané (1964). These investigators used an avoidance learning task identical to that used in the Lykken experiment. Sociopathic and nonsociopathic inmates from a penitentiary were used in the study. These subjects performed the avoidance task two times: once after receiving a drug called adrenalin and once with an injection of a placebo and not adrenalin. Adrenalin is a hormonal agent that is a sympathetic nervous system stimulant. An increase in sympathetic activity is viewed as a concomitant of anxiety, and so this drug was used to increase the anxiety level of subjects.

The results of this study, shown in the graph, demonstrated that, with the placebo that did not increase anxiety level, the sociopaths showed the same deficit in avoidance learning as was found in the Lykken experiment. However, when injected

The effects of adrenalin and placebo injections on avoidance learning in sociopathic and nonsociopathic inmates. Higher scores indicate better avoidance learning. (From Schachter & Latane 1964)

ADRENALIN AND LEARNING
Figure 13.1

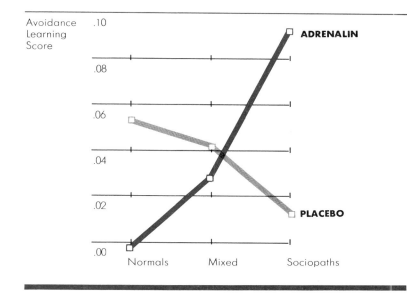

with adrenalin, the sociopaths learned to avoid the shock very effectively. If one is willing to assume that adrenalin-induced sympathetic activity produces the experience of anxiety, then these results support the hypothesis that an inadequate anxiety level in sociopaths causes their deficient avoidance learning ability. The data also further support the notion of an underaroused and anxiety-free sociopath.

There are some other data indicating that adrenalin may not be the only way of increasing the sociopath's avoidance learning ability. A study by Schmauk (1970) demonstrates that a stronger punishment than the relatively painful electric shock (used in the Lykken and Schacter and Latané studies) can have an effect on sociopaths. In Schmauk's experiment, the effects on avoidance learning of three different kinds of punishment were examined: electric shock, loss of money (quarters taken from an initial pile of forty), and social punishment (the experimenter saying ''wrong'' to the subject). Three groups of subjects were employed in this study—sociopathic inmates of a penitentiary, nonsociopathic inmates, and a group

of nonincarcerated normal subjects. The results of this study, shown in the second graph, indicate that when shock and social punishments are used, sociopaths again show a defect in avoidance learning. However, when the punishment was loss of money, the sociopaths learned to avoid better than all groups.

Thus, sociopaths can learn to avoid punishment not only when anxiety level is artificially increased by adrenalin, but also when the punishment becomes sufficiently meaningful and has an impact on them. Social punishment and physical punishment, such as electric shock, evidently lack the meaning and impact for sociopaths that they have for normal subjects. Money, on the other hand, which may be more relevant to their value system, may be especially important to them. Potential loss of money is therefore experienced as aversive and produces appropriate avoidance learning.

A number of other experimental studies support the presence of sympathetic nervous system underarousal in sociopaths. Hare (1976), in his review of the literature on sociopathy and physiological responding, concludes that sociopaths tend consistently to be physiologically less aroused than normal subjects. In studies where there is no doubt about the appropriate diagnosis of the subjects used, Hare finds differences. During resting periods, when subjects are not performing a task, sociopaths show lower GSR levels and fewer spontaneous GSR fluctuations than nonsociopaths. (GSR, galvanic skin response, is basically an index of sweat gland activity. An elevated activity level is associated with experiences of fear and anxiety.) Also, in response to exposure to intense or stressful stimulation, sociopaths demonstrate smaller GSR and heart rate responses than do nonsociopathic subjects. This evidence of physiological hyporesponsivity in sociopaths again supports clinical accounts of these persons' lack of anxiety, of emotional tension, and of arousal.

Steinberg and Schwartz (1976) conducted an interesting study that assessed whether psychopaths could learn voluntarily to modify their spontaneous GSR fluctuations using instructions and biofeedback. Subjects in this study were required both to increase and decrease the frequency of their spontaneous GSRs, first without biofeedback and then with biofeedback training. During the initial prefeedback period with instructions alone, psychopaths showed no voluntary GSR control, whereas nonpsychopathic subjects were able to

**AVOIDANCE
LEARNING
Figure 13.2**

Mean avoidance learning scores plotted for three subject groups across three punishment (physical, tangible, and social) conditions. (From Schmauk 1970)

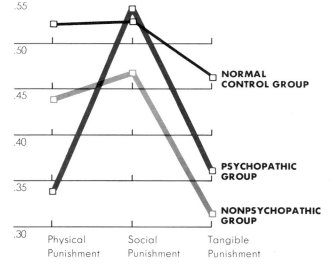

NORMAL
CONTROL GROUP

PSYCHOPATHIC
GROUP

NONPSYCHOPATHIC
GROUP

exert some control. However, after 16 minutes of biofeedback training, both groups were able to increase and decrease their GSRs to a comparable degree.

These results indicate that the initial inability of psychopaths voluntarily to respond physiologically is not an unalterable basis on which to distinguish psychopaths from nonpsychopaths. Rather, the differences between psychopaths and nonpsychopaths are dependent on their interaction with a particular situation. That psychopaths could learn some voluntary control suggests that their initial physiological hyporesponsivity is *not* an unalterable physiological deficit prohibiting their achievement of high levels of reactivity. Similarly, in the study by Schmauk (1970), psychopaths showed no learning deficits compared to nonpsychopaths in a particular situation—when money, rather than aversive stimulation, was used as a reinforcer.

Electrocortical concomitants of sociopathy. Although the sympathetic nervous system concomitants of sociopathy have been studied widely, very few studies have examined the brain-wave activity patterns of this group. Some consistent results, though, have been found. As Hare (1976) notes:

> Very few studies have been primarily concerned with the brain-wave activity of psychopaths. In most cases, the electroencephalogram (EEG) is obtained as part of a general survey of psychiatric patients, many of them somewhat uncertain diagnoses. Nevertheless, the results have been reasonably consistent. . . . Briefly, it appears that anywhere between 30 and 60 percent of diagnosed psychopaths exhibit some form of EEG abnormality, most usually widespread slow-wave activity. . . . In some cases, the highly aggressive forms of psychopathy may be associated with temporal abnormalities consisting of either slow-wave . . . or positive-spike . . . activity. (p. 342)

Hare (1976) suggests that the slow-wave activity often found in sociopaths can be viewed as consistent with the hypothesis that they tend to be cortically underaroused. Quay (1965) had earlier argued that the sociopath's impulsivity and need for excitement is due to a pathological need for stimulation because this person is cortically underaroused and in a continual condition of sensory deprivation. Sociopaths very quickly become bored

SOME EEG WAVEFORMS
Figure 13.3

These are examples of different forms of brain waves as recorded by an electroencephalogram. Traces (i) and (j) demonstrate positive spiking. (From *Psychopathy: Theory and Research*, by Robert D. Hare; copyright 1970 by John Wiley & Sons, Inc. Used by permission)

A 3—day—old infant

B 6—month—old infant

C 4—year—old child

D Adult, awake

s

E Adult, drowsy

F Adult, light sleep

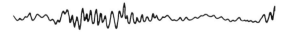

G Adult, deep sleep

H Adult, abnormal slow-wave

I 6/sec. positive spikes

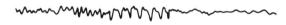

J 14/sec. positive spikes

and drowsy in situations that are unexciting and nonstimulating. Cleckley (1964) suggests that a dominant characteristic of a sociopath is boredom in situations that are not highly stimulating.

One study experimentally investigated whether sociopaths are stimulation-seekers who are highly susceptible to boredom. Orris (1967) compared the performance on a signal-detection task of three groups of subjects: sociopathic delinquents, subcultural delinquents, and neurotic delinquents. In this task, subjects were required to pay precise attention and report transient visual signals that were presented against a neutral background. The sociopaths performed consistently poorer on this task, indicating that they may be deficient in the ability to attend clearly to stimulation that is regular and somewhat monotonous. Orris also observed that the sociopathic group engaged in more self-stimulation (e.g., singing and talking) during the experiment than the other two groups. Many other experimental investigations also demonstrate that sociopaths show greater preference for novelty and complexity than nonsociopaths, possibly reflecting their need for stimulation. (cf. Hare 1970).

Hare (1976) has also suggested the significance of the slow-wave activity and positive spiking found in sociopaths.

> . . . the generalized slow-wave activity frequently found in psychopaths is consistent with the hypothesis that they tend to be cortically underaroused. . . . Since the psychopath's slow-wave activity is somewhat similar to that of normal children, it has been suggested that psychopathy may be related to delayed maturation of cortical processes. . . . In an earlier paper . . . it was suggested that the highly impulsive behavior of individuals with EEG abnormalities localized in the temporal lobes could be interpreted in terms of McCleary's concept of response preservation. This concept is based upon studies in which lesions in the limbic inhibitory mechanisms may result in perseveration of the most dominant response in any given situation, even though this response would ordinarily be inhibited. With respect to psychopathy, we might assume that the activity of these inhibitory mechanisms is periodically dampened, perhaps during states of high drive produced by sexual arousal, anger, etc. As a result, the dominant response in that particular situation (e.g., sexual or

CHROMOSOMES AND CRIME

A number of early investigators proposed that a tendency to engage in criminal behavior was an inherited trait. For example, Cesare Lombroso, who developed the "Italian School of Criminology" for the scientific analysis of crime and criminals (Lombroso-Ferrero 1911), suggested there were "born" criminal types who possessed anatomical "stigmatizing" features such as an unusually shaped head and jaw, low forehead, and eyebrows growing together above the bridge of the nose. These features, which were distinctively different from those of "normal" people, were considered to be characteristic of early "savage man." They were viewed as predisposing an individual to criminal behavior. This concept held that a person's proclivity toward crime was determined by his or her lineage and could be predicted by psychological and physiological anomalies.

This approach has long since been discarded. More recently, though, numerous investigations have suggested the importance of another inherited predisposing factor as a possible cause of criminal behavior. Indications are that the presence of an extra Y chromosome in males may be associated with violent criminal behavior. Within the nucleus of each human cell, there are twenty-three pairs of chromosomes. These chromosomes contain the "genetic code" that determines the traits we inherit and pass to our offspring. One chromosome pair determines an individual's sex and the later development of secondary sex characteristics. Male sex cells normally have one X and one Y chromosome; female cells have two X chromosomes. A genetic aberration that may occur in males is the presence of an additional Y sex chromosome. In the 1960s some evidence reported in the scientific literature indicated that men with this XYY chromosomal type tended to be very tall, aggressive, and often mentally dull. In the pioneering study in this area, Jacobs, Brunton, and Melville (1965) reported findings on a group of 197 mentally abnormal inmates of a special security institution who were diagnosed as having dangerous and violent criminal tendencies. It was found that seven members of this group, or 3.5 percent, possessed the XYY chromosome. The projected frequency in the normal population was only .13 percent. These initial findings generated a great deal of additional research of this chromosomal type. Not all these studies, however, paralleled the findings of the Jacobs et al. (1965) investigation.

In June 1969, the Center for Studies of Crime and Delinquency of the National Institutes of Mental Health conducted a national conference on this topic with experts from across the country participating. In their final report, participants concluded that it was premature to assume that this chromosomal aberration is a significant causal factor in aggressive, criminal behavior. The report, moreover, noted that some studies found the behavior of some men with this genetic anomaly to be *less* aggressive than that of normal males. The report also urged that the *XYY* chromosomal aberration not be made a basis for relieving offenders of legal responsibility for their criminal acts.

More recently, Jarvik, Klodin, and Matsuyama (1973) reported, on the basis of an extensive review of the research literature, that the frequency of *XYY*-aberrant males in the criminal population is approximately 2 percent. This is approximately 15 times the frequency found in the general male population. These figures lead them to conclude that, although the majority of crimes are committed by chromosomally normal males, the greater relative percentage of *XYY* individuals involved in such crimes suggests the importance of an extra Y chromosome as a possible predisposing factor in criminal-aggressive behavior. However, there still is not total agreement that such a relationship exists. Owen (1972) points out that the projected frequency in the general population is based primarily upon impressions from clinical data and may be greater than initially estimated. Moreover, some recent studies have not found the high rates of occurrence in criminal populations reported in earlier studies, raising the possibility that these earlier studies were in error. Needless to say, a great deal of additional research is required.

If future studies do confirm an association between the *XYY* chromosomal type and criminal behavior, an important question will be: "What is the biological process by which this chromoso-

mal type precipitates aggressive antisocial behavior?" Recent speculations suggest the following process: It is assumed that the Y chromosome is responsible for the production of the male hormone testosterone. It is suggested that an extra Y chromosome will generate a "double dose" or excessive amount of this hormone. Since some investigators have suggested a link between testosterone and aggression, it is speculated that the extra Y chromosome causes an even higher degree of aggression in these "double male" individuals.

One last point should be made. Even if future studies document that the *XYY* chromosomal type is associated with aggressive behavior, it will account for only about 2 percent of the criminal population. This indicates that environmental/learning factors still play the predominant role in this type of behavior. Moreover, one also must take into account the reports indicating that some *XYY* males turn out to be quiet, mild-mannered, and unaggressive. As Wiggens, Renner, Clore, and Rose (1976) indicate, the possibly higher frequency of *XYY* males in institutionalized settings may be due to an *indirect* relationship between the extra Y chromosome and behavior. That is, because this man is abnormally tall and often mentally dull, he provokes fear and so is readily labeled as aggressive/criminal. In this case, the *XYY* genetic effect would be indirect, with the aggressiveness merely representing the result of such individuals' selective social-learning history. This selective learning-history explanation could also be used to explain why some *XYY* types are mild-mannered and quite unaggressive. Moreover, there is some evidence to suggest that the representation of *XYY* types in criminal offenders is not much different than in other special groups, such as basketball players, who would be expected to have different learning histories. Future studies will need to be conducted to investigate whether the *XYY*-aggressiveness relationship is a direct or indirect one. Also, it would be beneficial to examine whether there is any one particular criminal group that is unusually violent because of the XYY aberration.

aggressive behavior) would occur, regardless of the consequences. (pp. 342–343)

It should be noted that positive spikes occur in the temporal lobe of the brain and consist of positive-polarity bursts of activity with frequencies of 6–8 and 14–16 cycles per second. Hare (1976) suggests that the EEG abnormalities in sociopaths thus are related to these persons' need for stimulation, their impulsive behavior, and their inability to inhibit behavior even in the face of negative consequences or punishment. These findings do not, however, tell us whether the underarousal is learned or is a genetic defect. Indeed, slow-wave activities or decreased GSR do not explain psychopathy but represent only physiological correlates.

THE FAMILY AND SOCIALIZATION A number of investigators have examined the role of the family and the socialization process in the development of sociopathic behavior. Gregory (1958), and more recently Hare (1970), have provided reviews of this research, which indicate that certain forms of early disturbance in family relationships, such as parental loss, parental rejection, and inconsistent and erratically punitive disciplinary techniques, may be important factors. For example, in a study conducted by Greer (1964), 60 percent of the sociopaths he studied had experienced a parental loss during childhood. This contrasted with only 28 percent for a group of neurotics and 27 percent for a group of normal subjects.

A host of other studies provide evidence for the importance of such factors. However, these data were gathered by means of retrospective reports; that is, information about early family experiences was obtained either from the sociopath being investigated or from parents, relatives, and friends long after the life events had actually occurred. Such data may be biased or unreliable because the individuals providing it may be unwilling or unable to recall the events accurately. There is one major investigation on sociopathy, however, that did not rely on retrospective reports. It is a study conducted by Robins (1966) in which very precise and detailed records were kept on children seen in a child guidance clinic. Ninety percent of an initial sample of these 584 children were located thirty years after their clinic referral and were interviewed by the investigators. An additional 100 control subjects who as children

were not seen by the clinic, but who lived in the same geographic area it served, were also followed-up in adulthood thirty years later. Because this investigation provides the most extensive data available to date on the development of sociopathy, we shall review the results in some detail.

Robins and her research colleagues interviewed the now-adult individuals in the clinic-referral group and the nonreferral control group. On the basis of the interviews, they were able to clinically assess and diagnose any maladjustments these individuals displayed. The adult problems were then correlated with the characteristics that these individuals displayed as children. The investigators could thus isolate the childhood characteristics that best predicted sociopathic behavior patterns in adulthood. Table 13.1 summarizes the data on family background and childhood characteristics of the sociopaths and the other clinic patients in this longitudinal study. As can be seen, sociopaths had childhood histories marked by aggressive, antisocial, impulsive, and sexual behavior.

Viewing the family backgrounds of these sociopaths and other patients, it is readily apparent that a large percentage of both groups came from impoverished homes and homes broken by divorce and separation. Most of the sociopaths, moreover, also had fathers who were either antisocial, sociopathic, or alcoholic. This relationship, in which a father's behavior predicts similar sociopathic behavior in his male or female offspring, is consistent with the findings by Andry (1957) and Marcus (1960) that maternal behavior or rejection are less predictive of delinquency development than is the personality of the father. Indeed, the important role of modeling in the development of social behavior (e.g., Bandura 1969) would suggest that a sociopathic father's modeling of antisocial behavior could produce similar learned behavior in his offspring.

Robins also found that the major results of having a sociopathic father were a lack of adequate discipline in the home and the presence of a great deal of parental discord. However, when discipline was adequate and there was an absence of parental discord, the probability was much lower that the child of an antisocial father would later be diagnosed as sociopathic. Robins therefore suggests that it is not merely parental loss or rejection that is related to sociopathy but the *circumstances* surrounding parental loss or rejection.

The relation between broken or discordant homes and delinquency or adult criminality so often interpreted in the literature as showing that broken homes "cause" delinquency or criminality may well be a spurious relationship occurring only because having an antisocial father simultaneously produces adult antisocial behavior in the children and marital discord between the parents. (Robins 1966, p. 179)

Although the results of the Robins study indicate the importance of circumstances surrounding early parental loss or rejection, Hare (1970) warns that one must be somewhat cautious in wholeheartedly accepting this and other socialization interpretations of sociopathy:

Another reason for being cautious about accepting the parental rejection and incon-

Antisocial Behavior
CHAPTER 13

From Robins 1966

CHARACTERISTICS OF SOCIOPATHS
Table 13.1

CHARACTERISTICS	SOCIOPATHS (N = 94)	OTHER PATIENTS (N = 342)	CHARACTERISTICS	SOCIOPATHS (N = 94)	OTHER PATIENTS (N = 342)
Male	85%	70%	Median age of onset	(7)[a]	(7)[a]
Referred for any antisocial behavior	95	66	Girls only	(13)[a]	(8)[a]
For theft	40	20	Juvenile court case	79	39
For sexual problems (girls only)	29	11	Sent to correctional institution	51	17
Symptoms			School retardation at referral	68	55
Theft	81	49	Final school level, eighth-grade graduate	62	36
Incorrigible	79	52	Antisocial toward		
Running away	71	39	Parents	73	50
Truancy	66	36	Teachers and other authority figures	83	57
Bad companions	56	36	Strangers	39	21
Sexual activity and excessive interest			Businesses	41	20
(Boys)	56	44	Family patterns		
(Girls)	79	62	Father sociopathic or alcoholic	53	32
Stay out late	55	35	Broken home, all causes	67	63
School discipline problems	53	31	Divorce and separation	44	33
Aggressive	45	26	Impoverished home	55	38
Reckless	35	23	Patient is only child	18	14
Impulsive	38	20	Patient is 1 of 4 children	27	17
Slovenly	32	17			
Enuretic	32	21			
Lack guilt	32	14			
Lying without cause	26	11			
Median age at referral	(14)[a]	(13)[a]			

[a]Figure expresses age in years.

sistent socialization interpretations of psychopathy is that most of the persons who come from what appear to be similarly disturbed backgrounds do not become psychopaths. Inconsistent socialization practices, for example, are related to a wide spectrum of later disturbances, including psychopathy and many forms of delinquent, neurotic, and psychotic behavior. Clearly, the gross type of disturbed family relationships generally discussed by most investigators are neither necessary nor sufficient conditions for the development of psychopathy. (p. 97)

In summary, the evidence suggests that a large percentage of sociopaths come from impoverished or broken homes and have experienced some form of parental loss or rejection. A more important socialization/child-rearing prediction of sociopathy, however, appears to be having a father who is sociopathic, antisocial, or alcoholic. These fathers appear to provide a model for antisocial behavior. As Hare (1970) notes, though, while the family experience may be an important factor in the development of sociopathy, it should not be viewed as providing the whole story of the development of this personality characteristic.

TREATMENT OF SOCIOPATHY

Traditional psychotherapeutic procedures have not been found to be effective in changing the behavior of sociopaths. Cleckley (1964) states:

> Over a period of many years I have remained discouraged about the effect of treatment on the psychopath. Having regularly failed in my own efforts to help such patients alter their fundamental pattern of inadequacy and antisocial activity, I had hoped for a while that treatment by others would be more successful. I have had the opportunity to see patients who were treated by psychoanalysis, by psychoanalytically oriented psychotherapy, by group and by milieu therapy, and by other variations of dynamic method. I have seen some patients who were treated for years. I have also known cases in which not only the patient but various members of his family were given prolonged psychotherapy. None

of these measures impressed me as achieving successful results. The psychopaths continued to behave as they had behaved in the past. (pp. 476–477)

Similarly, McCord and McCord (1964) reviewed a number of empirical studies that also reported discouraging treatment results for sociopaths. That traditional therapeutic techniques are not successful is not surprising because, as Hare (1970) notes, the sociopath lacks the requirements necessary for the psychotherapeutic process to be effective—e.g., the client being motivated towards changing behavior that he or she finds personally distressing and painful, and the establishment of an active interpersonal relationship between therapist and client. Moreover, most sociopaths see nothing seriously wrong with their behavior, which they often find extremely rewarding and exciting.

There is some evidence to indicate the possible effectiveness of two treatment approaches in modifying sociopathic behavior: (1) operant behavior modification techniques and (2) therapeutic communities. As we discuss the preliminary evidence, however, it is important to keep in mind that the studies lack adequate or appropriate control groups against which to make the necessary treatment-effectiveness comparisons. Moreover, many of the studies used a mixed group of sociopaths and delinquent/criminal subjects. Also, the sociopathic subject populations used were incarcerated, "unsuccessful" sociopaths. The evidence from these studies is therefore, at best, only mildly suggestive.

OPERANT BEHAVIOR MODIFICATION TECHNIQUES Davidson and Seidman (1974) have reviewed a series of studies in which behavior modification techniques were applied to juvenile delinquents. One such study was the Case I project (Cohen, Filipczak, & Bis 1967) undertaken at the National Training School for Boys, which utilized a controlled environment operant technique. The juvenile delinquent boys in this project could earn points, which later could be converted to money to buy desired goods, contingent on their successful completion of programmed instruction in academic subjects. Both scholastic achievement levels and educational achievement values were effectively raised in these boys. Like the work of Schmauk (1970), this program again demonstrates the effective use of tangible (monetary) incentives in shaping appropriate behavior in delinquents. Of course, we are assuming that a certain percentage of the delinquents in this project could be classified as sociopathic and so would benefit from this technique.

One can easily think of other types of operant programs that could be efficacious in altering deviant behavior of sociopaths within institutions. Buehler, Patterson, and Furniss (1966) assert that institutionalized delinquents positively reinforce each other's behavior. Using observational techniques in two institutions, they found over 70 percent positive reinforcement by peers of deviant behavior like breaking institutional rules, fighting, etc. In one of these institutions, they also found that the peer group punished socially conforming behavior more often than they rewarded it. To modify this situation, an operant program could be instituted in which individual incentives (such as monetary incentives) were made contingent on socially conforming, nondeviant behavior. In addition to requiring individuals to attain a certain criterion before receiving rewards, the program would require the peer group as a whole to attain a predetermined criterion. This would put pressure on the peer group to reward socially conforming behavior and punish deviant behavior. Such a program might modify and extinguish deviant behavior, since it would provide a "pay-off" for socially conforming behavior.

Trotter (1975) reports the use of a behavior modification program in which reinforcement procedures were employed with adult prisoners. The program was established at the Patuxent Federal Correctional Institution, in Jessup, Maryland, in January 1955. The treatment program was based on psychological learning principles and used a graded-tier system. Only volunteers participated. New inmates started at the bottom and earned more privileges as they worked their way up through four levels or stages. In Stage 1 of the program, the prisoner earned credits for behaviors such as keeping his cell neat, keeping clean, not complaining during daily counts, etc. The credits earned could later be used to purchase items in the commissary. After satisfactory completion of this first stage, the prisoners proceeded to Stage 2 in which more freedom and movement were provided in a type of "honor farm" setting. If the prisoner continued to respond by demonstrating socially acceptable behavior, he could move to Stage 3, which offered rehabilitation programs such as learning data processing techniques. Finally, at Stage 4, he was paid real money for the data-

Cory Wolinsky/Stock, Boston

Most prisons are not constructed for the benefit of the prisoners. They often become merely "human storehouses."

processing skills he learned while incarcerated.

The Patuxent program also uses an indeterminant sentence procedure, by which release from the institution depends on the approval of a committee of staff and outside professionals. The length of sentence is not set in advance. Release depends on the inmate's behavior being approved by the committee. This program has given evidence of producing a low recidivism rate. For example, in the ten-year period from 1955 to 1965 only 8 percent of those granted final release from the program returned to criminal behavior. Certain critics of the program, however, have argued that a low rate of recidivism is easy to obtain in any program using an indeterminant sentence procedure in which inmates can be kept incarcerated more or less indefinitely.

Programs such as this can be used successfully to modify behavior within the institutional setting. However, behavior modification techniques have received some bad publicity in recent years, being viewed as inhumane and manipulative. This viewpoint stemmed from a few occurrences in

Drugs

which drastic procedures such as the use of electric shock, administration of drugs that induce violent reactions, etc., were used to force compliance with the rules of the institution. On the basis of these rare occurrences, a great outcry was made against behavior modification techniques in general within the prison system.

In any therapeutic/rehabilitation program, it is important to ensure that treatment effects will not disappear soon after the interventions are terminated. The concern is not only to reduce certain behaviors in the institutional setting, but also to carry over the effect outside the institution. The prospect of achieving this generalization is probably extremely poor unless a certain amount of control over the individual, and his or her environment, can be maintained outside the prison setting. It is probably unrealistic to expect that an operant technique can change the total "personality structure" of the sociopath. The control of situational factors to prevent the expression of undesirable/ harmful sociopathic behaviors, and to reinforce socially accepted behaviors, may be the best and only possible treatment.

THERAPEUTIC COMMUNITIES Some treatment programs have attempted to change the sociopath's maladaptive behavior using the therapeutic community-milieu therapy concept. This concept, originally developed by Jones (1953), treats institutionalized settings as social systems that are structured so that inmates and staff can benefit from membership in it. An attempt also is made to sustain the personal integrity of inmates in such settings. In employing this basic concept with sociopaths, attempts have been made to completely restructure the social and psychological environment so as to achieve more appropriate socialization of their behavior. The controlled environment concept is similar to that used in the operant approach, but a variety of other therapeutic techniques are also employed. Hare (1970) has reviewed a number of these studies, one of which was conducted by McCord and McCord (1964).

McCord and McCord (1964), after reviewing the research on attempts to treat sociopathy, concluded that institution-based programs may be the only potential treatment strategies for this disorder. These investigators conducted a detailed study of the treatment effectiveness of one such institutional program at the Wiltwyck School for Boys in New York. This program, which they found to be therapeutically effective, stressed a loving,

permissive environment in which permissiveness was gradually replaced by concerted attempts to teach social responsibility and social control. In their study in 1954–1955, these investigators examined the response of different types of children to this treatment approach. They assessed 107 children: 15 of these children were identified as truly sociopathic personalities; 63 as behavior disorders who were delinquent but also displayed various neurotic traits, 23 identified as purely neurotic; and 6 as borderline psychotics. All were administered a series of tests and interviews in 1954 and were observed in standard behavior situations. Moreover, a sample of subjects who had recently arrived at the time of the first testing evaluation were retested in 1955 to attain a measure of the effects of the treatment program. Results of this program evaluation study indicated that sociopaths and subjects with behavior disorders responded most positively to the treatment. These individuals displayed an increase in internalized guilt, behaved less aggressively, and became less fearful of authority figures.

Another study, by Craft, Stephenson, and Granger (1964), assessed the therapeutic effectiveness of two different residential treatment programs at Balderton Hospital in England. Twenty-five sociopathic males between the ages of 13 and 25 were randomly assigned to one of two treatment groups. One program consisted of inmate self-governing procedures, intensive group psychotherapy, and the presence of tolerant staff members. The other program was more authoritarian in structure; it had a firm but sympathetic and understanding form of discipline and only superficial psychotherapy. Approximately 6–9 months after treatment began, subjects were allowed to obtain day jobs in the surrounding community but returned each night to the hospital. After one year of treatment, they were discharged. Psychological testing during treatment indicated that neither group showed significant personality or adjustment changes during the program. A one-year follow-up study after discharge, however, indicated that those subjects who were in the authoritarian program had been convicted of significantly fewer criminal offenses than those in the other group. The investigators concluded that for sociopaths a treatment program in a friendly but disciplined residential environment is more effective than a program of group psychotherapy in a permissive setting.

Finally, another promising program is *Achievement Place*. Originally developed in Kansas by Montrose Wolf, this program is now being used in more than 50 locations across the country. It is a group-home approach in which a small number (six to eight) of delinquent or predelinquent youths between the ages of 12 and 15 live together in a family-type environment. The youths are supervised by a couple known as *teaching parents*. The program has four major features: (1) a self-government system; (2) a behavioral skills training curriculum in which reinforcement, role playing, and modeling are employed to teach academic and social skills; (3) the development of a mutually reinforcing, warm relationship with the teaching parents; (4) a *token* economy in which the youths earn tokens for positive behavior that are exchangeable for privileges. The token economy is usually phased out after about a month, at which time the youths are placed on a merit system in which all privileges are free.

Wolf, Phillips, and Fixsen (1974) reported some preliminary evaluation data on one Achievement Place program. One group of youths randomly assigned to Achievement Place (n = 8) were compared with a control group receiving the usual community approach (n = 18). During the two years after the random assignment, 56 percent of the control group youths were institutionalized, as compared with only 12 percent of the Achievement Place youths. These results clearly show the positive impact of this type of program. Future evaluation studies can more thoroughly assess its long-term effectiveness.

These studies indicate the potential effectiveness of therapeutic community programs in the treatment of sociopathic disorders. However, as with operant behavior modification programs, one must interpret the significance of these studies with caution because of the use of a mixed group of criminal and patient types. What is needed in future investigations is a clearly delineated group

Courtesy of the Jewish Children's Bureau of Chicago

In a group home, a small number of youths live together in a family-like environment as a means of bringing about behavior change.

of sociopaths. Nevertheless, results do suggest that these therapeutic techniques may lead to the establishment of rapport with the sociopath, after which demands can more readily be made and social controls imposed. Such programs would at least improve on incarceration, which does little to reform the sociopath. In fact, while in traditional prison settings, sociopaths commit more offenses than other inmates and also spend more time in solitary confinement (Zax and Cowen 1972). Punishment alone clearly does not have a corrective impact on the behavior of sociopaths. A therapeutic community program may be a more effective alternative.

SECONDARY ANTISOCIAL BEHAVIOR

Secondary sociopathy and *neurotic sociopathy* have been the traditional terms used for this form of antisocial behavior. A potential problem with both terms, however, is the possibility of erroneously conveying the impression that the individual so labeled is basically a sociopath. As indicated earlier in this chapter, these individuals, unlike primary sociopaths, do experience guilt and remorse for their behavior. Their antisocial behavior is motivated primarily by neurotic or psychotic emotional disturbances or is the result of brain damage or mental retardation.

CAUSES AND STRESSORS

Brain damage or mental retardation can trigger antisocial behavior. For example, it has been found that in about 1 percent of the crimes committed by juvenile delinquents, brain pathology prompts a tendency towards episodes of violent antisocial behavior (Kiester 1974). Mental retardation or low intelligence can also be a precipitating factor because such persons may be unable to comprehend or appreciate the negative, antisocial consequences of their actions. They may also unwittingly become involved with gangs or with intellectually superior sociopaths who may use and exploit them. In approximately 5 percent of the juvenile delinquency cases, this factor of low intelligence seems to play a dominant role (Coleman 1976).

In about 6 to 10 percent of juvenile delinquent behavior, neurotic or psychotic disorders appear to be of causal significance (Coleman 1976). The antisocial behavior of these individuals reflects an underlying emotional maladjustment, rather than a dominant sociopathic personality. For example, in viewing delinquent behavior that is prompted by psychotic episodes, Bandura (1973) indicates that there is often a prolonged period of emotional turmoil and stress that eventually precipitates an outburst of violent behavior after extended frustration. Similarly, neurotic disorders may prompt certain antisocial behaviors, as in the case of the financially secure individual who shoplifts and steals items he or she does not need. Unlike the primary sociopath, this person may feel extremely guilty afterwards. The behavior is prompted by some neurotic conflict or stressor and is not due to the presence of a basic sociopathic personality attribute. The same causes and stressors discussed in the chapters on neurosis and psychosis can lead to an outburst of antisocial behavior.

TREATMENT

Because of the different precipitating causes of antisocial behavior in this group, it would be reasonable to expect that the type of treatment/ rehabilitation would differ from that provided to either the primary sociopath or, the dyssocial or subcultural delinquent/criminal (discussed in the next section). However, this is not always the case. When offenders are institutionalized, usually no differential rehabilitation is administered to different types of offenders. This may create additional problems for, say, the neurotic juvenile delinquent. By mixing nonviolent offenders who have committed minor crimes with hard-core "veteran" offenders or sociopaths who have committed repeated crimes of violence, the system may be providing learning experiences on how to become more sophisticated delinquents. These individuals may emerge from prison more criminal and less fit for society than when they first entered. If rehabilitation is a primary goal of the penal system, then one should not "lump together" the various types of offenders. Two alternatives are possible: (1) differential treatment/rehabilitation programs within the institutional setting; (2) probation and close supervision to help certain troubled individuals in their own environments either in lieu of or after a short period of institutionalization.

DIFFERENTIAL TREATMENT / REHABILITATION PROGRAMS A treatment program for juvenile delinquents that takes into account the different causes of antisocial behavior was developed by the Community Treatment Staff of the California Youth Authority. A classification and treatment-planning program called the "Interpersonal Maturity Level Classification" was formulated; it was an elaboration of a typology presented by Sullivan, Grant, and Grant (1957) that described a sequence of personality integration and interpersonal maturity in normal childhood development. The typology focused on the ways in which a delinquent is able to see himself or herself and the world, especially in terms of emotions and motivations associated with behavior. The system developed by the California Youth Authority takes into account interpersonal maturity level as well as delinquent subtypes in establishing an appropriate treatment program for each delinquent. A subcultural delinquent, for example, would be given a treatment regimen much different than that provided to a person displaying secondary antisocial behavior. This type of differential treatment program appears to be the only reasonable approach to deal therapeutically with the wide range of situational- and emotional-precipitated delinquent behaviors. Classification systems of this type will aid significantly in identifying the program needs of inmates not only in the area of counseling and psychotherapy, but also in vocational training and education. Because the number of professional staff has always been limited, and will probably always remain so, psychological treatment may be reserved for those persons assessed as particularly in need of this intervention technique. Para-professionals could be trained to effectively counsel and treat the less disturbed individuals.

At present, there is still a strong trend toward providing treatment/rehabilitation for juvenile offenders who are institutionalized. This is no longer true for adult offenders. The present trend for adults who require imprisonment is toward methods involving punishment and deterrence. This shift has been prompted by the high rate of recidivism. Even though the recidivism rate is as high for youthful offenders as for adults, society still views it as an obligation to attempt to "save" a youth. Society takes a harsher stance with the adult offender. Since the recidivism rate is high, many have concluded that rehabilitation with adults does not work. Schwartz (1975) has stated: "'Rehabilitation' in prison is at best a myth and at worst a fraud."

Legal and ethical issues. Even the therapeutic approach used in the Patuxent correctional institution (discussed earlier), which demonstrated some evidence of producing a low recidivism rate, has come under attack. Opponents have argued that this approach often overuses negative reinforcement-punishment procedures and abuses the indeterminate sentence procedure (Trotter 1975). The Patuxent program became a major focus of controversy and its continuation in its present form became doubtful. Many treatment professionals working within the prison system thus find themselves in a somewhat paradoxical position: Because of the high recidivism rate, they are accused of not providing effective treatment/rehabilitation. However, when an approach such as Patuxent is used, which has produced a low recidivism rate, they are criticized for using overly manipulative and inhumane techniques.

The complete elimination of rehabilitation programs — that is, relying only on time served as punishment for crimes — is considered too dramatic a step by many mental health professionals. Brown, Wienckowski, and Stolz (1975) argue that such a step would eliminate the opportunity for improvement in those prisoners who genuinely desire to participate. They suggest that it would be more advisable to build in safeguards for the inmates' rights rather than discard all such programs completely. They propose that each institu-

THE PATUXENT PROGRAM CONTROVERSY

The triggering incident in the controversy about the Patuxent program involved an inmate who was subjected to indefinite commitment. The inmate, Edward McNeil, was convicted of assault and attempted rape at the age of 19. He repeatedly denied the charges, but was given a sentence of not more than five years and sent to Patuxent for precommitment evaluation. He immediately began appealing the original conviction and also refused to cooperate with the evaluation procedures. Because of his lack of cooperation, the Patuxent staff did not diagnose him, but kept him in the receiving section without benefit of treatment. The institution asserted its right to hold him indefinitely without final court commitment.

After many appeals, the United States Supreme Court ordered McNeil's immediate release. At that time, he had been imprisoned for almost six years. If he had originally been sent to a regular prison, he would have been eligible for parole after *15 months*. The Supreme Court ruled that Patuxent could not hold noncommitment patients whose original sentences had expired. This was obviously a case of unjust imprisonment. It rightfully generated a great deal of public opinion against the use of indefinite sentence procedures in shaping inmates' behavior in a socially desirable direction. (This case summary is based on an article in the *American Psychological Association Monitor*, May 1975.)

tion establish a committee — composed of prison officials, prisoner representatives, and at least one lawyer who is knowledgeable in the area of civil liberties — that would determine the appropriateness of the methods and goals of proposed treatment programs. This committee would also monitor these programs when they are instituted. In addition, each possible participant in a program approved by the committee should be given the right not to participate without fear of losing privileges or receiving additional punishment. This proposal may provide an acceptable compromise between abandoning rehabilitation programs altogether

THE McNAGHTEN RULE AND THE DURHAM DECISION

In 1843, Daniel McNaghten assassinated Edward Drummond, secretary to the Prime Minister of England. McNaghten mistook Drummond for the Prime Minister himself, whom McNaghten had been commanded to kill "by the voice of God." He was found not guilty by the judges of England because he was declared "labouring under such a defect of reason, from disease of the mind, as not to know the nature and quality of the act he was doing; or, if he did know, that he did not know he was doing what was right." This led to the "McNaghten rule"—the "right and wrong" test of insanity that was widely adopted by courts in this country and is currently the most prevalent ruling. This rule, however, has been a source of controversy through the years because of the difficulty of determining whether an individual might be in some sense insane even though he or she knows "the difference between right and wrong."

In 1954, another milestone decision known as the "Durham decision" was handed down by a United States district court. It held that an "accused is not criminally responsible if his unlawful act was the product of mental disease or mental defect." This became known as the *Durham test*, which dictates that when a criminal act is the result of some form of mental illness, the individual should be hospitalized for treatment under the authority of a psychiatrist. The individual could be indefinitely committed to a hospital until "cured."

The Durham decision introduced a great number of difficulties into the criminal justice system. One basic problem is the question of whether a psychiatrist or other "expert" witnesses can adequately determine the state of mind of the accused. Thomas Szasz, a psychiatrist, has been the most outspoken critic of psychiatry playing a role in the judicial process. He points out the problems of such a system:

> . . . disregarding even the most obvious doubt concerning exactly what the expression "mental illness" is supposed to denote, it denotes a theory and not a fact. . . . To

believe that one's own theories are facts is considered by many contemporary psychiatrists as a symptom of schizophrenia. Yet that is what the language of the Durham decision does. It reifies some of the shakiest and most controversial aspects of psychiatry, i.e., those pertaining to what is "mental disease" and the classification of such alleged disease, and by legal fiat seeks to transform inadequate theory into "judicial fact". . . . Is Durham an improvement if it merely changes the "criminal" to a "patient"? (Szasz 1958, p. 190)

Another significant problem created by the Durham decision has to do with the civil rights of the individual declared mentally "insane" and incompetent to stand trial. Even though the individual is freed from legal responsibility for criminal behavior, he or she may be institutionalized for indefinite periods of time in a mental hospital or prison hospital. These periods of institutionalization may be longer than the time the person would have been confined in prison if the issue concerning sanity had not been raised. Moreover, as Szasz notes, this decision puts too much power in the hands of hospital psychiatrists, who become responsible for deciding when an individual is ready for discharge. Szasz also points out that the quality and effectiveness of treatment in mental hospitals are questionable.

Fortunately, many knowledgeable individuals in both the mental health and legal professions are aware of the difficulties and problems of the present system of determining legal responsibility. A number of recent court rulings have been made to curb possible abuses in the use of psychiatric examination and testimony in determining the mental status and competency of an offender to stand trial. A major task ahead for criminal law is the development of a system that is able to deal independently with the issues of legal guilt or innocence and the appropriate type of sentence (hospitalization or incarceration in prison).

and employing undue coercion to force prisoners into participating in them.

PROBATION/PAROLE AND CLOSE SUPERVISION Probation is widely used with juvenile offenders. Indeed, for many individuals, probation may be a better alternative to incarceration. The California Youth Authority conducted a five-year Community Treatment Project in which delinquents who had not been involved in serious or violent crimes (such as murder, rape, or arson) were given immediate probation and closely supervised in their own home communities. The results indicated that juvenile offenders treated in this program demonstrated a rehabilitation success rate of 72 percent. By contrast, a comparable group of delinquents who received institutional treatment and then were released on probation showed a rehabilitation success rate of only 48 percent (Blake 1967).

According to Coleman (1976), 90 percent of the females and 73 percent of the males who are committed as juvenile delinquents to the California Youth Authority were found to be eligible for such a community treatment program, indicating that it may be possible in most cases to modify maladaptive behavior within the community or family without having to resort to incarceration. However, again as Coleman (1976) notes, one apparently important factor in the success of the California project was a significant reduction in the supervision case loads of the probation officers involved. Programs patterned after this would similarly need additional personnel. However, since the rate of recidivism for juvenile offenders sent to correctional training schools has been estimated to be as high as 80 percent, the additional costs may be well worth it. There is also no reason to try a similar type of program with adult offenders.

DYSSOCIAL DELINQUENCY/CRIMINALITY

In many instances, individuals exhibit antisocial behavior not because they are sociopathic, emotionally disturbed, or brain-damaged, but because they were raised or are living in a delinquent/criminal subculture or environment that fosters and reinforces such behavior. For many of these persons, there also is an economic motivation in their criminal lifestyle as drug pushers, hired killers, burglars, and the like.

Traditionally, a clear distinction has been made between the *antisocial personality* (or sociopath) and *dyssocial behavior*. The former is labeled as a personality disorder; the latter is considered a behavior not normally associated with any significant personality disturbance. That is, the individual who engages in dyssocial behavior is not assumed to be psychologically abnormal. Cleckley (1964) has clearly distinguished between ordinary criminal behavior (i.e., dyssocial behavior) and sociopathic behavior. Dyssocial behavior is usually not characterized by the impulsive, reckless, callous quality typical of sociopathic behavior. Criminals usually consider the consequences of their behavior and work out goals associated with some pay-off, rather than acting impulsively.

Cloward and Ohlin (1960) have outlined three categories of dyssocial behavior: (1) The *criminal subculture* views success in crime as a positive form of behavior. Monetary gain is highly valued. The criminals involved are usually capable of maintaining normal interpersonal relationships and usually have strong loyalties to their organization or gang. The Mafia, as depicted in the film *The Godfather,* is an example of this criminal subculture. (2) The *conflict subculture* is one that values personal characteristics such as physical courage and violence. Exploits of violence against conventional society are highly valued. Street gangs or motorcycle gangs such as Hell's Angels are examples of this type of subculture. It is less stable than the criminal subculture, with members tending to leave when they grow older. (3) The *retreatist subculture* is usually organized around drug use. A primary goal of this subculture is to "turn on" to drugs and "turn off" to society. The crimes that are committed are usually to maintain the drug habit. The "hippie" drug communities that blossomed during the 1960s were examples of this retreatist subculture.

THE INCREASE IN VIOLENT CRIMES

According to the Uniform Crime Reports of the FBI (1975), violent crimes have increased significantly in the United States during the 1970s. Here are some of the figures: Murder up 76% from 1960 to 1970; up an additional 30% from 1970 to 1974. Aggravated assault up 117% from 1960 to 1970; up an additional 38% from 1970 to 1974. Forcible rape up 121% from 1960 to 1970; up an additional 50% from 1970 to 1974. Robbery up 224% from 1960 to 1970; up an additional 13% from 1970 to 1974.

The increase in crime has been especially noticeable in large urban areas. Along with this increase has come a reemergence of the street gang, more lethal now than in the past. The following short article by Daniel Rapoport reprinted from a 1976 issue of *Parade* Magazine, dramatizes this new "breed" of street gang, an example of the violence present in many urban areas today.

STREET GANGS ARE BACK WITH GUNS

Youth gangs in America today are more lethal than ever before. They are terrorizing greater numbers of people, employing deadlier weapons and proving harder to combat than gangs of the 1950s and 60s, according to a report recently handed the federal government. Most worrisome to local officials is that gang members have discovered the gun and have shifted a major part of their operations from the street to the school.

Efforts by cities to cope with the gangs, says the author of the report, have been failures.

"Many urban communities are gripped with hopelessness that anything can be done to curb the unremitting menace of the gangs," declares Walter B. Miller of Harvard's Center for Criminal Justice.

Miller, an anthropologist whose interest in and contact with gangs dates back to 1954, spent a year studying present-day gangs in the six cities that he concluded faced the worst gang problems—New York, Chicago, Los Angeles, Philadelphia, Detroit and San Francisco. His investigation was financed by the Justice Department's Law Enforcement Assistance Administration (LEAA) and constitutes what is believed to be the first national study of its kind. Among Miller's conclusions:

—Gang violence today is more lethal than during any previous period. The reason appears to lie in the "extraordinary increase in the availability and use" of guns by gang members.

—From 1972 through 1974 five of the six cities recorded 525 gang-related murders—about 25 percent of all juvenile homicides for those cities.

—Gangs can be found terrorizing elementary, junior and senior high schools. Says a Philadelphia junior high principal: "There is no point in trying to exaggerate the situation. The truth by itself is devastating."

—The six cities report from 760 gangs with 28,500 members to 2700 gangs with 81,500 members.

—Despite claims that American females are increasingly criminal and violent, urban youth gangs continue to be "a predominantly male enterprise." Gangs take an old-fashioned, traditional attitude toward sex roles. Girls carry weapons for boys, serve in female auxiliaries and frequently offer their impugned honor as the reason for a rumble between rival gangs.

Substantiating Miller's findings, Capt. Francis J. Daly, who commands the Youth Aid Division of the New York Police Department, says: "Ten years ago we had nothing in New York City. About 1971 it started up again in the Bronx." Although it has leveled off since then, Daly feels gang activity today is four times more violent than it was in the 1950s. "Weapons are much more available," says Daly. Another difference between now and the old days is that innocent people are more often the victims of gang criminality. In the old days they spent much more time on rumbles against each other. Now there are more robberies, burglaries and shakedowns against non-gang members.

NO CHEAP GUN

As for weapons, Miller's report finds that gangs are no longer satisfied with the homemade zip guns of 20 years ago or even "Saturday night specials." Instead, they want top-quality weaponry, such as the Smith & Wesson .38 used by many police departments.

Los Angeles Police Capt. William J. Riddle, commanding officer of the Juvenile Division, sees guns as a major contributor to the violence. "They're not that difficult to get," he says. "Every time a million more guns are sold to the public, more of them reach gangs and other criminals through such means as burglaries."

One of Miller's most alarming findings is that gangs have turned the public schools into battle grounds, attacking not only members of rival gangs, but also students who are non-members. He says that the shooting and killing of teachers by gang members has been reported in Chicago and Philadelphia.

Miller says this violence has led to "territorialization" of schools, meaning that gangs actually claim "ownership" of such areas as a cafeteria or a gym. "As owners of school facilities," he reports, "gang members have assumed the right to collect 'fees' from other students for a variety of 'privileges' which can be defined as passing through the hallways, using the gym, not being assaulted and of simply going to school."

INTIMIDATING THE SYSTEM

In some cases, he adds, school administrators seem helpless. A New York City source told him that some of the semi-autonomous school districts had "sold out," granting gangs the right to recruit among the student body in exchange for a promise of nonviolence.

Comments a Los Angeles youth worker: "The problem is out of hand. We've had three years of violence and killing in the schools with no real action by the authorities. All the schools in the inner city have large gang populations."

For the most part, Miller says, gang activity is confined to the slum areas of big cities. Gang members range in age from 12 to 21 and usually associate by ethnic background. Black and Hispanic gangs are more numerous than gangs of white youths from working-class families.

The newest and most surprising change that Miller discovered was the increase in the number of Asian-Americans involved:

"Accepted doctrine for many years has been that Oriental youths pose negligible problems in juvenile delinquency or gang activity. This accepted tenet has been seriously undermined by events of the 1970s—not only by the violent activities of the newly immigrated 'Hong Kong Chinese,' but by the development in several cities of gangs of Filipinos, Japanese and other Asian groups. The estimated number of Asian gangs is now almost equal to that of white gangs and may exceed their number in the near future."

WHAT THE FUTURE HOLDS

Miller is not overly optimistic about the future . . . barring some dramatic—and unlikely—move such as a massive program of federal help, Miller sees no immediate relief. His conclusion: "The likelihood that gang problems will continue to beset major cities during the next few years appears high."

Wisconsin Center for Film and Theater Research

THE GODFATHER © 1972, Paramount
Pictures. There are various criminal sub-
cultures that view success in certain types
of crime as a positive form of behavior.

**The criminals involved are usually ca-
pable of having loyal and loving family
relationships, as is shown in this film.**

CAUSES AND STRESSORS

Sutherland in the 1930s did some of the earliest
work indicating the importance of subcultural influences in the development of the professional
criminal (Sutherland & Cressey 1966). His pioneering study indicated that the basic socialization
process is very similar for everyone: the individual
comes to adopt the social/behavioral values and
standards that are modeled and emphasized by the
persons he or she interacts with on a repeated and
friendly basis. These persons are usually his or her
parents and peers. The person who grows up in a
subculture where antisocial behavior is the norm
learns certain criminal skills and internalizes certain
values and standards that are likely to be quite
different from those of the larger, conventional
society. The individual who may later become a
professional criminal acquires his or her training
through such learning experiences, values, and
rewards that the environment has provided. Is this
type of training, minus the emphasis on antisocial

criminal skills, basically any different than that
received by a legitimate professional? Sutherland
suggests that it is not. Indeed, social learning
theorists such as Bandura (1973) indicate that only
in rare exceptions (involving organic brain damage) is violent antisocial behavior not learned.

TREATMENT

Our discussion of treatment approaches for primary sociopathy and secondary antisocial behavior is applicable also to dyssocial sociopathy. In the
case of the subcultural delinquent/criminal, treatment need not be directed toward personality
restructuring or the modification of emotional
problems. Rather, social rehabilitation programs
need to be administered, preferably in the commu-
nity-family environment. Incarceration without an
attempt to deal with the situational-social factors
that precipitated the antisocial behavior is unlikely
to reform the criminal. Current high recidivism rates

Michael Abramson/Black Star

Often young people join gangs in a reaction against a conventional society that has given them a disadvantageous social position.

attest to this fact. Another point is that, for some individuals, a criminal lifestyle is the only realistic possibility, considering the social environment to which they will return and the potentially attractive and lucrative financial rewards of this profession.

Without major social efforts directed at reducing poverty and adequate educational, recreational, and job opportunities for disadvantaged individuals, it appears unrealistic to assume that any incarceration/rehabilitation method will be effective.

DIAGNOSIS AND ASSESSMENT

INTERVIEW/REFERRAL

Unlike many of the forms of psychopathology we have discussed, antisocial behavior in general can be diagnosed reliably because of the objective behavioral referent—the performance of a antisocial criminal act that brings an individual to the attention of the criminal justice system. Differentiating between the various causes of the antisocial behaviors is more difficult. To demonstrate the

obvious difficulties and resultant discrepancies in this differentiation process, Brodsky (1972) reviewed a number of studies of criminal offender diagnoses. Table 13.2, which summarizes some of these studies, reveals a wide range of results from psychiatric assessments of offenders. For example, four of the studies assessed over 80 percent of the sampled offenders as normal, while the other five studies show a wide range of much lower percentages classified as normal. These discrepancies most likely are due to the diverse diagnostic procedures and populations used. It is clear that a more standardized assessment procedure is needed.

In diagnosing sociopathy, the procedure used by Hare (1976) can serve as a prototype for other investigators and clinicians in this area; he uses it to select sociopaths for his research studies.

**EVALUATIONS
OF CRIMINALS**
Table 13.2

From Brodsky 1972

SOURCE	POPULATION	DIAGNOSIS	PERCENT
Glueck (1918)	608 Sing Sing prisoners	Psychotic or mentally deteriorated	12.0
		Normal	41.0
		Mentally retarded	28.1
Overholser (1935)	5,000 felons under Briggs Law in Mass.	Abnormal	15.0
		Normal	85.0
Bromberg & Thompson (1937)	9,958 offenders before Court of General Sessions, New York City	Psychotic	1.5
		Psychoneurotic	6.9
		Psychopathic personalities	6.9
		Feebleminded	2.4
		Normal or mild personality defects	82.3
Schilder (1940)	Convicted felons, Court of General Sessions of New York City	Psychotic	1.6
		Neurotic	4.2
		Psychopathic personalities	7.3
		Feebleminded	3.1
		Normal	83.8
Banay (1941)	Sing Sing prisoners	Psychotic	1.0
		Emotionally immature	20.0
		Psychopathic	17.0
		Normal	62.0
Poindexter (1955)	100 problem inmates	Mentally ill	20.0
		Normal	80.0
Schlessinger & Blau (1957)	500 typical prisoners	Character and behavior disorders	85.0
		Normal	15.0
Shands (1958)	1,720 North Carolina felon admissions to Central Prison	Psychotic	3.5
		Personality disorder	55.8
		Psychoneurotic	3.9
		Sociopathic personality	7.0
		Other	5.3
		No psychiatric disorder	4.7
		Transient personality disorder	19.8
Brodsky (1970)	32,511 military prisoners	Character and behavior disorders	77.1
		No psychiatric disease	21.3
		Miscellaneous disorders	1.6

In this procedure, the first step taken is a discussion of Cleckley's (1964) conception of sociopathy with the professional staff of the institution in which the research/evaluation is being conducted. This list of major features of sociopathy as delineated by Cleckley is reviewed with the staff:

1. Superficial charm and good intelligence.
2. Absence of delusions and other signs of irrational thinking.
3. Absence of nervousness or other neurotic manifestations.
4. Unreliability.
5. Untruthfulness and insincerity.
6. Lack of remorse or shame.
7. Antisocial behavior without apparent compunction.
8. Poor judgment and failure to learn from experience.
9. Pathologic egocentricity and incapacity for love.
10. General poverty in major affective reactions.
11. Specific loss of insight.
12. Unresponsiveness in general interpersonal relations.
13. Fantastic and uninviting behavior, with alcohol and sometimes without.
14. Sex life impersonal, trivial, and poorly integrated.
15. Failure to follow any life plan.

These criteria are used as a basis for diagnosing sociopathy. Based on information obtained from the staff, institutional and social history files, behavioral ratings by others, and information obtained during interviews, two or three global assessments on a 7-point scale are made of the degree to which the rater is confident that an inmate either does or does not fit these criteria for sociopathy. Thus, in this procedure, the raters collect and use as much information as is available. Sociopaths are defined as those individuals receiving a rating of 1 or 2; nonsociopaths are defined as those with a rating of 6 or 7. Subjects are also sometimes assigned to a "mixed" group, with ratings of 3–5. Hare indicates that these subjects would probably have been placed in the sociopathic group had more information been available on them.

Hare (1976) indicates that in his early studies, the raters used the 15-item Cleckley checklist before making the global rating. He notes, however, that he found the checklist was not really necessary, as long as the raters kept the concept of sociopathy clearly in mind when performing their global clinical assessments.

One potential shortcoming of the Hare assessment procedure is the subjective element involved in making the global ratings. Hare (1976) admits this as a possible fault, even though he has demonstrated replicable results in numerous studies using the procedure. Replication by independent investigators, however, is needed. Moreover, research is required to find the degree of agreement between this assessment procedure and psychometric inventories for assessing sociopathy (which we shall discuss in the next section). It would then be possible to determine what one technique, or combination of techniques, leads to the most reliable diagnosis. In addition, the use of physiological response measures in the assessment process needs to be examined. As discussed earlier, sociopaths tend consistently to be less aroused physiologically than nonsociopaths during resting periods and in response to intense or stressful stimulation. The routine assessment of physiological responding may prove to be a reliable diagnostic tool.

It can be assumed that most of the incarcerated individuals not diagnosed as sociopathic by the Hare assessment procedure will be either secondary antisocial or subcultural delinquents/ criminals. The differentiation between these two subtypes would be based on whether the individual's social history and present psychological functioning suggest the presence of a basic organic/ emotional precipitation of the antisocial behavior (secondary antisocial behavior), or whether environmental learning factors appear to be the predominant causal factor (subcultural delinquency/criminality). Unfortunately, there has been no thorough evaluation or construction of an equivalent assessment procedure for the assessment of these other two major forms of antisocial behavior.

TESTING

A commonly used and influential test for differentiating among various psychiatric groups, including sociopathy, is the Minnesota Multiphasic Personality Inventory (MMPI). A characteristic pattern is generally obtained for sociopaths that can be used to differentiate them from other clinical groups and normal subjects (e.g., Gilberstadt & Duker 1965; Dahlstrom & Welsh 1960). As the graph clearly shows, the two scales that differentiate best between sociopathic criminals and nonsociopathic criminals are the Psychopathic Deviate (Pd) scale and the Hypomania (Ma) scale. The Pd scale was developed to depict individuals who had shown notable difficulties in social adjustment, with past histories of delinquency and other forms of antisocial behavior. The Ma scale measures characteristics such as mild degrees of manic excitement characterized by excessive activity, easy distractibility, and elevated mood. Dahlstrom and Welsh (1960) describe persons with elevated Pd and Ma scale scores:

> Persons with the profile pattern show clear manifestations of psychopathic behavior, the hypomania seemingly energizing or activating the pattern related to . . . (the Pd scale). That is, these people tend to be overactive and impulsive, irresponsible and untrustworthy, shallow and superficial in their relationships. They are characterized by easy morals, readily circumvented consciences, and fluctuating ethical values. To satisfy their own desires and ambitions, they may expend great amounts of energy and effort, but they find it difficult to stick to duties and responsibilities imposed by others. In superficial contacts and social situations they create favorable impressions because of their freedom from inhibiting anxieties and insecurities. They are lively, conversational, fluent, and forthright; they enter wholeheartedly into games, outings, and parties, without being self-conscious or diffident. However, their lack of judgment and control may lead them to excesses of drinking, merrymaking, or teasing. They may be prone to continue activities so long that they exceed the proprieties, neglect other obligations, or alienate others. (p. 192)

As we have mentioned before, interpreting scores on the MMPI or any other single assessment test requires caution. The fact that an individual shows a profile pattern similar to that of a psychiatric group such as sociopathy does not necessarily mean that the person is actually a sociopath. It indicates only that the individual has answered a group of questions on the inventory in a manner in which a diagnosed sociopath might answer. Other causal factors, besides having a basic sociopathic personality trait, might cause this type of responding. Results of the test are only suggestive and should never be used as the sole basis for making a diagnosis. Additional supporting data, such as social history and behavioral ratings, are necessary before one can expect to make an accurate assessment.

A number of other psychometric inventories are used in the assessment of sociopathy. Lykken (1957) constructed the Activity Preference Questionnaire (APQ) to measure the degree of anxiety reactivity in individuals. This questionnaire consists

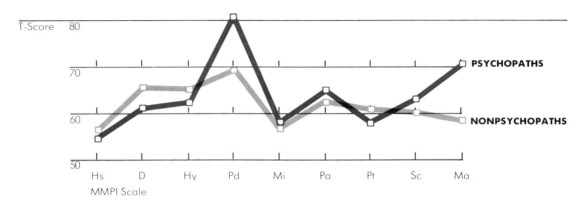

MMPI SCORES
Figure 13.4

Mean MMPI scores for 30 sociopathic and 30 nonsociopathic criminals. (From Hare 1970)

of 33 forced-choice paired items. One activity in
each pair is unpleasant in a frightening or embarrassing way; the other activity is designed to be
onerous but not frightening. The subject is requested to pick the member of each pair he or she
prefers as the lesser of two evils. Two examples of
these forced-choice items are:

1. (a) Having to cancel your vacation.
   (b) Standing on the ledge of the 25th
       floor of a building.
2. (a) Spending an evening with some boring
       people.
   (b) Being seen naked by a neighbor.

The extent to which an individual rejects the
unpleasant frightening alternatives is interpreted
as an index of the degree to which anxiety
determines his or her behavior. As might be
expected, Lykken (1957) found that sociopaths
demonstrated greater preference for the frightening items and showed less anxiety reactivity than
did either neurotic criminals or normal noncrim-
inals. A study by Rose (1964) of psychiatric
patients found similar results: Those subjects who
demonstrated low anxiety reactivity had APQ and
MMPI profile patterns indicative of sociopathy;
those patients with high anxiety reactivity scores
had MMPI profiles indicative of neuroticism.

The Taylor Manifest Anxiety Scale (Taylor
1953), which measures the degree to which an
individual reports experiencing symptoms of anxiety, has been used with some success in assessing
sociopathy. (see Hare 1970). Sociopaths typically
report less anxiety than nonsociopathic individuals.
Other inventories used include a series of scales
derived by factor analysis, developed by Quay and
colleagues (Quay & Parsons 1971), and the
Gough Delinquency Scale (Gough & Peterson
1952). As mentioned earlier, research is needed to
determine which one, or which combination, of
these various techniques is most reliable in assessing sociopathy and the other forms of antisocial
behavior.

The Porteus Maze Test (Porteus 1933) has
been used to differentiate between delinquent and
nondelinquent groups. This test consists of a series
of graded mazes, each progressively more difficult
than the one before. Porteus had claimed that this
test gauges factors such as foresight, judgment,
ability to delay gratification, and future time
perspective, and that therefore it is sensitive to
delinquency characteristics. A Qualitative (Q)
score measure was specifically developed to identify delinquents; it can be viewed as a measure of
the neatness associated with the execution of the
mazes. Riddle and Roberts (1977), in reviewing the
literature on the reliability of this test, found that
when Q scores of delinquent and normal groups
are compared, there are consistent and highly
significant differences. The Q score correctly identifies about 70 percent of delinquents sampled
and 70 percent of normals. Two other consistent
findings have been: (1) within a given group,
individuals with greater delinquent tendencies obtain higher Q scores than persons with less delinquent tendencies; (2) delinquents who tend to
recidivism obtain higher Q scores than do nonre-
cidivists. These findings are very impressive, demonstrating that the Porteus Maze Test does reliably
identify a great percentage of delinquents.

PROGNOSIS

Considering that the rate of recidivism for delinquents sent to training schools is sometimes estimated as high as 80 percent, innovations in the
treatment/rehabilitation process are obviously
sorely needed. The present prognosis for successful
modification of maladaptive antisocial behavior
can be described in one word—pessimistic. As long
as prisons remain human "storage factories" for
criminals, with the indiscriminate mixing of har-
dened violent offenders and nonviolent offenders,
it is not surprising that individuals return to society
more criminally inclined than before. What is
needed is the development of a general classification and rehabilitation program that is individualized to provide the most effective treatment/incar-
ceration program for the particular needs of
individuals. Moreover, long-range programs are
needed to prevent socially precipitated criminal
behavior due to factors such as poverty and
inadequate educational, recreational, and job opportunities for disadvantaged individuals. Such
programs require massive state and federal financial assistance, as well as a society that is willing to
support them.

SPONTANEOUS IMPROVEMENT OF SOCIOPATHY

Although most accounts of sociopathy convey rather pessimistic views concerning therapeutic improvement or rehabilitation, Robins (1966) has reported some interesting data that suggest the presence of spontaneous improvement in some sociopaths. She reported that approximately one-third of the sociopaths she studied showed a decrease in antisocial behavior with increasing age. The greatest improvement occurred most frequently between the ages of 30 and 40. That is, some sociopaths' antisocial behavior "burns out" as they get older. In explaining these results, Robins suggests that traditional psychotherapy may not be effective with the sociopath. The only effective approaches may be to wait for this "burning out" to occur, or to manipulate the sociopath's environment and use social controls as in therapeutic community and behavior modification programs. Indeed, Robins (1966) noted that those sociopaths who improved attributed their change to:

> . . . fear of further punishment or to loyalty to their spouses. Statistical association supported their explanation that marriage and brief sentences seemed related to im-

provement. While the current study offers no airtight demonstration for the powers of social control and fear of punishment as effective correctives to antisocial behavior, the positive relations found between social participation with spouse, sibling, friends, and neighbors and improvement makes it appear at least hopeful that supporting the pressures towards conformity in the sociopath's social environment and trying to prevent his becoming isolated from family, friends, and neighbors may be helpful in limiting his antisocial activities. Such goals at least appear more consistent with the current findings than do the goals of increased hospitalization or more psychotherapy, neither of which showed any positive association with improvement. If hospitalization and current psychotherapeutic techniques are not helpful, manipulation of the social environment may provide one hopeful alternative to patiently awaiting the "burning out" of antisocial interests, which frequently comes so late in life, if it comes at all, that enormous damage has been done both to the life of the patient and the lives of those with whom he interacts. (Robins 1966, p. 236)

SUMMARY

1. The terms *antisocial personality, psychopathy,* and *sociopathy* are used interchangeably to describe individuals who engage in chronic antisocial behavior. The major behavioral manifestations of this personality type are immaturity and inability to control impulses or delay gratification, lack of anxiety or guilt, lack of socialization, rejection of authority and discipline, failure to alter punished behavior, and inability to maintain meaningful interpersonal relationships.

2. The mere fact that a person engages in chronic antisocial behavior does not automatically label him or her a sociopath. *Sec-* *ondary antisocial behavior* is a category used to describe individuals who can experience guilt and remorse for their behavior, and whose antisocial behavior is motivated primarily by neurotic or psychotic emotional disturbances. For these individuals, the antisocial behavior is a symptom of a more basic underlying emotional problem. *Dyssocial* or *subcultural delinquency/criminality* is a category used to describe individuals who exhibit antisocial behavior because they were raised or are living in a delinquent subculture/environment that fosters and reinforces such behavior. They are merely

behaving in a manner suited to their own gang, group, or family.

3. Much of the experimental research on sociopathy has been based on sociopaths who were diagnosed while incarcerated for some criminal antisocial act. An important question that needs to be answered in future research is whether this incarcerated "unsuccessful" sociopath is similar to the "successful" sociopath who is making it quite successfully in society.

4. Experimental investigations of sociopaths have indicated that they show a deficit in learning to avoid punishment, possibly because of physiological underarousal. However, they can learn to avoid punishment when their anxiety level is artificially increased by a drug such as adrenalin, or under conditions where the punishment (e.g., financial loss) becomes sufficiently meaningful to have an impact on them. Also, the data indicating psychopaths or sociopaths can learn voluntarily to control spontaneous GSR activity suggest that their unusual physiological hyporesponsivity is *not* an unalterable physiological deficit prohibiting the achievement of high levels of reactivity.

5. EEG studies of sociopaths have demonstrated the presence of widespread slow-wave activity and positive spiking. These EEG abnormalities are viewed as consistent with the hypothesis that sociopaths tend to be cortically underaroused, and may be related to their need for stimulation, their impulsive behavior, and their inability to inhibit behavior even in the face of negative consequences or punishment.

6. Although research evidence suggests that a large percentage of sociopaths come from impoverished or broken homes and have experienced some form of parental loss or rejection, a more important predictor of sociopathy appears to be having a father who was sociopathic, antisocial, or alcoholic.

7. Traditional psychotherapeutic procedures have not been found to be effective in changing the behavior of sociopaths. There is some evidence suggesting the potential effectiveness of operant behavior modification techniques and therapeutic communities as ways of controlling situational factors to prevent the expression of undesirable sociopathic behaviors.

8. The use of (a) differential treatment/rehabilitation programs that take into account the different causes of antisocial behavior, and (b) probation and close supervision in lieu of institutionalization are two possible alternatives for dealing with secondary antisocial behavior. The high rate of recidivism indicates that the current common practice of "lumping together" the various types of offenders is not effective.

9. Incarcerating a dyssocial delinquent/criminal, without dealing with the situational-social factors that precipitated the antisocial behavior, is unlikely to successfully reform the criminal.

10. More standardized assessment procedures are currently needed to differentiate reliably between the various causes of antisocial behavior. The procedure used by Hare (1976) shows promise in diagnosing sociopathy reliably.

11. The Psychopathic Deviate (Pd) and Hypomania (Ma) MMPI profile pattern, the Activity Preference Questionnaire (APQ), the Taylor Manifest Anxiety Scale, the Gough Delinquency Scale, and a series of factor-analytically derived scales developed by Quay and colleagues are commonly used psychometric tests for the assessment of sociopathy. Research is needed to examine the relative effectiveness of these techniques and to determine which one, or which combination, is most reliable in assessing sociopathy and the other forms of antisocial behavior. The use of physiological responses may also prove to be a reliable assessment procedure. The Porteus Maze has been found to differentiate reliably between delinquents and nondelinquents.

12. The prognosis for successful modification of maladaptive antisocial behavior can be described as pessimistic at present. Innovations in the treatment/rehabilitation process are sorely needed.

13. Although most accounts of sociopathy convey rather pessimistic views concerning therapeutic improvement or rehabilitation, there is evidence of a decrease ("burning out") of antisocial behavior in some sociopaths with increasing age.

RECOMMENDED READINGS

Cleckley, H. *The Mask of Sanity.* (4th ed.) St. Louis: Mosby, 1964.

Davidson, W. S., & Seidman, E. Studies of behavior modification and juvenile delinquency: A review, methodological critique, and social perspective. *Psychological Bulletin,* 1974, *81,* 998–1011

Hare, R. D. *Psychopathy: Theory and research.* New York: Wiley, 1970.

Harrington, A. *Psychopaths.* New York: Simon and Schuster, 1972.

Jarvik, L. F., Klodin, V., & Matsuyama, S. S. Human aggression and the extra Y chromosome: Fact or fantasy? *American Psychologist,* 1973, *28,* 674–682.

Robins, L. N. *Deviant children grown up.* Baltimore, Md.: Williams & Wilkins, 1966.

Sutherland, E. H., & Cressey, D. R. *Principles of criminology.* (7th ed) Philadelphia: Lippincott, 1966.

BRAIN DYSFUNCTIONS AND SLEEP DISORDERS

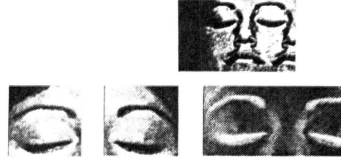

OVERVIEW In this chapter, we will consider two types of brain dysfunctions—organic brain syndromes and epilepsy (seizure disorders)—as well as sleep disorders. In the first section, on organic brain syndromes, we will examine organic brain problems induced by six different causes: (1) vitamin and nutritional deficiencies, (2) brain injuries, (3) circulation disturbances, (4) tumors, (5) cerebral infections, and (6) drugs and poisons. Because the last chapter will focus specifically upon old age reactions, this chapter will only touch lightly on organic brain syndromes that accompany aging. We will discuss the ways in which organic brain syndromes differ from functional psycho-pathologies in terms of impairment of memory,

intellectual functioning, judgment, orientation, and affect. We will also review methods of assessment and diagnosis of these syndromes.

In the section on epilepsy, we will discuss four types of seizure disorders: petit mal, grand mal, Jacksonian or focal, and psychomotor. It will be pointed out that in over three-quarters of all cases of epilepsy, the exact cause of the seizure is not known.

Finally, in the section on sleep disorders, we will discuss disturbances including insomnia, hypersomnia, narcolepsy, sleep apnea, nightmares, and sleepwalking. Although certain kinds of brain dysfunctions may be implicated in these problems, their exact causes are more complex.

DEMOGRAPHICS		USUAL AGE AT ONSET	PREVALENCE	SEX RATIO
	ORGANIC BRAIN SYNDROMES	May occur at any stage of life	Difficult to determine; estimates vary from 5 to 10% of population	Not known, although probably equal in males and females
	EPILEPSY	May occur at any stage of life, although onset is more common in childhood and adolescence	About 1% of population	More common in males than in females
	SLEEP DISORDERS	May occur at any stage of life, but more common in old age	Difficult to determine, although a recent survey indicated 14% of population had some kind of sleep disorder	Differs considerably from one disorder to the next

ORGANIC BRAIN SYNDROMES

SYMPTOM DESCRIPTION AND ETIOLOGY

Students of abnormal psychology often ask: "Are the abnormal behaviors caused by traumatic experiences or learning different from those caused by organic impairments of the brain?" Another question often asked: "Does a person's past experience—a patient's personality, for example—affect the nature of the abnormal behavior caused by organic damage to the brain?" That is, do individuals react differently to similar organic impairments? The answer to these questions is, in general, yes. For example, psychotic behaviors due to organic brain syndromes tend to have special features making them different from functional or nonorganic psychoses. Regarding the second question, a person's prior learned behaviors or personality do clearly influence the quality of an organic brain impairment. The term *premorbid personality* is used to refer specifically to the individual's behavioral inclinations or personality prior to the onset of brain impairment. As we will see, premorbid personality does influence the outcome (prognosis) of organic brain disorders.

The ways in which organic brain syndromes generally differ from functional psychopathologies can best be illustrated by examining the five chief characteristics of these syndromes.
1. Impairment of memory—immediate memory, recent memory, and remote memory.
2. Impairment of intellectual functioning.
3. Impairment of judgment.
4. Impairment of orientation.
5. Impairment of affect.

Before we describe each of these characteristics it is very important to recognize that diverse conditions such as tumors, circulatory disturbances, malnutrition, brain traumas, and other problems can produce any of them.

There are basically three types of *memory impairment* associated with organic brain syndromes. Impairment of *immediate* and *recent* memory is considered a hallmark of structural alterations in particular brain areas. (The *hippocampus* is a neural structure lying deep within the temporal lobes of the brain that has been suggested as playing a major role in immediate and recent memory. Alterations of this structure are thought to be tied to loss of these recall skills.)

Diagnosis of immediate and recent memory impairments often is made by asking the subject to repeat a phrase or passage after a given period of time. Immediate memory impairment is inferred if after a period of approximately five seconds, the subject cannot repeat what was said. Recent memory impairment is inferred after a period of approximately ten seconds has passed. Specifically, clinical psychologists often administer a *digit span test* to assess memory skills. The psychologist verbally gives the subject a sequence of numbers—5,8,2,4,9, for example—and then after a given period of time asks him or her to repeat the digits aloud. Inability to repeat five digits is sometimes considered to be a signal of bilateral hippocampal lesions or other organic impairments.

Remote memory impairment is assumed to involve dysfunction in some area other than the hippocampus. Loss of the ability to recall past events from one day to 25 years ago, for instance, is thought to be a signal of diffuse cortical impairment. It is noteworthy that "amnesia" due to psychological conflict, in contrast with amnesia that is organically induced, seems to be distinguished by failure to recall very specific events. This is usually not the case with organically induced impairments.

Because the organically brain-damaged individual may be unable to recall or remember certain things, he or she may at some time begin to employ a defense maneuver called *confabulation.* In this tactic, the person tries to fill in memory gaps with imagined experiences. Confabulation and remote memory impairment can be diagnosed by asking the individual certain questions. Linn (1975) gives as an example: "'Where were you last night?' This question is usually enough to elicit the phenomenon if it is present" (p. 804).

Impairment of any of the three types of memory produces major problems in the person's ability to cope with his or her environment. Dependency is greatly increased, and problem-solving skills are markedly reduced. When these conditions occur, and family members either do not have the time to devote to helping the person or find it too stressful, the person is likely to be institutionalized.

Impairment of intellectual functioning is often less noticeable, or more difficult for family members to detect, than other symptoms of organic brain syndromes. Nonetheless, it is associated with tissue damage to cortical areas of the brain. *Dementia* is the term sometimes used to refer to the

Modified from: *Aging and Organic Brain Syndrome,* McNeil Laboratories 1974, p. 12. (Cited in Mezey et al. 1975.)

MENTAL STATUS QUESTIONNAIRE (MSQ)
Table 14.1

QUESTION	PRESUMED TEST AREA
1. Where are we now?	Place
2. Where is this place located?	Place
3. What is today's date-day of month?	Time
4. What month is it?	Time
5. What year is it?	Time
6. How old are you?	Memory—recent or remote
7. What is your birthday?	Memory—recent or remote
8. What year were you born?	Memory—recent or remote
9. Who is president of the U.S.?	General information—memory
10. Who was president before him?	General information—memory

NO. OF ERRORS	PRESUMED MENTAL STATUS
0–2	Chronic brain syndrome, absent or mild
3–5	Chronic brain syndrome, mild to moderate
6–8	Chronic brain syndrome, moderate to severe
9–10	Chronic brain syndrome, severe
Non-testable	Chronic brain syndrome, severe

deterioration of mental functioning caused by organic impairment. Unlike the term *mental retardation*, which suggests that the person never had normal intellectual functioning, *dementia* refers to a late onset of the decline—the person once functioned normally intellectually, but no longer does so. Impairment is usually measured by giving the person an individual intelligence test.

Judgment impairment exists when a person loses the ability to solve ordinary day-to-day problems or comprehend basic social realities. Certain subtest scores from intelligence tests reflect judgmental deficits, but the specific site of neural damage is conjectural.

Orientation impairment is revealed when a patient is confused about the time, place, and setting in which he or she is living. The *Mental Status Questionnaire,* table 14.1, asks questions that are concerned with orientation, memory, and intelligence. Those questions asking the patient to tell where he or she is, the time, the place, and so on, determine the subject's "orientation." The number of errors on these questions is linked to the degree of organic impairment: 0–2 errors, absent to mild organic brain syndrome; 9–10 errors, severe organic brain syndrome (Mezey, Rauckhorst, & Stokes 1975).

Affect impairment is also a side-effect of severe brain damage. *Shallowness of affect* and *lability of affect* are terms applied to a person's emotions or mood when he or she underresponds to a situation that calls for the expression of emotion (shallowness) or when the mood fluctuates greatly (lability). For example, one 27-year-old man with severe frontal lobe brain damage showed almost no emotion when he was informed that his wife had been severely injured in a car accident (shallowness), but in other situations he would cry or laugh for no apparent reason (lability).

The clinical features of organic brain syndromes, then, often involve impairment of memory, orientation, judgment, intellectual functions, and affect. Indeed, the DSM-II notes that these five organic symptoms tend to be present in most brain-damaged patients ". . . regardless of whether the syndrome is mild, moderate, or severe" (p. 22). However, enormous individual variations are seen in organic brain syndromes. In fact, Lipowski (1975b) states that impairment of memory, orientation, judgment, and other symptoms are clearly exhibited only when brain damage is severe. Additionally, he argues that anxiety and

depression often accompany organic brain syndromes, two important symptoms not included in the "basic five."

CLASSIFICATION OF ORGANIC BRAIN SYNDROMES

Organic brain syndromes are often classified as either *acute or chronic*. In acute brain syndromes, some researchers state, the five basic symptoms are present, and the onset is sudden and the syndrome reversible. Generally speaking, organic brain syndrome induced by nutritional inadequacies or associated with drugs, alcohol, or poisons produce acute states rather than permanent conditions. Chronic brain syndromes, on the other hand, are thought to have a gradual onset and brain damage that is typically permanent or irreversible.

Lipowski (1975b) voices much concern about the ambiguity or misleading quality of the terms *acute* and *chronic*. He observes that there are organic brain syndromes that are irreversible yet have a sudden onset—carbon monoxide poisoning, for example—and there are also reversible syndromes that have gradual onsets. He suggests, among other things, that organic brain syndromes should be classified on the basis of reversibility or irreversibility. In chapter 19 we shall discuss several irreversible brain syndromes: progressive idiopathic dementia (senile psychosis), arteriosclerotic psychosis, and others.

ASSESSMENT AND DIAGNOSIS OF ORGANIC BRAIN SYNDROMES

Organic brain syndromes can be diagnosed by physical or histological (autopsy) exams; by such techniques as the *angiogram* (a brain X-ray procedure); by recording the brain waves; by observing overt behavior or motor skills (for example, seizures, drowsiness, confusion, language disturbances); by noting psychological or psychiatric complaints such as depression, anxiety, restlessness, dramatic alterations in personality and so forth; and by using *neuropsychological tests*.

NEUROPSYCHOLOGICAL ASSESSMENT The neuropsychological tests specifically designed for detecting brain damage give only hints that neurological impairment may exist (see chapter 5). Several tests are often used in the assessment of "organicity." For example, the Halstead-Reitan Test Battery, the Bender Visual-Motor Gestalt Test, and certain individual intelligence tests such as the Wechsler Intelligence Scale for Children-Revised (WISC-R), the Wechsler Adult Intelligence Scale (WAIS), and the Stanford-Binet have subtests that may *suggest* the possibility of neurological impairment. Clearly, however, certain scores on a psychological test never indicate unequivocally that a person has organic brain damage.

Neuropsychological assessment involves the close integration of both neurological and psychological assessment techniques in the search for behavioral manifestations or patterns of performance aberrations associated with specific brain disorders. Lezak (1976) provides a case study of brain dysfunction showing how the disciplines of neurology and psychology interact in assessment.

A CASE OF BRAIN DYSFUNCTION

A 29-year-old air force technician with an excellent health history had a "grand mal" seizure hours after a tempestuous quarrel with his wife. When he had a second seizure several weeks later, he went to the base hospital where a thorough neurological examination revealed no abnormality. The seizures increased in frequency and were then controlled fairly well by anticonvulsive drugs, but he was given a medical discharge from service and was seen as an outpatient by neurologists at regular intervals thereafter.

He made a rapid adjustment to civilian life, becoming an electronic parts inspector and then foreman, jobs which required a great deal of precision in visual judgment and adeptness in handling complex machinery and delicate parts. Approximately three years after his first seizure, his supervisor noticed that he was slowing down and becoming clumsy and inaccurate in his work. His employer requested that he obtain a medical evaluation and the patient returned for another neurological examination. His wife then reported to the neurologist that he was sleeping much of the time, that he had lost interest in his usual activities, and that his sexual performance had become unsatisfactory. Once again, there were

no "hard" neurological finds, but this time the patient was referred to a psychologist.

The patient was interviewed and given intellectual and personality tests. As expected from the history, the patient performed at "average" to "high average" levels (within the performance range of the upper 15 to 50% of the population) on almost all of the tests of intellectual ability, but scored lower on tasks involving organization, reproduction, and memory of complex visual perceptions. His personality test responses reflected a more than ordinary amount of preoccupation with physical concerns for a man his age but were otherwise unremarkable. Although the discrepancies between high and low test scores were not quite large enough to be statistically significant, they were sufficiently consistent to suggest an impairment pattern, particularly in the light of his having formerly excelled in work requiring fine visual discrimination and judgment.

Because of the psychological test pattern of impaired visual organization plus observations of slightly slurred speech and a barely perceptible flattening of the muscles on the left side of the nose and mouth, he was sent back to the neurologist with an urgent recommendation for further study of a possible right hemisphere tumor. He was operated on within the week for removal of a malignant tumor.

The patient lived two more years, becoming increasingly childish. His judgment deteriorated, self-control gave way to impulsivity and rapidly shifting emotional ups and downs, and he became unsteady, weak, and ultimately bedridden. The psychologist counseled his wife and two school-age children as they coped with role changes, added responsibilities, frustrations, and fears. The patient was tested several times during this period to give the family an objective picture of his changing strengths and limitations. After his death the widow continued to see the psychologist for vocational and personal counseling. (pp.11–12)

It is important to note that the behavior and psychological disorders associated with these organic brain syndromes, as well as the concomitant physical impairments, are greatly influenced by the following variables (based on Lipowski 1975b):

1. *Age of onset.* Various syndromes have greater side-effects when the person is

young and others have more harmful effects when the person is old. Malnutrition, for example, may create irreversible brain impairment in very young children, but rarely in adults.

2. *Individual differences* (biological, biochemical, genetic, temperamental, etc.).
3. *Individual differences* (psychological—past experiences, premorbid personality, etc.).
4. *Social isolation/social support* (the immediate environment in which the person is living—family, institution, etc.).

As Lipowski notes, all these variables and others not mentioned here must be '' . . . taken into account in planning diagnostic procedures and management of the patient'' (p. 21).

Pincus and Tucker (1974) mention three other factors that affect the clinical picture of an organic brain syndrome: (1) the amount of tissue destroyed; (2) the location of the area affected in the brain; and (3) the nature of the disease (tumor, head injury, stroke, and so on). They also cite *Lashley's hypothesis of equipotentiality*, which states in summary that the amount of brain tissue lost is more important than the location of the brain damage (Lashley 1929). The equipotentiality hypothesis, however, deals specifically with intellectual capacity and has not been completely tested in human subjects.

CAUSES AND STRESSORS

VITAMIN AND NUTRITIONAL DEFICIENCIES

It is common knowledge that severe head injuries, tumors, or other traumas can result in abnormal behavior and physical and intellectual impairment. But it is much less widely known that the restriction of vitamins, calories, and protein can also cause psychopathologies. We will discuss only the more significant vitamin and nutritional deficiencies related to organic brain syndromes.

VITAMIN B DEFICIENCY   Of all the vitamin groups, the B vitamins appear to play the most important role in brain metabolism and growth. Vitamin B_1 (thiamine) deficiencies in particular have been linked to alterations in personality. *Wernicke's encephalopathy* (also called *beriberi*) is a dysfunction produced by dramatic restriction of this vitamin. Symptoms include delirium, apathy, irritability, sleep disturbances, and personality changes. Commonly vitamin B_1 deficiencies occur in conjunction with vitamin B_2 (niacin) deficiencies. Vitamin B_2 depletions are related to the alcoholic disorder called *Korsakoff's psychosis*. That is, the Korsakoff reaction may be superimposed on Wernicke's encephalopathy, adding to the other symptoms memory impairments as well as other psychotic symptoms. In the United States, both these syndromes are sometimes seen in individuals with extremely poor diets, but are found more commonly in chronic alcoholics. The cause, simply stated, is that alcohol depletes the body and brain of vitamin B. (In other parts of the world, deficiencies such as beriberi are due primarily to inadequate diet.)

CALORIC AND PROTEIN DEFICIENCIES   The term *malnutrition* refers not only to those who are dramatically underfed, but also to those who are overnourished. Therefore, we will use the terms *undernourishment* and *deficiency* when considering insufficient intake of calories and protein.

It is becoming increasingly evident that undernourishment can induce central nervous system impairment. We cannot discuss undernourishment in detail, but simply note that dramatically reduced caloric intake or severe protein deficiency can cause neurological impairment.

Two general forms of undernourishment are nutritional marasmus and kwashiorkor. *Nutritional marasmus* occurs when an infant has a profound deficit of calories and protein. That is, neither carbohydrate nor protein intake is adequate. This condition is confined to infants and results in retardation of physical growth and intellectual impairment. (The term *marasmus* is used in another sense in chapter 16.) *Kwashiorkor* occurs in an infant or child when the diet is severely deficient in protein. In this deficiency, caloric intake from carbohydrates may be sufficient to give the child the appearance of being well fed, but irreversible neurological damage occurs from the lack of protein. Behaviorally, children with this condition are apathetic and moderately to severely retarded.

As we have noted, age of onset is an important variable in the outcome of organic brain syndromes. In the case of nutritional deficiencies, age is critically important. The earlier the child or infant is deprived of calories or protein, the more likely the syndrome is to be irreversible. By contrast, protein or caloric inadequacies in adults can most often be ameliorated by proper diet, and recovery generally follows. The harmful effects of vitamin deficiency and caloric and protein inadequacies can be reversed if the patient is not young and if the length of the deficiencies has not been great. Unfortunately we can give no exact critical period in which a reversible condition becomes irreversible.

TREATMENT The treatment of these deficiencies is rather obvious. When nicotinic acid therapy is employed in vitamin B deficiency, improvement is dramatic. In marasmus and kwashiorkor, the treatment strategy again is straightforward — supplying the subject with adequate calories and protein, but the prognosis is not as good unless the treatment is administered shortly after the deprivation.

BRAIN INJURIES

Head injuries are one of the most common causes of organic brain syndromes. Injuries to the brain result in a wide variety of physical and behavioral disorders. Because the brain has rather specialized regions that regulate particular behaviors, damage to different brain sites and different sorts of head injuries affect the clinical picture.

Peterson (1975) classifies head injuries into two general types: (1) *Closed* head injuries. The skull is not penetrated, but forces to the head nonetheless produce concussions, contusions, hemorrhages, and other pathological states. (2) *Open* head injuries. The skull and brain itself are penetrated by a bullet, bone matter, or other pointed object.

Of particular interest are injuries to the frontal lobe. The *frontal lobe syndrome* is the name often used to refer to a particular type of organic brain syndrome in which marked changes in personality occur. The frontal lobe syndrome has been known and reported in medical literature for centuries, and the symptoms reported in the past are similar to those reported in patients today who suffer from severe head injuries to the frontal area of the brain. Three symptoms seem to represent the frontal lobe syndrome:

1. Lack of initiative — a decrease in motor activity (Hacaen and Albert 1975).
2. Lack of concern — it has been said that these patients are possessed with "I don't give a damness."
3. Euphoria — inappropriate jokes and elation and silliness (Hacaen and Albert 1975).

Tumors and surgical intervention (frontal lobectomies and lobotomies), as well as head injuries, can induce symptoms similar to these three. The case study describes an accident-caused frontal lobe syndrome.

A CASE OF FRONTAL LOBE SYNDROME

At the age of 46, a successful salesman sustained a compound depressed fracture of the left frontal bone in a traffic accident. Treatment included débridement and amputation of the left frontal pole. Recovery was slow, and nine months after the injury he was referred for long-term custodial management. By this time, he had recovered motor function with only a minimal limp on the right side, had normal sensation, no evidence of aphasia, and normal memory and cognitive ability (IQ 118). Nonetheless, he remained under hospital care because of marked changes in personal habits.

Prior to the accident, the patient had been garrulous, enjoyed people, had many friends and talked freely. He was active in community affairs, including Little League, church activities, men's clubs, and so forth. It was stated by one acquaintance that the patient had a true charisma, "whenever he entered a room there was a change in the atmosphere, everything became more animated, happy and friendly."

Following the head injury, he was quiet and remote. He would speak when spoken to and made sensible replies but would then lapse into silence. He made no friends in the ward, spent most of his time sitting alone smoking. He was frequently incontinent of urine, occasionally of stool. He remained unconcerned about either and was frequently found soaking wet, calmly sitting and smoking. If asked, he would matter-of-factly state that he had not been able to get to the bathroom in time but that this didn't bother him. Because of objectionable eating habits he always ate alone on the ward. His sleep pattern was reversed; he stayed up much of the night and slept during the day. He did not resent being awakened or questioned. He could discuss many subjects intelligently, but was never known to initiate either a conversation or a request. (Benson & Blumer 1975, p. 156)

Damage or disease affecting the *temporal lobe*, especially the left temporal lobe, also produces significant changes in behavior. *Aphasia* is a language deficit that is related to temporal lobe damage. The symptoms, stated generally, involve the inability to understand and use language. Head injuries, tumors, seizures, and infectious disorders may produce acquired aphasia. There is also some evidence that lesions in the temporal lobe may result in marked changes in sexual behavior. Klüver and Bucy noted in 1939 that bilateral temporal lobe destruction produced, among other symptoms, altered sexual behavior. A few clinical studies have also shown that temporal damage in human subjects results in hypersexuality, disturbances in memory, and indifference.

Again, it is important to consider individual variables that affect the person's adaptation after an injury. His or her premorbid personality, the social environment to which the person returns, economic stability, age, and many other factors influence the clinical picture as well as the treatment and prognosis.

TREATMENT   Gilroy and Meyer (1975) point out a distinction between the treatment of closed head injuries and open ones. Closed head injuries call first for emergency treatment, mainly sustaining respiration and circulation. During the recovery phase, psychological counseling, rehabilitation of lost skills, and in some cases, treatment with anti-anxiety drugs may be required. On the other hand, treatment of open head injuries — a gunshot wound, for example — begins with surgery to remove the foreign material. Whether or not the patient is unconscious, and how long he or she is in a coma, also determine treatment. If unconsciousness extends beyond a few hours, damage to the brain is probably severe, and maintaining vital functions is the primary concern.

CIRCULATION DISTURBANCES

The brain is critically dependent on a supply of blood to provide its ten billion or so nerve cells with oxygen and glucose. Interruption of blood supply to the brain for even a few seconds can cause permanent damage. Blood supply decreases or interruptions can be caused by head injuries or tumors, by alterations in the circulatory system of the brain, and by other difficulties. Interruption of blood supply to the brain can produce profound changes or breakdowns in the body's vital functions, in sensory and motor functions, and in personality.

Blood supply interruptions resulting in nervous system disorders, physical disabilities, or organic brain syndromes are sometimes called *cerebrovascular disorders*. Not only are cerebrovascular disorders extremely serious for the individual, but they also are the third most common cause of death in the United States (Gilroy & Meyer 1975). Cerebrovascular disorders, for our purposes, are of two basic kinds: those resulting in the *rupture* of blood vessels, and those resulting in the *blockage* of blood vessels.

CEREBRAL ARTERIOSCLEROSIS   This term is often used generally to refer to both rupturing and blocking disorders. *Cerebral arteriosclerosis* is thought to be a degenerative process of blood vessels in the brain—essentially a hardening and narrowing of the brain's circulatory system—which produces several of the symptoms seen in organic brain syndromes. The hardening and narrowing of the vessels predisposes the person to ruptures and blockages. Researchers generally maintain that diet, lack of exercise, heredity, and in particular, high blood pressure play a major role in cerebral arteriosclerosis. In chapter 19 we use the term multi-infarct dementia or "arteriosclerotic psychosis" to refer to old age psychosis apparently induced by vascular problems.

CEREBRAL STROKES AND EMBOLISMS   A *cerebral stroke* (or *hemorrhage*) occurs very suddenly when a blood vessel in the brain ruptures. The behavior changes that follow a cerebral stroke depend mainly on the location of the hemorrhage. Depending on the area damaged, the patient may lose consciousness, become paralyzed, experience alterations in personality, or develop speech and language problems.

A *cerebral embolism* is a disorder of circulation caused by blockage of a blood vessel by some substance. The substance responsible for the embolism may be a blood clot or fatty deposits. The symptoms, as with strokes, have a very sudden onset and depend on the area of the brain affected. Often headaches, convulsions, confusion, and other symptoms occur.

TREATMENT   One treatment for cerebral arteriosclerosis and the two subvarieties of cerebrovascular disorders (strokes and embolisms) is to lower the patient's blood pressure. High blood pressure predisposes the person to cerebrovascular disorders. In addition, strokes and embolisms may require surgery to remove a clot, or drugs such as anticoagulant agents (Brain & Watson 1969). In other cases, *cerebral vasodilator drugs* are used to ''draw'' or ''pull'' blood away from a clotted or ruptured area to lessen further damage. Other predisposing conditions such as obesity, diabetes, or hypoglycemia also are treated.

CEREBRAL TUMORS

Tumors or *neoplasms* are abnormal tissue growths. They can develop in almost any part of the body, but the brain and its supporting tissue appear to be common sites. It has been estimated that 40 out of 100,000 people have brain tumors (Kurtzke, Kurland, & Goldberg 1971). The likelihood of tumor development increases significantly as we age; most stricken are between 20 and 60 years old.

Rather than giving the technical names of various sorts of tumors, we will discuss brain tumors that develop in certain areas of the brain and result in particular abnormal behaviors.

The following general symptoms are often reported with brain tumors: headaches, vomiting, seizures, impaired intellectual functioning, disturbances in language skills, alteration in consciousness, loss of memory, and loss of motivation. The region of brain destruction clearly influences the symptoms seen in the patient. Frontal lobe tumors are linked to personality changes, whereas parietal lobe tumors are associated with motor disturbances as well as sensory and tactile deficits. Temporal lobe tumors often produce language impairments, and in rare cases, aggressive behavior. However, specific abnormal behaviors are not always associated with tumors in specific brain areas. It has

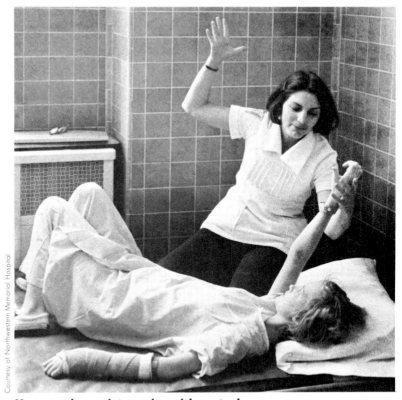

Here, a therapist works with a stroke victim.

often been assumed that organic brain syndromes, tumors included, exaggerate the individual's personality or behavior problems. Stated another way, if a given person is marginally adaptive, a brain tumor will exaggerate his or her unadaptive manner.

FRONTAL LOBE TUMORS   As we pointed out earlier, the *frontal lobe syndrome* can develop if this area of the brain is injured. Tumors can also produce this syndrome. Mild euphoria, lack of planning, inappropriate joking (*Witzelsucht*), regression or loss of social skills and moral behavior, and some deterioration in speech all are connected with frontal lobe tumors (Gilroy & Meyer 1975). Wolf, Munsat, and Dunne (1972) cite the following case:

> A 39-year-old woman was referred because of poor memory and decreasing vision. She had a history of heavy alcoholic intake. When seen in the office, she looked

and smelled as if she hadn't taken a bath in months. She joked and was inappropriately euphoric.

An angiogram disclosed a tumor in this woman's left frontal lobe. Wolf and his associates present her case because it is reversible and illustrates the importance of ''not passing off the demented alcoholic as suffering from chronic degenerative brain disease''(p. 229).

TEMPORAL LOBE TUMORS   Gilroy and Meyer (1975) point out that impairment of the temporal lobe—by circulatory disorders, tumors, injuries— often results in seizure activities. Indeed, the temporal lobe has a low threshold for epileptic activity. Aside from this fact, the temporal lobe is also associated with language functions; tumors principally in the left temporal area may produce severe aphasia. Auditory hallucinations can also occur if a tumor is present. Other temporal lobe tumor patients report very odd changes in self-awareness and orientation. For example, an individual may have a sudden feeling of intense familiarity in a strange place (*déjà vu*); or a familiar surrounding may suddenly seem entirely new and foreign (*jamais vu*). (Many persons who do not have brain tumors also have the *déjà vu* sensation.)

Most interestingly, the temporal lobe has been implicated in the regulation of violence and aggressive behavior. Moyer (1976) enumerates several investigations that suggest a relationship between temporal lobe tumors and violence-prone behavior. Perhaps the most remarkable case was that of the Texas mass murderer Charles Whitman, whose autopsy revealed a tumor in the interior of his temporal lobe.

THE CASE OF CHARLES WHITMAN

One of the most interesting features about the case of Charles Whitman is a letter that he wrote before killing his wife and his mother and then starting his shooting spree from atop the University of Texas library tower. The letter is used by some to support the notion that the tumor in Whitman's brain triggered his disturbing and ineffable alteration of consciousness and, ultimately, his impulsive rage.

I don't quite understand what it is that compels me to type this letter. Perhaps it is to leave some vague reason for the actions I have recently performed.

I don't really understand myself these days. I am supposed to be an average, reasonable and intelligent young man. However, lately (I can't recall when it started) I have been a victim of many unusual and irrational thoughts These thoughts constantly recur, and it requires a tremendous mental effort to concentrate on useful and progressive tasks. In March when my parents made a physical break I noticed a great deal of stress. I consulted a Dr. Cochrum at the University Health Center and asked him to recommend someone that I could consult with about some psychiatric disorders I felt I had. I talked with a doctor once for about two hours and tried to convey to him my fears that I felt overcome [sic] by overwhelming violent impulses. After one session I never saw the doctor again and since then I have been fighting my mental turmoil alone, and seemingly to no avail. After my death I wish that an autopsy would be performed on me to see if there is any visible physical disorder. I have had some tremendous headaches in the past and have consumed two large bottles of Excedrin in the past three months. It was after much thought that I decided to kill my wife Kathy, tonight after I pick her up from . . . . I love her dearly and she has been a fine wife to me as any man could ever hope to have. I cannot rationally pinpoint any specific reason for doing this. I don't know whether it is selfishness or if I don't want her to face the embarrassment my actions would surely cause her. At this time, though, the prominent reason in my mind is that I truly do not consider this world worth living in, and I am prepared to die, and I do not want to leave her to suffer alone in it. I intend to kill her as painlessly as possible.
Charles Whitman

TREATMENT   There are currently three basic treatments for tumors: (1) chemotherapy—drugs that slow or retard tumor growth; (2) radiation therapy; and (3) surgery. Gilroy and Meyer point out that the effectiveness of the treatment depends on the type of tumor (malignant/nonmalignant) and its location. Early detection of the tumor enhances the chances of recovery.

CEREBRAL INFECTIONS

Various behavior disorders are due to bacterial and viral infections that affect brain tissue. There are two major types of brain infections which we will consider in this section: encephalitis and cerebral syphilis.

ENCEPHALITIS   The term *encephalitis* means an inflammation of the brain tissue. There are a number of different varieties of this viral disease. *Epidemic encephalitis* is a contagious form that was especially widespread in the United States and Europe during and immediately following World War I. Today, this form is almost totally under control in the developed countries; it is still, however, fairly common in certain areas of Asia and Africa. This form of encephalitis, because it is marked by lethargy, drowsiness, and prolonged periods of sleep, came to be known as "sleeping sickness." Along with the marked lethargy, a high fever usually appears immediately after infection. Other characteristics associated with the disorder are hyperactivity, irritability, and restlessness between periods of sleep. The infected person may also suffer convulsions, delirium, and disorientation, and may experience frightening hallucinations. In severe forms of this disorder, extended coma and death can occur. There can also be significant post-infection effects, especially in children, who are most susceptible to the disease. A child who may have been friendly, cooperative, and cheerful before the infection may become hyperactive, impulsive, irritable, and a serious discipline problem afterward. The child may demonstrate marked moral deterioration and, for example, start lying and cheating. These problems can significantly interfere with the development of an emotionally stable personality; the behavior may continue into adulthood so that the individual remains undisciplined, impulsive, and moody.

Although epidemic encephalitis is almost nonexistent in the Western world today because the virus responsible for it has been controlled, other types of encephalitis, caused by different viruses, still occur with some regularity. Most of these are classified under the category known as *unspecified encephalitis*. The diseases, usually transmitted by mosquitos and ticks, produce the same types of symptoms as epidemic encephalitis.

The third major form this disease can take is *meningococcal meningitis,* a viral infection that inflames the *meninges* or membrane covering of the brain and spinal cord. Initially, the patient displays delirium, disorientation, depression, irritability, and difficulties in concentration and memory. He or she may later remain depressed and irritable. Recovery from this disease is usually complete, but some patients may have permanent sensory or motor dysfunctions if the infection was severe and permanent brain damage occurred. If the disorder occurs in infants and is especially severe, it can cause mental retardation.

CEREBRAL SYPHILIS   The discovery of the role that syphilis can play in abnormal behavior was the basis for the medical-disease model of abnormal behavior. This dreaded and once widespread venereal disease (which some historians feel was introduced into Europe by members of Columbus's crew who had contracted it from women in the West Indies) could not be effectively treated until relatively recently. Until the recent advances in antibiotic therapies, syphilis led to significant psychological and physiological impairments and ultimately death in those afflicted. Before the development of antibiotic therapies, more than one-fourth of admissions to mental institutions were thought to be the result of syphilis (Millon & Millon, 1974).

Before doctors realized the relationship between this disease and psychological impairment, it was viewed primarily as a type of smallpox and skin disease and was commonly called the "Great pox" (or Spanish pox or French pox). The usual symptoms demonstrated when the especially virulent form of the disease was first introduced into Europe were skin rash, high fever, delirium, and bone ulcers, which occurred during the early stages of the disease. The disease itself is a bacterial infection of the central nervous system in which the syphilitic *spirochete* bacteria (*Treponema pallidum*) initially enters the body through mucous membranes such as those in the lining of the mouth and genitals, or through small abrasions or breaks in the skin. It is almost always contracted from an infected person during sexual intercourse or oral-genital contact. It can also be transmitted from mother to child during the fetal development period (this form is called *congenital syphilis*).

The disease routinely progresses in four stages. As soon as the spirochetes enter the body, they begin to multiply rapidly. The first stage occurs from approximately ten days to a month after contraction of the disease. A sore or pimple that feels hard to the touch (*hard chancre*) develops at the place of infection (usually the genitals or mouth). This sore disappears in about a month, even if untreated, and the infected person may erroneously assume that he or she merely had a minor skin irritation that is now completely cleared up. The second stage occurs one or two months after the initial development of the hard chancre. A copper-colored skin rash develops over the entire body. This skin rash may look like measles or small pox, explaining why the disease was known as the "pox." The rash may be accompanied by fever, headache, indigestion, and loss of appetite. The third stage is the latent stage during which these overt physical symptoms disappear. The disappearance of these symptoms may again lead the person to believe the disease is cured, and he or she may not seek out, or may discontinue, treatment. However, although overt symptoms disappear, the spirochetes continue to multiply internally and destroy tissues and organs, especially blood vessels and neural brain cells, resulting in permanent degeneration and damage. Finally, *the fourth stage* occurs 5 to 20 or even 30 years after the initial infection and manifests itself in a wide variety of possible organic symptoms that represent the accumulated damage produced during the previous stages: heart attacks due to destruction of heart tissue and vasculature; blindness; motor tremors and gross motor uncoordination due to nerve cell damage, resulting in the loss of balance and an unsteady gait (*locomotor ataxia*); speech disturbances resulting in slurred speech; convulsions and the loss of consciousness. During this stage the *Argyll Robertson sign* is readily observed, in which the pupils of the eyes fail to respond to light.

General paresis is the term used when syphilis causes mental disturbances through destruction of brain tissue; it was once called "general paralysis of the insane." Significant psychological disturbances manifest themselves in this stage of the disease. Initially, the infected person becomes careless and inattentive. Personal habits start deteriorating, so that a formerly neat person now becomes sloppy and unconcerned about personal appearance. The person also displays social tactlessness, dull or inappropriate affect, and memory defects. As the disease progresses and reaches the terminal stages, the individual may no longer be able to care for himself or herself, may become inattentive and unconcerned about everything, and may lead more or less a vegetative existence. The final result is a total breakdown of functioning that leads to death.

Meningovascular syphilis is a much rarer form of cerebral syphilis in which the organic damage is initially concentrated in the blood vessels and meninges of the brain rather than in the brain neural tissue itself (the term *meningoencephalitis syphilis* is used when the primary damage is to the brain cells). Usually, there is not the initial marked deterioration of behavior and psychological functioning that is normally found in general paresis, because destruction of brain cells is less in the early stages. In the later stages, however, the symptoms are similar because the brain cells are now being directly damaged.

Still another form of syphilis is *juvenile paresis*, the result of congenital syphilis transmitted from mother to child during fetal development. It is general paresis that occurs during childhood and adolescence. Besides the progressive mental and physical deterioration that can occur, it at one time accounted for a high infant mortality rate and physical afflictions at birth. Before the development of effective antibiotic treatment, congenital syphilis accounted for more than one-half of all blindness in children at birth, and was the largest cause of stillbirths and of deaths in the first few years of life (Coleman 1976).

TREATMENT Because the virus causing encephalitis can be effectively treated with antibiotics, most patients make a complete and satisfactory recovery. In some individuals, however, especially children, there may be some significant residual side-effects from severe cases. In such cases, some form of rehabilitation/psychological/educational treatment will be needed to deal with such aftereffects as hyperactivity, loss of self-control, and decreased learning ability.

When penicillin, discovered in the 1940s, was found to treat syphilis effectively, there was a dramatic drop in the number of cases of this disease. As a result, many people assumed that this medical problem was solved. However, starting in the 1960s there was a significant increase in the number of venereal disease cases reported in the United States, so that syphilis is once again a serious medical problem. This is unfortunate and unnecessary, because the disease is treatable and can be completely cured if caught in the early stages. However, the longer the case is untreated, the greater the permanent neurological and psychological damage that can occur. Many individuals, however, do not seek treatment because of inadequate information concerning the disease or because of the social stigma attached to it.

The prevention or early detection and treatment of the disease is an attainable goal. Currently, education of the public about syphilis and other forms of venereal disease (VD) is being provided by governmental, educational, and religious agencies. Many states now provide free diagnosis and treatment, and most require physical tests or examinations (Wasserman test) before marriage as a way of preventing its spread. With a comprehensive approach such as this, and with the medical means to treat it, syphilis can be controlled as a public health problem.

DRUGS AND POISONS

The *blood-brain barrier* is a protective mechanism in the brain that acts to screen the flow of harmful substances from the bloodstream into the brain and subsequently into the rest of the central nervous system. At the same time that it screens out harmful substances, it allows free flow of substances that are essential for bodily functioning and health. There are times, however, when factors such as oxygen deprivation or excessive amounts of a toxic metal or gas can impair the effective functioning of the blood-brain barrier. Such impairment can significantly interfere with normal brain functioning and, in severe cases, cause brain damage and even death.

METAL AND GAS POISONING   Many common metals and gases are toxic and, if ingested, can produce brain dysfunctions ranging from temporary mild symptoms (such as the clouding of consciousness) to permanent brain damage. The heavy metals lead and mercury, for instance, if ingested or absorbed through the skin, can cause physical pains such as abdominal cramps and nausea, difficulties in concentration and memory, impaired coordination, emotional difficulties, hyperactivity and irritability, and psychotic-type hallucinations and delusions. Excessive amounts can cause convulsions, paralysis, and death. Lead poisoning can be a significant problem for young children who, if near old lead-based paints or crumbling plaster falling from walls in old buildings, are likely to eat or chew these substances; they may also chew on toys and other objects painted with lead-base paints. These children may develop mental retardation.

Commonly, metal poisoning results from accidents or constant exposure to these substances in industrial settings or in water polluted by industrial waste. In a number of instances, mercury-contaminated fish taken from waters polluted by mercury waste from factories have produced serious brain damage in people who, unaware of the danger, ate the fish. In other cases, workers in metal and chemical plants, constantly exposed to these toxic substances, have developed brain disturbances ranging from mild dysphoria to significant disturbances of sensory, motor, and psychological functioning.

Gases such as carbon monoxide and carbon disulfide can also cause serious brain damage. Carbon monoxide, which is emitted from automobile exhaust fumes, is an especially dangerous gas because it is odorless, tasteless, and invisible, and can cause a fast and painless death before the individual becomes aware of its presence. Each year, there are numerous suicides by carbon monoxide poisoning. In unsuccessful attempts, permanent brain damage can occur.

DRUGS   In chapter 10 on alcoholism and other drug use disorders, we pointed out the psychological and physiological disturbances that can result from the chronic abuse of drugs. We also noted that withdrawal from drugs can be painful, especially from alcohol, opium and its derivatives, and barbiturates. These disturbances can be considered forms of organic brain syndromes because of the effects the drugs have on neural tissue. It should also be pointed out that many over-the-counter nonprescription sleeping pills consist of compounds containing *bromides*. High doses of bromides are toxic and can cause psychotic-type hallucinations and delusions and even permanent brain damage if appropriate medical treatment is not administered. (We will discuss some additional serious side-effects of sleeping pills in the last section of this chapter, which reviews the major forms of sleep disturbances.)

TREATMENT   It is obvious that if significant gas, metal, or drug poisoning produces irreversible brain damage, there is no treatment that can totally restore the individual's premorbid psychological and physiological functioning. At best, treatment can merely help the individual accept and possibly compensate for the brain-related disturbances. For milder and reversible forms, treatment can help the individual deal with the temporary symptoms. Of course, in any form of poisoning, appropriate medical treatment must be administered to neutralize the harmful substances in the bloodstream and the central nervous system.

EPILEPSY

SYMPTOM DESCRIPTION AND ETIOLOGY

Epilepsy is a Greek word that means "seizure." Most forms of epilepsy are associated with a period of unconsciousness and involuntary movements. Such seizures, or convulsive states, are associated with many of the organic brain syndromes we have discussed in this chapter. Infectious diseases, vascular accidents, tumors, tissue degeneration, and toxins all can cause epileptic symptomatology. In this section, we will discuss *idiopathic* forms of epilepsy; that is, epilepsy in which the cause of the seizure is not known. Approximately 77 percent of all cases of epilepsy are idiopathic (Kolb 1973).

About two million Americans suffer from epilepsy. It usually has its initial onset before the age of 20. There are many misconceptions and unfortunate myths about epilepsy, and epileptics are often viewed by the uninformed as having a form of insanity or mental retardation. However, this is not at all true. Most of the time, that is, between seizures, the epileptic suffers no serious disturbance of psychological functioning. Most epileptics have the same intellectual capability as the general population, and no greater incidence of brain dysfunction. Indeed, a number of notable and successful historical figures, including Julius Caesar and Feodor Dostoyevsky, were epileptics.

Epilepsy is not associated with an elevated incidence of major personality disturbance, and there is no distinctive "epileptic personality" (Tizard 1962). However, mild personality disturbances often occur with a greater than average frequency in epileptic patients. This appears to be a socially learned concomitant of the disorder rather than an intrinsic component of it. Many epileptics, for instance, encounter a great deal of social humiliation and stigmatism in connection with their disorder. They may be overprotected by concerned parents and may develop feelings of inadequacy and low self-esteem that interfere with the development of adequate interpersonal relationships and self-concept. These mild personality disturbances are especially common in the *psychomotor* form of epilepsy. Some investigators have sug-

gested that patients with temporal lobe epilepsy are more likely to engage in hyperactive and aggressive behaviors (e.g., Gibbs 1958). However, in a recent survey of the research evidence, Gunn and Fenton (1971) found no support for this suggestion.

It is unfortunate that some employers still hesitate to hire epileptics because they erroneously assume that these individuals have regularly occurring convulsive seizures. With the appropriate medication, the majority of epileptics remain symptom free, and their job performance is not affected.

The *epileptic seizure* process is associated with a neurological state characterized by a spontaneous and massive discharge of groups of brain cells. This discharge may be localized to specific areas or widespread across a number of cortical areas. During a seizure, about 85 percent of epileptics show distinctive abnormalities in the EEG tracing recorded from the affected brain area. If the seizure affects motor regions of the brain, for example, the individual typically exhibits tremors and uncontrollable physical activity. If the visual area is affected, the person may experience visual hallucinations. There is a wide range of stimuli that can trigger a convulsive episode, including psychological stress, fatigue, or a metabolic disturbance such as low blood sugar (hypoglycemia). For some individuals, an apparent innocuous stimulus such as certain musical notes or tunes, or the flickering of lights at a certain frequency, may produce a seizure by triggering an unusual biophysical sensitivity. For example, in a patient known by one of the authors, the tune "Stardust" would reliably trigger a convulsive seizure. In another patient, the voice of a local radio disc jockey consistently provoked seizures. In such cases, it appears that these stimuli activate specific sensitive and vulnerable areas of the brain, triggering a local discharge of brain cell firing that then spreads into a full-fledged convulsive seizure. In many cases, the stimuli triggering the seizure are not known.

In most forms of epilepsy in which the individual loses consciousness, there is a brief warning or *aura* of the oncoming convulsion. Auras may take different forms, ranging from a diffuse apprehensiveness, to sensations such as distinct unpleasant odors or sounds in the ear, to specific physical symptoms such as dizziness, abdominal cramps, or uncontrollable twitching of the legs or arms.

The various forms of idiopathic epilepsy are differentiated on the basis of symptomatology, not etiology, because the precise causes of the various types have not been delineated. We will discuss four of the major forms. However, not all types of epilepsy are described by these four categories, nor are these categories mutually exclusive. Some patients may display a mixture of several forms of epilepsy.

PETIT MAL EPILEPSY

In this type of epilepsy, which is characterized by a minor or small (*petit*) seizure, no aura, convulsions, or total loss of consciousness is involved. There is only a momentary disturbance of consciousness, lasting on the average of 10 to 15 seconds. During these brief episodes, which can occur as often as 20 times a day, the individual momentarily loses awareness of the immediate surroundings, ceases whatever he or she is doing, stares ahead in a trance-like state, and then resumes his or her activities without knowing what transpired during the brief seizure state. It has been traditional to include two specific types of seizure attacks under the petit mal category: (1) *akinetic* attacks, marked by a sudden loss of muscle tonus that causes the person to fall to the ground if unsupported, or to drop objects, or to nod his or her head; and (2) *myoclonic* attacks, marked by momentary muscle contractions and/or motor jerking.

GRAND MAL EPILEPSY

This is the most clinically dramatic form of epilepsy, with a generalized seizure throughout the entire brain. It involves convulsions, loss of consciousness and, in the majority of cases, the experience of an aura before the seizure. The grand mal seizure usually has four stages: (1) The *aura* phase, which signals the impending convulsion. (2) The *tonic* phase, which marks the actual beginning of the seizure—the muscles become rigid, the individual loses muscle control and falls with arms and trunk extended, the eyes remain open but the pupils dilate, and the individual loses consciousness. This phase usually lasts about one minute. (3) The *clonic*

The Bettmann Archive

Julius Caesar is one of a number of notable historical figures who were epileptic.

phase, in which the muscles alternately contract and relax, producing violent spasms, contortions, and jerking movements. A frothy saliva may appear around the mouth. The jaws are vigorously opened and closed, and there is a danger that the person will bite or swallow the tongue. (Those nearby should take precautions to prevent this from happening, such as inserting a tongue-depressor in the person's mouth.) This phase also lasts approximately one minute. (4) The *coma* phase, in which the individual remains unconscious but the muscles relax. The individual then gradually regains consciousness but usually remains somewhat confused, feels sleepy, and may have a headache for some time. When fully recovered, the individual has no memory of the events that transpired after the start of the tonic phase. This type of seizure can occur as frequently as several times a day or as infrequently as once every few years.

JACKSONIAN OR FOCAL EPILEPSY

In Jacksonian or focal epilepsy, the seizure is limited to a certain sensory or motor portion of the

DOSTOYEVSKY ON EPILEPSY

He remembered among other things that he always had one minute just before the epileptic fit (if it came on while he was awake), when suddenly in the midst of sadness, spiritual darkness and oppression, there seemed at moments a flash of light in his brain, and with extraordinary impetus all his vital forces suddenly began working at their highest tension. The sense of life, the consciousness of self, were multiplied ten times at these moments which passed like a flash of lightning. His mind and his heart were flooded with extraordinary light; all his uneasiness, all his doubts, all his anxieties were relieved at once; they were all merged in a lofty calm, full of serene, harmonious joy and hope. But these moments, these flashes, were only the prelude of that final second (it was never more than a second) with which the fit began. That second was, of course, unendurable. Thinking of that moment later, when he was all right again, he often said to himself that all these gleams and flashes of the highest sensation of life and self-consciousness, and therefore also of the highest form of existence, were nothing but disease, the interruption of the normal condition; and if so, it was not at all the highest form of being, but on the contrary must be reckoned the lowest. And yet he came at last to an extremely paradoxical conclusion. "What if it is disease?" he decided at last. "What does it matter that it is an abnormal intensity, if the result, if the minute of sensation, re-membered and analysed afterwards in health, turns out to be the acme of harmony and beauty, and gives a feeling, unknown and undivined till then, of completeness, of proportion, of reconciliation, and of ecstatic devotional merging in the highest synthesis of life?" These vague expressions seemed to him very comprehensible, though too weak. That it really was "beauty and worship," that it really was the "highest synthesis of life" he could not doubt, and could not admit the possibility of doubt. It was not as though he saw abnormal and unreal visions of some sort at that moment, as from hashish, opium, or wine, destroying the reason and distorting the soul. He was quite capable of judging of that when the attack was over. These moments were only an extraordinary quickening of self-consciousness—if the condition was to be expressed in one word—and at the same time of the direct sensation of existence in the most intense degree. Since at that second, that is at the very last conscious moment before the fit, he had time to say to himself clearly and consciously, "Yes, for this moment one might give one's whole life!" then without doubt that moment was really worth the whole of life.

From *The Idiot,* by Fyodor Dostoyevsky, translated by Constance Garnett. Copyright 1935 by Modern Library, Inc.

body. It is initially localized to a specific part of the body, but this circumscribed muscular twitching or tingling sensation then spreads to the rest of the body. The individual is conscious as those initial symptoms appear, but then usually loses consciousness. Often this type of seizure is a prelude to a full-blown grand mal seizure.

PSYCHOMOTOR EPILEPSY

In this type of epilepsy, the seizure state is preceded by an aura. The seizure itself usually consists of nothing more than a clouding of consciousness and loss of contact with reality that lasts anywhere from a few seconds to a few minutes. During the seizure period, the individual may appear quite normal and commonly will engage in an organized and mechanical sequence of activities. When the seizure ends, he or she will resume the interrupted behavior and will be amnesic for the episode. For example, in the middle of an important business meeting, a man may suddenly leave the room, return to his office down the hall, and begin mechanically to organize things on his desk. In a few minutes, he may return to the meeting and become reinvolved in the discussion as if he had never left, with no awareness of his activities during the previous few minutes.

TREATMENT

Fortunately, most cases of epilepsy can be controlled successfully with anticonvulsive drug medication. A new anticonvulsive drug recently introduced into this country from Europe—*valproic acid*—appears to be extremely effective in eliminating seizures even in very severe cases of epilepsy. Along with chemotherapy, it is also beneficial to administer some form of educational/ psychological treatment aimed at aiding the epileptic to better understand the disorder, and helping him or her deal with any feelings of inferiority and negative self-image that may have developed because of others' attitudes toward the disorder. Such treatment will help to ensure that the epileptic will make an effective educational, interpersonal, and occupational adjustment. Only in rare cases in which severe seizures are frequent and highly disruptive, and cannot be effectively controlled with medication, will surgery be considered to remove the portion of the brain involved. Such surgery is a last resort when everything else fails.

One interesting and potentially valuable use of biofeedback techniques has been in the area of epilepsy. Although this research is still in a very early stage of evaluation and development, preliminary evidence suggests that biofeedback may prove to be an alternative or adjunct to drug medication in controlling seizures. The notion behind the use of biofeedback training is that by teaching a patient to suppress the characteristic electrical brain pattern associated with an attack, or by training him or her to generate an EEG brain pattern incompatible with the seizure pattern, it may be possible to suppress or reduce the incidence of seizures. A number of preliminary studies have reported the successful reduction of seizures in epileptics with the use of EEG biofeedback training procedures (e.g., Finley, Smith, & Etherton 1975; Sterman & Friar 1972). However, there has also been some research that did not find any reduction in seizures with the use of EEG biofeedback (e.g., Kaplan 1975). A great deal of additional research is needed before any widespread clinical application, in order to demonstrate unequivocally that EEG biofeedback does produce significant clinical improvement.

DISORDERS OF SLEEP

SYMPTOM DESCRIPTION AND ETIOLOGY

Sleep is as natural as breathing and is just as necessary. Most people take sleep for granted, having no difficulties at all associated with this natural act. For many others, however, disturbances associated with sleep create significant problems. At the outset, we should note that the exact causes of these disturbances are not fully understood. Sleep itself is still somewhat of a mystery. Much more research is needed to understand the adaptive functions it serves. In this section, we will review a number of common sleep disturbances.

On the basis of EEG recordings from the brain, four distinct stages of sleep have been delineated, ranging along a continuum from light sleep during *Stage 1* to deep sleep during *Stage 4*. These four stages occur with regular cyclic variation during the course of the night—every 90 or so minutes. Between each four-stage cycle, at the beginning of Stage 1, is the REM or *rapid eye movement* phase, during which there is a high frequency of eye movements. This REM sleep period, which also came to be known as *paradoxical sleep,* was found by Aserinsky and Kleitman (1953) to be the period during sleep when dreaming is likely to occur.

Most sleep researchers believe that if any Stage 4 deep sleep or REM sleep is missed one night, it will be made up the next night. Consistently missing these phases of sleep usually causes the person to become tense and irritable and may even trigger a mental breakdown in some marginally adjusted individuals. Many investigators suggest that the disturbed sleep patterns usually found in depression, schizophrenia, and other forms of psychopathology play an important role in these disorders. As new sleep research is designed and carried out, more definitive answers may soon be available.

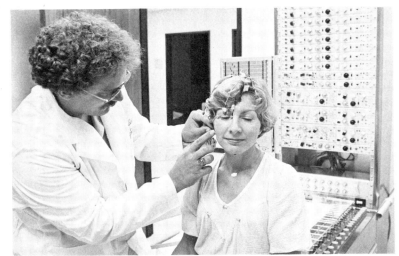

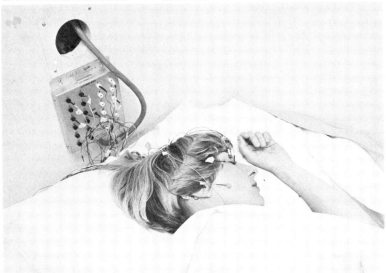

Sleep research laboratories are beginning to investigate systematically the basic mechanisms and disorders of sleep. Here, electrodes have been attached to the subject's scalp to record brain wave activity during sleep.

INSOMNIA

Insomnia is a very common sleep disturbance, affecting about 20 million Americans to some degree. One needs only to look at the vast number of sleeping pills sold each year to verify the prevalence of this disorder. All of us have experienced periods during which we found it extremely difficult to fall asleep. For the insomniac, however, this is a chronic problem. Throughout history,

insomnia has been a problem for many people — Abraham Lincoln and Theodore Roosevelt were well-known insomniacs. The severity of insomnia varies greatly from one insomniac to the next, ranging from very mild to very severe cases. Fortunately, even severe cases are never fatal. However, insomniacs who consistently lose a great deal of sleep will, besides feeling fatigued after a number of sleepless or restless nights, often display symptoms of anxiety and depression. One of the greatest problems associated with insomnia is the great amount of worry it produces in insomniacs who cannot sleep when they feel they should — worrying, though, merely makes the problem worse.

HYPERSOMNIA

Whereas insomniacs have difficulty falling asleep, *hypersomniacs* find it very difficult to stay awake. They need a great deal of sleep to act and feel their best. This can create problems for an individual who, needing more than ten hours of sleep a day, may not be able to participate in all the necessary activities of living. They may also start feeling guilty about excessive sleepiness-laziness that is not their fault. A well-known form of periodic hypersomnia is the *Kleine-Levin* syndrome, in which recurrent periods of excessive sleeping can last several days and involve as much as 18–20 hours of sleep per day. Other symptoms usually associated with this syndrome are excessive hunger and overeating. Although the exact cause of this syndrome is not known, most investigators suggest that it is probably due to some dysfunction of the hypothalamus (e.g., Gallinek 1967).

NARCOLEPSY In this unusual form of hypersomnia, the individual periodically suffers from a sudden and overpowering seizure of sleepiness and cannot stay awake. These sudden sleeping attacks usually last from a few minutes to up to a half hour. Although they may occur at any time and anywhere, they are usually triggered by boring and monotonous activities. One common accompanying symptom is *cataplexy,* or the complete loss of muscle tone. Emotional arousal or stress usually precipitates attacks of cataplexy, during which the individual loses complete control of his or her muscles and falls limply to the ground. Such an attack may be particularly embarrassing if it occurs in the middle of a conversation or while engaged in some activity such as making love.

Although the exact cause of narcolepsy is not currently known, it appears to be associated with an abnormality of the REM stage sleep process. When narcoleptics have an attack, they fall immediately into REM-stage sleep, during which there is a significant decrease in muscle tone (Rechtschaffen, Wolpert, Dement, Mitchell, & Fisher 1963). Research is needed to isolate the brain mechanisms that prompt this sudden onset of sleep into the REM period.

SLEEP APNEA

Sleep apnea involves the inability to breathe for a short time while sleeping. The individual, after falling asleep, may stop breathing for one or two minutes and then suddenly take a few violent breaths after being aroused by the sudden shortage of oxygen, after which he or she will fall asleep again. Many individuals are not aware they suffer from apnea, having no memory for the momentary awakenings when they gasp for air. These individuals may complain of hypersomnia because they are always tired because of the frequent awakenings and must spend a great deal of additional time sleeping. Or they may complain of insomnia because of the frequent awakenings caused by the constant need to gasp for air during an attack. The cause of this disorder is not known. It should also be noted that it has been suggested as a possible cause of *crib death* (Sudden Infant Death Syndrome), in which perfectly healthy infants suddenly die during sleep because of apparent respiratory failure.

NIGHTMARES

All of us have experienced nightmares or "bad dreams" at some time in our lives. They occur most frequently in children and appear to occur most often during REM sleep. A *night terror* or *pavor nocturnis* is a particularly severe variety of bad dream. When it occurs, the child shows marked physiological changes and intense fear and emotion. He or she will scream vigorously and may appear to be fighting or running from some terrifying person or situation. Even when awakened, the child may continue to scream and remain disoriented and confused for a while. When the child is fully awake, he or she usually does not remember any details of the dream.

For the majority of children, bad dreams do not cause any significant or long-lasting problems. They appear merely to reflect a transient response to some stress. For those children who chronically experience frequent and severe nightmares or night terror, they may reflect significant fear and anxiety the child is harboring. In such cases, this anxiety or fear may have to be dealt with.

SLEEPWALKING

Sleepwalking or *somnambulism* was discussed in chapter 6 when we discussed hysterical reactions. Contrary to what the movies show, people who are sleepwalking do not do so with arms outstretched and eyes closed. The somnambulist walks about with eyes opened, moving about in a relatively rigid manner. Sleepwalking is not a serious problem, and most authorities do not recommend psychotherapy or drugs in dealing with it. Rather, they merely recommend locking the doors and removing dangerous objects at night if one is living with a known somnambulist.

TREATMENT

Unfortunately, sleeping pills are often prescribed by many physicians for insomnia. We say "unfortunately" because these sleep-inducing drugs—commonly containing barbiturates—usually have the effect of merely worsening the insomniac's problem in the long run. Although such drugs may help the patient temporarily, a dependency and increased tolerance can develop so that larger and larger doses are needed to produce the same desired effect. Earlier in this chapter, we noted the potential harm produced by an excessive intake of *bromides*, which are contained in sleeping pills. Another of the effects of such drugs is to decrease the amount of Stage 4 and REM sleep, which are the most important and necessary stages of sleep. If the insomniac suddenly stops taking the drug, severe nightmares may occur because of overcompensation for the missed REM sleep. The insomniac soon finds himself taking a wide variety of different pills but is still not able to get to sleep easily. Such drug dependency is a serious problem. Only a gradual withdrawal from sleep-inducing medication will allow the person to get any sleep.

Because of the problems recently found to be associated with the use of drugs in treating insomnia, a great deal of research has been directed at finding effective nondrug therapy techniques for dealing with this sleep disorder. Recent investigations have demonstrated the effectiveness of certain behavior therapy methods in the treatment of sleep-onset insomnia. For example, standard muscle relaxation training (discussed in earlier chapters) has been found to be effective (e.g., Borkovec, Kaloupek & Slama 1975), as well as stimulus-control methods (e.g., Bootzin 1973). Borkovec, Slama, and Grayson (1977) have summarized such self-control methods:

> Stimulus-control procedures . . . assume that sleep is a conditioned behavior that will or will not occur depending on the association of bed-related stimuli with behaviors that are either compatible or incompatible with sleep. The patient is instructed to observe a regular sleep schedule (retiring and awakening at the same time each day, avoiding daytime naps) and to avoid engaging in sleep-incompatible behaviors in the presence of bed-related stimuli (e.g., watching television, eating, or studying in bed). Sometimes the patient is also told to leave the bedroom within 10 minutes after retiring if he or she has not yet fallen asleep, return when drowsy, and repeat this procedure as often as necessary. The latter technique guarantees that only sleep-compatible behaviors are occurring in bed and that rapid sleep onset becomes associated with bed stimuli. (p. 391)

There is not yet any cure for hypersomnia or narcolepsy. The only treatment that appears to decrease the frequency of these attacks in some people is the regular administration of stimulant drugs such as *Ritalin*. Of course, along with this form of chemotherapy, some form of counseling/educational therapy should be administered so that the individual learns to understand the biological nature of the disorder and adjust to the problem.

Sleep apnea is also incurable at the present time. Moreover, no known drug appears to effectively treat this disorder.

Nightmares and sleepwalking, as mentioned earlier, usually are not serious disorders and as a result do not require any treatment. However, as we indicated, if nightmares are very frequent and severe, then some form of treatment may need to be administered to deal with anxiety or stresses that may be prompting these bad dreams. However, the percentage of such cases is low.

SUMMARY

1. Differences between organic brain syndromes and functional psychopathologies are usually observed in the areas of impairment of *memory, intellectual functioning, judgment, orientation,* and *affect.* Enormous individual differences exist, however, in the degree to which all five variables are seen in a specific case of organic brain syndrome.

2. Organic brain syndromes are diagnosed by a number of procedures: physical or histological (autopsy) exams, by use of the angiogram, the recording of brain wave activity, by observing overt behavior and motor skills, and by use of neuropsychological techniques such as the Halstead-Reitan test battery.

3. The behavioral, psychological, and physical impairments produced by organic brain syndromes are greatly influenced by variables such as age of onset, individual differences in psychological and biological functioning, and the degree of social isolation/social support, the amount of tissue destroyed, the location of the area affected in the brain, and the nature of the disease (e.g., tumor, head injury, stroke, etc.).

4. Deficiencies of vitamins (especially the vitamin B group), calories, and proteins can also produce certain organic brain syndromes.

5. Head injuries are one of the most common causes of organic brain syndromes. Such injuries are usually classified into one of

two general headings: (a) *closed head* injuries, in which the skull is not penetrated but force to the head produces concussion, hemorrhage, and other pathological states; (b) open head injuries, in which some object penetrates the skull and brain.

6. Interruption of the blood supply to the brain can cause permanent brain damage. Such blood supply interruptions to the brain are referred to as *cerebrovascular disorders.* These disorders are the third most common cause of death in this country. There are two major forms: *cerebral arteriosclerosis,* which involves the hardening and narrowing of the arteries of the brain; and *cerebral strokes* (hemorrhage of blood vessels) and *embolisms* (blockage of blood vessels by some substance).

7. Tumors or neoplasms are abnormal tissue growths. They can develop in most any part of the body, but the brain and its supporting tissue appear to be a common site. The location of the brain tumor determines the degree and type of impairment evidenced.

8. There are various brain disorders that are caused by bacterial and viral infections that affect brain tissue. Two major types of brain infections are *encephalitis* and *cerebral syphilis.*

9. The *blood-brain barrier* is a protective mechanism of the brain that acts to screen the flow of harmful substances from the bloodstream into the brain and subsequently into the rest of the central nervous system. Due to factors such as oxygen deprivation or the presence of excessive amounts of toxic metals, gas, or drugs, the effective functioning of this blood-brain barrier can be impaired, resulting in significant interference with brain functioning and, in severe cases, permanent brain damage and even death.

10. *Epilepsy* is a Greek word that means "seizure." Most forms of epilepsy are associated with a period of unconsciousness and involuntary movements. Approximately three-quarters of all cases of epilepsy are *idiopathic,* that is, of unknown cause.

11. The various forms of idiopathic epilepsy are differentiated on the basis of symptomatology, not etiology. The *petit mal* type is characterized by a minor or small seizure, with no aura, convulsions, or total loss of consciousness. The *grand mal* type is the most clinically dramatic form, involving a generalized seizure throughout the entire brain. There are convulsions and a loss of consciousness. The *Jacksonian* or *focal* type is characterized by the seizure being limited to a certain sensory or motor portion of the body. In *psychomotor* epilepsy, the seizure itself usually is no more than a clouding of consciousness and loss of contact with reality that lasts anywhere from a few seconds to a few minutes. Fortunately, most epilepsy cases can be effectively treated and controlled with anticonvulsive drugs.

12. Certain disturbances associated with sleep can create significant problems for an individual. *Insomnia* is a very common sleep disturbance that affects millions of Americans. Whereas insomniacs have difficulty falling asleep, *hypersomniacs* have difficulty remaining awake. *Narcolepsy* is an unusual form of hypersomnia in which the individual periodically suffers from a sudden and overpowering seizure of sleepiness and cannot stay awake. *Sleep apnea* involves the inability to breathe for a short time while sleeping. Another common sleep disturbance is *nightmares.* Although all of us have experienced nightmares or "bad dreams," certain individuals experience frequent and especially frightening nightmares. Finally sleepwalking or *somnambulism* is another disorder of sleep which we reviewed.

Borkovec, T. D., Slama, K. M., & Grayson, J. B. Sleep, disorders of sleep, and hypnosis. In D. C. Rimm and J. W. Sommervill (Eds.), *Abnormal psychology.* New York: Academic Press, 1977.

Lezak, M. D. *Neuropsychological assessment.* New York: Oxford University Press, 1976.

Lipowski, Z. J. Organic brain syndromes: Overview and classification. In D. Benson & D. Blumer (Eds.), *Psychiatric aspects of neurologic disease.* New York: Grune & Stratton, 1975.

Pincus, J. H., & Tucker, G. *Behavioral neurology.* New York: Oxford University Press, 1974.

RECOMMENDED READINGS

15

MENTAL RETARDATION

OVERVIEW In this chapter, we will discuss mental retardation. Mental retardation can be seen as a medical, social, educational, or psychological problem. It is not a single syndrome, but affects a heterogeneous group of people in a variety of ways. Classification, definition, and treatment of mental retardation have always been problematic, dependent to a great degree on social attitudes. We will begin by examining some historical approaches to mental retardation and then discuss the problems involved in defining and assessing this disorder. Both the DSM-III and the American Association on Mental Deficiency (AAMD) offer definitions of mental retardation, but their criteria for defining the disorder have been criticized. The use of standard IQ tests will therefore be questioned; problems with these tests include cultural and language bias, difficulties in assessing social adequacy, and the use of an arbitrary cutting score. Another issue to be covered involves the classification of levels of mental retardation (educable, trainable, and profound or custodial) in terms of education and schooling.

In the second part of the chapter we will examine a number of clinical forms of mental retardation. All these have a somatic basis and cause profound retardation. Mild retardation is the subject of a separate discussion. We will discuss possible causes and stressors that may apply at various stages of life. Finally, the chapter concludes with a look at some educational, therapeutic, and preventive approaches to mental retardation.

WHAT IS MENTAL RETARDATION?

Mental retardation is quite unlike any of the psychopathologies we have discussed in previous chapters. First, mental retardation can be viewed as a psychological problem, a medical problem, an educational problem, or a social problem—or as all of these. Second, mental retardation does not appear to be a uniform syndrome taking in a homogeneous group of individuals; rather, it appears to be an extremely varied syndrome affecting a heterogeneous group. Third, those who are mentally retarded may also have other psychopathologies in addition to being mentally handicapped. All these reasons lead us to conclude that mental retardation is much more complex and varied than the stereotypes suggest. Before we consider the major issues, let us look first at the historical trends in dealing with mental retardation.

HISTORICAL ATTITUDES

The first written references to the problem of mental retardation come from the time of ancient Greece and Rome, though it was probably known much earlier. From the Greco-Roman period through the Middle Ages, the mentally handicapped were often subjected to the worst possible treatment. If a retarded person did survive infancy or childhood (in ancient Rome and Sparta, legend and folklore recount that a mentally retarded infant was to be cast into a river), life often held in store only mockery, ridicule, neglect, and immeasurable suffering. Some few were fortunate enough to be cared for by enlightened and compassionate persons; others lived out their lives wandering aimlessly, eating garbage, sleeping in the streets; others, perhaps more fortunate, became jesters, clowns, or side-show freaks, traveling about in circuses entertaining the public and royalty. In general, public reaction to the mentally retarded, and professional concern for these people, depended in part upon the prevailing view of what caused retardation. Often the retarded were thought to be workers of Satan; but just as often they were seen as special agents of God (a Yiddish proverb reads: "A complete fool is half prophet"). For years the mentally dull were viewed as being insane, and not until the late 1700s did clinicians start to suggest that mental retardation was not a form of insanity. Esquirol (1772–1840) was one of the first to draw a distinction between "idiocy" and insanity; he, however, believed that "acquired idiocy" was often the result of excessive masturbation. For centuries, no major efforts were made to educate or rehabilitate the retarded.

DEFINITIONS OF MENTAL RETARDATION

One of the first attempts to define and analyze mental retardation was made by Alfred Binet (1857–1911), commonly thought of as the father of intelligence testing. About 1904, the French Minister of Public Instruction requested that Binet devise a method that could differentiate normal children from retarded children. Binet and an associate, Victor Henri, had earlier developed several mental tests that could detect individual differences in memory and other skills. The Minister now wanted Binet to continue his work, refining it to a point at which he could regularly test children for placement in special classes. Another colleague, Theodore Simon, was also to work with Binet on the development of a formal intelligence test. Binet's test, of course, became the prototype of later intelligence tests, and the IQ or *intelligence quotient* was to become the major criterion for establishing the categorical diagnosis of mental retardation. Not only did Binet and his colleagues introduce intelligence testing, a procedure enabling the assignment of a single score to a retarded person, but these men also showed that retardation was not an all-or-none phenomenon.

Definitions and criteria for mental retardation have changed little since the time of Binet, and most definitions still rely heavily on "measured intelligence." Although newer criteria and classification systems are being developed, the principal criterion is still a low score on an intelligence test.

Prehm (1974) states that five concepts or criteria have been used most widely in the definitions of mental retardation:

1. Mental retardation originates *early in life*, during the developmental period. Retardation is distinguished from *dementia*, which resembles it; dementia, though, has its onset after the developmental period, usually at 17 or 18 years of age.

DEMOGRAPHICS	USUAL AGE AT ONSET	PREVALENCE	SEX RATIO
ORGANIC MENTAL RETARDATION	Apparent prior to or at birth	Approximately 1% of population	Male-female ratio approximately 2 to 1
CULTURAL OR FAMILIAL MENTAL RETARDATION	Typically diagnosed at the beginning of formal schooling (6 yrs.)	Between 1 and 3%	Not known

2. Mental retardation involves *subnormal intelligence*. Intelligence test scores falling below a given "cutting score" or arbitrary designation, point to mental retardation, according to this definition.

3. Mental retardation involves *social inadequacy*. This criterion is a remnant of a European tradition stating that those who could not manage their own affairs, fend for themselves, count to 20, or manage their money were to some extent retarded. Obviously, on this basis, some people with low IQs appear to be socially adequate, while some with high IQs appear to be socially inadequate! We will deal later with the problems of reliably measuring "social adequacy."

4. Mental retardation involves an *hypothesized* or *inferred organic cause*. Central nervous system damage has been inferred in all cases of mental retardation, both mild and profound; it should be noted, however, that neurological damage cannot be detected in approximately 80 percent of all retardates.

5. Mental retardation is *incurable*. This criterion has appeared in many definitions of mental retardation, and surely seems to be one of the most inaccurate of the traditional criteria. As we shall see, some forms of mental retardation are not curable; others do respond to remediation; and some can be prevented and ameliorated.

Two recent definitions of mental retardation still retain three of these five criteria, but the last two have been deleted. The first definition is made by the American Psychiatric Association, in the new DSM-III; the second definition is proposed by the American Association on Mental Deficiency.

THE DSM-III DEFINITION The new DSM-III refers to mental retardation as a syndrome manifested by three chief characteristics:

1. *Subnormal intellectual functioning*—defined by an IQ score of more than two standard deviations below the mean. (The mean for the IQ test is 100, and the standard deviation is usually 15 or 16 points, depending on the test used; thus, two standard deviations would be a departure from the mean of at least 30 to 32 IQ points—an IQ below 70.)

2. *Deficits in adaptive behavior*—defined by social responsibility and independent functioning, taking into consideration age and cultural factors. (DSM-III acknowledges that adaptive behavior is vague and hard to define and may require "clinical judgment" to determine general adaptation.)

3. *Onset prior to age 18*—if the person has symptoms that resemble retardation, but they have their onset after the last developmental stage (adolescence), then the disorder is called *dementia*.

THE AAMD DEFINITION The American Association on Mental Deficiency (AAMD) has published the most widely accepted definition of mental retardation. The AAMD definition generally offers the same three criteria as the DSM-III. These were specified in the *Manual on Terminology and Classification in Mental Retardation* (Grossman 1973):

> Mental Retardation refers to significantly subaverage general intellectual functioning existing concurrently with deficits in adaptive behavior, and manifested during the developmental period. (p. 11)

Unlike the American Psychiatric Association's conceptual definition of "adaptive behavior," the

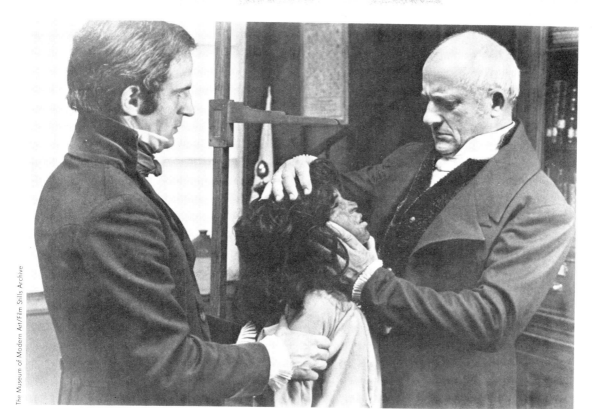

The Museum of Modern Art/Film Stills Archive

L'ENFANT SAUVAGE (The Wild Child) 1970, Francois Truffaut. In this film, the "Wild boy of Aveyron" is depicted as **retarded and unsocialized. But many modern clinicians believe the child was autistic.**

AAMD has developed an *Adaptive Behavior Scale* for this criterion (Nihara, Foster, Shellhaas, & Leland 1974). This scale is designed to quantify adaptive behavior and so make this criterion more objective. The scale can be administered by someone without detailed training; for example, the rater scores the subject on the dimensions shown in table 15.1

Both the DSM-III and the AAMD, then, use essentially the same three criteria for determining retarded intellectual functioning: IQ deficits (scores below 70) and adaptive or social inadequacies, both beginning within infancy, childhood, or adolescence. Several criticisms can be made of such definition systems.

PROBLEMS OF DEFINITION   First, IQ cutting scores—"below 70"—are arbitrary. Further, one person with an IQ of 65 may have widely different types of skills or deficits than another person with the same score; these persons are not as equal as the score suggests. The fact is that a single score does not convey all of the information about a person's intellectual functioning. Although the single score is not to be discarded, viewing a profile of the person's intellect is much more revealing and

often suggests that in certain given areas, a particular "retarded" child may be very close to normal.

Second, adaptive behavior scales are not viewed as being adequate. Clausen (1972), for one, proposed that behavioral measures should not be part of the criteria for retardation until an instrument is developed that can accurately gauge behavior adaptation. Others have pointed out that the current Adaptive Behavior Scale does not have norms on which to compare children of various ages and social classes; the current norms are based on institutionalized children.

Finally, the two chief criteria, low IQ and failures in adaptive behavior, do not always vary together; as we noted previously, one person may have a low IQ but adequate adaptive responses, while another may have a high IQ and poor adaptive behavior. The possibility of low correlations between the two measures in certain cases suggests that, in fact, these two criteria are measuring something other than retardation. Further, adaptive behavior fluctuates more than IQ, and so a given person with a low IQ may be judged retarded because of temporary fluctuations in adaptive behavior.

AAMD REVISED ADAPTIVE BEHAVIOR SCALE
Table 15.1

This scale contains two major parts, with the first comprising 10 behavioral dimensions and 21 subcategories. (Nihara et al. 1974)

I. Independent Functioning
- A. Eating
- B. Toilet use
- C. Cleanliness
- D. Appearance
- E. Care of clothing
- F. Dressing and undressing
- G. Travel
- H. General independent functioning

II. Physical Development
- A. Sensory development
- B. Motor development

III. Economic Activity
- A. Money handling and budgeting
- B. Shopping skills

IV. Language Development
- A. Expression
- B. Comprehension
- C. Social language development

V. Numbers and Time

VI. Domestic Activity
- A. Cleaning
- B. Kitchen duties
- C. Other domestic activities

VII. Vocational Activity

VIII. Self-Direction
- A. Initiative
- B. Perseverance
- C. Leisure time

IX. Responsibility

X. Socialization

The second part of the Adaptive Behavior Scale involves 13 dimensions of problem behaviors and one dimension dealing with medication:

- I. Violent and Destructive Behavior
- II. Antisocial Behavior
- III. Rebellious Behavior
- IV. Untrustworthy Behavior
- V. Withdrawal
- VI. Stereotyped Behavior and Odd Mannerisms
- VII. Inappropriate Interpersonal Manners
- VIII. Unacceptable Vocal Habits
- IX. Unacceptable or Eccentric Habits
- X. Self-Abusive Behavior
- XI. Hyperactive Tendencies
- XII. Sexually Aberrant Behavior
- XIII. Psychological Disturbances
- XIV. Use of Medications

FAULKNER ON IDIOCY

Benjamin. Born Maury, after his mother's only brother: a handsome flashing swaggering workless bachelor who borrowed money from almost anyone, even Dilsey although she was a Negro, explaining to her as he withdrew his hand from his pocket that she was not only in his eyes the same as a member of his sister's family, she would be considered a born lady anywhere in any eyes. Who, when, at last even his mother realized what he was and insisted weeping that his name must be changed, was rechristened Benjamin by his brother Quentin (Benjamin, our lastborn, sold into Egypt). Who loved three things: the pasture which was sold to pay for Candace's wedding and to send Quentin to Harvard, his sister Candace, firelight. Who lost none of them because he could not remember his sister but only the loss of her, and firelight was the same bright shape as going to sleep, and the pasture was even better sold than before because now he and TP could not only follow timeless along the fence the motions which it did not even matter to him were humanbeings swinging golfsticks, TP could lead them to clumps of grass or weeds where there would appear suddenly in TP's hand small white spherules which competed with and even conquered what he did not even know was gravity and all the immutable laws when released from the hand toward plank floor or smokehouse wall or concrete sidewalk. Gelded 1913. Committed to the State Asylum, Jackson 1933. Lost nothing then either because, as with his sister, he remembered not the pasture but only its loss, and firelight was still the same bright shape of sleep.

From *The Sound and the Fury*, by William Faulkner. Copyright 1939 by William Faulkner.

LEVELS OF MENTAL RETARDATION

Mental retardation, as a concept, is a categorical label; it separates people into two distinct groups—retarded and not retarded. But measured intelligence and adaptive ratings—the major criteria—are both reported as continuous numerical data. For example, measured intelligence (IQ score) is a number falling somewhere between two extreme points: an IQ of near zero to an IQ over 150. Assigning scores from this continuum implies that there exist widely varying levels of intellectual functioning—not just two groups labeled "bright" and "dull." But the categorical term *mental retardation* assumes that there is a point, a cutting score, at which mental retardation commences. This is indeed a dilemma that will not go away.

To elaborate upon this quandary, let us consider the Wechsler Intelligence Scale for Children—Revised, the WISC-R (1974). (The WISC-R is an individually administered intelligence test intended for children 6 through 16 years of age; a child receives three IQ scores—verbal IQ, performance IQ, and a full scale [combination] IQ.) Measured intelligence on the WISC-R can range from a high of about 160 points to a low of about 40 IQ points. At what point, then, does one receive the label "mentally retarded" or "mentally deficient"? The WISC-R manual states that persons scoring 69 and below are considered in the mentally deficient category. Yet what is the actual difference between a score of 68 and a score of 71? Could a group of clinical psychologists distinguish between the two persons scoring 68 and 71 if they did not know the IQ scores? Could a special educator or teacher tell the difference? It seems doubtful that they could.

One procedure to lessen this dilemma is to specify "levels" or degrees of mental retardation.

The Museum of Modern Art/Film Stills Archive

CHARLY © 1968, Selmur. If it is inferable from this film that mental retardation is not permanently remediable, the inference is misguided. Several therapeutic techniques have proved effective in raising the learning abilities of retarded persons.

Table 15.2 shows how the WISC-R deals with this problem.

EDUCATIONAL LABELING Another, more recent, means for "labeling" those who score below a given point is to refer to *what can be expected of them.* Educational diagnosticians and school psychologists often place the retarded into one of two

| IQ | CLASSIFICATION | PERCENT INCLUDED | |
		THEORETICAL NORMAL CURVE	ACTUAL SAMPLE[a]
130 and above	Very Superior	2.2	2.3
120–129	Superior	6.7	7.4
110–119	High Average (Bright)[b]	16.1	16.5
90–109	Average	50.0	49.4
80–89	Low Average (Dull)[b]	16.1	16.2
70–79	Borderline	6.7	6.0
69 and below	Mentally Deficient[b]	2.2	2.2

INTELLIGENCE CLASSIFICATIONS Table 15.2

[a]The percents shown are for Full Scale IQ, and are based on the total standardization sample (N = 2200). The percents obtained for Verbal IQ and Performance IQ are essentially the same.
[b]The terms *High Average (Bright), Low Average (Dull),* and *Mentally Deficient* correspond to the terms *Bright Normal, Dull Normal,* and *Mental Defective,* respectively, used in the *WPPSI, WAIS,* and 1949 *WISC* manuals. (WISC-R, 1974, p. 26)

THE EARLY TEACHERS: ITARD AND SEGUIN

Jean Itard (1774–1838) is most often associated with one of the strangest clinical studies known —the education of a "wild boy." Itard was a physician-director at the Asylum for the Deaf and Dumb, at Paris during the early 1800s. Through a series of complex referrals, he was given custody of a boy who had been discovered living as an animal in the forest of Aveyron in France. Describing Itard's new patient, Édouard Séguin (1864) later wrote:

> This naked boy was marked with numerous scars; he was nimble as a deer, subsisting on roots and nuts, which he cracked like a monkey, laughing at the falling snow, and rolling himself with delight in this white blanket. . . . He seemed about 17 years of age.

Prior to placement with Itard, this boy was known as the "wild boy [l'enfant sauvage] of Aveyron." He could not speak; at times he walked on all fours; and to say the least, he was oblivious to human communication. All of Paris had seen the wild boy; he was exhibited for some time in Paris by Sicard, providing amusement and fright to those who came to watch him tear off his clothes and growl at onlookers.

Several qualified specialists of the day saw the wild boy and pronounced him an "idiot." But Itard was unmoved by these assertions. He stated quite simply that the boy was "entirely untaught." Itard worked with the "wild boy" for six years and succeeded in developing some language skills in him. His method of teaching had been borrowed from Jacob Peréire, a Spanish clinician who had worked with deaf-mute children. Peréire believed that through the *sense of touch*, the mentally dull as well as the deaf-mute children could learn to speak. It has been reported that Peréire taught deaf children to speak certain phrases, with particular accents, to perfection. No doubt his work influenced Itard and those who were to follow.

Of those who came next, probably none did more to foster an interest in teaching and rehabilitating the mentally handicapped than Edouard Séguin (1812–1880). Séguin's educational procedure was called *psycho-physiological training*. Described simply, this procedure involved a progressive series of stimulation: first, for example, the child would learn "animal movements," then imitation and obedience, words, ideas, faces, moral expressions, and participating in moral feelings. Exercise, hand-training, tactile impressions, and all sorts of sensory training formed the building blocks of intelligence, according to Séguin. The retarded could be helped, he believed, by moving patiently through a series of increasingly difficult tasks. Séguin thus suggested to those concerned that "idiots" could in fact learn.

categories: *educable mentally retarded* (EMR) and *trainable mentally retarded* (TMR). A third category is reserved for those with the most severe varieties of retardation, who would not be a concern of the school system: *profoundly mentally retarded* (PMR), or custodial retarded. The case study on page 372 describes the behavior and symptoms of a person in this category.

Table 15.3 illustrates how Chinn, Drew, and Logan (1975) arrange the terminology (label), corresponding IQ range, and corresponding educational expectation for four levels of IQs.

It seems that the major shortcoming of the labels *EMR, TMR,* and *PMR* (custodial) is that the three groups are vastly different from one another. In particular, *EMRs* contrasted with profound retardates present a difference so obvious that it is hard to believe only an adjective (*educable / trainable / profound*) separates them. The label suggests that they are more similar than different because the noun is the same: *mentally retarded*. Indeed, it seems easier for teachers, special educators, psychologists, and parents, as well as the child, to forget the adjective (*educable* or whatever) and remember only the noun—*retarded*. These labels only worsen the dilemma of the cutting score. As we will see, a new trend is to drop the label "mental retardation" unless the individual specifically falls within the profound or custodial range.

FREQUENCY

The frequency of mental retardation cannot be considered apart from the problems of definition that currently exist. Since there is no agreement on what retardation is or how it is to be defined (many disagree with the DSM-III and AAMD criteria), the prevalence of mental retardation can only be roughly estimated. In 1970, the President's Task Force on Mental Retardation stated that approximately 6 million people in the United States were retarded; this represents approximately 3 percent of the population. However, some researchers find this percentage too high. Tarjan, Wright, Eyman, and Keeran (1973), for example, suggest that because of the higher mortality rate of mentally retarded populations (excluding mild or EMRs), the invalidity of using IQ alone to assess retardation, and the possibility that certain retarded individuals are no longer labeled retarded after leaving school, the true frequency of retardation is more likely to be 1 percent.

One comprehensive epidemiological investigation of mental retardation was conducted in Riverside, California, between 1963 and 1965 (Mercer 1973; Mercer and Lewis, in press). Basi-

Courtesy J. R. Mercer

J. R. Mercer has worked for an end to discriminatory intelligence testing.

cally, this investigation found the frequency of retardation to be lower than the estimated 3 percent. Mercer and Lewis (in press) also reported

TERMINOLOGY	APPROXIMATE IQ RANGE*	EDUCATIONAL EXPECTATION
Dull-normal	75 or 80 to 90	Capable of competing in school in most areas except in the strictly academic areas where performance is below average. Social adjustment which is not noticeably difficult from the larger population although in the lower segment of adequate adjustment. Occupational performance satisfactory in nontechnical areas, with total self-support highly probable.
Educable	50 to 75 or 80	Second- to fifth-grade achievement in school academic areas. Social adjustment that will permit some degree of independence in the community. Occupational sufficiency that will permit partial or total support when an adult.
Trainable	20 to 49	Learning primarily in the areas of self-help skills, very limited achievement in areas considered academic. Social adjustment usually limited to home and closely surrounding area. Occupational performance primarily in sheltered workshop or an institutional setting.
Custodial	Below 20	Usually unable to achieve even sufficient skills to care for basic needs. Will usually require nearly total care and supervision for duration of lifetime.

*IQ ranges represent approximate ranges, which vary to some degree depending on the source of data consulted. (From Chinn et al. 1975, p. 14)

CLASSIFICATION BY EDUCATIONAL EXPECTATION
Table 15.3

A CASE OF PROFOUND RETARDATION

Raymond is a 23-year-old white male of slender body build. Physically, Ray is somewhat above average in height but is below average in weight. Although he does not present noticeable signs of retardation, he does have a vacant stare that tends to give an impression of dullness. Ray has never spoken a word but on rare occasions does grunt.

Characteristically, Ray is noted for his hyperactivity. When indoors, he spends much time pacing to and fro, going first into the playroom area then out again. When the door to the playground is open Ray goes in and out an average of 75 to 100 times during an eight-hour period. Frequently, he displays tropistic-like behavior and stares directly into the sun for short periods. During these periods, Ray is frequently smiling and seems to enjoy such an occupation. While staring into the sun, Ray stands and rocks to and fro on tiptoe. His only object of attachment is a rubber ball about 6 inches in circumference. When seated he can bounce the ball against the wall very rapidly. When another patient takes his ball away, Ray will frequently try in a very primitive and infantile manner to recover his loss. However, he cannot display even the slightest outward aggressive behavior. Another of Ray's spontaneous actions, unless stopped by the attendant, is to go through the motions of copulation. About this, Ray shows no concern regarding privacy. He never attempts to conceal this activity. Another frequent activity in which Ray delights is to drink from one of the urinals or commodes. Unless guarded carefully, Ray will do this as often as ten times per hour. Invariably when he succeeds in drinking from the commodes, he appears pleased. The tell-tale sign of a recent success, of course, is that Ray's hair is wet. Ray is not toilet trained—he wets and soils both day and night and may, on any given day require his clothing to be changed up to 5 or even 10 times. Each soiling, of course, requires a shower.

Feeding is a problem with Ray too. He cannot feed himself without help and in chewing, he often drools as much as half his intake, thus requiring special bibs or else clean clothes following each meal. In regard to food preference, Ray possesses little discrimination. Very often he will eat match sticks, broom straws, fecal material, dirt or even vomit.

In regard to sensory efficiency, Ray's most outstanding capability would be in the area of motor skills. He has no known visual problem although this is suspect. Intellectual functioning, based upon the Vineland Social Maturity Scale, is estimated, in terms of IQ, simply as "below 19." Hearing seems to be mildly impaired and his pain threshold is very high. This is based upon reports from the staff physicians and dentists who remark that the ordinary shots, dental drilling, or other generally painful stimuli simply do not get through since he never squeals, whimpers or in

these critical findings concerning tests and testing procedures.

1. Males of all ages scored lower on the adaptive behavior scales than females.
2. There were no differences in adaptive behavior scores for children from differing socioeconomic and ethnic minority backgrounds.
3. There were no sex differences on IQ scores.
4. There was "overlabeling" of persons from lower socioeconomic backgrounds as retarded.
5. There was "underlabeling" of persons from higher socioeconomic backgrounds as retarded.
6. Those who were labeled retarded in the higher socioeconomic backgrounds were more likely to exhibit physical disabilities.
7. Black and Spanish-surname children who were tested by a school psychologist (who was invariably white) were more likely than Anglo children to score less than 79.
8. Many parents were concerned about stigmatization and limited educational programs offered children who had been labeled.
9. School-age children were "overlabeled" as retarded, while those who were preschoolers or out of school were underlabled.

(These data are adapted from Mercer and Lewis, in press).

any manner reacts, except to smile. On one occasion while on a home visit from the institution Ray received severe burns when he grabbed a hot steam pipe and held it for several minutes. His mother reported that had she not noticed him being very quiet, he would have had his flesh burned to the bone. In the institution Ray must be guarded to prevent his slipping into a shower and scalding himself since he has absolutely no awareness of danger and in the opinion of the professional staff, no realization of pain sensation.

Ray has been diagnosed as profoundly retarded, IQ below 19, with a post-infectious etiology. He has now been in residence at the _____ State School since the age of seven. His attendants describe him as "happy and little trouble." He never bites others and seems very self-reliant. Since his admission Ray has had only one illness—measles at age 13. Occasionally, Ray will bite himself but this occurs mainly when he is not permitted to get into the shower or to do some other act that will endanger his life. The attendants report their only major problem is to keep him from common dangers. He seems bent at all times on engaging in self-destructive activities. His greatest pleasure, and the main way of telling whether Ray is ill or well, is his belching. This Ray carries out simultaneously with his rocking, and aerophagia (air-swallowing) is continual. Only when ill does Ray reduce these activities. (Cited in Cleland 1978, pp. 195–196)

The "frequency" of mental retardation, then, depends directly on how this problem is defined. Further, the instrument used and the cutoff level established both influence the recorded frequency of mental retardation. Many clinicians and researchers are therefore suggesting that the cutting score or cutoff level for retardation be lowered, a process that would obviously lower the frequency. As Mercer and Lewis (in press) suggest, if the cutting score or cutoff level were lowered, fewer persons from lower socioeconomic and ethnic backgrounds would be stigmatized with the label of mild mental retardation. It appears that many clinicians are reserving the term "mentally retarded" for those with IQs of 50 and below.

EARLY IQ TESTS—WHAT DO THEY MEASURE?

Intelligence testing and adaptive behavior assessment have been described for use with school-age children. Perhaps you wonder how early an IQ test can be given to a child or infant.

After an infant is about 2 months of age, a few psychological tests can be used. Some of these so-called "infant IQ" tests purport to measure the infant's intelligence, but what these tests appear to be measuring is the child's "sensorimotor performance," only one dimension of intelligence. Thomas (1970), for example, states that sensorimotor scores obtained during infancy are not highly predictive of later intelligence scores. Hence, infant scores must be viewed with considerable reservation, particularly if attempts are being made to use these scores to forecast behavior well in the future. In short, before the age of 3 years or even 4 in some instances, IQ test scores are very unreliable.

ASSESSMENT METHODS

So far we have discussed retardation as it is inferred from psychometric or behavioral tests. Assessment techniques, however, need not involve IQ tests or adaptive behavioral scales. The choice of assessment or diagnostic procedures depends on *when* in the life cycle they are employed (Chinn et al. 1975). That is, the assessment procedures to be employed depend in part on the age of the subject. Assessment procedures may be employed before birth, immediately after birth, during late infancy, during childhood, and at later stages of development.

ASSESSMENT BEFORE BIRTH In some cases, it is possible to predict with considerable accuracy whether or not certain fetuses will become retarded as infants or children. One of the most common prebirth assessment procedures is *amniocentesis*. This medical procedure is most commonly undertaken after the fourteenth week of gestation. Briefly, the procedure involves making a surgical puncture into the amniotic sac of the pregnant woman and withdrawing a sample of amniotic

CAN TESTING BE FAIR?

In 1969, in Monterey County, California, complaints on behalf of twelve Mexican-American children were filed against a local school district. The complaint charged that these children had been placed in special classes for retarded children on the basis of IQ tests that were given in English. (The IQ tests were the two most commonly used tests of intelligence, the WISC-R and the Stanford-Binet.) One illustration of the injustice and inappropriateness of giving Spanish-speaking children English-language IQ tests is shown by the case of *Diana* v. *California State Board of Education*. When Diana was given an individual IQ test, she scored in the retarded (mild) range. Yet when Diana was retested by a Spanish-speaking psychologist, her score was almost 50 points higher! The suit called for an elimination of standardized IQ tests alone as a measure of retardation. The plaintiffs wanted, first, the inclusion of a child's adaptive behavior; second, if the child was to be tested for intelligence, the test would be in the child's language—not necessarily the psychologist's.

In 1970, the San Francisco School Board was presented with a petition from the Association of Black Psychologists, who argued that many black children had been unfairly labeled as retarded because tests given to black schoolchildren were not measuring intelligence but familiarity with white culture. This group of psychologists recommended a moratorium on intelligence testing until more culturally fair instruments could be developed. As it now stands, it is now illegal in some states to give intelligence tests for the purpose of placement in special classes. On February 5, 1975, for instance, the California Board of Education demanded a halt to IQ testing for EMR placement. A court injunction followed the Board's demand. In another suit, *Larry P.* v. *Wiles Riles,* a federal district court ruled that "IQ testing" was indeed prejudicial to black children (*APA Monitor* 1977).

Black children and Spanish-speaking children still are overrepresented in EMR classes, a fact that strongly suggests that current IQ tests are definitely culturally biased. One recent effort has been to develop a test that takes into account sociocultural backgrounds and linguistic origins—one that is racially and culturally nondiscriminatory. The test is called *SOMPA* (Mercer & Lewis, in press), which stands for *System Of Multicultural Pluralistic Assessment.* This instrument, published by the Psychological Corporation, has novel subtest scales such as *sociocultural scales* (assessing family size, family structure, socioeconomic status, urban acculturation); *health history inventories* (assessing prenatal/postnatal stressors, traumas encountered, disease and illness experienced); and most important, an *Adaptive Behavior Inventory for Children* (ABIC). The ABIC provides the examiner with an "adaptive topography" of the child's present coping skills, in the context of five social systems encountered by children. Generally, items on the SOMPA are answered by an observer who knows the child rather well—mothers often answer questions about the child's adaptation at home: "Does the child get along with mother, father, grown-ups, etc.?" "Does he or she fear the dark, read books, purchase things with money, avoid dangerous things, etc.?" (Mercer and Lewis in press).

The SOMPA also incorporates the Wechsler scales (an IQ test) because Mercer and Lewis believe that, properly used, standardized IQ tests can help certain children. As they state:

. . . assessment should be for the purpose of educating children, not for the purpose of labeling and placing them. The individually administered standardized test [WISC-R, Stanford-Binet] is the most reliable approach currently available. . . . (p. 150)

Thus the SOMPA follows a multidimensional approach, assessing not only intelligence but cognitive abilities, perceptual-motor development and physical health, social systems within the community and school, and vital features of the child's sociocultural background. Since an educational decision will probably be made in school, with or without standardized tests, this new comprehensive method (SOMPA) seems far superior to current assessment procedures. It remains for research to bear out or reject this optimism.

fluid. The fluid is cultured for approximately two weeks, at which time the sloughed-off cells are examined for possible genetic or chromosomal defects. About 40 genetic disorders can be detected by amniocentesis; in connection with mental retardation, Down's syndrome, Lesch-Nyhan syndrome, Tay-Sachs disease, and several others can be detected. Because amniocentesis can often detect genetic abnormalities well before birth, therapeutic abortions are then possible. If selected fetus abortions were performed, Down's syndrome, for example, could be lessened by at least 20 percent (Howell 1973).

Another recent medical technique for diagnosing physical and mental defects is the use of *ultrasound*. In this procedure high frequency sound waves are bounced off the fetus; in a very real way, this procedure resembles *sonar,* since sound waves pass through the amniotic fluid, reach an object (the fetus), then return as sound waves that can be converted into an image or profile of the fetus. The image can be displayed on a type of oscilloscope, revealing any fetal deformities.

ASSESSMENT AT BIRTH Apgar (1953) developed a type of physical or reflexive rating scale (called the *Apgar*) which can be used to evaluate vital signs in newborns. The Apgar has five dimensions that are scored with either a zero, 1, or 2, depending on the extent and development of vital signs in the newborn. Heart beat, respiration,

muscle tone, reflex irritability, and color, for example, are dimensions (signs) that can be scored. Zero is the poorest score; 2 is the highest or best score. The scoring typically is done within five minutes after birth. Not only can physical normality in the neonate often be determined, but the effects on the infant of drugs the mother has taken also can be assessed. If a newborn has excellent vital signs, he or she will typically receive a score approaching 10; a score of 2 for all or almost all the dimensions. Chinn (1974) has noted that when compared with neonates who have excellent Apgar scores— scores between 7 and 10—those who have scores below 3 have three times more neurological difficulties. In some cases, neurological difficulties are associated with particular varieties of mental retardation.

One of the most obvious methods for diagnosing certain types of mental retardation—nearly always the severe or profound types—is to examine the newborn for physical deformities. Numerous physical signs, in addition to those assessed by the Apgar, correlate with central nervous system damage in general and mental retardation in particular. Chamberling (1975) suggests that the head circumferences of all infants should be measured because some forms of mental retardation— macrocephalus or macrocephaly, for example— can be detected early by such measurement. *Transillumination* of the skull may also suggest hydrocephaly (hydraencephaly) (see page 379).

SYMPTOM DESCRIPTION AND ETIOLOGY

As we noted at the beginning of the chapter, mentally retarded persons represent a very heterogeneous group, both because there are many levels of retardation and because retarded persons may have additional personality or behavior defects superimposed on the retardation. Nevertheless, it is possible to give a general portrayal of certain clinical forms of mental retardation.

Zigler (1967) suggests that mentally retarded persons can be divided into two general groups, based on both their measured IQ and on the presence or absence of a biological or organic cause. Zigler's view is called the *two-group hy-*

pothesis. First, he suggests the existence of a group called the *familial* or *cultural-familial type.* This type includes individuals who have no known organic cause for their mild retardation; they score between 50 and 70 IQ points. Second, Zigler suggests the existence of an *organic type.* These individuals have somatic or biochemical defects thought to cause their retardation; they score, on the average, lower than 50. The important point, Zigler suggests, is that the first group is essentially from the same genetic pool as normal and bright individuals; retardation in the cultural-familial group is thought to be caused by cultural, psychological, or environmental stressors. We will discuss causes and stressors—organic, genetic, and cultural-familial—in a later section.

Most of the major clinical forms of mental retardation have definite *somatic* features; that is, physical or biochemical symptoms exist that can be measured or detected. The types of mental retardation we will describe here are the more severe or profound variety. These clinical forms make up a very small proportion of mentally retarded, if we still employ the cutting score of 70. As we have noted, mental retardation with a biological or somatic etiology falls within the IQ range from 50 down to 25 and lower, but a much more sizable group of retardates score between 50 and 70. In approximately 75 to 80 percent of the cases of mental retardation, no specific biological defect can account for the disorder.

DOWN'S SYNDROME (MONGOLISM)

Langdon Down, in 1866, made the first elaborate efforts to describe and explain a variety of retarded persons who, he claimed, physically resembled the ethnic group called "Mongols." Regrettably, the term "mongol" was applied to children who were retarded and fitted a characteristic description; e.g., slanting eyes, a small

rounded skull, flabby hands, a protruding tongue, a cleft between the first and second toe, and incurved fifth digits. It was an unfortunate term to use because no actual link exists between this form of mental retardation and the Mongoloid race. Later, the name *mongol* was changed to *mongoloid*, and more recently it has been called "Down's syndrome."

In addition to the physical features, many developmental lags exist: motor development is very retarded—some are unable to walk until age 7 or 8; speech is very slow to develop; reproductive organs, as well as other internal organs, are typically underdeveloped. Because of the internal organ defects, at least 25 percent of Down's syndrome children die of congenital heart problems during infancy (Allen & Sherard 1975), and by the age of 5 almost 50 percent will have died.

When given an individualized intelligence test, the Down's syndrome child usually scores in the moderate to severe range (20 to 50); however, a few have scored much higher. Carr (1970) notes that, curiously, some Down's syndrome children, when tested during infancy, differ very little from normals; yet when tested again, at age 2 or 3, they have fallen well behind the average child. The apparent normal scores made by these retarded children may be accounted for by two phenomena: (1) infant tests cannot sample enough behavior to predict future developmental levels; or (2) neurological deterioration progresses—the brain becomes smaller—as these children grow older (Kirman 1974). Down's syndrome is one of the more common varieties of organic retardation; its causes will be discussed later. The following case tells of a Down's syndrome child who grew to adolescence.

**ZIGLER'S
DISTRIBUTIONS**
Figure 15.1

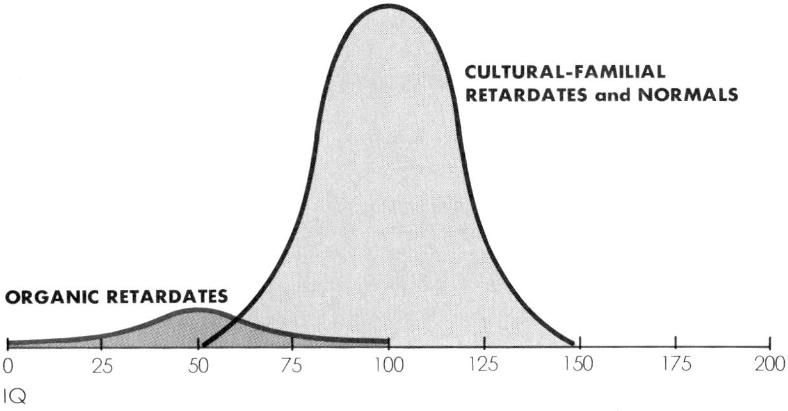

CULTURAL-FAMILIAL
RETARDATES and NORMALS

ORGANIC RETARDATES

0   25   50   75   100   125   150   175   200
IQ

A CASE OF DOWN'S SYNDROME

Chick is an eighteen-year-old Down's syndrome boy who lives at home with his parents. He is an only child, born to his parents when they were in their late forties. For some reason the diagnosis of Down's syndrome was not made until Chick was over two years old, despite the fact that his features were clearly those of a Down's child. When told that their child had Down's syndrome, his parents would not accept the diagnosis, particularly his mother. She was convinced that her son was not mentally retarded and went to a succession of physicians seeking a different diagnosis.

Chick was kept at home, where he was protected by his mother. Other children were occasionally allowed to play with Chick in his home, but his mother berated them if they wanted to stop playing with him or got into arguments with him.

When it was time for Chick to begin school his mother insisted that he be placed in a regular kindergarten class. Her request was granted after a long and heated exchange with school officials. At the end of kindergarten the school again recommended that Chick be placed in the program for the mentally retarded. Again his mother refused, and he was placed in the first grade, where he became the object of ridicule of the other children. The teacher objected to the fact that Chick was not toilet-trained because she had to deal with his wetting or soiling every day. Chick's mother insisted that these were merely "accidents" and that he was toilet-trained. She hired a tutor to work on reading with Chick, but little progress was made.

By the end of the first semester Chick's mother was at the elementary school daily. According to school officials she interfered constantly, catching the teacher during her breaks to discuss Chick and reprimanding children who she felt were picking on Chick. One day Chick undressed in the restroom and came walking out in the hall naked. This prompted the principal to insist that he be withdrawn from school unless the parents would place him in the program for the mentally retarded if his psychological workup warranted such placement. Since that time Chick has been enrolled in programs for the TMR and EMR in six different elementary schools. He was enrolled in the EMR program on a trial basis when his mother argued that he was much brighter than the TMR children.

By now Chick is very aggressive; he taunts and teases other children constantly. His behavior has made him a problem in the TMR program and he has had difficulty in any situation involving cooperative work or play. His teachers are now concerned that he will be unable to function in a sheltered workshop later on because he causes trouble so frequently.

The prognosis is poor for Chick. His parents are now approaching seventy and both are in poor health. It is very tempting to attribute his aggressive behavior to his mother's treatment, but regardless of the source, it will prove a problem in placing him in any setting where coopera-

Bruce Roberts, Rapho/Photo Researchers

While Down's syndrome children may have certain characteristic features, they may differ widely in physical appearance and personality.

tion in living or working is required. (MacMillan 1977, pp. 126–127)

PHENYLKETONURIA (PKU)

PKU is an organic retardation that occurs very rarely—approximately once in 15,000 births. Yet there is great interest in PKU. Concern over this infrequently occurring disorder arises from the fact that if diagnosed and treated early enough, it can, in some cases, be ameliorated by following a diet

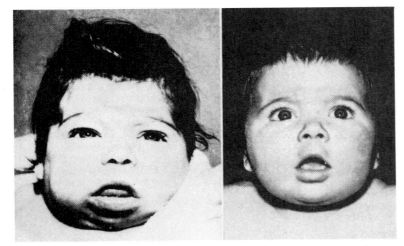

Iodine therapy, used to treat mental retardation caused by malfunctioning thyroid, often shows dramatic results, as in this infant.

free of the amino acid *phenylalanine.* PKU typically is diagnosed through the detection of phenylpyruvic acid in the urine or from blood tests.

In most humans, Menkes (1975) states, phenylalanine is an essential dietary element "necessary for protein synthesis." But in particular individuals, because of an inborn error in metabolism, phenylalanine cannot be converted into another substance; it accumulates in the blood and cerebrospinal fluid, impairing myelinization and resulting generally in central nervous system degeneration.

Like other persons with organic mental retardation, phenylketonurics usually have IQs below 50, although a very wide range of scores is found. For example, some phenylketonurics have near-normal intelligence scores. Thus, high phenylalanine levels in the blood or urine do not always suggest mental retardation.

The symptoms displayed by infants or children with PKU provide an interesting contrast with other retardates. PKU children are often much more aggressive and hyperactive than the other organic retardates (Johnson 1969). In addition to their aggressivity, they tend to be seizure-prone, irritable, distractible, and very retarded in language and motor development.

If PKU is detected early, preferably before the age of 3 months, significant improvements in intelligence can be made by following a diet low in phenylalanine. Dietary restrictions can cease after the age of 5 or 6 years. However, discontinuance of the diet may result in behavior abnormalities and a recurrence of seizures (Cytryn & Lourie 1975).

PKU is transmitted genetically. Both parents must be carriers of the autosomal recessive genes, although the parents are asymptomatic or normal.

TAY-SACHS DISEASE

Near the end of the nineteenth century, two researchers, Warren Tay and Bernard Sachs, described a new type of mental retardation observed during infancy. In this form of infantile retardation, which occurs predominantly in those of Jewish ancestry (at a rate of about one in every 5,000 births), neurological and ophthalmological problems emerge by at least the sixth month of life. One of the first symptoms to be noticed is extreme motor retardation; for example, the baby may be unable to raise its head or turn over. Furthermore, seizures are common, and by the end of the first year of life optic atrophy, leading to blindness, has begun to develop. Accompanying these defects are gross intellectual retardation, emaciation, hearing loss, and paralysis. Berg (1974) points out that death usually occurs between the second and fourth year.

Tay-Sachs disease is often diagnosed by a "cherry-red" spot in the area of the retina. It may also be diagnosed before birth through amniocentesis. The cause of this variety of mental retardation is unknown, and at present no treatment can change its course (Brain & Watson 1969).

CRETINISM (CONGENITAL HYPOTHYROIDISM)

The term *cretin* has an interesting origin, which is briefly described by Wilkening (1973):

> Ancient Christian refugees who settled in remote areas of the Pyrenees developed hypothyroidism because of lack of iodine in the water. Their goitrous condition, with open mouths and slow thinking, caused the natives to contemptuously label these foreigners "Chrétien" ["Christian"], which became "cretin" over the years. (p. 54)

For years, "cretin" has meant deformed idiot. Cretinism, as we know it today, refers to a type of mental retardation caused by impairment of thyroid functioning. For example, a pregnant woman whose diet is deficient in iodine may give birth to an infant with cretinism—congenital hypothyroidism. Although the infant with cretinism may appear normal shortly after birth unless thyroid extract is given, the child's intellectual development will be retarded, and a number of other symptoms may emerge. If untreated, for instance, these infants usually become very apathetic and listless, and their bone development will also be severely delayed.

Mental and physical retardation associated with cretinism can be ameliorated if therapy is started very early, yet the prognosis for increments in intelligence vary considerably; that is, some respond with marked increases in mental ability while others do not.

HYDROCEPHALY (HYDROCEPHALUS)

Unlike several of the other organic forms of mental retardation, hydrocephaly is often recognizable at birth because of the enlargement of the baby's head and "prominent scalps, veins, and turning down of the eyes ('rising sun sign')" (Brain & Walton 1969). Hydrocephaly—meaning "water-head" or "water-brain"—is a rare form of mental retardation occurring when a blockage or failure in absorption prevents cerebrospinal fluid from flowing out of the ventricles located deep within the brain, or when fluid is trapped in the subarachnoid spaces surrounding the cortex. This interference with fluid circulation raises the pressure within the brain cavity, pushing the soft skull outward and often compressing the cortex.

In the infantile variety of hydrocephaly, symptoms usually include seizures, cerebral palsy, blindness, and sometimes gross mental retardation. Gradations of hydrocephaly do exist, producing various degrees of mental and physical impairment. For example, Tredgold and Soddy (1963) described two types of hydrocephaly: those who were severely retarded—usually bedridden and untrainable—and a less severe form. In some cases, excessive fluid may be drained or diverted from the cranial cavity, preventing extensive retardation.

CAT-CRY SYNDROME (CRI DU CHAT)

One of the most severe forms of organic retardation is cri du chat, or the cat-cry syndrome. Infants with this variety of retardation, in addition to profound retardation, have a characteristic "cat-like cry," caused by abnormalities of the larynx. This syndrome often has two additional physical characteristics: microcephaly (small head) and low-set ears. There is no known treatment.

TURNER'S SYNDROME

Turner's syndrome (when a person has 45 chromosomes instead of 46) does not always result in mental retardation, and when it does, the retardation is very mild. Indeed, this is one of the only forms of mild mental retardation that has a known organic or genetic etiology. This syndrome occurs only in females; instead of the normal two X chromosomes, they have only one X. (The male counterpart is Klinefelter's syndrome.) Typically the female with this syndrome has great difficulty with space-form discrimination or space-form perception in general. Because the syndrome may result in mild retardation, it is usually not detected until schooling begins. Often, however, it may not be detected until adolescence when the secondary sexual characteristics fail to develop. Since internal genitalia (ovaries) fail to develop, women with Turner's syndrome are sterile. There is no treatment for the retardation, although the administration of female hormones produces some secondary sexual characteristics that make the woman physically more normal.

KLINEFELTER'S SYNDROME

The corresponding genetic abnormality in males, which also may cause mild mental retardation, is Klinefelter's syndrome. Normal males have an XY chromosomal pattern, but in Klinefelter's syndrome an extra X is found: XXY. This chromosome configuration occurs very rarely. Approximately half of these males appear physically normal; others are eunuchoid. Between 25 and 50 percent are mildly retarded. All Klinefelter males are sterile.

MILD MENTAL RETARDATION

The largest group of mentally retarded persons—about 75 percent—are the cultural-familial type, who are only mildly retarded. Generally, the IQ scores for this group fall between 50 and 70; this group, educationally speaking, is referred to as "educable." It is often assumed that EMRs will be unable to profit sufficiently from regular school programs, though it is also held that this group can learn most academic subjects, most social skills, and minimal occupational roles. These points are still highly controversial. The DSM-III states:

> Individuals in the mild level . . . during the pre-school period (age 0–5) can develop social and communication skills, have minimal retardation in sensorimotor areas, and often are not distinguished from normal children until later age. During the school age period they can learn academic skills up to approximately the sixth grade level by their late teens. . . . During the adult years over 21, they can usually achieve social and vocational skills adequate for minimum self support, but may need guidance and assistance when under unusual social or economic stress.

MacMillan (1977) has examined the evidence about adult adjustment of EMRs or mildly retarded persons. MacMillan divides the research findings about former EMRs into two groups: investigations that presented an optimistic view and investigations that presented a pessimistic view. Briefly, the optimistic view contends that EMRs for the most part vanish into the larger society, escape labeling, and manage to do quite well. By contrast, the pessimistic view contends that adult EMRs do more poorly than nonretarded persons who are matched with respect to socioeconomic background; they abound, these studies note, in the unskilled and service-oriented occupations. The pessimistic studies (Gozali 1972; Heber & Dever 1970;) point to a lower annual income for EMRs. MacMillan, however, warns us not to make too much of these findings because serious methodological flaws exist: e.g., some investigators used different cut-off scores to define mild mental retardation. MacMillan, admitting that the data are conflicting, nevertheless states:

> . . . it would appear that former EMRs do adjust at some level. In the majority of cases they do avoid designation as mentally retarded as adults, they do find work unless economic conditions are poor, they do marry and raise families, and they do provide housing and food for their families. (p. 326)

CAUSES AND STRESSORS

Various causes and stressors have been thought to play a role in the development of mental retardation. For the most part, however, the causes of mental retardation are not known (Stern 1973). As we have noted earlier, genetic factors may be involved in certain types of retardation. Various sorts of environmental factors also may result in retardation. In still other instances, the development of certain forms of mental retardation may require small genetic effects combined with special environmental stressors. PKU, for example, is genetically determined, but special environments (diets low in or saturated with phenylalanine) can make a difference. We will discuss five categories of stressors or possible causal agents that may account for different types of mental retardation: genetic defects (chromosomal and metabolic defects), prenatal stressors, perinatal stressors, postnatal physical stressors, and postnatal psychological-social stressors. This list parallels rather closely the categories given in the AAMD *Manual:*

1. Following infection and intoxication.
2. Following trauma or physical agents.
3. With disorders of metabolism or nutrition.
4. Associated with gross brain disease (postnatal).

5. Associated with disease and conditions due to unknown prenatal influence.
6. With chromosomal abnormality.
7. Gestational disorders.
8. Environmental influences.
9. Following psychiatric disorder.
10. Other conditions.

GENETIC AND CHROMOSOMAL DEFECTS

In 1959, the psychiatrist Jerome Lejeune discovered that children with Down's syndrome had 47 rather than the customary 46 chromosomes. This finding led to a more thorough examination of chromosomal configurations in other varieties of retardation. Aside from Down's syndrome, however, only a few other forms of mental retardation have a chromosomal aberration—cat-cry syndrome, trisomy 13, trisomy 18, trisomy 22, and both Turner's and Klinefelter's syndromes, all of which have sex chromosome anomalies.

Trisomy is one of the more common types of chromosomal aberration that lead to mental retardation. The name "trisomy" comes from an error in chromosomal matching. Normally, a person receives 23 chromosomes from each parent, making a total of 46 chromosomes in each cell. In proper cell division, the chromosomes are matched in pairs. But in Down's syndrome, the person receives *three* chromosomes (*trisomy*) 21. The other 22 chromosome pairs may be normal, but the extra chromosome gives the person 47 chromosomes in all, not the normal 46. (Trisomy means a three-bodied or three-paired set of chromosomes.)

Any of the 23 chromosome pairs can have errors. In trisomies 13, 18, and 22, the errors (again, three matching chromosomes instead of two) occur on chromosome 13, 18, or 22. On the whole, trisomies, especially trisomy 21, are much

---

Down's syndrome can be detected prenatally by amniocentesis, a procedure that involves searching fetal cells found in the amniotic fluid for chromosomal abnormalities. Here, an extra chromosome appears in position 21, indicating that the child will have Down's syndrome.

CHROMOSOMES OF A DOWN'S SYNDROME CHILD
Figure 15.2

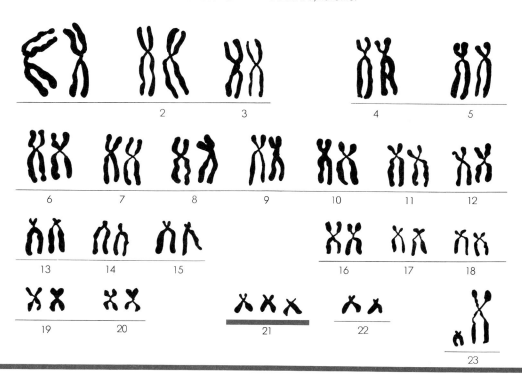

more likely to occur if the mother is over age 35. Approximately half the children with trisomy 21 (Down's syndrome) are born to older mothers.

These types of chromosomal aberrations are caused for the most part by *mutations*; that is, some error changes the genetic material. For example, in the trisomies, mutations occur when the egg or sperm is developing. On the other hand, there are mental retardations induced by dominant and recessive gene defects, not necessarily mutations. PKU is a disorder of amino acid metabolism that is transmitted recessively (an *autosomal recessive* trait). "Recessive" means that both parents must be carriers of PKU genes (though they themselves are not retarded) in order for this condition to appear in the offspring. If PKU were caused by a dominant gene, only one parent would have to be a carrier.

Maple syrup urine disease (Menkes syndrome), in which the infant's urine has a distinctive maple syrup-like odor (caused by hydroxybutyric acid), is also an inborn metabolic disorder resulting from a single recessive gene. (Most of the genetically transmitted metabolic disorders, PKU, maple syrup disease, Hartnup disease, etc., can be detected shortly after birth by examining the urine.)

There are a few autosomal *dominant* disorders that result in retardation, though these forms of mental retardation are exceedingly rare. *Tuberous sclerosis, Epiloia* (minute types of brain tumors), and *Marfan's syndrome* are disorders that are transmitted by a single dominant gene. It is rare, however, for both parents to be carriers of the same lethal gene. Finally, little is known about the cause of cell division problems that produce genetic and chromosomal defects. Such factors as advanced maternal age and radiation exposure do indeed increase the risk of cell division difficulties.

PRENATAL STRESSORS

Prenatal stressors are physical or environmental conditions that retard normal fetal development during gestation. These are examples of prenatal stressors that may contribute to certain forms of mental retardation:

1. Malnutrition in a woman during her pregnancy may adversely affect the neonate's neurological growth. For example, Winick and Rosso (1973) found that severe protein malnutrition in pregnant rats resulted in

their producing offspring with reduced numbers of neurons.

2. Maternal infection can affect the offspring's physical as well as neurological potential: syphilis in the pregnant woman often causes mental retardation in the offspring; German measles (rubella) in the affected pregnant woman also can result in fetal deformities and subsequent mental retardation.

3. Various drugs taken by a pregnant woman can often adversely affect the neonate. For example, certain prescription medication, such as barbiturates, various antibiotics, and some tranquilizers may have serious side-effects on the fetus; LSD and other drugs taken during pregnancy may also have deleterious consequences on the offspring; heroin addiction in a woman can be passed on to the fetus; finally, chronic use of alcohol by a pregnant woman may retard the fetus's mental and physical growth.

PERINATAL STRESSORS

Perinatal stressors refer to conditions at birth or during the birth process that hamper or retard normal development. *Prematurity* is a perinatal stressor and is associated with neurological impairment in the neonate. In general, low birth weight infants (premature ones) are more likely to be retarded than are nonpremature neonates. Paradoxically, as Cytryn and Lourie (1975) relate, improved obstetrical procedures have brought about a higher survival rate of premature infants, who in turn are more likely to have neurological impairments.

POSTNATAL PHYSICAL STRESSORS

Postnatal physical stressors refer to aversive physical conditions following birth that may adversely affect the infant. A host of potential stressors of this sort exist: cerebral trauma or head injuries, acute protein-calorie malnutrition, infectious diseases. One of the more serious stressors is acute protein-calorie malnutrition.

A problem primarily in underdeveloped nations, severe infant malnutrition is becoming increasingly linked with mental and physical retardation. Acute protein-calorie malnutrition has two essential features. First, if an infant has a diet much too low in calories, his or her intellectual and physical growth may be severely restricted. This condition, characterized by great weight loss and apathy, is sometimes termed *nutritional marasmus*. (Compare this with *marasmus* described in chapter 16.) Second, if the infant's diet has an abundance of carbohydrates, which many third-world nations provide, but a drastic deficiency of protein, then a disorder called *kwashiorkor* occurs. The symptoms of kwashiorkor often include profound indifference, withdrawal, loss of appetite, numerous physical symptoms, and mental retardation. Kwashiorkor, a Ghanaian word, means ''the sickness of the deprived child.'' Ironically, because of the high carbohydrate intake, the disease is disguised by obesity in the afflicted child; that is, although the infant or child may be 20 to 40 percent underweight, a protruding stomach conceals the advanced symptoms of undernourishment from observers. The child appears to be well-fed. Although kwashiorkor has almost always been associated with low income third-world countries, it has sometimes been found in certain areas of the United States.

Little research in the area of human malnourishment has been conducted using a control group. One study was carried out in South Africa by Stoch (1967). In this investigation, it was found that severely undernourished infants and children (0 to 24 months of age) scored significantly lower on IQ tests when compared with a matched group of children who had adequate diets.

In cases of acute protein-calorie malnutrition, it is generally held that the earlier the age of undernourishment, the more severe will be the retardation. Chase and Martin (1970) reported that malnourished infants treated at 4 months of age recovered while those treated at 12 months did not. In animal studies, similar results have been obtained. Dobbing (1972) has noted that malnourishment of experimental animals during weaning retards brain growth irreversibly.

Finally, since malnourishment has been shown to decrease myelinization in the brain (*Nutritional Review* 1970), and since children in lower socioeconomic classes may experience more malnourishment, then it is quite possible that the overrepresentation of mild or familial retardation in the lower class is in part attributable to nutri-

tional factors. Yet much more research is needed in this area to clarify the relationship between early malnourishment and neural efficiency.

POSTNATAL PSYCHOLOGICAL/SOCIAL STRESSORS

Postnatal psychological or *social stressors* are adverse psychological or social conditions following birth that may retard the infant. Unlike the physical stressors, which can be observed and measured reliably, psychological or social stressors are difficult to verify. Let us make a careful distinction between *physical-environmental* stressors and *psychological-environmental* stressors. Brain injuries due to trauma or disease (rubella), for example, are environmental stressors of the physical kind because they originate within the environment — that is, they are not the consequence of genetic endowment. The stressors to be discussed in this section also arise within the infant's environment, but within the psychological or social environment. Here we will summarize several studies and mention psychological and social environments that may retard intellectual growth. In the main, if these environments do retard intellectual growth, they do so only to a mild degree. From another standpoint, it is possible to argue that these environments do not produce retarded children at all, but children with different kinds of abilities. Their abilities would permit them to do well on tasks other than passing IQ tests.

A definite correlation exists between socioeconomic class and intelligence, as measured by our current IQ tests. On the whole, many research studies find a significant excess of mild mental retardation in the lower classes (Stein & Susser 1960; Rutter, Tizard, & Whitmore 1970; Birch, Richardson, Baird, Horobin, & Illsley 1970; Heber and Dever 1970). A few investigations have shown that families producing mildly retarded children exhibit distinguishing characteristics: for example, the parents themselves have very little education; language and verbal communication seem to be less frequent than in higher class families; and the number of siblings is relatively large. Hess and Shipman (1965) found striking differences between socioeconomic classes with respect to verbal output or verbal communication between parents and children. One notion to explain the lower IQ scores of mildly retarded persons is that they generally emerge from backgrounds that are lan-guage-impoverished compared with middle class environments. Although this notion is not a demon-strated empirical fact, the particular IQ test items failed by many persons classed as mildly retarded suggest that they do most poorly on language and verbal skills. Indeed, Levenstein (1969) claims that 17-point average IQ gains in the child have been produced by stimulating mother-child verbal inter-actions over a half-year period.

Overall, certain families appear to provide environments that make it difficult for their children to learn the skills necessary for doing well on verbal sections of current IQ tests. But Birch and his associates (1970) see the high prevalence of mild retardation in the lower classes as being associated with more than just poor language training; the

Birch analysis of family characteristics reveals a host of environmental stressors, both physical and psychological, that are associated with mental retardation. Vernon (1972) expresses a similar point:

> More often than not there is a syndrome of mutually interacting adverse factors, for ex-ample, poverty, poor nutrition and health, overcrowded home, lack of intellectual stimulation, inferior language background, lack of parental interest in education, . . . [and] poor schooling. (p. 33)

Mild mental retardation, then, is not at present viewed as being caused by any single factor; rather, a number of conditions, including biased IQ tests, cooperate to enhance this problem.

EDUCATION, TREATMENT, AND PREVENTION OF MENTAL RETARDATION

Broadly stated, there are at least three ways in which the problem of mental retardation can be faced: first, by attempting to educate retarded persons; second, by attempting to alter the essence of retardation through biochemical, behavioral, or psychological procedures; and third, by attempting to prevent retardation from occurring in the first place. As we shall see below, these approaches have their advocates and their critics; we shall review a few strengths and weaknesses of each.

EDUCATION OF THE MENTALLY RETARDED

The early teachers of the mentally retarded—Itard, Séguin and others—were mainly interested in the retarded person's ability to learn. Thus, since the beginning of any formal study of retardation, education—the teaching of skills, for example—has been a key element. Yet after the early work by Itard and Séguin, the emphasis shifted away from education and toward confinement and institution-alization. Indeed, for more than 130 years, institu-tionalization or "residential care" has been the chief way of dealing with most retardates. Land-mark court decisions have certainly changed this

trend, and now it again appears that education has become a chief goal.

Although many important cases have been heard in this area, no case or bill seems to have stirred up so much controversy as the passage of Public Law 94–142 in November, 1975, by both the House and the Senate. PL 94–142 is con-sidered by many to be the "Bill of Rights" for the handicapped. It is an ambitious law, dealing not only with the mentally retarded, but also with all handicapped children. Here are a few of the major points of PL 94–142:

1. The person has the right to free and appro-priate public education.
2. The person is to be protected from nondis-criminatory testing and labeling—where a single criterion is used. The law specifies that evaluations and testing are not to be culturally or racially discriminatory. For ex-ample, the test must be given in a language the child can understand.
3. The person must have an "individualized educational plan" developed; this plan must include the handicapped child's cur-rent level of performance, annual goals for the child, and specific educational services.
4. The person must be in a "least restrictive" environment. So that handicapped children

THE "RIGHT TO TREATMENT": WYATT V. *STICKNEY*

The case of *Wyatt* v. *Stickney,* more commonly called the "Partlow-Alabama case," was initially filed on behalf of institutionalized mentally retarded children at Partlow State School and Hospital for the Mentally Retarded in Alabama. The plaintiff (Wyatt) claimed that Partlow was a warehouse, unconcerned for either his psychological or his physical well-being. A federal judge reviewed the evidence and, on April 13, 1972, ruled that mentally retarded persons have a constitutional right to rehabilitative treatment. The suit noted that, in fact, Wyatt was unable to receive reasonable treatment while committed. Thus, the *Wyatt* v. *Stickney* case is a "right-to-treatment" case; further, the court ruled that patients do have the right to refuse certain sorts of treatment: shock treatment, lobotomy, major surgery, and certain medications. Regarding the education of retarded patients, the court ruled that they must receive education services for at least six hours a day. However, other institutions have appealed these educational standards. Ennis (1975) makes this ironic point:

> Dr. Stickney [the chief person at Partlow] stipulated to most of the criteria that were demanded by the plaintiff. . . . However, after this occurred, Dr. Stickney was dismissed by the Alabama Mental Health Board in September 1972, and replaced by a nonmedical associate commissioner who joined the state in appealing the case. (pp. 102–103)

are not deprived of their rights, the environment must not be one that removes normal privileges, such as education; thus, placement in certain types of segregated education classes may be viewed as restrictive.

Public Law 94–142 also deals with the "place" in which the retarded person will receive his or her education. The "place" is an environment that is to be "least restrictive." This feature of the law relates directly to the two major trends in educating retarded and handicapped persons: (1) placing them in segregated special education classes, or (2) placing them in normal classes with nonhandi-

capped children. Over the years, retarded and handicapped persons have been segregated into special, self-paced classes. The rationale for placing EMRs in these classes is clear: They will learn better if they receive special attention and instruction, moving at a pace at which they can adjust. The second approach—leaving them in the regular classroom—is called *mainstreaming* or *normalization.* The rationale for *not* placing EMRs in special classes also is clear: They will learn best, not have their rights violated, not suffer damage to self-esteem if they are not segregated. Nirje (1969) explains mainstreaming (normalization) in this way:

> . . . normalization . . . means making available to the mentally retarded patterns and conditions of everyday life which are as close as possible to the norms and patterns of the mainstream of society. (Cited in Cleland 1978)

What does the evidence say about the effectiveness or ineffectiveness of special education as compared with mainstreaming? MacMillan (1977) comments on *efficacy studies* (which compare the effectiveness of both groups); he cites various studies suggesting that being labeled as an EMR, and therefore segregated, results in overall bad feelings of those labeled (Gozali 1972). In particular, placing a child in a special segregated learning unit may very well alter the child's own expectations as well as the teacher's expectations for the child (Yoshida 1974; Meyers, MacMillan, & Yoshida, 1974, cited in MacMillan 1977). In one clinician's words, these children develop "failure identities" that will for most of their lives restrict their aspirations and achievements.

BIOCHEMICAL THERAPY, PSYCHOTHERAPY, AND BEHAVIOR THERAPY

Mordock (1975) notes that over the years there have been many dubious reports of miracle cures for mental retardation, brain disorders, and related problems. During the 1940s (Mordock reports) there were articles in popular magazines claiming that "scientists" had finally produced a cure for feeble-mindedness. (The article most widely read appeared in the September 1947 issue of *Reader's Digest,* entitled "They Are Feeble-minded No Longer.") This so-called cure was a novel educational procedure, which later proved to be rela-

Bruce Roberts, Rapho/Photo Researchers

Here, a Down's syndrome child is comforted as he receives an injection of an isotope that aids in the identification of substances in body tissues.

tively useless. Sometime later, *glutamic acid* was offered as a panacea for retardation. Then followed the controversial "patterning" procedures of Doman and Delacto, in which the patient goes through a complex series of primitive movements (creeping and crawling), then gradually progresses to more sophisticated motor skills. Basically, patterning involved having the child or adult go through movement characteristic of the stage at which the patient had been developmentally arrested.

In addition, megavitamins, hormones, and other biochemical memory drugs have been offered as cures, but supporting evidence is lacking. Recently, some evidence has suggested that a pituitary gland substance, *vasopressin*, when inhaled, may elevate memory; so far, however, no one has shown that vasopressin will elevate IQ. In general, biochemical cures, at this time, seem extremely remote for the severe forms of mental retardation.

Psychotherapy has also been attempted with some mentally retarded persons, not necessarily in an effort to ameliorate the retardation, but rather to help the person emotionally. As the DSM-III notes, mentally retarded individuals sometimes exhibit additional psychopathological complications superimposed on their retardation. In fact, DSM-III states that the prevalence of psychiatric disorders in mentally retarded children is three to four times greater than in children in the general population. Efforts have been made to deal with these accompanying psychopathologies: drugs, psychotherapy, behavior therapy, and other change strategies have been tried. Unfortunately, no evidence exists for the effectiveness of "talking therapies" (psychotherapy) with retarded individuals. Behavior therapy procedures are used within the classroom for the purpose of helping the children learn basic skills and for managing problem behaviors if they arise. Behavior therapy employs various reinforcement procedures (social reinforcement, tangible reinforcement, negative consequences) to manage problem behaviors, but these techniques cannot cure mental retardation.

PREVENTION

Prevention of mental retardation is a *public health* concept. Public health procedures involve providing people with services that will reduce their susceptibility to disease. In the case of mental retardation, public health procedures are aimed at strengthening the *host*—the mother, the family, or the community—so that mental retardation will be lessened. Here we will consider four types of prevention:

1. Prevention of prenatal stressors.
2. Prevention of perinatal stressors.
3. Prevention of postnatal stressors.
4. Prevention of gene and chromosome defects.

First, prevention of the prenatal and perinatal stressors associated with mental retardation specifically involves promoting physical health in a woman during her pregnancy. Promoting maternal health, through adequate diet and good obstetric and pediatric care, is believed to be one means for preventing certain types of mental retardation. Second, prevention of both physical and psychological postnatal stressors is also significant. Providing the infant with a good diet (high in protein) and a sound verbal and emotional environment may prevent some milder forms of retardation.

On the other hand, preventing mental retardation also has some controversial aspects: genetic counseling and eugenics. *Genetic counseling* is one method for identifying parents who may give birth to *high-risk children*. Very often, genetic counseling simply involves telling parents the probability of their having a retarded child. For example, the risk of having a second child with Down's syndrome is one in three (Cytryn & Lourie 1975). In other cases, genetic counseling may involve complex biochemical screening to determine if the parents are carriers of genetic disorders. *Amniocentesis* is one tool used in genetic counseling.

The ethical and legal questions reach their high point with the topic of eugenics. *Eugenics* is the science of improving the genetic pool for a given species. In the main, two methods of eugenics are thought to affect the human gene pool: *negative eugenics* and *positive eugenics*. In its extreme form, negative eugenics creates this scenario: a mentally retarded person should be discouraged from marrying another retarded person or, at least, from having children. In certain countries, compulsory sterilization or castration of retarded persons has been enforced in an effort to eliminate retardation. Positive eugenics, on the other hand, involves selectively breeding "bright" or "superior" individuals. In such a scheme, the extremely intelligent (determined by IQ tests?) would be encouraged or rewarded for having children. (Few psychologists would want to determine whether or not given couples should be encouraged to have children.) A variant of positive eugenics is *eutelegenesis* (Lerner 1968). This futuristic procedure (which is now possible) involves artificially inseminating a female with injections of semen from a male "judged to be superior." Other fanciful thinkers have suggested that traditional human reproduction may be replaced by *cloning*. Defective individuals will cease being created, a few futurists have argued.

There are profound problems with eugenics in general. For instance, no one knows what qualities (high measured IQ, resistance to schizophrenia, etc.) will be useful for survival over a long span of time. Geneticists would insist that the human gene pool have diversity, while some politicians might someday insist on genetic uniformity.

Through some very detailed calculations, one geneticist has estimated that eutelegenesis could raise the IQ .04 points a year. In 100 years only a 4 point gain would have occurred!

Lerner (1968), in his text *Human Evolution and Society*, points out that eugenics will not eliminate retardation. He cites a study which suggests that nine years of schooling "would be twice as effective as one hundred years of selection . . . "(p. 271). Further, he notes that it is "folly" to attempt to purge the human race of detrimental mutations. As he puts it, negative eugenics could work if it were not for the fact that:

. . . all of us are carriers of, on the average, several detrimental mutations. Thus, eugenics based on heterozygous screening on a scale large enough to be of significance would not lead to improvement but rather to termination of mankind on earth. (p. 179)

Each year the list of treatable and preventable forms grows. Early detection of certain types of retardation, coupled with genetic counseling, promises to reduce the number of victims.

SUMMARY

1. Mental retardation was one of the earliest recognized abnormal behaviors. In the early 1800s, Jean Itard, Edouard Séguin, and other physicians began to classify various types of retardation. Attempts were also made to educate retarded persons during this time.

2. Modern definitions of retardation are based on three criteria: (a) mental retardation originates early in life (before the end of adolescence, usually during fetal development and infancy); (b) mental retardation involves subnormal scores on an intelligence test; (c) mental retardation involves social inadequacy, typically measured by a

standardized instrument such as the SOMPA or the AAMD Adaptive Behavior Scale. The AAMD (American Association of Mental Deficiency) and the DSM-III (*Diagnostic and Statistical Manual*) both employ these three criteria. An IQ score below 70 is often used as the cutting score between mental retardation and "borderline" or dull-normal IQs.

3. Many classification systems have been developed that break retardation down into levels or degrees of impairment. One of the more common systems used in the 1960s and 1970s is the one employed in special education: *educable mentally retarded* (IQs

generally between 50 to 75); *trainable mentally retarded* (IQs ranging from roughly 20 to 49); and custodial or *profound mentally retarded* (IQs below 20). All three groups have corresponding educational expectations.

4. The prevalence or frequency of mental retardation depends on how broadly "retardation" is defined. Many researchers have claimed that the frequency is about 3 percent of the population. More recently, however, researchers such as Mercer maintain that biased and culturally unfair tests are responsible for this figure. She suggests that with culturally fair tests, the frequency would be somewhere in the neighborhood of 1 percent.

5. Mental retardation can be assessed or gauged by many different techniques and at different times within the life span. During fetal development, a few medical techniques can detect severe organic retardation in some fetuses. *Amniocentesis* is one procedure used to check for chromosome and genetic defects that might cause mental retardation. The *Apgar scoring system* is a procedure for checking the physical and reflexive condition of a newborn by assessing heart beat, respiration, muscle tone, reflex irritability and responsivity, and color. If a newborn does not show good Apgar signs, the probability of mental retardation is greater. IQ tests (psychometric instruments used with infants) given before age 3 are not highly reliable or valid as predictors of later intellectual behavior.

6. Zigler has suggested that there are two general forms of mental retardation: the *cultural-familial type* and the *organic type*. The cultural-familial variety has an unknown etiology, although Zigler and others assume that this sort of retardation is a consequence of environmental factors. The organic variety usually stems from some organic (genetic or neurologic) defect. The causes of organic retardation are not understood in many cases; as a rule it is much more severe than the cultural-familial type.

7. *Down's syndrome* (mongolism or trisomy 21) is one of the more common kinds of organic or genetic retardation; it is a severe form of mental retardation caused in part by an extra chromosome 21 —thus *trisomy*

21. Many of these children are born to older mothers. Persons with Down's syndrome have additional physical impairments and thus have a short life expectancy.

8. *Phenylketonuria* (PKU) is a genetically recessive variety of organic or genetic retardation, in which an inherited biochemical defect interferes with the ability to oxidize phenylpyruvic acid (phenylalanine). The phenylalanine interacts with other biochemicals, and the brain and central nervous system are damaged. PKU can be detected very early, and special diets may prevent retardation.

9. *Tay-Sachs disease* is a rare genetic disorder, most common in persons of Jewish descent. It apparently is transmitted by a single recessive gene. It occurs at a rate of about 1 in 5,000 births. Retardation is severe, and there is no cure or treatment at this time.

10. *Cretinism* is an organic variety of mental retardation which in most cases appears to be extensive if the disorder is not detected early and supplemental thyroid treatment given.

11. *Hydrocephaly* (also *hydrocephalus*) is a rare form of organic retardation. The cause is usually unknown. The symptoms include severe to mild retardation with accompanying physical impairments such as seizures and cerebral palsy. The large head is directly a result of the accumulation of cerebrospinal fluid that has been trapped in the subarachnoid spaces or has failed to flow out of the ventricles. The pressure of the fluid compresses the brain and pushes the skull outward. In some cases the fluid may be drained and damage minimized.

12. *Cat-cry syndrome* (Cri du chat) is a severe but rare form of inherited organic retardation. Infants with this variety of retardation sometimes emit a "cat-like" cry, the result of deterioration and changes in the larynx.

13. *Turner's syndrome* is a chromosomal disorder of females that sometimes (but not always) results in mild mental retardation. Those affected have two rather than one X chromosome.

14. *Klinefelter's syndrome* is a chromosomal disorder of males that may or may not result in mild mental retardation. In this disorder a male has an extra X chromosome,

giving him an *XXY* configuration. About 25 to 50 percent of Klinefelter males are mildly retarded.

15. *Mild mental retardation,* with the exception of a few organic or chromosomal disorders, is a consequence of cultural or environmental factors. These persons' IQs range between 50 and 75.

16. The causes of many forms of mental retardation are not yet known. Several major stressor conditions do seem to play an etiological role: *genetic defects* such as extra chromosomes; *prenatal stressors, perinatal stressors, postnatal physical stressors,* and *postnatal psychological-social stressors.*

17. Trisomies (a third or extra chromosome) are involved in several varieties of mental retardation. Mutations and defective genes also contribute to retardation.

18. *Prenatal stressors* involve physical or environmental conditions that may adversely affect the intellectual and physical development of the fetus. They include maternal malnutrition, infection, and maternal drug use.

19. *Perinatal stressors* are adverse events occurring after the prenatal period—during birth. Prematurity and low birth weight are linked to mental retardation and other abnormalities.

20. *Postnatal physical stressors* refer to adverse physical conditions which occur after birth or during infancy, such as head injuries, infant malnutrition, and infant infectious diseases.

21. *Postnatal psychological/social stressors* are adverse psychological or social factors that may emerge during the critical period of infancy and are thought to account for most mild retardation. These stressors may take the form of faulty parent-child interactions, poor verbal and language skills used by parents, neglect, and other psychological factors. Some research has shown that increasing verbal interactions between the mother and child may elevate the child's intelligence.

22. In recent years various pieces of legislation have been passed in an effort to educate and help mentally retarded and handicapped citizens. The *Wyatt* v. *Stickney* case was a landmark case that mandated that mentally retarded persons have constitutional rights to rehabilitative treatment, not just custodial care. *Public Law 94–142* also stresses that handicapped individuals should be treated in a "least restrictive environment." Further, it is intended to protect children from discriminatory IQ testing and labeling; it requires school systems to develop and implement an "individualized educational plan" for handicapped children.

23. *Biochemical therapy* has so far been unimpressive in altering the course of organic mental retardation. In a few varieties of mental retardation, special diets may halt retardation, but this is to be viewed more as prevention than cure.

24. *Psychotherapy* has been used with mentally retarded persons, but only to help them adjust better to their limitations.

25. *Behavior therapy* has been used mainly to alter or reduce the frequency of behavior problems that sometimes may accompany mental retardation.

26. *Prevention* is a public health concept that attempts to reduce stressor conditions before they result in mental retardation. Good prenatal care, genetic counseling, sound verbal and emotional environments may be planned and may well reduce the incidence of retardation.

MacMillan, D. L. *Mental retardation in school and society.* Boston: Little, Brown, 1977.

Mordock, J. B. *The other children. An introduction to exceptionality.* New York: Harper & Row, 1975.

Rosen, M., Clark, G. R., & Kivitz, M. S. (Eds.). *The history of mental retardation.* Volumes 1 & 2. Baltimore: University Park Press, 1976.

RECOMMENDED READINGS

PART 3

DEVELOPMENTAL FEATURES OF PSYCHOPATHY

16

ABNORMAL BEHAVIORS ASSOCIATED WITH CHILDHOOD

OVERVIEW In this first chapter of Part III we shall focus on abnormal behaviors associated with early and late childhood. The discussion is divided into two broad sections: the first section presents a number of clinical syndromes associated with childhood; the second section examines special problem behaviors that may or may not be considered psychopathological.

Within the clinical syndrome section these disorders are examined, along with the frequency, symptom descriptions, causes and stressors, and treatment approaches for each one: marasmus and anaclitic depression; early infantile autism; childhood psychosis; and childhood hyperactivity. In the special problem behaviors section we will look at these behaviors: school phobia, enuresis, stuttering, tics and self-stimulatory behaviors. We will also discuss children's reactions to childhood bereavement and grief.

HISTORICAL ATTITUDES

The past provides little information concerning mental illnesses that occur during infancy and childhood. Rie (1971) observes, "The study of disordered behavior in children, . . . awaited the slow development of an inclusive concept of childhood" (p. 3). Despert (1970) explains that one reason for the neglect in studying infant and childhood disorders was that as late as the sixteenth century, children were not differentiated medically from adults. Nevertheless, there were those who did become interested in disordered behavior in children, and by the nineteenth century several historical steps had been taken in psychopathology: Esquirol in the 1830s differentiated mentally retarded children from psychotic ones; Griesinger (1867) proposed that intellectually normal children could be insane and suggested "masturbatory insanity" as a "unique disorder of youth." Finally, Hermann Emminghaus (1887), in his book *Psychic Disturbances of Childhood*, dealt with statistical epidemiological investigation of childhood behavior problems. In this text Emminghaus specified several conditions believed to produce abnormality. Alexander and Selesnick (1966) describe Emminghaus's approach:

> He divided the psychoses into those resulting from physical causes, such as disease of the brain, and those caused by psychological factors, such as excessive fear or anxiety. Emminghaus noted that poor home conditions, poor education, and unhealthy social situations produced mental illness in children. (p. 374)

Some time later, about 1905, the psychoanalyst Sigmund Freud wrote articles dealing with childhood disorders. During the early 1920s Arnold Gesell began studying normal development of children. But it was only during the 1930s and 1940s that modern categories of psychoses were applied to the very young.

SYMPTOM DESCRIPTION AND ETIOLOGY

EARLY INFANTILE AUTISM

> Of all [of Victor's] senses the ear appeared least sensitive. It was found, nevertheless, that the sound of a cracking walnut or other favourite eatable never failed to make him turn around . . . yet this same organ showed itself insensible to the loudest of noises and the explosion of firearms. (J.M.G. Itard, 1799)

In chapter 15, the case of a "wild boy" found living like an animal in the Aveyron forest in France was used to illustrate mental retardation and its treatment by Itard. Yet many modern clinicians, after reading about Itard's wild boy, are convinced that the child was not retarded, but *autistic*. Wing (1972), in particular, believes that Victor was abandoned by his parents because he was autistic and hard to manage. We will never know for sure, yet Victor's fascination with various objects and sounds, coupled with his complete oblivion to other stimuli, does seem to point toward autism.

Almost a hundred years after Itard's work, John Haslam published a book in which he mentioned a 5-year-old boy who displayed very odd behaviors. In 1919, still another report emerged: Witner published an article describing a 2½-year-old boy whose behavior was highly bizarre. Witner's description resembled modern portrayals and clinical descriptions of early infantile autism. Not until 1943, however, was *early infantile autism* acknowledged as a clinical entity independent of mental retardation, muteness, and childhood schizophrenia. In that year, America's first child psychiatrist, Leo Kanner, wrote a paper describing a small group of children who were profoundly aloof and affectionateless and showed a striking failure to develop language, despite what he thought was their normal or high intellectual ability.

THE DEPRESSED INFANTS

Marasmus was once the name pediatricians gave to a wasting-away process seen in some institutionalized infants. These babies showed such symptoms as stunted growth, poor muscle bulk, and apparent intellectual inertia, and the process was first thought to be strictly a nutritional disorder. (*Nutritional marasmus* is due to protein-calorie deficiency.)

But Spitz (1946) asserted that marasmus was actually a form of grief or depression caused by the lack of mothering. He renamed the disorder *anaclitic depression*. *Anaclisis* is a psychoanalytic term meaning "to depend upon, or to be attached, or to lean upon" an earlier established love object—the mother. Instead of attributing the progressive weight loss to faulty nutrition, Spitz suggested that the infant was depressed because of inadequate mothering; the apathy and refusal to eat (*anorexia*) represented an extreme form of negativism to an unresponsive caretaker. Although Spitz has been harshly criticized for the poor design of his famous study and the generalizations he made from his observations, other, better designed, investigations of institutionalized infants bear out his essential findings.

Several important laboratory studies have induced a form of depression in animals. Kaufman and Rosenblum (1967), for instance, noted that monkeys separated from their mothers resembled anaclitically depressed human infants. Harlow and Harlow (1971) reported that social isolation had pernicious effects on infant monkeys; some of the infant monkeys refused to eat, one dying of self-induced starvation, and others had to be force-fed. Ferster (1966) also conducted work related to depression in laboratory animals. Although he did not apply his findings to a theory of anaclitic depression, he suggested that two environmental stressors tend to induce a "reduced frequency" of behavior in most any organism. One stressor involves the amount of behavior re-

quired for the organism to alter its environment. If, for example, a large number of correct responses are necessary to alter the environment (that is, to bring about reinforcement or terminate an aversive stimulus), then the frequency of responses may be drastically reduced. Indeed, the behavioral definition of depression used in laboratory settings usually is "reduced frequency of responding."

Applying Ferster's view, anaclitic depression may be induced by the infant's inability to alter the environment. That is, the infant has a limited repertoire of responses to begin with, and these are further reduced when attempts to produce reinforcement or remove aversive conditions fail to alter the environment. Engel (1962) also points out that the infant's unsuccessful attempts to "produce the good satisfying mother" culminate in reduced behavior and withdrawal.

A second environmental stressor noted by Ferster is a "sudden change in the environment" of the organism. Thus separation from the mother (perhaps Ferster's "sudden change") or any other significant alteration in the environment would reduce the frequency of the infant's responses.

Most of the speculation about marasmus or infantile depression proposes that the cause is not biological or biochemical, but psychogenic or environmental. It is agreed that the cause of depression (or reduced frequency of behaviors) lies in specific events. Basically, the traumatic event is separation from the mother.

Pinneau (1955), however, is critical of the maternal deprivation position, especially as proposed in Spitz's study. Pinneau noted that Spitz's infants had begun to deteriorate well before the time of the actual separation from the mother. This observation suggests that it was not the mother's presence or absence or unresponsiveness that induced the deterioration, but the indelible stimulus restriction of the institutional setting.

FREQUENCY Early infantile autism is an exceedingly rare psychopathology. An initial epidemiological survey conducted in Middlesex (England) found that approximately four children in every 10,000 were diagnosed as autistic; a Danish study showed the same incidence. American re-

ports, too, generally agree: Schreibman and Koegel (1975) place the incidence at four in 10,000; Oppenheim states that the incidence is between two to five cases per 10,000.

Another component of the incidence of early infantile autism is its sex ratio: males outnumber females 3 or 4 to 1 (Rimland 1964; Rutter 1968; DSM-III 1978).

SYMPTOMS OF EARLY INFANTILE AUTISM

Wing (1972) observed that each autistic child is unique, ". . . and is different in many ways from other children with the same diagnosis" (p. 11). But despite the uniqueness of the autistic child, autists do exhibit distinctive symptoms. Kanner (1943) noted that the most striking and characteristic feature of these children is their "extreme autistic aloneness." (*Autism* itself is a psychiatric term meaning "private" or "detached." It was coined initially by the Swiss psychiatrist Eugen Bleuler and was used by him to describe the characteristic withdrawn nature of adult schizophrenics.) Kanner proposed four cardinal symptoms of early infantile autism. For the most part, these symptoms represent some of the current criteria for diagnosing this syndrome:

1. *Social aloofness* and indifference to people.
2. *Resistance to changes* in certain environments of the child (*maintenance of sameness*).
3. *Failure to adopt normal language usage* (particularly speech).
4. *Preoccupation with manipulation of various sorts of objects* (stones, radios, electric motors, etc.)

In addition to these cardinal features, Kanner also proposed that these children were paradoxically endowed with good intelligence as well as "strikingly intelligent physiognomies" (p. 247).

Since Kanner's publication of these cardinal features, other clinicians and researchers have confirmed most of his findings. Disagreement has focused principally on Kanner's declaration that autistic children typically are intelligent and look bright (Rutter 1968; Rutter & Bartak 1971; Wing 1972). For example, many assert that in terms of intelligence, autistic children may either be normal, retarded, or gifted.

Modern diagnostic systems are based mainly on clinical findings, but traces of Kanner's cardinal features are still evident. DSM-II, the 1968 version, contained no description of early infantile autism. The new DSM-III (draft 1978) does contain information about this syndrome, giving five operational criteria for infantile autism:

1. Onset usually prior to 30 months but up to 42 months.
2. Lack of responsiveness to other human beings ("autism").

The behavioral psychologist O. I. Lovaas here talks with an autistic child. Autistic children often begin to use language normally and then abruptly stop.

3. Gross deficits in language development.
4. If speech is present, peculiar speech patterns such as immediate and delayed echolalia, and pronoun reversals.
5. Peculiar interest or attachments to animate or inanimate objects.

Some of the verbal and language problems of the autistic child are illustrated in this case study.

A CASE OF AUTISM

One remarkable case of autism was a 10-year-old boy named Don. Oppenheim (1974) recounts that Don, at the time of this interview (at the Rimland School for Autistic Children), was completely nonverbal; like many autistic children, Don could write his thoughts rather clearly, but he could not relate them verbally. Here is a verbatim transcription of Don's written replies to oral questions asked of him:

Q: How come you didn't do what I asked you to? Didn't you understand, or what?

DON: I don't know what the trouble is, really, not understanding or the fact that somehow I'm not ever sure that I'm right.

Q: How do you mean, "not sure you're right?"

DON: Not sure that I'm understanding what means what. Meanings of words have always mixed me up.

Q: I'm talking to you in words *now*. Are you mixed up about the meaning of what I'm saying?

DON: No.

Q: Well, then—in what situation do words mix you up, then?

DON: They mix me up in situations where when the need to think interrupts the thing that needs to be done. (Cited in Oppenheim 1974, pp. 93-94)

Oppenheim admits to being rather baffled by Don's remarks and the interpretations that can be made of his writings. She states, "The nearest we can come to an interpretation of this problem is that it seems to represent a kind of 'I can't think when I'm in motion' situation" (p. 94).

Autistic children often have great problems with speech in general; they may be able to understand the spoken word, but are unable to speak what they think. Comprehension, then, apparently is not as much of a problem as performance and speaking.

The age of onset for symptoms of infantile autism varies, but in most cases the fourth or fifth month heralds the beginning of the major disturbing symptoms. At about this time, parents start to notice significant behavioral excesses and deficits. The father and mother may observe that their child does not respond when being picked up or cuddled. Autistic infants frequently go stiff or limp when being held; others cry or pull away from their parents. Another distressing symptom is the *gaze-aversion*. The autistic child is often noted for her or his refusal to make eye contact. One of the most rewarding responses an infant typically makes to the father or mother is the social smile; yet with the autistic infant only a pebble or stone may receive a

smile. When the infant does glance at another person, people report that the child appears to "look right through them."

CAUSES AND STRESSORS The etiological theories of infantile autism can be arbitrarily placed into two categories: psychogenic theories and biogenic theories. The *psychogenic theories* suggest that autism is essentially a learned reaction, or an unadaptive response to early traumatic and rejecting experiences. The *biogenic theories* suggest that infantile autism is caused by subtle central nervous system defects; these hypothesized defects are further believed to be caused either by unknown genetic errors or physical damage to the brain during prenatal development.

Psychogenic position I: Bettelheim. Bruno Bettelheim (1967) suggests that the stressor conditions producing infantile autism are mainly psychological; he asserts that the parents unconsciously wish the child did not exist, and, according to his hypothesis of *affective conspiracy*, communicate this wish to their infant. The *affective conspiracy model* suggests that the mother, in particular, is an *emotional refrigerator*, rebuffing the infant's natural tendency to get close and be intimate. Critics seriously question this conspiracy position. DesLauriers and Carlson (1969), for example, wonder how an "infant" could *sense* the inferred destructive and ejecting attitudes of the parents? They raise this interesting point:

> One is left to seriously wonder why an infant, who from the very first hours of his life senses the destructive attitude of a mother who wishes he did not exist and, in consequence, turns away from and blots out such a destructive experience, would not end up in marasmus and possibly die rather than live on forever as an autistic child? (p. 41)

To restate their question, why does one child become anaclitically depressed when rejected or abandoned emotionally, while the other becomes autistic?

Again, Bettelheim states that parental rejection, indifference, and lack of love during critical periods of development are so overwhelming that the infant decides to renounce reality and retreat to a world of fantasy. Autism as he views it is a protective barrier. The child becomes an empty fortress and withdraws into a subhuman form of existence.

Other psychoanalytic clinicians have sup-

Mike Manney/Black Star

Bruno Bettelheim suggests that stressor conditions producing autism are mainly psychological.

ported Bettelheim's claim that autism is a reaction to parental pathology. Margaret Mahler, for example, says that the autistic child's refusal to use the personal pronoun "I" correctly—they often use "you" in its place—is an indicator of the child's lack of self-hood.

Psychogenic position II: Ferster. A behavioral psychologist, not a psychoanalyst like Bettelheim, Ferster uses different terms. Yet both believe that autism is chiefly a result of environmental events. Specifically, Ferster (1961) proposes that early infantile autism as well as childhood schizophrenia is a consequence of a disastrous early reinforcement history.

Ferster argues that infantile autism is basically a disorder of behavior deficits: deficits in language and interpersonal skills. That is, the appropriate or desired behaviors have not been reinforced by the parents. Ferster and other behavioral psychologists use data from animal research to support the learning position. It is true indeed, that bizarre laboratory conditions can produce a type of autism in monkeys (Harlow & Harlow 1971), yet there is absolutely no evidence that similar conditions produced human autism.

In the Harlow pit study, an horrendously contrived stainless steel compartment was used to restrict climbing behaviors and stimulation in monkeys. This devastating confinement did produce a counterpart of human autism: rocking, self-stimulation, reduced exploratory behavior, and increased self-aggression. But certainly no one has reported a human environment that in any way approaches Harlow's pit. In fact, Mordock (1975), arguing Ferster's claims are unsupported, states that "no one has demonstrated that abnormal patterns of reinforcement existed in these children's background" (p. 226). Just as retrospective data are challenged when used to support psychoanalytic positions, retrospective data dealing with reinforcement history must equally be questioned. How does Ferster know the reinforcement history was defective?

Biogenic position I: Rimland. Rimland (1964) has written perhaps the most thorough text on early infantile autism. After having reviewed all the hypothesized causes of this disorder and stating that the psychogenic views were "pernicious," he postulated that autism is a consequence of neurologic impairment in the brain stem. This hypothesized defect yields a child who cannot "relate new stimuli to remembered experience" (p. 79).

Rimland, whose own child is autistic, refers to "the heavy burden of shame and guilt . . . "that parents feel when they learn what psychogenic theorists believe: that they, the parents, are principally responsible for the autistic condition. It is interesting to note, as Rimland does, that two forms of mental retardation that result from organic impairments—Heller's disease and PKU—were for many years considered to be functional psychoses. We can guess that many parents were blamed for inducing these reactions.

Motivated as a scientist, and perhaps as a parent, and wishing to present another side to the etiology of autism, Rimland has researched the area and has listed nine points (table 16.1) that he believes support the biogenesis of autism.

Specifically, Rimland (1964) states that the reticular formation—a center in the brain that is thought to regulate consciousness, attention, and alertness—has been damaged because of an hereditary susceptibility to oxygen injury. He presents data to support his conclusion showing that a high proportion of these children were administered medical oxygen soon after birth. Rimland says, "Oxygen in excess of an infant's tolerance can in some cases produce or simulate infantile autism" (p. 114).

A curious but fascinating feature of Rimland's theory states that autistic children are veritably geniuses "gone awry." That autistic children do have brighter than average parents is supported by a few studies (he refers to Keeler's 1957 study); for example, a fairly large percentage of the parents examined had status occupations and advanced college degrees. Other investigations challenge this particular part of Rimland's position. Nevertheless, he argues that autistic infants are potentially gifted, but are damaged by oxygen excesses. Infants, he emphasizes, "differ enormously" in response to conditions of over-oxygenation or under-oxygenation. This oxygen intolerance thesis, blended with the hypothesized superior intellectual potential of the infant, is summarized in this statement by Rimland (1964):

> If a potentially very intelligent child, whose brain was continuing to develop at a rapid rate, were exposed to atmospheric oxygen (or worse yet, to relatively high concentrations of medical oxygen) while the vasculature was still immature, damage to the vasculature of his brain could result. (p.129)

BIOGENESIS OF INFANTILE AUTISM
Table 16.1

Rimland 1964, pp. 51–52

1. Some clearly autistic children are born of parents who do not fit the autistic parent personality pattern.
2. Parents who do fit the description of the supposedly pathogenic parent almost invariably have normal, non-autistic children.
3. With very few exceptions, the siblings of autistic children are normal.
4. Autistic children are behaviorally unusual "from the moment of birth."
5. There is a consistent ratio of three or four boys to one girl.
6. Virtually all cases of twins reported in the literature have been identical, with both twins afflicted.
7. Autism can occur or be closely simulated in children with known organic brain damage.
8. The symptomatology is highly unique and specific.
9. There is an absence of gradations of infantile autism which would create "blends" from normal to severely afflicted.

Simply, Rimland views the autistic child as a potentially brilliant child who has neurological impairments; the bizarre symptoms represent the attempts of a brain-damaged latent genius to make sense out of his or her world.

Biogenic position II: DesLauriers and Carlson. DesLauriers and Carlson (1969) propose that autism is caused by an inborn organic imbalance existing in the arousal system. According to these writers, normal people have two states of arousal, but no imbalance between them. Autistic children, on the other hand, have an inborn imbalance. The *two-arousal hypothesis* was first proposed by Routtenberg (1966, 1968) as a model of how the brain arouses and activates the neocortex. Without such activation or arousal, learning and memory would not be adequate.

Arousal system I is an "activating-drive-energy" system. Arousal system II is a "reward-positive incentive" system. The first system motivates or moves the organism; the second provides for the feelings of pleasure, pain, and reinforcement in general. Structurally, system I is the *reticular formation*; system II is the *limbic area*. According to DesLauriers and Carlson (1969), system I and system II are in disequilibrium in the autistic child, reflecting an imbalance between reticular and limbic areas.

Basically two conditions of disequilibrium can exist: System I can be too high, thus suppressing system II. When this occurs, very little learning can take place, but because of a high energy level, aimless, repetitive, and stereotyped responses prevail. It is noteworthy that many clinicians suggest the existence of two varieties of early infantile autism: the hyperactive/hypersensitive variety, and the hypoactive/hyposensitive variety. It is the hyperactive/hypersensitive variety that is thought to be caused by high arousal of system I and the suppression of system II. When system I is dominant, or in "ascendancy,"

> . . . it would mean that the organism, while capable of altering and attending to new novel stimuli, and while capable of emitting responses, would be severely limited in (if not almost incapable of) establishing any associations between responses and rewards, since System II would be . . . incapable of suppressing the drive energy long enough for such association to become established or consolidated. (DesLauriers & Carlson 1969, p. 62)

System II can be higher than system I. In this case a hypoactive/hyposensitive autistic infant exists. Initially, the parents may report that their baby is normal but later, however, the child starts to exhibit "quiet stereotypes." As DesLauriers and Carlson put it, "If he rocks, it is persistent but quiet. He may stand at the wall quietly scratching for long periods of time (p. 65)." The autistic infant, according to the foregoing comments, is not responding to parental rejection or environmental impoverishment, as Bettelheim and Ferster suggest, but is responding to sensory and affective deprivation engendered by an inborn organic imbalance between the two arousal systems. This position is similar to Rimland's but acknowledges that infantile autism is an affective disorder.

DesLauriers and Carlson's theory holds that the vast majority of all impinging stimuli remain forever new and novel for the autistic child. Reality is perceived as a type of "white noise," a senseless array of stimuli.

Although structural anomalies have yet to be detected in the brains of autistic children, biochemical abnormalities have been recently reported. Goldstein, Mahanand, and Lee (1976) found low levels of dopamine (a neurotransmitter) in a sample of autistic children. Lake, Ziegler, and Murphy (1977) subsequently confirmed the Goldstein findings. Investigators have also reported imbalances in other neurotransmitter substances such as serotonin. But it is possible that these chemical anomalies may be effects rather than causes of autism. Yet as we shall see shortly, the beneficial consequences of biochemical therapy (in particular megavitamins) with some autistic children suggest a possible biochemical basis of this syndrome.

BETTELHEIM'S TREATMENT APPROACH

Parentectomy is the principle behind Bettelheim's treatment procedure, though he does not use this term. According to Bettelheim, the autistic child *must* be removed from his or her parents—thus parentectomy, a complete separation from home and family, is the hallmark of this approach.

In 1944 Bettelheim established the Orthogenic School at the University of Chicago. This institution was created as a residential treatment center for severely disturbed children who, Bettelheim believed, needed to be removed from a rejecting home environment and placed in a therapeutic surrounding. Aside from the initial parentec-

tomy, the school's fundamental characteristics are to treat the children with complete acceptance and permissiveness. Since Bettelheim maintains that the parents have rejected their child and have not fulfilled his or her needs, the usual therapeutic techniques include satisfying the child's infantile strivings. Because of the totally accepting environment of the school, it is reasoned that the child's trust in the therapist ultimately will flourish.

However, as no one has been able to replicate Bettelheim's specific therapeutic milieu, or to agree on definitions of autism or cure, the effectiveness of the method has not been confirmed.

BEHAVIOR MODIFICATION APPROACH

As Ferster is not the only behavioral psychologist involved in working with autistic children, we will not focus specifically on his techniques but on several different procedures.

Behaviors not frequently observed in an infant or child's repertoire can sometimes be shaped into existence through using various reinforcement procedures. *Positive reinforcement* may be used to increase the frequency of desired behaviors in autistic children. Eye-contact, for example, can be reinforced by following it with candy or other reinforcers. *Negative reinforcement* may also be used to increase the frequency of desired behaviors. In positive reinforcement, desirable behavior is increased by following the desired target behavior with a positive event; in negative reinforcement, desirable behavior is increased when the desired target behavior produces the termination or avoidance of a negative event—for instance, a shock can be terminated or avoided if a desired behavior occurs first.

Lovaas and colleagues (1974) have established rather complex social behaviors in autistic and schizophrenic children with both positive and negative reinforcement. The child may be reinforced for imitating or copying what the therapist does—perhaps performing some social behavior. The child typically is reinforced initially for a very simple imitative response—standing up, or clapping his or her hands. Gradually, more complex tasks are modeled by the therapist, and now only those complex tasks imitated by the child are reinforced occasionally. Lovaas has produced such complex activities as hand-washing, brushing the hair, playing tag, and kicking a ball by using positive reinforcement procedures.

Particular negative reinforcement proce-

Some therapists try to crack the "affective barrier" in autistic children by repeatedly presenting them with positive stimuli.

dures may lessen inappropriate or self-injurious behaviors and strengthen socially desired behaviors. Although there are many ethical considerations involved in using these procedures, especially with children, some evidence shows that they can eliminate or produce certain behaviors. Lovaas and his associates (1974) demonstrated how aversive conditioning (a negative reinforcement procedure) can be used to strengthen social behaviors in an autistic child:

> Pain [an electric shock] was induced by means of an electric grid on the floor upon which the children stood. The shock was turned on immediately following pathologi-

cal behaviors. It was turned off or withheld when the children came to the adults who were present. (p. 109)

The target behavior—turning or moving toward humans—was strengthened because it terminated the shock. An intriguing positive feature also arises out of this procedure: the adults present when the shock is terminated (usually the therapists) take on positive reinforcing properties; it is as if they have "saved" the child from the shock.

Indeed, Lovaas hypothesized that parents normally become positive reinforcing agents because they are often associated with the removal of stress. Parents commonly provide their children with comfort when they are in pain, or help eliminate the pain. Thus, though in a contrived and artificial way, the therapist in this aversive procedure comes to be perceived as a stress-reducing stimulus as the autistic child moves toward him or her.

We should recognize that behavior modification procedures do not cure early infantile autism. Although more supporting evidence exists for behavior modification than for most other forms of treatment, these behavior methods often focus only on small components of the child's total response possibilities. For example, self-mutilating behavior may be diminished, yet the child may remain autistic in many other ways. Another therapy approach attempts to help the whole child; it uses some behavior therapy methods along with ordinary human contact, education methods, and affection.

BIOCHEMICAL APPROACH (ORTHOMOLECULAR THERAPY)

Because Rimland and several other theorists have proposed an underlying biological or biochemical defect in autism, it follows that they would recommend biochemical efforts to manage autistic children. This is indeed the case. In his 1964 book, Rimland made some rather general statements about the potential benefit of oxygen, carbon dioxide, LSD, deanol, and nicotinic acid (vitamin B_3). Since the publication of *Infantile Autism* in 1964, Rimland and several other independent investigators have focused more sharply on *megavitamin therapy*, an approach often called *orthomolecular therapy*. Sagor (1974), paraphrasing the chemist Linus Pauling, defines orthomolecular therapy as "the treatment of mental illness by the provision of the optimum molecular composition of the brain" (p. 83). As a rule, orthomolecular therapy involves giving massive doses of specific vitamins to establish the optimum molecular composition of the nervous system.

In a 1969 publication, Rimland proposed that megavitamin supplements of nicotinic acid and vitamin C dramatically improved the behavior of approximately 80 percent of those taking the vitamins. But this investigation did have numerous methodological defects. Cott (1972) also reported impressive results with megavitamin treatment. Most recently, Rimland and other investigators using megavitamin regimes have turned their attention particularly to the administration of high levels of vitamin B_6 (pyridoxine). In particular, Rimland, Callaway, and Dreyfus (1978) found that they could predict with great accuracy which children were given vitamin B_6 and which were given placebos by analyzing a behavioral checklist that had been filled out by the parents of the autistic children. This study was double-blind to insure against experimenter bias, meaning that the principal investigators (Rimland and Callaway), as well as the parents and autistic children, did not know whether they were receiving vitamin B_6 or an inactive ingredient. For example, Rimland and Callaway correctly determined when the autistic children were on placebos and when they were on vitamin B_6 for 11 of 15 children. Again, the researchers made this correct judgment only from a knowledge of scores on a behavior checklist.

Rimland and his associates admit that many variables were uncontrolled in this particular investigation. Moreover, they acknowledge that the behavior checklist filled out by the parents had unspecified reliability. Further still, not all of the children in this investigation received the same doses of vitamin B_6. Nevertheless, their findings seem promising. Finally, Rimland and his group caution us that vitamin B_6 is not a cure for autism. In their words, it "seems a safe agent of potential value in the management of autistic-type children" (p. 475).

Finally, Mordock (1975) has suggested that we exercise great caution in evaluating some of the megavitamin studies. Not responding directly to the Rimland data, Mordock reminds us that many so-called "miracle cures" have later proved to be useless. Glutamic acid was once such a promised miracle cure for the feebleminded. Indeed, Mordock insists that glutamic acid and megavitamin regimes will not be the last of the miracle cures. Surely it seems perilous indeed to say that autism or schizophrenia, as Pauling once suggested, is a "brain scurvy" ameliorable by massive doses of vitamins. But it also seems perilous to make blank condemnations of biochemical therapies. Only further research will clarify these opposing points.

MULTISTRATEGY APPROACHES Two similar approaches are included in this category: those of DesLauriers and Carlson and of Oppenheim. Both methods use more than one single guiding principal: they both employ behavior or learning theory procedures, as well as tactile and kinesthetic stimulation, affection, control, and rather standard teaching techniques.

DesLauriers and Carlson. This treatment approach is based on these theorists' hypothesis of imbalance in the two-arousal system. Generally, they contend that the affective system (system II) is too weak, resulting in sensory and affective deprivation. Again, this defect is "an inborn limitation." Since the autistic child cannot receive the sensory messages or affective stimulation normally given by the environment, therapeutic strategy involves the application of "impactful affective stimulation," to activate system II (the reward area, or limbic system).

They describe two conditions under which an autistic child can learn: (1) learning can occur through "excessive repetition" or "repeated encounters with the same stimulus situation" (p. 35); (2) learning can occur if the thing to be learned is presented with a "strong affective" or emotional climate.

Aside from these two conditions, DesLauriers and Carlson also note that the hyperactive/hypersensitive child and the hypoactive/hyposensitive child are to be treated differently. The former must be presented with *mild* tactile, proprioceptive, and kinesthetic stimulation. Conversely, the hypoactive/hyposensitive child must be *bombarded* with high affective stimulation; that is, tactile, proprioceptive, and kinesthetic modalities (near-receptors) must be pelted, at the same time as stimuli are being repeated. That is, DesLauriers and Carlson believe that the best way to reach the autistic child is through sensory and preverbal modes. Only by beginning at this basic level can the affective barrier be surmounted. They claimed that their method was highly efficient, helping most of the children improve; but unfortunately, their research project had to be terminated for lack of funds (Oppenheim 1974). No others have reestablished their precise methods.

Rosalind Oppenheim (1974) began developing methods for treating autistic children because she had a severely afflicted autistic son. After unsuccessful attempts to get help for her son, she began to teach him herself. Although she initially encountered seemingly insurmountable difficulties (he could not talk, would not look at her, etc.), she discovered that certain things did work. Briefly, these are the important points Oppenheim makes:

1. The crucial *first* step is the establishment of *control*. By this she means that the child must be required to perform the command or task you have shown him or her; e.g., if the child will not do what you command, physically show the child—"literally use his hands to put him through the activity."
2. The teacher must convey to the child that she or he is in control.
3. Much of the initial teaching must be conducted by touch.
4. The child must not be permitted to engage in autistic behaviors during the learning sessions.
5. The child must be required to *attend* to the lesson materials (Oppenheim explains in detail how to accomplish this goal).
6. Every activity during which the child engages in nonautistic behaviors must be praised and reinforced.
7. The physical setting should be quiet and relatively isolated.
8. The curriculum taught should resemble normal school curriculum.
9. The autistic child must be required to repeat the same task over and over again—drilling is a key feature. (Adapted from Oppenheim 1974)

Generally, Oppenheim's approach is behaviorally oriented, but it also makes use of touch, affection, drill, and standard teaching devices. Her program has been implemented at the Rimland School for Autistic Children (of which she is the director). She has presented clinical cases showing the effectiveness of her method in helping these children learn to speak, write, read, and develop important social skills.

CHILDHOOD PSYCHOSIS

Childhood psychosis refers to a cluster of bizarre symptoms exhibited by children between about 3 and 12 years of age. The most common subcat-

CHILDHOOD PSYCHOSIS OR INFANTILE AUTISM?

Prior and colleagues (1975) used a statistical procedure to reduce a large array of symptoms observed in psychotic children into more manageable categories. After the analysis, two classes of psychotic children were identified: those whose symptoms appeared in infancy, and those whose symptoms emerged after age 2. The early onset class resemble very closely Kanner and Rimland's descriptions of early infantile autism. They developed their strange behaviors before 2 years of age, while the childhood onset group had a brief period of seemingly normal development, then rapidly regressed into an autistic state.

Common features did prevail for both the early and late onset children. For one, both displayed a basic "indifference to people." However, the early onset group was regarded as more disturbed on several behavioral dimensions.

Bender (1970) maintains that early onset psychoses and childhood psychoses belong to the same group; that is, the early onset disorders such as early infantile autism are actually a subcategory of childhood schizophrenia. But other researchers, such as Rimland (1964), argue that the two disorders are separate clinical entities. Rimland specifically points out the higher ratio of males seen in the early autistic group. Currently, the majority of researchers in the field view the two disorders as different clinical entities.

egory of childhood psychosis is *childhood schizophrenia*.

As with many other psychopathologies, the criteria for determining childhood psychosis are ambiguous and too inclusive. Prior (1975) and her associates state that childhood psychosis is "a blanket term currently used to describe a multitude of disorders ranging from developmental retardation to schizophrenia" (p. 321). However, a very broad cluster of behaviors seems to be characteristic for psychotic children.

FREQUENCY OF CHILDHOOD PSYCHOSIS   As with many disorders, the frequency or incidence of childhood psychosis depends on how those reporting the data define the syndrome. Diagnostic criteria or standards are not at all consistent from investigator to investigator.

For instance, to accept the contention (Bender 1970) that early infantile autism and childhood schizophrenia are the same basic disorder would clearly increase the frequency. But by and large, childhood psychosis, even including both early and late onset disorders, is much rarer than adult psychotic reactions. Until quite recently, the literature of psychopathology held that schizophrenia could not occur before puberty. More recently however, some data have been collected showing that a small percentage of children treated are psychotic. Shaw and Lucas (1970) reported that approximately 4 percent of the children evaluated in one clinic were labeled as psychotic. These authors also cite other studies that, in summary, indicate that as high as 10 percent of the children evaluated exhibited psychotic symptoms. Finally, diagnostic error (or differential diagnosis) may account for the varying frequencies reported by different investigators. For instance, mentally retarded children often have been labeled as autistic or psychotic.

SYMPTOMS OF CHILDHOOD PSYCHOSIS Because childhood schizophrenia is the most prevalent form of childhood psychosis, the symptoms we will describe refer to childhood schizophrenia. But we must recognize, as Goldfarb (1974) does, wide individual differences among these children. Psychotic children form a diverse group. Goldfarb (1974) notes that they vary considerably in adaptive skills and neurological functioning. Longitudinal studies have also demonstrated that these children differ in emotional and intellectual growth (Goldfarb 1970, 1974).

Many investigators have found a common cluster of symptoms characterizing psychotic children. Perhaps the most widely cited set of criteria was given by Creak (1961) and his co-workers in England. This group listed nine basic symptoms of childhood psychosis; Goldfarb also has confirmed them in the children he observed in the United States:

1. Gross and sustained impairment of emotional relationships with people.
2. Apparent unawareness of personal identity.
3. Pathological preoccupation with and attachment to particular objects.

4. Resistance to any change in the environment.
5. Abnormal perceptual experiences, even though sensory functions are almost normal.
6. Acute, excessive, and illogical anxiety.
7. Speech defects and arrests, or failure to use language appropriately.
8. Distorted movements or bizarre stereotyped behaviors — twirling, toe-walking, hand-flapping.
9. A history of serious retardation, yet with some unusual or near normal abilities in certain areas.

The DSM-III proposes a diagnostic category referred to as *atypical childhood psychosis*, which apparently will represent childhood schizophrenia and childhood psychosis. Atypical childhood psychosis is distinguished from early infantile autism by age of onset; the atypical syndrome emerges after 30 months but prior to 12 years of age. Children with this diagnosis will exhibit some of these symptoms: gross impairment of emotional relationships, self-mutilation (head-banging, severe biting, etc.), strange speech and vocal anomalies, lack of appropriate fear, unexplained panic, and several others. Although the DSM-III states that atypical childhood psychotics do not exhibit delusions, hallucinations, and incoherence — behaviors that are seen in adult schizophrenia — other clinicians disagree about the absence of hallucinations. The case study of Tyrone illustrates some of these symptoms.

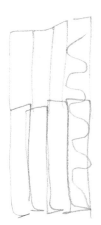

A CASE OF CHILDHOOD PSYCHOSIS

Tyrone is a black male who has been in and out of the Children's Unit of Creedmoor State Hospital from the age of 7 on. . . . At nine years [Tyrone] was anxious and disturbed. He complained of an object inside of him that went back and forth and knocked his back. It made him do bad things and got him in trouble. He was not sure of the nature of the object but thought it was a person. . . . It makes him do bad things like run away, and set fires. It tells him to kill himself or abandon his baby brother on a subway so a man could come along and kill him. He doesn't listen when it tells him to do really bad things. . . .

A month later he said the object inside of him was a grasshopper that walks inside of him and may leave some night when he is asleep. (Bender 1970, p. 98)

CAUSES AND STRESSORS The biogenic and psychogenic theories discussed in connection with early infantile autism generally apply also to childhood psychosis. We will include a discussion of the *family pathology model* (a variant of the psychogenic position) and an *interactional model* (a combination of the psychogenic and biogenic positions).

For years the mother alone was seen as the principal environmental agent inducing psychosis in an offspring; the so-called *schizophrenogenic mother* supposedly had pathological behaviors that turned the child into a psychotic. A more recent position suggests that producing a psychotic child requires teamwork and efforts by the entire family. The *family pathology theorists* or *family interactionists* (Vogel & Bell 1960; Haley 1973; Laing & Esterson 1970; Wolman 1970) assert that overall disturbances in the family may result in schizophrenia or psychosis in a given child. Wolman, for instance, leans toward a *disruptive view* — that is, disruption in the relationship between father and mother predisposes the child to psychosis. Wolman (1970) states that "Whenever a child was schizophrenic, his parents inadvertently hated one another and used the child emotionally" (p. vii). On the other hand, it could reasonably be argued that having a schizophrenic child might cause some parents to hate one another. Rejecting this interpretation, Wolman maintains that childhood schizophrenia is an environmentally induced "irrational struggle for survival" resulting in part from failing husband-wife bonds. No empirical support, however, has causally linked husband-wife hatred with schizophrenia in the offspring.

Another family pathology view is the *conspiracy model*. R.D. Laing has for a number of years been the principal spokesperson for this view. In many of his writings, he suggests that schizophrenia is a consequence of the family's discounting or minimizing a particular child's efforts to be a separate and whole self. The pathological family fails to "endorse" many of the child's experiences, according to Laing, and so the child does not receive, in the long run, confirmation of his or her unacceptable experiences. In Laing's

MAGICAL HALLUCINATIONS

Although the cluster of symptoms in adult psychosis is by no means clear-cut, even more imprecise descriptions exist for childhood psychosis. For instance, much controversy surrounds the question of whether psychotic children hallucinate. One widely used psychiatry text asserts that hallucinations are not experienced by psychotic children. Other texts and clinicians, most notably Loretta Bender (1970), contend that schizophrenic children, and even some nonpsychotic children, occasionally hallucinate. The bulk of evidence now seems to suggest that hallucinations can and do occur in psychotic children. But the quality or "content" of children's hallucinations differs from the content of adult hallucinations. Blatt and Wild (1976) make the point that "Hallucinations occurring in patients at a higher developmental level are apt to involve real people who have meaning to the patient" (p. 20). Children, on the other hand, have hallucinations "not anchored to real objects in the environment. . . ." That is, the things perceived in the hallucination are not only sheer fantasy, but do not usually even have counterparts in reality.

Bender (1970) gives us a more elaborate contrast between adult and childhood psychotic experiences:

words, the child becomes a "divided self." Searles (1959) was an early theorist who also advocated a type of conspiracy view. Searles described six "modes of driving the other person crazy":

1. Point out areas of the other's personality of which he may be unaware or that are inconsistent with his ideal or actual self-image.
2. Stimulate the person sexually in settings where attempts to gratify the efforts would be disastrous.
3. Simultaneously or rapidly alter stimulation and frustration.
4. Relate to the other person simultaneously on two unrelated levels (sexual advances during an intellectual political discussion).
5. Switch erratically from one emotional wave length to the other while discussing the same topic.

> The hallucinations of childhood . . . have specific characteristics different from those of adults. They are introjected and rarely projected. The inner voice of conscience, God, the Devil, angels, the good, bad or dead parents, are inside the child, impulses are directed by a voice in the child's head.
>
> I have heard children speak of a Jack Hammer pounding on the brain and heart that urged the boy to kill; a tape recorder in the head of an 11-year-old since he was six or seven which played back things that had happened to him and made him do things he didn't want to do and not do things he wanted to do; a gorilla inside of a boy that told him to kill himself; a baby eagle in a boy's belly that came out at night through his toenails to teach him to fly. (p. 96)

Bender goes on to point out that the hallucination is a function of the child's inner life, and hence a function of the stage of development he or she has reached. Since the child's cognitive skills are much less developed than the adult's, the psychotic experiences seem to be dominated by magical or mysterious animal powers.

6. Switch topics while maintaining the same emotional wave length (e.g., discuss life-and-death issues in the same manner as trivial matters).
(Adapted in part from Mishler & Waxler 1965)

The final family position is what we term the *equilibrium model:* the person or child goes mad to save the family from collapsing (Vogel & Bell 1960). Haley (1973) is one of the foremost spokespersons for this model. Most simply stated, this model maintains that many psychopathologies in a child are sustained or initiated because the child's disturbing behaviors actually enhance family stability and equilibrium. Haley describes this view:

> When child and parents cannot tolerate becoming separated, the threatened separa-

tion can be aborted if something goes wrong with the child. By developing a problem that incapacitates him socially, the child remains within the family system. The parents can continue to share the child as a source of concern and disagreement, and they find it unnecessary to deal with each other without him. The child can continue to participate in a triangular struggle with his parents, while offering himself and them his "mental illness" as an excuse for all difficulties. (p. 43)

Turning this around, we could say that the parents keep the child "mad" or encourage deviance so they will not have to deal with their own problems. In any case, there is no way of knowing whether the problems seen between the parents or in the family were caused *by* a schizophrenic child or *caused* a schizophrenic child.

The *interactional model* or *diathesis-stress model* is a combination of the genetic and environmental positions. It states that psychosis is in part genetically determined, but the genetic contribution to psychosis is "switched on" or activated by certain environmental stressors. First, we should note that some genetically jinxed children, whose parents and siblings are psychotic, often become "notably successful adults" (Blatt & Wild 1976). Two eminent genetic researchers, Gottesman and Shields (1972), contend that genetics alone is "not sufficient to account for schizophrenia." What they do suggest is that harmful genes may not be triggered until certain stressors are encountered. The dependence of the genetic contribution on environmental stressors may explain why one individual develops psychosis in childhood, another during adolescence, and another not at all. For example, a high-risk child who is somehow spared environmental stressors of great magnitude during childhood (the child does not lose a parent early in life, for instance), may not develop a disorder until another major stressor occurs late in his or her life.

To single out one condition or stressor—the either/or approach—is in Clarke and Clarke's (1974) words, "dated and in many ways ridiculous."

TREATMENT METHODS Since most of the therapeutic methods used with autistic infants have also been applied to the treatment of childhood psychosis, here we will simply consider a broad description of treatment and intervention methods.

© 1978 by Betty Medsger

Methods of treatment for the disturbed child include many kinds of therapy, the goal of which is getting the child to notice people.

Treatment and intervention methods depend largely on the extent of deterioration or retardation in the psychotic child. Unlike the adult schizophrenic, who already has mastered the developmental tasks of childhood, the disturbed child not only has to learn normal skills (the developmental tasks), but also to attempt to eliminate or lessen disturbing behaviors. Wolman (1970) notes that treatment for the most deeply disturbed child usually focuses on a rudimentary skill: trying to develop in the child a recognition of other people. To paraphrase Wolman, the psychotic child is intolerant of human contact, and so must learn to tolerate people. Rather than trying to eliminate specific behavioral excesses and deficits—speech difficulties, odd mannerisms—the therapist must initially shift his or her efforts toward getting the child to notice people. This lowest level of treatment resembles the therapy efforts of DesLauriers and Carlson described for autism. The therapist tries to break through the affective barrier, luring

the child out of his or her shell by employing all types of devices: music, rhythm, activities, eating, pleasurable stimulation of the child's sense organs (Wolman 1970; DesLauriers & Carlson 1969).

CHILDHOOD HYPERACTIVITY

In 1845, a German physician, Heinrich Hoffman, wrote a poem describing a "fidgety boy" who could never sit still. Hoffman's description was surely one of the earliest and it was not until the 1930s that *hyperactivity* was more formally described as a clinical syndrome (Kramer & Pollnow, 1932). About ten years after Kramer and Pollnow described the syndrome, Strauss reported on a group of brain-injured children who, despite normal IQs, displayed problems in learning, lacked inhibitions, and exhibited the classic symptoms of excitability and distractibility. At that time, children showing the symptoms were labeled as "Strauss syndrome children."

Although early accounts suggest that hyperactivity has been around for some time, such reports of hyperactivity were not common prior to extended and lengthy compulsory education. Renshaw (1974) makes this important observation about the relationship between the reported frequency of hyperactivity and the confining classroom:

> Although the 20th century is recognized as the age of the emergent individual, it has also demanded increased conformity of the individual child to the subculture of the classroom. Little latitude exists in the modern schoolroom for deviant behavior of even moderate degree. It is not surprising, therefore, that the greatest peak of recognition of the "hyperactive" child is between five and seven years of age, when the child is expected to conform to the norms of other children. . . . (p. 3)

Other reasons also may contribute to the increase of reported hyperactivity. For one, teachers are now very aware of the term and the ease with which its "diagnosis" can be made.

FREQUENCY OF HYPERACTIVITY Renshaw (1974) estimates that about 3 million children, roughly 8 percent of all schoolchildren, are hyperactive. Wender (1973) suggests that there are many more; according to him, at least 5 million hyperactive children exist in this country. The DSM-III (draft 3, 1978) has a new category called *attention deficit disorders,* one form being associated with hyperactivity. Its authors note that the disorder is common and state that as many as 3 percent suffer from hyperactivity. Why the discrepancies? For one, most researchers use different criteria and assessment procedures. Some people define hyperactivity very loosely, so that the number of children said to be suffering from this behavior problem is large indeed. In one California community an ''epidemic of hyperactivity'' was reported (Bruck 1976)—many teachers, the school psychologist, and a physician thought they saw the symptoms of hyperactivity in almost every child. In this particular situation, Ritalin (a stimulant medication used to lessen motor excitability) was widely prescribed. One parent said at the height of the so-called epidemic, ''You can't find anyone in this town who doesn't either have a kid on it [Ritalin] or knows somebody who has'' (Bruck 1976). Considering these problems, the current statistics on hyperactivity must be viewed cautiously. Since it has been almost in vogue to label inattentive, fidgety students as ''hyperactive,'' realistic estimates cannot be offered at this time.

SYMPTOMS OF HYPERACTIVITY Renshaw (1974) has proposed a cluster of symptoms frequently thought to depict a hyperactive child over age 5. Examples of the symptoms include:

1. Ceaseless, purposeless activity.
2. Short attention span.
3. Highly distractible.
4. Poor concentration.
5. Heedless of danger or pain.
6. Accident-prone; clumsy; poor motor coordination.
7. Speech problems.
8. Sleep disturbances.
9. Perceptual difficulties.

Renshaw lists 22 specific symptoms and further points out that it is simple to recognize hyperactivity if at least half the 22 symptoms are occurring *persistently.* Hyperactive children, unlike psychotic or autistic ones, do not have problems of failing to regard people as people.

As we previously noted, the proposed DSM-III associates an attention deficit syndrome with hyperactivity. These are some of the diagnostic criteria:

1. Difficulty sustaining attention.
2. Frequent ''forgetting'' of demands made, or task assigned.
3. Sloppy work in spite of reasonable efforts to perform adequately.
4. Frequent calling out of turn in class or making noises.
5. Difficulty waiting for one's turn in games, or in group situations.

A typical case of hyperactivity, illustrating a number of these symptoms, is described in the case study.

A CASE OF HYPERACTIVITY

Ron is a 6-year-old boy who was referred by the school for his hyperactive behavior. The teacher reports that he was extremely restless, so much so that he could not be weighed by the school nurse; she was afraid he would damage the scales because of his persistent ''bouncing.'' His mother describes him as a ''sweet boy,'' but counters with, ''he is going ninety miles an hour all the time.'' In addition to learning problems, caused primarily by the fact that he will not sit still for a minute, Ron is very accident-prone. He has had bicycle falls too numerous to mention, with almost daily bruises and abrasions. His father said: ''When I come home from work, I sometimes have a hard time recognizing him, a new cut here, a bandage on his face, or a cast on his leg.''

Ron was placed on 5 mg of methylphenidate a day, and the parents and teachers were to evaluate the boy on the *Conner's Abbreviated Teacher's Questionnaire* and the *Conner's Abbreviated Parent's Questionnaire.* Although it is possible that variables other than the drug could have accounted for Ron's improvement, he did show marked inhibition of several disturbing behaviors, though his school work did not improve.

CAUSES AND STRESSORS Theories concerning the cause of hyperactivity come from either the *biogenic* (organic) or *psychogenic* (environmental) view. Most of the theorizing about cause has emerged from the biogenic position.

Biogenic views. In 1937 Bradley noted that Benzedrine, a CNS stimulant, had an apparent positive effect on hyperactive children; that is, some of these children became calmer after ingesting the stimulant drug. This important observation led not only to the most widely used treatment approach for hyperactivity, but also to much theorizing about possible neurological damage. Neurological damage was postulated because of the paradoxical reaction to stimulants. It remains unclear why some hyperactive children apparently become calmer after receiving stimulant medication such as Ritalin. A few investigators speculate that hyperactivity is caused by basic cortical underarousal (cortical inhibition), a condition that leads to impulsivity and poor impulse control. Thus various stimulants ostensibly elevate cortical activity and enable better inhibitions of responses. This apparent drug reaction paradox (stimulants making certain individuals calmer) might be understood easier if you will recall that alcohol is a depressant, yet can make many people more excited and impulsive. Indeed, depressants lower cortical arousal and may lead to loss of impulse control in some individuals. In fact, administering alcohol or other cortical depressants to hyperactive children would be contraindicated. Based on Bradley's findings and subsequent observations by Strauss, biogenic theorists have maintained that subtle impairment in the central nervous system is responsible for hyperactivity.

Paul Wender, a leading biogenic theorist, suggested the *Wender hypothesis* (Wender 1971, 1973). It states that hyperactivity, in its extreme form, is a consequence of biochemical imbalances of particular *neurotransmitters*. The neurotransmitting chemicals in the brain, collectively called *catecholamines* or *monamines*, include norepinephrine, epinephrine, dopamine, and serotonin. Specifically, Wender suggests that a deficiency in dopamine (a deficiency in the brain stem) adversely alters inhibitory behaviors. Hyperactivity is thus a failure of inhibitory responses. Wender further argues that as the child grows, natural changes take place in catecholamine levels, thus explaining in part why hyperactivity decreases during adolescence. Stimulants may be effective because they alter catecholamines.

On the other hand, Dubey (1976), in a survey of the research on catecholamine differences in hyperactive and normal children (as detected through urinalysis), states that the vast majority of hyperactive children do not manifest biochemical abnormalities. Another point for the biogenic view is that hyperactive males consistently outnumber females approximately 4 to 1.

Psychogenic theories. In opposition to the biogenic theories, Paternite and colleagues (1976) found a relationship between socioeconomic status, parenting styles, and severity of hyperactive symptoms. They noted that styles of parenting (hostility, inconsistency, affection, etc.) were good predictors of symptom severity. Clarkson and Hayden (1972) have suggested that hyperactivity may be an overreaction to a very adverse home environment. Wender (1971), though fundamentally a biogenic theorist, calls attention to the role that psychological stress may play in hyperactivity. He believes, for example, that placing a child in a foster home or trying to force a child to do academic work beyond his or her capacity may engender this disorder.

TREATMENT AND INTERVENTION METHODS
The two basic treatment approaches we will consider are stimulant medication and behavior modification.

Before discussing treatment methods, we must recognize the problem of defining ''cure,'' ''improved,'' or other terms suggesting that the person is responding satisfactorily to treatment. Should, for instance, a clinician say that a hyperactive child is ''improved'' if, following medication, the child has elevated blood pressure, delayed physical growth, or a greater chance of seizures? It seems reasonable that claims for the effectiveness of treatment should be weighed against possible side-effects. Only after evaluating *long-term* improvements should pronouncements about the effectiveness of a treatment method be made.

For a time, the most common treatment of hyperactive behavior was to give various dosages of methylphenidate, commercially called Ritalin. Although Ritalin is effective in lessening overt symptoms in some children, questions have been raised about its positive effects on increasing learning and achievement. Rie and his associates (Rie et al. 1976) contend that Ritalin actually ''masks'' other problems. Research by this group suggests that the drug produces no gains in learning or achievement when children are compared with placebo or control groups.

Simmons (1975) points out three reasons for

seeking treatment methods other than drugs. First, drugs produce significant side-effects. Second, drugs suppress behavior, but do not add important and necessary adaptive responses to the child's repertoire. These adaptive behaviors and necessary skills must be learned. Third, drugs are not effective with a "significant number of hyperactive children." Simmons and numerous other clinicians and researchers thus prefer the use of behavior modification.

Perhaps the most useful behavior modification method is a general procedure called *contingency management*. Contingency management involves the "contingent administration of rewarding (reinforcing) consequences or events" (Rimm & Masters 1974). For instance, the hyperactive child is reinforced for appropriate behaviors (paying attention or sitting still) while the hyperactive symptoms are not reinforced (Patterson et al. 1965). Aversive consequences may be combined with positive reinforcers to lessen hyperactive symptoms (Lovaas & Willis 1974). While the child is given social praise or tangible reinforcers for appropriate behavior, he or she may lose the reinforcers already collected (response cost) or be separated or isolated from others for a short period (time out) for committing the hyperactive behaviors.

SPECIAL SYMPTOMS AND REACTIONS OF CHILDHOOD

Two reasons exist for including a separate section on special symptoms and reactions of childhood. First, the childhood psychopathologies discussed in the first section were characterized by a cluster of symptoms (syndrome); four of the disorders discussed here, however—school phobia, enuresis, stuttering, tics, self-stimulatory behavior—have only one predominant symptom. Second, childhood grief reactions would have been inappropriate in the first section because they may well be a normal response to a grievous event—the loss of a parent or loved one.

SCHOOL PHOBIA

As defined in chapter 6, a *phobia* is an intense but unwarranted fear of some object or situation. Somatic symptoms such as nausea, refusal to eat, vomiting, and abdominal pains may accompany the fear or anxiety. While children may develop animal phobias and transportation phobias (Kessler 1966), school phobia is the most common.

Specifically, a school phobia consists of anxiety, panic, and often abdominal pains that develop when the child is faced with having to go to school. Bakwin and Bakwin (1972) remark that the fear is usually related to a particular teacher, classmate, or anticipation of an exam.

CAUSES The hypothesized causes of school phobia are rather simple. Learning theorists, for instance, hold that the phobia has been acquired because it is reinforcing to avoid school. Stated differently, the school setting is perceived as aversive; any behavior that keeps the child from the dreaded situation will be reinforced or strengthened. Somatic complaints (such as nausea) are also thought to be learned, for they reduce the likelihood that the child will have to go to school. Another etiological thesis states that going to school is feared because the child has not learned to "separate" from his or her mother. The child is pathologically attached to her, and the prospect of separation engenders anxiety and panic. Bakwin and Bakwin write:

> In the majority of cases the school phobia is based on separation anxiety, a pathological emotional state in which child and parent, usually the mother, are involved in a mutually hostile, dependent relationship; the outstanding characteristic of which is an intense need to be together. (pp. 369–370)

TREATMENT The anxiety associated with phobias is often dealt with by behavior modification techniques. Three techniques are *systematic desensitization*, a broad category of procedures referred to as *contingency management techniques*, and *modeling*. As described earlier, in systematic desensitization, an anxiety-arousing stimulus (school) is paired with a physiological state "incompatible with anxiety." (One state incompatible with anxiety is relaxation.) Let us look at the steps involved

A THOUSAND CLOWNS © **1965, United Artists. Some children avoid going to school because it frightens them, others avoid it because it bores them. The truancy** **of the boy in this film is attributed to the conflict between the values of his home and those of his school.**

in systematic desensitization as applied to school phobia. First, the child receives training in deep muscle relaxation. Second, he or she, with the help of the therapist, constructs an *anxiety hierarchy*, a list of the most feared and least feared "scenes." Here is a five-item anxiety hierarchy:

1. Being in a classroom filled with other children. (*Most feared scene*)
2. Walking in the halls of the school.
3. Standing outside the school.
4. Approaching the school in the car.
5. Leaving the house for school. (*Least feared scene*)

Finally, the desensitization procedure begins. The child is instructed to "imagine" the least feared stimulus while deeply relaxed. After the child has demonstrated that the weak scene (leaving the house for school) no longer produces anxiety, he or she moves to the next higher anxiety-arousing

stimulus. This procedure is continued until the most feared scene can be encountered with relatively little anxiety.

It is difficult to teach some children how to relax. If this is the case, a *contingency management* technique can be used, in which reinforcers (both positive and negative) are dispensed "contingent upon" the performance or elimination of a given behavior. For example, a contingency contract could state that the child would go to school and, for doing this, he or she would be rewarded. In the contingency management program called *token economy*, tokens are earned by the child for attending school. The tokens collected can later be exchanged for back-up reinforcers such as prizes, privileges, free time, and the like.

Modeling can also be used to lessen phobic fears. With this technique, a child learns to engage in a given behavior by observing other children doing it. It is possible that a child can learn to perform a given behavior even by seeing it on film (O'Conner 1969, 1972; Evers & Schwarz 1973). One group of isolated and phobic children watched a short film depicting children who were not withdrawn or afraid of others. The short film was effective in developing new responses in those who saw it.

ENURESIS

Enuresis is defined as the occurrence of "persistent" bed-wetting after the age of 5. The most important point to keep in mind before labeling a child enuretic is that the definition of enuresis depends to a great extent on the child's age. Infants and very young children, for instance, wet their beds, yet are not enuretic. Thus far, bed-wetting is the only reaction that occurs normally up to a certain age and thereafter is considered abnormal. Care must be taken before this label and subsequent treatment are applied.

Another point is whether the child has ever had bladder control. If a 5- or 6-year-old has displayed bladder control for, say, two or three years and then relapses, the label can be applied. On the other hand, labeling by itself does no good; it could even be harmful. The purpose in specifying that a problem exists is so that intervention methods can be started immediately.

Bed-wetting should be taken seriously. Baller (1975) tells us that bed-wetters often feel very guilty, think they are deviant and odd, and thus hold a low view of themselves. He cites evidence of changes in self-concept after successful treatment.

CAUSES The etiological theories explaining enuresis are numerous; a few of the more popular ones are that it is an inherited defect; that it is a result of poor toilet-training; and that it is a symptom of an underlying problem, that is, it is emotionally induced.

The first view suggests that enuretics have an organic impairment or infection in the urinary tract; that is, a defect in the bladder, urethra, or kidneys. The preponderance of male enuretics (about three to two) is often used as evidence for this organic defect view. The observation that drugs may have some effect in lessening bed-wetting also is used to support the organic view. In this connection, the drug of choice has been *imipramine,* an antide-

pressant that has been shown to be effective in certain cases. Why is an antidepressant effective? According to a few theorists, the reason is that the drug reduces anxiety. In one etiological view, conflict (anxiety) is thought to play some role in bed-wetting.

Another organic or hereditary theory states that enuresis tends to "run in the family." Young (1963), for example, found that approximately 50 percent of a sample of 320 enuretic children had relatives who were also enuretic. Bakwin and Bakwin (1972) cite studies conducted in Israel and twin studies that strongly imply that heredity plays a part in enuresis.

The second view claims that enuresis is learned. Or, more specifically, that it is unwittingly "taught" by the parents. Baller remarks that "a high pecentage of bed-wetting can accurately be attributed *directly and exclusively* to a child's being 'taught' to urinate while asleep" (p. 4). To further explain this interesting view, Baller remarks that many parents keep up the practice of placing the child on the toilet while he or she is still asleep. Obviously this procedure is intended to help the child learn to urinate in the appropriate place. But what appears on the surface to be good parenting actually trains the child to urinate while he or she is still drowsy. Rather than taking a sleeping child to the bathroom, he or she should be awakened before being gotten out of bed.

The third theory states that enuresis is emotionally induced. Stated differently, this position suggests that enuresis is a symbolic expression of some underlying conflict. Psychoanalysts have traditionally taken this point of view. They contend that bed-wetting is a symptom of repressed desires or conflict. The repressed desire, it is thought, involves repressed sexual material; bed-wetting has been called a symbolic form of masturbation. The psychoanalytic view also states that bed-wetting may represent an expression of hostility or aggression; analytically inclined theorists have called it "revenge wetting." Finally, it has been suggested that bed-wetting is simply a consequence of being depressed and unhappy. Sperling (1974) quotes the remarks of a persistently enuretic 5-year-old who said, "People sometimes do these things because they are unhappy. They do it to make themselves feel happy" (p. 317).

The psychoanalytic view, in short, does not view enuresis as an organic defect or an accident of learning, but as a symbol of some unconscious wish. Treatment based on this model therefore aims at uncovering the unconscious motivation, not at alleviating the symptom.

TREATMENT An effective treatment based on learning theory was developed by Mowrer and Mowrer (1933, 1938). The *Mowrer procedure* was the prototype for conditioning treatments of enuresis. The apparatus used in this "bell-and-blanket" method consists of a liquid-sensitive gauze on which the child sleeps. When the discharge of urine contacts the liquid-sensitive gauze, an alarm (a bell) is sounded that arouses the child. How this procedure teaches the child to wake up before he or she urinates is still a matter of some dispute. Mowrer asserted that bladder distention, a stimulus, occurs prior to the alarm; after many pairings with the alarm, bladder distention takes on the awakening qualities of the aversive sound. A contrasting view claims that the child learns to wake up in order to avoid the alarm. Regardless of why or how the child learns to wake up prior to bed-wetting, the method is very effective.

STUTTERING

Travis (1971) defines stuttering in these words:
[a] disturbance of rhythm and fluency of speech by an intermittent blocking; convulsive repetition; or prolongation of sounds, syllables. . . .

CAUSES As usual, the etiological theories of stuttering are divided between biogenic or psychogenic causes. The *biogenic* view suggests that stuttering results from organic impairment in the central nervous system. Support for this position again comes from the overrepresentation of males among stutterers (three to eight times more prevalent than females). In addition, it is often noted that stuttering is seen uniformly throughout the world, implying that culture makes little difference (Sheehan 1975).

The *psychogenic* position maintains that stuttering is learned behavior. One particular learning theory model was proposed by Bloodstein (1975): the *anticipatory struggle hypothesis*. This hypothesis proposes that the stutterer behaves as though he or she has "acquired a belief in the difficulty of speech. . . ." For example, the child takes for granted that he or she will fail in speaking.

Bloodstein further notes that stuttering occurs primarily in social situations and "becomes intensified when [he or she feels] socially ill at ease, tense, insecure, or uncomfortable . . ." (p. 18). Since the stutterer can, in certain situations, speak rather fluently, it is the anticipation of failure and the struggle not to fail (*anticipatory struggle*) that undermines normal speaking. As Polow (1975) remarks, the person does not stutter so much when he or she feels confident. The harder the person tries, the more likely he or she is to fail.

Bloodstein offers several antecedent environmental conditions that may cause a child to develop a poor self-concept and a belief in his or her inability to speak. Parents often demand perfection, or they may seem overconcerned about their child's speech.

TREATMENT Treatment based on the anticipatory struggle hypothesis involves counseling with the parents to lessen environmental pressures. Other essentials of treatment are (1) desired speech patterns should be reinforced; (2) the child's anxiety about stuttering should be reduced by bringing the problem out in the open; (3) the child should recognize that other persons do not always speak perfectly; (4) the child should not avoid the opportunity to speak. Sheehan (1975) similarly suggests that the key element in therapy is "avoidance-reduction." That is, the stutterer should not try to avoid speaking, but should make every effort to speak when it is appropriate to do so. The stutterer should, therefore, talk more, not avoid activities because of the possibility that he or she will stutter. As Sheehan puts it, "Don't let stuttering keep you from taking part in life."

TICS AND SELF-STIMULATORY BEHAVIORS

A *tic* is a meaningless, repetitive, involuntary motor activity. They usually include such motor activities as persistent eye-blinking, twitching, shrugging the shoulders, grimacing, and so on. One question always raised is whether the tic is the main problem or merely represents some underlying difficulty. Kessler (1972) suggests that persistent tic-like behaviors usually indicate emotional difficulties.

CAUSES Specific etiological theories about tics include learning theory positions and a psychoanalytic position. The *tension-reduction hypothesis,* one learning viewpoint, implies that tics reduce tension or anxiety and so are continued. According to Bandura (1969), tics can be acquired by accident; that is, under stress, certain responses may be made by chance and be found to reduce tension. This position, however, appears to overlook the initial stressors that produce the "random" motor activity.

Another learning theory dealing with tics is *modeling.* This notion suggests simply that tics are learned by watching or imitating others. This view is circular, though, because it does not tell us how the "model" developed the tic.

Finally, the psychoanalytic position is an elaboration of Kessler's position that tics are emotionally induced symbolic activities expressing some underlying wish or conflict. The explanation is virtually identical to the one given for bed-wetting — both actions are thought to release either repressed sexual or destructive impulses.

TREATMENT   Treatment of a tic depends chiefly on the orientation of the clinician. The behaviorist might use *massed practice* (also referred to as negative practice), in which the tic is performed intentionally for a long time. For instance, a child with a shoulder-shrugging tic would be instructed to practice shrugging his or her shoulders for one hour without stopping. Massed practice is perhaps the most effective treatment approach.

Psychoanalysts, on the other hand, argue that eliminating the symptom without getting at the underlying cause will not help the child in the long run. Treating the symptom alone (the behavioral approach) only shifts the "energy" to some other activity or symptom. This is referred to as *symptom substitution.* Although this argument sounds plausible, Bandura (1969) cites numerous studies to refute the symptom substitution idea. Nevertheless, psychoanalytic therapy involves uncovering repressed material that is thought to provide the motivation for the tic.

Finally we should note that not all tics are psychogenically induced. Certain illnesses (encephalitis, for instance) can produce tic-like mannerisms.

SELF-STIMULATORY BEHAVIOR   Another type of stereotyped motor activity, resembling the tic, is *self-stimulatory behavior.* While there are normal forms of self-stimulatory behavior (nail-biting and thumbsucking, for instance), pathological exam-

ples are often seen in very disturbed children. For example, head-banging, body-rocking, hair-pulling, and specific self-mutilation may represent pathological forms of self-stimulatory behaviors if they occur persistently.

The difference between self-stimulatory behaviors and tics is that the former behaviors are more elaborate and less likely to be confused with a reflex. A few theorists even speculate that certain forms of self-stimulatory behavior symbolize subclinical or incomplete suicide. Tics are rarely viewed in this light.

Learning theorists see self-stimulatory behaviors as having been acquired because of their effects on the environment: these behaviors can control other people. Obviously, children could use these behaviors to get attention. But as with tics, it is also possible that self-stimulatory activities reduce anxiety and tension.

Treatment of self-stimulatory behaviors range from tranquilizing drugs to behavior modification techniques. The behavior modification procedures employed depend on the age of the child and whether or not the behaviors are self-destructive. Obviously, massed practice would not be used for treating head-banging or other damaging stereotyped activities. Aversive methods have been used with great success.

CHILDHOOD BEREAVEMENT AND GRIEF REACTIONS

Quite apart from what has been discussed thus far, below we shall examine the stresses of bereavement and grief reactions in children. The reactions discussed here are not necessarily viewed as psychopathological. It is unclear, for example, whether the delayed reaction to bereavement is a necessary way for some children to deal with death, or whether it is an unadaptive response. The purpose for including this section is that bereavement is often associated with emotional difficulties. While little hard empirical evidence exists in this area, hopefully the following section should give you a view of a new area being studied in abnormal behavior.

Reactions to the death of a loved one depend in large measure on the age of the bereaved individual. For example, a child's reactions to the death of a parent differ considerably from an adult son or daughter's reactions to the loss of a parent.

Just why children's reactions to loss are different will be discussed shortly.

Let us begin by defining bereavement and grief. *Bereavement* refers to the condition or state of having a loved one die. *Grief*, on the other hand, refers to the reaction to the loss, great sorrow and acute mental anguish.

Erich Lindemann was one of the first clinicians to point out that bereavement induces a characteristic grief process. After counseling with many of the survivors who had lost a spouse or relative in the disastrous Coconut Grove nightclub fire, Lindemann (1944) observed that bereavement often produced hostility, guilt, depression, sleep disturbances, and similar symptoms. Since Lindemann's work, other clinicians have also documented a rather consistent set of stages passed through by adult mourners: shock, denial, apathy, grief, recovery. (The adult stages are more fully described in chapter 19.)

Children, however, do not go through these stages of the grief process. Davidson (1975) tells us that the child's typical reaction to the death of a parent is "denial." But while adults also experience denial, very young children, those under age 5, seem unable to understand the meaning of death itself. Are children capable of denying something they do not understand? To be sure, one's conception of death follows a developmental pattern, and one's conception of death also determines how he or she reacts to a loss. Thus, denial in an adult is surely not the same thing as absence of grief in children. Perhaps what adults infer as *denial*—because the child may not openly weep, for instance—may simply be the child's bewilderment about death. Those who have seen small children at the funeral of a parent may have noticed them laughing and giggling after the service. Is this "inappropriate" reaction denial or mystification about death? Ruitenbeek (1973), recalling events from his childhood, gives this impression of how his youthful peers reacted toward death.

> [As] children we did not comprehend the totality and finality of death. It created a certain excitement among us and it was something to be curious about, sometimes even to be envious about. I remember that in grade school the father of one of my classmates died and, first of all, my friend did not appear for a few days in school (an unexpected vacation!). Then, when he did come back he had something special which the others in our class did not have . . .

> the teacher gave him more attention and consideration than the rest of us. (p. 2)

Maria Nagy (1948, 1959) revealed some interesting things about children's developmental conceptions of death. Before age 5, the child does not conceive of death as permanent. "It's like sleep," a 4-year-old stated. After age 5, however, the child begins to see death as a "thing," a skeleton, a dead body, a ghost. Not until late childhood or early adolescence does the child start to recognize that death is inevitable and final. We must also keep in mind that children differ widely in their exposure to death. The death of a pet, funeral services of relatives—all play some part in forming the child's view of this phenomenon. Too early an exposure to funerals may sensitize a child.

Against this background, let us make our main point: Bereavement during childhood is often said to predispose the individual to psychopathology later in life. For example, several studies show that children who have lost a parent have a greater liability to adult psychopathology: antisocial behavior, depression, suicide (Brown 1961; Archibald et al. 1963; Greer 1964; LeShan 1966). While other investigators have challenged these claims (Morrison et al. 1974), the issue of whether childhood bereavement produces adult psychopathology still remains.

At the heart of this question is the hypothesized *delayed-response phenomenon* (Pincus 1974). In simple terms, the delayed-response hypothesis states that reactions to stressful events (as the death of a parent during childhood) do not always occur immediately, but may instead emerge many years later. Though the child may not openly express grief at the time, later, as an adult, this person may fear establishing new relationships or feeling concern for others (Pincus 1974). For example, Hetherington (1973) claims that young girls whose fathers died would later be more disposed to exhibit severe sexual anxieties and discomfort in the presence of males.

Pincus and others see "unresolved grief" as the principal stressor provoking the delayed response phenomenon. Describing her patients who failed to mourn, Pincus remarks:

> In each of them, unresolved grief led to a defense against emotional commitment, a denial of feeling, and an improvishment of the personality. Such severely denied mourning requires therapeutic help. (pp. 173–174)

Here we should point out that unresolved grief may not be the only explanation for the delayed-response phenomenon. When a parent dies, the whole family structure is permanently altered. Frequently the widowed parent becomes depressed, and the child may react to this upsetting behavior. The remaining parent may later remarry, and the child will have to adjust to this significant change. The delayed response, then, could be a result of events following the death and have little to do with the so-called denial of mourning.

Warning signs for unresolved grief or for a bereaved child needing help have been offered by Hendin (1973):

1. The child who appears to show no grief at all may be in trouble and have problems later in life.
2. If a child maintains an unshakable fixation on the lost love object, if he [or she] continues to believe that the dead person will return for more than a week or so, he [or she] may need aid to give up [the] fantasy and deal with the reality of the situation.
3. If a child ceases to function in school or turns to severe delinquent activities.
4. If a child whose anger leads him [or her] to strike out at society by stealing or other illegal and unsocial acts also needs help. (p. 156)

Finally, another thing to consider is that the delayed-response phenomenon can be prompted by exposing a child to traumatizing funeral services. Schowalter (1975) believes that children should not be taken to funerals before 7 or 8 years of age. While adults may tolerate or even appreciate the "fake life" appearance of the deceased, it may be terrifying to a small child. Moriarty (1967), for instance, describes the case of a depressed and suicidal woman who could remember very little about her mother (the mother died before the child was 3) except her mother's cemetery service. The shoveling of dirt on her mother's coffin was still vividly recalled some 25 years later. Because of those events, this woman was obsessed about death and had enduring fears that she would be bereaved again.

Schowalter maintains that children should be gradually exposed to death, for this process may desensitize them somewhat from the fear of funerals. He contends:

> Children who have been active in arranging funerals for pets or who have discovered dead animals often seem better able to experience their passive role at the funeral. (p. 92)

As for children who supposedly repress grief, little evidence exists for what therapists should do. Grief therapy for adults consists chiefly of encouraging the bereaved to accept the death and openly express his or her sorrow, but similar therapy with children who do not yet understand death is questionable.

SUMMARY

1. The study of childhood psychopathologies is a relatively recent activity. *Marasmus* and *anaclitic depression* were two of the first diagnostic labels specifically applied to disturbed children. Marasmus consisted of physical deterioration, apathy, and intellectual underdevelopment. Spitz asserted that marasmus (he later changed the name to anaclitic depression) was a type of infantile grief response to the loss of or abandonment by the mother.

2. *Early infantile autism* is considered by many to be the first specific clinical syndrome used to describe profoundly disturbed children. Kanner identified and named this syndrome in the early 1940s. The major symptoms consist of indifference to others, resistance to change in the environment, defects in language and preoccupation with mechanical objects. There exist two basic etiological theories of autism: the biogenic and the psychogenic. The psychogenic theories suggest that particular parent-child interactions or the child's reinforcement history are faulty. Bettelheim and Ferster's views are both psychogenic. The biogenic

theories suggest that an underlying anatomical or biochemical defect is responsible for this syndrome. The treatment approaches are Bettelheim's "parentectomy" (removing the child from his or her parents); behavior modification; multistrategy approaches (consisting of tactile stimulation and repetitive task presentation); and biochemical methods.

3. *Childhood psychosis* refers to a type of autism or schizophrenia that has its onset approximately after age 3 and before age 12. The symptoms resemble those of autism, but make their appearance later in life. The etiological theories and treatment approaches are similar for both childhood psychosis and early infantile autism.

4. *Childhood hyperactivity* is a syndrome characterized by purposeless activity, a short attention span, poor concentration, perceptual difficulties, and other symptoms. The biogenic theories of hyperactivity state that there are biochemical imbalances in the brain. The psychogenic theories propose that this syndrome is a reaction to faulty parenting or to certain other environmental stresses. Treatment methods consist of giving stimulant medication (Ritalin is a commonly used drug) and employing behavior modification procedures.

5. *School phobia* is a special problematic behavior involving a child who exhibits anxiety or reports that he or she is afraid to go to school or attend a particular class. The etiological positions for this reaction are mainly psychogenic. Anxiety management techniques, such as systematic desensitization and modeling, have been employed with this reaction.

6. *Enuresis* refers to persistent bed-wetting after the age of approximately 5. Theories of the causes of enuresis include biological and psychological positions. The biogenic theory views enuresis as a medical problem, a result of impairment of the bladder, urethra, or kidney. Drugs may be given to reduce anxiety or to affect the bladder or kidney and thereby lessen the tendency for bed-wetting. The psychogenic theory views enuresis as the result of faulty learning, or as a consequence of emotional stress. The "bell-and-blanket method," Mowrer's procedure, is a conditioning procedure that signals the sleeping child that he or she has wet the bed; the signal eventually becomes associated with bladder distention and usually results in the child's awakening to these sensations.

7. *Stuttering* is a disturbance in speech, characterized mainly by prolongation and blocking of speech sounds. There are both biogenic and psychogenic views of stuttering. The biogenic positions, in general, suggest that some organic impairment in the speech centers in the brain is responsible for the problem. The psychogenic positions argue that stuttering is a learned response, a reaction to emotional stress. Treatment often involves reinforcing desired speech patterns as well as encouraging the stutterer not to avoid speaking situations. There is often an effort to get the person to feel less anxiety about the problem.

8. *Tics* refer to meaningless, repetitive motor activities. Twitching or persistent eye blinking are two examples. Tics are believed to have some tension reducing benefit. They may be acquired accidentally by modeling. *Massed practice* is one procedure used to reduce the frequency of certain tics. This procedure involves having the person deliberately practice the tic response at a very high rate and for a rather long duration. *Self-stimulatory behavior* is also a stereotypical motor activity like the tic, but self-stimulatory behavior is usually a more elaborate or complex set of responses. Treatment of self-stimulatory behavior often involves the application of behavior modification procedures.

9. Children often react differently to loss and bereavement than do adults. Children are less able to handle and express grief. Some theorists argue that bereavement or loss of a parent during early childhood traumatizes the child, inducing or contributing to psychopathologies later in life. This notion has little empirical support, however. The *delayed response phenomenon* deals with this unsupported claim; briefly, it suggests that unresolved grief causes abnormal behavior, but there is a delayed reaction to the grief because the child is unable to express and resolve his or her feelings of loss.

Baller, W. R. *Bed-wetting: Origins and treatment.* New York: Pergamon, 1975.

Erickson, M. T. *Childhood psychopathology.* Englewood Cliffs, NJ: Prentice-Hall, 1978.

Gardner, W. I. *Children with learning and behavior problems.* Boston: Allyn & Bacon, 1978.

Goldfarb, W. *Growth and change of schizophrenic children: A longitudinal study.* New York: Wiley, 1974.

Mahler, M. S., Pine, F., & Bergman, A. *The psychological birth of the human infant: Symbiosis and individuation.* New York: Basic, 1975.

Rimland, B. *Infantile autism.* New York: Appleton-Century-Crofts, 1964.

17

ABNORMAL BEHAVIORS ASSOCIATED WITH ADOLESCENCE

OVERVIEW In this chapter we will look at a number of behavior problems that typically have their onset during adolescence. Adolescence is defined as the period from approximately age 10 to age 20.) We will begin with two eating disorders, *anorexia nervosa* and *bulimia;* for each, we examine the frequency, major symptoms, causes and stressors, and treatment strategies. Another important problem in adolescence is suicide and other life-threatening behaviors (LTB). Although depression and suicide were discussed in an earlier chapter, this problem has special importance in adolescence. We will discuss the major symptoms of life-threatening behavior, the frequency of adolescent suicide, and means for detecting suicidal motives and lethality; we also give an example

of a "psychological autopsy" form and review treatment and suicide prevention strategies. Another problem behavior in adolescence is drug abuse; although drug abuse was also discussed in an earlier chapter, here we will discuss it as it specifically relates to adolescence. The last two problems we will examine are academic or work inhibition and the emancipation disorder, two new problems described in the proposed DSM-III.

Adolescence is a stage of development that takes place roughly between the chronological ages of 10 and 20 years. This stage is often thought to have characteristic behaviors, social circumstances and opportunities, and physiological and biological changes. Adolescence is also considered a period of great stress and turmoil. It is a time of "growing up," and demands and new expectations on the individual account for most of the stresses associated with this stage of development. As with most other stages in the life cycle, abnormal behaviors do arise during adolescence.

The abnormal behaviors described in this chapter may also manifest themselves in childhood or adulthood, but characteristically have their *onset* during adolescence. We should also stress that many adolescents with psychopathologies do not exhibit just a single set of behaviors; they may have not only an adolescent onset disorder but also other abnormal behaviors. A suicide attempt may lead to a diagnosis of depression, but the depression may be linked, for instance, with a psychosexual deviation. A multiple pattern or diverse set of symptoms often characterizes individual psychopathology. In this chapter, then, we describe various abnormal behaviors in the *context* of adolescence.

SYMPTOM DESCRIPTION AND ETIOLOGY

In this section we follow rather closely the classification system and diagnostic procedures proposed in the new DSM-III. DSM-III acknowledges great overlaps in its classification system. For example, schizophrenia, dyshomophilia, and somatoform disorders all may be seen in adolescents, yet they are not classified as adolescent problems. The DSM-III, as well as this section, groups together a set of behavior problems that typically arise during adolescence.

ANOREXIA NERVOSA

Anorexia nervosa is a type of psychophysiological disorder characterized by the inability or refusal to eat. It occurs most often in adolescent females. Accompanying the refusal to eat is a delay or absence of menstruation (amenorrhea), as well as profound weight loss. Anorexia nervosa is not a new syndrome. In 1694, Richard Morton reported two cases of adolescent children who showed classic signs that are the essential features seen today: a marked reduction in food intake and resulting emaciation. Morton reported on one adolescent who he described as being "like a skeleton clad only with skin" (Wicklund 1973).

FREQUENCY OF ANOREXIA NERVOSA   It has been estimated that approximately one in 100,000 adolescents is anorectic. Approximately 95 percent of those who are anorectic are female. An interesting demographic fact is that anorexia nervosa is predominantly a middle class or upper class phenomenon. One clinician says this is so because these social classes place a high value on "leanness."

SYMPTOMS OF ANOREXIA NERVOSA   The anorectic adolescent girl typically begins to lose weight by self-imposed restriction of food. Oddly enough, she may start to diet to improve her appearance when, by no standards, would others classify her as overweight. Indeed, this young woman often has a very distorted body image (Kron et al. 1977). She thinks she is fat when she is not, and, after becoming very emaciated following irrational fasting, she may be totally unaware that she is exceedingly thin. The DSM-III gives these six criteria for identifying anorexia nervosa:

1. Refusal to maintain body weight over a minimal normal weight for age and height.
2. Weight loss of at least 25 percent of original body weight, or if under eighteen years of age, weight loss from original body weight plus projected weight gain expected on pediatric growth charts may be combined to comprise the 25 percent.
3. Disturbance of body image with inability to accurately perceive body size.
4. Intense fear of becoming obese. This fear does not diminish as weight loss progresses.
5. No known medical illness that would account for weight loss.
6. Amenorrhea (in females).

A few of these symptoms are illustrated dramatically in the case study.

The anorectic often suffers from a distorted self image.

A CASE OF ANOREXIA NERVOSA

This 20-year-old female student came to the physician weighing 65 pounds, hardly able to stand, and unable to assume an upright position without crawling up her legs with her hands. In spite of this she insisted on going out in the coldest weather and braving any kind of storm. She had several attacks of pulmonary collapse and had many infections which, however, she resisted well in spite of her unwillingness to accept medical attention or to enter a hospital. Her primary com-

plaint was the loss of weight and inability to eat. Especially was she unable to eat in the presence of any other person. With some rationalization or other she would always contrive to eat alone, ingesting food with caloric value insufficient to maintain life. During the middle of the night, however, even in spite of the most intense control that she could muster, she would go into the kitchen, open the icebox and eat everything in sight. This included raw meat, and at times she would eat a whole raw chicken or raw lamb chops. Sometimes after filling herself with this food, she would contrive to vomit by sticking her finger down her throat; but most of the time she permitted the food to pass into her intestines, and suffered severe cramps while her abdomen was distended with food and gas. She would take cathartics in order to push the food through and prevent it from being assimilated, and therefore had very frequent, severe diarrheas.

Under treatment the patient made some progress, although the strength of her ego was always a question. This is true of most cases of anorexia nervosa: that they resemble very closely the schizophrenic in their ego deficiencies. It was so difficult to teach her the meaning of her internal impulses that it seemed no success could be attained; gradually, however, she began to act as though she understood what was going on around her and that the difficulties arose within herself. She ultimately weighed 120 pounds, moved out of the city, was quite successful in her work, and finally married and settled down with a university teacher in another city. (Grinkers & Robbins 1954, pp. 197–198)

CAUSES AND STRESSORS The causes suggested for anorexia nervosa fall in two categories: psychogenic theories and biogenic theories. Psychogenic theories regarding anorexia are mainly psychoanalytic views. For example, one psychoanalytic theory contends that anorexia nervosa is a symptom of the child's refusal to grow up — a type of protest. In this connection, some psychoanalytic theorists believe that anorectic adolescents have much in common with *borderline syndrome adolescents*. In the borderline syndrome, pathological dependency and odd behaviors exist that resemble both neuroses and schizophrenia (thus the term "borderline"). Anorectic adolescents, then, have been viewed as highly dependent persons who fear separation and independence from parents. Further, both anorectic individuals and borderline individuals tend to be shy, tense, and hypochondriacal; it is often believed that both have been overprotected.

Other analytic theories have approached this problem in a different way. Because weight loss is profound, and such severe emaciation is generally associated with undernourishment and death, a few clinicians have suggested that anorexia nervosa is really a form of *subintentional suicide*. That is, they believe this behavior disorder to be motivated by self-destructive urges. Thus far, however, no empirical evidence exists to support any of these theories.

By contrast, the biogenic positions contend that anorexia nervosa has a biological or genetic origin. Some evidence does show an association between certain abnormal chromosome patterns and anorexia in females (Kron et al. 1977). In particular, chromosome configuration XO (a condition called *gonadal dysgenesis* or Turner's syndrome) is associated significantly with anorexia. Another investigation revealed that gonadal dysgenic individuals exhibit symptoms of passivity, dependency, and, in the researcher's words, "psychoinfantilism" (Kihlbom 1969). Further research is required before a more complete understanding of the etiology of anorexia nervosa is achieved.

TREATMENT   Almost every technique imaginable has been tried with anorectic patients (Bliss 1975). Lobotomies, hormone injections, drugs, isolation, electroconvulsive therapy, behavior modification, hospitalization, insulin coma, and even "gentle reasoning" have been tried with these patients. In addition to physical methods, family therapy and individual psychotherapy (insight therapy) have been employed with varying degrees of success and failure. Perhaps no single therapy has emerged because there are different causes of this disorder and different levels of severity. Discussing the diverse group of individuals who exhibit anorexia, Bliss (1975) states:

> There are those patients who are clearly schizophrenic . . . they harbor delusional convictions about food, believing it to be contaminated or poisoned. Then there are deeply depressed patients whose dysphoric state leads to a loss of appetite. . . . [There] is a group of adolescents, many overweight, who become desperately concerned about their weight, feel self-con-

scious and ugly, and they diet excessively to escape obesity. (p. 1655)

The differing features of anorexia nervosa make it unlikely that a single therapy can be proposed. To date, no highly effective treatment strategy exists for this problem. A number of strategies are being tried, but the evidence supports none in particular.

BULIMIA

Bulimia is another eating disorder that commonly arises during adolescence. The term comes from the Greek word *boulimia,* which roughly means "to hunger." As an abnormal eating pattern, bulimia refers specifically to voracious, episodic eating binges. These binges may or may not result in obesity. One thing the binges do bring about, however, is an irrational fear that one cannot control one's insatiable cravings and consumption of foods. The bulimiac not only feels driven to eat, but after episodes of gorging feels depression, guilt, and other negative thoughts.

SYMPTOMS OF BULIMIA   The DSM-III lists several features associated with bulimia. The bulimic adolescent may have a history of intermittent drug abuse; alcohol, barbiturates, and stimulants are frequently abused by this group. Like anorectic adolescents, the bulimic teenager—again, usually female—is often obsessed with her body image, and she is also overly concerned with how others perceive her body. Indeed she is in a vicious circle: she has an insatiable urge to eat, but is hypersensitive about the consequences.

In the case study, many of the same features appear as in the case of anorexia. Perhaps in some instances the only difference between anorexia nervosa and bulimia is weight gain or weight loss—those with anorexia nervosa become severely underweight, but in bulimia, obesity may develop.

A CASE OF BULIMIA

Della C. is an 18-year-old female who was referred to a psychiatrist because of her apparent addiction to certain foods. Della would indulge in eating binges at least once a week. These binges invariably occurred late in the evening. On most occasions, she would "secretly" buy and consume as much as three gallons of chocolate ice cream, a feat that would seem to set some sort of record for a rather small girl. Following the ice-cream eating orgy, Della would then try and drink a large amount of water, a process that she says always made her vomit up the ice cream. Vomiting, she admitted, was not induced so that she could continue to eat, but rather to abate the guilt that followed the binges.

For several days following the binges, Della would fast, but then she would make up for her abstinence with another fit of gluttony. At one point, Della's small frame (5' 3") supported 156 pounds. Later, however, Della's weight decreased to about normal for her height, although she was still bulimic.

The DSM-III lists several operational criteria for bulimia:

1. An episodic pattern of binge eating, . . . accompanied by (a) an awareness of disordered eating patterns, with a fear of not being able voluntarily to stop eating; and (b) depressive moods and negative afterthoughts following the gorging.
2. The bulimic person must have at least three of the following symptoms:
   a. Rapid consumption of food during the eating episode.
   b. Ingestion of high caloric food during the episode.
   c. Clandestine eating binges.
   d. Following the binges, abdominal pain, sleep, social interruption, or self-induced vomiting.
   e. Repeated efforts to lose weight—diets, cathartics, vomiting.
   f. Cyclical patterns of gluttony and fasting. (Adapted in part from DSM-III, draft 2, 1978)

FREQUENCY OF BULIMIA   The DSM-III and a few other sources suggest that bulimia is not too uncommon in adolescent females. At this time, however, sound estimates of the frequency are not available.

CAUSES AND STRESSORS   Unfortunately no information is available concerning the possible causes of bulimia. Although a parent or sibling may

be obese, no predisposing factors or stressors have been found, according to the DSM-III. It is not even known at this time whether, like obesity, bulimia is more common in lower social classes than in middle and upper classes; or whether, like anorexia nervosa, it is mainly a middle class disorder. To be sure, much more research is needed in connection with this problem.

TREATMENT   Since bulimia does not follow a pattern like that of simple overeating (obesity), it seems doubtful whether appetite reducing methods would be effective; many bulimic persons are not, in fact, overweight. There seems to be no published evidence demonstrating a systematic and effective means for dealing with this problem. While private clinicians may have dealt with some bulimics with success, these data have yet to be made public.

ADOLESCENT SUICIDE AND LIFE-THREATENING BEHAVIORS

Can there be any greater enigma in life than a young person's decision to end it? Suicide is often an incomprehensible act. A famous suicidologist, Edwin Shneidman, suggests that there is no single reason for suicide (Shneidman 1976). He states that a dozen people may kill themselves for a dozen different reasons. A common theme or motivation, however, is the desire to "escape" from something painful.

The concept of suicide is not limited to self-murder. Some contend that suicide is simply the ultimate form of self-destructive behavior. This approach suggests, then, that there are degrees or levels of self-destructive behavior. The term *life-threatening behavior* (LTB) is used to represent a class of actions that are less lethal than suicide. Weisman (1976) lists these types of life-threatening behaviors:

1. *Self-injury and intoxication*—includes non-suicidal overdoses of drugs, frequent alcohol abuse, and other repetitive acts that result in trauma.
2. *Rash, regretted, incautious, or bizarre acts*—unskilled use of dangerous tools, instruments, and the automobile; where there is real danger, these people may show very poor judgment, which creates a death-related setting.

3. *Significant omissions*—omits medication, disregards medical or other professional advice.
4. *Significant excesses*—gross overeating, starvation diets, chronic alcoholism.
5. *Countertherapeutic behavior*—rebellions against rules, roles, and requirements during hospitalization.

In the late 1930s, in his book *Man Against Himself*, Karl Menninger described how completed suicide, the ultimate act, is on a continuum with lesser self-destructive behaviors such as alcohol addiction, drug abuse, self-mutilation, polysurgery (exhibited by those who seek doctors who will operate on them), and other self-destructive acts. This profound point of Menninger's, that there exist degrees or symbolic acts of suicide, certainly seems to apply to particular adolescent actions.

According to Jarvis and colleagues (1976), the occurrence of *self-injury*, a life-threatening behavior, is a function of both the age and the sex of the person engaging in limited self-destruction. Adolescence is a high point for both self-injury and attempted suicide. But female adolescents are more likely to engage in self-injury, while adolescent males are more likely to commit suicide. It is not clear whether self-injury is a stepping stone to attempted suicide or to completed suicide; females injure themselves and *attempt* suicide, while males more often complete suicide. However, as was mentioned in an earlier chapter, males may more often complete suicides because they tend to use lethal methods, ones that are likely to result in death. Specifically, males are likely to use guns, and females to take an overdose of pills. Others insist that attempted suicide is a different phenomenon than completed suicide—that is, there are different motivations for the two acts. The case study illustrates some of the characteristic actions in adolescent suicide.

Lynn McLaren, Rapho/Photo Researchers

Adolescence is considered a period of great stress. New expectations and limited access to status account for most of the stresses associated with this stage.

A CASE OF SUICIDE

Paul C. killed himself with a 22 caliber pistol. He shot himself through the head in his motel room, which was occupied at the time by several other musician-friends. According to those who witnessed the shooting, Paul was sitting in a chair "fooling around" with the gun, raised it to the side of his head and, without a word, fired it.

Paul's death was ruled a gun accident by the local medical examiner. Those present were baffled. There appeared to be no reason for his actions. He did not seem depressed; in fact he had been doing what he had wanted to do, playing in a rock band.

It is noteworthy, however, that Paul had twice mentioned that he often thought of suicide. Once he took an overdose of Seconal capsules, about 50 in all. On another occasion he mentioned having obsessive and intrusive thoughts about running his car into a speeding train; he said he almost tried it one night but the car he was in belonged to someone else. It is also interesting that these self-destructive thoughts emerged very shortly after the death of his father.

FREQUENCY OF ADOLESCENT SUICIDE Although suicide is not a leading cause of death for those between 10 and 14 years of age, between

A PSYCHOLOGICAL AUTOPSY FORM

1. Identifying information for victim: name, age, address, marital status, religious practices, occupation, and other details.
2. Details of the death, including the cause or method and other pertinent details.
3. Brief outline of victim's history: siblings, marriage, medical illnesses, medical treatment, psychotherapy, previous suicide attempts.
4. "Death history" of victim's family: suicides, cancer, other fatal illnesses, ages at death, and other details.
5. Description of the personality and life style of the victim.
6. Victim's typical patterns of reaction to stress, emotional upsets, and periods of disequilibrium.
7. Any recent (from last few days to last 12 months) upsets, pressures, tensions, or anticipations of trouble.
8. Role of alcohol and drugs in (a) overall life style of victim and (b) in his or her death.
9. Nature of victim's interpersonal relationships (including physicians).
10. Fantasies, dreams, thoughts, premonitions, or fears of victim relating to death, accident, or suicide.
11. Changes in the victim before death: habits, hobbies, eating, sexual patterns, and other life routines.
12. Information relating to the "life side" of victim (upswings, successes, plans).
13. Assessment of intention, i.e., role of the victim in his or her own demise.
14. Rating of lethality.
15. Reactions of informants to victim's death.
16. Comments, special features, etc. (Shneidman 1976, p. 353)

ages 15 and 19 it becomes the fourth leading cause of death, exceeded only by accidents, homicides, and malignant tumors (U.S. Public Health Service, National Center for Health Statistics, 1974). Of the approximately 25,000 suicides reported in one year, 4,000 were committed by the adolescent group. Another interesting statistic shows that in the last 20 years adolescent suicide has increased nearly 250 percent. Still the picture of the frequency of adolescent suicide is incomplete. Suicide is notoriously underreported, and many so-called accidents clearly involve elements of intentionality. Yet if there is any question of intentionality, a medical examiner virtually always rules the death accidental. This is partly because a ruling of suicide may be viewed as harmful to the family. In addition, some automobile "accidents" may involve intentionality, but in such cases, intentionality would be virtually impossible to prove. The automobile is thus an ideal instrument for intentional self-destruction.

ASSESSING THE SUICIDE MOTIVE Another reason why suicides are classically underreported is that suicide motives are not easy to determine. Even if a gun is in the person's hand, or the body is at the base of a high building, was it an accident or was it intentional? The difficult step in determining suicide deals with just this point: attributing intentionality to an act after the person is dead. Even if a suicide note is found, can we be sure that the person who wrote it really wanted to die? Could he or she have wished to be discovered in time? Was the effort a "cry for help" rather than a real desire to die? Several researchers have sought ways to reveal intentionality and assess *lethality* in suicide attempts.

Edwin Shneidman worked for many years on developing a method for understanding why people commit suicide and whether a given death is accidental or intentional. He was instrumental in developing the first *psychological autopsy* technique, a procedure that helps the coroner or medical examiner to determine whether a person's death was accidental.

The psychological autopsy is basically a life history chart of major events in the victim's life. The data making up the psychological autopsy are taken from close survivors or relatives of the victim. Prodromal symptoms (warning signs) may be revealed, depending on the intentionality of the death.

Another problem concerning suicide is the evaluation of the seriousness or *lethality* of attempts. Weisman and Worden (1972) developed a "Risk-Rescue-Rating" that would enable them to rate an attempt behaviorally and then calculate the risk of death. Scores of lethality can range from very low levels to very high levels. Worden (1976) states:

Any suicide attempt entails a calculated risk. Because it takes place in a psychosocial context, survival may depend upon resources for rescue as well as upon the specific form of the attempt. Jumping off a relatively high bridge into the water has about the same level of risk whether it is done at 3 o'clock in the afternoon or 3 o'clock in the morning. However, the possibilities for rescue are reduced in the early morning hours when darkness may obscure the act and fewer people are around to effect a rescue. (p. 140)

Thus a suicide attempt can be rated according to the degree of *risk* in the method used (e.g., sleeping pills or a gun) and the likelihood of *rescue*, the chances that someone would have stopped the person from carrying out the suicide.

Worden and other suicidologists contend that the *lethality* dimension — that is, whether or not death will occur following an attempt — can be assessed by the risk-rescue rating. Worden and his group studied 40 patients who had made suicidal attempts. The researchers calculated risk-rescue scores and then attempted to determine whether prodromal symptoms or personality factors were related to high lethality scores among these patients. In contrasting high lethal and low lethal attempters, Worden says:

> If we construct a composite picture contrasting persons who made high-level lethal attempts with persons who made low-level lethal attempts, we find that high-level attempts are associated with persons who had expected serious injury or death from the attempt. These persons had few friends and showed a lifelong difficulty in getting along with others. Any relationships they had could be defined as mutually destructive. A mental illness history, sometimes with accompanying psychosis, was frequently present. Homicidal thoughts, impulses, and frequent outbursts of rage were often found. Often they were the only or oldest child coming from a small family. (p. 153)

PRODROMAL SYMPTOMS OF ADOLESCENT SUICIDE Because the actual act of suicide has only one symptom — self-destruction — we will examine symptoms that are shown prior to suicide or suicide attempts. These *prodromal* symptoms are based mainly on clinical data gathered from suicide investigations in general, not just adolescent suicides.

The majority of persons who commit suicide give a number of warnings. First, approximately eight out of ten suicides make threats or attempt suicide (Shneidman and Farberow 1965). Second, it has been reported that once an individual has decided to commit suicide, he or she may become very withdrawn (Shneidman 1976). In addition to these two prodromal signs, the person intent on suicide often begins to give away his or her possessions, a sign of resignation and hopelessness about the future.

Although most of the clues to suicide have emerged from investigations of adult male suicides, a few of these conditions may also warn of adolescent suicide potential: (1) crippling physical disability; (2) early rejection by the father; (3) heavy drug use; (4) verbal statements about one's own worthlessness or the absence of hope or purpose in life; and (5) major setbacks or failures in social, academic, or family affairs. We discussed etiological theories of suicide in the earlier chapter on depression and suicide; see chapter 8 for causes and stressors.

TREATMENT AND SUICIDE PREVENTION In the chapter on affective disorders we discussed therapies aimed at ameliorating depression. In addition to those methods, specific therapies may be employed with an adolescent who has threatened to kill himself or herself, or who has actually attempted suicide. *Family therapy* is often suggested for a suicidal adolescent. It is a group psychotherapeutic procedure that assumes the family is the patient. The suicidal adolescent is seen as the symptom-bearer of pathology in the family. Thus, the mother, father, siblings, and the suicidal individual are seen together by a therapist. Family sessions are principally aimed at identifying stressors that provoke the threats or attempts. Communication patterns among the members are clarified, and new coping techniques are explored.

Crisis intervention in suicide provides immediate psychological help. The rationale for crisis intervention is based on the idea that people can face situational stress so great that help and support are needed as soon as possible. Korchin (1976) gives these immediate goals of crisis intervention:

1. To relieve present distress, e.g., anxiety, confusion, and hopelessness;

ALTERED STATES OF CONSCIOUSNESS: SUICIDE AND FEELING OF REBIRTH

SAN FRANCISCO (UPI)—Six of ten known survivors of suicidal leaps from the Golden Gate and Bay bridges said they sensed spiritual rebirth during the fall, according to a psychiatrist who interviewed them.

Dr. David H. Rosen of the Langley Porter Neuropsychiatric Institute said that persons who would not try to take their lives elsewhere would leap from the famous spans.

One survivor, whose experience Rosen discussed in the Western Journal of Medicine, said of the leap:

"I felt like a bird flying—total relief. In my mind I was getting away from one realm and into another. Even now I'm still symbolically looking for the better world—I'm still in that place between the bridge and the water."

2. To restore the client or patient to previous level of functioning;
3. To help the client, his or her family, or other related person in learning what personal actions are possible and the community resources available;
4. To understand the relation of the existing crisis with past crises and problems; and,
5. To develop new attitudes, behaviors, and coping skills (adapted from Korchin, 1976, p. 507).

In crisis intervention, support must be given immediately. Often the telephone will play a major role in suicide prevention, since some who are going to commit suicide or attempt to commit suicide will first call a suicide prevention center. Most of these centers operate 24 hours a day and have a "hot line." The caller most often speaks with a highly trained volunteer or professional. The staff person generally attempts to maintain contact with the caller, finding out as much information as possible, assessing the "lethality" of the threat, and also assessing the caller's reasons for wanting to commit suicide. In addition to telephone hot lines, some centers have emergency teams who drive immediately to crisis situations to deter or aid the person

attempting suicide (Fox 1976). Some have suggested that England's declining suicide rate is partly a consequence of numerous suicide prevention services in that country.

DRUG PROBLEMS OF ADOLESCENCE

In chapter 10, we discussed alcoholism and drug abuse, including such major issues as excessive use, physiological dependence, psychological dependence, and definitions of addiction and abuse. Here we will expand on certain points made earlier as they specifically relate to adolescence.

It is common knowledge that many adolescents are using alcohol and other drugs. It is difficult, however, to determine whether this great interest and use are an expression of a desire to enhance life and expand consciousness, or to restrict awareness and obscure reality. The wide variety of drugs used by adolescents suggests that there is no single motive for their use. Stimulant drugs can be used for increasing alertness and endurance, for recreation, or for easing social situations. Other substances have a deadening effect, filtering out much of the noise and stress of life. Still other compounds can give the user a new and exciting perception of ordinary and trivial things. One 17-year-old user said that he would ingest LSD, then go to his garage and stare in fascination for hours at an ordinary crack in the garage floor. Various clinicians and researchers have even suggested that using drugs in general provides the individual with a "purpose" and identity (Cuskey & Edington 1975). Finally, drugs may be taken by adolescents to lessen psychological pain, inspire artistic ability, or end a life.

FREQUENCY OF ADOLESCENT DRUG USE In a study using a large sample (1,094) of high school students, the following incidence of drug use was reported by Gould and colleagues (1977):
- 75 percent had used alcohol.
- 50 percent had used marijuana.
- 33 percent had used hashish.
- 18 percent had used amphetamines.
- 12 percent had usd LSD.
- 6 percent had used cocaine.

The Gould study also noted that multiple or sequential drug use was widespread in this student sample. Approximately 58 percent had used two different drugs; 44 percent had used three or more.

SYMPTOMS OF DRUG ABUSE   No single representative set of symptoms exists for the misuse of drugs. *Physiological withdrawal* can indicate addiction, but certain substances such as marijuana and cocaine do not produce common withdrawal signs. Thus, in many cases the yardstick for unadaptive use of drugs is *psychological dependency* (see chapter 10).

It is important to note that drug use or drug abuse among adolescents is often a transitory affair rather than a chronic pattern. With the exception of marijuana, use of drugs is temporary for adolescents and younger adults.

For some adolescents, various substances can bring about or amplify abnormal behavior. For instance, cocaine, a derivative of coca leaves, is a stimulant that produces alertness, muscular vigor, feelings of euphoria, and suppression of appetite. But in addition to these symptoms, prolonged cocaine users can develop *cocaine psychosis*, an acute paranoid schizophrenia. (Snyder 1974). However, many believe that an individual's premorbid personality — his or her response style prior to the ingestion of the chemical — contributes profoundly to the psychopathology. The *private meaning* of the drug experience is also defined and determined by social circumstances and the setting in which the drug is taken (Weil 1972; Lennard et al. 1972).

In a study contrasting high-dose methamphetamine ("speed") abusers with psychedelic abusers (LSD), it was reported that "speed freaks" tend to be violent and physically aggressive whereas "acidheads" tend to be nonviolent and rather passive (Smith 1969). The differences between these two groups are attributed to personality characteristics prior to drug use (premorbid personality); that is, individuals who are inclined to be violent would also be more inclined to use methamphetamines.

Suicide is also related to drug abuse. Menninger and many other clinicians have suggested that drug abuse is a form of suicide — a chronic suicide. As noted in a previous section, alcoholism and drug abuse may be prodromal clues to suicide. Suicide rates among narcotic addicts, for instance, are 20 to 50 times greater than among the general population (Glatt et al. 1967).

Just as it has been suggested that people with certain personality characteristics seek special types of drugs, it has also been reported that most suicides among drug abusers typically involve certain drugs, the *soporifics* (sleep-inducing agents) — opiates, barbiturates, and alcohol (Cus-

Paul Sequiera, Rapho/Photo Researchers

Certain individuals can attain a degree of prestige, status, and identity by taking drugs.

key & Edington 1975). We should point out that many drugs other than the soporifics can result in death, but apparently many users of LSD, heroin, and amphetamines do not have the intention of dying. (Cuskey and Edington believe that most heroin overdoses are accidental. Overdoses of barbiturates, however, would signal intentionality.) Cuskey and Edington assert, in fact, that alcohol and barbiturate use may encourage some people to commit suicide. Chronic barbiturate use can be viewed as "slow suicide." Cuskey and Edington (1975) state:

> Slow suicide, in effect, need not be total death; it may be temporary surcease, sleep, or relaxed intoxication; or unconsciousness taken to the borderline of death. . . . (p. 150)

Thus, the characteristic sensations of the soporifics — sleep, drowsiness, and annihilation of thought — phenomenologically resemble death much more than the characteristic sensations of heroin or amphetamines.

CAUSES AND STRESSORS   Cuskey and Edington (1975) provide an excellent list of possible reasons why young people may use and abuse drugs. They suggest, first, the possibility of *risk-taking motive*. Drugs are often taken for the thrill and danger involved. In a related sense, drugs can be taken in the pursuit of novelty and drama (Lennard et al. 1972). Second, drug use may reflect a *courting of death*. This is the view that drug use is a subclinical or subintentional expression of the desire to die. Third, drug use may provide the user with *control over life;* that is, being able to "turn on" provides the user with a feeling of mastery and control. Drug use can fill the void in an adolescent's life by giving him or her a new identity or role. A degree of prestige and status may even be attached to the drug-taking identity (Cuskey & Edington 1975). Fourth, drugs are used as a *coping strategy*. Anxiety, tension, depression, and other uncomfortable sensations can be temporarily obliterated by the effects of drugs.

Another motivation in drug use is the individual's desire for intimacy and companionship (Lennard et al. 1972). Adolescents with deficits of interpersonal skills may find that using drugs creates the impression that they are socially adept. For those with these expectations, drugs can generate feelings of warmth and closeness to others, but there are disadvantages in bypassing the learning of social skills. Lennard and his colleagues put it this way:

> When one attains intimacy by means of drugs, one by-passes the usual phases of relationships and interaction that occur on the road to true intimacy. . . . The pseudo-intimacy established with drugs is likely to vanish with the elimination of the drug. . . . (p. 50)

Treatments for alcoholism and other forms of drug abuse are discussed in chapter 10.

OTHER ADOLESCENT ONSET PROBLEMS

In this concluding section, we will present two general problems of adolescence that are described and discussed in the new DSM-III. Although clinicians have reported behavior problems similar to these two reactions, thus far only the DSM-III has assigned them status as a "disorder."

IDENTITY DISORDER

DSM-III states that the major feature of this problematic reaction is the adolescent's uncertainty about his or her identity, and most important for diagnosis, severe subjective distress regarding this uncertainty. Identity is viewed in general terms in this disorder: identity deals with issues such as "Who am I?" "What am I going to do with my life?" "By what values and standards should I live?" and many similar issues.

William Glasser, a psychiatrist and founder of reality therapy, wrote a book called *The Identity Society* (1972) that deals with many identity issues.

Glasser maintains that most young people in our society no longer strive for goals as younger people in past generations had. Rather, today "roles" are sought before "goals." To illustrate this contrast, Glasser says that "almost everyone is personally engaged in a search for acceptance as a person rather than as a performer of a task" (p. 10). Unfortunately for many of us, it is not "who we are" that counts, but rather "what we do for a living." Our identity is inordinately tied to our occupational role, a role that, to say the least, is vulnerable.

Thus, adolescents often experience profound distress over the tasks of making a career choice because there is uncertainty about what these careers are really like, and over whether or not they have access into educational prerequisites for these careers. The DSM-III says a problem may become "chronic" if the person is unable to establish a career commitment or if, on another dimension, he or she fails to form lasting emotional attachments because of shifts in jobs and interpersonal relationships.

THE BLACKBOARD JUNGLE © 1955, Metro-Goldwyn-Mayer. Antisocial behavior in adolescents is not necessarily a sign of sociopathy. A delinquent often exhibits antisocial behavior as an expression of emancipation from dependence and as an identity tactic. Such behavior is clearly seen in this film.

EMANCIPATION DISORDER

The new DSM-III states that the chief feature of this new syndrome is great difficulty in separating emotionally from parental supervision and control and becoming able to make independent decisions. It can occur either in adolescents or young adults. The DSM-III gives these operational criteria for the *emancipation syndrome.*

1. Recent assumption of a situation in which the patient is more independent of parental control or supervision.
2. The patient regards the change as desirable.
3. Symptomatic expression of a conflict over independence is manifested by two or more of the following:
   a. Difficulty in making independent decisions commensurate with a new situation.
   b. Increased dependence on parental advice.
   c. Newly developed and unwarranted concern about parental possessiveness.
   d. Adoption of values deliberately in opposition to those of parents.
   e. Rapid development of markedly dependent peer relationships.
   f. Homesickness that the individual finds inconsistent with a conscious wish to be away from home.
4. The condition is not secondary to any other mental disorder.

J. Berndt/Stock, Boston

One of the significant stressors for adolescents is finding meaningful roles in society. Lack of access to status positions, according to sociologists like Robert Merton, often results in problem behaviors.

To an extent, the *emancipation disorder* resembles the "borderline syndrome," which we discussed earlier in this chapter. Haley (1973) calls these dependent, overattached adolescents "peripheral people." They are not yet complete individuals, for they have not really learned to separate or detach from their parents. The analyst Marget Mahler asserts that a major stressor for children and adolescents is learning to separate and be relatively independent from their parents. Mahler sees this separation as a major step in the process of individuation and identity as an adult (Mahler, Pine, Bergman 1975). To describe the emancipation syndrome briefly: it seems that, for these people, any major break with the parents that signals the beginning of independence results in anxiety, depression, and similar reactions. For example, going away to college, moving away to start a new job, joining the service, or even getting married may trigger the symptoms. Such experiences and reactions certainly are common, however, and it should be stressed that these symptoms do not constitute a mental disorder. Etiological theories and treatment methods are not offered for these newly appointed syndromes because of the meager experimental research data dealing with these topics. In fact, it is anticipated that many researchers and clinicians will not view these last "disorders" as highly pathological or abnormal. It will probably be argued that identity and emancipation problems are more akin to "crises" or "stages" than to disorders.

SUMMARY

1. Adolescence is a stage of development that takes place between the chronological ages of 10 and 20 and is generally associated with characteristic behaviors, social circumstances, physiological changes, and rather characteristic abnormal behaviors.
2. *Anorexia nervosa* is an abnormal behavior usually associated with adolescence. Its major symptoms are a marked reduction in food intake, great loss of weight, and distorted body image. Anorexia nervosa occurs in approximately one adolescent in 100,000. Approximately 95 percent of the anorectic individuals are females. There are numerous theories proposed that attempt to account for this syndrome: the disorder has been associated with a type of pathological dependency (the borderline syndrome); others speculate that the pathological abstinence is actually a form of subintentional or subclinical suicide; finally, a few studies have found an association between some anorectic persons and a chromosome dysfunction called Turner's syndrome (XO configuration). No particular treatment for this syndrome has been shown to be consistently effective. Many different therapeutic strategies have been employed, but thus far, none seems to stand out as highly effective.
3. *Bulimia*, like anorexia nervosa, is an eating disorder associated with adolescence. This syndrome is characterized by voracious, episodic eating binges, followed usually by guilt and depression over unrestrained eating. Additionally, there is apprehension and anxiety that one will not be able to control the impulse to eat. Weight gain may occur, and the individual will overreact and become hypersensitive to minor changes in

weight. No particular prevalence has been stated for bulimia, but DSM-III states that this disorder is not uncommon in adolescent females. No formalized etiological theory has been provided. Moreover, no systematized and consistently effective treatment strategies have been reported at this time.

4. Although the probability of suicide increases rather markedly in middle and old age, adolescence is still a period of some risk. The term *life-threatening behavior* (LTB) was used in this chapter to refer to a special group of behaviors less lethal than suicide. Intoxication, reckless driving, heavy drug use, starvation diets, and other risky activities have been categorized as LTBs. Suicide is the fourth leading cause of death among people between 15 and 19 and appears to be increasing in this age group. Exact figures for the number of suicides committed are unavailable for one main reason: it is difficult if not impossible to determine intent in many instances. In many cases, however, motives can be assessed by a *psychological autopsy*. This is an assessment tool that resembles an interview; relatives who knew the deceased are questioned about factors that may reflect the deceased's wish to die. For instance, heavy drug use and depression may signal the possibility that the individual could have taken his or her life. The *prodromal symptoms* (early warning signs) of suicide may include such things as heavy drug use, ver-bal statements of worthlessness, major setbacks such as social or academic failures. If the potential suicide is identified in time, often family therapy, individual therapy, or crisis intervention (which would often lead to these therapies) may dissuade the person from ending his or her life.

5. Drug abuse during adolescence is a major problem. A few studies have suggested that drug use or multiple or sequential drug use is widespread. The causes of drug use and abuse are numerous and speculative at best. It has been suggested that drug use or abuse may represent some of the following motives: risk-taking, courting of death, controlling or coping with life. Other theorists propose that drugs may be used to enhance intimacy and companionship, or to appear to cover up one's interpersonal deficits.

6. In addition to several other adolescent problems, the new DSM-III discusses *identity disorder* and *emancipation disorder*. The identity disorder is characterized by distress over decisions regarding career choice, friendship patterns, and values in general. Often this is coupled with failure to complete tasks. In the emancipation disorder the adolescent or young person experiences great distress over having to make independent decisions. The person may become more dependent on parental advice, but paradoxically overconcerned about their possessiveness.

Glasser, W. *The identity society.* New York: Harper & Row, 1972.

Guardo, C. J. *The adolescent as individual: Issues and insights.* New York: Harper & Row, 1975.

Haley, J. *Uncommon therapy.* New York: Ballantine, 1973.

Lennard, H. L. et al. *Mystification and drug misuse.* New York: Perennial Library, 1972.

Shneidman, E. S. *Suicidology: Contemporary developments.* New York: Grune & Stratton, 1976.

RECOMMENDED READINGS

18

ABNORMAL BEHAVIORS ASSOCIATED WITH THE FAMILY

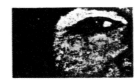

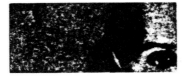
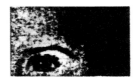

OVERVIEW In this chapter, we will examine issues related to abnormal behavior and the family. Our main thrust will be directed at describing a rather new area of abnormal psychology: one that describes psychopathology in the context of the family.

The chapter will begin with a brief historical view of the family: how early families began, functions of the family, and how families are changing will be examined. Part of this background section will also discuss the life cycle of a family.

The second section of this chapter will describe characteristics of dysfunctional or abnormal families. Part of this general discussion will consider topics such as child abuse with subtopics on the battered child syndrome and sexually abusive families. The chapter will conclude with a general discussion on family and group therapies.

THE FAMILY

HISTORICAL PERSPECTIVES

Attributing our social problems and individual psychopathologies to the family is nothing new. Philosophers, statesmen, the Bible, and other sources of authority have argued that the family environment determines the offspring's behavior. At one time it was fashionable in sociology to view the family as an organism susceptible to disease and dysfunction (Laing & Esterson 1970). At other times the influence of family environment was minimized. Freud, for example, stressed the importance of particular experiences with a given parent or a particular traumatic episode, but discounted the dynamic influence of the family entity on abnormal behavior. Gradually there emerged a renewed interest in the family as a chief stressor in individual development. Historically, perhaps the first widely known theorist to emphasize the significance of the family experience on psychopathology was the psychoanalyst Alfred Adler. Adler noted that a child's *birth order* (oldest, middle, or youngest) influenced his or her personality development. He asserted, for example, that because of particular parenting styles and interactions among siblings, the first-born was inclined to be more deviant than later-born siblings. Adler also suggested that alcoholics, neurotics, and sexual deviants were more often first-born, but later studies failed to support his idea (Hall & Lindzey 1978). Nevertheless, Adler and other theorists created a new interest in the family as one stressor that induces psychopathology.

This relatively new area, one that considers psychological dysfunctions within the framework of the family, has been called "family process," "family dynamics," and "family therapy." Again, the main thrust of this perspective is that abnormal behavior is best conceived and managed within an organizational system. In the extreme sense, this viewpoint sees the family as the patient and the vehicle by which behavior change is to be accomplished.

Later we will consider dysfunctional families and individual psychopathologies that relate to the family. To provide perspective, we will first look at the possible origin and functions of the family.

FAMILY BEGINNINGS

The human family existed in prehistory. Like other higher mammals, humans who banded together into groups had a much greater chance of surviving as individuals and sustaining the species. Chances of gratifying the human biological needs to get food, secure shelter, and find a mate were enhanced by living with large clusters of people. No one knows exactly the composition of those early families. What seems reasonable is that a father was not always present or an essential element in the early family (Tiger & Fox 1971). Although the adult male's contribution to impregnation was obviously necessary (though not necessarily understood), after impregnation the father was dispensable if other adult humans were present to provide care for dependent members. What was essential for the early families was the banding together of adults, probably blood relatives, to protect the mother-child unit. Those early families were probably *extended families*. That is, the family was composed of brothers, sisters, a mother, a father, and probably aunts, uncles, and grandparents. It is unlikely that the *nuclear family* (mother, father, and offspring) was the most typical type because, as we have stated, the father was dispensable. Only in recent times has the nuclear family flourished. The anthropologists Lionel Tiger and Robin Fox make this point:

> It is nonsense to assume that the only kind of "parental" bond possible in the human species is between sexual partners. There is another bond more fundamental in some ways, and just as logical—the bond between brother and sister. This is an asexual bond that grows up over the years and is in some sense ready-made for the task of parental care. It does not involve the setting up of a new and risky contractual relationship, but can draw on already existing trust and deeply developed obligations. In some human societies, the weight of responsibility for a woman and her children rests with her brothers. Her sex life is separate from her parental role. (Tiger and Fox 1971, p. 70)

The family then, appears to have developed, in part, to care for the mother-child bond, with or without the father.

FAMILY FUNCTIONS

A family is more than just a group of people living together. Most psychologists, anthropologists, and sociologists note that it has a number of functions. For instance, Howells (1975) suggests that authorities generally agree on these functions: (1) to satisfy affectional needs of family members; (2) to provide a socially sanctioned setting for gratification of sexual desires and reproduction; (3) to protect and care for dependent members; and (4) to transmit society's values and the culture to the offspring.

Before we elaborate on family functions and how they have changed, it must be stressed that little empirical data exist concerning exactly how families operate and whether the members of the family are content with the effectiveness of this unit for fulfilling the functions. Therefore the findings of family studies must be interpreted with care. In addition, family studies are beset with methodological problems that preclude the making of definite statements about the family's role in causing psychopathologies.

The function of the family seems to have changed markedly in the last hundred years or so, and it is continuing to change. In fact, some critics of the family argue that this unit is ineffectual and destructive and that changes will ultimately be beneficial (Cooper 1970). Except for reproduction and a sanctioned location for sexual contact, the family continues to decline in many of the roles and activities it once performed (Peacock & Kirsch 1970; Williams & Wirths 1965). The typical family unit of the past was quite self-sufficient and autonomous in most areas. Many families could maintain themselves without the assistance of schools, churches, factories, corporations, or governmental agencies. Most importantly, each member of the family was almost always an indispensable component. Offspring were of great economic benefit, since adolescents and even very young children provided essential labor. Autonomy, dependency on one another, and cooperation highlighted many of these families. The members were not necessarily happy and content with their role and structured time in these autonomous groups,

but the pre-industrial, pre-urban family was durable and stable.

Obviously, much has changed. In industrialized-urban areas, family members have become comparatively dispensable. Children rarely make significant economic contributions as they once did. Work is done outside the home, rather than within the family unit. The educating function of the parents has clearly been displaced by schools. Over the last 50 years various social and governmental programs have been developed that in one way or another have replaced or lessened the need for family functions, thus reducing the members' contribution. With both parents working in many cases, their functions have become much more abstract than before. Regarding the importance of education and socialization, Peacock and Kirsch (1970) describe the function loss of parents with these words:

> [The] family in modern society has decreased its contribution to the education of the child—just about the only important function still served by the modern family. Children enter nursery school at an increasingly early age. Eventually, the task of educating the child for an unknown future may simply prove too much for the parents, and the child's education may be placed fully in the hands of specialized and bureaucratized organizations. . . . The parent might then be merely a pal, entrusting the difficult task of educating the child in skills, knowledge, character, and ethics to the experts. (p. 287)

There is no empirical evidence that loss of family functioning leads directly or indirectly to individual psychopathology. It may be appealing to suggest that weakening family ties and role loss of parents and adolescents can engender individual psychopathologies, but there is no hard evidence to substantiate this line of thought.

In the following section we shall consider dysfunctional families. It is often argued that dysfunctional families induce abnormal behavior in their offspring, but few theories have been proposed that explain why there are dysfunctional families. Could declining family function have any bearing on dysfunctional families? If the answer is yes, then it would have to be explained why there are dysfunctional families and healthy families. The notion of declining family function applies to all families, not just dysfunctional ones. Dysfunctional families do indeed have problems carrying out certain functions, but this may be because the parents themselves are suffering from psychopathology. Thus, more research describing differences between healthy and unhealthy families will have to be conducted before the role of declining family function can be evaluated with any degree of accuracy.

THE FAMILY LIFE CYCLE

Just as the individual follows a life cycle of growth and decline, so does the family (Haley 1973; Howells 1975; Glick 1977). Glick (1977) mentions these stages: marriage, birth of first and last child, marriage of last child, and death of one spouse. Haley has listed six similar stages we will examine: courtship, marriage, childbirth and rearing, middle marriage, weaning, and retirement and old age. As we will see, Haley also describes particular stressors and problems that correspond to each of the six stages.

The *courtship* stage involves behaviors involved in securing a marriage partner or mate. Haley suggests that a particular type of individual may find the courtship period extremely stressful because he or she lacks emotional independence from the parents. For instance, a young adult who has never become sufficiently independent from his or her family does not select a mate; rather, the mate is indirectly selected by the family. Haley writes:

> Even when young people select mates out of spite because their parents oppose the choice, they are still caught up in the parental involvement, because the choice is not an independent one. What was once thought of as a "neurotic choice of partners" evidently involves a family decision process. (p. 30)

Marriage is the second stage, and it introduces all sorts of possible stressors. Perhaps the most important one is *disillusionment*. Disillusionment simply means that a person has expectations that are unmet after the marriage has existed for a while. That is, a newly married person may discover that things are not as he or she imagined. Indeed, love, escape from parents, and idealism corrupt rational decision making about the mate (Putney & Putney 1972). Many newlyweds, particularly those who

marry to escape from troubled homes, often blow out of proportion the positive features they believe their mate possesses. Haley states that "[young] people who marry largely to escape from their families may find, once they are married, that the reason for their marriage has disappeared" (p. 32).

In connection with Haley's point, Mueller and Pope (1977) found that women from families that were intact (no divorces) tended to marry low-risk mates. That is, these women married older males, those having higher social status, and those not previously divorced. In a real sense, these women were not "running" from their families; thus their selection of mates was rational. Mueller and Pope also mentioned what is referred to as the *transmission hypothesis*. This hypothesis suggests that disruptive marital behaviors are learned and transmitted from parents to children. The children in turn will be more likely to engage in family disruptions and produce unstable marriages. Mueller and Pope (1977) explain that "parental marital instability leads to high-risk mate selection outcomes for the children, which in turn results in their higher marital dissolution rates" (p. 91).

The third period in the life cycle of a family is *childbirth and rearing*. As Haley notes, the birth of a child creates many new roles: mother, father, grandparents, uncles, and aunts. Most importantly, the birth may create new problems as the mates start to evaluate each other's effectiveness in their new roles. For example, prior to the birth, the "husband" may be evaluated by his wife in terms of how much fun he is or how easy he is to get along with; but after the birth the "father" now has to prove himself according to new standards. The "wife," now a "mother," must also meet new expectations. Haley points out that following the birth of a child, many women develop psychiatric symptoms such as depression because of shifts in roles and expectations. He gives an example of a women in her twenties who became very depressed shortly after the birth of her first child. She experienced bouts of persistent weeping, feelings of worthlessness, and other symptoms. Ordinarily, one might look at this woman's background to explain the depression, or hypothesize some biochemical imbalance, but from the family perspective this is not the approach. Instead, she would be considered in the context of her family, in particular, in her relationships with her husband and the birth of her child. Haley describes the husband and his role in precipitating her depression.

He was an amiable young man who appeared reluctant to leave his original family and take on adult responsibilities. He worked for his father, and he seemed unable to oppose his mother and support his wife when an issue came up. By becoming incapacitated, the wife had forced her husband to take more responsibility in the marriage. (p. 158)

This case hints at an important assumption: that emotional illness or psychopathology often adds stability to a family unit. We shall demonstrate later that ultimately this process is unadaptive.

For Haley, the major potential stressor of the childbirth and rearing stage occurs when the child starts school. The child is beginning slowly to drift away from the parents, becoming a bit more autonomous. For some parents, this budding independence can be a problem. Another problem is that the family now has the child on "display." He or she, in a sense, acts as a family "representative," and difficulties at school over the child's misbehavior for instance, can create family dissension about how to raise children. At this stage, often one parent begins to side with the child over difficulties the child is having. Haley suggests that some families have difficulty in getting past this stage. That is, they continue to interact in a triangle: mother and child against father, or vice versa.

The fourth period in the family life cycle is *middle age*. Howells (1975) calls this stage in the life cycle the *phase of consolidation*, and while it may be a time of pleasure, many problems occur. Howells lists some possible concerns during this stage: general difficulties with adolescents, emerging sexual behavior of the children, high earning power required of the parents to support the children, and clashes with the growing children on values.

Power struggles also characterize this period. For example, Haley says, "a wife wants her husband to be more dominating—but she'd like him to dominate her the way she tells him to" (p. 190). Ackerman (1970) gives us one illustration of a middle-age family with a deviant adolescent whose behavior, according to Ackerman, is a consequence of a power struggle.

If mother said white, father said black. Father terrorized mother with his explosive tantrums. She in turn took vengeance in sly, covert ways. She emasculated him. She declared openly for years that he was under-

sexed. She allied both boys (adolescents) with her against father; she made it three against one. The father felt rejected and exiled. He then turned about to become seductive with his younger son, John. He carried on an open flirtation with him. John became the second woman for his father, substituting for mother. Mother in turn trained her older son, Henry, to be her fighting arm against father. (p. 89)

The boy, John, obviously had developed concerns over his own heterosexuality, a reflection, according to the family perspective, of family discord.

Again, we must stress that family theorists insist that the family is vulnerable to all sorts of outside stressors. Economic problems, for instance, can disturb interactions among family members, which in turn may result in individual emotional difficulties. We shall examine this point later.

The fifth stage is the *weaning stage* (Haley 1973). Howells (1975) calls this period the *phase of contraction*. Regardless of the name one uses, this period is described similarly by many theorists. It is a time characterized by a loss of involvement with children, a need for new interests by the wife, and, if the family is fortunate, new prosperity (Howells 1975).

In chapter 17, we mentioned the concept of the *borderline syndrome* (Masterson 1972). The major symptoms of this syndrome is a pronounced conflict between an adolescent's yearning for independence and autonomy and his or her fear of parental abandonment. (DSM-III calls this problem the emancipation disorder.) This same conflict often is observed in certain parents as their children grow up and leave home. Indeed, being weaned from one's children is a difficult task, and for some parents it creates major problems. Haley (1973) describes this weaning stage and the problems it often brings:

Sometimes the turmoil between parents comes when the oldest child leaves home, while in other families the disturbances seems to become progressively worse as each child leaves, and in others as the youngest is about to go. In many cases, parents who have watched their children leave one by one without difficulty suddenly have difficulty when one particular child reaches that age. In such cases, the child has usually been of special importance in the marriage. He may have been the one through whom the parents carried on most

AGGRESSION AND CHILDREN OF DIVORCE

When a woman is divorced and charged with raising an adolescent male (who soon may become the new "man of the house"), Tooley (1976) suggests that shortly after the father actually leaves the family begins a *post-divorce* period. This post-divorce period is a time of great stress. She writes:

> The children are angry at the father for leaving, and angry at the mother for "making him leave." They can infuriate her by idealizing him, which in turn makes them wonder if she might "divorce" them also.

Tooley also suggests that in this post-divorce period antisocial behavior, especially overt aggression, often surfaces. It is maintained that many of these divorced women have been unaccustomed to being aggressive in dealing with frustrations and situations that call for assertion. For example, she may now find that she is required to be assertive in dealing with a repair-man who has not done his job adequately. But Tooley claims that after the divorce her young son takes on the burden of being the aggressor on behalf of his family.

But this young boy's response to his mother's frustration is misdirected. Rather than specifically dealing with the repairman, for example, the boy displays his aggressive reaction in antisocial acts against the neighbors, teachers, and other outsiders.

Taking a slight digression, we should point out that the only child of a divorced mother often fares much more poorly than do children having siblings (Kelley and Wallerstein 1977). Seemingly, emotional difficulties and antisocial behavior, of the sort mentioned above, may be less if a child has other siblings to support him or her in the post-divorce period. Nevertheless, some evidence supports the notion that divorce may be a factor in producing antisocial behavior in the offspring.

---

of their communication with each other, or the one they felt most burdened by and were held together in their common concern and care for him.

A marital difficulty that may emerge at this time is that the parents find they have nothing to say to each other and nothing to share. They have not talked to each other about anything except the children for years. (pp. 42, 47)

Thus, it should be noted that a son or daughter may represent a "negative bond" that has held the parents and family together for years (Abrams & Kaslow 1977). Yet ultimately that son or daughter will leave home. Apparently the departure of a child can be interpreted by the parents as a sort of "death." In this case they would go through a period of grief. Or the departure, as Haley notes above, could unmask hidden conflicts.

Cooper (1970), Richter (1974), and other family theorists, as we have noted, believe that some parents and some families stifle the growth of their progeny because of a symbiotic attachment. Richter (1974), for instance, suggests that particular families "have to turn one or another of their members into a failure [the victim develops a psychopathology] in order to put an end to the tension [the daughter or son's growth] within the group" (p. 54). This interesting notion of "scapegoating" will be reviewed again in the section on dysfunctional families. Children, then, can reduce family discord by remaining dependent upon the family. Clearly, however, this would not occur if the family were the sort that encouraged autonomy and independence in its members.

Retirement and old age is the final stage in the life cycle of the family. We will mention this stage here only briefly because aging and retirement are the central subjects of chapter 19.

In 1965, Richard Williams and Claudine Wirths published a volume called *Lives Through the Years*. This investigation examined the lives of 168 elderly women and men over a period of five and a half years. Among other things, they delineated six coping life styles used by the elderly. They are (1) world of work, (2) familism, (3) living alone, (4) couplehood, (5) easing through life, and (6) living fully. Each of these styles has successful and unsuccessful examples. Here we will just mention familism as a style that relates to families and their functions.

Although we noted earlier that the family as a unit is losing many of its functions, Williams and Wirth found that almost a third of the elderly people they studied adopted *familism* as a means of coping. They define this style in terms of decisions the person makes. If familism is the style, the person makes all of his or her decisions in relation to the family. The predominant values center on the family, and this person spends, in general, almost all of his or her time with children, siblings, or parents.

The least successful older persons described by Williams and Wirth were always dependent, with varying degrees of emotional stability. The most successful ones, by contrast, were described as autonomous and independent. The least successful who adopted the familism style were preoccupied by relations with their mothers and fathers (if living), daughters, sons, siblings, and so forth. They describe a classic case of familism in an aging mother:

> Lack of success in aging is illustrated by the case of the anxious mother, who was becoming increasingly dependent on a relationship with her young son. This is a major reason for lack of success in aging and in life in general. When the aging person depends on another, the control of the aged

one's life space is placed in the hands of another person who may or may not contribute action energy that is appropriate or acceptable from the standpoint of the ager. In this instance, the mother, by needing to give to the child, was demanding more action energy from him than he was willing or able to give as time passed. As he matured, he did not want to have her continue to give to him, and he was unwilling to respond with action energy that permitted her to give him more and more. Thus, when anyone absolutely must have a large amount of energy put into his action system to maintain him, and that energy is not forthcoming, for whatever reason, he is at once in a precarious state, which, if not remedied, may result in total personal disorganization. (p. 165)

We should point out that familism would rarely be unadaptive if our culture stressed the maintenance of extended families (families composed of a variety of persons—mother, father, grandparents, aunts, uncles, children, etc.). Since mobility and weakened family ties are current realities, however, nuclear families prevail.

DYSFUNCTIONAL FAMILIES

Family theorists often make these assumptions regarding the family and psychopathology:

1. The family can become dysfunctional or ''sick.''
2. The family, by analyzing transactions and interactions among its members, is a fruitful setting for studying abnormal behavior.
3. An individual (the symptom-bearer) may become emotionally disturbed to keep the family together or in its state of equilibrium.
4. The family, as a group, can be treated with psychotherapeutic techniques.

THE STUDY OF FAMILY PATHOLOGY

The first assumption—that a family can become dysfunctional—is the major structure on which this

chapter is based. Although little empirical evidence exists, many clinical studies have been conducted that provide us with some understanding of this new area for studying abnormal behavior. The trend in clinical psychology has been to focus on classifying, attempting to determine etiology, and trying to treat *individual* abnormal reactions. Recently, however, clinical psychology has broadened to include study of healthy and abnormal families.

We will examine several different family studies. One in particular, conducted by Lewis and colleagues (1976), was a seven-year project aimed principally at finding characteristics of healthy families. Detailed interviews and videotapes of 44 families were done. This study suggests characteristic differences between pathological and optimal family systems. The families studied in the Lewis investigation were placed in one of three categories according to psychological health: *se-*

verely disturbed families, *mid-range or mildly dysfunctional* families, and *optimal or healthy* families. For our purposes we will contrast only the severely disturbed and the healthy groups.

The psychological health of the families considered was measured in terms of five qualities that we will elaborate on: (1) power structure of the family; (2) degree of family individuation; (3) acceptance of separation and loss; (4) perception of reality; and (5) affect. In addition to discussing the Lewis study, we will touch on other investigations that deal with family stressors and dysfunctional family systems.

POWER STRUCTURE In a family, the *power structure* refers to who controls or dominates the family. Family power structures may be very difficult or very easy to detect. In some, no member may be clearly dominant or submissive, while in others, the power structure may clearly be in the hands of one member. In most of the severely disturbed families, the father has little power (Beavers 1976). The Lewis study, of which Beavers was a part, is not the first to report this finding. As we noted in earlier chapters, the dominant mother / weak father power structure has often been connected with alcoholism, homosexuality, and schizophrenia. More recent studies, however (e.g., Wild et al. 1977), have found that fathers of male schizophrenics were more dominant within their families than were the fathers of two control groups.

In contrast to the power structure observed in very dysfunctional families (those having schizophrenic offspring), some studies suggest that healthy families have a clear hierarchy of power, often with the father in a type of leading role. Theodore Lidz (1963), however, describes a family type called *marital skew*, in which one partner is inordinately dominant and overbearing. Lidz, a psychotherapist who works with schizophrenic patients and their families, claims that this pattern of power plays some role in precipitating pathological behavior in an offspring (schizophrenia in particular). Finally, Wild and colleagues (1977) noted that their control group families (presumably healthy families) had no clearly dominant members. This appears to be in marked contrast to several other earlier studies. But it could be that father-dominance is high in one group of families and low in another group because various research teams use different definitions of dominance. (Wild and colleagues used length of time talking as a measure of dominance.) Another possible expla-

nation for the discrepancies found in power is that there are many varieties of dysfunctional families.

FAILURE OF INDIVIDUATION The second quality measured in the families investigated was the *degree of individuation*—how much a family tolerates its members to be unique or become autonomous and independent. Lewis and his group suggest that the most severely disturbed families, in contrast to the mid-range dysfunctional and the healthy families, do not tolerate individuation. Simply put, individuation is not tolerated in severely dysfunctional families. Regarding this intolerance, Beavers (1974) concludes:

> The members of these disturbed families behave as if human closeness is found by thinking and feeling just like one another; therefore, individuation is tantamount to rejection and exclusion. (p. 58)

Luthman and Kirschenbaum (1974), describing a dysfunctional family type called the *repressive family*, make exactly this same point:

> The covert rule in the [repressive] family is that everyone must feel the same way about everything. Any expression of individuation will make other family members feel hurt and inadequate. (p. 160)

That is, the very disturbed families encourage conformity or sameness of emotional expression. Unique interpretations or independent thinking is discouraged. Indeed, a few theorists speculate that those who attempt to become independent and show their autonomy will be "ganged up on" by the family. Berke (1971), for example, suggests that the most healthy member of a disturbed family—the one attempting to assert his or her autonomy—often becomes the scapegoat or the "crazy" member of that family:

> Often, we find that a person who is labelled insane is the sanest member of his or her family. . . . The reason why the person will be labelled insane [by the family] is because he will be trying to escape from the "crazy" or disturbing relationship—the shared behavior patterns within the family. (pp. 275–276)

This quote again suggests intolerance of individuation—a family member's independent behaviors will be condemned and labeled as deviant by the family. In this usage, a family could label a member as "crazy" simply by discounting his or her behavior or, as Wild and colleagues (1977) found, by simply not talking very much to that person.

On the other hand, dysfunctional family behavior can be looked at in another way: rather than say that the family causes abnormal behavior in a particular member, it can be argued just as reasonably that the member provokes dysfunctional family behavior.

In healthy families, individuation is presumably encouraged, though little empirical data exist to support this claim. We observed in chapter 17 that secure and healthy parents can usually separate from their adolescent children without undue emotional traumas. To be sure, one of the critical developmental tasks for the growing child (and for the growing adult-parents) is to achieve individuation. This task, from the parents' viewpoint, is accomplished when they can "let go" of their children. Unfortunately, there are no clear demarcation lines to suggest at what age the parents' daughter or son is an independent adult (Haley 1973). It is certainly untrue to suggest that the legal age of adulthood signals weaning of parents from children. It appears that parents who themselves were given freedom to be autonomous pass on the same general behaviors to their offspring, but parents who, as children, had their individuation stifled do the same to their sons and daughters.

Several theorists have proposed that *separation-individuation* is related to the so-called adolescent *borderline syndrome* (a form of symbiotic psychosis). Many clinicians believe the child's self-image and feelings of being in control of his or her thinking and feelings are related to the mother's or father's encouragement of the child's potential individuality. Regarding individuality, Beavers (1974) used the term "I-ness" to refer to behaviors that a child makes that express his or her feelings and thoughts. "I-ness" is related to feelings of controllability and the perception that one is responsible for one's actions.

SEPARATION   The third quality measured in the family by Lewis and associates was the various family reactions to *separation* and *loss*. Severely dysfunctional families cling together in a symbiotic defense against any major change or loss of a member from the family. Healthy families, by contrast, tend to deal with the separation or loss of a loved one. In this connection, there is some evidence that healthier persons do not have a *repressed grief reaction* following the death of a loved one. In general, the reaction to separation

seems to be part of a failure to successfully pass through the earlier weaning stage.

LOSS OF REALITY CONTACT   The Lewis study found the greatest difference between the unhealthy and healthy families on the measure of *reality contact*. Simply defined in a family setting, a family or its members would be considered to have little reality contact if they were "blind to" or ignored extremely pathological behavior in a family member—particularly in the parents. The severely dysfunctional families have a *mythology system* (beliefs about family members that go unchallenged) that is virtually delusional. Beavers (1976) gives the example of a mother who by all standards is disintegrated and incompetent, but still is viewed by the family as "capable" in times of stress. The myths of the severely disturbed groups stand in marked contrast to actual behaviors. Laing and Esterson (1971) also insist that the disturbed families they interviewed had family myths that were firmly held by the group but bore no appropriate relation to how most others perceived the family. In one family, an adolescent catatonic girl became pregnant, and the whole family distorted and exaggerated the consequences of her pregnancy:

> The whole family was choked with its sense of shame and scandal. While emphasizing this to Ruby [the adolescent daughter] again and again, they told her that she was only imagining things when she thought that people were talking about her. Their lives began to revolve round her. They fussed over her and, at the same time, accused her of being spoiled and pampered. When she tried to reject their pampering they told her that she was ungrateful and that she needed them, she was still a child, and so on. (p. 135)

In place of denial, healthy families tend to be readily capable of detecting disturbing behavior in a family member if it exists. The healthy family also believes that the troubled person can be helped. Healthy families do have a set of myths, but they tend to be "gentle and humorous." "Father is a bull in a china shop" (a gentle myth) is certainly very different than "father is inadequate" or "mother is always capable."

AFFECT   The last quality measured in the families was *affect* (their feelings expressed). One dimen-

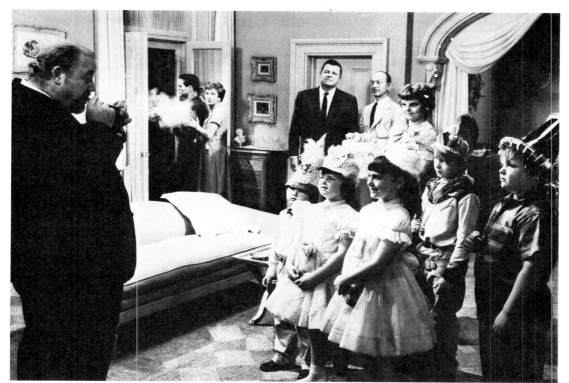

CAT ON A HOT TIN ROOF © 1958,
Metro-Goldwyn-Mayer. Unhealthy families often establish elaborate myth systems to keep the family together. One such system, which includes the common myth that the father is all-powerful and all-knowing, is portrayed in this film.

sion of affect was *expressiveness*, which means open and direct disclosure of feelings as opposed to no expression—withdrawal. Other behaviors that make up affect include the *mood* of the family—humorous, hostile, depressive, apathetic, caustic, or negative. Clearly these moods are hard to define behaviorally, but with much practice in viewing videotaped families, raters can polish their skills at arriving at consistent scores.

Healthy families tend to exhibit behaviors that are interpreted as being supportive, tender, humorous, warm and, in general, positive. By contrast, the severely disturbed families displayed a negative mood. For example, open hostility, cynicism, expression of despair, and sarcastic remarks characterized the severely disturbed families.

Let us look at a few other viewpoints that help form a picture of disturbed family dynamics.

DISTURBED FAMILIES Luthman and Kirschenbaum (1974) have described three basic dysfunctional families: the *repressive* family, the *delinquent* family, and the *suicidal* family.

The *repressive family* resembles Lewis's se-

verely disturbed groups. The term "repressive" is quite fitting, for members of these families discount or disqualify their own feelings and those of other members. For example, during interviews with these families, a child may display bizarre behavior, yet the parents and other family members would ignore the behavior or make ineffectual attempts to control it. (Luthman and Kirschenbaum provide no evidence, however, about what the parents did outside an interview setting.) Luthman and Kirschenbaum use the term "survival myths" to refer to a type of family defense mechanism employed by the family to deal with conflicts. The survival myth of repressive families was simply to deny troubled behaviors and feelings that existed.

We should not conclude that the family's or parents' behaviors cause a particular family member to behave bizarrely. Although this interpretation is plausible, it is just as reasonable, based on data gathered thus far, that having a severely disturbed child can shape the parents to develop survival myths. The data gathered on family pathology leave us with the classic chicken-and-egg problem: which came first, the dysfunctional family or the disturbed individual members?

The second family is the *delinquent family*. According to Luthman and Kirschenbaum, ''the function of the identified patient [usually an adolescent family member] is to act out the impulses of one parent.'' The predominant symptoms in the patient are usually antisocial behaviors: aggression or promiscuous sexuality. Thus the name ''delinquent family'' actually refers to the intentions and values of the family that are acted out by the child, the identified patient (Luthman and Kirschenbaum 1974). For a moment let us back up a bit and give an example of how this particular type of reasoning emerged. In psychoanalytic speculation, early during the 1950s, the *Johnson and Szurek hypothesis* was often cited as a possible means to account for sociopathic or psychopathic behavior emitted in offspring. As the hypothesis goes, the sociopathic youngster became this way in order to act out the unconscious or covert wishes of a particular parent (Johnson & Szurek 1952; 1954). For instance, if the parent has subtle hostilities (perhaps even fantasies) or unexpressed deviances, the child will somehow pick up the cues from the parent and amplify or carry out these deviances. Tooley (1976) later gathered data that lend indirect support for the Johnson and Szurek thesis.

Finally, a six-year follow-up of female criminals' recidivism rates also lends support to the notion that family psychopathology is tied to antisocial behavior. Martin, Cloninger, and Guze (1978), for example, could best predict recidivism in female criminals by examining familial psychopathologies such as antisocial behavior and alcoholism in the women's homes.

The *suicidal family* is the third type of family briefly described by Luthman and Kirschenbaum. Simply stated, this family often is self-destructive. Drug addiction, alcoholism, and suicide are often behaviors modeled by disturbed parents, and these actions often become behavior styles copied by other family members.

CHILD ABUSE

Withhold not correction from the child, for if thou beatest him with the rod, he shall not die. Thou shall beat him with a rod, and shalt deliver his soul from Hell.

Proverbs 23: 13–14.

In this section we shall cover two forms of child abuse, the *battered child syndrome* and *sexually abusive families*. In addition to these two family psychopathologies, *child abuse* includes physical neglect of the child (undernourishment, for example), subtle emotional neglect of a child, overt rejection of a child, and ultimately, murder.

Child abuse has been placed in the chapter on families because the etiology of child abuse and its treatment deal with the family as a whole, not just on the abused child or a single abuser. We will view child abuse as a complex family pathology, a learned set of responses.

Since the beginning of time children have been crippled, mutilated, and murdered by their parents. Unwanted or handicapped infants or children, as history records, have all too frequently been severely abused or abandoned. Indeed, many societies have encouraged or disregarded child abuse. *Infanticide* (killing an infant) and *filicide* (killing a child) were often accepted without societal penalties (Bakan 1971; Roberts 1974; Walters 1975). As Walters (1975) and others note, much literature—the Bible, fairy tales, folklore, nursery rhymes, and so forth—catalogues the horrors perpetrated against children. It is amazing how often infanticidal impulses are revealed in literature. The *Medea syndrome* (Medea, daughter of the king of Colchis, killed her children when her husband, Jason, left her) has been a common theme in literature as well as in real people's lives.

Only very recently in human history have laws been established protecting the child. In fact, societies and organizations opposing cruelty to animals were established well before demands were voiced for better treatment of children.

Lord and Weisfeld (1974) describe the case of ''Mary Ellen,'' one of the first efforts to help an abused child:

A CASE OF CRUELTY

In 1874, a church worker was visiting an elderly woman in a tenement house in New York City and she learned that a little girl, Mary Ellen, who lived in the tenement, was beaten every day. In addition to the physical abuse, the church worker was told that the girl was seriously malnourished. The worker tried to interest such public agencies as the police department and the district attorney's office in doing something about the abuse of Mary Ellen. There was nothing that could be done, the church worker was told, since there was nothing illegal about the beating and starving of Mary Ellen. There were no laws at all, in the United States, for the protection of children in such situations.

In a probably desperate and certainly creative effort, the church worker appealed to the American Society for the Prevention of Cruelty to Animals. Her appeal was based on the premise that Mary Ellen was a member of the animal kingdom and that the treatment of the little girl constituted illegal cruelty to this "human animal." The American Society for the Prevention of Cruelty to Animals brought a suit which led to the child being removed from her home. One year after this incident, the New York Society for the Prevention of Cruelty to Children was organized. (p. 66)

But these authors go on to note that this church worker's efforts, while praiseworthy, had little effect in arousing public sentiment against child abuse. It took more than 80 years from the case of Mary Ellen for child abuse to be recognized on a wide scale.

In 1955 two pediatric radiologists asserted that many injuries (multiple fractures and subdural hematoma) suffered by children were caused purposely by parents (Woolley & Evans 1955, cited in Radbill 1968). It was Wolley and Evans's announcement of the possibility that some parents deliberately injured their children that finally brought child abuse to public attention.

BATTERED CHILD SYNDROME

Building on the assertions of Wolley and Evans, Henry Kempe, a pediatrician, introduced the term *battered child syndrome* in 1961. This syndrome involves persistent physical abuse of a child, resulting typically in significant tissue damage, broken bones, or death. More precisely, this syndrome may be defined as clinical injuries found

from X-ray examination, physical examination, or autopsy (Lord & Weisfeld 1974).

ASSESSMENT PROCEDURES Typically, the family doctor, a pediatrician, or a school nurse is the first to suspect that a child has been physically abused. In these cases, after many previous assaults, the child is ultimately taken to a doctor or hospital with burns, bruises, broken bones, hematomas, cuts, or other injuries. But since many of these injuries could be either accidental or deliberate, many physicians are afraid to question further to see if felonious assault has occurred.

Separating accidental from deliberate injuries or death rest on one main feature: previous injuries detected. The battered child represents one who has been persistently abused. Recidivism is the hallmark for diagnosis. Chronic hematoma (swelling and internal bleeding) may create suspicion in the pediatrician. Most important, X-ray studies and other medical evaluations may reveal if there were other injuries that have healed. Repeated traumas, deliberately inflicted by the parents or other adults, point to the battered child syndrome. The two case studies provided by Kaplun and Reich (1976) both illustrate a fairly common pattern in which child abuse occurs.

TWO CASES OF CHILD ABUSE

Case 1. Mrs. A was 17 when she and Mr. A married, a month after she had become pregnant with her son, Juan. After two years her husband, whom she described as an abusive alcoholic, left her four months pregnant and in need of public assistance. Mrs. A's caseworker saw her as a sweet-tempered, affectionate young woman overburdened with home responsibilities. The little boy seemed happy, bright, and friendly. Mr. A made unexpected home visits, having been told by his mother that his wife had an addicted paramour. On one such visit there was a quarrel in the course of which Mrs. A slashed her husband with a kitchen knife. She spent a night in jail on his complaint.

A week later Mrs. A brought Juan, now 3, to a nearby hospital (one of the finest teaching institutions in the city) with bruises, burns, and a leg fracture, caused, she said, by a fall from a crib against a hot radiator. During the hospitalization the child was asked about this, and said that Mommy had beaten him and burned his heels with a cigarette. Because of Mrs. A's constant visits to the hospital, with home-cooked food, the hospital concluded that the father, who visited separately, had coached the child to make false statements, and Mrs. A was allowed to take him home. Psychiatric evaluation was considered unnecessary because the public assistance caseworker concurred in this view. Eight months later the child was brought back with a swollen eye, attributed by Mrs. A to a boiler explosion in the home.

Four months later Juan was murdered. Mrs. A first stated that the massive injuries, which the postmortem report said were the result of blunt force, were caused by a convulsion the child had on a mattress with a broken spring. When a police investigation disclosed that the mattress was in good condition, Mrs. A said that her 18-year-old paramour, by whom she was pregnant, had done the killing during her absence from the apartment. The young man, who had a criminal history, was released after passing a lie detector test. The two surviving siblings were taken from Mrs. A. Social workers observed that Mrs. A showed "inappropriately flat affect" when discussing the killing and that she arranged a costly funeral. (pp. 809–810)

Case 2. Miss C, a soft-spoken and ladylike person, had her first out-of-wedlock child, a girl, when she was 16. Following the birth she continued living with her mother, to whom she seemed attached. When she became pregnant again at 17, she asked that the coming child be placed so she could go to business school. This was done. In the next year Miss C did not once visit the baby, Victor, but continued relationships with men, one of whom beat her so badly that her mother called the police. Miss C made such a good impression on the foster-home social worker that she arranged a trial discharge of Victor to Miss C and her mother. A few weeks later two teen-age boys whom Miss C often entertained in her apartment entered it in her absence and found the baby brutally beaten. They brought him to a hospital, where he died. The 2-year-old girl seemed unharmed.

It turned out that the child was murdered by Miss C's latest paramour, Mr. M, a drug addict with a prison record and a period in a mental hospital. when he was arrested he attempted suicide. Miss C tried to protect Mr M first by saying that the baby had choked on food and

then by saying that an aunt of Mr. M's had done the killing and that he was the finest man she had ever known. She discussed Victor's death "entirely without affect." Shortly after the murder Miss C's mother found her in bed with a girl. Both were under the influence of drugs—not the first time her involvement with narcotics had come to the agency's attention. Miss C verbalized an interest in psychiatric help at this point but broke all appointments that were made for her. (p. 811)

The case of Victor is a rather common battering situation in which the mother's lover beats the child while the biological mother either encourages him to do so or does not protest. Indeed, many clinicians have noted that when the mother's lover stops beating the child the mother may "goad him" until he resumes the mistreatment (Walters 1975). Kaplun and Reich (1976) found that adult males rarely beat their own children. That is, the boyfriend is much more likely to beat or abuse other women's children. The women in these cases apparently are not only attracted to this sort of man but will often faithfully defend them and protest their innocence. Also it is rare to find one parent who batters his child while the other parent violently protests the abuse. Somehow these adults manage to "select" those who are inclined to be abusers.

FREQUENCY   The incidence or frequency of the battered child syndrome is not known. Because of problems in separating accidental from deliberate injuries, only a sketchy picture of the number of maltreated children can be drawn. Other factors also stand in the way of knowing how many children are battered. For instance, many injured children may never be brought to treatment. Or the child may die and the injuries be attributed to an accident. Only those children who are severely and persistently beaten, yet do not die, are likely to be detected as abuse cases. Mild or episodic battering usually escapes discovery.

Gil (1968) reports that throughout the United States during 1967, estimates of battering from 14 states totaled 2,937 cases. That would be approximately 37 cases reported for every one million persons. More recent estimations on this syndrome in particular are unavailable.

Regarding filicide or child murder, a New York City investigation reported that between 1968 and 1969, 140 children were murdered by their parents (Kaplun & Reich, 1976). But these researchers go on to point out that one out of four child deaths is claimed to be accidental, "although review of some of these 'accidental' deaths indicates that the possibility of homicidal assault cannot be excluded" (p. 809).

ETIOLOGICAL THEORIES There are at least seven specific etiological theories of child abuse, although a few of these overlap. They state that:

1. Child abuse is a result of cultural heritage.
2. Child abuse is a consequence of individual or adult psychopathology—alcoholism, for example.
3. Child abuse is a set of learned behaviors and projection.
4. Child abuse is caused by social-ecological stresses.
5. Child abuse is a result of family pathology.
6. Child abuse is an indirect consequence of brain dysfunction in a particular parent or paramour.
7. Child abuse is determined by a combination of stressors.

(These etiological theories have been extracted from the following sources: Bakan 1971; Walters 1975; Lord & Weisfeld 1974; Kaplun & Reich 1976.)

The *cultural heritage* view holds that we have inherited a tradition in which children are regarded as property, with few if any rights. Bakan (1971) calls this whole notion "parental immunity." Interpreted, this means that we have inherited a cultural tradition that parents have the right to do what they please to their offspring. Coupled with the notion of parental immunity is the fact that our society is basically a violent one. One parent stated that her child is a safe target for her to ventilate or release her frustrations through battering, because chidren are very unlikely to report their parents to the authorities.

The second view, *individual psychopathology*, simply maintains that battering is a result of a mental illness or psychiatric disorder in a particular parent or adult. Alcoholism in the father, for example, is often associated with the battered child syndrome. But although a few parents who batter or kill their children may be psychotic or deeply disturbed, many more who do so have no apparent psychopathology other than the beating behavior itself. Those who have murdered children, however, often exhibit these prehomicidal symptoms: alco-

A parent who batters a child may be expressing self-hatred.

holism, narcotic use, and criminal involvement (Kaplun & Reich 1976).

The *learning view* asserts that child abuse is a set of behaviors acquired from experience in the abuser's childhood. In the main, abusing parents were often battered or neglected as children. Simply put, child abuse is thought to be learned through observation or modeling. Parents who batter their children will often have children who in turn batter their offspring.

An interesting offshoot of the learning position is what we call *projective battering*. In this case, a father, for example, may batter his child because he sees in his child the alienated and despised elements of himself (projection). For example, a father may beat a child because he views the child as a demanding and selfish creature—the same qualities the parent believes he himself possesses. In this way, battering, at least from a phenomenological or experiential level, may in some cases be viewed as a form of self-hatred or scaled-down suicide.

The fourth position contends that particular *social-ecological factors* incite child abuse. This position is definitely related to the learning position, but it further suggests that certain external or extrafamilial stressors provoke abuse. For instance, many studies have argued that lower class families are more inclined to be citadels of abuse. Poor housing, unemployment, lack of recreational

SEXUAL ABUSE: A MISLEADING TERM?

In this section we should note that sexual abuse, incest, pedophilia, and rape overlap and therefore cannot be adequately differentiated. In fact, the confusion may even have negative side-effects as we shall point out shortly. While slight differences do exist among the meanings of these terms, their applications are usually arbitrary.

First, sexual abuse is a term widely used in the literature dealing with child abuse and family problems. More often than not, sexual abuse is used rather than incest or rape. As we noted previously, the distinction between incest and pedophilia rests chiefly on whether or not the aggressor is related to the abused child. Further, incest most often refers to sexual intercourse, whereas pedophilia can refer to intercourse or lesser sex-

ual contact. Also proving to be a problem in differentiating these terms is the issue of force. Rape, with the exception perhaps of statutory rape, involves actions where the aggressor violently compels the victim to have intercourse. But rape is rarely applied to forced sexual acts within the family context.

Sexual abuse, then, is a loosely defined term referring to sexual contact between a parent and a child, where force may or may not be used. Further, sexual intercourse may not be the sexual activity engaged in. Yet this term, sexual abuse, may be unfortunately applied in many cases. For example, if a parent has forcible sexual encounters with his or her child (indeed, force would be difficult to define) sexual abuse would be a

activities, and general restriction and limited access to options, it is reasoned, contribute to abuse. One recent study found that approximately 70 percent of families involved in filicide were living in extreme poverty and were known to welfare agencies (Kaplun & Reich 1976).

The fifth view holds that particular *family dynamics* or *interactions* among family members contribute to child abuse. Although this position overlaps with some of the others, it emphasizes the role of interpersonal communication and interaction as the stressor. One of the most common observations made is that battered children are often unwanted or illegitimate.

Related specifically to interactional problems is the "scapegoating" phenomenon. Many mothers say they batter a particular child after the child "rejects" them. This means that a mother's sense of self-worth may be lessened or destroyed by having a baby who cries incessantly or a child who misbehaves. She interprets this behavior as a rejection of her. In frustration she batters the child. This view clearly resembles the projection theory offered earlier.

Still in other situations, the lover of a divorced or single mother may batter her child because he feels the child is interfering with the relationship between him and the mother—the child is demanding too much of her attention.

Again, it is provocative how many of these women admire and defend their lovers after the beatings, almost as if the mothers wished the child to be beaten.

The sixth etiological theory is the only biogenic one. It suggests that subtle *brain damage*—for instance, tumors, head injuries, brain lesions, hormonal malfunctions, temporal lobe seizures, and so on—predisposes an individual to lose impulse control and therefore under certain stressful conditions to batter a child. Although there is no specific empirical support linking battering with brain dysfunction, there is evidence showing that brain dysfunction in particular sites in the central nervous system can result in the inhibition of impulse control and extreme outbursts of violence (Moyer 1976).

Each of these views may be accurate for particular individuals and families. It is also reasonable to assume that a number of stressors must interact in order for battering to emerge in its full-blown form. It seems that there are *high-risk* conditions for battering which include multiple stressors:

1. The child to be battered is unwanted or illegitimate.
2. A nonbiological father or paramour resides in the family.
3. One or both of the parents is an alcoholic.

poor term to apply because laws do not always protect children from acts defined as sexual abuse. What seems to be the unfortunate state of affairs, legally speaking, is that family membership can often protect the violator from prosecution on more serious charges. Thus, while sexual assault on an unrelated child would be called rape (a very serious offense), if the same assault occurs within the context of the family, the milder term sexual abuse is often applied.

The problem may nevertheless be insoluble in many instances because the child will not or is afraid to report the abusing parent. Still, the term sexual abuse seems rather mild when applied to a pathological parent who for all intents and purposes has raped the child.

4. One or both of the parents, as children, were themselve abused.
5. The parent has nowhere to turn for help in dealing with frustrations.

SEXUALLY ABUSIVE FAMILIES

In contrast to the battered child syndrome, very little information is available on sexual abuse of children. Therefore, much of our discussion necessarily is based on clinical data and speculation. Since virtually no literature exists on this subject (Walters 1975), information concerning frequency and assessment techniques is meager.

There are two reasons why sexual abuse of children is discussed in this chapter rather than in those on childhood problems or psychosexual deviations. For one, sexual abuse is not a disorder of children, but rather a pathology of the family or particular parent. For another, the focus is not just on the violator or deviant (as it was in the psychosexual deviations chapter), but on the child or victim and his or her interactions with the family. Sexual abuse also differs from *incest* in certain ways, as we previously explained.

Sexually abusive behavior is defined as a family pathology, not a childhood disorder. Spe-

cifically, sexual abuse commonly involves a male violator who demands sexual activities with a child; this typically occurs in the family environment.

ASSESSMENT PROCEDURES There are no typical physical indications to suggest that a child has been sexually abused by a parent, except in cases where vaginal examinations of the female child can be made. The absence of clinical clues or symptoms for detecting sexual abuse creates substantial problems in discovering those children who are in need of help. Unlike the battered child syndrome, where there may be physical symptoms and X-ray evidence of abuse, sexual abuse has no comparable indicators.

But if there are not always physical signs, what about verbal reports from the child? Will children tell authorities or even the uninvolved parent or sibling that they are being sexually abused by the other parent? Here again, we do not know. Quite often a child who is being sexually molested by a parent will be afraid to speak out about the episode to anyone—not just to a social worker or outside source, but even to other members of her family. She may be terrified thinking what her father might do to her. However, in a few cases one abused child will report the sexual encounters to protect a younger sister whom, she fears, might next be sexually molested.

FREQUENCY As we have explained, no accurate estimate can be made of the number of sexual abuses against children by parents. *Pedophilia* statistics are not helpful, for pedophilia is not the same sort of problem. It is likely to involve someone outside the immediate family, whom the child may be more willing to report. Incest statistics (discussed in chapter 11) are of some use in establishing sexual contact among relatives, but sexual abuse is slightly different than incest. It may be considered a subvariety of incest, but always involving the father or mother and with the child participating against his or her will. Sexual abuse of children is most often a family problem, and when it is detected it quickly becomes a family secret that might never be divulged (Walters 1975). Hence, the reported cases of sexual abuse are thought to be extreme situations and unrepresentative of the true problem.

SYMPTOMS The three case studies of sexually abusive behavior involve both parents. The first case is by far the most common type of sexual abuse and, broadly speaking, may be termed incest. The second is one of the very rare accounts of adult female sexual abuse with a small child. The third case, also involving an adult female parent, is surely more common than the second.

Sexually abusive behavior occurs when a parent forces a child to have any type of sexual contact. This may involve coitus, oral genital contact, masturbation, or even petting. The child enters into the sexual encounter completely against his or her will. These sexual violations are exceedingly difficult to prosecute, thus in many cases the child remains in the home with the violating parent.

THREE CASES OF SEXUAL ABUSE

Case 1. Mr. L, age 44, was a power company employee. Mr. L's wife had taken a psychology course in a junior college and calmly told the instructor, after class, that her husband often masturbated and had intercourse with their 6-year-old daughter. The instructor told the student that she should protect the child by getting some intervention in this situation from a local mental health agency. Ultimately, the father was required to leave his home, but no therapy was directed toward the child or the mother, who appeared to be *not* greatly disturbed by these events.

Case 2. Ms. R was a single parent with a 3-year-old boy. She would rub his penis against her genitals and had done this since the child was a few months old. She was reported to the police for allegedly teaching the boy to perform cunnilingus on her. She did not deny the charge. (Walters 1975, p. 127)

Case 3. Mrs. D, age 36, had slept and had intercourse with her son, age 14, for about 3 years. After the boy was questioned by a social worker and revealed the episodes, Mrs. D confirmed his report. Her husband, an army officer, had been stationed away from home for the last five years.

ETIOLOGICAL THEORIES In discussing the topic here, we are considering sexual abuse of children as a family disturbance. Specifically, the relationship between the husband and wife is believed to be dysfunctional. For instance, the mother may not discourage sexual activities between the child and father. This reaction is partly due to the way the

sexual encounters begin; that is, the sexual contact between the daughter and father may begin gradually and escalate into more intimate contact. The mother would probably be more inclined to protest the father's advances if he suddenly started having overt sexual contact. Instead he may begin by holding, petting, and masturbating, and ultimately have intercourse with the child. Walters (1975) puts it this way:

> The play progresses over a period of years, and this is an important point. The abuse does not develop overnight, and instances of a father's attacking a daughter sexually with no prior involvement are extremely rare. Often the father and daughter have been engaging in various forms of sexual behavior over the years. They may begin by sleeping together; then the daughter is asked to fondle the father's penis or to masturbate him; as the daughter matures he may fondle her genitalia; and finally there is intercourse. (p. 125)

Many etiological positions have implicated the mother as an indirect source of the father's abuse of the child. Some theorists insist that some women push the father into incestuous contact so that they will not have to have intercourse. Others claim that the father is pathological—that is, he is immature and can only feel adequate and masculine with a child. Still other clinicians argue that the daughter entices the father (in particular, a stepfather).

In spite of the meager data on sexually abusive families, especially in connection with theories about cause, certain conditions apparently may precipitate this behavior:

1. Persistent occasions in which the mother sleeps with her male child, and the father is either unconcerned or absent.
2. Gradual physical contact between a father and his growing daughter.
3. A mother who denies or seems to be indifferent to the father's physical advances toward the child.
4. Alcoholism in the father.
5. In general, a disturbance in sexual relationships—certainly brought on by other problems—between the parents.

Clearly, these predisposing conditions may not be causal at all, but rather they may be symptoms of some other family or individual pathology. (Compare the discussions on pedophilia and incest in chapter 11.)

FAMILY AND GROUP THERAPIES

Group therapy does not imply a specific technique, but simply the treatment of more than one client or patient at a time. Family therapies are similar. Richter (1974), for example, writes that family therapy is not a specific or single type of therapy, " . . . but rather a number of relatively different methods" (p. 112). Family therapies, therefore, may include techniques drawn from psychoanalysis, transactional analysis, behavior therapy, and many others. Several obvious features differentiate family therapy from individual therapy and contribute to the increasing use of family therapy.

In family therapy, the therapist works with a social system—with either the entire family or with two or three members at a time. As we mentioned earlier, the "symptom-bearer" or "identified patient" is not viewed as the principal patient in a family perspective. Instead, the entire family may be viewed as the patient. Family therapy is based on a broader perspective called *general systems theory*. General systems theory always views the individual in terms of a social support system—the family, community, or other group. General systems theory assumes that a person's behavior cannot be viewed in isolation from various support systems within which he or she lives. Gottman and Leiblum (1974) suggest that the initial stages in therapy involve recognizing the problem in regard to the social system (family, school, peer group) in which the behavioral problem occurs.

CONJOINT FAMILY THERAPY

Virginia Satir (1967) developed a family therapy procedure called *conjoint family therapy*. "Conjoint" means joined together or unified; in this usage, it refers to the bringing together of the entire family to work out problems. These are a few of the many important points Satir makes about conjoint family therapy:

1. This therapy approach is aimed essentially at treating the entire family system, not just the identified patient.
2. Seeing a family together, how they communicate and behave toward each other, can reveal problems that otherwise could have been overlooked in individuals.
3. People stop growing and developing adap-

tive behaviors because of dysfunctional family systems.

Satir (1967) describes what she calls *family system games*, which represent modes of family interaction. The games are stated in the form of interaction rules the family members use to communicate or relate with one another. She contends that the following rules or styles represent almost any family system:

1. The first interactional rule dictates that a person is to handle differences by eliminating himself or herself. In other words, the person always *agrees* with others in the system regardless of how he or she really feels.
2. The second rule is that one may handle differences by eliminating the others, by always *disagreeing*, finding fault, and blaming.
3. In the third rule, one eliminates both self and other by always being irrelevant, changing the subject, etc., so that both one's self and others find it impossible openly to negotiate differences.
4. The fourth rule permits the inclusion of both self and other in the system, i.e., a person negotiates openly and clearly and permits others to do the same (pp. 185-186).

One of the goals of conjoint family therapy, of course, is to have each family member adopt the fourth rule of communication.

Many steps are involved in conjoint family therapy; we will briefly summarize the main ones. *Diagnosis* phase occurs first. At this opening stage the therapist attempts to identify the family problem. This may, for example, involve making family members aware of their own individual communication styles. Satir asks many questions in order to bring about this awareness. Also in the first stage is the development of a *family life chronology*. This history-taking step familiarizes the therapist with the milestones from the family's past. Every family has had many joint experiences that may affect the general attitude of the family; the family life chronology might include deaths in the family, childbirth, departure of a member, significant job changes and so on.

In the second stage, the therapist focuses on

Domestic court judges often recommend family therapy in an effort to encourage healthy communication between family members.

the behavior problem that brought the family to therapy. An attempt is made to get every family member to give his or her interpretation of the problem. Satir states:

> The therapist helps children to understand their parents and to understand themselves as children. . . . [The therapist] asks children to explain a parent's behavior, in order to . . . add other possible interpretations. (p. 152)

Another goal of conjoint family therapy is to enhance the family's communication skills. If family members do not know how to express their feelings or how to make other people experience them the way they wish, many difficulties will arise. For example, Laing and colleagues (1966) make this important point:

> I may so act as to induce the other to experience me in a particular way. A great deal of human action has as its goal the induction of particular experiences in the other of oneself. I wish to be seen by the other as

generous, or tough, or fair-minded. However, I may or may not know what it is that I have to do to induce the other to interpret my action and experience me as I desire. . . . (p. 19)

Satir and other therapists see that one problem is getting others to experience us the way we want to be experienced—for no one likes to be misinterpreted. Satir gives an illustration from therapy of miscommunication between husband and wife.

HUSBAND: She never comes up to me and kisses me. I am always the one to make the overtures.

THERAPIST: Is this the way you see yourself behaving with your husband?

WIFE: Yes, I would say he is the demonstrative one. I didn't know he wanted me to make overtures.

THERAPIST: Have you told your wife that you would like this from her—more open demonstration of affection?

HUSBAND: Well, no, you'd think she'd know.

WIFE: No, how would I know? You always said you didn't like aggressive women.

HUSBAND: I don't, I don't like *dominating* women.

WIFE: Well, I thought you meant women who make the overtures. How am I to know what you want?

THERAPIST: You'd have a better idea if he had been able to *tell* you.

In sum, the objective of conjoint family therapy is to treat the entire family as the patient by improving their communication patterns. The method is effective communication training, and the explicit goal is to make family members into *functional communicators.* The functional communicator, by contrast with the *dysfunctional communicator,* does not send vague and incomplete messages to other members. Functional communicators engage in clear and direct talk, and and this style opens up communication and induces others to respond similarly.

PARENTS ANONYMOUS

While conjoint family therapy is used to treat a broad range of family problems, *Parents Anonymous* is aimed specifically at helping parents who physically or sexually abuse their children. Parents Anonymous sessions have been formed in various parts of the country by groups of parents who are battering or abusing their children or have done so in the past. Commonly these groups are led by a reformed child abuser.

These people may assemble once or twice a week for several hours to discuss their feelings and motivations for abuse. The sessions typically involve a great outpouring of emotion, and in many cases, parents reveal stressful situations that prompt their abusing actions. Since the listeners, acting as both client and therapist, are also abusers, they can provide sympathy and support for one another. Most important, out of these sessions the participants discover coping behaviors other than battering. Although Parents' Anonymous, at this writing, is too new to have solid empirical support, many participants, as well as their children, report that the sessions have stopped the battering and abusive activities.

What seems to be a very important function of Parents Anonymous is their toll-free answering service which acts as a crisis intervention center. If a parent feels the need to begin battering a child, he or she can call the center. Just this simple option—being able to call someone—may be enough to halt the battering sequence temporarily. The center may refer the caller to an agency or therapist that can help. Unfortunately, funding for such services is always difficult to acquire.

Walters (1975), in his description of group treatment strategies for abusers, suggests that group members should do three things: (1) identify when they are under stress; (2) identify children's behaviors that create difficulties; and (3) help one another find appropriate or alternate behaviors for dealing with their children.

SUMMARY

1. In recent years there has been renewed interest in the family and its role in the development of individual psychopathology. Alfred Adler was one of the first psychotherapists to stress the importance of family experience in the development of psychopathology in the family member.

2. Family units have no doubt existed since the beginning of human history. These early families were more than likely *extended families,* composed of grandparents, mother, father, sisters and brothers.

3. To a large degree, families have lost many of their traditional functions. The education of the child and many other forms of socialization have been taken over by agencies other than the family. It is not known whether or not declining family functions contribute to individual psychopathology.

4. The family, just like the individual, has a life cycle or series of stages through which it progresses. Haley describes these six stages that most families tend to follow: courtship, marriage, childbirth and rearing, middle marriage, weaning, and retirement and old age. Each of these stages is associated with particular demands or stressors. Families cope differently as they progress within each stage.

5. A new trend in clinical psychology is to focus on the family as a unit. Like the individual, the family can become dysfunctional or abnormal. Lewis described three categories of psychological health by which a family could be classified: severely disturbed families, mid-range or mildly dysfunctional families, and optimal or healthy families.

6. Five qualities or traits were used to assess families and place them in the three categories previously mentioned: *power structure, degree of individuation, separation, reality contact,* and *affect.*

7. *Power structure* refers to who controls or dominates the family. In severely disturbed families, according to the Lewis study, the fathers have little power. In healthy families, however, Wild and colleagues found there were no clearly dominant members.

8. *Degree of individuation* refers to the extent that a family tolerates its members to become autonomous and independent. The more severely disturbed families interviewed in the Lewis study did not permit individuation in its members. Dysfunctional families encourage conformity and sameness of emotional expression.

9. Lewis investigated the reactions of various families to separation and loss. Very disturbed families could not cope with weaning periods or loss of a loved one.

10. *Loss of reality* contact was another trait of dysfunctional families. Dysfunctional families develop ways of thinking (mythology

systems) that distort and deny abnormal behavior committed by family members.

11. *Affect* was the final measure assessed by Lewis. Expressiveness was a particular dimension of affect or mood. Healthy families tended to express supportive behaviors, while unhealthy families tended to express hostile and cynical behaviors.

12. *Child abuse* has two forms, and both deal with dysfunctional families: the *battered child syndrome* and *sexually abusing family syndrome*.

13. The *battered child syndrome* is a term that was coined in 1961 by Henry Kempe. It refers to persistent physical abuse of a child that may result in physical injury or death.

14. The key to assessing the battered child syndrome is repeated injuries seen in a child. It is very difficult for a physician to discriminate between accidental and intentional injuries, but repeated injuries may suggest deliberate abuse.

15. The prevalence of battering is unknown, but reported cases have exceeded approximately 3,000 a year. This figure is surely an underestimate because many physicians and health authorities are reluctant to report cases unless the cases are clearly indicative of deliberate abuse.

16. No single theory of child abuse can explain most of the reported cases. Instead, a number of theories have been offered: child abuse is a result of cultural heritage; child abuse is a consequence of individual or adult mental illness; child abuse is a set of learned behaviors; child abuse is the result of projection; child abuse is caused by social-ecological stresses, such as poor housing and poverty in general; child abuse is a consequence of some underlying family pathology; child abuse is an indirect consequence of brain impairment in the abusing adult; and, child abuse is multidetermined.

17. In the sexually abusive family, one member, typically the father or paramour, violates a child sexually. The prevalence of sexual abuse is unknown.

18. Sexual abuse of children, from the perspective of this chapter, is viewed as a symptom of family disturbance, for example, a disturbed relationship between husband and wife.

19. Family and group therapies are considered to be the treatment of choice for family dysfunctions. Family therapists treat the whole family, not just the identified patient. *Conjoint family therapy* is a variety of family therapy. Virginia Satir, its founder, asserts that symptoms in a client, the identified patient, result from faulty family communications. The main objective or goals of conjoint family therapy is to have the family members communicate openly and clearly. The first stage of therapy involves determining the nature of the problem in the symptom-bearer (the identified patient). The second major stage involves training the family how to communicate more effectively, that is, learning how to express their feelings so that they will not be misunderstood or falsely interpreted.

20. *Parents Anonymous* is an organization that attempts to help parents who are child abusers. This organization typically puts a group of abusers in contact with one another and provides a means for them to share their problems and possible ways for changing their behavior. Group contact with those having similar difficulties is thought to assist the individual abuser in identifying stressors that prompt abusive behaviors.

RECOMMENDED READINGS

Cooper, D. *The death of the family.* New York: Vintage, 1970.

Haley, J. *Uncommon therapy.* New York: Ballantine, 1973.

Manocchio, T., & Petitt, W. *Families under stress.* London: Routledge & Kegan Paul, 1975.

Richter, H. E. *The family as patient.* New York: Farrar, Straus & Giroux, 1974.

Walters, D. R. *Physical and sexual abuse of children.* Bloomington: Indiana University Press, 1975.

ABNORMAL BEHAVIORS ASSOCIATED WITH OLD AGE

19

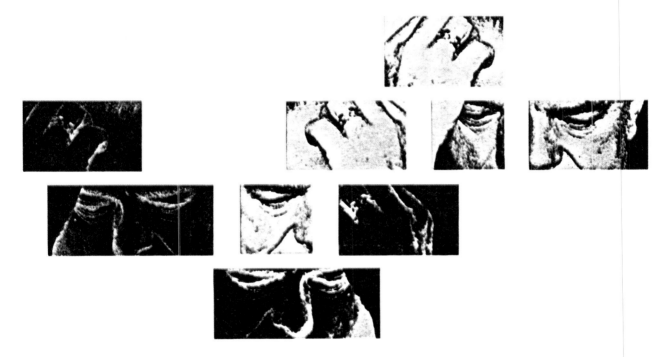

OVERVIEW In this final chapter we will examine two basic issues: aging and the clinical syndromes associated with advanced age. In looking at aging itself, we will discuss biological aging, social aging, and psychological aging, and the characteristic changes associated with each. We will also look at some of the special stressors associated with the senium (old age). Four basic stressors will be featured: retirement shock, bereavement, isolation, and leisure time; we will focus mostly on bereavement and grief research.

The second major section of this chapter presents clinical syndromes of two basic types: progressive idiopathic dementia and multi-infarct dementia. We will discuss and describe the chief characteristics of these syndromes, as well as the onset, course, prevalence, and treatment. Finally we will look at various kinds of treatment and therapy efforts, including institutionalization (nursing home care), psychological and occupational therapies, drug therapies, and home help services and rehabilitation.

AGING: WHAT IS IT?

No one seems to know what aging is or how to define it. Yet we are *all*, whether we admit it or not, concerned about this unknown but unavoidable phenomenon. We do know some things about aging—it is clearly related to the passage of time; it is clearly related to increased chances of developing illnesses; it is absolutely linked with death. Busse and Pfeiffer (1977) suggest that *aging* is a biological process that is associated with a decline of efficiency and functioning, a process that sooner or later results in death. Aging, in fact, is very difficult to separate from disease. Although diseases do exist in childhood, nevertheless disease is an impairing process that strikingly resembles aging (Vogel 1977). Unlike disease, however, aging moves along at a steady pace, often not causing noticeable symptoms or feelings until substantial retrograde alterations in the body have occurred.

We will look at aging from three standpoints: *biological aging, social aging,* and *psychological aging.* With each of these processes, we hope to show characteristic changes that become apparent in the *senium* (old age).

BIOLOGICAL AGING

Biological aging refers to a process of physical decline over a rather extensive period of time. This decline is gradual, destructive, and irreversible. As we noted earlier, aging closely resembles disease or illness in that both are destructive processes. Yet diseases of most kinds are reversible. Aging is not. Biological aging involves an inexorable wearing down or wasting away of virtually every system in the body; muscles, tissues, cells, organs, all show irreversible retrograde alterations. Initially the alterations can be detected only by microscopic observation. Later, however, the retrograde changes can be detected by simply looking at the person.

At the cellular level, the structure of certain cells begins an early demise. Connective tissue called *collagen*, a substance that binds muscles and organs together, gradually loses its elasticity. Collagen, so to speak, resembles a sort of body glue. The alterations in collagen over the years

have prompted some gerontologists to suggest that in old age we literally "come unglued." The changes are very slow but inevitable. At about age 40, lines on the face become more evident. The skin becomes less firm and more transparent. Yet still the glaring symptoms of aging may be disguised somewhat by cosmetics and dress. By about 60, however, and sooner in some individuals, the overt signs have become obvious. The eyes have lost some of their color; the hair has become grayer and more sparse; benign lesions called *lentigo senilis* commonly start to appear on the back of the hands; and there is a shrinking of muscle tissue and a general stiffening of joints. An age-related bone disease (osteoporosis) also tends to start emerging in the 60s and 70s. Osteoporosis exists when bones become porous and brittle. This subjects the individual not only to broken bones, but perhaps the falls that accompany many broken bones—that is, the bones break and then the fall occurs.

Blood flow also begins to decrease rapidly in later years. Insufficient blood supply is no doubt one of the most serious problems of aging. Blood supply is vital because the brain in particular depends on two essential brain elements: oxygen and glucose. The reason for the decrease in blood flow is not completely understood. One factor is that the cerebrovascular system has begun to become clogged with age, thus lessening blood flow. Yet blood pressure in most individuals increases as they grow older. While the increase in pressure elevates the chance of strokes and artery hardening, it paradoxically assures the brain of a reduced but essential blood supply.

The most vital organ, the brain, is clearly the structure most affected by the ravages of time. Even at birth, nerve cells or neurons within the central nervous system have started to decline in number. It has been estimated that the brain loses some 100,000 of its 10 billion or so cells daily. After the age of 30, other gerontologists suggest, we lose about one percent of our neurons yearly (Vogel 1977). By age 75, a sizable proportion of the neurons have died. It is generally believed that depopulation of central nervous system neurons is a result of decreases in blood flow. Other unknown factors certainly enhance the depopulation process.

With the loss of brain cells, our sensory

Barbara Alper/Stock, Boston

Many elderly people remain quite active. Others disengage quite early in the senium.

processes diminish. Hearing, especially for high-pitched sounds, starts to decline shortly after the tenth year of life (this applies more in urban areas); impairment of vision also begins gradually in early life and accelerates with age. Finally, reaction time slows considerably after adolescence and early adulthood.

Although biological aging occurs in everyone, individual variations in the rate and extent of these changes are quite striking. For example, some 70-year-olds are healthier and may look younger than others who are only 50. Many elderly people stay active well into the 80s and 90s. In fact, certain individuals may show improvement in some areas as they age. Troll (1973) observes:

> The one function that clearly decreases throughout maturity and old age is speed, and anything involving speed. Slowing down starts in the twenties or at least the

thirties. On the other hand, capacities that involve accumulation and storage of experience, e.g., vocabulary and information, show increases throughout the life span until just before death. (p. 100)

Even though neural loss is striking over a lifetime, for the most part specific problematic symptoms do not exist for everyone. On the whole, the brain can apparently maintain much of its normal functioning despite neural depopulation.

SOCIAL AGING

Social aging refers to the changes in roles or the loss of roles that occurs during late adulthood. Phillips (1957) listed nine role changes (stressors) that apply to many older persons in our society. Although the list is more than 20 years old, it still has relevance today:

1. Retirement from full-time employment.
2. Withdrawal from active community and organizational leadership.
3. Breaking up of marriage through the death of one's mate.
4. Loss of an independent household.
5. Loss of interest in distant goals and plans.
6. Acceptance of dependence upon others for support or advice and management of funds.
7. Acceptance of a subordinate position to adult offspring or to social workers.
8. Taking up of memberships in groups made up largely of old people.
9. Acceptance of planning in terms of immediate goals. (pp. 212–213)

Social aging, then, is chiefly a function of significant role changes. These changes are often problematic and stressful because they entail a loss of status and a loss of companionship. Thus we age not only biologically, but socially as well.

Perhaps the most cited social theory of aging is the *disengagement* theory (Cumming & Henry 1961). Cumming (1976) defines her theory this way:

> The disengagement theory proposes that under certain conditions normal aging is a mutual withdrawal or "disengagement" between the aging person and others in the social system to which he belongs. (pp. 19–21)

CALCULATING LIFE EXPECTANCIES

In about 1832, Benjamin Gompertz, an English insurance actuary, discovered a mathematical law. *Gompertz's law* stated that a person's chance of dying doubles every eight years, irrespective of the environment. Simply put, this meant that a man of 100 would have a chance of dying approximately 1,000 times greater than that of a young man of 25. Indeed, if we kept the physiology of a 15-year-old indefinitely, our average life expectancy would be more than 20,000 years! (Strehler 1978).

But there are some rather subtle inconsistencies in Gompertz's law, especially if we think of the difference between life expectancy today and life expectancy in prehistory. Before we point out the subtle inconsistency, let us define two terms: *life expectancy* and *life span.*

Life expectancy is defined as the average duration of life (Schulz 1978). Life expectancy seems to be a function of both genetic endowment and exposure to environmental stressors such as disease. By contrast, *life span* is the theoretical limits of life; that is, under ideal conditions, the potential to exist for some number of years. As a generalization, many *gerontologists* (those who study aging) believe that our life span potential is somewhere between 80 and 100 years, individual differences aside. But most of us do not reach the end of our potential life span.

Most of us live to an average age of about 70 (life *expectancy*). If you inspect the life expectancies in the table, you will notice that human life expectancy has been strikingly different at different periods in history. It has ranged from about 18 years during prehistory to 71 years during the early 1970s. We should again stress that while people in prehistory had a life *expectancy* of 18, their life *span* was about the same as ours. In fact, there have been individuals throughout history who, for unknown reasons, have approached the upper limits. In ancient Rome, where life expectancy was 22 years, life spans of 70 years were often recorded.

The discrepancies between life expectancies centuries ago and today can be attributed mainly to the decrease in a few basic diseases, a partial violation of Gompertz's Law. As certain diseases were controlled, life expectancy gradually began to approach the theoretical life span. For example, people who lived even during the early 1900s were often victims of several very deadly diseases: influenza and pneumonia. (Tuberculosis was perhaps a third major deadly illness at that time.) Since these diseases have been held in check to some extent, we are now living longer. But our longer life expectancy has its negative side-effects, and two different deadly problems have now emerged: cancer and heart disease. While the death rate from pneumonia, influenza, and tuberculosis has dramatically dropped, deaths due to cancer have increased by about 150 percent since the 1900s; heart disease claims almost 50 percent more people now.

Besides physical diseases typical of aging, our longer life expectancy also raises the probability that we will experience new social, psychological, and biological stressors that influence the development of late onset psychopathologies. It is obvious, for example, that senile dementia was not a problem in prehistory, simply because very few people lived to be old enough. Today, with increasing life expectancy and with more people reaching the senium, we are witnessing a rise in late onset psychopathologies, which, of course, are impossible to predict. Even so, charts like this one can help you estimate your life expectancy.

LIFE EXPECTANCIES

From Lerner, M. "The demography of death." In E. S. Shneidman (Ed.), *Death: Current perspectives.* Palo Alto, Ca.: Mayfield, 1976, p. 140. (Cited in Schulz 1978)

TIME PERIOD	AVERAGE LIFE SPAN IN YEARS
Prehistory	18
Ancient Greece	20
Ancient Rome	22
Middle Ages, England	33
1620 (Massachusetts Bay Colony)	35
19th century England, Wales	41
1900 USA	47.3
1915 USA	54.5
1954 USA	69.6
1967 USA	70.2
1971 USA	71

This is a rough guide for calculating your personal longevity. The basic life expectancy for males is age 67 and for females it is age 75. Write down your basic life expectancy. If you are in your 50s or 60s, you should add ten years to the basic figure because you have already proven yourself quite durable. If you are over age 60 and active, add two more years. From Schulz 1978.

BASIC LIFE EXPECTANCY
Decide how each item below applies to you and add or subtract the appropriate number of years from your expectancy.

1. FAMILY HISTORY
Add 5 years if 2 or more of your grandparents lived to 80 or beyond. _____

Subtract 4 years if any parent, grandparent, sister, or brother died of heart attack or stroke before 50. Subtract 2 years if anyone died from these diseases before 60. _____

Subtract 3 years for each case of diabetes, thyroid disorders, breast cancer, cancer of the digestive system, asthma, or chronic bronchitis among parents or grandparents. _____

2. MARITAL STATUS
If you are married, add 4 years. _____

If you are over 25 and not married, subtract 1 year for every unwedded decade. _____

3. ECONOMIC STATUS
Subtract 2 years if your family income is over $40,000 per year. _____

Subtract 3 years if you have been poor for greater part of life. _____

4. PHYSIQUE
Subtract one year for every 10 pounds you are overweight. _____

For each inch your girth measurement exceeds your chest measurement deduct two years. _____

Add 3 years if you are over 40 and not overweight. _____

5. EXERCISE
Regular and moderate (jogging 3 times a week), add 3 years. _____

Regular and vigorous (long distance running 3 times a week), add 5 years. _____

Subtract 3 years if your job is sedentary. _____

Add 3 years if it is active. _____

6. ALCOHOL
Add 2 years if you are a light drinker (1-3 drinks a day). _____

Subtract 5 to 10 years if you are a heavy drinker (more than 4 drinks per day). _____

Subtract 1 year if you are a teetotaler. _____

7. SMOKING
Two or more packs of cigarettes per day, subtract 8 years. _____

One to two packs per day, subtract 4 years. _____

Less than one pack, subtract 2 years. _____

Subtract 2 years if you regularly smoke a pipe or cigars. _____

8. DISPOSITION
Add 2 years if you are a reasoned, practical person. _____

Subtract 2 years if you are aggressive, intense, and competitive. _____

Add 1-5 years if you are basically happy and content with life. _____

Subtract 1-5 years if you are often unhappy, worried, and often feel guilty. _____

9. EDUCATION
Less than high school, subtract 2 years. _____

Four years of school beyond high school, add 1 year. _____

Five or more years beyond high school, add 3 years. _____

10. ENVIRONMENT
If you have lived most of your life in a rural environment, add 4 years. _____

Subtract 2 years if you have lived most of your life in an urban environment. _____

11. SLEEP
More than 9 hours a day, subtract 5 years. _____

12. TEMPERATURE
Add 2 years if your home's thermostat is set at no more than 68° F. _____

13. HEALTH CARE
Regular medical checkups and regular dental care, add 3 years _____

Frequently ill, subtract 2 years. _____

PERSPECTIVE LIFE CYCLE

A key ingredient in successful aging and maintenance of life satisfaction is the development of a mature *life perspective*. A perspective refers to a mental point of view or picture, and so one's life perspective is a mental view of where one has been—a picture of the past—and where one is going. Butler and Lewis (1977) call this picture an "inner sense of the life cycle." The beginning of this inner sense starts, according to Robert Kastenbaum (1973), when the child makes two important discoveries: first, that there is a future (futurity or future time), and second, that he or she is mortal.

Butler and Lewis give us a more precise description of the perspective:

It is a subjective feel for the life cycle as a whole, its rhythm, its variability, and the relation of this to the individual's sense of himself [or herself]. This inner sense seems to be a necessary personal achievement in order for the individual to orient himself [or herself] wherever he [or she] happens to comprehend his [or her] own eventual end. (p. 138)

Kastenbaum (1973) goes farther and describes a *mature* life perspective:

A mature life perspective is the type that permits a person to make constructive use of his [or her] past experiences without capitulating in that direction either. (p. 74)

Disengagement, then, refers to a phase of social aging in which the person gradually gives up social roles and relationships. It involves a type of "retreat." Even achievement is slowly abandoned. The person becomes less involved with other persons and does not take part in as many activities as before. But as with biological aging, disengagement does not begin during old age (65 years or so). Cumming points out that typically it begins to emerge gradually during middle age.

Part of the reason for the abandonment of achievement, a feature of disengagement, is that the older person recognizes that his or her life is limited. Striving for superiority and distant goals (engagement) demands that the person believe he or she has a future. The belief that one's life will be over soon may account for the association of disengagement and old age.

In the United States, the socially defined period for the beginning of old age or senescence falls between 65 and 74 (Butler & Lewis 1977). Generally, individuals lose status and roles, or their access to reinforcement, when they cross this arbitrary age threshold. The assigning of status according to age—the denial of reinforcement opportunities based chiefly on age—is called *ageism*. As one senior citizen puts it, "One of the doctrines of ageism is that old people know nothing. It's part of the image with which we have to cope."

Age discrimination (ageism), many gerontologists contend, influences biological aging. It best represents the notion of social aging. Indeed, ours is a society that abhors the thought of old age. The elderly are often avoided (even by doctors) as if they were evil or tainted.

But before modern advances in medicine and the subsequent extension of life expectancy, old persons in many societies were valued for the fact that they had reached advanced years. Old age was itself an achievement. In most modern societies, this is not the case. Youth is now worshiped. The veneration for the older person has been replaced by a societal "gerontophobia," a fear of aging. Only a few industrialized nations, such as Japan, still revere the elderly (Palmore 1978).

In social gerontology there is a small ongoing debate about the benefits or disadvantages of disengagement. Some theorists suggest that disengagement is the natural and adaptive way to age. Others disagree. One opposing theory, the activity theory, suggests that social aging is most natural and adaptive if one stays active and involved. Research has shown, however, that various styles of adaptive aging exist: some people maintain a high degree of life satisfaction and are disengaged; others remain active and involved and report a high degree of life satisfaction. Most certainly, the culture as a whole, as well as the individual's immediate environment and physical health, determine life satisfaction regardless of activity or disengagement.

Broadly stated, psychologists have suggested that those who make successful adjustments during senescence have a realistic picture of themselves in terms of where they are within the life cycle.

Other general traits found in successful adjustment to aging include some rather obvious ones: intelligence, physical energy, and financial stability.

It is important to realize that it is becoming more difficult to develop a realistic life perspective, especially concerning one's mortality or death. A reason for this has been offered by Kastenbaum and Aisenberg (1972), who claim that the average man or woman today is "insulated from the perception of death."

To better understand social aging, we can examine two general types of societies that create different atmospheres and conditions for old people. These societal structures or societies were called *Gesellschaft* and *Gemeinschaft* types by Ferdinand Tönnies. These societal types can be contrasted in terms of the kinds of interactions between people, the stability of the culture, and the motivation of the people:

As you can see, the *Gesellschaft* society resembles very closely the modern way of living in a large American or western European city. Since this social structure emphasizes productivity and speed in accomplishing tasks, biologically older individuals will not fare too well. Further, the *Gesellschaft* society is characterized by a very specialized labor force, a high degree of automation, unions, bureaucratic involvement, and occupational obsolescence. Not only does the *Gesellschaft* society poorly prepare young people for times of occupational retirement and abundance of leisure time, but the old person has virtually no value or prestige in this setting.

By contrast, the *Gemeinschaft* society prevailed in many primitive, nonindustrialized settings. Cultures with this structure typically emphasized traditional roles; the norms were rather clear-cut; there was family solidarity; and the society or culture was agriculturally oriented. We speak of this latter society in the past tense because more and more societies are becoming like the *Gesellschaft* structure.

TWO TYPES OF SOCIETIES

GEMEINSCHAFT	GESELLSCHAFT
Rural setting.	Urban setting.
Shared values & strong social bonds.	Few shared values and weak social bonds.
Group interests.	Self-interests.
High intimacy among inhabitants.	Low intimacy (high mobility).

Alexander Leaf (1973) notes that most centenarians (those living to be 100 or more) live in *Gemeinschaft* societies. The Caucasus Mountains in the U.S.S.R., for example, represent a *Gemeinschaft* society. The mountain people of this region define youth as extending into the eighties. It has been noted that these people do not have a phrase "old people." Outsiders observe that this society provides its members with continued purpose, feelings of control over their lives, and dignity well beyond the time in which our society "benches" its elderly. Perhaps their extended definition of youth prevents people from being stigmatized as old and useless. There clearly is such a thing as "age-role identification." Leaf, as well as many other gerontologists, takes the view that "control" over one's life, or "usefulness," is critical. He suggests that the old die quickly once they lose useful roles in their community.

To summarize, in a *Gemeinschaft* society, biologically older individuals retain their status and usually their work activities. In *Gesellschaft* societies, forced retirement and loss of status are the rule. We should not overlook the possibility that genetic endowment, diet, exercise, or other factors also may account for the longer life span of the centenarians. In fact, the reason these very old people retain their status may be their ability to do some work. Not all *Gemeinschaft* societies produce people who live for great periods of time. We are a long way from determining the contributions of exercise, diet, genetic endowment, and the social environment in exact terms.

PSYCHOLOGICAL AGING

The third dimension of aging involves *psychological aging*. To a large degree, psychological aging results from the combined effects of both biological and social aging; that is, biological alterations (especially in the brain) and changes in social roles bring about psychological experiences that can be labeled "old." Psychological aging involves degenerative changes in emotions, memory, learning ability, judgment, intelligence, and mood that are associated with the senium.

Because of the enormous amount of information that relates to psychological aging, we will focus selectively on the alterations in emotional reactions as a person ages.

Elderly people's emotional reactions to biological and social aging typically include some of the following: anxiety, depression, guilt (lowering of self-esteem), anger, and feelings of powerlessness or lack of control. Although these emotions and feelings surely occur during other stages of the life span, much evidence, as we shall see, suggests that they intensify with age.

Anxiety is a common emotional reaction that most normal people experience under stressful conditions. In the elderly such feelings are often exaggerated and persistent. Anxiety may be evoked by the fear of death (thanatophobia), the fear of being abandoned, of becoming an invalid, or of not having the income to live at one's accustomed level. When an elderly person frequently reports anxiety, it is often misinterpreted as a sign of senility (Butler & Lewis 1977).

Perhaps the most common emotional reaction reported by older persons is *depression*. Although depression occurs often in young adults, it is frequently considered to be the hallmark of psychological aging. Post (1962), for example, notes that depression is the most commonly reported complaint among elderly persons. Many British gerontologists insist that neurotic disorders in old persons (anxiety) are actually expressions of depression, not anxiety. In this case, neurotic disorders would be treated by dealing with the underlying depression and not the anxiety (Whitehead 1974).

Because depression increases with age, and suicide is very frequently a consequence of depression, we should expect that suicide rates increase with age. This is indeed the case: 25 percent of all suicides are committed by people over 65 (Butler & Lewis 1977). One curious fact

is that only 1 to 2 percent of elderly blacks commit suicide (Hicks 1977).

Guilt is another emotional reaction commonly expressed during old age. As with depression, the acknowledgment of guilt may lead some to label an individual as senile or emotionally disturbed. But there appears to be some justification for the emergence of these feelings. Butler and Lewis (1977) make the point that "Old age is a time of reflection and reminiscence that can evoke a resurgence of past conflicts and regrets" (p. 43). Guilt may emerge when the older person considers his or her past and the deeds and acts that were not accomplished. This often results in a lowering of self-esteem. Guilt, depression, anxiety, and other negative emotions may occur in part because of a shortened *life perspective*.

With a shortened life perspective, little planning for future accomplishments is possible. The elderly frequently wonder whether they achieved their potential in youth. Everyday problems, economic pressures, loneliness, and other difficulties may be interpreted as evidence of personal shortcomings, and so feelings of guilt arise.

A corollary emotional reaction to both depression and guilt is *rage* or *anger*. Rage expressed at an early age may be said to be a result of frustration. Yet in older people the expression of rage is often thought to be an irrational and meaningless emotion, not a response to an appropriate frustrating event. Rage is only infrequently interpreted as an appropriate response to what Butler and Lewis call the "inhuman treatment" of some of our elderly. Actually there exist in aging specific frustrating events that should elicit anger. For example, economic hardship, the onset of illness, mental deterioration, failing of memory, and many other events can evoke rage.

Finally, both *feelings of powerlessness* and *loss of control* are often experienced by the older person. These emotions or perceptions are related to depression and seem particularly to be evoked by involuntary confinement in an institution. In a more extreme sense, Seligman (1975) contends that perceived lack of control may precipitate a psychogenic death.

SENESCENCE AND ITS STRESSORS

Every man knows how useful it is to be useful. No one seems to know how useful it is to be useless.   Chuang-Tzu

Like all the previous discussed stages, senescence has associated stressors and psychopathologies. Here we shall discuss four basic stressors of senescence: retirement shock, bereavement, isolation, and leisure time. Most of these stressors were previously mentioned by Phillips (1957).

First, let us define a stressor. A stressor refers to any condition, biological or environmental, that induces psychopathology. Although there obviously are biological stressors caused by the aging process (decreases in brain efficiency, for example), we shall focus on psychological or social stressors.

RETIREMENT SHOCK

Perhaps the most common social stressor occurring during senescence is retirement. *Retirement shock* involves either the thought of retiring or the act of retiring itself. Bromley (1971), for example, claims that the period immediately preceding retirement may be more stressful than actual retirement. Back and Guptill (1966) attempt to explain why retirement is so critical:

> The principal means of self-identification for the adult male in today's Western society is derived from his work activity . . . the loss of the work role due to retirement is considered one of the major crises in the process of aging. (p. 120)

Retirement shock occurs when one who has invested his or her identity and esteem in work discovers that he or she is occupationally obsolete. Because our feelings of usefulness and control are principally derived from our occupational role, loss of this role is a major stressor. Cobb and Kasl (1972), for example, showed that more than half of the men who lost their jobs because of plant closures developed major psychological and physical problems. Even men in their 40s and 50s showed increases in blood pressure, ulcers, and arthritis when laid off or forced to retire.

But forced retirement or layoffs do not affect everyone in the same way. Butler and Lewis (1977) have noted that some individuals look forward to retirement:

> . . . some groups cannot retire fast enough, usually those holding tedious, assembly line type or heavy labor type jobs. [This group] . . . shows some improvement, not decline, in health as a result of retirement. (p. 302)

Most gerontologists believe that the worker's atti-

Drawing by Cresci; © 1978 by Modern Maturity

"Now that you're retired, George, you've got to learn to relax."

tude toward retirement determines to a large degree whether or not retirement is a stressor. Simpson and colleagues (1966) tell us that "if one is committed to his work he will be unfavorably disposed toward retirement." Further, these writers contend that if a worker has attained some of his or her goals and aspirations, retirement will be less threatening.

Another important influence on the shock of retirement is the question of retirement income. It is believed that the size of the gap between pre-retirement income and retirement income is very important. For example, for an individual who has made a great deal of money prior to retirement and become accustomed to living at a high level, a drastically reduced income following retirement could be very stressful.

A possible way to lessen retirement shock has been offered by Bromley (1971), a British gerontologist. He suggests that preparation for retirement is essential for successful adjustment:

> The financial and leisure problems of retirement can be met only by long-term planning. Many do not face up to the problem soon enough, and enter retirement inadequately prepared. Preparation means . . . putting money aside, buying and disposing of personal property and real estate, attending to health needs, getting information and advice about leisure-time interests. (p. 73)

BEREAVEMENT AND GRIEF

The death of a loved one is perhaps the darkest hour in human experience. The "perils of survivorship" can be so harsh that many psychologists, gerontologists, and physicians sometimes view the experience as a sort of illness. It is no longer mere speculation that bereavement is emotionally and physically a disruptive event; within the last few years many studies have revealed the association of recent bereavement and physical illnesses in the survivor. The death of a close loved one is so stressful and frustrating because it is an irretrievable loss. We shall review a few of the classic studies dealing with bereavement, but should point out that numerous methodological problems exist with most of these investigations. We should not ignore this kind of research, however; rather, we should examine these studies critically, looking for other possible interpretations but not minimizing the terrible plight of a grievous loss.

Toynbee (1968) points out also that bereavement is not the only sort of crisis that leaves numbed survivors; there is, in his words, "premature death of the spirit," meaning that the brain or mind of an individual can die (senility is an example he uses) yet his or her body lives on. This death-of-the-mind in a loved one is also an incalculable and grievous event. It may indeed be more appalling to see one's spouse or dear friends lose their grasp of reality than to witness their physical demise. Speaking of both physical death and death of the spirit, Toynbee says:

> There are always two parties to a death;
> the person who dies and the survivors who
> are bereaved.

Erich Lindemann was a pioneer in developing crisis intervention methods in his work with those who were bereaved by the tragic 1942 fire at the Coconut Grove nightclub in Boston, which killed 499 people. In a classic article written in 1944, Lindemann discussed the symptomatology of bereavement and the steps physicians should take (*postvention*) to head off further debilitation. Lindemann noted that the survivor may experience loss of muscular power, tightness in the throat, subjective distress and anxiety, a need to cry, shortness of breath, and an empty feeling in the stomach. The article written by Lindemann was one of the first to suggest a link between grief and ensuing physical illness.

Courtesy of the National Institute on Aging

Robert Butler, a psychiatrist and gerontologist, has for a number of years criticized society's treatment of older people.

Schulz (1978) has summarized grief research and listed characteristic phases in *normal grief* and *morbid grief reactions*. *Normal grief* consists of three major phases: initial response, intermediate phase, and recovery phase. Each of these phases has component parts. For example, during the *initial* stages of survivorship, the bereaved may react with shock and disbelief. Physically she or he may experience numbing sensations: feeling cold, dazed, or that it is a bad dream that will soon be over. Next the *intermediate* phase occurs, which is a time of selective remembering (or "obsessional review") of meaningful things about the deceased. A second part of the intermediate phase is what Schulz calls a "search for meaning for the death": "His death can't be in vain; there must be some reason for my suffering." Also during this second phase the mourner begins searching for the deceased (Pincus 1974, Oates 1975; Schulz 1978): For example, a man who has recently been bereaved may set the table for him and his wife or may wait at a familiar spot for her return. In a very real sense, denial of the death is being maintained. Soon, however, the flood walls will break and the reality of the tragedy comes into full awareness. Animal grieving reactions are similar:

Members of lower species protest at the loss of a loved object and do all in their power to seek and recover it; hostility, externally directed, is frequent; withdrawal, rejection of a potential new object, apathy, and restlessness are the rule. (Bowlby 1961, cited in Schulz 1978)

Finally the *recovery stage* triumphs. Acceptance of the death is generally complete, and the bereaved now recognizes that "dwelling on the past is fruitless" (Schulz 1978). Schulz points out that the recovery stage usually starts by the beginning of the second year after the death. Others suggest that there is no timetable for grieving (Oates 1975).

Briefly, pathological or *morbid grief reactions* follow closely these same stages, but the grief reactions are more intense and more sustained. Schulz describes several of Lindemann's early observations concerning morbid grief responses. He suggested that the characteristic feature of morbid grief is a delay in accepting the fact that the person is dead. For example, the bereaved may initially exhibit no noticeable grief reactions. They may even seem cheerful and exceedingly composed in light of the circumstances. As we discussed in connection with children's grief, *delayed grief reactions* are a symptom of heavy denial, denial that cannot be maintained indefinitely. Normal grief thus differs from morbid grief in that the latter is characterized by a delay of acceptance; ultimately, however, these people do work through their grief and reach the stage of recovery. Oates (1975) comments that even in normal recovery, selective memories still occur. Anniversaries, birthdays, and Christmas often once again trigger grieving thoughts.

Some clinical evidence suggests that successful recovery from bereavement requires open weeping and acceptance, as opposed to denial of the death (Oates 1975). Unresolved grief is viewed by many clinicians as an unadaptive and serious response (Pincus 1974). Although there is no immunity from the shock of the loss of a loved one, mourning (weeping) appears to have therapeutic elements. A bereaved patient testifies to the cathartic effect of weeping: "When I cry, I am emptying my emotional bladder and it brings as real a relief as elimination" (Davidson 1975, p. 45).

As we mentioned, some research evidence suggests that bereavement is associated with physical illness and increased mortality rates

George Malave/Stock, Boston

Too much leisure time becomes stressful if one's identity and purpose in life was inordinately tied to a work role.

(Maddison and Viola, 1968). Thomas Holmes and R. H. Rahe (1967) followed the medical histories and records of a large sample of individuals (600) over many years; they found that the frequency of illness and disease—ranging from strokes and cancer to colds, flu, accidents, etc.—was correlated significantly with the occurrence of "life change units" According to these investigators, high totals of "life change units" predispose the person to illness or disease. Rahe (1975) also reports that many other investigators have since confirmed the initial Holmes-Rahe study. Again, as we mentioned in chapter 7, the list of "life change units" has various values—for example, bereavement or death of a spouse receives a score or value of 100. Holmes and Rahe consider this the most serious life change unit. The higher the number assigned to the life change event, the greater are one's chances of developing some sort of physical problem; in other words, Holmes and Rahe contend that a direct relationship exists between the magnitude of life change units and the incidence of physical illness. On Holmes and Rahe's scale, life change units are additive; this means that lesser life change units can add up and accumulate to a high stress score. They suggest 200 life change units as the point at which major illnesses have a high probability of occurring.

A criticism leveled particularly at the life change unit research of Holmes and Rahe is that the self-administered questionnaire filled out by each subject is not reliable (Sarason et al. 1975). According to Sarason and his associates, the self-administered questionnaire is the major source of information about a subject's recent life changes and his or her reported illnesses. But if subjects are retested with this questionnaire, different scores emerge. Since the instrument used by Holmes and Rahe is unreliable, Sarason suggests that the interpretations made by Holmes and Rahe (that stressor events enhance illness) are hazardous.

Aside from Holmes and Rahe's correlational study, other investigations suggest that the chances of developing cancer increase dramatically in those who suffer a loss (bereavement) (LeShan 1966). In a particular investigation involving 4,486 English men, Michael Young and colleagues (1963) reported a 40 percent increase in the mortality rate among the bereaved during the first half year after the loss. Holmes and Rahe noted that widows and widowers have about a ten times higher death rate in general than persons of the same age who have not been bereaved. An American study conducted at Johns Hopkins Medical School in 1956 by Kraus and Lilenfeld (1959) also demonstrated that mortality rates among young widowed persons were significantly greater than the rate for a nonwidowed group. The relationship between marital status and mortality is summarized by them:

> Married people experienced a lower mortality rate from all causes than did single persons, the widowed, and the divorced for every specific age group in each sex and color. . . . The relative excess mortality in the not-married categories compared to the married group was greater at the younger ages. . . . The relative excess mortality in the not-married categories was consistently greater in males than in females. (p. 207)

Many other studies have supported the general findings that bereavement on the one hand, and family or marital ties on the other, affect mortality rates (Lynch 1977). Kobrin and Hendershot (1977) summarized numerous investigations dealing with family ties and mortality and they report that not only are the rates lower for those who are married, but are lower still for those who are married and have children.

Many interpretations are possible for the link between bereavement or family ties and mortality rate. One area of speculation, the *selection hypothesis*, states that healthy individuals tend to select one another for mates. Another view, the

protection hypothesis, states that social interactions somehow protect individuals from certain stresses and illnesses (Kobrin & Hendershot 1977). A third and related view suggests that the shock of bereavement alters the body's immune response system, making the person susceptible to particular diseases. A fourth psychogenic view, related especially to bereavement, suggests that those who are bereaved commit a type of "subintentional suicide." For example, they fail to eat properly, their sleep is disturbed, and they neglect their health in general. As yet, however, there is no conclusive proof for any of these explanatory notions.

ISOLATION

Isolation refers to certain environments where the individual experiences reduced social interaction and involvement with others. Isolation is a psychological stressor because it may provoke further withdrawal and disengagement. Two stressors in the senium especially seem to enhance isolation: bereavement and deterioration of physical health. Clearly the bereaved older individual loses a major source of social involvement and communication. Physical illness and injury for example, limit or restrict social contact. Even institutionalization may exacerbate social isolation. Since many who are confined to nursing homes also have limited social skills and physical mobility, chances for interacting in a meaningful manner are not great. Further, nursing homes and state geriatric institutions draw from a very diverse population. This means that the experiential background of the residents may be so diverse that finding things in common with other patients could be difficult (Gustafson, 1973).

Lastly, failing physical health, causing reduced mobility, drastically restricts the ability of the person to engage and become active.

LEISURE TIME

> [Too] much leisure is apt to be tedious except to those who have considerable intelligence, activities and interests.
> *Bertrand Russell*

Leisure time is a stressor when an individual does not have enough activities (hobbies or work, for example) to occupy his or her time. A surplus of leisure time, according to Berne (1964), violates one of our basic needs: the need to have our time structured. (Berne called this need "structure hunger.") Thus, a superabundance of unstructured time is an aversive stimulus. People escape from or avoid it by doing meaningful work or engaging in approved activities. But for the elderly, opportunities for working and getting involved are reduced.

Unlike work, leisure time and unemployment have no clear social values. Being industrious, working, or saving money do have social value, and so prestigious standing is assigned to these acts. But our society does not consider it an achievement to have leisure time (when you are old), nor does it value playing or spectatorship. Indeed, what Gregory Stone (1972) calls the "ghosts of work" stigmatize the occupationally inactive. As he views this issue, there are "ghosts

of work" in most every segment of our society, persistently spreading the gospel that virtue is achieved only through work. Lurking about, these ghosts cry out that work is the chief component of human dignity. We might call this work-obsession the "anti-leisure ethic"—all play and no work is bound to be bad. Years ago Lord Chesterfield revealed this anti-fun or -leisure ethic when he said:

> To play a good game of billiards is a sign of a well-rounded education, but to play too good a game of billiards is a sign of a misspent youth.

So, while the active or employed may enjoy some leisure time and still retain status, leisure becomes a burden and loses its meaning when there is too much of it.

CLINICAL SYNDROMES OF THE SENIUM: SYMPTOM DESCRIPTION AND ETIOLOGY

In this section we shall cover a broad variety of late onset psychopathologies. Some of these clinical syndromes arise in the *presenium* (before the age of 65), others in the *senium* (after 65). Apart from a few mild abnormal reaction patterns, the syndromes we shall discuss are collectively referred to as *dementias*. Dementias typically have five characteristic features: (1) memory impairment, (2) intellectual impairment, (3) judgment impairment, (4) orientation impairment (confused, wandering), and (5) affect impairment (shallow or shifting moods). Dementias may also be *acute* (temporary) or *chronic* (irreversible and permanent).

The new DSM-III no longer makes a distinction between the symptomatology of presenium dementias and senium dementias; the only distinction is time of onset. Traditionally, abnormal psychology texts and classification systems have listed presenile dementias (Alzheimer's disease, Pick's disease, Huntington's chorea) and senile dementias separately; DSM-III has abandoned this practice, saying that all these should be classified under a single clinical category called *progressive idiopathic dementia* (senile or presenile onset). We shall attempt to incorporate the traditional viewpoint with the newer DSM-III system. In addition, the DSM-III has a second category with rather different characteristics; this second syndrome is

called *multi-infarct* dementia. We shall discuss these along with other syndromes.

PROGRESSIVE IDIOPATHIC DEMENTIAS

Progressive idiopathic dementia has been referred to in the past by various names: *senile dementia, senile psychosis,* or popularly but imprecisely, *senility.* Generally, it has been classified as a mental disorder having a definite organic etiology; that is, it is in the category of brain dysfunctions.

The cardinal features of this syndrome entail the basic features of dementia—impairments of memory, judgment, intelligence, orientation, and affect. Chronic (irreversible) dementia has its onset at about age 70–75. The onset is rather slow in most cases; in the early stages, the individual may experience only memory defects. The spouse or friends may first notice short-term or recent memory failures, but recall of distant experiences (long-term memory) is not impaired. Slowly and insidiously other symptoms emerge. The person becomes easily confused in familiar surroundings. He or she may no longer be able to find the way home. Aimless wandering and restlessness (pacing) become obvious and highly irritating to those living with this person. More symptoms are now superimposed on those just described; there are problems with attention, so that the person may no longer be able to watch television or read. Intellectual functioning falls sharply. The person shows even more pronounced disinterest in her or his environment. During intermediate stages the person may be unable to recognize even close friends and family members and cannot answer simple questions such as "Who are you?" "Who am I?" "Who is your husband?" "Who is your son?" Names and dates utterly confuse these people. In the final stages, according to the DSM-III, the individual may become mute, inattentive, and grossly uncooperative. Death typically occurs approximately five years after onset.

A CASE OF PROGRESSIVE IDIOPATHIC DEMENTIA

The sister of a 68-year-old white married female called Duke University Medical Center and related the following information. Her sister (the patient) had developed difficulty with her memory, especially over the past three years. The condition had worsened over the six months prior to her call and the family had become increasingly disturbed. The patient lived with her 78-year-old husband and had two married sisters with whom she had frequent (almost daily) contact. The husband (a "loner") had very little social outlets other than the sisters of the patient and their husbands. The patient and her husband had had no children.

The patient had a previous history of "nervousness" and this had been especially manifested by periodic outbursts at her employers which led to some difficulties during her working years. One of these outbursts precipitated her premature retirement 8 years ago. The patient was described by her sister and her husband as being very sensitive and shy, but with a very quick temper. Recently they noticed that she did not wish to be left in the house alone and would follow the husband out to his garden toward dusk and scold him severely for not joining her in the house. She also could not remember places that she had visited over many years, though she continued to enjoy visiting. This woman, known for her very quick mind and her meticulous habits, had begun to ask the same question over and over again and to take less interest in her

usual household activities (in particular cooking and housekeeping). She also demonstrated less pride in her appearance (which was particularly troublesome to the husband and the sisters). The husband was very concerned that he could not leave his wife without supervision. Both the husband and two sisters expressed a sense of helplessness at not being able to provide their loved one with the care and help that they felt she needed.

The patient said she had some problems with her nerves and did have a definite problem with her memory. She did not speak spontaneously and answered most questions with either "I don't know" or "Things are all right." She was alert and approximately oriented to time. No severe depression or anxiety was noted. Her physical health was excellent for her age. (Case provided by Dan Blazer, M.D.)

This disorder has an organic etiology, but no clear-cut evidence exists as to predisposing factors. The DSM-III states that in most cases there is evidence of cortical atrophy, widened cortical sulci, and enlarged ventricles in the brain. Senile plaques, neurofibrillary tangles, and other neural degenerative changes occur (Vogel 1977).

Approximately 2 to 4 percent of the population over 65 develop the symptoms of dementia. It apparently is more common in women than in men, but this may in part be related to available statistics. Those admitted to hospitals are more likely to be women, since they are less likely than men to be married to someone younger who can care for them privately. A 75-year-old woman typically is widowed, whereas men of this age are not so likely to be. Thus, when a woman of this age becomes rather demented, there may be no one to care for her; married men of the same age may be exhibiting these symptoms but be cared for at home. Therefore these statistics (more women than men) should be viewed with some reservation.

PRESENIUM SYNDROMES Progressive idiopathic dementia may have a presenium onset or a senium onset. For example, *Alzheimer's disease* is a presenium syndrome, but appears to be the same disorder. In fact, inspection of insults to the brain (biopsy diagnosis) reveals that Down's syndrome, Alzheimer's disease, and senile dementia all have nearly identical lesions (Vogel 1977). Neurofibrillary tangles, senile plagues, and other neural

PROGERIA

Perhaps the most baffling, tragic, and bizarre of all aging disorders is *progeria*. In this exceedingly rare disease, insidious aging begins in a child of 3 to 4 years of age and progresses at an awesome pace. The progeric child physically deteriorates, becoming wrinkled and gray; the eyes protrude, the skin becomes almost opaque; yet mental alertness does not seem to diminish, and so the child is fully conscious of his or her plight (Rosenfeld 1976). By 13 or 14 the child resembles an old man or woman, and death occurs during early adolescence.

degenerations exist for all three. On a positive note, Vogel notes the absence of these degenerative changes in many older people, which suggests to him that ". . . all central nervous systems are not created alike" (p. 237). Nonetheless, Alzheimer's disease does occur much earlier than most forms of senile diseases. In some cases it has emerged in 40-year-old subjects. Death usually comes in five to ten years in these cases.

Pick's disease is another presenium dementia, but there is some confusion as to whether it is variety of progressive idiopathic dementia. For example, Whitehead (1974) points out that those with Pick's disease suffer no great loss of memory, which is typical of early onset progressive idiopathic dementia. Impairment of speech, some intellectual dullness and personality changes, rather than pronounced intellectual changes, seem to be the chief characteristics of Pick's disease. Whitehead elaborates on the deteriorating personality of an individual with this disease:

> A very tidy person may become ill-dressed, and a pillar of society take to drink, theft and sexual experimentation. Blunting of the emotions is common, and child-like behavior with a tendency to play silly games or tell schoolboy jokes is not uncommon. (p. 71)

There has been some evidence that the frontal and temporal lobes are affected in Pick's disease. But other histopathological examinations do not find conclusive results because of the inaccessibility of maximally affected brain areas (Wang 1977). Death typically follows in two to fifteen years after the early onset (Butler & Lewis 1977).

Huntington's chorea is another, very rare, inherited presenile dementia, in which most of the five organic brain symptoms are present. The onset can be as early as age 30, and the major symptoms include confusion, progressive intellectual deterioration, and rapid involuntary jerking (chorea).

Huntington's chorea is a fatal condition, but some victims survive for 20 or 30 years. Because the dementia cannot be reversed, treatment has thus far been aimed at reducing the chorea.

This disorder is thought to be transmitted genetically. Interestingly, this presenile dementia is virtually nonexistent in England and Europe, but more common in the United States. It has been suggested that the bad genes responsible came from three brothers who emigrated to the United States in the seventeenth century (Brain & Watson 1969).

Jakob-Creutzfeld's disease is a presenile dementia that seems to run in particular families. In addition to slow but progressive mental deterioration, there are symptoms of Parkinsonism; that is, the patient shows muscular rigidity, tremors, or spastic weakness of the limbs. Death usually occurs within two to three years (Brain & Watson 1969).

Pitt (1974) has commented that "this disease might be a congenital disease transmitted by a 'slow' virus, which takes almost a lifetime to show its effects."

PARAPHRENIA (SENIUM ONSET SCHIZOPHRENIA)

Paraphrenia is an infrequently observed functional psychosis that resembles paranoid schizophrenia or the paranoid state. The essential difference is that paraphrenia has its onset during senescence. The paraphrenic patient, as Bromley (1971) notes, has a history of seclusiveness and suspicion of others. These traits are amplified by the aging process, resulting in a late onset schizophrenia. Pitt (1974) states that paraphrenics tend to be "female, solitary, partially deaf, and eccentric. . . . " Many other gerontologists have also noted the high incidence of deafness in these patients.

The major symptoms of paraphrenia (patients are usually women) include auditory halluci-

AUDEN ON AN OLD PEOPLES' HOME

All are limitory, but each has her own
nuance of damage. The elite can dress and de-
cent themselves,
        are ambulant with a single stick, adroit
to read a book all through, or play the slow
movements of
        easy sonatas. (Yet, perhaps, their very
carnal freedom is their spirit's bane: intelligent
        of what has happened and why, they are
obnoxious
to a glum beyond tears.) Then come those on
wheels, the average
        majority, who endure T.V. and, led by
lenient therapists, do community singing, then
        the loners, muttering in limbo, and last
the terminally incompetent, as impeccable,
        improvident, unspeakable as the plants
they parody. (Plants may sweat profusely but
never
        sully themselves.) One tie, though, unites
them: all
appeared when the world, though much was
awry there, was more
        spacious, more comely to look at, its Old
Ones
with an audience and secular station. (Then a
child,

in dismay with Mamma, could refuge with
Gran
to be revalued and told a story.) As of now,
        we all know what to expect, but their gen-
eration
is the first to fade like this, not at home but
assigned
        to a numbered frequent ward, stowed out
of conscience
as unpopular luggage.
                As I ride the subway
        to spend half-an-hour with one, I revisage
who she was in the pomp and sumpture of her
hey-day,
        when week-end visits were a presumptive
joy,
not a good work. Am I cold to wish for a speedy
        painless dormition, pray, as I know she
prays,
that God or Nature will abrupt her earthly function?

Reprinted from *Epistle to a Godson and Other
Poems* by W. H. Auden, by permission of Random
House, Inc. © 1970, W. H. Auden.

nations, delusions that she is being watched and
spied on, and the belief that men want to rape and
seduce her. Pitt describes how these women may
respond to their delusions by barricading themselves in their rooms, with many bolts and locks
fastened to the door to hold off the imaginary
enemies.

Unlike those with progressive idiopathic dementia, individuals with paraphrenia may live for
many years after the onset. Shock treatment and
antidepressant drugs have been used (Bromley
1971).

MULTI-INFARCT DEMENTIA

The second major type of dementia is *multi-infarct
dementia*. The term *infarct* roughly means a dying
portion of tissue caused by an obstruction of the

blood supply; the root of the word means "stopped
up" or "clogged." The clinical category *multi-infarct dementia* is the new term used in DSM-III and
other sources to refer to dementia that is linked
directly to clear-cut vascular or vessel disturbances
in the brain. Specifically, a succession of small
strokes (multi-infarct) has destroyed a sufficient
amount of neural tissue to produce dementia
(DSM-III). In the past, this reaction was often called
"organic brain syndrome with cerebral arteriosclerosis." In England it is still called "arteriosclerotic psychosis."

Multi-infarct dementia has some noteworthy
differences from idiopathic dementia. First, intellectual deterioration may not be complete as it is
with the idiopathic variety; that is, the person with
multi-infarct dementia may have what is called
"patchy deterioration." Certain functions are apparently unaffected. The second major difference is
that multi-farct dementia has a much more sudden

onset and follows an erratic course, rather than uniform deterioration. In addition, clinical symptoms often reported include complaints of dizziness; blackouts and headaches; slurring of speech; depression, confusion, and wide emotional fluctuations (lability); weakness of the limbs; and involuntary muscle tremors and rigidity (Parkinsonism).

As with the other dementias, the exact cause of multi-infarct dementia is not completely understood. Some gerontologists and geropsychiatrists believe that genetics is involved; others claim that diet (high fat and high sugar intake), little exercise, smoking, hypertension, and environmental stress may predispose an individual to this disorder.

In marked contrast to cases of progressive idiopathic dementia, those with multi-infarct dementia appear to have a varied prognosis. Some patients with this syndrome may die shortly after the initial stroke, while others, if their blood pressure is brought down, may live on for 10 to 15 years after the onset. Treatment efforts at this time seem to be more promising for multi-infarct dementia, mainly because the nature of the damage is better understood. For example, since this syndrome is linked in many cases to hypertension, control of this problem lessens the chances for additional strokes. In some cases, anticoagulant drugs have been administered. We shall discuss other treatment possibilities in the next section.

A CASE OF CONFUSED ORIENTATION

NURSE: Good morning Mrs. E. Did you have a nice rest last night?

MRS. E: Dear Sue, where have you and your brothers been? I have made lunch and have been waiting for you kids.

NURSE: Mrs. E, Do you know where you are?

MRS. E: Who are you? I hate the abusive treatment I've been getting here. I want my kids.

NURSE: Your sister is coming by to see you this afternoon, Mrs. E. Won't that be nice?

MRS. E: I don't have a sister. Where is Sue? I know all sorts of things. I am still a very good teacher. Have you handed in your work? I taught kids your age and I must get back to work.

TREATMENT AND THERAPY EFFORTS

INSTITUTIONALIZATION

The term *institutionalization* broadly refers to full-time, long-term, residential care. Institutionalization further involves comprehensive care; that is, many services are provided. Care may be given at a state geriatric hospital (usually a wing or section of a state mental hospital), a private nursing home, or other health facilities. As the most widely used facility is the private nursing home, we will focus on this sort of institutionalization.

The subject of nursing homes provokes certain natural reactions—some people have concluded that nursing homes are dumping grounds for those who are no longer wanted. A related reaction is that there is no justifiable reason for placing a person in such a facility. But there are many other considerations. Admitting a relative with dementia to a nursing home is usually the last resort taken by a family. At that point, other family members are desperate; after the dementia is full blown, the disoriented behaviors often become so distracting that the spouse or other family members cannot cope. Full-time care is needed. In other cases, the person who has become demented was living alone; these people are in danger of coming to serious harm. They may leave the stove on, forget to turn off the water, wander around town at night, and in general show no sign of being able to meet their own basic needs. Others who have brain syndromes may squander a life's savings in a short time, then have no money to feed and clothe themselves. When conditions such as these develop, and they do for a small percentage of elderly persons, then institutionalization may be the only alternative. Goldfarb (1977) makes this important point:

> Well-intentioned advocates of keeping old people out of congregated residential settings are often unaware of, or ignore, the high proportion of the elderly ill, impaired, or disabled who have no protective family; family members may be dead, ill, alienated, or emotionally incapable of provid-

ing protective care. Studies of the pathways to institutions show that the very old, the very ill, and the severely impaired are not "dumped" by families but find their way into institutions as a last resort after heroic efforts have been made to keep them in their own or a relative's home. (p. 266)

Admitting a person to an institution surely is one of the more traumatic decisions for a family or a spouse to make. Guilt of the highest level is often experienced by family members who agree to the institutionalization. But only the uninformed and inexperienced can say categorically that institutionalization is bad. No doubt it is the last resort in many cases, but unfortunately, it may be the only alternative for some families.

Nursing homes, as almost everyone knows, have been severely criticized, and rightly so in many cases. Yet all nursing homes are not guilty of the charges leveled against them. Generalizations are almost impossible, for nursing homes vary remarkably with respect to physical plant, food service, social programs, medical staff, and administration. In some cases the care provided is excellent; in other cases patients are actually abused (Brown 1977). But some patients do receive good medical services, social services, psychological counseling, and the basic necessities.

The therapeutic methods available in nursing homes cover a broad range of services: occupational therapy, physical therapy, recreational activities, psychotherapy, drug therapy, behavior modification, reality orientation, and other methods. None of these methods is enough by itself.

DRUG THERAPY

Medication may be given both in institutional settings and on an out-patient basis. In describing some of the drugs that are often used with geriatric patients, we shall attempt to describe fairly both their benefits and their negative side-effects.

Many geropsychiatrists (psychiatrists who are trained specifically for working with abnormal or psychopathological problems in the senium) divide drugs into three main categories (Whitehead 1974; Pitt 1974):

1. *Tranquilizers* (used to treat anxiety, agitation, mania, psychotic behavior).

2. *Sedatives and hypnotics* (used principally to induce sleep or combat insomnia).
3. *Antidepressives* (used to treat mood disorders, particular depression).

Tranquilizers are widely prescribed for elderly people who are confused, especially those who are agitated and manic. One of the most widely used drugs is Librium; Valium, a stronger tranquilizer, may also be given. These drugs do have some calming effects, but in time many patients seem to build up a tolerance. The side-effects are not too serious for most patients, however. For those patients who are more seriously disturbed, drugs such as Mellaril and Haldol are used extensively. Most tranquilizers cause drowsiness but Haldol may also produce Parkinsonism symptoms (muscle spasms, tremors). These symptoms are sometimes called "extrapyramidal effects," because they appear to affect the extrapyramidal pathways that descend from the brain conveying motor impulse control. The face in particular may show signs of tremors and drooping caused by high doses of antipsychotic drugs; these side-effects are referred to as *tardive dyskinesia*. Haldol does appear, however, to control manic and psychotic behavior to some extent. Some individuals, however, seem to be made worse by antipsychotic drugs.

The *phenothiazines* are potent tranquilizing and antipsychotic drugs. Unfortunately, they may have more serious side-effects than Haldol. In some patients, for example, blood pressure may drop sharply (hypotension), further reducing vital blood flow through the brain. Tardive dyskinesia is a common problem with the use of phenothiazines.

Second, *sedatives* and *hypnotics* are extensively used by elderly persons who have problems sleeping. Initially, the sedatives and hypnotics may aid the person to sleep, but eventually dosage has to be increased, which can produce serious side-effects. Both physical and psychological dependence can occur, and sudden withdrawal from these drugs is dangerous. Further, hypnotics or sedatives such as the barbiturates increase the risk of self-poisoning or attempted suicide. Commonly used sedative-hypnotic medications are: secobarbital, phenobarbital, mutabarbital, chloral hydrate, methaqualone, and flurazepam. Some geropsychiatrists feel it is better never to start medicating older people with potent hypnotics.

Because depression is a frequently occurring problem in the senium and in certain late onset psychopathologies, *antidepressants* are often prescribed. Antidepressants used with elderly patients typically come from three subcategories: *tricyclic antidepressants* (imipramine is a common one); *monoamine oxidase inhibitors* (MAO); and *lithium carbonate.* Each has special benefits and side-effects, but for the most part they all decrease depressive moods to some extent. In addition, antidepressants often have tranquilizing effects. The side-effects, however, may be serious. Lithium carbonate can adversely alter electrolyte balance in older patients; the tricyclics may be contraindicated for patients with cardiac or heart problems. Additionally, tricyclics may induce seizures because they lower the seizure threshold. The MAOs can exacerbate hypertension, a common disorder in many older patients.

Finally, we should mention that substances other than tranquilizers, sedatives and antidepressives are often given to older persons with organic impairment. For example, megavitamin regimes are often used in combination with other drugs. Vasodilators, such as *Hydergine* are sometimes prescribed; Hydergine is supposed to increase the flow of blood through the brain, thereby enhancing neurologic functioning. Various Vitamin B supplements (nicotinic acid in particular) are often given for the purpose of increasing circulation. It should be recognized that at this time no evidence has emerged to demonstrate the direct benefit of vitamins or vasodilators on brain syndromes.

Biochemical treatment for dementias is not highly effective, but there are at present no alternatives to treat gross symptoms. The side-effects are no doubt serious, yet in many cases, patients not treated with some of these drugs may do serious harm to themselves. Finally, drug therapy seems best if coupled with supportive environmental efforts such as occupational therapy, recreational activities, and visits from relatives and friends. Figure 19.1 shows treatment methods that should be available for older people with problems. It is important to note that multiple treatments are often prescribed.

HOME HELP SERVICES AND REHABILITATION

Not all patients with progressive idiopathic dementia or multi-infarct dementia are institutionalized. Some communities provide what are sometimes called *home help services* to those people who wish to keep the ill person at home. Many communities are funded to provide trained volunteers or paid

HARRY & TONTO © **1974, 20th Century-Fox. This film is atypical of a genre that until recently has generally characterized aged persons as foolish and unattractive. To a large extent, popular films reflect popular prejudices.**

nurses to supervise and care for the person. Home help is sometimes the only alternative for families who wish to institutionalize a seriously demented relative, but find they cannot afford it. The cost of nursing home care, unless a family is on welfare or has very little income and so can receive public aid, is very high, even with Medicare and Medicaid. Good nursing home care, Scott (1978) reports, costs the patient or family between $600 and $1,200 a month. Scott also notes that the present system of financing nursing home care needs to be overhauled, because those with incomes above the poverty level may exhaust their entire savings caring for the person. Home help services then become a viable alternative if they are available. Again, however, those who have incomes above the poverty level may have to spend $10 to $20 dollars a day for home help care.

For persons not too seriously disturbed, some rehabilitation efforts can be made. Many of those with multi-infarct problems may also be paralyzed

Developmental
Features of
Psychopathology
PART 3

from a stroke; rehabilitation and physical therapy are often tried, and in many cases the patient can regain the use of his or her limbs. Others may be taught again to dress and care for themselves.

Rehabilitation, Pitt (1974) writes, may not restore ability lost through various dementias, but the patient may learn to make the best of the abilities remaining.

TREATMENT METHODS
Figure 19.1

Typical treatment methods used with various problem behaviors. Note that many of the treatment methods are used concurrently. (From Whitehead 1974)

	ECT	Drug Treatment	Behavior Therapy	O.T.	Social Therapies	Milieu Therapy	Group Psycho-therapy	Individual Psycho-therapy
PSYCHOTIC DEPRESSION	Major	Major		Important	Important	Important	Possible	Possible
MANIA AND HYPOMANIA	Major	Major		Important	Important	Important	Possible	Possible
PARAPHRENIA	Possible	Major		Major	Major	Major	Major	Possible
NEUROTIC DEPRESSION		Major		Important	Important	Major	Major	Possible
ANXIETY STATES		Major	Important	Possible	Possible	Possible	Major	Major
PHOBIC STATES		Major	Major	Possible	Possible	Possible	Major	Major
OBSESSIONAL COMPULSIVE STATES	Possible	Major	Major				Major	Major
PSYCHOSOMATIC DISORDERS		Possible					Major	Major
SEXUAL PROBLEMS			Major				Major	Major
PERSONALITY DISORDERS						Important	Major	Major
ORGANIC BRAIN DISEASES				Important*	Major	Major	Important	Important

Note: In the "ORGANIC BRAIN DISEASES" row the shading appears under Drug Treatment (light), O.T. (dark), Social Therapies (dark), Milieu Therapy (dark), Group Psychotherapy (light), Individual Psychotherapy (light).

Legend:
- ▓ Major Treatment for Condition
- ▒ Other Important Treatment for Condition
- ☐ Treatment of Possible Use

A number of other investigators have demonstrated the potential effectiveness of behavior therapy techniques with neurotic depression, psychosomatic disorders, and personality disorders in children and young adults. Although Whitehead has not indicated this in his chart, there is no reason to suspect these techniques would not benefit geriatric patients as well.

SUMMARY

1. Aging is a process associated with declining efficiency and functioning. It resembles disease to some degree, but aging is irreversible. Aging seems to be caused by a combination of genetic and environmental factors. There are three types of aging: *biological aging, social aging, psychological aging.*

2. *Biological aging* refers to alterations specifically affecting the skin, musculature, sense organs, bones, central nervous system, and all other physical components of the body. Individuals do not age at the same rate.

3. *Social aging* occurs when the individual adopts or is assigned to various age-related roles. Retirement or becoming a grandparent, for instance, requires adopting new roles and social behaviors. *Disengagement* is a particular theory of social aging, which suggests that the older person gradually relinquishes social roles and occupational activities. Disengagement is thought to be in part a coping mechanism by which the person gradually becomes accustomed to both reduced physical powers and reduced social involvement.

4. *Psychological aging* refers to retrograde alterations in emotions, memory, and learning ability, along with increased frequency of certain negative emotions such as depression. The increases in anxiety, depression, guilt, and other negative emotions are related to increased exposure to various environmental stressors and biological changes.

5. During *senescence* or the *senium,* certain sorts of social and environmental stressors appear to increase. Four important stressors are retirement, bereavement, isolation, and leisure time. Bereavement and retirement seem to be the most stressful of the four.

6. Various *dementias* have their onset during the senium. Dementia is often defined by the presence of five major impairments: those of memory, intelligence, judgment, orientation, and affect. Two major types of dementias exist during old age: *progressive idiopathic dementia* (early onset, prior to old age; late onset, after age 65) and *multi-infarct dementia.*

7. Progressive idiopathic dementia is still often called *senile dementia* or *senile psychosis.* This disorder has a rather gradual onset, follows a steady course of intellectual and cognitive degeneration, and terminates in death.

8. Multi-infarct dementia has a sudden onset (mainly because of the small strokes); this disorder does not always cause the extensive intellectual and cognitive alterations that are exhibited by patients with progressive idiopathic dementia. Multi-infarct dementia is often called *cerebral arteriosclerosis* or arteriosclerotic psychosis. Multi-infarct dementia appears to be a vascular disorder, while the other form of dementia appears to be a degenerative or neuron loss disorder. There is no cure for either disorder, although the prognosis is much better for multi-infarct dementia.

9. *Institutionalization* is one way of dealing with profoundly confused elderly persons. Institutionalization may take place in a geriatrics ward of a state mental hospital or in a private nursing home. Institutionalization, for the most part, does not involve just custodial care. Often efforts are made to rehabilitate certain patients; recreational activities as well as reality orientations are provided.

10. *Drug therapy* is frequently used with confused elderly patients. Drug therapy may be given in conjunction with other strategies such as psychotherapy, institutionalization, or ordinary home care.

11. Three general categories of drugs are often used to treat confused older individuals: *tranquilizers,* which are subdivided into mild anti-anxiety drugs and the more powerful antipsychotic tranquilizers such as Haldol and the phenothiazines; *sedatives* and *hypnotics,* which are used to treat sleep impairments; and *antidepressants.* All biochemical interventions have side-effects, although in many cases they provide the only alternative.

12. Many older patients who experience confu-

sion and profound dementia may be cared for at home. In the initial stages of dementia, home care may be satisfactory, but if deterioration becomes profound, the unaffected spouse or family member may find that the care is too great for her or him to provide.

RECOMMENDED READINGS

Butler, R. N., & Lewis, M. I. *Aging and mental health*. St. Louis: C. V. Mosby, 1977.

Busse, E. W., & Pfeiffer, E. *Behavior and adaptation in late life*. Boston: Little, Brown, 1977.

Cox, H. *Focus: Aging* (annual edition). Guilford, Conn.: Dushkin Publishing Group, 1978.

Huyck, M. H. *Growing older*. New York: Spectrum Books (Prentice-Hall), 1974.

Kart, C. S., Metress, E. S., & Metress, J. F. *Aging & health: Biologic and social perspectives*. Menlo Park, Cal.: Addison-Wesley, 1978.

Pincus, L. *Death and the family: The importance of mourning*. New York: Vintage Books, 1974.

Schulz, R. *The psychology of death, dying, and bereavement*. Menlo Park, Cal.: Addison-Wesley, 1978.

GLOSSARY

ACUTE SCHIZOPHRENIA Schizophrenia characterized by a rapid onset of schizophrenic symptoms, with the patient having had little previous hospitalization.

ADDICTION See *Drug addiction*.

ADRENOCHROME An adrenalin-like substance that, when present in large amounts, is converted into its metabolite adrenolutin rather than its normal product, dihydroxy-N-methylindole; it is assumed by some to produce symptoms of schizophrenia.

ADRENOLUTIN A metabolite of adrenochrome that is assumed by some to produce schizophrenic symptomatology.

ADULT EGO STATE In transactional analysis, the rational component of the personality, which appraises the environment objectively and functions accordingly.

AFFECT A subjective feeling or emotional tone, often accompanied by bodily expressions noticeable to others; the term is synonymous with emotion.

AFFECT IMPAIRMENT A side-effect of certain forms of psychopathology in which inappropriate feelings or emotions are displayed.

AFFECTIVE DISORDERS In DSM-III, a category that includes disorders characterized by severe alterations of mood.

AGEISM The assigning of status according to age and the denial of reinforcement opportunities chiefly because of age (age discrimination).

AKINETIC A type of petit mal epileptic seizure marked by a sudden loss of muscle tone that causes the person to fall if unsupported.

ALARM REACTION According to Selye, the response of a person to a stressful situation, which marks the beginning of *diseases of adaptation*.

ALCOHOLIC PSYCHOSIS A form of alcoholism that leads to brain damage and appearance of psychotic-type behavior.

ALCOHOLISM A behavioral disorder characterized by excessive and continuous consumption of alcoholic beverages, resulting in psychological dependence on alcohol.

ALPHA ALCOHOLISM A pattern of problem drinking (described by Jellinek) in which an individual relies on alcohol as the primary means of relieving bodily or emotional stress and discomfort.

ALTERNATING PERSONALITY A multiple personality in which two personalities or identities alternate with one another, each having amnesia for the thoughts and behavior of the other.

ALTRUISTIC SUICIDE As defined by Durkheim, self-annihilation that is felt to be the proper response to an accepted value system of the culture because it serves a social purpose; the suicide missions of the Japanese kamikaze pilots during World War II are an example.

ALZHEIMER'S DISEASE An early onset dementia marked by a progressive destruction of tissue that results in slurring of speech, involuntary muscular movements, and gradual intellectual impairment.

AMBIVALENT AFFECT An emotional state in which both positive and negative emotions are expressed simultaneously toward a single person or event.

AMENTIA A term used to refer to mental retardation.

AMNESIA A hysterical dissociative reaction characterized by partial or total loss of memory of past experiences.

AMNIOCENTESIS A pre-birth assessment procedure in which amniotic fluid is removed and tested in order to detect and predict certain genetic or chromosomal defects.

AMYGDALA An area of the brain (part of the lymbic system) involved with aggression and other emotions.

ANACLITIC DEPRESSION A psychoanalytic term referring to profound sadness of an infant who is separated from its mother for a prolonged period.

ANECTINE A muscle-paralyzing drug used in *aversion therapy* for drug abuse.

ANGIOGRAM A brain X-ray procedure used to diagnose organic brain damage.

ANOMIC SUICIDE As defined by Durkheim, self-annihilation triggered by the person's inability to cope with sudden changes in the normal functioning of his or her social situation.

ANOMIE PERSPECTIVE A social theory contending that when the norms governing behavior become vague and ambiguous (normlessness) deviance occurs.

ANOREXIA NERVOSA A type of psychophysiological disorder, found predominantly in adolescent females, characterized by the inability or refusal to eat and a resultant profound weight loss.

ANTABUSE (DISULFIRAM) A chemical that interferes with the metabolic processing of alcohol; it is used in aversion therapy with alcoholics.

ANTIDEPRESSANT A drug used to treat mood disorders, particularly depression.

ANTISOCIAL PERSONALITY A diagnosis applied to individuals who have repeated conflicts with society, are selfish, have a lack of anxiety and guilt, and are incapable of loyalty to others. The term is synonymous with "sociopath" and "psychopath."

ANXIETY A generalized state of fear and apprehension.

ANXIETY ATTACK Acute episode of intense anxiety in which the individual cannot identify the source of the threat.

ANXIETY DISORDER In DSM-III, a category that includes problem behaviors associated with a significant degree of subjective feelings of anxiety.

ANXIETY NEUROSIS (free-floating anxiety). Disorder characterized by chronic anxiety and apprehension that does not appear to have any specific cause.

APGAR TEST A type of physical rating scale used to evaluate vital signs in newborns.

APHASIA Loss or impairment of the ability to use language because of hypothesized brain pathology: *executive*, difficulties in speaking or writing; *receptive*, difficulties in understanding written or spoken language.

ARBITRARY INFERENCE The tendency of an individual to draw a conclusion illogically from an experience or situation that is not supported by a sufficient amount of real evidence.

ARGYLL-ROBERTSON SIGN A sign occurring during the fourth stage of syphilitic infection, in which the pupils of the eye fail to respond to light.

ASSERTION TRAINING A behavior therapy procedure for helping individuals express themselves more directly in interpersonal relationships.

ASSOCIATIVE TECHNIQUE A type of projective technique in which the subject is instructed to respond to a stimulus with the first word, image, or thought that comes to mind. The Rorschach Inkblot Test is an example.

ASTHMA A psychophysiological disorder of the bronchial system caused by narrowing of the airways and increased secretion of mucus, which in turn causes wheezing, coughing, and general difficulty in breathing.

ATYPICAL AFFECTIVE DISORDERS In DSM-III, a category of affective disorders that cannot be classified as "episodic affective disorders" or "chronic affective disorders."

AUGMENTERS Individuals who show an increase in the size of the *cortical evoked potential* as stimulus intensity increases.

AURA (1) Signal or warning of an impending epileptic convulsion, in the form of dizziness or an unusual sensory experience. (2) A subjective sensation alerting an individual to the impending onset of a migraine headache.

AUTISM Extreme self-interest or fantasy employed to avoid communication and to escape external reality. See also *Infantile autism*.

AUTONOMIC NERVOUS SYSTEM Part of the peripheral nervous system that regulates endocrine glands, smooth muscle, and heart muscle; it also initiates physiological responses to emotion via two divisions, the *sympathetic* and the *parasympathetic*.

AVERSION THERAPY Form of behavior therapy in which aversive stimulation or punishment is used to eliminate unwanted behavior.

AVOIDANCE CONDITIONING A method in which a neutral stimulus is paired with a noxious one, resulting in avoidance of the previously neutral stimulus.

B

BASE RATE Pre-therapy level of behavior against which post-therapy level is measured to evaluate efficacy of treatment.

BATTERED CHILD SYNDROME A term referring to persistent physical abuse of a child, typically resulting in significant tissue damage, broken bones, or death.

BERIBERI A dysfunction of the brain produced by dramatic restriction of B vitamins (also called Wernicke's encephalopathy).

BETA ALCOHOLISM A pattern of problem drinking (described by Jellinek) that involves physical complaints and complications, such as cirrhosis of the liver or gastritis.

BIOFEEDBACK A term referring to procedures used to train individuals to gain voluntary control over their physiological responses.

BIOLOGICAL AGING The process of physical decline over a rather extensive period of time.

BIOLOGICAL PERSPECTIVE A group of viewpoints in which physical or organic factors are assumed to account for abnormal behavior.

BIPOLAR AFFECTIVE DISORDER An affective disorder that, according to the DSM-III, is characterized by both mania and depression.

BLOOD-BRAIN BARRIER A protective mechanism of the brain that acts to screen the flow of harmful substances from the bloodstream into the brain and subsequently into the rest of the nervous system.

BORDERLINE SYNDROME A pronounced conflict between the yearning for independence and autonomy and the fear of parental abandonment.

BRADYKININ A pain-threshold chemical thought to be a precursor of a migraine headache; it is released at the site of the dilated vessels, causing an inflammatory reaction.

BRIQUET'S SYNDROME In DSM-III, a category used to describe a chronic disorder characterized by frequent and multiple somatic complaints unattributable to any real physical illness; also called "somatization disorder."

BROAD-SPECTRUM BEHAVIOR THERAPY A term used to emphasize the fact that most behavior therapists employ several different treatment procedures for a specific disorder in an attempt to deal effectively with all the important controlling or causal variables.

BROCA'S AREA   A portion of the left cerebral hemisphere said to control motor speech.

BROMIDES   A substance (potassium bromide) used in many "over-the-counter" nonprescription sleeping pills; if taken in high doses, bromides are toxic and can cause psychotic-type hallucinations, delusions, and permanent brain damage unless appropriate medical treatment is given.

BULIMIA   An eating disorder characterized by voracious episodic eating binges.

C

CANNABIS SATIVA   Indian hemp plant from which marijuana and hashish are derived.

CATAPLEXY   A rare symptom that accompanies *narcolepsy* and involves complete loss of muscle tone.

CATATONIC IMMOBILITY (CATATONIA)   Rigidity of posture maintained for long periods with accompanying muscular rigidity, trancelike state of consciousness, and *waxy flexibility*.

CATATONIC SCHIZOPHRENIA   A psychotic disorder characterized by symptoms of stuporous immobility (catatonic immobility) that sometimes alternate with excited agitation.

CAT-CRY SYNDROME (*CRI DU CHAT*)   A severe form of organic retardation in infants, characterized by "cat-like cries" due to laryngeal abnormalities. Other abnormalities include low-set ears, microcephaly, and profound retardation.

CATECHOLAMINE HYPOTHESIS   Schildkraut's theory, which suggests that too little norepinephrine produces an understimulation of nerve fibers and thus the underexcitability of depression.

CATHARTIC METHOD   Therapy procedure introduced in the nineteenth century by Joseph Breuer whereby a patient, under hypnosis, relives traumatic childhood events.

CENTRAL NERVOUS SYSTEM   The part of the nervous system including the brain and spinal cord through which all sensory impulses are transmitted and from which motor impulses pass; supervises activities of the complete nervous system.

CEREBELLUM   The largest part of the hindbrain, responsible for balance and the fine control of muscle movements.

CEREBRAL ARTERIOSCLEROSIS   A cerebrovascular disorder involving the hardening and narrowing of arteries of the brain, which predisposes the person to ruptures and blockages.

CEREBRAL EMBOLISM   A cerebrovascular disorder of circulation due to blockage of a blood vessel by a blood clot or fatty deposits.

CEREBRAL HEMISPHERE   The outermost section of the brain, composed of two large sections of cerebral cortex or grey matter.

CEREBRAL STROKE   A sudden cerebrovascular disorder that occurs when a blood vessel in the brain ruptures; the term is synonymous with "cerebral hemorrhage."

CEREBRAL VASODILATOR DRUGS   Drugs used to "draw" or "pull" blood away from a clotted or ruptured area and so lessen further damage.

CEREBROVASCULAR DISORDERS   Interruptions of the blood supply to the brain: two basic kinds are those resulting in the *rupture* of blood vessels and those resulting in the *blockage* of blood vessels.

CHEMOTHERAPY   The use of drugs in the treatment of a disorder.

CHILDHOOD SCHIZOPHRENIA   A childhood psychosis, occurring after age 5, marked by *hallucinations* and other perceptual distortions, impairment of emotional relationships with others, and distorted body movements.

CHLORDIAZEPOXIDE HYDROCHLORIDE (LIBRIUM)   A compound used as a tranquilizer in the treatment of various psychoneuroses and alcoholism.

CHLORPROMAZINE (THORAZINE)   Major tranquilizer used to control the symptoms of agitation and thought disturbances commonly found in schizophrenia.

CHOICE TECHNIQUE (ORDERING TECHNIQUE)   A type of projective technique in which the individual chooses from stimuli according to some specified criterion such as correctness or attractiveness.

CHRONIC AFFECTIVE DISORDERS In DSM-III, a category of affective disorders in which there exists long-standing (at least two years) manifestation of symptoms.

CHRONIC SCHIZOPHRENIA Schizophrenia characterized by a gradual onset of schizophrenic symptoms, with the patient usually having been hospitalized for more than two years.

CLANG ASSOCIATION In schizophrenia, a sentence or statement made up of an illogical series of rhyming words chained together simply because they rhyme.

CLASSICAL CONDITIONING Pavlov's basic learning method, whereby a neutral stimulus is paired repeatedly with another stimulus (the unconditioned stimulus or UCS) that elicits a certain unconditioned reflexive response (UCR). After repeated pairings, the neutral stimulus becomes a conditioned stimulus (CS) and evokes the same or similar response (the conditioned response or CR).

CLIENT-CENTERED THERAPY A form of psychotherapy, developed by Carl Rogers, that emphasizes the importance of understanding the client's subjective feelings and experiences and encouraging an increase in the client's awareness of current motivations for actions.

CLONIC PHASE State of violent spasms, contortions, and jerking movements during a grand mal epileptic attack.

CLOSED HEAD INJURIES Injuries caused by forces that do not penetrate the skull, such as concussions, contusions, and hemorrhages.

COCAINE ("COKE") A stimulant drug extracted from the leaves of the coca plant. The drug produces a state of extreme euphoria, increases energy level and sleeplessness, and reduces tension and depression.

CO-CONSCIOUS A term used to describe the subconscious but totally aware state of the subordinate personality (or personalities) that can exist in a multiple personality hysterical dissociative reaction.

COLLAGEN Connective tissue that binds muscles or organs together, but gradually loses its elasticity as age increases.

COMA PHASE State in which the individual remains unconscious but the muscles relax; it is the last phase of the grand mal epileptic attack.

COMMITMENT A legal procedure required for the mandatory placement of an individual in a mental institution.

COMPETENCY A legal decision as to whether an individual is capable of understanding and adhering to responsibilities such as participating in his or her own legal defense.

COMPLETION TECHNIQUE A type of projective technique in which the respondent is requested to complete an incomplete project in any manner he or she wishes. The Rotter Incomplete Sentence Test is an example.

CONFABULATION A maneuver used by an individual to fill in memory gaps with imagined experiences.

CONFLICT SUBCULTURE A subculture that encourages dyssocial behavior by the value placed on personal characteristics such as physical courage and violence.

CONGENITAL SYPHILIS One form of the infection caused by the syphilitic spirochete bacteria if it has been transmitted from mother to child during the fetal development period.

CONSTRUCT A concept inferred from observable behavior. "Ego" or "id" are constructs inferred from certain overt behaviors.

CONSTRUCTION TECHNIQUE A type of projective technique in which an individual is required to create or construct something, such as a story or picture. The Thematic Apperception Test is an example.

CONTENT ANALYSIS An assessment technique that provides a basis for quantifying verbal behavior.

CONTIGUITY THEORY A learning theory that assumes a learned connection has been made between two stimuli because they have occurred at approximately the same time, or between a stimulus and a response because they have occurred contiguously.

CONTINGENCY MANAGEMENT A behavior modification procedure involving the contingent administration of rewarding (reinforcing) consequences or events.

CONVERSION A defense mechanism in which unacceptable impulses are converted into physical symptoms that may be symbolic representations of the repressed thoughts or impulses.

CORTICAL EVOKED POTENTIAL (CEP) A type of electrical activity in the brain that is stimulated by incoming sensory signals; the higher the intensity of the incoming stimulus, the larger the CEP response.

COUNTERCONDITIONING Relearning by eliciting a new response from a particular stimulus.

COVERT SENSITIZATION A verbal or cognitive method in which unpleasant events are imagined simultaneously as the abnormal behavior is imagined.

CRETINISM A congenital hormone imbalance caused by a thyroxine deficiency and marked by mental retardation and physical disabilities.

CRIMINAL RESPONSIBILITY A legal decision on whether a criminal act committed by an individual was the direct result of some type of mental illness; if so, the individual would not be held responsible for his or her actions.

CRIMINAL SUBCULTURE A subculture that encourages dyssocial behavior by viewing success in crime as a positive form of behavior.
of behavior.

CULTURAL BIAS A term applied to the theory that items on most intelligence tests are more familiar to middle-class children than to their lower class peers, resulting in higher-level performances by the middle-class children.

CULTURAL-FAMILIAL RETARDATION Mild mental retardation with no known organic cause, but with evidence of similar limitations found in at least one of the parents or siblings.

CULTURAL HERITAGE As related to child abuse, the assumption that the inherited tradition of viewing children as property with few if any rights may be a contributory factor.

CULTURAL RELATIVISM Judgments based on the acceptable behavior patterns and normative expectations of a given society.

CYPROTERONE ACETATE A chemical that acts as an anti-androgen compound, thereby mimicking the female hormone, estrogen. Mimics castration with regard to sexual arousal.

D

DEGREE OF FAMILY INDIVIDUATION The amount of uniqueness a family will tolerate in its members.

DÉJÀ VU A sudden feeling of intense familiarity in a strange place or situation.

DELAYED RESPONSE PHENOMENON The hypothesis that some reactions to stressful events do not occur immediately, but instead emerge many years later.

DELIRIUM TREMENS (DTs) A psychotic-type reaction that can occur in the excessive drinker either during a period of abstinence or withdrawal from alcohol or during periods of extensive drinking. Symptoms include disorientation in place and time, hallucinations, and tremors.

DELTA ALCOHOLISM A pattern of problem drinking (described by Jellinek) that includes individuals who cannot abstain from drinking but can regulate the amount they drink.

DELUSIONS A belief contrary to reality, firmly held in spite of evidence to the contrary; common in paranoid disorders. *Of grandeur*, belief that one is an especially important or powerful person; *of persecution*, belief that one is being plotted against or oppressed by others; *of control*, belief that one is being manipulated by some external force; *Hypochondriacal*, belief that one is afflicted by some bizarre somatic disorder.

DEMENTIA Noticeable progressive deterioration of mental functioning occurring after adolescence.

DEMENTIA PRAECOX An older term for schizophrenia, used to describe what was thought to be an incurable and progressive deterioration of mental functioning beginning in adolescence.

DEMOGRAPHIC FACTOR Vital or social statistical information about an individual or sample group used to make determinations such as vulnerability to suicide.

DEMONOLOGY Belief that a person's abnormal behavior is caused by an "evil spirit" dwelling inside his or her body.

DEPENDENT VARIABLE In a psychological experiment, the measured behavior that is expected to change with the manipulation of the independent variable.

DEPERSONALIZATION NEUROSIS Neurotic reaction characterized by feelings of personal alienation and little sense of purpose and control over one's life.

DEPRESSION Emotional state marked by great sadness and apprehension; feelings of worthlessness and guilt; withdrawal from others; loss of sleep, appetite, and sexual desire; and either lethargy or agitation.

DEPRESSIVE DISORDER An affective disorder that, according to the DSM-III, is characterized by dominant behavioral symptoms of depression.

DEPRESSIVE NEUROSIS Neurotic reaction characterized by persistent dejection and despondency, usually precipitated by some environmental setback or interpersonal loss.

DIATHESIS-STRESS THEORY As applied in psychopathology, a paradigm that assumes an individual genetically predisposed toward a disorder will be profoundly affected by exposure to environmental stresses, and will manifest abnormal behavior.

DIAZEPAM (VALIUM) A tranquilizer used especially to relieve anxiety and tension, and as a muscle relaxant.

DIGIT SPAN TEST A numerical test to assess memory skills that requires repeating digits.

DISEASES OF ADAPTATION According to Selye, the variety of physiological symptoms that appear when physiological resources are demobilized or exhausted because of prolonged stress.

DISENGAGEMENT The phase of social aging in which the person gradually gives up social roles and relationships.

DISORIENTATION A state of mental confusion with regard to time, place, and the identity of the self, other persons, and objects.

DISPLACEMENT An ego defense mechanism in which aggressive or sexual instincts are shifted from a possibly dangerous object or concept to a safe one.

DISSOCIATIVE DISORDERS In DSM-III, a category that includes disorders characterized by alterations in consciousness, such as amnesia.

DOPAMINE HYPOTHESIS The assertion that an excessive amount of dopamine (an important neurotransmitter substance in the brain, involved in the chemical transmission of nerve impulses) causes a psychotic reaction such as schizophrenia.

DOUBLE BIND Situation in which an individual receives inconsistent messages for performing a given act; believed by some theorists to cause schizophrenia.

DOUBLE-BLIND METHOD An experimental method, used in drug research, in which neither the experimenters nor the subjects know whether the drug administered is active or inert (placebo).

DOWN'S SYNDROME (MONGOLISM) A form of mental retardation caused by an extra chromosome (trisomy 21). Distinctive physical characteristics are slanting eyes, flat nose, small rounded skull, and a protruding tongue.

DRUG ADDICTION Physiological dependence on a drug through continual use; characterized by *withdrawal* symptoms and increased *tolerance*.

DURHAM TEST The result of the 1954 "Durham decision," this test dictates that when a criminal act is the result of some form of mental illness, the individual should be hospitalized for treatment under the authority of a psychiatrist.

DYSHOMOPHILIA In DSM-III, a term used to refer to an individual who experiences distress, feels guilty, or becomes depressed because of his or her homosexuality.

DYSPAREUNIA Painful sexual intercourse experienced by the female.

DYSSOCIAL OR SUBCULTURAL DELINQUENCY/ CRIMINALITY   A term describing the behavior of individuals who exhibit antisocial behavior because of prolonged exposure to a delinquent subculture/environment that fosters and reinforces such behavior. This behavior is not normally associated with any significant personality disorder.

E

ECOLOGICAL PERSPECTIVE   A social theory that assumes a strong association between environmental conditions and increased rates of mental illness and crime.

EDEMA   The term used when the body tissues (such as walls of the blood vessels) become filled with fluid.

EGO   In psychoanalytic theory, the rational part of the personality, which mediates between the demands of the id, superego and reality.

EGO DEFENSE MECHANISMS (EDMs)   In psychoanalytic theory, a set of mental operations unconsciously adopted to protect the ego from anxiety by bringing about compromise among conflicting impulses or by reducing awareness of them.

EGOISTIC SUICIDE   As defined by Durkheim, self-annihilation committed because the individual feels extreme alienation from society and therefore lacks support during periods of stress.

ELECTROCONVULSIVE THERAPY (ECT)   Treatment that produces a convulsion by passing electric current through the brain, sometimes useful in alleviating profound depression.

ELECTROLYTES   Electrically charged particles that carry an electrical current from one nerve fiber to the next.

EMANCIPATION DISORDER   In DSM-III, a syndrome characterized by the individual's great difficulty in emotionally separating himself or herself from parental supervision and control so that independent decisions can be made.

EMOTION   See *Affect.*

ENCEPHALITIS   Inflammation of brain tissue caused by a number of agents, the most important being several viruses carried by insects.

ENDOGENOUS   Attributed to internal causes.

ENURESIS   The occurrence of persistent bedwetting after the age of 5.

EPIDEMIC ENCEPHALITIS   A contagious form of encephalitis marked by lethargy, drowsiness, and prolonged periods of sleep; also known as "sleeping sickness."

EPIDEMIOLOGY   The study of epidemic diseases; specifically, a survey study approach based on clinical case history statistics and on direct assessment of psychopathology in the general population.

EPILEPSY   An altered state of consciousness accompanied by sudden changes in the usual rhythmical electrical activities of the brain, resulting in seizures. See also *grand mal, petit mal, Jacksonian,* and *psychomotor epilepsy.*

EPILEPTIC SEIZURE   A process associated with a neurological state in which a spontaneous and massive discharge of groups of brain cells occurs.

EPILOIA   A genetic disorder marked by minute brain tumors and seizures.

EPISODIC AFFECTIVE DISORDERS   In DSM-III, a category of affective disorders in which there are periods of depression, mania, or bipolar reactions that may last for a short period of time (less than two years).

ESSENTIAL HYPERTENSION   A psychophysiological disorder characterized by chronically elevated blood pressure for which no organic cause is known.

EUGENICS   The science of improving the genetic pool for a given species.

EXCLUSIVE HOMOSEXUAL   A term used to refer to an individual who restricts his or her sexual and erotic experiences to the same sex.

EXHIBITIONISM   Deliberate exposure of genitals in situations where such exposure is inappropriate.

EXISTENTIALISM A philosophical approach to psychotherapy that stresses the importance of finding meaning and purpose through the individual's subjective experiences and freedom of choice.

EXISTENTIAL NEUROSIS Similar to *depersonalization neurosis*, this disorder is characterized by an intense sense of emptiness and lack of fulfillment even though the individual is performing effectively in society.

EXOGENOUS (REACTIVE) Attributed to external causes.

EXPERIMENTAL METHOD A powerful research technique for determining the causal relationship between variables; it involves the manipulation of an *independent variable* and the measurement of a *dependent variable*. Subjects may be randomly assigned or matched and placed in an experimental or control group.

EXPRESSIVE TECHNIQUE A type of projective technique in which an individual is asked to express himself or herself freely in some way, as in painting.

F

FACTITIOUS DISORDER In the DSM-III, a disorder characterized by physical or psychological symptoms that are not real, but are produced by the patient and are under his or her voluntary control.

FALSIFICATION Filling in memory gaps by making up stories or misapplying old reminiscences, especially prevalent in Korsakoff's psychosis.

FAMILY RISK STUDIES Genetic studies that assess each member of a family to determine whether the prevalence of a given psychopathology exceeds that found in the general population.

FETISHISM A sexual deviation in which an individual is aroused sexually by holding, tasting, smelling, or viewing the fetish item, usually while masturbating.

FILICIDE The killing of a child.

FIXATION In psychoanalytic theory, the arrest of psychosexual development at a particular stage because of too much or too little gratification at that stage.

FLAT AFFECT A deviation in emotional response wherein virtually no emotion is expressed regardless of the stimuli.

FOCAL EPILEPSY See *Jacksonian epilepsy.*

FOLIE À DEUX See *Shared paranoid disorder.*

FORCED-CHOICE TECHNIQUE A question format used to control for social desirability by presenting equivalent response alternatives.

FREE ASSOCIATION A basic tool of psychoanalytic therapy in which the patient is free to verbalize any thoughts and feelings without fear of the therapist structuring or criticizing his or her remarks. The assumption is that repressed material will eventually emerge.

FRIGIDITY Repulsion by the female toward having sexual contact with a male; it is usually accompanied by orgasmic dysfunction.

FRONTAL LOBE Forward section of each cerebral hemisphere; associated with motivation, personality, affect, reasoning, and other higher mental processes.

FRONTAL LOBE SYNDROME A type of organic brain syndrome in which marked personality changes occur—lack of initiative, lack of concern, and euphoria—because of lesions to the frontal lobe.

FUGUE STATE A hysterical dissociative reaction in which the individual develops amnesia and flees to a new locality, but appears normal to others.

FUNCTIONAL BEHAVIORAL ANALYSIS An approach used to measure behavior and its situational determinants directly.

G

GAMES In transactional analysis, the term for the ulterior or unconscious transactions between people that are designed to acquire *strokes.*

GAMMA ALCOHOLISM A pattern of problem drinking (described by Jellinek) in which increased tissue tolerance to alcohol develops, so that the individual must consume greater and greater amounts to produce the same desired effects.

GENDER IDENTITY DISORDER A term used to describe the feelings of some adults that, as children, they shared the behaviors, attitudes, and values of the opposite sex.

GENERAL PARESIS The term used when syphilis causes mental disturbances through its destruction of brain tissue.

GENERAL SYSTEMS THEORY A type of family therapy in which the individual and his or her behavior is always viewed in terms of the various support systems within which he or she lives.

GENETICS The study of heredity and accompanying attempts to demonstrate how physical or behavioral characteristics of offspring are acquired from their parents.

GODIVA PRINCIPLE The idea that some individuals become sexually attracted to those activities and objects that are viewed as illicit, illegal, or immoral.

GRAND MAL EPILEPSY The most severe form of epilepsy, involving loss of consciousness, violent convulsions, and in most cases, the experience of an aura before the seizure.

H

HALLUCINATION A sensory experience that occurs in the absence of any stimulation from the environment.

HALLUCINOGENS (PSYCHEDELICS) Drugs such as LSD and mescaline that have the ability to produce potent hallucinatory effects and profound subjective experiences.

HARD CHANCRE Associated with the first stage of syphilis, a sore or pimple that feels hard to the touch, and develops at the place of infection (usually the genitals or mouth).

HEBEPHRENIC SCHIZOPHRENIA A psychotic disorder marked by silliness, incoherent speech, hallucinations, delusions, and considerable psychological deterioration.

HIERARCHY An arrangement or ordering of most-feared to least-feared events, used in systematic desensitization.

HIGH-RISK STUDY A method of investigation, used especially in the study of schizophrenia, in which persons who have a greater-than-average risk of becoming abnormal are observed and examined extensively.

HIPPOCAMPUS A neural structure lying deep within the temporal lobes of the brain; it has been suggested as playing a major role in immediate and recent memory.

HOMOSEXUALITY Sexual activity or desire directed toward an individual's own sex.

HUNTINGTON'S CHOREA A fatal presenium dementia passed on by a single dominant gene. Symptoms include rapid involuntary jerking of the limbs, mental deterioration, confusion, and psychotic behavior.

HYDROCEPHALUS A brain disorder caused by an overabundance of cerebrospinal fluids in the ventricles of the brain, producing various degrees of mental retardation and physical impairment.

HYPERACTIVITY A childhood disorder characterized by the inability to inhibit movement in situations where inactivity is required, along with short attention span and problems with speech and perception.

HYPERSOMNIA A sleep disorder in which an individual has extreme difficulty in staying awake.

HYPOCHONDRIACAL NEUROSIS Disorder in which the individual is preoccupied with his or her own bodily functions and presumed illnesses.

HYPOTHALAMUS An area beneath the cortex that regulates many of the body's functions, as well as the activity of the pituitary gland.

HYSTERICAL NEUROSIS　In the DSM-II, a disorder characterized by complaints of some organic physical illness when there is no actual organic evidence to explain symptoms. Two types: *conversion* and *dissociative*. In DSM-III, hysterical neurosis is replaced by *dissociative disorders* and *somatoform disorders*.

I

IATROGENIC　Medically induced drug abuse in which an individual first takes a prescribed drug for a legitimate medical purpose and then gets "hooked" on it.

ID　In psychoanalytic terms, the totality of biological drives present at birth that constantly struggle for gratification.

IDIOPATHIC　Describes a disorder for which there is no known cause, as in "idiopathic epilepsy."

IMIPRAMINE　An antidepressant drug used to treat depression and *enuresis*.

IMMEDIATE MEMORY IMPAIRMENT　A diagnosis applied to an individual who, after a period of approximately five seconds, cannot repeat what was said.

IMPOTENCE　Failure by the male to achieve an erection sufficient enough to engage in intercourse.

INAPPROPRIATE AFFECT　Emotional responses that are out of context, such as laughter when hearing sad news.

INCEST　The occurrence of sexual activities between blood relatives.

INCLUSIVE HOMOSEXUAL (BISEXUAL)　A term used to refer to an individual who periodically has sexual and erotic experiences with both sexes.

INCOHERENCE　In schizophrenia, a thought disorder in which verbal expression is marked by fragmented thoughts, *neologisms,* and jumbled phrases.

INDEPENDENT VARIABLE　In a psychological experiment, the variable that is under the control of the experimenter and is expected to have an effect on the subjects as measured by changes in the dependent variable.

INDICANT FALLACY　The false assumption that, through observance of physiological responses, a clearly defined relationship can be established between a specific psychological state and physiological responding, as in the use of the lie detector test.

INDIVIDUAL RESPONSE STEREOTYPY　A constitutional predisposition to respond physiologically to a situation in a particular way, with consistent activation of certain physiological systems or organs.

INDOLEAMINES　One of two major compound groups of neurotransmitters in the brain, containing the substances serotonin and tryptamine, which have been implicated in mood and emotion changes.

INFANTICIDE　The killing of an infant.

INFANTILE AUTISM　A infant onset disorder characterized by extreme aloneness, mutism or echolalic speech, and preservation of sameness.

INFERIORITY COMPLEX　Intense feelings of inadequacy and insecurity that tend to dominate an individual's entire life, thus producing a constant need to strive for adjustment.

INSOMNIA　The basic inability to fall asleep, a common sleep disturbance that can produce symptoms of anxiety and depression because of extreme fatigue.

INTAKE INTERVIEW　The initial diagnostic interview, the most frequently used procedure for assessment of abnormal behavior.

INTELLIGENCE QUOTIENT (IQ)　An index of relative general intelligence, commonly derived from either Stanford-Binet or Wechsler intelligence tests.

INVOLUTIONAL MELANCHOLIA　An affective disorder characterized by profound sadness, occurring typically in women after menopause (involutional period).

J

JACKSONIAN EPILEPSY (FOCAL EPILEPSY) A form of epilepsy in which muscle spasms are limited to a certain sensory or motor portion of the body.

JAKOB CREUTZFELD'S DISEASE A *presenium* dementia thought to be congenital; marked by progressive mental deterioration, muscular rigidity, tremors, and spastic limb weakness.

JAMAIS VU A feeling that occurs when familiar surroundings suddenly seem entirely new and foreign.

JUVENILE PARESIS A result of congenital syphilis, and marked by the same progressive mental and physical deterioration as in general paresis.

K

KLEIN-LEVIN SYNDROME A form of periodic hypersomnia in which recurrent periods of excessive sleeping can last several days and involve as much as 18 to 20 hours of sleep per day.

KLINEFELTER'S SYNDROME A genetic abnormality, limited to males who have an extra *X* chromosome, marked by sterility and possible mental retardation and physical abnormalities.

KLÜVER-BUCY SYNDROME Heightened but indiscriminate sexual behavior caused by a *bilateral lobectomy* of the temporal lobes.

KORSAKOFF'S PSYCHOSIS A chronic brain disorder related to alcoholism and caused by dramatic restrictions of B vitamins; symptoms include loss of recent memories and associated confabulation.

KWASHIORKOR A form of undernourishment found in an infant or child who has had insufficient protein; the result is irreversible neurological damage even though, because of an adequate intake of carbohydrates, a child may appear to be well fed.

L

LA BELLE INDIFFERENCE The term applied to the unconcerned attitude of hysterics toward their symptoms.

LABELING PERSPECTIVE A social theory that states that a person's deviance increases once he or she is labeled and defined as being different.

LABILITY OF AFFECT A term applied to frequent fluctuations in a person's emotions or mood.

LASHLEY'S HYPOTHESIS OF EQUIPOTENTIALITY A theory dealing specifically with intellectual capacity, stating that the amount of brain tissue lost is more important than the specific location of the brain damage.

LATENT STAGE The third stage of syphilis, during which overt physical symptoms such as rash, fever, and loss of appetite disappear.

L-DOPA A chemical that the body converts to dopamine when ingested.

LEARNED HELPLESSNESS A concept referring to the passive acceptance of environmental events because of the perception that one cannot control them by one's behavior.

LEARNING MODEL (BEHAVIOR MODEL) As applied in abnormal psychology, a set of assumptions that abnormal behavior is a learned response; therefore, behavior should be dealt with rather than inferred underlying causes.

LESBIAN A female who is motivated in adult life by a primary erotic, psychological, emotional, and social attraction to, and interest in, other females.

LIBIDO In psychoanalytic terms, the instinctual sexual energy of the *id* that strives for immediate sexual gratification.

LIFE CHANGE UNITS (LCUs) A score of total ratings of stress produced by recent life events; high scores are found to be associated with significant health problems.

LIMBIC SYSTEM Borderline area between the old and new brain, intimately involved in emotion and drive-motivated behavior.

LITHIUM CARBONATE A drug found to be highly effective in the treatment of both mania and depression.

LOCOMOTOR ATAXIA Gross motor uncoordination occurring during the fourth stage of syphilitic infection, characterized by loss of balance and an unsteady gait.

LOGOTHERAPY A form of existential therapy used in aiding an individual to find meaning and purpose for his or her existence.

LOOSE ASSOCIATION In schizophrenia, a type of thought disorder wherein the individual has difficulty in sticking to one topic and tends to drift toward associations evoked by a past idea.

M

MAGNIFICATON AND MINIMIZATION The tendency of an individual to make grossly inaccurate judgments about the significance of events and the effect of his or her behavior on them.

MAJOR AFFECTIVE DISORDERS Disabling mood disturbances listed in the DSM-II classification system as manic-depressive illnesses and involutional melancholia.

MALLEUS MALEFICARUM ("*THE HAMMER OF WITCHES*"). A text written in the fifteenth century by two well-known and respected Dominican monks to provide rules for identifying and punishing witches.

MANIA Emotional state characterized by intense elation of mood not attributable to any specific stimuli.

MANIC-DEPRESSIVE PSYCHOSIS An affective disorder characterized by moods of euphoria and profound sadness that appear either alternately (circular type), almost simultaneously (mixed type), or individually (manic type or depressed type).

MANIC DISORDER An affective disorder that, according to the DSM-III, is characterized by an extreme mood elevation.

MAPLE SYRUP URINE DISEASE (MENKES' SYNDROME) A genetic disorder resulting from a single recessive gene and marked by a maple syrup-like odor in the infant's urine.

MARITAL SKEW A family type in which one partner is inordinately dominant and overbearing.

MASOCHISM A term used to refer to a sexual response in which the individual derives sexual pleasure from receiving pain.

MASTURBATORY CONDITIONING A behavior therapy technique for increasing heterosexual arousal.

MEDIAL FOREBRAIN BUNDLE A structure located in the hypothalamus which, when stimulated, is thought to be the physiological basis for pleasure, with norepinephrine as the primary transmitter.

MEDIATOR An unobservable inferred construct that is hypothesized to account for certain behaviors.

MELANCHOLIC One of Hippocrates' four temperamental categories; it is characterized by depression and was thought to be caused by an overabundance of black bile.

MEMORY IMPAIRMENTS Impairments associated with organic brain syndrome that result in the inability to recall past events; three basic types are immediate, recent, and remote.

MENINGES The three layers of non-neural tissue (membranes) that envelop the brain and spinal cord: the dura mater, the arachnoid, and the pia mater.

MENINGOCOCCAL MENINGITIS A viral infection that inflames the *meninges*.

MENINGOENCEPHALITIS SYPHILIS A form of cerebral syphilis in which organic damage is initially concentrated in the brain cells.

MENINGOVASCULAR SYPHILIS A rare form of cerebral syphilis in which the organic damage is initially concentrated in the blood vessels and meninges of the brain rather than in the brain neural tissue.

MENTAL RETARDATION Below-normal intellectual functioning, usually revealed in early childhood and associated with poor social adjustment.

MENTAL STATUS QUESTIONNAIRE A diagnostic test concerned with assessing orientation, memory, and intelligence, used in geriatric setting to diagnose or assess dementia or organic brain syndrome.

MESCALINE   A hallucinogenic drug.

METHADONE (DOLOPHINE)   A synthetic drug that has a heroin-like effect on pain, but does not produce euphoria; widely used as a treatment for heroin addicts.

MIGRAINE HEADACHES   Cardiovascular disorders that are thought to result from severe dilation or stretching of the blood vessels in the brain. *Common migraine* appears to be directly tied to some specific environmental stress. *Classic migraine* occurs periodically, preceded by prodromal visual symptoms such as zig-zag lines in the visual field. *Cluster headache* is characterized by a series of closely spaced attacks followed by a lengthy remission.

MILIEU THERAPY   Treatment procedure in which the entire clinical facility is used as a "therapeutic community," with as few restraints as possible placed on the freedom of the patients.

MODELING   Learning by observing and imitating the behavior of others.

MONGOLISM   See *Down's syndrome.*

MONOMANIA   A broad diagnostic category used in the 1800s to refer to disorders in which the person appeared normal except for one area of deviance.

MULTIAXIAL ASSESSMENT   A procedure used by the DSM-III in which individuals are assessed on each of five axes: psychiatric syndrome present; evaluation of patient's past personality and developmental disorders; determination of possible non-mental medical disorders; severity of psychosocial stressors; and highest level of adaptive functioning during the past year.

MULTIDIMENSIONAL PERSONALITY INVENTORY   A comprehensive test directed at obtaining multifaceted personality descriptions to use in the description and diagnosis of abnormal behavior.

MULTI-INFARCT DEMENTIA (CEREBRAL ARTERIOSCLEROSIS)   In DSM-III, a dementia directly linked to clear-cut vascular or vessel disturbances in the brain.

MULTIPLE PERSONALITY   An extreme and rare hysterical dissociative reaction in which there are two or more completely distinctive and well-developed behavior-personality organizations.

MUNCHAUSEN SYNDROME   A chronic factitious disorder listed in DSM-III. The patient exhibits factitious (not real) physical symptoms but can obtain and sustain multiple hospitalizations.

MUTATIONS   Genetic errors after conception that change the genetic material.

MYOCLONIC   A type of petit mal epileptic seizure marked by momentary muscle contractions and/or motor jerking.

MYTHOLOGY SYSTEM   Belief about a particular family member that goes unchallenged.

N

NARCOLEPSY   A form of hypersomnia in which an individual periodically suffers from a sudden and overpowering seizure of sleepiness and cannot stay awake.

NEEDS   Internal motivators of behavior, such as a need for achievement, aggression, or abasement.

NEOLOGISM   In schizophrenia, a word that the individual makes up and uses in speech.

NEOPLASM   See *Tumor.*

NEURASTHENIC NEUROSIS   Disorder characterized by chronic fatigue, weakness, and lack of enthusiasm, none of which can be attributed to illness.

NEUROKININ   A pain-threshold chemical released at the site of the dilated vessels, causing an inflammatory reaction; it is thought to be a precursor of a migraine headache.

NEUROPSYCHOLOGICAL ASSESSMENT   A method of searching for behavioral manifestations or patterns of performance abnormalities that are associated with specific brain disorders.

NEUROTIC PARADOX   The continual performance of neurotic behaviors despite their self-defeating nature.

NEUROTIC TRIAD   The frequent overlapping of categories found in neurotics tested by the MMPI, with hypochondriasis, depression, and hysteria scales standing highest in the profile.

NIGHT TERROR (PROCTOR NOCTURNIS) A particularly severe variety of bad dreams occurring most frequently in children.

NOREPINEPHRINE A catecholamine that is an important neurotransmitter of the central nervous system and the sympathetic nervous system.

NOSOLOGY A systematic classification of diseases.

NUTRITIONAL MARASMUS A form of undernourishment found in infants who have had a profound deficit of carbohydrates and protein, resulting in retardation of physical growth and intellectual impairment.

O

OBSERVATIONAL LEARNING A learning theory based on the assumption that behavior can be acquired by observing and imitating the behavior of others.

OBSESSIVE-COMPULSIVE NEUROSIS Disorder in which persistent unwanted thoughts, urges, or actions are ever present and uncontrollable, even though the individual recognizes them as irrational.

OPEN HEAD INJURIES Injuries to the head in which the skull and the brain are penetrated, as by bullet, sharp object, or bone matter.

OPERANT BEHAVIOR A voluntary response that ''operates'' on the environment in order to bring about changes in it.

OPERANT CONDITIONING A learning method concerned with developing new behaviors by eliciting a desired response and subsequently reinforcing it to increase the probability that it will occur more frequently.

OPIATES Major *opium* derivatives: codeine, morphine, and heroin.

OPIUM A bitter, brownish, addictive narcotic drug made from the dried juice of the opium poppy.

ORAL EROTICISM A personality characteristic caused by fixation at the oral stage of psychosexual development and associated with great dependency on external sources to provide emotional gratification.

ORAL STAGE In psychoanalytic theory, the first psychosexual stage, extending into the second year of life, during which the mouth is the principal pleasure zone.

ORGANIC BRAIN SYNDROME A mental disorder in which intellectual or emotional functioning, or both, are impaired because of a pathological dysfunction of the brain.

ORGANIC RETARDATION The label applied to individuals with limited mental capacity who have measurable or detectable anatomical or biochemical deficits.

ORGASMIC DYSFUNCTION The inability of a woman to reach a climax during intercourse.

ORTHOMOLECULAR THERAPY The treatment of mental illness with megavitamin therapy to maintain the optimum molecular composition of the brain.

OVERGENERALIZATION The tendency of an individual to draw erroneous conclusions about his or her overall ability or worth, solely on the basis of a single incident.

OVERINCLUSION See *Loose association.*

P

PARADOXICAL SLEEP See *Rapid Eye Movement phase.*

PARANOIA A disorder characterized by a well-systemized and logical delusional system consisting of delusions of grandeur and/or persecution, although the individual's basic personality structure remains intact.

PARANOID CERTAINTY The paranoid schizophrenic's assuredness about his or her false beliefs or suspicions, despite evidence to the contrary.

PARANOID SCHIZOPHRENIA A psychotic disorder involving systematized delusions as well as hallucinations, ideas of reference, and withdrawal from society.

PARANOID STATE   A disorder characterized by transient paranoid delusions usually precipitated by some specific stress.

PARAPHILIAS   A category (DSM-III) of sexual deviations that includes fetishisms, zoophilia, pedophilia, dyshomophilia, exhibitionism, voyeurism, sexual masochism, sexual sadism, and others.

PARAPHRENIA   A senium psychosis resembling paranoid schizophrenia, with symptoms of auditory hallucinations and paranoid delusions.

PARASYMPATHETIC DIVISION   The part of the *autonomic nervous system* that is dominant during nonarousal conditions. It regulates the internal activities of breathing, heart rate, blood pressure, stomach and intestinal activity, and elimination.

PARENTAL PROGRAMMING   In transactional analysis theory of illness, the early processing of particular messages and instructions given by the parents to the child, which later becomes a decisive factor in determining the child's behavior.

PARENTECTOMY   An early procedure to treat autistic children involving the complete separation of a child from his or her home and family because the home is highly dysfunctional.

PARENT EGO STATE   In transactional analysis, the collection of neurological "tapes" of parental attitudes and feelings as recorded in childhood.

PARENTS ANONYMOUS   A type of group therapy for abusive parents.

PEDOPHILIA   A sexual deviation in which an adult desires or engages in sexual relations with a child defined legally as under age.

PEEPING   A type of voyeurism in which the person has no legal right to be at the location from which he observes.

PEPSIN   An enzyme in the stomach that digests proteins and, with hydrochloric acid, is the primary active agent in gastric digestive juices.

PEPSINOGEN   A stomach secretion converted to the enzyme *pepsin*. It is often viewed as a cause of ulcers.

PERINATAL STRESSORS   Conditions during birth that hamper or retard normal development.

PERIPHERAL NERVOUS SYSTEM   Nerve fibers outside the brain and spinal cord (*central nervous system*) that connect the central nervous system with the outside world via receptors and effectors.

PETIT MAL EPILEPSY   A form of epilepsy in which a momentary disturbance of consciousness occurs; no aura, convulsion, or total loss of consciousness is involved.

PHENOMENAL FIELD   In the phenomenological approach, a term used to describe all the perceptions and experiences within a person that are available to his or her awareness.

PHENOMENOLOGY   In psychology, the view that the subject's immediate perception determines behavior.

PHENOTHIAZINE   A major tranquilizing drug that is highly effective in alleviating the symptoms of schizophrenia because of its apparent ability to block dopamine receptors in the dopamine tract.

PHENYLKETONURIA (PKU)   A rare genetic disorder that causes severe mental retardation, due to a deficiency in a liver enzyme, phenylalanine hydrorylase. It may be ameliorated if diet is restricted soon after the disorder is detected.

PHOBIA   Intense irrational fear of some specific object or situation that presents no real danger.

PHOBIC NEUROSIS   Disorder characterized by an intense irrational fear of an object or situation.

PHRENOLOGY   A forerunner of the organic approach to abnormal behavior, this pseudo-science attributed personality traits to the conformation and "bumps" of the skull.

PHYSICAL GENETICS   The study of the way heredity correlates with physical or biological qualities.

PHYSIOGNOMY   A pseudo-scientific forerunner of the organic approach to abnormal behavior, in which an individual's personality was assessed by studying his or her facial expressions and structure and classifying them accordingly.

PHYSIOLOGICAL DEPENDENCE   Type of drug dependence in which withdrawal symptoms occur when the drug is discontinued.

PICK'S DISEASE   A presenium dementia marked by speech impairment, reduced intellectual functioning, and changes in personality.

PLACEBO   Any substance or technique that is used deliberately to produce a specific effect on a person's behavior because he or she expects a change, although the placebo is without a known specific activity for the evaluated condition.

PLACEBO EFFECT   The nonspecific, psychological, or psychophysiological effect produced by placebos.

PLEASURE PRINCIPLE   In psychoanalytic theory, the principle by which the id functions in seeking immediate gratification of needs regardless of reality.

POLYGENIC EFFECTS   The effect produced when environmental factors combine with genetic factors to predispose a person to psychopathology.

POSTNATAL PHYSICAL STRESSORS   Aversive physical conditions following birth that may adversely affect the infant.

PRE-ALCOHOLIC PHASE   The first of four stages leading to alcoholism described by Jellinek; characterized by social drinking intermixed with occasions of heavy drinking to reduce tension.

PREFRONTAL LOBECTOMY   Radical psychosurgical procedure in which much of the frontal lobe is removed.

PREFRONTAL LOBOTOMY   Psychosurgical procedure in which nerve fibers connecting the frontal lobes to the thalamus and limbic system are severed.

PREFRONTAL TOPECTOMY   Psychosurgical procedure in which selected areas of the frontal lobe are removed.

PREMATURE EJACULATION   Inability of the male to postpone his orgasm long enough to achieve a mutually satisfactory sexual relationship.

PREMORBID ADJUSTMENT OR PERSONALITY   The individual's behavior inclinations or personality characteristics prior to the onset of physical or psychological impairment.

PRENATAL STRESSORS   Physical or environmental conditions before birth that retard normal development, such as malnutrition and maternal infection.

PRESENIUM   Occurring before the age of 65.

PRESSES   As evaluated on the TAT, environmental determinants of behavior such as physical danger or rejection by a loved one.

PROCTOR NOCTURNIS   See *Night terror.*

PRODROMAL PHASE   The second stage leading to alcoholism described by Jellinek; marked by excessive drinking and occasional blackouts.

PROGERIA   A rare disease that causes extremely rapid aging and death in children.

PROGRESSIVE IDIOPATHIC DEMENTIA (SENILE DEMENTIA)   A DSM-III category referring to an organic mental disorder brought on by progressive deterioration of the brain caused in part by aging and unknown processes; marked by impaired judgment, memory, intelligence, orientation, and affect.

PROJECTION   An ego defense mechanism whereby one's own unacceptable feelings are attributed to others.

PROJECTIVE BATTERING   In child abuse cases, the individual's real aggressive feelings about himself or herself are projected to the child.

PROJECTIVE TEST   A psychological assessment device employing a set of stimuli for which the cultural pattern of responding is not well-defined, on the assumption that unstructured material will allow unconscious aspects of an individual's personality to surface.

PROVOKED ANXIETY METHOD   An aversion therapy technique used in the treatment of exhibitionism.

PSEUDO CORIOLIS EFFECT   A chemical-induced nausea technique.

PSYCHEDELIC See *Hallucinogens.*

PSYCHOANALYSIS A term applied to the therapeutic method pioneered by Freud, which relies mainly on free association and dream interpretation, the analysis of resistance, and transference. The ultimate goal is to give the patient insight into his or her unconscious conflicts, motives, and impulses.

PSYCHODYNAMICS A term generally used to refer to mental energies or mental forces, for example, id, ego, and superego.

PSYCHOLOGICAL AGING A term used to refer to the effects of both *biological* and *social aging*, which cause degenerative changes in emotions, memory, learning ability, judgment, intelligence, and mood.

PSYCHOLOGICAL AUTOPSY A thorough analysis of an individual's suicide through the examination of notes and interviews with friends and family to determine why that person took his or her life.

PSYCHOMOTOR EPILEPSY Form of epileptic seizure in which the individual loses contact with the environment but appears conscious and performs some routine, repetitive act or engages in more complex activity.

PSYCHOPATHY See *Antisocial personality.*

PSYCHOPHYSIOLOGICAL DISORDER (PSYCHOSOMATIC DISORDER). A disorder characterized by physical symptoms caused by emotional factors but linked to actual tissue damage, usually in one organ system.

PSYCHOPHYSIOLOGICAL TRAINING A learning procedure that uses progressive stimulation to enhance the learning capacity of the mentally retarded individual.

PSYCHOSEXUAL DYSFUNCTIONS Category of disorders that includes inhibited sexual desire, inhibited sexual excitement, frigidity, impotence, inhibited female orgasm, inhibited male orgasm, and premature ejaculation.

PSYCHOSOMATIC DISORDERS See *Psychophysiological disorders.*

PSYCHOSURGERY A surgical technique in which various neural pathways in the brain are removed or disconnected in order to change behavior.

PSYCHOTIC DEPRESSIVE REACTION A mood disorder characterized by the occurrence of an extreme depressive mood precipitated by some event or experience in the individual's environment.

PSYCHOTOMIMETIC DRUGS Drugs thought to produce effects similar to the symptoms of a psychosis.

Q

QUALITATIVE Describing differences in kind, rather than differences in intensity or amount.

QUANTITATIVE Capable of being measured.

R

RAPID EYE MOVEMENT (REM) PHASE (PARADOXICAL SLEEP) A period during Stage 1 of sleep when there is a high frequency of eye movement; it has been found to be the period during sleep when dreaming is likely to occur.

REACTION FORMATION Ego defense mechanism in which the individual develops attitudes or behaviors that are opposite to his or her real repressed wishes.

REACTIVE See *Exogenous.*

REALITY PRINCIPLE In psychoanalytic theory, the driving force of the ego concerned with awareness of the demands of the environment and adjustment of behavior to meet those demands.

RECENT MEMORY IMPAIRMENT A diagnosis applied if, after a period of ten seconds, the subject cannot repeat what was said.

REDUCERS Individuals who do not show a marked increase in their cortical evoked potential as stimulus intensity increases.

REGRESSION An ego defense mechanism in which anxiety is avoided by a retreat to the behavior patterns of an earlier developmental stage.

REINFORCEMENT THEORY A learning theory that assumes many maladaptive behaviors are maintained or shaped into existence because reinforcers, either by accident or by intention, follow the problem behavior.

RELIABILITY The degree to which a test, measurement, or classification system produces the same scientific observation each time.

REM PHASE SLEEP See *Rapid Eye Movement phase*.

REMOTE MEMORY IMPAIRMENT A diagnosis applied to an individual who is unable to recall past events from one day to 25 years ago, a characteristic that is thought to imply diffuse cortical impairment.

REPARENTING A transactional analysis procedure involving erasing the original *Parent* tapes and replacing these tapes with new data.

REPRESSION An ego defense mechanism in which unacceptable thoughts and impulses are pushed into the unconscious.

REPRESSIVE FAMILY A dysfunctional family type in which every member must feel the same about everything.

RESISTANCE In psychoanalytic therapy, the process that occurs when the patient consciously attempts to prevent repressed material from being revealed in the session.

RESPONSE ACQUIESCENCE The tendency of an individual to agree with test items no matter what their content.

RESPONSE DEVIATION The tendency of an individual to answer questions in an uncommon way, regardless of their content.

RESPONSE DISSIMULATION See *Response deviation*.

RESPONSE HIERARCHY The arranging of a series of responses according to the probability that a particular stimulus will elicit them.

RESPONSE SET (BIAS) A particular test-taking attitude that causes an individual to respond consistently to items on the test, regardless of what the items actually say.

RETICULAR FORMATION SYSTEM (RETICULAR ACTIVATING SYSTEM) Network of fibers and nuclei in the core of the brainstem, which serves as an important arousal mechanism as well as a regulator of other vital functions such as sleep, memory and attention.

RETREATIST SUBCULTURE A subculture that encourages a form of dyssocial behavior in which the individual's primary goal is centered on drug use.

REVERSAL DESIGN (ABAB DESIGN) An experimental design common in operant research, in which behavior is measured during a baseline period (A), during a treatment-induced period (B), during reintroduction to baseline period conditions (A), and finally during reintroduction of the treatment period (B).

RITALIN A stimulant drug used in the treatment of hypersomnia, narcolepsy, and some forms of hyperactivity.

S

SADISM A sexual deviation in which the individual derives sexual pleasure from inflicting pain on others.

SADOMASOCHISM A sexual deviation in which the individual derives sexual pleasure from inflicting or receiving pain.

SAMPLE APPROACH The assessment of observable behavior and how it is affected by alterations and specific conditions.

SCHIZOAFFECTIVE PSYCHOSIS A psychotic disorder characterized by disturbances of both mood and thought process.

SCHIZOID PERSONALITY A personality disorder description applied to individuals who demonstrate certain schizophrenic symptomatology but only to a mild degree.

SCHIZOPHRENIA   A group of psychotic disorders characterized by major disturbances in thought, emotion, and behavior—illogical thoughts; faulty attention and perception; bizarre motor activity; impaired perceptual and emotional connections; flat, inappropriate, ambivalent, or labile affect; reduced tolerance for stress of interpersonal relations prompting social isolation.

SCHIZOPHRENICNESS   Signs of schizophrenia.

SCHIZOPHRENOGENIC MOTHER   A term used to describe the cold, conflict-inducing mother who is alleged to make her children schizophrenic.

SCHIZOPHRENOGENICNESS   Describing behavior that tends to create schizophrenia in others because of faulty communication patterns that make it difficult for the listener to fully comprehend what is being said.

SCHIZOTAXIA   An assumed neural defect in potential schizophrenics that genetically predisposes them to develop the disorder.

SCHIZOTYPY   An altered personality structure or makeup found in schizotaxic individuals, which is assumed to be caused by common everyday stress.

SCRIPT   A term used in transactional analysis to describe parental injunctions given to the child on how to think, feel, and behave.

SECONDARY GAINS   Reinforcement, such as attention or sympathy, that is offered in addition to the protection the individual receives through avoiding some unwanted situation.

SEDATIVE   A drug that is commonly used to treat sleep disorders, particularly insomnia.

SELECTIVE ABSTRACTION   The tendency of an individual to draw a conclusion illogically on the basis of only one of several elements of a multifaceted situation.

SENIUM   The period after the age of 65.

SENIUM PSYCHOSIS   A psychosis specifically associated with the senium period.

SEPTUM   A structure in the hypothalamus that inhibits the activity of the medial forebrain bundle.

SEROTONIN   A neurotransmitter substance found in the brain; its cell structure closely resembles that of LSD (D-Lysergic acid diethylamide).

SEXUAL MOTIVATION   The urge for sexual activity.

SHALLOWNESS OF AFFECT   A term applied to a person's emotions or mood when he or she underresponds to a situation that calls for the expression of emotion.

SHARED PARANOID DISORDER (FOLIE À DEUX, OR DOUBLE INSANITY)   A relatively rare form of paranoia in which two people (e.g., husband and wife or two sisters) develop similar paranoid delusions.

SIGN APPROACH   The assessment of behaviors that are viewed as indirect symptoms of underlying dispositions and motives.

SIMPLE SCHIZOPHRENIA   A psychotic disorder characterized by the reduction of attachment to, and interest in, external objects and individuals; delusions and hallucinations are infrequent.

SLEEP APNEA   A sleep disorder involving the inability to breathe for a short time while sleeping.

SOCIAL AGING   A term used to refer to changes in roles or loss of roles that occur during late adulthood.

SOCIAL DESIRABILITY RESPONSE SET   The tendency of an individual to answer items in the direction that is most socially acceptable, regardless of whether the answers are true.

SOCIOLOGICAL PERSPECTIVE   A sociological orientation that takes into account the effects of cultural context, group factors, and physical environment as predispositions of behavior.

SOCIOPATHY   See *Antisocial personality*.

SOMATIZATION   An ego defense mechanism in which anxiety is converted into a bodily symptom.

SOMATOFORM DISORDERS   In DSM-III, a category including disorders that suggest the presence of some organic physical illness with no known organic underpinnings, See also *Hysterical neurosis*.

SOMNAMBULISM   Sleepwalking.

SPECIFIC-ATTITUDES THEORY   Hypothesis that certain attitudes are associated with certain psychophysiological disorders; for example, the person who feels deprived and seeks revenge may develop ulcers.

SPECIFIC RESPONSE PATTERN APPROACH
See *Weak organ/system theory.*

SPIROCHETE   Any of a group of nonflagellated, slender, spiral-shaped bacteria; specifically, the microorganism that causes syphillis.

SPONTANEOUS IMPROVEMENT   A term applied when a disorder improves without the patient receiving any treatment.

STATE ANXIETY   Momentary anxiety that is situationally specific.

STATISTICAL SIGNIFICANCE   The probability that the differences found between treatment and control groups would occur on a chance basis alone.

STATUTORY RAPE   Sexual intercourse with a minor.

STRESS   A response that strains the psychological or physiological capability of an organism.

STRESS-RESPONSE SYNDROME   Overarousal of the sympathetic division of the nervous system, induced by severe emotional stress and marked by physiological changes and subjective feelings of anxiety.

STROKING   A transactional analysis term used to describe the giving or imparting of recognition (*strokes*), whether verbally or physically.

STRUCTURED TEST   An assessment test in which an individual chooses from a number of provided responses, allowing the test to be scored objectively.

STUTTERING   A disturbance of rhythm and fluency of speech by an intermittent blocking.

SUCCINYLCHOLINE (SCOLINE)   A drug used to induce muscular paralysis.

SUPEREGO   In psychoanalytic theory, the "moral" or "conscience" part of the personality that determines prohibitions and values and checks the performance of the ego.

SUPPRESSION   An ego defense mechanism in which an impulse is satisfied by turning it into a socially desired behavior.

SYMPATHETIC DIVISION   The part of the *autonomic nervous system* that becomes dominant during arousal and heightens bodily responses, causing physiological changes such as increases in blood pressure, heart rate, sweat gland activity, and blood flow to skeletal muscles.

SYSTEMATIZED DELUSIONS   A highly organized set of mistaken beliefs that has become the dominant focus of a paranoid individual's life.

SYSTEMATIC DESENSITIZATION   A behavior therapy procedure used to help a person overcome fears or anxieties; an incompatible relaxation response is introduced simultaneously with the fear-evoking stimuli.

T

TARAXEIN   A protein substance in the blood serum of schizophrenics, proposed by Heath to be responsible for the psychosis.

TAY-SACHS DISEASE   A genetic disorder of lipid metabolism, resulting in severe mental retardation, muscular deterioration, convulsions, blindness, and death in about the third year of life.

TEMPORAL LOBE   Either of the large areas in each cerebral hemisphere situated below the lateral sulcus and in front of the occipital lobe; the left temporal lobe is generally associated with language functions.

TETRAHYDROCANNABINOL (THC)   Active chemical component in both hashish and marijuana.

THALAMUS   The thalamus relays and receives messages to and from other areas of the brain.

THANATOS   In psychoanalytic theory, the death instinct which, if directed inward, would prompt an individual to take his or her own life.

THORAZINE Trade name for the drug chlorpromazine.

THOUGHT DISORDER The primary symptom of schizophrenia, associated with readily observable characteristics such as incoherence, delusions, and loose associations.

THOUGHT STOPPING A behavior therapy procedure in which a subject tells himself or herself to stop thinking intrusive thoughts. It is used with clients who experience distress because of uncontrollable obsessive thoughts.

TIC A meaningless, repetitive, involuntary motor activity such as blinking or twitching.

TIME SERIES ANALYSIS A time-study method used to assess statistically whether a causal relationship exists between specific variables.

TOKEN ECONOMY A *behavior modification* procedure based on *operant conditioning* principles, in which patients are given tokens, such as poker chips, contingent on performing some socially adaptive behavior. The tokens themselves can then be exchanged for desirable items and activities such as extra recreational time.

TOLERANCE A physiological condition in which greater and greater amounts of an addictive drug are required to produce the same effect.

TONIC PHASE State of rigid muscle tension and suspended breathing that marks the beginning of a grand mal epileptic attack.

TRAIT ANXIETY A stable and characteristic high level of anxiety.

TRANSACTIONAL ANALYSIS (TA) A form of interpersonal analysis and therapy aimed chiefly at describing behavior in terms of three ego states—Child, Parent, and Adult.

TRANSFERENCE In psychoanalytic therapy, the process by which the patient projects toward the therapist emotions and attitudes that actually apply to another significant person in the patient's life.

TRANSITORY HOMOSEXUAL (SPORADIC HOMOSEXUAL) An individual who for a short period of time engages in exclusive homosexuality but later returns to heterosexual relationships.

TRANQUILIZER A drug used to treat anxiety, agitation, mania, or psychotic behavior.

TRANSMISSION HYPOTHESIS The inference that disruptive marital behaviors are learned and transmitted from parents to children who therefore become more likely to engage in family disruptions and produce unstable marriages.

TRANSSEXUAL An individual who persistently feels discomfort with his or her own anatomical sex.

TRANSVESTITE An individual who achieves sexual gratification by dressing in the clothes of the opposite sex.

TREMORS Involuntary trembling of muscles.

TREPHINING (TREPANNING) An ancient surgical procedure in which a portion of the skull of a person who was behaving peculiarly was chipped away to allow the "evil spirits" to escape.

TREPONEMA PALLIDUM The medical term for the syphilitic spirochete, which invades the body through the mucous membranes after being contracted during either intercourse or oral-genital contact with an infected person.

TRISOMY A condition in which there are three rather than the usual two chromosomes in the twenty-first pair, causing mental retardation.

TRYPTAMINE A neurotransmitter substance found in the brain; an indoleamine.

TUMOR (NEOPLASM) An abnormal growth; tumors in the brain can be malignant and destroy the brain tissue directly, or benign and disrupt functioning by increasing intracranial pressure.

TURNER'S SYNDROME A chromosome disorder limited to females in which only one X chromosome is present. Characteristics include difficulty in space-form perception, sterility, and, in some cases, varied degrees of mental retardation.

U

ULCER A break in the skin or mucous membrane resulting in tissue disintegration; generally regarded as a psychophysiological disorder.

ULCERATIVE COLITIS Ulceration and inflammation of the colon.

ULTRASOUND PROCEDURE A pre-birth assessment technique for diagnosing physical and mental defects; high-frequency sound waves are bounced off the fetus and then converted into images, thereby revealing fetal deformities.

UNDOING An ego defense mechanism in which the individual carries out some act designed to make up for his or her misdeeds by "undoing" them.

UNIDIMENSIONAL TEST A test designed to measure one particular facet or dimension of personality.

UNSOCIALIZED-AGGRESSIVE Describing a syndrome in which the individual displays primary psychopathic behavior, such as inadequate guilt feelings, defiance of authority, malicious mischief, assaultive tendencies, and cruelty.

UNSPECIFIED ENCEPHALITIS A type of encephalitis usually transmitted by mosquitoes and ticks; it produces the same types of symptoms as epidemic encephalitis.

UNSTRUCTURED TEST A psychological assessment device that allows an individual to respond freely rather than choose from already provided responses.

V

VAGINISMUS Irregular and involuntary contractions of the vaginal muscles prior to or during intercourse, making insertion of the penis extremely difficult or impossible.

VALIDITY A term describing the accuracy of the statements or predictions that can be made about a disorder once it is classified. As applied to psychiatric diagnosis: *predictive* validity, the extent to which predictions can be made about the future behavior of patients with the same diagnosis; *concurrent* validity, the extent to which previously undiscovered symptoms or behavior patterns are found among patients with the same diagnosis; *etiological* validity, the extent to which a disorder in a number of individuals is found to have the same cause or causes.

VALPROIC ACID A new and extremely effective anticonvulsive drug recently introduced into the United States from Europe.

VALUE-CONFLICT PERSPECTIVE A social theory that contends that crime and other forms of deviant behavior are chiefly the consequence of learning a different set of values than those that govern normal behavior.

VASOPRESSIN A pituitary gland substance that may elevate memory when inhaled.

VICARIOUS EMOTIONAL CONDITIONING A term used to denote the learning of an anxiety response through modeling.

VOYEURISM (SCOPTOPHILIA) The act of looking at a particular person to attain some level of sexual gratification.

VULNERABILITY A diathesis-stress concept that takes into account the intermixing of genetic, physiological, developmental, learning, and stress factors in the etiology of schizophrenia.

W

WAXY FLEXIBILITY A stage of catatonic immobility in which the individual's limbs can be moved into a variety of positions, where they will remain for long periods of time.

WEAK ORGAN / SYSTEM THEORY (SPECIFIC RESPONSE PATTERN APPROACH) Hypothesis that specific physiological response patterns to situations, including stressful ones, are inherited.

WERNICKE'S AREA A portion of the left cerebral hemisphere said to control speech processing.

WERNICKE'S ENCEPHALOPATHY See *Beriberi*.

WITHDRAWAL SYMPTOMS Wide range of negative psychological and physiological reactions resulting from the body's attempt to readjust to the absence of a drug.

WORD SALAD In schizophrenia, a total disorganization of speech in which there are no associative links between words or thoughts.

REFERENCES

Abel, G., Barlow, D. H., Blanchard, E. B., & Guild, D. The components of rapists' sexual arousal. *Archives of General Psychiatry*, 1977, *34*, 895-903.

Abraham, K. Notes on the psychoanalytic investigation and treatment of manic-depressive insanity and allied conditions (1911). In *Selected papers on psychoanalysis*. New York: Basic Books, 1960.

Abrams, J. C., & Kaslow, F. Family systems and the learning disabled child: Intervention and treatment. *Journal of Learning Disabilities*, 1977, *10*, 27-31.

Abramson, L. Y., & Sackeim, H. A. A paradox of depression: Uncontrollability and self-blame. *Psychological Bulletin*, 1977, *84*, 838-51.

Abramson, L. Y., Seligman, M. E. P., & Teasdale, J. D. Learned helplessness in humans: critique and reformulation. *Journal of Abnormal Psychology*, 1978, *87*, 49-74.

Ackerman, N. W. *Family process*. New York: Basic Books, 1970.

Adler, G. Methods of treatment in analytic psychology. In B. B. Wolman (Ed.), *Psychoanalytic techniques*. New York: Basic Books, 1967.

Akers, R. L. Problems in the sociology of deviance: Social definitions and behavior. *Social Forces*, June 1968, 455-65.

Akiskal, H. S., & McKinney, W. T. Depressive disorders: Towards a unified hypothesis. *Science*, 1973, *182*, 20-29.

Aldrin, E., & Warga, W. *Return to earth*. New York: Random House, 1973.

Alexander, A. B. Systematic relaxation and flow rates in asthmatic children: Relationship to emotional precipitants and anxiety. *Journal of Psychosomatic Research*, 1972, *16*, 405-10. 10.

Alexander, F. *Psychosomatic medicine: Its principles and applications*. New York: Norton, 1950.

Alexander, F. *Fundamentals of psychoanalysis*. New York: Norton, 1963.

Alexander, F., and Selesnick, S. *The history of psychiatry*. New York: Harper & Row, 1966.

Allen, N., & Sherard, E. S. Developmental and degenerative diseases of the brain. In T. W. Farmer (Ed.), *Pediatric neurology*. New York: Harper & Row, 1975.

Altschule, M. D. *The development of traditional psychopathology*. New York: Wiley, 1976.

American Psychiatric Association. *American psychiatry*. New York: Columbia University Press, 1944.

American Psychiatric Association. *Diagnostic and statistical manual of mental disorders* (DSM-II). (2nd ed.) Washington, D.C.: *American Psychiatric Association*, 1968 (DSM-III).

Amir, M. *Patterns in forcible rape*. Chicago: University of Chicago Press, 1971.

Anastasi, A. *Psychological testing*. (3rd ed.) New York: Macmillan, 1968.

Anderson, O. D., Parmenter, R., & Liddell, H. S. Some cardiovascular manifestations of experimental neuroses in sheep. *AMA Archives of Neurological Psychiatry*, 1935, *34*, 330-54.

Andry, R. G. Faculty paternal- and maternal-child relationships, affection and delinquency. *British Journal of Delinquency*, 1957, *8*, 34-48.

Annent, J. *Feedback and human behavior*. Baltimore: Penguin Books, 1969.

Anthony, W. A. Psychological rehabilitation: A concept in need of a method. *American Psychologist*, 1977, *32*, 658-62.

APA Monitor. I.Q. tests on trial. *APA Monitor*, 1977, vol. 8, no. 11. Washington, D.C.: American Psychological Association.

Apgar, V. A proposal for a new method of evaluation of the newborn infant. *Anesthesia and Analgesia*, 1953, *32*, 260-67.

Archibald, H. C., Bell, D., Miller, C., and Tuddenham, R. D. Bereavement in childhood and adult psychiatric disturbance. *Psychosomatic Medicine*, 1963, *24*, 82-88.

Aserinsky, E., & Kleitman, N. Regularly occurring periods of eye motility and concomitant phenomena during sleep. *Science*, 1953, *118*, 273-74.

Atthowe, J. M. Treating the hospitalized patient. In W. E. Craighead, A. E. Kaldin, & M. J. Mahoney (Eds.), *Behavior modification: Principles, issues, and applications*. Boston: Houghton Mifflin, 1976.

Auden, W. H. *Old peoples' home*. Costa Mesa, Cal.: Concept Media, 1973.

Ayllon, T., & Azrin, N. H. *The token economy: A motivational system for therapy and rehabilitation*. New York: Appleton-Century-Crofts, 1968.

Bachrach, A. J. *Psychological research*. New York: Random House, 1972.

Back, K. W., & Guptill, C. S. Retirement and self-rating. In I. H. Simpson & J. C. McKinney (Eds.), *Social aspects of aging*. Durham, N.C.: Duke University Press, 1966.

Bakal, D. A. Headache: A biopsychological perspective. *Psychological Bulletin*, 1975, *82*, 369-82.

Bakan, D. *Slaughter of the innocents*. San Francisco: Jossey-Bass, 1971.

Bakwin, H., & Bakwin, R. M. *Behavior disorders in children*. Philadelphia: W. B. Saunders, 1972.

Bales, R. F. Cultural differences in rates of alcoholism. *Quarterly Journal of Studies on Alcohol*, 1946, 6, 480-99.

Ball, J. C., & Chambers, C. D. (Eds.) *The epidemiology of opiate addiction in the United States*. Springfield, Ill.: Charles C Thomas, 1970.

Baller, W. R. *Bed-wetting: Origins and treatment*. New York: Pergamon Press, 1975.

Ban, T. *Recent advances in the biology of schizophrenia*. Springfield, Ill.: Charles C Thomas, 1973.

Bandura, A. Influence of models' reinforcement contingencies on the acquisition of imitative responses. *Journal of Personality and Social Psychology*, 1965, 1, 589-95.

Bandura, A. *Principles of behavior modification*. New York: Holt, Rinehart & Winston, 1969.

Bandura, A. Psychotherapy based upon modeling principles. In A. E. Bergin & S. L. Garfield (Eds.), *Handbook of psychotherapy and behavior change: An empirical analysis*. New York: Wiley, 1971.

Bandura, A. *Aggression: A social learning analysis*. Englewood Cliffs, N.J.,: Prentice-Hall, 1973.

Bandura, A., & Walters, R. H. *Social learning and personality development*. New York: Holt, Rinehart & Winston, 1963.

Bannister, D., Salmon, P., & Lieberman, D.M. Diagnosis-treatment relationships in psychiatry: A statistical analysis. *British Journal of Psychiatry*, 1964, 110, 726-32.

Barber, T. X., DiCara, L. V., Kamiya, J., Miller, N. E., Shapiro, D., & Stoyva, J. M. *Biofeedback and self control: An Aldine Annual on the regulation of bodily processes and consciousness*. Chicago: Aldine, 1976.

Bard, P. A. A diencephalic mechanism for the expression of rage with special reference to sympathetic nervous system. *American Journal of Physiology*, 1928, 84, 490-515.

Barker-Benfield, G. J. *The horrors of the half-known life: Male attitudes toward women and sexuality in nineteenth-century America*. New York: Harper & Row, 1976.

Barlow, D. H. Increasing heterosexual responsiveness in the treatment of sexual deviation: A review of the clinical and experimental evidence. *Behavior Therapy*, 1973, 4, 655-71.

Barlow, D. H. The treatment of sexual deviation: Towards a comprehensive behavioral approach. In K. S. Calhoun; H. E. Adams, & K. M. Mitchell (Eds.), *Journal of Applied Behavior Analysis*, 1973, 6, 355-66.

Barlow, D. H., Reynolds, E. J., & Agras, S. Gender identity change in a transsexual. *Archives of General Psychiatry*, 1973, 28, 569.

Barraclough, B. M., Nelson, B., Bunch, J., & Sainsbury, P. The diagnostic classification and psychiatric treatment of 100 suicides. *Proceedings of the Fifth International Conference for Suicide Prevention*, London, 1969.

Barrett, W. *Irrational man. A study in existential philosophy*. New York: Anchor Books, 1962.

Bateson, G., Jackson, D., Haley, J., & Weakland, J. Toward a theory of schizophrenia. *Behavioral Science*, 1956, 1, 251-64.

Bazell, R. J. Drug abuse: Methadone becomes the solution and the problem. *Science*, 1973, 179, 772-75.

Beavers, W. R. A theoretical basis for family evaluation. In J. M. Lewis, W. R. Beavers, J. T. Gossett, & V. A. Phillips (Eds.), *No single thread: Psychological health in family systems*. New York: Brunner/Mazel, 1976.

Beck, A. T. *Depression: Clinical experimental, and theoretical aspects*. New York: Harper & Row, 1967.

Beck, A. T. The development of depression: A cognitive model. In R. J. Friedman & M. M. Katz (Eds.). *The psychology of depression: Contemporary theory and research*. Washington, D.C.: Wiley, 1974.

Beck, S. J. *Rorschach's Test I: Basic processes*. (3rd ed.) New York: Grune & Stratton, 1961.

Becker, E. *The denial of death*. New York: Free Press, 1972.

Becker, J. *Affective disorders*. Morristown, N.J.: General Learning Press, 1977.

Bellack, A. S., & Hersen, M. *Behavior modification*. Baltimore: Williams & Wilkins, 1977.

Bender, L. The maturation process and hallucinations in children. In W. Keup (Ed.), *Origin and mechanisms of hallucinations*. New York: Plenum Press, 1970.

Bennett, E. L., Rosenzweig, M. R., & Diamond, M. C. Rat brain: Effects of environmental enrichment on wet and dry weights. *Science*, 1968, 163, 825-26.

Benson, D., & Blumer, D. Personality changes with frontal and temporal lobe lesions. In D. Benson & D. Blumer (Eds.), *Psychiatric aspects of neurologic disease*. New York: Grune & Stratton, 1975.

Benson, H. *The relaxation response*. New York: Avon Books, 1975.

Benson, H., Shapiro, D., Tursky, B., & Schwartz, G. E. Decreased systolic blood pressure through operant conditioning techniques in patients with essential hypertension. *Science*, 1971, 173, 740-42.

Benson, H. J., & Wallace, R. K. Decreased drug abuse with transcendental meditation. A study of 1,862 subjects. In C. J. D. Zarafonetis (Ed.), *Drug abuse—Proceedings of the International Conference*. Philadelphia: Lea & Febiger, 1972.

Bentler, P. M., Shearman, R. W., & Prince, V. Personality characteristics of male transvestites. *Journal of Clinical Psychology*, 1970, 126, 287-91.

Berg, J. M. Etiological aspects of mental subnormality: Pathological factors. In A. M. Clarke & A. D. B. Clarke (Eds.), *Mental deficiency: The changing outlook*. New York: Free Press, 1974.

Berger, S. M. Conditioning through vicarious instigation. *Psychological Review*, 1962, 69, 450-66.

Bergin, A. E. The evaluation of therapeutic outcomes. In A. E. Bergin & S. L. Garfield (Eds.), *Handbook of psychotherapy and behavior change: An empirical analysis*. New York: Wiley, 1971.

Bergler, E. *Homosexuality. Disease or way of life?* New York: Collier Books, 1967.

Berke, J. An interview with Dr. Joseph Berke. In R. Boyers and R. Orrill (Eds.), *R. D. Laing and antipsychiatry*. New York: Harper & Row, Perennial Library, 1971.

Berne, E. *Games people play*. New York: Grove Press: 1964.

Berne, E. *What do you say after you say hello?* New York: Grove Press, 1972.

Bernstein, D., & McAlister, A. The modification of smoking behavior: Progress and problems. *Addictive Behaviors*, 1976, 1, 89-102.

Berry, J. C. Antecedents of schizophrenia, impulsive character and alcoholism in males. Paper presented at the American Psychological Association, Washington, D.C., 1967.

von Bertalanffy, L. *Robots, men and mind.* New York: Braziller, 1967.

Berzins, J. I., Ross, W. F., & Monroe, J. J. A multivariate study of the personality characteristics of hospitalized narcotic addicts on the MMPI. *Journal of Clinical Psychology,* 1971, *27,* 174-81.

Bettelheim, B. *The empty fortress.* New York: Free Press, 1967.

Bieber, I., Dain, H. J., Dince, P. R., Drellich, M. G. Grand, H. C., Gundlach, R. H., Kremer, M. W., Rifkin, A. H., Wilbur, C. B., & Bieber, T. B. *Homosexuality: A psychoanalytic study.* New York: Random House, 1962.

Birch, H. G., Richardson, S. A., Baird, D., Horobin, G., & Illsely, R. *Mental subnormality in the community: A clinical and epidemiological study.* Baltimore: Williams & Wilkins, 1970.

Blachly, P. H. An "electric needle" for aversive conditioning of the needle ritual. *International Journal of the Addictions,* 1971, *6,* 327-28.

Blake, B. G. A follow-up of alcoholics treated by behavior therapy. *Behavior Research and Therapy,* 1967, *5,* 89-94.

Blake, G. Community treatment plan aids delinquents. Five year experiment. *Los Angeles Times,* Jan. 26, 1967, I, 6.

Blanchard, E. B., Libet, J. M., & Young, L. D. Apneic aversion and covert sensitization in the treatment of a hydrocarbon inhalation addiction: A case study. *Journal of Behavior Therapy and Experimental Psychiatry,* 1973, *4,* 383-87.

Blaney, P. H. Contemporary theories of depression: Critique and comparison. *Journal of Abnormal Psychology,* 1977, *86,* 203-23.

Blatt, S. J., & Wild, C. M. *Schizophrenia: A developmental analysis.* New York: Academic Press, 1976.

Bleuler, M. The offspring of schizophrenics (trans. by S. M. Clemens). *Schizophrenia Bulletin,* 1974, *8,* 93-108.

Bliss, E. L. Anorexia nervosa. In A. M. Freedman, H. I. Kaplan, & B. J. Sadock (Eds.), *Comprehensive textbook of psychiatry/II,* Vol. 2. Baltimore: Williams & Wilkins, 1975.

Block, J. *The challenge of response sets.* New York: Appleton-Century-Crofts, 1965.

Bloodstein, O. Stuttering as tension and fragmentation. In J. Eisenson (Ed.), *Stuttering.* New York: Harper & Row, 1975.

Blum, G. S. *The Blacky pictures: A technique for the exploration of personality dynamics.* New York: Psychological Corporation, 1950.

Boisen, A. T. Types of dementia praecox— A study in psychiatric classification. *Psychiatry,* 1938, *2,* 233-36.

Bootzin, R. Stimulus-control of insomnia. Paper presented at the American Psychological Association, Montreal, August 1973.

Borkovec, T. D., Kaloupek, D. G., & Slama, K. M. The facilitative effect of muscle tension release in the relaxation treatment of sleep disturbance. *Behavior Therapy,* 1975, *6,* 301-9.

Borkovec, T. D., Slama, K. M., & Grayson, J. B. Sleep, disorders of sleep, and hypnosis. In D. C. Rimm & J. W. Somervill (Eds.), *Abnormal psychology.* New York: Academic Press, 1977.

Boudin, H. M. Contingency contrasting as a therapeutic tool in the deceleration of amphetamine use. *Behavior Therapy,* 1972, *3,* 604-8.

Bowlby, J. Processes of mourning. *International Journal of Psychoanalysis,* 1961, *317,* 44.

Boyers, R., & Orrill, R. *R. D. Laing and antipsychiatry.* New York: Harper & Row, Perennial Library, 1971.

Brady, J. V., Porter, R. W., Conrad, D. G., & Mason, J. W. Avoidance behavior and the development of gastroduodenal ulcers. *Journal of Experimental Analysis of Behavior,* 1958, *1,* 69-73.

Brady, J. V., & Nauta, W. J. H. Subcortical mechanisms in emotional behavior: affective changes following septal forebrain lesions in the albino rat. *Journal of Comparative and Physiological Psychology,* 1953, *46,* 339-46.

Braginsky, B. M., Braginsky, D. D., & Ring, K. *Methods of madness: The mental hospital as a last resort.* New York: Holt, Rinehart & Winston, 1969.

Brain, W. R., & Watson, J. N. *Brain's diseases of the nervous system.* London: Oxford University Press, 1969.

Braucht, G. N., Brakarsh, D., Follingstad, D., & Berry, K. L. Deviant drug use in adolescence: A review of psychosocial correlates. *Psychological Bulletin,* 1973, *79,* 92-106.

Brodsky, S. L. *Psychologists in the criminal justice system.* Marysville, Ohio: American Association of Correctional Psychologists, 1972.

Broen, W. E., & Storms, L. H. Lawful disorganization: The process underlying a schizophrenic syndrome. *Psychological Review,* 1966, *73,* 265-79.

Broen, W. E. *Schizophrenia: Research and theory.* New York: Academic Press, 1968.

Bromberg, W. *From shaman to psychotherapist.* Chicago: Henry Regnery, 1975

Bromley, D. B. *The psychology of human aging.* Baltimore: Penguin Books, 1971.

Brown, B. S., Wienckowski, L. A., & Stolz, S. B. *Behavior modification: Perspective on a current issue.* National Institute of Mental Health, 1975 (DHEW publication no. ADM 75-202).

Brown, F. Depression and childhood bereavement. *Journal of Mental Science,* 1961, *107,* 754-77.

Brown, G. W. Length of hospital stay and schizophrenia: A review of statistical studies. *Acta Psychiatry et Neurology Scandinavia,* 1960, *35,* 414-30.

Brown, J. A. C. *Freud and the post-Freudians.* Baltimore: Penguin, 1972.

Brown, R. N. A bill of rights for nursing home patients. *Trial,* 1977, *5.*

Bruck, C. Battle lines in the Ritalin war. *Human Behavior,* 1976, *8,* 25-33.

Buchsbaum, M. S. Average evoked response augmenting/reducing in schizophrenia and affective disorders. In D. X. Freedman (Ed.), *The biology of the major psychoses: A comparative analysis.* New York: Raven Press, 1975.

Budzynski, T. H., Stoyva, J. M., Adler, C. S., & Mullaney, D. J. EMG biofeedback and tension headache: A controlled outcome study. *Psychosomatic Medicine,* 1973, *35,* 484-96.

Buehler, R., Patterson, G. R., & Furniss, J. The reinforcement of behavior in institutionalized settings. *Behavior Research and Therapy,* 1966, *4,* 157-67.

Burgess, E. P. The modification of depressive disorders. In R. D. Rubin & C. M. Franks (Eds.), *Advances in behavior therapy, 1968.* New York: Academic Press, 1969.

Burrows, G. M. Commentaries on insanity. London: Underwood, 1828.

Buss, A. H. Psychopathology. New York: Wiley, 1966.

Busse, E. W., & Pfeiffer, E. Behavior and adaptation in late life. Boston: Little, Brown, 1977.

Butler, R. Aging's best advocate...an interview with Robert Butler. APA Monitor, March 1976.

Butler, R. N., & Lewis, M. I. Aging and mental health. (2nd ed.) St. Louis: C. V. Mosby, 1977.

Button, A. D. The genesis and development of alcoholism: An empirically based schema. Quarterly Journal of Studies on Alcoholism, 1956, 17, 671-75.

Caffey, E. M., Galbrecht, C. R., & Klett, C. J. Brief hospitalization and aftercare in the treatment of schizophrenia. Archives of General Psychiatry, 1971, 21, 81-86.

Calder, N. The Mind of Man: An Investigation Into Current Research on the Brain and Human Behavior. New York: Viking Press, 1971.

Cameron, N. Paranoid conditions and paranoia. In S. Arieti (Ed.), American handbook of psychiatry. New York: Basic Books, 1959.

Campbell, D., Sanderson, R. E., & Laverty, S. G. Characteristics of a conditioned response in human subjects during extinction trials following a single traumatic conditioning trial. Journal of Abnormal and Social Psychology, 1964, 68, 627-39.

Campbell, D. T., & Stanley, J. C. Experimental and quasi-experimental designs for research. Chicago: Rand McNally, 1970.

Cannon, W. B. Bodily changes in pain, hunger, fear, and rage. (2nd ed.) New York: Academic Press, 1929.

Carlson, N. R. Physiology of behavior. Boston: Allyn & Bacon, 1977.

Carr, J. Mongolism: Telling the parents. Developmental Medical Child Neurology, 1970, 12, 213-21.

Cattell, R. B. The culture-free intelligence test. Champaign, Ill.: IPAT, 1949.

Cautela, J. R. The treatment of alcoholism by covert sensitization. Psychotherapy: Theory, research, and practice, 1970, 1, 83-90.

Cawley, R. H. The present status of physical methods of treatment of schizophrenia. In A. Coppen & A. Walk (Eds.), Recent developments in schizophrenia: A symposium. London: Headly Brothers, 1967.

Chamberling, H. R. Mental retardation. In T. W. Farmer (Ed.), Pediatric neurology. New York: Harper & Row, 1975.

Chapman, L. J. Schizomimetic conditions and schizophrenia. Journal of Consulting and Clinical Psychology, 1969, 33, 646-50.

Chapman, L. J., & Chapman, J. D. Disordered thought in schizophrenia. Englewood Cliffs, N.J.: Prentice-Hall, 1973.

Chase, H. P., & Martin, H. Undernutrition and child development. New England Journal of Medicine. 1970, 282, 933-39.

Chesney, M. A., & Shelton, J. L. A comparison of muscle relaxation and electromyogram biofeedback treatments for muscle contraction headache. Journal of Behavior Therapy & Experimental Psychiatry, 1976, 7, 221-25.

Chesser, E. Strange loves: The human aspects of sexual deviation. New York: William Morrow, 1971.

Chilton, B. Psychosexual development in twins. Journal of Biosocial Sciences, 1972, 4, 277-86.

Chinn, P. L. Child Health Maintenance: Concepts for family-centered care. St. Louis: C. V. Mosby, 1974.

Chinn, P. L., Drew, C. P., & Logan, D. R. Mental Retardation: A life cycle approach. St. Louis: C. V. Mosby, 1975.

Chu, F. D., & Trotter, S. The mental health complex. Part I: Community mental health centers. (Part I of the task force report of the National Institutes of Mental Health.) Washington, D.C.: Center for Study of Responsive Law, 1972.

Churchill, W. Homosexual behavior among males. New York: Hawthorn Books, 1967.

Chusid, J. G. Correlative neuroanatomy and functional neurology. Los Altos, Cal.: Lange Medical Publications, 1970.

Clarke, A. M., & Clarke, A. D. B. Mental deficiency: The changing outlook. New York: Free Press, 1974.

Clarkson, F. E. & Hayden, B.S. The relationship of hyperactivity in a normal class setting with family background factors and neurological status. Proceedings of the Annual Convention of the American Psychiatric Association, 1977, Vol. 7, (Part 2), 559-60.

Clausen, J. A. Quo vadis, AAMD? Journal of special education, 1972, 6, 51-60.

Cleary, T. A., Humphreys, L. G., Kendrick, S. A., & Wesman, A. Educational uses of tests with disadvantaged students. American Psychologist, 1975, 30, 15-41.

Cleckley, H. The mask of sanity. (4th ed.) St. Louis: C. V. Mosby, 1964. (5th ed., 1976)

Cleland, C. C. Retardation: A developmental approach. Englewood Cliffs, N.J.: Prentice-Hall, 1978.

Clements, F. E. Primitive concepts of disease. University of California Publications in American Archaeology and Ethnology, 1932, 32, 185-252.

Cline, D. W., & Chosey, J. J. A prospective study of life changes and subsequent health changes. Archives of General Psychiatry, 1972, 27, 51-53.

Cloward, R. A., & Ohlin, L. E. Delinquency and opportunity. Glencoe, Ill.: Free Press, 1960.

Cobb, S., & Kasl, S. V. Some medical aspects of unemployment. Industrial Gerontology, 1972, 8, 111.

Cochrane, R., & Robertson, A. The life events inventory: A measure of the relative severity of psycho-social stressors. Journal of Psychosomatic Research, 1973, 17, 135-39.

Cohen, H. L., Filipczak, J., & Bis, J. S. Case I: An initial study of contingencies applicable to special education. Silver Spring, Md.: Educational Facility Press-IBR, 1967.

Cohen, M., Baker, G., Cohen, R. A., Fromm-Reichman, F., & Weigart, E. V. An intensive study of twelve cases of manic-depressive psychosis. Psychiatry, 1954, 17, 103-37.

Cohen, M., Garofalo, R., Boucher, R., & Seghorn, T. The psychology of rapists. In S. A. Pasternack (Ed.), Violence and victims. New York: Spectrum Publications, 1975.

Cohen, M. E., Robins, E., Purtell, J. J., Altman, M. W., & Reid, D. E. Excessive surgery in hysteria. Journal of the American Medical Association, 1953, 151, 977-86.

Colby, K. M. Appraisal of four psychological theories of paranoid phenomena. *Journal of Abnormal Psychology*, 1977, 86, 54-59.

Coleman, J. C. Abnormal psychology and modern life. (5th ed.) Glenview, Ill.: Scott, Foresman, 1976.

Coltrera, J. T., & Ross, N. Freud's psychoanalytic technique—from the beginning to 1923. In B. B. Wolman (Ed.), *Psychoanalytic techniques*. New York: Basic Books, 1967.

Combs, A., & Snygg, D. *Individual behavior. A perceptual approach to behavior*. New York: Harper & Row, 1959.

Conger, J. J. Proceedings of the American Psychological Association, Incorporated, for the year 1974: Minutes of the annual meeting of the council of representatives. *American Psychologist*, 1975, 30, 620-651.

Conner, T., & Kremer, E. Methadone maintenance—is it enough? *International Journal of the Addictions*, 1971, 6, 279-98.

Cooper, D. *The death of the family*. New York: Vintage Books, 1970.

Cooper, J. E., Kendell, R. E., Gurland, B. J., Sharpe, L., Copeland, J. R. M., & Simon, R. J. *Psychiatric diagnosis in New York and London: A comparative study of mental hospital admission*. (Maudsley Monograph 20) London: Oxford University Press, 1972.

Coopersmith, S. Adaptive reactions of alcoholics and nonalcoholics. *Quarterly Journal of Studies on Alcohol*, 1964, 27, 262-78.

Coppen, A. The biochemistry of affective disorders. *British Journal of Psychiatry*, 1967, 113, 1237-64.

Costello, C. G., & Belton, G. P. Depression: Treatment. In C. G. Costello (Ed.), *Symptoms of psychopathology*. New York: Wiley, 1970.

Cott, A. Megavitamins: The orthomolecular approach to behavioral disorders and learning disabilities. *Academic Therapy Quarterly*, 1972, 7, 245-58.

Cowen, E. L. Social and community interventions. *Annual Review of Psychology*, 1973, 24, 423-72.

Cox, H. *Focus: Aging*. (Annual Edition). Sluice Dock, Guilford, Conn.: Dushkin Publishing Group, 1978.

Craft, M., Stephenson, G., & Granger, C. A controlled trial of authoritarian and self-governing regimes with adolescent psychopaths. *American Journal of Orthopsychiatry*, 1964, 34, 543-54.

Creak, E. M. Schizophrenic syndrome in childhood. Progress report of a working party. *Cerebral Palsy Bulletin*, 1961, 3, 501-4.

CRM. *Abnormal psychology: Current perspectives*. New York: Random House, 1976.

Cumming, E., & Henry, W. E. *Growing old: The process of disengagement*. New York: Basic Books, 1961.

Cumming. E. Further thoughts on the theory of disengagement. In C. S. Kart and B. B. Manard (Eds.), *Aging in America*. Port Washington, N.Y.: Alfred Publishing, 1976.

Curran, J. P. Skills training as an approach to the treatment of heterosexual-social anxiety: A review. *Psychological Bulletin*, 1977, 84, 140-57.

Cuskey, W. R., & Edington, B. M. Drug abuse as self-destructive behavior. In A. R. Roberts (Ed.), *Self-destructive behavior*. Springfield, Ill.: Charles C Thomas, 1975.

Cytryn, L., & Lourie, R. S. Mental retardation. In A. M. Freedman, H. I. Kaplan, & B. J. Sadock (Eds.), *Comprehensive textbook of psychiatry/II. Vol. 2*. Baltimore: Williams and Wilkins, 1975.

Dahlstrom, W. G., & Welsh, G. S. *An MMPI handbook*. Minneapolis: University of Minnesota Press, 1960.

Dahlstrom, W. G., Welsh, G. S., & Dahlstrom, L. E. MMPI handbook. Vol. 1: Clinical Interpretations (Revised Edition). Minneapolis: University of Minnesota Press, 1972.

Dalessio, D. J. *Wolff's headache and other head pain*. New York: Oxford University Press, 1972.

Davidson, G. W. *Living with dying*. Minneapolis: Augsburg, 1975.

Davidson, W. S. Studies of aversive conditioning of alcoholics: A critical review of theory and research methodology. *Psychological Bulletin*, 1974, 81, 571-81.

Davidson, W. S., & Seidman, E. Studies of behavior modification and juvenile delinquency: A review, methodological critique, and social perspective. *Psychological Bulletin*, 1974, 81, 998-1011.

Davis, A. *Social class influences upon learning*. Cambridge: Harvard University Press, 1948.

Davis, K. B. *Factors in the sex life of twenty-two hundred women*. New York: Harper & Brothers, 1929.

Davis, N. J. *Sociological constructions of deviance*. Dubuque, Iowa: William C. Brown, 1975.

Davison, G. C., & Neale, J. M. *Abnormal psychology: An experimental clinical approach*. New York: Wiley, 1974.

DeCourmelles, F. *Hypnotism* (trans. by Laura Enser). London: Routledge and Kegan Paul, 1891.

Dekker, E., Pelser, H. E., & Groen, J. Conditioning as a cause of asthmatic attacks. *Journal of Psychosomatic Research*, 1957, 2, 97-108.

Delgado, J. M. R. *Physical control of the mind*. New York: Harper & Row, 1969.

Depue, R. A. An activity-withdrawal distinction in schizophrenia: Behavioral, clinical, brain damage, and neurophysiological correlates. *Journal of Abnormal Psychology*, 1976, 85, 174-85.

Depue, R. A., & Evans, R. The psychology of depressive disorders. In B. A. Maker (Ed.). *Progress in experimental personality research*. New York: Academic Press, 1975.

DesLauriers, A. M., & Carlson, C. F. *Your child is asleep*. Homewood, Ill.: Dorsey Press, 1969.

Despert, J. L. *The emotionally disturbed child*. New York: Anchor Books, 1970.

DISCUS (Distilled Spirits Council of the United States). *Scientific Advisory Council Report*, (1960-1975) of the Alcoholism Research Grant Program. Washington, D.C., 1976.

Dobbing, J. *Growth and development of the human brain*. Philadelphia: W. B. Saunders, 1972.

Dohrenwend, B. P., & Dohrenwend, B. S. *Social status and psychological disorder*. New York: Wiley, 1969.

Dole, V. P., & Nyswander, M. E. A medical treatment for diacetylmorphine (heroin) addiction: A clinical trial with methadone hydrochloride. *Journal of the American Medical Association,* 1965, *193,* 646-50.

Dole, V. P., Nyswander, M. E., & Warner, A. Successful treatment of 750 criminal addicts. *Journal of the American Medical Association,* 1968, *206,* 2708-11.

Dubey, D. R. Organic factors in hyperkinesis: A critical evaluation. *American Journal of Orthopsychiatry,* 1976, *4,* 453-56.

Dunham, P. J. *Experimental psychology: Theory and practice.* New York: Harper & Row, 1977.

DuPont, R. L., & Katon, R. N. Development of a heroin-addiction treatment program: Effect on urban crime. *Journal of the American Medical Association,* 1971, *216,* 1320-24.

Durkheim, E. *Suicide* (1897; trans. by J. A. Spaulding & G. Simpson). New York: Free Press, 1951.

Dutton, G. The growth pattern of psychotic boys. *British Journal of Psychiatry,* 1964, *110,* 101-3.

Ebel, H. Agoraphobia no exception to a "family system approach to psychiatric disorders. *Behavior Today,* 1978, *30,* 6.

Eccles, J. C. *The understanding of the brain.* New York: McGraw-Hill, 1977.

Edwards, A. L. The relationship between the judged desirability of a trait and the probability that the trait will be endorsed. *Journal of Applied Psychology,* 1953, *37,* 90-93.

Edwards, A. L. *Edwards personal preference schedule.* New York: Psychological Corporation, 1959.

Eisenson, J. *Stuttering.* New York: Harper & Row, 1975.

Elder, S. T., Ruiz, Z. R., Deabler, H. L., & Dillenkoffer, R. L. Instrumental conditioning of diastolic blood pressure in essential hypertensive patients. *Journal of Applied Behavior Analysis,* 1973, *6,* 377-82.

Ellenberger, H. F. *The discovery of the unconscious.* New York: Basic Books, 1970.

Ellis, A. *Reason and emotion in psychotherapy.* New York: Lyle Stuart, 1962.

Ellis, A. Frigidity. In A. Ellis & A. Abarbanel (Eds.). *The encyclopedia of sexual behavior.* New York: Jason Aronson, 1973.

Ellis, A., & Abarbanel, A. *The encyclopedia of sexual behavior.* New York: Jason Aronson, 1973.

Engel, G. L. *Psychological development in health and disease.* Philadelphia: W. B. Saunders, 1962.

Ennis, B. The impact of litigation on the future of state hospitals. In J. Zusman, & E. F. Bertsch (Eds.), *The future role of the state hospital.* Lexington, Mass.: D. C. Heath, 1975.

Epstein, H. A sin or a right? *New York Times Magazine,* Sept. 8, 1974, 91-94.

Erickson, M. T. *Childhood psychopathology.* Englewood Cliffs, N.J.: Prentice-Hall, 1978.

Essman, W. B. Neurochemical changes in ECS and ECT. *Seminars in Psychiatry,* 1972, *4,* 67-79.

Evans, R. B. Childhood parental relationships of homosexual men. *Journal of Consulting and Clinical Psychology,* 1969, *33,* 129-35.

Evers, W. L., & Schwarz, J. C. Maintaining social withdrawal in preschoolers: The effect of filmed modeling and teacher praise. *Journal of Abnormal Child Psychology,* 1973, *1,* 248-56.

Exner, J. E., Jr. *The Rorschach systems.* New York: Grune & Stratton, 1974.

Eysenck, H. J. The effects of psychotherapy: An evaluation. *Journal of Consulting Psychology,* 1952, *16,* 319-24.

Eysenck, H. J. Psychiatric diagnoses as a psychological and statistical problem. *Psychological Reports,* 1955, *1,* 3-17.

Eysenck, H. J. *Dynamics of anxiety and hysteria.* London: Routledge & Kegan Paul, 1957.

Eysenck, H. J. *The structure of human personality.* (2nd ed.) London: Methuen, 1960.

Eysenck, H. J. *The effects of psychotherapy.* New York: International Science Press, 1966.

Fairweather, G. W. *Methods in experimental social innovation.* New York: Wiley, 1967.

Fairweather, G. W., Sanders, D. H., Cressler, D. L., & Maynard, H. *Community life for the mentally ill.* Chicago: Aldine, 1969.

Faris, R. E. L., & Dunham, H. W. *Mental disorders in urban areas.* Chicago: University of Chicago Press, 1939.

Farberow, N. L., Shneidman, E. S., & Leonard, C. Suicide among general medical and surgical hospital patients with malignant neoplasms. Veterans Administration, Department of Medicine & Surgery, *Medical Bulletin,* Feb. 25, 1963, 1-11.

Feinbloom, D. H. *Transvestites and transsexuals.* New York: Delacorte Press/ Seymour Lawrence, 1976.

Feldman, G. M. The effect of biofeedback training on respiratory resistance of asthmatic children. *Psychosomatic Medicine,* 1976, *38,* 27-34.

Feldman, M. P., & MacCulloch, M. J. *Homosexual behavior: Therapy and assessment.* Oxford, Eng.: Pergamon Press, 1971.

Fenichel, O. *The psychoanalytic theory of neuroses.* New York: Norton, 1945.

Fenichel, O. Ten years of the Berlin Psychoanalytic Institute, 1920-1930. (1930). *Collected Papers,* edited by H. Fenichel and D. Rapaport. 2 Vols. New York: Norton, 1953-54.

Ferster, C. B. Positive reinforcement and behavioral deficits of autistic children. *Child Development,* 1961, *32,* 437-56.

Ferster, C. B. Classification of behavioral pathology. In L. Krasner & L. P. Ullmann (Eds.), *Research in behavior modification.* New York: Holt, Rinehart & Winston, 1965.

Ferster, C. B. Animal behavior and mental illness. *The Psychological Record,* 1966, *16,* 345-56.

Finch, J. R., Smith, J. P., & Pokorny, A. D. Vehicular studies. Paper presented at the American Psychological Association, 1970.

Finley, W. W., Smith, H. A., & Etherton, M. D. Reduction of seizures and normalization of the EEG in a severe epileptic following sensorimotor biofeedback training: Preliminary study. *Biological Psychology,* 1975, *2,* 189-203.

Fisher, S., & Cleveland, S. E. *Body image and personality.* Princeton, N.J.: Van Nostrand, 1958.

Fontana, A. Familial etiology of schizophrenia: Is a scientific methodology possible? *Psychological Bulletin,* 1966, *66,* 214-28.

Fox, R. The recent decline of suicide in Britain: The role of the samaritan suicide prevention movement. In E. S. Shneidman (Ed.), *Suicidology: Contemporary developments.* New York: Grune & Stratton, 1976.

Frank, J. D. *Persuasion and healing.* New York: Schocken Books, 1961.

Frank, L. K. Projective methods for the study of personality. *Journal of Psychology,* 1939, *8,* 389-413.

Frankl, V. E. Paradoxical intention: A logotherapeutic technique. *American Journal of Psychotherapy,* 1960, *14,* 520-35.

Frankl, V. E. *Man's search for meaning.* Boston: Beacon Press, 1962.

Frederiks, V. A. M. Disorders of attention in neurological syndromes (Sensory extinction syndromes: The hyperkinetic syndrome). In P. J. Vinkin & G. W. Bryun (Eds.), *Handbook of clinical neurology.* New York: American Elsevier, 1969.

Freed, E. X. Anxiety and conflict: Role of drug dependent learning in the rat. *Quarterly Journal of Studies on Alcohol,* 1971, *32,* 13-29.

Freud, S. *The problem of anxiety.* New York: Norton, 1896.

Freund, K., McKnight, C. K., Langevin, R., & Cibiri, S. The female child as a surrogate object. *Archives of Sexual Behavior,* 1972, *2,* 119-33.

Friar, M., & Beatty, J. Migraine: Management by trained control of vasoconstriction. *Journal of Consulting and Clinical Psychology,* 1976, *44,* 46-53.

Friedman, R., & Iwai, J. Genetic predisposition and stress- induced hypertension. *Science,* 1976, *193,* 161-92.

Friedman, M., & Rosenman, R. H. *Type A behavior and your heart.* New York: Alfred Knopf, 1974.

Fromm-Reichman, F. Notes on the development of treatment of schizophrenics by psychoanalytic psychotherapy. *Psychiatry,* 1948, *11,* 263-73.

Fromm-Reichman, F. *Psychoanalysis and psychotherapy: Selected papers,* ed. by D. M. Bullard. Chicago: University of Chicago Press, 1974.

Fuchs, C. Z., & Rehm, L. P. A self-control behavior therapy program for depression. *Journal of Consulting and Clinical Psychology,* 1977, *45,* 206-15.

Gallinek, A. The Kleine-Levin syndrome. *Diseases of the Nervous System,* 1967, *28,* 448-51.

Gardner, W. I. *Children with learning and behavior problems.* Boston: Allyn & Bacon, 1978.

Gartrell, N. K., Loriaux, D. L., & Chase, T. N. Plasma testosterone in homosexual and heterosexual women. *American Journal of Psychiatry,* 1977, *10,* 1117-18.

Gatchel, R. J. The therapeutic effectiveness of voluntary heart rate control in reducing anxiety: A case report. *Journal of Consulting and Clinical Psychology,* 1977, *45,* 689-91.

Gatchel, R. J. Biofeedback and the modification of fear and anxiety. In R. J. Gatchel & K. P. Price (Eds.), *Clinical applications of biofeedback: Appraisal and status.* Elmsford, N.Y.: Pergamon Press, 1979.

Gatchel, R. J., Hatch, J. P., Watson, P. J., Smith, D., & Gaas, E. Comparative effectiveness of voluntary heart-rate control and muscular relaxation as active coping skills for reducing speech anxiety. *Journal of Consulting and Clinical Psychology.* 1978, *45,* 1093-1100.

Gatchel, R. J., McKinney, M. E., & Koebernick, L. F. Learned helplessness, depression, and physiological responding. *Psychophysiology,* 1977, *14,* 25-31.

Gatchel, R. J., & Proctor, J. D. Physiological correlates of learned helplessness in man. *Journal of Abnormal Psychology,* 1976, *85,* 27-34.

Gatchel, R. J., & Proctor, J. D. Effectiveness of voluntary heart rate control in reducing speech anxiety. *Journal of Consulting and Clinical Psychology,* 1976, *44,* 381-89.

Gebhard, P. H. Fetishism and sadomasochism. In M. S. Weinberg (Ed.), *Sex research.* New York: Oxford University Press, 1976.

Gebhard, P. H., Gagnon, J. H., Pomeroy, W. B., & Christenson, C. V. *Sex offender.* London: Heinemann, 1965.

Geer, J. H. The development of a scale to measure fear. *Behavior Research and Therapy,* 1965, *3,* 45-53.

Gibbs, F. A. Abnormal electrical activity in the temporal regions and its relationship to abnormalities in behavior. *Research Publication of the Association for Research on Nervous and Mental Diseases,* 1958, *36,* 278-94.

Giese, H. (Ed.). *Die sexuelle perversion.* Frankfurt: Akademische Verlagsgesellschaft, Akademische Reihe, 1967.

Gil, D. G. Incidence of child abuse and demographic characteristics of persons involved. In R. E. Helfer & H. Kempe (Eds.). *The battered child.* Chicago: University of Chicago Press, 1968.

Gilberstadt, H. A modal MMPI profile type in neurodermatitis. *Psychosomatic Medicine,* 1962, *24,* 471-76.

Gilberstadt, H., & Duker, J. *A handbook for clinical and actuarial MMPI interpretation.* Philadelphia: W. B. Saunders, 1965.

Gilroy, J., & Meyer, J. S. *Medical neurology.* New York: Macmillan, 1975.

Glasser, W. *The identity society.* New York: Harper & Row, 1972.

Glassocote, R. M., Sanders, D., Forstenzer, H. M., & Foley, A. R. (Eds.). *The community mental health center: An analysis of existing models.* Washington, D.C.: American Psychiatric Association, 1964.

Glatt, M. M., Pittman, D. J., Gillespie, D. G., & Hillis, D. R. *The drug scene in Great Britain.* London: Edward Arnold, 1967.

Glazer, H. I., Weiss, J. M., Pohorecky, L. A., & Miller, N. E. Monoamines as mediators of avoidance-escape behavior. *Psychosomatic Medicine,* 1975, *37,* 535-43.

Glick, P. C. Updating the life cycle of the family. *Journal of Marriage and Family,* 1977, *39,* 5-13.

Glover, B. Control of the sexual deviate. *Federal Probation,* 1960, *24,* 38-45.

Glueck, S., & Glueck, E. *Physique and delinquency.* New York: Harper & Row, 1956.

Goldberg E. M., & Morrison, S. L. Schizophrenia and social class. *British Journal of Psychiatry,* 1963, *109,* 785-802.

Goldblatt, P. B., Moore, M. E., & Stunkard, A. J. Social factors in obesity. *Journal of the American Medical Association,* 1965, *192,* 1039.

Goldfarb, A. I. Institutional care of the aged. In E. W. Busse & E. Pfeiffer (Eds.), *Behavior and adaptation in late life.* Boston: Little, Brown, 1977.

Goldfarb, W. A. A follow-up investigation of schizophrenic children treated in residence. *Psychosocial Process,* 1970, *1,* 9.

Goldfarb, W. A. *Growth and change of schizophrenic children: A longitudinal study.* New York: Wiley, 1974.

Goldfried, M. R., & Davison, G. C. *Clinical behavior therapy.* New York: Holt, Rinehart & Winston, 1976.

Goldfried, M. R., & Kent, R. N. Traditional versus behavioral assessment: A comparison of methodological and theoretical assumptions. *Psychological Bulletin,* 1972, *77,* 409-20.

Goldfried, M. R., Stricker, G., & Weiner, I. B. *Rorschach handbook of clinical and research applications.* Englewood Cliffs, N.J.: Prentice-Hall, 1971.

Goldstein, A. P., & Stein, N. *Prescriptive psychotherapies.* New York: Pergamon Press, 1976.

Goldstein, B. *Human sexuality.* New York: McGraw-Hill, 1976.

Goldstein, M., Mahanand, D., Lee, J., et al., Dopamine - beta - hydroxylase and endogeneous total five - hydroxyindole levels in autistic patients and controls. In M. Coleman (Ed.), *The Autistic Syndromes.* Amsterdam: North Holland Pub. Co., 1976.

Goodwin, D. W. Is alcoholism hereditary? *General Psychiatry,* 1969, *126,* 191-98.

Goodwin, D. W., Crane, J. B., & Guze, S. B. Alcoholic ''blackouts; A review and clinical study of 100 alcoholics. *American Journal of Psychiatry,* 1969, *126,* 191-98.

Goodwin, D. W., Schulsinger, F., Hermansen, L., Guze, S. B., & Winokur, G. Alcohol problems in adoptees raised apart from alcoholic biological parents. *Archives of General Psychiatry,* 1973, *28,* 238-43.

Goodwin, D. W., Schulsinger, F., Moller, N., Hermansen, L., Winokur, G., & Guze, S. B. Drinking problems in adopted and nonadopted sons of alcoholics. *Archives of General Psychiatry,* 1974, *31,* 164-69.

Gorsuch, R. L., & Butler, M. C. Initial drug abuse: A review of predisposing social psychological factors. *Psychological Bulletin,* 1976, *83,* 120-37.

Goshen, C. E. *Documentary history of psychiatry.* New York: Philosophical Library, 1967.

Gottesman, L. E. The mental hospital's role in developing programs for geriatric residents. In J. Zusman and E. F. Bertsch (Eds.), *The future role of the state hospital.* Lexington, Mass.: Lexington Books, 1975.

Gottesman, I., and Shields, J., Schizophrenia and genetics. A twin-study vantage point. New York: Academic Press, 1972.

Gottman, J. M. N-of-one and N-of-two research in psychotherapy. *Psychological Bulletin,* 1973, *80,* 93-105. 105.

Gottman, J. M., & Leiblum, S. R. *How to do psychotherapy and how to evaluate it.* New York: Holt, Rinehart & Winston, 1974.

Gough, H. G., & Peterson, D. R. The identification and measurement of predispositional factors in crime and delinquency. *Journal of Consulting Psychology,* 1952, *16,* 207-12.

Gould, L. C., Berberian, R., Kasl, S. V., Thompson, W. D., & Kleber, H. D. Sequential patterns of multiple-drug use among high school students. *Archives of General Psychiatry.* 1977, *34,* 216-22.

Gozali, J. Perception of the EMR special class by former students. *Mental Retardation,* 1972, *10,* 34-35.

Grace, W. J., & Graham, D. T. Relationship of specific attitudes and emotions to certain bodily diseases. *Psychosomatic Medicine,* 1952, *14,* 242-51.

Graham, D. T. Some research on psychophysiologic specificity and its relation to psychosomatic disease. In R. Roessler & W. S. Greenfield (Eds.), *Physiological correlates of psychological disease.* Madison: University of Wisconsin Press, 1962.

Graham, D. T. Psychosomatic medicine. In N. S. Greenfield & R. A. Sternbach (Eds.), *Handbook of psychophysiology* New York: Holt, Rinehart & Winston, 1972.

Graham, D. T., Kabler, J. D., & Graham, F. K. Physiological responses to the suggestion of attitudes specific for hives and hypertension. *Psychosomatic Medicine,* 1962, *24,* 159-69.

Graham, D. T., Lundy, R. M., Benjamin, L. S., Kabler, J. D., Lewis W. C., Kunish, N. C., & Graham, F. K. Specific attitudes in initial interviews with patients having different ''psychosomatic'' diseases. *Psychosomatic Medicine,* 1962, *24,* 257-66.

Graham, D. T., Stern, J. A., & Winokur, G. Experimental investigation of the specificity hypothesis in psychosomatic disease. *Psychosomatic Medicine,* 1958, *20,* 446-57.

Grayson, H. M., & Olinger, L. B. Simulation of ''normalcy'' by psychiatric patients on the MMPI. *Journal of Consulting Psychology,* 1957, *21.* 73-77.

Green, R., and Money, J. (Eds.). *Transsexualism and sex reassignment.* Baltimore: Johns Hopkins Press, 1969.

Greenfield, N. S., & Sternbach, R. A. *Handbook of psychophysiology.* New York: Holt, Rinehart & Winston, 1972.

Greer, S. Study of parental loss in neurotics and sociopaths. *Archives of General Psychiatry,* 1964, *11,* 177-80.

Greer, S., & Morris, T. Psychological attributes of women who develop breast cancer: A controlled study. *Journal of Psychosomatic Research,* 1975, *19,* 147-53.

Gregory, I. An analysis of familial data on psychiatric patients: Parental age, family size, birth order and ordinal position. *British Journal of Preventive Social Medicine,* 1958, *12,* 42-59.

Griesinger, W. *Mental Pathology and Therapeutics.* Trans. by C. L. Robertson and J. Rutherford. London: New Sydenham Society, 1867.

Griffith, J. D., Cavanaugh, J., Held, N. N., & Oates, J. A. Dextroamphetamine: Evaluation of psychotomimetic properties in man. *Archives of General Psychiatry,* 1972, *26,* 97-100.

Griffiths, P. D., Merry, J., & Browning, M. Homosexual women: An endocrine and psychological study. *Journal of Endocrinology,* 1974, *63,* 549-56.

Grinkers, R. R., & Robbins, F. P. *Psychosomatic case book.* New York: Balkiston Co., 1954.

Grinspoon, L., Ewalt, J. R., & Shader, R. Psychotherapy and pharmacotherapy in chronic schizophrenia. *American Journal of Psychiatry,* 1968, *124,* 1645-52.

Grob, G. N. *Mental institutions in America: Social policy to 1875.* New York: Free Press, 1973.

Grossman, H. J. (Ed.). *Manual on terminology and classification in mental retardation.* Washington, D.C: American Association on Mental Deficiency, 1973.

Gruzelier, J. H., & Venables, P. H. Evidence of high and low levels of physiological arousal in schizophrenics. *Psychophysiology,* 1975, *12,* 66-73.

Guardo, C. J. The adolescent as individual: Issues and insights. New York: Harper & Row, 1975.

Guilford, J. P. Personality. New York: McGraw Hill, 1959.

Gundlach, R., & Riess, B. F. Self and sexual identity in the female: A study of female homosexuals. In B. F. Riess (Ed.), New directions in mental health. New York: Grune & Stratton, 1968.

Gunn, J., & Fenton, G. Lancet, June 5, 1971, 1173-76.

Guntrip, H. Schizoid phenomena, object relations, and the self. New York: International Universities Press, 1969.

Gustafson, E. Dying: The career of the nursing-home patient. Journal of Health and Social Behavior, 1973, 13, 226-35.

Gutheil, T. and Avery, N. Multiple overt incest as family defense against loss. Family Process, 1977, 16, 105-116.

Hacaen, H., & Albert, M. L. Disorders of mental functioning related to frontal lobe pathology. In D. Benson, & D. Blumer (Eds.), Psychiatric aspects of neurologic disease. New York: Grune & Stratton, 1975.

Haertzen, C. A. Subjective drug effects: A factorial representation of subjective drug effects on the Addiction Research Center Inventory. Journal of Nervous and Mental Diseases, 1965, 40, 280-89.

Haertzen, C. A., & Hooks, N. T. Changes in personality and subjective experience associated with the chronic administration and withdrawal of opiates. Journal of Nervous and Mental Diseases, 1969, 148, 606-14.

Haley, J. Uncommon therapy. New York: Ballantine Books, 1973.

Hall, C. S., & Lindzey, G. Theories of personality. New York: Wiley, 1978.

Halstead, W. C. Brain and intelligence. Chicago: University of Chicago Press, 1947.

Hambling, J. Psychosomatic aspects of arterial hypertension. British Journal of Medical Psychology, 1952, 25, 39-47.

Hamilton, M. A rating scale for depression. Journal of Neurology, Neurosurgery, and Psychiatry, 1960, 23, 56-62.

Hammen, C. L., & Glass, D. R. Depression, activity, and evaluation of reinforcement. Journal of Abnormal Psychology, 1975, 84, 718-21.

Hanson, D. R., & Gottesman, L. I. The genetics, if any, of infantile autism and childhood schizophrenia. Journal of Autism and Childhood Schizophrenia, 1976, 6, 209-340.

Hare, R. D. Psychopathy: Theory and research. New York: Wiley, 1970.

Hare, R. D. Psychopathy. In P. H. Venables & M. J. Christie (Eds.), Research in psychophysiology. New York: Wiley, 1976.

Harlow, H. F., & Harlow, M. Psychopathology in monkeys. In H. D. Kimmel (Ed.), Experimental psychopathology: Recent research and theory. New York: Academic Press, 1971.

Harlow, H. F., & Suomi, S. J. Induced depression in monkeys. Behavioral Biology, 1974, 12, 273-96.

Harrington, A. Psychopaths. New York: Simon and Schuster, 1972.

Harris, T. A. I'm ok, you're ok. New York: Harper & Row, 1967.

Hathaway, S. R., & McKinley, J. C. MMPI manual, New York: Psychological Corporation, 1943.

Hauser, R. Rapid smoking as a technique of behavior modification: Caution in the selection of subjects. Journal of Consulting and Clinical Psychology, 1974, 42, 625-30.

Hawkins, R., & Tiedeman, G. The creation of deviance: Interpersonal and organizational determinants. Columbus, Ohio: Merrill, 1975.

Haynes, S. N., Griffin, P., Mooney, D., & Parise, M. Electromyographic biofeedback and relaxation instructions in the treatment of muscle contraction headaches. Behavior Therapy, 1975, 6, 672-78.

Health Research Group. Through the mental health maze. Washington, D. C: Health Research Group (Dept. P, 2000 P Street, N.W., Room 708).

Heath, R. G. A biochemical hypothesis on the etiology of schizophrenia. In D. D. Jackson (Ed.), The etiology of schizophrenia. New York: Basic Books, 1960.

Heath, R. G., Martens, S., Leach, B. E., Cohen, M., & Angel, C. Effect on behavior in humans with the administration of taraxein. American Journal of Psychiatry, 1957, 114, 14-24.

Heber, R. F., & Dever, R. B. Research on education and habilitation of the mentally retarded. In H. C. Haywood (Ed.), Social-cultural aspects of mental retardation. New York: Appleton-Century-Crofts, 1970.

Heilbrun, A. B. An empirical test of the modeling theory of sex-role learning. Child Development, 1965, 36, 789-99.

Henderson, D. J. Incest. In A. M. Freedman, H. I. Kaplan, & B. J. Sadock (Eds.), Comprehensive textbook of psychiatry/ II. Vol. 2. Baltimore: Williams & Wilkins, 1975.

Hendin, D. Death as a fact of life. New York: Norton, 1973.

Hernandez-Peon, R., O'Flaherty, J. J., & Mazzuchelli-O'Flaherty, A. L. Sleep and other behavioral effects induced by acetylcholine stimulation of basal temporal cortex and striate structures. Brain Research, 1967, 4, 243-67.

Herrnstein, R. J. Doing what comes naturally. American Psychologist, 1977, 32, 1013-16.

Hess, R. D., & Shipman, V. C. Early experience and the socialization of cognitive modes in children. Child Development, 1965, 36, 869-86.

Hess, W. R. Stammganglein-Reizversuche, 10. Tagung der Deutschen Physiologischen Gesellschaft Frankfurt am Main. Berichten über die Gesamte Physiologie, 1928, 42, 554-55.

Heston, L. L. Psychiatric disorders in foster home reared children of schizophrenic mothers. British Journal of Psychiatry. 1966, 112, 819-25.

Hetherington, E. M. Girls without fathers. Psychology Today, 1973, 6, 46-47.

Hettlinger, R. Human sexuality: A psychosocial perspective. Belmont, Cal.: Wadsworth, 1975.

Hicks, N. Life after 65. Black Enterprise Magazine. 1977.

Higgins, R. L., & Marlatt, G. A. The effects of anxiety arousal on the consumption of alcohol by alcoholics and social drinkers. Journal of Consulting and Clinical Psychology, 1973, 41, 426-33.

Higgins, R. L., & Marlatt, G. A. Fear of interpersonal evaluation as a determinant of alcohol consumption in male social drinkers. Journal of Abnormal Psychology, 1975, 84, 644-51.

Hill, M. J., & Blane, H. T. Evaluation of psychotherapy with alcoholics: A critical review. Quarterly Journal of Studies on Alcohol, 1967, 28, 76-104.

Hill, R. G. *The abandonment of restraints.* London: Simpkin, Marshall, 1839.

Hite, S. *Sexual honesty. By women for women.* New York: Warner Books, 1974.

Hite, S. *The Hite report: A nationwide study of female sexuality.* New York: Dell Books, 1976.

Hoffer, A. The adrenochrome theory of schizophrenia: A review. *Diseases of the Nervous System,* 1964, *25,* 173-78.

Hokanson, J. E., & Burgess, M. The effects of three types of aggression on vascular processes. *Journal of Abnormal and Social Psychology,* 1962, *65,* 446-49.

Holland, R., Cohen, G., Goldenberg, M., Sha, J., & Leifer, A. I. Adrenaline and noradrenaline in the urine and plasma of schizophrenics. *Federation Proceedings,* 1958, *17,* 378.

Hollingshead, A. B., & Redlich, F. C. *Social class and mental illness.* New York: Wiley, 1958.

Holloway, W. H. Transactional analysis: An integrative view. In G. Barnes, (Ed.), *Transactional Analysis After Eric Berne.* New York: Harper's College Press, 1977.

Holmes, T. H., & Rahe, R. H. The social readjustment rating scale. *Journal of Psychosomatic Research,* 1967, *11,* 213-18.

Hooker, E. Male homosexuality in the Rorschach. *Journal of Projective Techniques,* 1958, *22,* 33-54.

Horowitz, M. J. Flashbacks: Recurrent intrusive images after the use of LSD. *American Journal of Psychiatry,* 1969, *126,* 147-51.

Horowitz, M. J. *Stress response syndrome.* New York: Jason Aronson, 1976.

Howell, R. R. Prenatal diagnosis in the prevention of handicapping disorders. *Pediatric Clinics of North America,* 1973, *20,* 141.

Howells, J. G. *Principles of family psychiatry.* New York: Brunner/Mazel, 1975.

Hunt, M. *Sexual behavior in the 1970s.* New York: Dell Books, 1974.

Husek, T. R. and Alexander, S. The effectiveness of the anxiety differential in examination of stress situations. *Educational Psychology Measurement,* 1963, vol. 23, 309-18.

Huyck, M. H. *Growing older.* New York: Spectrum Book (Prentice-Hall), 1974.

Hyden, H., & Lange, P. W. Correlation of the S-100 brain protein with behavior. In J. Gaito (Ed.), *Macromolecules and behavior.* (2nd ed.) New York: Appleton-Century-Crofts, 1972, 131-43.

International Classification of Diseases. (8th rev.) Adapted for use in the U.S. Public Health Service Publication no. 1693. Washington, D.C.: U.S. Government Printing Office, 1968.

Iversen, S. D., & Iversen, L. L. *Behavioral pharmacology.* New York: Oxford University Press, 1975.

Jacob, T. Family interaction in disturbed and normal families: A methodological and substantive view. *Psychological Bulletin.* 1975, *82,* 33-65.

Jacobs, P. A., Brunton, M., & Melville, M. M. Aggressive behavior, mental subnormality, and the XYY male. *Nature,* 1965, *208,* 1351-52.

Jacobson, E. *Progressive relaxation.* Chicago: University of Chicago Press, 1938.

Jahoda, M. *Current concepts of positive mental health.* New York: Basic Books, 1958.

Jarvik, L. F., Klodin, V., & Matsuyama, S. S. Human aggression and the extra Y chromosome: Fact or fantasy? *American Psychologist,* 1973, *28,* 674-82.

Jarvis, G. K., Ferrence, R. G., Johnson, F. G., & Whitehead, P. C. Sex and age patterns in self-injury. *Journal of Health and Social Behavior,* 1976, *17,* 146-55.

Jellinek, E. M. Phases of alcohol addiction. *Quarterly Journal of Studies on Alcohol,* 1952, *13,* 673-78.

Jellinek, E. M. *The disease concept of alcoholism.* Highland Park, N.J.: Hillhouse Press, 1960.

Jenkins, R. L. Diagnosis, dynamics, and treatment in child psychiatry. *Psychiatric Research Reports,* 1964, *18,* 91-120.

Jenkins, R. L. Psychiatric syndromes in children and their relation to family background. *American Journal of Orthopsychiatry,* 1966, *36,* 450-57.

Jenkins, R. L. The varieties of children's behavioral problems and family dynamics. *American Journal of Psychiatry,* 1968, *124,* 1440-45.

Johnson, A. M., & Szurek, S. A. The genesis of antisocial acting-out in children and adults. *Psychoanalytic Quarterly,* 1952, *21,* 323.

Johnson, A. M., & Szurek, S. A. Etiology of antisocial behavior in delinquents and psychopaths. *Journal of the American Medical Association,* 1954, *154,* 814.

Johnson, R. C. Behavioral characteristics of phenylketonurics and matched controls. *American Journal of Mental Deficiency,* 1969, *74,* 17-19.

Jones, B. E., Bobillier, P., & Jouvet, M. Effets de la destruction des neurones contenant des catecholamines du mesencephale sur le cycle veillesommeils du chat. *Comptes rendus de la Societe de Biologie, Paris,* 1969, *163,* 176-79.

Jones, I. H., & Frei, D. Provoked anxiety as a treatment of exhibitionism. *British Journal of Psychiatry,* 1977, *131,* 295-300.

Jones, M. *The therapeutic community.* New York: Basic Books, 1953.

Jones, M. C. Personality correlates and antecedents of drinking patterns in adult males. *Journal of Consulting and Clinical Psychology,* 1968, *32,* 2-12.

Jones, M. C. Personality antecedents and correlates of drinking patterns in women. *Journal of Consulting and Clinical Psychology,* 1971, *36,* 61-69.

Jourard, S. M. *The transparent self.* New York: Van Nostrand- Reinhold, 1971.

Kahn, R. L. Stress: From 9 to 5. *Psychology Today,* 1969, *3,* 34-38.

Kaij, L. *Alcoholism in twins: Studies on the etiology and sequels of abuse of alcohol.* Stockholm: Alcuquist & Wiksell, 1960.

Kallmann, F. J. The genetic theory of schizophrenia: An analysis of 691 schizophrenic twin index families. *American Journal of Psychiatry,* 1946, *103,* 309-22.

Kanfer, F. H., & Saslow, G. Behavioral diagnosis. In C. F. Franks (Ed.), *Behavior therapy: Appraisal and status*. New York: McGraw-Hill, 1969.

Kanner, L. Autistic disturbances of affective contact. *The Nervous Child*, 1943, *2*, 217-50.

Kantor, R. E., Wallner, J. M., & Winder, C. L. Process and reactive schizophrenia. *Journal of Consulting Psychology*, 1953, *17*, 157-62.

Kaplan, B. J. Biofeedback in epileptics: Equivocal relationship of reinforced EEG frequency to seizure reduction. *Epilepsia*, 1975, *16*, 477-85.

Kaplun, D., & Reich, R. The murdered child and his killer. *American Journal of Psychiatry*, 1976, *7*, 809-13.

Karlen, A. *Sexuality and homosexuality*. New York: Norton, 1971.

Karpman, B. *The sexual offender and his offenses*. New York: Julian Press, 1963.

Kart, C. S., Metress, E. S., & Metress, J. F. *Aging and health. Biologic and social perspectives*. Menlo Park, Cal.: Addison-Wesley, 1978.

Karush, A., Daniels, G. E., O'Connor, J. F., & Stern, L. O. The response to psychotherapy in chronic ulcerative colitis. *Psychosomatic Medicine*, 1969, *31*, 201-26.

Kastenbaum, R. The foreshortened life perspective. In V. M. Brantl & Sister Marie R. Brown (Eds.), *Readings in gerontology*. St. Louis: C. V. Mosby, 1973.

Kastenbaum, R., & Aisenberg, R. *The psychology of death*. New York: Springer, 1972.

Katchadourian, H. A., & Lunde, D. T. *Fundamentals of human sexuality*. New York: Holt, Rinehart & Winston, 1972.

Kaufman, I. C., & Rosenblum, L. A. The reaction to separation in infant monkeys: Anaclitic depression and conservation- withdrawal. *Psychosomatic Medicine*, 1967, *29*, 648-75.

Kazdin, A. E. Covert modeling, model similarity, and reduction of avoidance behavior. *Behavior Therapy*, 1974, *5*, 325-40.

Kazdin, A. E. *Behavior modification in applied settings*. Homewood, Ill.: Dorsey Press, 1975.

Kelley, J. B., & Wallerstein, J. S. Brief interventions with children in divorcing families. *American Journal of Orthopsychiatry*, 1977, *47*, 23-39.

Kessler, J. *Tics and self-stimulatory behavior*. In B. B. Wolman (Ed.) *Manual of Child Psychopathology*, New York: McGraw/Hill, 1972.

Kessler, J. *Psychopathology of childhood*. Englewood Cliffs, N.J: Prentice-Hall, 1966.

Kety, S. S. Recent biochemical theories of schizophrenia. In D. D. Jackson (Ed.), *The etiology of schizophrenia*. New York: Basic Books, 1960.

Kety, S. S. Neurochemical aspects of emotional behavior. In P. Black (Ed.), *Physiological correlates of emotion*. New York: Academic Press, 1970.

Kety, S. S. Commentary. *Journal of Nervous and Mental Disorders*, 1971, *153*, 323.

Kety, S. S., Javoy, F., Thierry, A. M., Julou, L., & Glowinski, J. A sustained effect of electroconvulsive shock on the turnover of norepinephrine in the central nervous system of the rat. *Proceedings of the National Academy of Sciences*, 1967, *58*, 1249-54.

Kety, S. S., Rosenthal, D., Wender, P. H., & Schulsinger, F. Mental illness in the biological and adoptive families of adopted schizophrenics. *American Journal of Psychiatry*, 1971, *128*, 302-6.

Kiester, E. Explosive youngsters. What to do about them. *Today's Health*, 1974, *52*, 49-53.

Kiev, A. Prognostic factors in attempted suicide. *American Journal of Psychiatry*, 1974, *131*, 987-90.

Kihlbom, M. Psychopathology of Turner's Syndrome. *Acta Paedopsychiatri*, 1969, *36*, 75-81.

Kinsey, A. C., Pomeroy, W. B., & Martin, C. E. *Sexual behavior in the human male*. Philadelphia: W. B. Saunders, 1948.

Kinsey, A. C., Pomeroy, W. B., Martin, C. E., & Gebhard, P. H. *Sexual behavior in the human female*. Philadelphia: W. B. Saunders, 1953.

Kirman, B. H. Individual differences in the mentally subnormal. In A. M. Clarke & A. D. B. Clarke (Eds.), *Mental deficiency: The changing outlook*. New York: Free Press, 1974.

Kleinmuntz, B. *Personality measurement: An introduction*. Homewood, Ill.: Dorsey, 1967.

Kleinmuntz, B. *Essentials of abnormal psychology*. New York: Harper & Row, 1974.

Klopfer, B., Ainsworth, M., Klopfer, W. G., & Holt, R. R. *Developments in the Rorschach technique*. Vol. 1. *Techniques and Theory*. Yonkers-on-Hudson, N.Y: World Book, 1954.

Kobrin, P. E. and Hendershot, G. E. Do family ties reduce mortality—evidence from the United States, 1966-1968. *Journal of Marriage and the Family*, 1977, *39*, 737-45.

Kohn, M. L. Social class and schizophrenia: A critical review. In D. Rosenthal & S. S. Kety (Eds.), *The transmission of schizophrenia*. Elmsford, N.Y.: Pergamon Press, 1968.

Kolb, L. *Noyes' modern clinical psychology*. Philadelphia: W. B. Saunders, 1973.

Kolodny, R. C., Masters, W. H., Hendryx, J., & Toro, G. Plasma testosterone and the semen analysis in male homosexuals. *New England Journal of Medicine*, 1971, *285*, 1170-74.

Kolvin, I. Aversive imagery therapy in adolescents. *Behavior Research and Therapy*, 1967, *5*, 245-48.

Kopp, S. B. The character structure of sex offenders. *American Journal of Psychotherapy*, 1962, *16*, 64-70.

Korchin, S. J. *Modern clinical psychology: Principles of intervention in the clinic and community*. New York: Basic Books, 1976.

Kovacs, M., Beck, A. T., & Weissman, A. Hopelessness: An indicator of suicidal risk. *Suicide*, 1975, *5*, 95-103.

Kraepelin, E. *Lehrbuch der Psychiatrie*. Germany, 1883.

Kraines, S. H. Manic-depressive syndrome: A physiologic disease. *Diseases of the Nervous System*, 1966, *27*, 3-19.

Kramer, F., & Pollnow, H. Ueber eine Hyperkinetische Erkrankung im Kinesaltar. *Monastschr. Psychiat. Neurol.*, 1932, *82*, 1-40.

Krasner, L. Assessment of token economy programmes in psychiatric hospitals. In N. H. Miller & R. Porter (Eds.), *Learning theory and psychotherapy*. London: CIBA Foundation, 1968.

Kraus, A. S., & Lillienfeld, A. M. Some epidemiological aspects of the high mortality rate in the young widowed group. *Journal of Chronic Diseases*, 1959, *10*, 207-17.

Kretschmer, E. *Physique and character*. New York: Harcourt Brace, 1925.

Kreuz, L. E., Rose, R. M., & Jennings, J. Suppression of plasma testosterone levels and psychological stress. *Archives of General Psychiatry*, 1972, *26*, 479-82.

Kron, L., Katz, J. L., Gorzynski, G., & Weiner, H. Anorexia nervosa and gonadal dysgenesis: Further evidence of a relationship. *Archives of General Psychiatry,* 1977, 3, 332-35.

Kurtzke, J. F., Kurland, L. T., & Goldberg, I. D. The numerical impact of the major neurologic and sense organ disorders. *Transactions of the American Neurological Association,* 1971, 96, 265.

Kushlick, A., & Blunden, R. The epidemiology of mental subnormality. In A. M. Clarke & A. D. B. Clarke (Eds.), *Mental deficiency: The changing outlook.* New York: Free Press, 1974.

Lacey, J. I. The evaluation of autonomic responses: Toward a general solution. *Annals of the New York Academy of Science,* 1956, 67, 123-64.

Lacey, J. I. Somatic response patterning and stress: Some revisions of activation theory. In M. H. Appley & R. Trumbull (Eds.), *Psychological stress.* New York: McGraw-Hill, 1967.

Laing, R. D. *The politics of experience.* Baltimore: Penguin, 1967.

Laing, R. D. *The divided self.* New York: Pantheon, 1969.

Laing, R. D., & Esterson, A. *Sanity, madness and the family.* Baltimore: Penguin Books, 1970.

Laing, R. D., Phillipson, H., & Lee, A. R. *Interpersonal perception. A theory and a method of research.* New York: Harper & Row, Perennial Libary, 1966.

Lake, C. R., Ziegler, M. G., & Murphy, D. L. Increased norepinephrine levels and decreased dopamine beta hydroxylase activity in primary autism. *Archives of General Psychiatry,* 1977, 34, 566-72.

Lamon, S., Wilson, G. T., & Leaf, R. C. Human classical aversion conditioning: Nausea versus electric shock in the reduction of target beverage consumption. *Behavior Research and Therapy,* 1977, 15, 313-20.

Lang, P. J. Fear reduction and fear behavior: Problems in treating a construct. In J. M. Shlieu (Ed.), *Research in psychotherapy,* Vol. 3. Washington, D.C.: American Psychological Association, 1968.

Lang, P. J. Autonomic control or learning to play the internal organs. *Psychology Today,* October 1970, 4, 37-41.

Lang, P. J. The application of psychophysiological methods to the study of psychotherapy and behavior modification. In A. E. Bergin & S. L. Garfield (Eds.), *Handbook of psychotherapy and behavior change: An empirical analysis.* New York: Wiley, 1971.

Lang, P. J., & Buss, A. H. Psychological deficit in schizophrenia: II. Interference and activation. *Journal of Abnormal Psychology,* 1965, 70, 77-106.

Lang, P. J., Rice, D. C., & Sternbach, R. A. Psychophysiology of emotion. In N. Greenfield & R. Sternbach (Eds.), *Handbook of psychophysiology.* New York: Holt, Rinehart & Winston, 1972.

Lanyon, R. I., & Goodstein, L. D. *Personality assessment.* New York: Wiley, 1971.

Laschet, U. Antiandrogen in the treatment of sex offenders: Mode of action and therapeutic outcome. In J. Zubin and J. Money (Eds.), *Contemporary sexual behavior: Critical issues in the 1970s.* Baltimore: Johns Hopkins Press, 1973.

Lashley, K. S. *Brain mechanisms and intelligence.* Chicago: University of Chicago Press, 1929.

Lazarus. A. A. *Behavior therapy and beyond.* New York: McGraw-Hill, 1971.

Lazarus, A. A. Multimodal behavioral treatment of depression. *Behavior Therapy,* 1974, 5, 549-54.

Lazarus, A. A. Behavior therapy approach. In C. A. Loew, H. Grayson, & C. H. Loew (Eds.), *Three psychotherapies.* New York: Brunner/Mazel, 1975.

Lazarus, A. A., Davison, G. C., & Polefka, D. Classical and operant factors in the treatment of a school phobia. *Journal of Abnormal Psychology,* 1965, 70, 225-29.

Lazarus, A. A., & Rosen, R. C. Behavior therapy techniques in the treatment of sexual disorders. In J. K. Meyer (Ed.), *Clinical management of sexual disorders.* Baltimore: Williams and Wilkins, 1976.

Leaf, A. Every day is a gift when you are over 100, *National Geographic,* 1973, Vol. 143, 93-119.

Leff, J. P. Assessment of drugs in schizophrenia. *British Journal of Clinical Pharmacology,* 1976, Supplement, 75-78.

Lehmann, H. E. Pharmacotherapy of schizophrenia. In P. H. Hock & J. Zubin (Eds.), *Psychopathology of schizophrenia.* New York: Grune & Stratton, 1966.

Lemere, F., & Voegtlin, W. L. An evaluation of the aversion treatment of alcoholism. *Quarterly Journal of Studies on Alcohol,* 1950, 11, 199-204.

Lemert, E. M. *Social pathology.* New York: McGraw-Hill, 1951.

Lennard, H. L., Epstein, L. J., Bernstein, A., & Ranson, D. C. *Mystification and drug misuse,* New York: Perennial Library, 1972.

Leon, G. R. *Case histories of deviant behavior.* Boston: Holbrook, 1977.

Leonard, C. V. Depression and suicidality. *Journal of Consulting and Clinical Psychology,* 1974, 42, 98-104.

Lerner, I. M. *Heredity, evolution and society.* San Francisco: W. H. Freeman, 1968.

LeShan, L. An emotional life history pattern associated with neoplastic disease. *Annals of the New York Academy of Science,* 1966.

Lesser, R. Behavior therapy with a narcotics user: A case study. *Behavior Research and Therapy,* 1967, 5, 251-52.

Lester, D., & Beck, A. T. Suicidal intent, medical lethality of the suicide attempt, and components of depression. *Journal of Clinical Psychology,* 1975, 31, 11-12.

Leukel, F. *Essential of physiological psychology.* St. Louis: C. V. Mosby, 1978.

Levenstein, P. Cognitive growth in preschoolers through stimulation of verbal interaction with mothers. Paper presented at the 46th annual meeting of the American Orthopsychiatric Association. New York, 1969.

Levis, D. J. Learned helplessness: A reply and alternative S-R interpretation. *Journal of Experimental Psychology: General,* 1976, 105, 47-65.

Levy, D. M. Use of play technique as experimental procedure. *American Journal of Orthopsychiatry,* 1933, 3, 266-77.

Lewinsohn, P. H. A behavioral approach to depression. In R. J. Friedman & M. M. Katz (Eds.), *The psychology of depression: Contemporary theory and research.* Washington, D.C.: Winston-Wiley, 1974.

Lewinsohn, P. H., & Graf, M. Pleasant activities and depression. *Journal of Consulting and Clinical Psychology,* 1972, 41, 215-68.

Lewinsohn, P. H., Shaffer, M., & Libet, J. A behavioral approach to depression. Paper presented at the American Psychological Association, 1969.

Lewis J. M., Beavers, W. R., Gossett, J. T., & Phillips, V. A. *No single thread: Psychological health in family systems.* New York: Brunner/Mazel, 1976.

Lezak, M. D. *Neuropsychological assessment.* New York: Oxford University Press, 1976.

Liberman, R. P., & Raskin, D. E. Depression: A behavioral formulation. *Archives of General Psychiatry*, 1971, *24*, 515-23.

Lichtenstein, E., & Penner, M. Long-term effects of rapid smoking treatment. *Addictive Behaviors*, 1977, *2*.

Liddell, H. S. Conditioned reflex method and experimental neurosis. In J. McV. Hunt (Ed.), *Personality and the behavior disorders.* New York: Ronald, 1944.

Liddick B. Male impotence. Troubled sex - perform or panic. *San Francisco Chronicle*, Aug. 18, 1972, quoting G. L. Ginsberg, W. A. Frosch, and T. Shapiro.

Lidz, T. *The Family and Human Adaptation.* New York, International University Press, 1963.

Liebert, R. M., & Spiegler, M. D. *Personality: Strategies for the study of man.* Homewood, Ill.: Dorsey Press, 1974.

Lindemann, E. Symptomatology and management of acute grief. *American Journal of Psychiatry*, 1944, *101*, 141-48.

Lindsley, D. B., & Sassaman, W. H. Autonomic activity and brain potentials associated with "voluntary control of the pilomotors. *Journal of Neurophysiology*, 1938, *1*, 342-49.

Lindzey, G. *Projective techniques and cross-cultural research.* New York: Appleton-Century-Crofts, 1959.

Linn, L. Clinical manifestations of psychiatric disorders. In A. M. Freedman, H. I. Kaplan, & B. J. Sadock (Eds.), *Comprehensive textbook of psychiatry/II.* (2nd ed.). Baltimore: Williams and Wilkins, 1975.

Lipowski, Z. J. Psychophysiological cardiovascular disorders. In A. M. Freedman, H. I. Kaplan, & B. J. Sadock (Eds.), *Comprehensive textbook of psychiatry/II.* (2nd ed.) Baltimore: Williams and Wilkins, 1975.

Lipowski, Z. J. Organic brain syndromes: Overview and classification. In D. Benson & D. Blumer (Eds.), *Psychiatric aspects of neurologic disease.* New York: Grune & Stratton, 1975.

Lipowski, Z. J. Psychosomatic medicine in the seventies: An overview. *American Journal of Psychiatry*, 1977, *134*, 233-43.

Lipp, M. R., Looney, J. G., & Spitzer, R. L. Classifying psychophysiologic disorders: A new idea. *Psychosomatic Medicine*, 1977, *39*, 285-87.

Little, K. B., & Shneidman, E. S. Congruencies among interpretations of psychological test and anamnestic data. *Psychological Monographs*, 1959, *73*, (6, Whole No. 476).

Lloyd, R. W., & Salzberg, H. C. Controlled social drinking: An alternative to abstinence as a treatment goal for some alcohol abusers. *Psychological Bulletin*, 1975, *82*, 815-42.

Loew, C. A., Grayson, H., & Loew, G. H. Frigidity: The case of June. In C. A. Loew, H. Grayson & G. H. Loew (Eds.). *Three psychotherapies.* New York: Brunner/Mazel, 1975.

Lombroso-Ferrero, C. *Criminal man.* New York: Putnam, 1911.

Loraine, J. A., Adamopoulos, D. A., Kirkham, E. E., Ismael, A. A., & Dove, G. A. Patterns of hormone excretion in male and female homosexuals. *Nature*, 1971, *234*, 552-55.

Loraine, J. A., Ismael, A. A., Adamopoulos, P. A., & Dove, G. A. Endocrine function in male and female homosexuals. *British Medical Journal*, 1970, *4*, 406.

Lord, E., & Weisfeld, D. The abused child. In A. R. Roberts (Ed.), *Childhood deprivation.* Springfield, Ill.: Charles C Thomas, 1974.

Lovaas, O. I., Freitag, G., Gold, V. J., & Kassorla, I. C. Recording apparatus for observation of behaviors of children in free play settings. *Journal of Experimental Child Psychology*, 1965, *2*, 108-20.

Lovaas, O. I., & Willis, T. *Behavioral control of a hyperactive child.* Unpublished manuscript, 1974.

Lovaas, O. I., Freitas, L., Nelson, K., & Whalen, C. The establishment of imitation and its use for the development of complex behavior in schizophrenic children. In O. I. Lovaas & B. D. Bucher (Eds.). *Perspectives in behavior modification with deviant children.* Englewood Cliffs, N.J.: Prentice-Hall, 1974. Pp. 143-49.

Lovibond, S. H., & Caddy, G. Discriminated aversive control in the modification of alcoholics' drinking behavior. *Behavior Therapy*, 1970, *1*, 437-44.

Lubin, B. Adjective checklists for the measurement of depression. *Archives of General Psychiatry*, 1965, *12*, 57-62.

Lucas, C., Sainsbury, P., & Collins, J. G. A social and clinical study of delusions in schizophrenia. *Journal of Mental Health*, 1962, *108*, 747-58.

Lukianowicz, N. Incest. *British Journal of Psychiatry*, 1972, *120*, 301.

Luria, A. R. *The mind of a mnemonist.* New York: Discus Books, 1969.

Luthman, S. G., & Kirschenbaum, M. *The dynamic family.* New York: Science and Behavior Books, 1974.

Lykken, D. T. A study of anxiety in the sociopathic personality. *Journal of Abnormal Psychology*, 1957, *55*, 6-10.

Lykken, D. T. Psychology and the lie detector industry. *American Psychologist*, 1974, *29*, 725-39.

Lynch, J. *The Broken Heart: The Medical Consequences of Loneliness.* New York, Basic Books, 1977.

MacAndrew, C. The differentiation of male alcoholic outpatients from nonalcoholic psychiatric outpatients by means of the MMPI. *Quarterly Journal of Studies on Alcohol*, 1965, *26*, 238-46.

McAlister, A. Helping people quit smoking: Current progress. In A. Enelow (Ed.), *Applying behavioral science to cardiovascular disease.* New York: American Heart Association, 1975.

McCandless, B. R. *Children: Behavior and development.* New York: Holt, Rinehart & Winston, 1967.

McClelland, D. C., Atkinson, J. W., Clark, R. A., & Lowell, E. L. *The achievement motive.* New York: Appleton, 1953.

McClelland, D. C., David, W. N., Kalin, R., & Wanner, E. *The drinking man.* New York: Free Press, 1972.

McClure, C. M. Cardiac arrest through volition. *California Medicine,* 1959, *90,* 440-41.

McConaghy, N., & Barr, R. F. Classical, avoidance, and backward conditioning treatment of homosexuality. *British Journal of Psychiatry,* 1973, *122,* 156-62.

McCord, W., McCord, J., & Guderman, J. Some current theories of alcoholism. A longitudinal evaluation. *Quarterly Journal of Studies on Alcohol,* 1959, *20,* 727-49.

McCord, W., & McCord, J. *The psychopath: An essay on the criminal mind.* New York: Van Nostrand-Reinhold, 1964.

McDermott, S. *Female sexuality: Its nature and conflicts.* New York: Simon and Schuster, 1970.

McFall, R. M., & Lillesand, D. V. Behavior rehearsal with modeling and coaching in assertive training. *Journal of Abnormal Psychology,* 1971, *77,* 313-23.

McFall, R. M., & Marston, A. An experimental investigation of behavior rehearsal in assertive training. *Journal of Abnormal Psychology,* 1970, *76,* 295-303.

McFall, R. M., & Twentyman, C. T. Four experiments on the relative contributions of rehearsal, modeling, and coaching to assertion training. *Journal of Abnormal Psychology,* 1973, *81,* 199-218.

McGhie, A., & Chapman, J. S. Disorders of attention and perception in early schizophrenia. *British Journal of Medical Psychology,* 1961, *34,* 103-16.

McGinn, N., Harburg, E., Julius, S., & McLeod, J. Psychological correlates of blood pressure. *Psychological Bulletin,* 1964, *61,* 209-19.

McGlothlin, W. H., Sparkes, R. S., & Arnold, D. O. Effect of LSD on human pregnancy. *Journal of the American Medical Association,* 1970, *212,* 1483-87.

Machover, K. *Personality projection in the drawing of the human figure.* Springfield, Ill.: Charles C Thomas, 1948.

MacIver, R. M. *The ramparts we guard.* New York: Crowell-Collier/MacMillan, 1950.

MacLean, P. D. A triune concept of the brain and behavior: Lecture I. Man's reptilian and limbic inheritance. Lecture II. Man's limbic brain and the psychoses. Lecture III. New trends in man's evolution. Cited in Lennart Levi (Ed.), *Emotions: Their parameters and measurement.* New York: Raven Press, 1975.

MacLean, P. D. Sensory and perceptive factors in emotional functions of the triune brain. In Lennart Levi (Ed.), *Emotions: Their parameters and measurements.* New York: Raven Press, 1975.

MacMillan, D. L. *Mental retardation in school and society.* Boston: Little, Brown, 1977.

McNamee, H. B., Mello, N. K., & Mendelson, J. H. Experimental analysis of drinking patterns in alcoholics: Concurrent psychiatric observations. *American Journal of Psychiatry,* 1968, *124,* 1063-71.

McNeil, E. B. *The quiet furies.* Englewood Cliffs, N.J.: Prentice-Hall, 1967.

McWilliams, S. A., & Tuttle, R. J. Long-term psychological effects of LSD. *Psychological Bulletin,* 1973, *79,* 341-51.

Maddi, S. R. *Personality theories: A comparative analysis.* Homewood, Ill.: Dorsey Press, 1972.

Maddison, D., & Viola, A. The health of widows in the year following bereavement. *Journal of Psychosomatic Research,* 1968, *12,* 297.

Maddox, G. L. Drinking prior to college. In G. L. Maddox (Ed.), *The domesticated drug: Drinking among collegians.* New Haven, Conn.: College and University Press, 1970.

Maher, B. A. *Principles of psychopathology.* New York: McGraw-Hill, 1966.

Mahler, M. S., Pine, F., & Bergman, A. *The psychological birth of the human infant. Symbiosis and individuation.* New York: Basic Books, 1975.

Malan, D. H. The outcome problem in psychotherapy research: A historical review. *Archives of General Psychiatry,* 1973, *29,* 719-29.

Malmo, R. B. *On emotions, needs, and our archaic brain.* New York: Holt, Rinehart & Winston, 1975.

Malmo, R. B., & Shagass, C. Physiologic study of symptom mechanisms in psychiatric patients under stress. *Psychosomatic Medicine,* 1949, *11,* 25-29.

Manocchio, T., & Petitt, W. *Families under stress.* London: Routledge & Kegan Paul, 1975.

Manson, M. P. *The Alcadd test.* Beverly Hills, Cal.: Western Psychological Service, 1949.

Manson, M. P. *The Manson evaluation.* Beverly Hills, Cal.: Western Psychological Service, 1948.

Marcus, B. A dimensional study of a prison population. *British Journal of Criminology,* 1960, *1,* 130-53.

Margolese, M. S. Homosexuality: A new endocrine correlate. *Hormonal Behavior,* 1970, *1,* 151-70.

Mark, V. H., & Ervin F. R. *Violence and the brain.* New York: Harper & Row, 1970.

Marks, I. M. Management of sexual disorders. In H. Leitenberg (Ed.), *Handbook of behavior modification and behavior therapy.* Englewood Cliffs, N.J.: Prentice-Hall, 1976.

Marks, I. M., & Gelder, M. G. Transvestism and fetishism: Clinical and psychological changes during faradic aversion. *British Journal of Psychiatry,* 1967, *113,* 711-29.

Marks, P. A., & Seeman, W. *The actuarial description of abnormal personality.* Baltimore: Williams & Wilkins, 1963.

Marlatt, G. A. The Drinking Profile: A questionnaire for the behavioral assessment of alcoholism. In E. J. Mash & L. G. Terdal (Eds.), *Behavioral therapy assessment: Diagnosis, design, and evaluation.* New York: Springer-Verlag, 1977.

Marlatt, G. A., Demming, B., & Reid, J. B. Loss of control drinking in alcoholics: An experimental analogue. *Journal of Abnormal Psychology,* 1973, *81,* 233-41.

Marmor, J. (Ed.) *Sexual inversion: The multiple roots of homosexuality.* New York: Basic Books, 1965.

Marmor, J. Frigidity, dyspareunia, and vaginismus. In A. M. Freedman, H. I. Kaplan, & B. J. Sadock (Eds.), *Comprehensive textbook of psychiatry/II.* Baltimore: Williams & Wilkins, 1976.

Marmor, J. Sexual disorders...homosexuality and sexual orientation disturbances. In A. M. Freedman, H. I. Kaplan & B. J. Sadock (Eds.), *Comprehensive textbook of psychiatry/II.* Vol. 2. Baltimore: Williams & Wilkins, 1975.

Marquart, D. I., & Bailey, L. L. An evaluation of the culture-free test of intelligence. *Journal of Genetic Psychology,* 1955, *86,* 353-58.

Martin, R., Cloninger, R., & Guze, S. Female criminality and the prediction of recidivism. *Archives of General Psychiatry,* 1978, *35,* 207-14.

Maslow, A. H. *Toward a psychology of being.* Princeton, N.J.: Van Nostrand, 1968.

Masserman, J. H. *Behavior and neurosis.* Chicago: University of Chicago Press, 1943.

Masters, W. H., & Johnson, V. E. *Human sexual response.* Boston: Little, Brown, 1966.

Masters, W. H., & Johnson, V. E. *Human sexual inadequacy.* Boston: Little, Brown, 1970.

Masterson, J. F. *Treatment of the borderline adolescent: A development approach.* New York: Wiley, 1972.

Matthews, W. B., & Miller, H. *Diseases of the nervous system.* Oxford: Blackwell, 1972.

May, P. R. A. *Treatment of schizophrenia: A comparative study of five treatment methods.* New York: Science House, 1968.

Mednick, S. A. Breakdown in individuals at high-risk for schizophrenia: Possible predispositional perinatal factors. *Mental Hygiene.* 1970, *54,* 50-63.

Mednick S. A., & Schulsinger, F. Some premorbid characteristics related to breakdown in children with schizophrenic mothers. In D. Rosenthal and S. S. Kety (Eds.), *The transmission of schizophrenia.* Elmsford, N.Y.: Pergamon Press, 1968.

Mednick, S. A., & Schulsinger, F. A learning theory of schizophrenia: Thirteen years later. In M. Hammer, K. Salyinger, & S. Sutton (Eds.), *Psychopathology: Contributions from the social, behavioral, and biological sciences.* New York: Wiley, 1973.

Meehl, P. E. The cognitive activity of the clinician. *American Psychologist,* 1960, *15,* 19-27.

Meehl, P. E. Schizotaxia, schizotypy, schizophrenia. *American Psychologist,* 1962, *17,* 827-38.

Mehlman, B. The reliability of psychiatric diagnosis. *Journal of Abnormal and Social Psychology,* 1952, *47,* 577-78.

Meichenbaum, D. Clinical implications of modifying what clients say to themselves. University of Waterloo Research Reports in Psychology no. 42, December 19, 1972.

Meininger, J. *Success through transactional analysis.* New York: Signet Books, 1973.

Meissner, W. W., Mack, J. E., & Semrad, E. V. Theories of personality and psychopathy: I. Freudian school, In A. M. Freedman, H. I. Kaplan, & B. J. Sadock (Eds.), *Comprehensive textbook of psychiatry/II,* Vol. 1. Baltimore: Williams & Wilkins, 1975.

Meltzoff, J., & Kornreich, M. *Research in psychotherapy.* New York: Atherton, 1970.

Mendels, J. The prediction of response to electroconvulsive therapy. *American Journal of Psychiatry.* 1967, *124,* 153-59.

Mendels, J. *Concepts of depression.* New York: Wiley, 1970.

Mendels, J., & Cochrane, C. Syndromes of depression and the response to ECT. Cited in J. Mendels, *Concepts of depression.* New York: Wiley, 1970.

Mendelson, J. H. Ethanol-1-C^{14} metabolism in alcoholics and nonalcoholics. *Science,* 1968, *159,* 319-20.

Menkes, J. H. Disorders of amino acid metabolism. In M. M. Cohen (Ed.), *Biochemistry of neural disease.* New York: Harper & Row, 1975.

Menninger, K. A. *Man against himself.* New York: Hart-Davis, 1963.

Menninger, K. A., Mayman, M., & Pruyser, P. *The vital balance.* New York: Viking Press, 1963.

Mercer, J. R. The myth of 3% prevalence. In R. K. Eyman, C. E. Meyers, & G. Tarjan (Eds.), *Sociobehavioral studies in mental retardation.* Monographs of the American Association on Mental Deficiency, 1973, No. 1.

Mercer, J., & Lewis, J. *System of multicultural pluralistic assessment.* New York: Pychological Corporation, in press.

Merton, R. K. Social structure and anomie. *Social theory and social structure.* New York: Macmillan, 1968.

Messick, S., & Jackson, D. N. Acquiescence and the factorial interpretation of the MMPI. *Psychological Bulletin,* 1961, *58,* 299-305.

Meyer, J. K. *Clinical management of sexual disorders.* Baltimore: Williams & Wilkins, 1976.

Meyers, C. E., MacMillan, D. L., & Yoshida, R. K. Preliminary findings on the decertification of inner city EMR's. Paper presented at the Annual Joint Convention, American Academy of Mental Retardation and the American Association on Mental Deficiency, Toronto, June, 1974.

Mezey, K. D., Rauckhorst, L. M., & Stokes, S. *Physical assessment of the aged person.* Spring Valley, N.Y.: Blue Hill Educational Systems, 1975.

Miller, N. E. Theory and experiment relating psychoanalytic displacement to stimulus response generalization. *Journal of Abnormal and Social Psychology,* 1948, *43,* 155-78.

Miller, N. E. Learning of visceral and glandular responses. *Science,* 1969, *163,* 434-45.

Miller, P. M. Behavioral assessment in alcoholism research and treatment: Current techniques. *International Journal of the Addictions,* 1973, *8,* 831-37.

Miller, P. M., & Eisler, R. M. Alcohol and drug abuse. In W. E. Craighead, A. E. Kazdin, & M. J. Mahomey (Eds.), *Behavior modification: Principles, issues, and applications.* Boston: Houghton Mifflin, 1976.

Miller, P. M., & Hersen, M. Quantitative changes in alcohol consumption as a function of electrical aversive conditioning. *Journal of Clinical Psychology,* 1972, *28,* 590-93.

Miller, W. R. Alcoholism scales and objective assessment methods: A review. *Psychological Bulletin,* 1976, *83,* 649-74.

Miller, W. R., & Seligman, M. E. P. Depression and the perception of reinforcement. *Journal of Abnormal Psychology,* 1973, *82,* 62-73.

Millon, T. Reflections on Rosenhan's "On being sane in insane places." *Journal of Abnormal Psychology,* 1975, *84,* 456-61.

Millon, T., & Millon, R. *Abnormal behavior and personality: A biosocial learning approach.* Philadelphia: W. B. Saunders, 1974.

Minckler, J. *Introduction to neuroscience.* St. Louis: C. V. Mosby, 1972.

Mirsky, I. A. Physiologic, psychologic, and social determinants in the etiology of duodenal ulcer. *American Journal of Digestive Diseases,* 1958, *3,* 285-314.

Mischel, W. *Personality and assessment.* New York: Wiley, 1968.

Mischel, W. Toward a cognitive social learning reconceptualization of personality. *Psychological Review,* 1973, *80,* 252-83.

Mischel, W. *Introduction to personality.* (2nd ed.) New York: Holt, Rinehart & Winston, 1976.

Mishler, E., & Waxler, N. E. Family interaction processes and schizophrenia: A review of current theories. *Merrill-Palmer Quarterly of Behavior and Development,* 1965 (October), *4,* 11.

Mishler, E., & Waxler, N. E. *Interaction in families: An experimental study of family processes and schizophrenia.* New York: Wiley, 1968.

Mitchell, K. R., & Mitchell, D. M. Migraine: An exploratory treatment application of programmed behavior therapy techniques. *Journal of Psychosomatic Research,* 1971, *15,* 137-57.

Mohr, J. W. Phases in group treatment of immature adolescent offenders. *Reporting Day,* fall, 1962, 13-22.

Mohr, J. W., Turner, R. E., & Jerry, M. B. *Pedophilia and exhibitionism.* Toronto: University of Toronto Press, 1964.

Money, J. Components of eroticism in man: The hormones in relation to sexual morphology and sexual desire. *Journal of Nervous and Mental Diseases,* 1961, *132,* 239-48.

Money, J., & Tucker P. *Sexual signatures: On being a man or a woman.* Boston: Little, Brown, 1975.

Moore, N. Behavior therapy in bronchial asthma: A controlled study. *Journal of Psychosomatic Research,* 1965, *9,* 257-76.

Mordock, J. B. *The other children: An introduction to exceptionality.* New York: Harper & Row, 1975.

Moreno, J. L. *The theatre of spontaneity.* New York: Beacon House, 1947.

Moriarty, D. *The loss of loved ones.* Springfield, Ill.: Charles C Thomas, 1967.

Morin, S. F. Heterosexual bias in psychological research on lesbianism and male homosexuality. *American Psychologist,* 1977, *32,* 629-37.

Morrison, J. R. Changes in subtype diagnosis of schizophrenia: 1920-1966. *American Journal of Psychiatry,* 1974, *131,* 674-77.

Morrison, J. R., Hudgens, R. W., & Barchha, R. G. Life events and psychiatric illness. In M. J. Feldman, P. J. Handal, H. S. Barhal, et al. (Eds.), *Fears related to death and suicide.* New York: MSS Information Corp., 1974.

Mosher, L. R. Psychiatric heretics and extramedical treatment of schizophrenia. In R. Canero, N. Fox, & L. Shapiro (Eds.), *Strategic intervention in schizophrenia: Current developments in treatment.* New York: Behavioral Publications, 1974.

Mowrer, O. H. Apparatus for the study and treatment of enuresis. *American Journal of Psychology,* 1933, *51,* 163-66.

Mowrer, O. H. On the dual nature of learning - A reinterpretation of "conditioning and "problem-solving." *Harvard Educational Review,* 1947, *17,* 102-48.

Mowrer, O. H., & Mowrer, W. M. Enuresis, a method for its study and treatment. *American Journal of Orthopsychiatry,* 1938, *8,* 436-59.

Moyer, K. E. *The physiology of aggression.* New York: Harper & Row, 1976.

Mueller, C. W., & Pope, H. Marital instability: A study of its transmission between generations. *Journal of Marriage and the Family,* 1977, *39,* 83-92.

Mullen, F. G., Jr. Treatment of dysmenorrhea by professional and student behavior therapists. Paper presented at Association for the Advancement of Behavior Therapy, Washington, D.C. 1971.

Munroe, R. *Schools of psychoanalytic thought.* New York: Dryden Press, 1955.

Murray, E. J., Auld, F., Jr., & White, A. M. A psychotherapy case showing progress but no decrease in the discomfort-relief quotient. *Journal of Consulting Psychology,* 1954, *18,* 349-53.

Murray, H. A. *Explorations in personality.* New York: Oxford University Press, 1938.

Mussen, P. H., & Naylor H. K. The relationship betwen overt and fantasy aggression. *Journal of Abnormal and Social Psychology,* 1954, *49,* 235-40.

Myers, J. K., & Bean, L. L. *A decade later.* New York: Wiley, 1968.

Nagy, M. The child's view of death. *Journal of Genetic Psychology,* 1948, *73,* 3-27.

Nathan, P. E., & Harris, S. L. *Psychopathology and society.* New York: McGraw-Hill, 1975.

Nathan, P. E., & O'Brien, J. S. An experimental analysis of the behavior of alcoholics and nonalcoholics during prolonged experimental drinking: A necessary precursor of behavior therapy? *Behavior Therapy,* 1971, *2,* 455-76.

Neale, J. M., & Cromwell, R. L. Attention and schizophrenia. In B. A. Maher (Ed.), *Progress in experimental personality research.* Vol. 5. New York: Academic Press, 1970.

Neale, J. M., Kopfstein, J. H., & Levine, A. Premorbid adjustment and paranoid status in schizophrenia: Varying assessment techniques and the influence of chronicity. Paper presented at the American Psychological Association, Honolulu, 1972.

Neuman, C. P., & Tamerin, J. S. The treatment of adult alcoholics in one hospital: A comparison and critical appraisal of factors related to outcome. *Quarterly Journal of Studies on Alcohol,* 1971, *32,* 82-93.

Newmark, C. S., Frerking, P. A., Cook, L, & Newmark, L. Endorsement of Ellis' irrational beliefs as a function of psychopathology. *Journal of Clinical Psychology,* 1973, *29,* 300-02.

Nieschlag, E., & Loriaux, D. L. Radioimmunoassay for plasma testosterone. *Z. Klip. Chem. Klin. Biochem.,* 1972, *10,* 164-68.

Nihara, K., Foster, R., Shellhaas, M., & Leland, H. *AAMD adaptive behavior scale revised.* Washington, D.C.: American Association of Mental Deficiency, 1974.

Nirje, B. The normalization principle and its human management implication. In R. B. Kugel & W. Wolfensberger (Eds.), *Changing patterns in residential services for the mentally retarded.* Washington, D.C.: Presidents Committee on Mental Retardation, 1969.

Nunnally, J. C., Jr. *Psychometric theory.* New York: McGraw-Hill, 1967.

Nutritional Review. Malnutrition and myelination. *Nutritional Review,* 1970, *28,* 110-11.

Nyback, H., Borzecki, Z., & Sedvall, G. Accumulation and disappearance of catecholamines formed from tyrosine-C in mouse brain; effect of some psychotropic drugs. *European Journal of Pharmacology,* 1968, *4,* 395-402.

Oates, W. E. The other side of anxiety. Nashville, Tenn.: Graded Press, 1975.

O'Connor, J. F., Daniels, G., Karush, A., Moses, L., Flood, C., & Stein, L. The effects of psychotherapy in the course of ulcerative colitis - A preliminary report. American Journal of Psychiatry, 1964, 120, 738-42.

O'Connor, R. D. Relative efficacy of modeling, shaping, and the combined procedures for modification of social withdrawal. Journal of Abnormal Psychology, 1972, 79, 327-34.

O'Connor, R. D. Modification of social withdrawal through symbolic modeling. Journal of Applied Behavior Analysis, 1969, 2, 15-22.

Ogden, E., & Shock, N. W. Voluntary hypercirculation. American Journal of the Medical Sciences, 1939, 198, 329-42.

Oppenheim, R. C. Effective teaching methods for autistic children. Springfield, Ill.: Charles C. Thomas, 1974.

Orris, J. P. Visual monitoring performance delinquents. Unpublished master's thesis, University of Illinois, 1967.

Osmond, H., & Smythies, J. Schizophrenia: A new approach. Journal of Mental Science, 1952, 98, 309-15.

Owen, D. R. The 47, XYY male: A review. Psychological Bulletin, 1972, 78, 209-33.

Palmore, E. What can the USA learn from Japan about aging? In H. Cox (Ed.), Focus: Aging. Sluice Dock, Guilford, Conn.: Dushkin Publishing Group, 1978.

Paternite, C. E., Loney, J., & Langhorne, J. Relationship between symptomatology & SES-related factors in hyperkinetic/MBD boys. American Journal of Orthopsychiatry, 1976, 2, 291-301.

Patterson, C. H. Theories of counseling and psychotherapy. New York: Harper & Row, 1973.

Patterson, G. R., Jones, R., Whittier, J., & Wright, M. A. A behavior modification technique for the hyperactive child. Behavior Research and Therapy, 1965, 2, 217-26.

Paul, G. L. Insight vs. desensitization in psychotherapy. Stanford: Stanford University Press, 1966.

Paul, G. L. Chronic mental patient: Current status - future directions. Psychological Bulletin, 1969, 71, 81-94.

Pavlov, I. P. Conditioned reflexes: An investigation of the physiology activity of the cerebral cortex. London: Oxford University Press, 1927.

Peacock, J. L., & Kirsch, A. The human direction: An evolutionary approach to social and cultural anthropology. New York: Appleton-Century-Crofts, 1970.

Penfield, W., & Jasper, M. Epilepsy and the functional anatomy of the human brain. Boston: Little, Brown, 1954.

Peters, J. E., & Stern, R. M. Specificity of attitude hypothesis in psychosomatic medicine: A reexamination. Journal of Psychosomatic Research, 1971, 15, 129-35.

Peterson, G. C. Organic brain syndromes associated with brain trauma. In A. M. Freedman, H. I. Kaplan, & B. J. Sadock (Eds.), Comprehensive textbook of psychiatry/II. (2nd ed.) Vol. 2, Baltimore: Williams and Wilkins, 1975.

Phillips, B. S. A role theory approach to adjustment in old age. American Sociological Review, 1957, 22, 212-17.

Phillips, L. Case history data and prognosis in schizophrenia. Journal of Nervous and Mental Diseases, 1953, 117, 515-25.

Pincus, J. H., & Tucker, G. Behavioral neurology. New York: Oxford University Press, 1974.

Pincus, L. Death and the family: The importance of mourning. New York: Vintage Books, 1974.

Pinneau, S. R. The infantile disorders of hospitalism and anaclitic depression. Psychological Bulletin, 1955, 52, 429-52.

Pitt, B. Psychogeriatrics. London: Churchill Livingston, 1974.

Podlesny, J. A., & Raskin, D. C. Physiological measures and the detection of deception. Psychological Bulletin, 1977, 84, 782-99.

Pokorny, A. D. Myths about suicide. In H. L. P. Resnik (Ed.), Suicidal behaviors. Boston: Little, Brown, 1968.

Polivy, J., Schueneman, A. L., & Carlson, K. Alcohol and tension reduction: Cognitive and physiological effects. Journal of Abnormal Psychology, 1976, 85, 595-600.

Pollack, E. S., & Taube, C. A. Trends and projections in state hospital use. In J. Zusman & E. F. Bertsch (Eds.), The future role of the state hospital. Lexington, Mass.: Lexington Books, 1975.

Polow, N. G. A stuttering manual for the speech therapist. Springfield, Ill.: Charles C Thomas, 1975.

Pomerleau, O. F., & Pomerleau, C. S. Break the smoking habit: A behavioral program for giving up cigarettes. Champaign, Ill.: Research Press, 1977.

Porteus, S. D. The maze test and mental differences. Vineland, N.J.: Smith, 1933.

Post, F. The significance of affective symptoms in old age: A follow-up study of one hundred patients. London: Oxford University Press, 1962.

Prehm, H. J. Mental retardation: Definition, classification, and prevalence. In P. Browning (Ed.), Mental retardation. Springfield, Ill.: Charles C Thomas, 1974.

Pribram, K. H., & Gill, M. Freuds project reassessed. New York: Basic Books, 1976.

Price, K. P. The pathological effects in rats of predictable and unpredictable shock. Psychological Reports, 1972, 30, 419-26.

Price, K. P. The application of behavior therapy to the treatment of psychosomatic disorders: Restrospect and prospect. Psychotherapy: Theory, Research and Practice, 11, summer, 1974, 138-55.

Price, R. H. Abnormal behavior: Perspectives in conflict. New York: Holt, Rinehart & Winston, 1972.

Prince, V., & Bentler, P. M. Survey of 504 cases of transvestism. Psychological Reports, 1972, 31, 903.

Prior, M., Perry, D., & Gajzago, C. Kanners' syndrome or early-onset psychosis: Taxonomic analysis of 142 cases. Journal of Autism and Childhood Schizophrenia. 1975, 5 (1), 71-80.

Purcell, K., Brady, K., Chai, H., Muser, J., Molk, L., Gordon, N., & Means, J. The effect on asthma in children of experimental separation from the family. Psychosomatic Medicine, 1969, 31, 144-64.

Purdey, S. B. The erotic in literature. In H. A. Katchadourian and D. Lunde (Eds.), Fundamentals of human sexuality. New York: Holt, Rinehart & Winston, 1972.

Putney, S., & Putney, G. *The adjusted American: Normal neuroses in the individual and society.* New York: Harper & Row, 1972.

Quay, H. C. Psychopathic personality as pathological stimulation seeking. *American Journal of Psychiatry,* 1965, *122,* 180-83.

Quay, H. C., & Parsons, L. B. *The differential behavioral classification of the juvenile offender.* Washington, D.C.: Bureau of Prisons, 1971.

Rachman, S. Clinical applications of observational learning, imitation, and modeling. *Behavior Therapy,* 1972, *3,* 379-97.

Radbill, S. X. A history of child abuse and infanticide. In R. E. Helfer & H. Kempe (Eds.), *The battered child.* Chicago: University of Chicago Press, 1968.

Rahe, R. H. Life changes and near-future illness reports. In L. Levi (Eds.), *Emotions: Their parameters and measurement.* New York: Raven Press, 1975.

Raines, G. N., & Rohrer, J. H. The operational matrix of psychiatric practice: I. Consistency and variability in interview impressions of different psychiatrists. *American Journal of Psychiatry,* 1955, *111,* 721-33.

Rapoport, D. Street gangs are back with guns. *Parade Magazine,* May 2, 1976.

Rappaport, M. Competing voice messages: Effects of message load and drugs on the ability of acute schizophrenics to attend. *Archives of General Psychiatry,* 1967, *17,* 97-103.

Raskin, A. A guide for drug use in depressive disorders. *American Journal of Psychiatry,* 1974, *131,* 181-85.

Ratliff, R. G., & Stein, N. H. Treatment of neurodermatitis by behavior therapy: A case study. *Behavior Research and Therapy,* 1968, *6,* 397-99.

Ray, O. S. *Drugs, society, and human behavior.* St. Louis: C. V. Mosby, 1974.

Rechtschaffen, A., Wolpert, E. A., Dement, W. C., Mitchell, S. A., & Fisher, C. Nocturnal sleep of narcoleptics. *Electroencephalographica Clinica Neurophysiologica,* 1963, *15,* 599-609.

Rees, L. The importance of psychological, allergic, and infective factors in childhood asthma. *Schizophrenia Bulletin,* 1964, *8,* 7-11.

Reitan, R. M. Certain differential effects of left and right cerebral lesions in human adults. *Journal of Comparative and Physiological Psychology,* 1955, *48,* 474-77.

Reitan, R. M. Psychological deficits resulting from cerebral lesions in man. In J. M. Warren & K. Akert (Eds.), *The frontal granular cortex and behavior.* New York: McGraw-Hill, 1964.

Renshaw, D. C. *The hyperactive child.* Chicago: Nelson-Hall, 1974.

Reynolds, B. S. Psychological treatment models and outcome results for erectile dysfunction: A critical review. *Psychological Bulletin,* 1977, *84,* 1218-38.

Richmond, J. B., & Lustman, S. L. Autonomic function in the neonate: I. Implications for psychosomatic theory. *Psychosomatic Medicine,* 1955, *17,* 269-75.

Richter, H. E. *The family as patient.* New York: Farrar, Straus & Giroux, 1974.

Riddle, M., & Roberts, A. H. Delinquency, delay of gratification, recidivism, and the Porteus maze tests. *Psychological Bulletin,* 1977, *84,* 417-25.

Rie, H. E. Historical perspective of concepts of child psychopathology. In H. E. Rie (Ed.), *Perspectives in child psychopathology.* Chicago: Aldine-Atherton, 1971.

Rie, H. E., et al. Effects of Ritalin on underachieving children: A replication. *American Journal of Orthopsychiatry,* 1976, *4,* 313-22.

Riess, B. F. New viewpoints on the female homosexual. In V. Franks & V. Burtie (Eds.), *Women in therapy.* New York: Brunner/Mazel, 1954.

Rimbaud, Arthur. *Poèmes.* Paris: Laruelle, 1886.

Rimland, B. *Infantile autism.* New York: Appleton-Century-Crofts, 1964.

Rimland, B. Psychogenesis versus biogenesis: The issues and the evidence. In S. C. Plog & R. B. Edgerton (Eds.), *Changing perspectives in mental illness.* New York: Holt, Rinehart & Winston, 1969.

Rimland, B. The effect of high dosage levels of certain vitamins on the behavior of children with severe mental disorders. In D. R. Hawkins & L. Payling (Eds.), *Orthomolecular psychiatry.* San Francisco: W. H. Freeman, 1971.

Rimland, B., Callaway, E., & Dreyfus, P. The effect of high doses of vitamin B6 on autistic children: A double-blind crossover study. *American Journal of Psychiatry,* 1978, *4,* 472-75.

Rimm, D. C., & Masters, J. C. *Behavior therapy: Techniques and empirical findings.* New York: Academic Press, 1974.

Roberts, A. R. *Childhood deprivation.* Springfield, Ill.: Charles C Thomas, 1974.

Robins, E., Munoz, R. A., Martin S., & Gentry, K. A. Primary and secondary affective disorders. In J. Zubin & F. A. Freyhan (Eds.), *Disorders of mood.* Baltimore: Johns Hopkins Press, 1972.

Robins, L. N. *Deviant children grown up.* Baltimore: Williams & Wilkins, 1966.

Robbins, R. H. (Ed.), *The encyclopedia of witchcraft and demonology.* New York: Crown, 1959.

Rodgers, D. A., & McClearn, G. E. Mouse strain differences in preference for various concentrations of alcohol. *Quarterly Journal of Studies on Alcohol,* 1962, *23,* 26-33.

Roe, A., Burks, B. S., & Mittelmann, B. Adult adjustment of foster children of alcoholic and psychotic parentage and the influence of the foster home. *Memorial Section on Alcohol Studies,* no. 3. New Haven, Conn.: Yale University Press, 1945.

Rogers, C. R. *Counseling and psychotherapy: Newer concepts in practice.* Boston: Houghton Mifflin, 1942.

Rogers, C. R. *Client-centered therapy.* Boston: Houghton Mifflin, 1951.

Rogers, C. R. The actualizing tendency in relation to ''motives'' and to consciousness. In M. R. Jones (Ed.), *Nebraska symposium on motivation.* Lincoln: University of Nebraska Press, 1963, Pp. 1-24.

Rogers, C. R., & Dymond, R. F. (Eds.) *Psychotherapy and personality change: Coordinated studies in the client-centered approach.* Chicago: University of Chicago Press, 1954.

Rokeach, M. *The three Christs of Ypsilanti.* New York: Alfred Knopf, 1964.

Rooth, G. Exhibitionists around the world. *Human Behavior,* May 1974, *3* (5), 61.

Rorer, L. G. The great response-style myth. *Psychological Bulletin,* 1965, *63,* 129-56.

Rorschach, H. *Psychodiagnostics*. Berne, Switz.: Huber, 1942.

Rose, R. J. Preliminary study of three indicants of arousal: Measurement, interrelationships, and clinical correlates. Unpublished doctoral dissertation, University of Minnesota, 1964.

Rosen, D. H. *Lesbianism: A study of female homosexuality*. Springfield, Ill.: Charles C. Thomas, 1974.

Rosen, E., & Gregory, I. *Abnormal psychology*. Philadelphia: W. B. Saunders, 1965.

Rosen, G. *Madness in society*. Chicago: University of Chicago Press, 1968.

Rosen, M., Clark, G. R., & Kivitz, M. S. (Eds.) *The history of mental retardation*. Vols. 1 and 2. Baltimore: University Park Press, 1976.

Rosenfeld, A. Prolongevity. *Smithsonian*, 1976, *7*, 40-47.

Rosenhan, D. L. On being sane in insane places. *Science*, 1973, *179*, 250-58.

Rosenthal, D. The heredity-environment issue in schizophrenia: A summary of the conference and present status of our knowledge. In D. Rosenthal & S. S. Kety (Eds.), *The transmission of schizophrenia*. Elmsford, N.Y.: Pergamon Press, 1968.

Rosenthal, D. *Genetic theory and abnormal behavior*. New York: McGraw-Hill, 1970.

Rosenthal, D., Wender, P., Kety, S. S., Welner, J., & Schulsinger, F. The adopted-away offspring of schizophrenics. *American Journal of Psychiatry*, 1971, *128*, 307-11.

Rosenzweig, N. A mechanism in schizophrenia. *Archives of Neurology and Psychiatry*. 1955, *74*, 544.

Rosenzweig, M. R., Bennett, E. L., & Diamond, M. C. Chemical and anatomical plasticity of brain: Replication and extensions, 1970. In J. Gaito (Ed.), *Macromolecules and behavior*. (2nd ed.) New York: Appleton-Century-Crofts, 1972. Pp.205-78.

Rosenzweig, S. The picture-association method and its application in a study of reactions to frustration. *Journal of Personality*, 1945, *14*, 3-23.

Rotter, J. B., & Rafferty, J. E. *Manual for the Rotter incomplete sentences blanks* (College Form). New York: Psychological Corporation, 1950.

Rouen, T. Treatise cited in R. H. Robins (Ed.), *The encyclopedia of witchcraft and demonology*. New York: Crown, 1959.

Routtenberg, A. Neural mechanisms of sleep: Changing view of reticular formation function. *Psychological Review*, 1966, *73*.

Routtenberg, A. The two arousal hypothesis: Reticular formation and limbic system. *Psychological Review*, 1968, *75*.

Ruchs, C. Z., & Rehm, L. P. A self-control behavior therapy program for depression. *Journal of Consulting and Clinical Psychology*, 1977, *45*, 206-15.

Ruitenbeek, H. M. *The interpretation of death*. New York: Jason Aronson, 1973.

Rutter, M. Concepts of autism: A review of research. *Journal of Child Psychology and Psychiatry*, 1968, *9*, 1-25.

Rutter, M., & Bartak, L. Causes of infantile autism: Some considerations from recent literature. *Journal of Autism and Childhood Schizophrenia*, 1971, *1*, 20-32.

Rutter, M., Tizard, J., & Whitmore, K. *Education health and behaviour*. London: Longmans, 1970.

Rychlak, J. F. *Introduction to personality theory*. Boston: Houghton Mifflin, 1973.

Saghir, M., & Robins, E. *Male and female homosexuality*. Baltimore: Williams & Wilkins, 1973.

Sagor, M. Biological bases of childhood behavior disorders. In W. C. Rhodes & M. L. Tracy (Eds.), *A study of child variance*. Vol 1 *Conceptual models*. Ann Arbor: Univeristy of Michigan Press, 1974.

Sahakian, W. S. *Psychology of personality: Readings in theory*. Chicago: Rand McNally College Publishing Co., 1977.

Sahakian, W. S. *History and systems of psychology*. New York: Wiley, 1975.

Salter, A. *Conditioned reflex therapy*. New York: Farrar, Straus, 1949.

Salter, A. *Conditioned reflex therapy*. New York: Capricorn Books, 1961.

Salzinger, K. *Schizophrenia: Behavioral aspects*. New York: Wiley, 1973.

Santamaria, B. A. G. Dysmenorrhea. *Clinical Obstetrics and Gynecology*, 1969, *12*, 708-23.

Sarason, I. G. *Personality: An objective approach*. New York: Wiley, 1972.

Sarason, I. G., de Monchaux, C., & Hunt, T. Methodological issues in the assessment of life stress. In L. Levi (Ed.), *Emotions. Their parameters and measurement*. New York: Raven Press, 1975.

Sarason, S. B. *The clinical interaction*. New York: Harper, 1954.

Sarbin, T. R. The scientific status of the mental illness metaphor. In S. C. Plog & R. B. Edgerton (Eds.), *Changing perspectives in mental illness*, New York: Holt, Rinehart and Winston, 1969.

Sarbin, T. R., & Allen, V. L. Role theory. In G. Lindzey and E. Aronson (Eds.), *The handbook of social psychology*. Vol. 1. Reading, Mass.: Addison-Wesley, 1968.

Sarbin, T. R., & Juhasz, J. B. *The historical background of the concept of hallucinations*. Unpublished manuscript, University of California, Berkeley, 1966.

Sargent, J. D., Green, E. E., & Walters, E. D. Preliminary report on the use of autogenic feedback training in the treatment of migraine and tension headaches. *Psychosomatic Medicine*, 1973, *35*, 129-35.

Satir, V. *Conjoint family therapy*. Palo Alto, Cal.: Science and Behavior Books, 1967.

Schachter, S. Some extraordinary facts about obese humans and rats. *American Psychologist*, 1971, *26*, 129.

Schacter, S., & Latané, B. Crime, cognition, and the autonomic nervous system. In D. Levine (Ed.), *Nebraska symposium on motivation*. Vol. 12. Lincoln: University of Nebraska Press, 1964.

Schanche, D. A. If you're way, way down or up too high... *Today's Health*, 1974, *52*, 39-41.

Scheff, T. J. *Labeling madness*. Englewood Cliffs, N.J.: Prentice-Hall, 1975.

Schiff, A. F. Rape. *Medical Aspects of Human Sexuality*, 1972, *6* (5), 76-84.

Schiff, J. L., Fishman, J., Mellor, K., Schiff, A., & Schiff, S. *The cathexis reader*. New York: Harper & Row, 1975.

Schildkraut, J. J. The catecholamine hypothesis of affective disorders: A review of supporting evidence. *American Journal of Psychiatry*, 1965, *122*, 509-22.

Schmauk, F. J. Punishment, arousal, and avoidance learning in sociopaths. *Journal of Abnormal Psychology*, 1970, *76*, 325-55.

Schmidt, H., & Fonda, C. The reliability of psychiatric diagnosis: A new look. *Journal of Abnormal and Social Psychology*, 1956, *52*, 262-67.

Schofield, M. *Sociological aspects of homosexuality*. Boston: Little, Brown, 1965.

Schou, M. Lithium in psychiatric therapy and prophylaxis. *Journal of Psychiatric Research*, 1968, *6*, 67-95.

Schowalter, J. E. Children and funerals. In O. S. Margolis, H. C. Raether, A. H. Kutscher, R. J. Volk, I, K. Goldberg, & D. J. Cherico (Eds.), *Grief and the meaning of the funeral*. New York: MSS Information Corp., 1975.

Schreibman, L., & Koegel, R. Autism: A defeatable horror: How parents can treat their troubled children. *Psychology Today*, March 1975.

Schultz, J. H., & Luthe, W. *Autogenic training: A psychophysiological approach in psychotherapy*. New York: Grune and Stratton, 1959.

Shultz, R. *The psychology of death, dying, and bereavement*. Reading, Mass.: Addison-Wesley, 1978.

Schur, E. M. *Labeling deviant behavior*. New York: Harper & Row, 1971.

Schwartz, H. Danger ahead in get-tough policy. *Los Angeles Times*, May 25, 1975, IV, p. 5.

Scott, J. P., & Fuller, J. L. *Genetics and the social behavior of the dog*. Chicago: University of Chicago Press, 1965.

Scott, M. P. The nursing home dilemma, Part III: Coping with the cost. *Better Homes and Gardens*, April 1978, Pp. 82-88.

Searles, H. The effort to drive the other person crazy: An element in the actiology and psychotherapy of schizophrenia. *British Journal of Medical Psychology*, 1959, *32*, 1-18.

Seguin, E. Origin of the treatment and training of idiots (1864). In M. Rosen, G. R. Clark, & M. S. Kivitz (Eds.), *The history of mental retardation: Collected papers*. Vol. I. Baltimore: University Park Press, 1976.

Seligman, M. E. P. *Helplessness: On depression, development and death*. San Franciso: W. H. Freeman, 1975.

Seligman, M. E. P., & Maier, S. F. Failure to escape traumatic shock. *Journal of Experimental Psychology*, 1967, *74*, 1-9.

Selye, H. *The stress of life*. New York: McGraw-Hill, 1956.

Selzer, In Miller, W. R. Alcoholism Scales and Objective Assessment Methods: A review. *Psychiatric Bulletin*, 1976, Vol. 83, Pp. 649-74.

Semelaigne, R. *Les grands alienists français*. Paris: Stein & Neil, 1894.

Serber, M. Shame aversion therapy. *Journal of Behavior Therapy and Experimental Psychiatry*, 1970, *1*, 213-15.

Shagass, C. Experimental neurosis. In A. M. Freedman, H. I. Kaplan, & B. J. Sadock (Eds.), *Comprehensive textbook of psychiatry/II*. Vol. I. Baltimore: Williams & Wilkins, 1975.

Shakow, D. Psychological deficit in schizophrenia. *Behavioral Science*, 1963, *8*, 275-305.

Shapiro, A. K. Placebo effects in medicine, psychotherapy, and psychoanalysis. In A. E. Bergin & S. L. Garfield (Eds.), *Handbook of psychotherapy and behavior change: An empirical analysis*. New York: Wiley, 1971.

Shaw, B. F. Comparison of cognitive therapy and behavior therapy in the treatment of depression. *Journal of Consulting and Clinical Psychology*, 1977, *45*, 543-51.

Shaw, C. R., & Lucas, A. *The psychiatric disorders of childhood*. New York: Appleton-Century-Crofts, 1970.

Shaw, D. M. Mineral metabolism, mania, and melancholia. *British Medical Journal*, 1966, *2*, 262-67.

Sheehan, J. G. Conflict theory and avoidance-reduction therapy. In J. Eisenson (Ed.), *Stuttering*. New York: Harper & Row, 1975.

Sheldon, W. H. *Varieties of human physique*. New York: Harper & Bros., 1940.

Shneidman, E. S. Suicide notes reconsidered. *Psychiatry*, 1973, *36*, 379-94.

Shneidman, E. S. (Ed.), *Suicidology: Contemporary developments*. New York: Grune & Stratton, 1976.

Shneidman, E. S. & Farberow, N. L. Some facts about suicide: Causes and prevention. Public Health Service Publication no. 852. Washington, D.C.: U.S. Government Printing Office, 1965.

Shneidman, E. S., & Farberow, N. L. The logic of suicide. In E. S. Shneidman, N. L. Farberow, & R. E. Litman (Eds.), *The psychology of suicide*. New York: Science House, 1970.

Shoben, E. J., Jr. Toward a concept of the normal personality. *American Psychologist*, 1957, *12*, 183-89.

Shoham, S. G. *Social deviance*. New York: Gardner Press, 1976.

Sidman, M. *Tactics of scientific research*. New York: Basic Books, 1960.

Siegelman, M. Adjustment of homosexual and heterosexual women. *British Journal of Psychiatry*, 1972, *120*, 477-81.

Siegler, M., Osmond, H., & Mann, H. Laing's models of madness. In Robert Boyers (Ed.), *R. D. Laing & antipsychiatry*. New York: Perennial Library, Harper & Row, 1971.

Simmons, J. Behavioral management of the hyperactive child. In D. P. Cantwell (Ed.), *The hyperactive child*. New York: Spectrum Publications, 1975.

Simpson, I. H., Back, K. W., & McKinney, J. C. Orientation toward work and retirement, and self-evaluation in retirement. In I. H. Simpson & J. C. McKinney (Eds.), *Social aspects of aging*. Durham, N.C.: Duke University Press, 1966.

Sines, J. O., Cleeland, C., & Adkins, J. The behavior of normal and stomach lesion susceptible rats in several learning situations. *Journal of Genetic Psychology*, 1963, *102*, 91-94.

Skinner, B. F. "Superstition" in the pigeon. *Journal of Experimental Psychology*, 1948, *38*, 168-72.

Skinner, B. F. *Science and human behavior*. New York: Macmillan, 1953.

Skinner, B. F. *Verbal behavior*. New York: Appleton-Century-Crofts, 1957.

Skinner, B. F. *Beyond freedom and dignity*. New York: Knopf, 1971.

Skultans, V. *Madness and morals*. London: Routledge and Kegan Paul, 1975.

Slater, E., & Shields, J. Genetic aspects of anxiety. In M. H. Lader (Ed.), *Studies of anxiety*. Ashford, Eng.: Headley Brothers, 1969.

Sloane, R. B., Staples, F. R., Yorkston, W., Cristol, A., & Whipple, K. *Behavior therapy versus psychotherapy*. Cambridge: Commonwealth Publication, Harvard University Press, 1974.

Slotnick, B. M., McMullen, M. F., & Fleischer, S. Changes in emotionality following destruction of the septal area in albino mice. *Brain, Behavior, and Evolution*, 1974, *8*, 241-52.

Smith, D. E. The characteristics of dependence in high-dose methamphetamine abuse. *International Journal of the Addictions*, 1969, *4*, 453-59.

Snyder, S. H. Madness and the brain, New York: McGraw-Hill, 1974.

Snyder, S. H., & Pert, C. B. Opiate receptor: Demonstration in nervous tissue. Science, 1973, 179, 1011-14.

Sobell, M. B., & Sobell, L. C. Individualized behavior therapy for alcoholics. Behavior Therapy, 1973, 4, 49-72.

Solomon, R. C. Phenomenology and existentialism. New York: Harper & Row, 1972.

Solomon, R. L., & Wynne, L. C. Traumatic avoidance learning: The principles of anxiety conservation and partial irreversibility. Psychological Review, 1954, 61, 353-85.

Sotile, W. M., & Kilmann, P. R. Treatments of psychogenic female sexual dysfunctions. Psychological Bulletin, 1977, 84, 619-33.

Sperling, M. The major neuroses and behavior disorders in children. New York: Jason Aronson, 1974.

Spielberger, C. D. The effects of anxiety on complex learning and academic achievement. In C. D. Spielberger (Ed.), Anxiety and behavior. New York: Academic Press, 1966.

Spitz, R. Authority and masturbation. Psychoanalytic Quarterly, 1952, 21, 490-577.

Spitz, R. A. Anaclitic depression. In A. Freud (Ed.), The psychoanalytic study of the child. Vol. 2. New York: International Universities Press, 1946.

Spitzer, R. L. The mental status schedule: Potential use as a criterion measure in psychotherapy research. American Journal of Psychotherapy, 1966, 20, 156-64.

Spitzer, R. L. On pseudoscience in science, logic in remission, and psychiatric diagnosis: A critique of Rosenhans "On being sane in insane places." Journal of Abnormal Psychology, 1975, 84, 442-52.

Spitzer, R. L., & Endicott, J. DIAGNO II: Further developments in a computer program for psychiatric diagnoses. American Journal of Psychiatry, 1969, 125, 12-21.

Spitzer, R. L., & Endicott, J. Automation of psychiatric case records. International Journal of Psychiatry, 1970, 9, 604-21.

Squire, L. R., & Davis, H. P. Cerebral protein synthesis inhibition and discrimination training: Effects of extent and duration of inhibition. Behavioral Biology, 1975, 13, 49-57.

Srole, L., Langner, T. S., Michael, S. T., Opler, M. K., & Rennie, T. A. C. Mental health in the metropolis: The midtown Manhattan study. New York: McGraw-Hill, 1962.

Stachnik, T. J. The case against criminal penalties for illicit drug use. American Psychologist, 1972, 27, 637-42.

Standard and Poor. Tobacco: Basic analysis. Standard and Poor's Industry Surveys, May 22, 1975, 105-20.

Staples, F. R., Sloane, R. B., Whipple, K., Cristol, A. H., & Yorkston, W. Process and outcome in psychotherapy and behavior. Journal of Consulting and Clinical Psychology, 1976, 44, 340-50.

Starkey, M. L. The devil in Massachusetts. New York: Doubleday, 1961.

Steffen, J. J., Nathan, P. E., & Taylor, H. A. Tension-reducing effects of alcohol: Further evidence and some methodological considerations. Journal of Abnormal Psychology, 1974, 83, 542-47.

Stein, Z., & Susser, M. W. The families of dull children: Classification for predicting careers. British Journal of Preventive Social Medicine, 1960, 14, 83-88.

Steinberg, E. P., & Schwartz, G. E. Biofeedback and electrodermal self-regulation in psychopathy. Journal of Abnormal Psychology, 1976, 85, 408-15.

Steiner, C. Scripts people live. New York: Grove Press, 1974.

Sterman, M. B., & Friar, L. Suppression of seizures in an epileptic following sensorimotor EEG feedback training. Electroencephalography and Clinical Neurophysiology, 1972, 33, 89-95.

Stern, C. Principles of human genetics. (3rd ed.) San Francisco: W. H. Freeman, 1973.

Sternbach, R. A. Principles of psychophysiology. New York: Academic Press, 1966.

Stewart, D. S., & Mickunas, A. Exploring phenomenology. Chicago: American Library Association, 1974.

Stoch, M. B. The effect of undernutrition during infancy on subsequent brain growth and intellectual development. South African Medical Journal, 1967, 1027-30.

Stoller, R. J. Sex and gender: On the development of masculinity and femininity. New York: Science House, 1968.

Stoller, R. J. Gender identity. In A. M. Freedman, H. I. Kaplan, & B. J. Sadock (Eds.), Comprehensive textbook of psychiatry/II. Baltimore: Williams & Wilkins, 1976.

Stone, G. Introduction. In G. Stone (Ed.), Games, sports and power. New Brunswick, N.J.: Transaction Books, 1972.

Strehler, B. L. A new age for aging. In H. Cox (Ed.), Focus: Aging. Sluice Dock, Guilford, Conn.: Dushkin Publishing Group, 1978.

Sturup, G. K. Correctional treatment and the criminal sexual offender. Canadian Journal of Correction, 1961, 3, 250-65.

Sullivan, C., Grant, M., & Grant, J. P. The development of interpersonal maturity: Application to delinquency. Psychiatry, 1957, 20, 373-85.

Sullivan, P. L., & Welsh, G. S. A technique for objective configural analysis of MMPI profiles. Journal of Consulting Psychology, 1952, 16, 383-88.

Summit, R., and Kryso, J. Sexual abuse of children: A clinical spectrum. American Journal of Orthopsychiatry, 1978, 48, Pp. 237-51.

Sutherland, E. H. Principles of criminology. Philadelphia: Lippincott, 1939.

Sutherland, E. H., & Cressey, D. R. Principles of criminology. (7th ed.) Philadelphia: Lippincott, 1966.

Sutherland, E. H., & Cressey, D. R. The theory of differential association. Principles of criminology. (8th ed.) Philadelphia: Lippincott, 1970.

Szasz, T. S. Psychiatry, ethics, and the criminal law. Columbia Law Review, 1958, 58, 182-98.

Szasz, T. S. The myth of mental illness. New York: Norton, 1961.

Szasz, T. S. The age of madness. Garden City, N.Y.: Anchor Books, 1973.

Szondi, L. Schicksalsanalyse. Basel, Switz.: Benno Schwabe, 1944.

Tannenbaum, F. Crime and the community. Boston: Ginn, 1938.

Tarjan, G., Wright, S. W., Eyman, R. K., & Keeran, C. V. Natural history of mental retardation: Some aspects of epidemiology. American Journal of Mental Deficiency. 1973, 77, 369-79.

Task Force on Nomenclature and Statistics of the American Psychiatric Association. *Diagnostic and statistical manual of mental disorders*, (DSM-III). (3rd ed.) *Draft*. Washington, D.C.: American Psychiatric Association, 1978.

Taube, C. A., & Redick, R. Utilization of mental health resources by persons diagnosed with schizophrenia. HEW publication no. (HSM) 73-9110. Rockville, Md.: National Institutes of Mental Health, 1973.

Taylor, J. A. A personality scale of manifest anxiety. *Journal of Abnormal and Social Psychology*, 1953, 48, 285-90.

Thigpen, C. H., & Cleckley, H. M. *Three faces of Eve*. New York: McGraw-Hill, 1957.

Thimann, J. Conditioned-reflex treatment of alcoholism. II. The risk of its application, its indications, contraindications, and psychotherapeutic aspects. *New England Journal of Medicine*, 1949, 241, 406-10.

Thomas E., & Balter, A. Learned helplessness: Amelioration of symptoms by cholinergic blockade of the septum. Cited in M. E. P. Seligman, *Helplessness*. San Francisco: W. H. Freeman, 1975.

Thomas, H. Psychological assessment instruments for use with human infants. *Merrill Palmer Quarterly*, 1970, 16, 179-223.

Thompson, C. M. *Interpersonal psychoanalysis: The selected papers of Clara M. Thompson*. New York: Basic Books, 1964.

Thompson, I. G., & Rathod, N. H. Aversion therapy for heroin dependence. *Lancet*, 1968, 2, 382-84.

Tiger, L., & Fox, R. *The imperial animal*. New York: Holt, Rinehart & Winston, 1971.

Tittle, C. R. Labelling and crime: An empirical evaluation. In W. R. Gove (Ed.), *The labelling of deviance*. New York: Halsted Press, 1975.

Tizard, B. The personality of epileptics: A discussion of the evidence. *Psychological Bulletin*, 1962, 59, 196-210.

Tomkins, S. S. The Tomkins-Horn picture arrangement test. *Transactions of the New York Academy of Science*, 1952, 15, 46-50.

Tooley, K. Antisocial behavior and social alienation post divorce: The "man of the house" and his mother. *American Journal of Orthopsychiatry*, 1976, 46, 33-42.

Tourney, G., & Hatfield, L. M. Androgen metabolism in schizophrenics, homosexuals, and normal controls. *Biological Psychiatry*, 1973, 6, 23.

Tourney, G., Petrilli, A. J., & Hatfield, L. M. Hormonal relationships in homosexual men. *American Journal of Psychiatry*, 1975, 132, 288-90.

Toynbee, A. *Mans concern with death*. New York: McGraw-Hill, 1968.

Tracey, D. A., & Nathan, P. E. Behavioral analysis of chronic alcoholism in four women. *Journal of Consulting and Clinical Psychology*, 1976, 44, 832-42.

Travis, L. *Handbook of speech pathology*. New York: Appleton-Century-Crofts, 1970.

Tredgold, R. F., and Soddy, K. *Tregold's Mental Retardation*. Baltimore: Williams & Wilkins, 1963.

Tripp, C. A. *The homosexual matrix*. New York: McGraw-Hill, 1975.

Troll, L. Eating and aging. In V. Brantl & Sister Marie R. Brown (Eds.), *Readings in gerontology*. St. Louis: C. V. Mosby, 1973.

Trotter, S. Patuxent: "Therapeutic" prison faces test. *APA Monitor*, 1975, 6, 12.

Trouton, D. S., & Maxwell, A. E. The relation between neuroses and psychoses. *Journal of Mental Science*, 1956, 102, 1-21.

Truax, C. B., & Mitchell, K. M. Research on certain therapist interpersonal skills in relation to process and outcome. In A. E. Bergin & S. L. Garfield (Eds.), *Handbook of psychotherapy and behavior change: An empirical analysis*. New York: Wiley, 1971.

Tryon, R. C. Experimental behavior genetics of maze learning and a sufficient polygenic theory. *American Psychologist*, 1963, 18, 442.

Turnbull, J. W. Asthma conceived as a learned response. *Journal of Psychosomatic Research*, 1962, 6, 59-70.

Turner, R. J., & Wagonfeld, M. O. Occupational mobility and schizophrenia. *American Sociological Review*, 1967, 32, 104-13.

Ullmann, L. P., & Krasner, L. *Psychological approach to abnormal psychology*. Englewood Cliffs, N.J.: Prentice-Hall, 1975.

Uniform Crime Reports. U.S. Dept. of Justice, Federal Bureau of Investigation. Washington, D.C.: U.S. Government Printing Office, 1975.

Urmson, J. O. *The concise encyclopedia of Western philosophy and philosphers*. New York: Hawthorne Books, 1960.

Valenstein, E. S. *Brain control*. New York: Wiley, 1973.

Velten, J. A laboratory task for indication of mood states. *Behavior Research and Therapy*, 1968, 6, 473-82.

Venables, P. H. A short scale for rating "activity-withdrawal" in schizophrenics. *Journal of Mental Science*, 1957, 103, 197-99.

Venables, P. H. Psychophysiological studies of schizophrenic pathology. In P. H. Venables & M. J. Christie (Eds.), *Research in psychophysiology*. New York: Wiley, 1975.

Vernon, P. E. *Intelligence and Cultural Environment*. Methuen: 1972.

Vogel, E., & Bell, N. The emotionally disturbed child as the family scapegoat. In E. Vogel & N. Bell (Eds.), *A modern introduction to the family*. New York: Free Press, 1960.

Vogel, F. S. The brain and time. In E. W. Busse and E. Pfeiffer (Eds.), *Behavior and adaptation in late life*. Boston: Little, Brown, 1977.

Volkmann, R., & Cressey, D. R. Differential association and the rehabilitation of drug addicts. *American Journal of Sociology*, 1963, 64, 129-42.

Walker, R. N. Body build and behavior in young children: I. Body build and nursery school teachers' ratings. *Monographs of the Society for Research in Child Development*, 1962, 27, serial no. 84.

Walters, D. R. *Physical and sexual abuse of children. Causes and treatment*. Bloomington: Indiana University Press, 1975.

Wang, H. S. Organic brain syndromes. In E. W. Busse & E. Pfeiffer (Eds.), *Behavior and adaptation in late life.* Boston: Little, Brown, 1977.

Watson, J. B., & Rayner, R. Conditioned emotional reactions. *Journal of Experimental Psychology,* 1920, *3,* 1-14.

Waxenberg, S. E., et al. The role of hormones in human behavior: I. Changes in female sexuality after adrenalectomy. *Journal of Clinical Endocrinology and Metabolism,* 1959, *19,* 193-202.

Wechsler, D. *Manual for the Wechsler intelligence scale for children - revised.* New York: Psychological Corporation, 1974.

Weil, A. *The natural mind. A new way of looking at drugs, and the higher consciousness.* Boston: Houghton Mifflin, 1972.

Weinberg, M. S., & Williams, C. J. *Male homosexuals: Their problems and adaptations.* New York: Oxford University Press, 1974.

Weiner, B. "On being sane in insane places: A process (attributional) analysis and critique. *Journal of Abnormal Psychology,* 1975, *84,* 433-41.

Weiner, H., Thaler, M., Reiser, M. F., & Mirsky, I. A. Etiology of duodenal ulcer: I. Relation of specific psychological characteristics to rate of gastric secretion (serum pepsinogen). *Psychosomatic Medicine,* 1957, *19,* 1-10.

Weinstock, H. J. Successful treatment of ulcerative colitis by psychoanalysis: A survey of 28 cases with follow-up. *Journal of Psychosomatic Research,* 1962, *6,* 243-49.

Weisman, A. D. Thanatology. In A. M. Freedman, H. I. Kaplan, & B. J. Sadock (Eds.), *Comprehensive textbook of psychiatry/II.* (2nd ed.) Vol. 2. Baltimore: Williams & Wilkins, 1975.

Weisman, A. D., & Worden, J. W. Risk-rescue rating in suicide assessment. *Archives of General Psychiatry,* 1972, *26,* 553-60.

Weisman, A. D., et al. Lethality factors and the suicide attempt. In E. S. Shneidman (Ed.), *Suicidology: Contemporary developments.* New York: Grune & Stratton, 1976.

Weiss, J. M. Effects of coping response on stress. *Journal of Comparative and Physiological Psychology,* 1968, *65,* 251-60.

Weiss, J. M. Effects of predictable and unpredictable shock on development of gastrointestinal lesions in rats. *Proceedings, 76th Annual American Psychological Association,* 1968, 263-64.

Weiss, J. M. Effects of coping behavior in different warning signal conditions on stress pathology in rats. *Journal of Comparative and Physiological Psychology,* 1971, *77,* 1-13.

Weiss, J. M., Glazer, H. I., Pohorecky, L. A., Briek, J., & Miller, N. E. Effects of chronic exposure to stressors on avoidance-escape behavior and on brain norepinephrine. *Psychosomatic Medicine,* 1975, *37,* 522-34.

Wender, P. H. *Minimal brain dysfunction in children.* New York: Wiley, 1971.

Wender, P. H. *The hyperactive child.* New York: Crown, 1973.

Werman, D. S. On the occurence of incest fantasies. *Psychoanalytic Quarterly,* 1977, *46,* Pp. 245-55.

West, D. J. *Homosexuality.* Harmondsworth (Middlesex), Eng.: Penguin Books, 1968.

Whalen, R. E. Sexual motivation. *Psychological Review,* 1966, *73* (2), 151-63.

Whaley, D. L., & Malott, R. W. *Elementary principles of behavior.* New York: Appleton-Century-Crofts, 1971.

Whitehead, J. A. *Psychiatric disorders in old age.* New York: Springer, 1974.

Wicklund, J. D. Helen: A case of anorexia nervosa. In M. F. Freehill (Ed.), *Disturbed and troubled children.* Flushing, N.Y.: Spectrum Publications, 1973.

Wickramasekera, I. A technique for controlling a certain type of sexual exhibitionism. *Psychotherapy: Theory, Research and Practice,* 1972, *9,* 207-10.

Wiggens, J. S., Renner, I. E., Clore, G. L., & Rose, R. J. *Principles of personality.* Reading, Mass.: Addison-Wesley, 1976.

Wikler, A. Conditioning factors in opiate addiction and relapse. In D. M. Wilmer & G. G. Kassebaum (Eds.), *Narcotics.* New York: McGraw-Hill, 1965.

Wilcoxon, L. A., Schrader, S. L., & Nelson, R. E. Behavioral formulations of depression. In W. E. Craighead, A. E. Kayden, & M. J. Mahoney (Eds.), *Behavior modification: Principles, issues, and applications.* Boston: Houghton Mifflin, 1976.

Wild, C. M., Shapiro, L. N., & Abelin, T. Communication patterns and role structure in families of male schizophrenics. *Archives of General Psychiatry,* 1977, *34,* 50.

Wilkening, H. E. *The psychology almanac: A handbook for students.* Monterey, Cal.: Brooks/Cole Publishing Co., 1973.

Williams, J. G., Barlow, D. H., & Agras, W. S. Behavioral measurement of severe depression. *Archives of General Psychiatry,* 1972, *27,* 330-33.

Williams, R., & Wirths, C. *Lives through the years: Styles of life and successful aging.* New York: Atherton, 1965.

Williams, T. R. *Introduction to socialization. Human culture transmitted.* St. Louis: C. V. Mosby, 1972.

Wilson, C. *The occult.* New York: Random House, 1971.

Wilson, C. *Introduction to the new existentialism.* London: Hutchinson, 1966.

Wilson, M., & Greene, R. Personality characteristics of female homosexuals. *Psychological Reports,* 1971, *28,* 407-12.

Wing, L. *Autistic children.* New York: Brunner/Mazel, 1972.

Winick, M., & Rosso, P. Effects of malnutrition on brain development. *Biology of Brain Dysfunction,* 1973, *1,* 301-17.

Winnick, C. The desexualized society. *The Humanist,* December 1969.

Winokur, G. Genetic principles in the clarification of clinical issues in affective disorders. In A. J. Mandell & M. P. Mandell (Eds.), *Psychochemical research in man.* New York: Academic Press, 1969.

Wisocki, P. A. The successful treatment of a heroin addict by covert conditioning techniques. *Journal of Behavior Therapy and Experimental Psychiatry,* 1973, *4,* 55-61.

Witt, G. M., & Hall, C. S. The genetics of audiogenic seizures in the house mouse. *Journal of Comparative and Physiological Psychology,* 1949, *42,* 58-63.

Wittkower, E. D., & Dudek, S. Z. Psychosomatic medicine: The mind-body-society interaction. In B. Wolman (Ed.), *Handbook of general psychology.* Englewood Cliffs, N.J.: Prentice-Hall, 1973.

Wittman, P. A scale for measuring prognosis in schizophrenic patients. *Elgin State Hospital Papers,* 1941, *4,* 20-23.

Witzig, J. S. The group treatment of male exhibitionists. *American Journal of Psychiatry*, 1968, *125*, 75-81.

Wolberg, L. R. *The technique of psychotherapy*. New York: Grune & Stratton, 1967.

Wolf, M. M., Phillips, E. L., & Fixsen, D. L. Achievement Place: Phase II. Final report for Grant MH 20030 (May 1, 1971 - April 30, 1974). Center for Studies of Crime and Delinquency, National Institutes of Mental Health, 1974.

Wolf, S. M., Munsat, T. L., & Dunne, P. B. *Neurology case studies*. Flushing, N.Y.: Medical Examination Publishing Co., 1972.

Wolf, S., & Wolf, H. G. *Human gastric functions*. New York: Oxford University Press, 1947.

Wolff, C. *Love between women*. New York: St. Martin's Press, 1971.

Wolman, B. B. *Children without childhood: A study of childhood schizophrenia*. New York: Grune & Stratton, 1970.

Wolpe, J. *Psychotherapy by reciprocal inhibition*. Stanford: Stanford University Press, 1958.

Wolpe, J. Conditioning inhibition of craving in drug addiction: A pilot experiment. *Behavior Research and Therapy*, 1965, *2*, 285-88.

Woodruff, R. A., Goodwin, D. W., & Guze, S. B. *Psychiatric diagnosis*. New York: Oxford University Press, 1974.

Woodworth, R. S. *Personal data sheet*. Chicago: Stoelting, 1919.

Wooley, D. W. *The biochemical bases of psychoses*. New York: Wiley, 1962.

Wooley, P. V., & Evans, W. A. Significance of skeletal lesions in infants resembling those of traumatic origin. *Journal of the American Medical Association*, 1955, *56*, 163.

Worden, J. W. Lethality factors and the suicide attempt. In E. S. Shneidman (Ed.), *Suicidology: Contemporary developments*. New York: Grune & Stratton, 1976.

World Health Organization. *Report of the international pilot study of schizophrenia. Vol. 1*. Geneva: WHO, 1973.

Wyden, P., & Wyden, B. *Growing up straight*. New York: Signet Books, 1968.

Wynne, L. C. Methodological and conceptual issues in the study of schizophrenics and their families. In D. Rosenthal and S. S. Kety (Eds.), *The transmission of schizophrenia*. Elmsford, N.Y.: Pergamon Press, 1968.

Yoshida, R. K. Effects of labeling on elementary and EMR teacher's expectancies for change in a student's performance. Unpublished doctoral dissertation, University of Southern California, 1974.

Young, G. C. The family history of enuresis. *Journal of the Royal Institute of Public Health*, August 1963, 197-201.

Young, M., Benjamin, B., & Wallis, C. Mortality of widowers. *Lancet*, 1963, *2*, 454.

Zax, M., & Cowen, E. L. *Abnormal psychology: Changing conceptions*. New York: Holt, Rinehart & Winston, 1973.

Ziegler, F. J., Imboden, J. B., & Meyer, E. Contemporary conversion reactions: A clinical study. *American Journal of Psychiatry*, 1960, *116*, 901-10.

Zigler, E. Familial mental retardation: A continuing dilemma. *Science*, 1967, *155*, 292-98.

Zigler, E., & Levine, J. Premorbid adjustment and paranoid-nonparanoid status in schizophrenia: A further investigation. *Journal of Abnormal Psychology*, 1961, *63*, 69-77.

Zigler, E., & Phillips, L. Psychiatric diagnosis and symptomatology. *Journal of Abnormal and Social Psychology*, 1961, *63*, 69-75.

Zilboorg, G., & Henry, G. *A history of medical psychology*. New York: Norton: 1941.

Zimbardo, P. G. *Shyness*. Reading, Mass.: Addison-Wesley, 1977.

Zubin, J. Classification of the behavior disorders. *Annual Review of Psychology*, 1967, *18*, 373-406.

Zubin, J., Salzinger, S., Fleiss, J. L., Gurland, B., Spitzer, R. L., Endicott, J., & Sutton, S. Biometric approach to psychopathology: Abnormal and clinical psychology - statistical, epidemiological, and diagnostic approaches. *Annual Review of Psychology*, 1975, *26*, 621-71.

Zubin, J., & Spring, B. Vulnerability - A new view of schizophrenia. *Journal of Abnormal Psychology*, 1977, *86*, 103-26.

Zuckerman, M., & Lubin, B. *Manual for the multiple affect adjective check list*. San Diego: Educational and Industrial Testing Service, 1965.

Zung, W. K. A self-rating depression scale. *Archives of General Psychiatry*, 1965, *12*, 63-70.

CREDITS

NAME INDEX

SUBJECT INDEX

FREDERICK MEARS
Professor and chairman of the Department of Psychology at Texas Eastern University at Tyler. He received his Ph.D. in psychometry and research and statistical methodology from the University of Northern Colorado in 1970 and took postdoctoral training in clinical psychology at the University of Arkansas Medical School. He had an internship in school psychology and also received postdoctoral internship and clinical training in clinical gerontology. His current research interests are in psychopathology within the life span. He has published in the areas of sexual deviations, epidemiology and predictions of senium psychopathologies, and nondiscriminatory intelligence testing. He is at present a consultant in geriatric settings and in various school districts.

ROBERT J. GATCHEL
Associate professor of psychology at the University of Texas at Arlington and clinical associate professor of psychiatry at the University of Texas Health Science Center at Dallas. He received his B.A. from the State University of New York at Stony Brook in 1969, and his Ph.D. in clinical psychology from the University of Wisconsin in 1973. His current research interests are in the areas of clinical applications of biofeedback and the psychophysiology of emotion. His biofeedback research is presently being supported by a grant from the National Institute of Health. He is a reviewer and active contributor to many professional journals such as the *Journal of Abnormal Psychology, Journal of Consulting and Clinical Psychology*, and *Psychophysiology*. In addition to his teaching and research, he is a practicing clinical psychologist.